THE GREEN GUIDE

Ph. Gajic/MICHELIN

When a man is tired of London, he is tired of life;
for there is in London all that life can afford.

Dr Samuel Johnson 1777

London

Travel Publications

Hannay House, 39 Clarendon Road
Watford, Herts WD17 1JA, UK
☎ (01923) 205 240 - Fax (01923) 205 241
www.ViaMichelin.com
TheGreenGuide-uk@uk.michelin.com

Manufacture française des pneumatiques Michelin
Société en commandite par actions au capital de 304 000 000 EUR
Place des Carmes-Déchaux – 63 Clermont-Ferrand (France)
R.C.S. Clermont-Fd B 855 200 507

Dépôt légal décembre 2001 – ISBN 2-06-100353-2 – ISSN 0763- 1383
Printed in Fance 03-04/4.3

Typesetting, printing and binding: IME à Baume-les-Dames
Graphics: Christiane Beylier, Paris 12e arr.

Cover design: Carré Noir, Paris 17e arr.

THE GREEN GUIDE: Spirit of Discovery

Leisure time spent with The Green Guide is also a time for refreshing your spirit, enjoying yourself, and taking advantage of our selection of fine restaurants, hotels and other places for relaxing: immerse yourself in the local culture, discover new horizons, experience the local lifestyle. The Green Guide opens the door for you.

Each year our writers go touring: visiting the sights, devising the driving tours, identifying the highlights, selecting the most attractive hotels and restaurants, checking the routes for the maps and plans.

Each title is compiled with great care, giving you the benefit of regular revisions and Michelin's first-hand knowledge. The Green Guide responds to changing circumstances and takes account of its readers' suggestions; all comments are welcome.

Share with us our enthusiasm for travel, which has led us to discover over 60 destinations in France and other countries. Like us, let yourself be guided by the desire to explore, which is the best motive for travel: the spirit of discovery.

Contents

Practical Points

Insights and Images

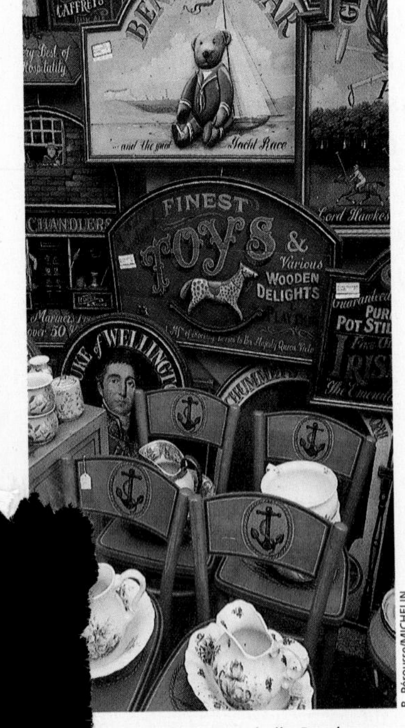

B. Pérousse/MICHELIN

Antique shop, Portobello Road

Eurasia Press/PHOTONONSTOP

Globe Theatre

Selected Sights

D. Ball/PHOTONONSTOP

Millennium Dome

B. Morandi/MICHELIN

Trooping the Colour

Maps and Plans

Companion publications

City Plans

Michelin Plan of London **34** (Scale 1 : 8000 – 1cm : 80m), also available as a spiral-bound **atlas**, includes main thoroughfares, one-way streets, main car parks, post offices and the most important public buildings in the city, an alphabetical street index and maps of the underground network

Regional Maps

Michelin map **504** – South East Midlands East Anglia (Scale 1 : 400 000 – 1cm = 4km – 1in : 6.30 miles) covers the main regions of the country, the network of motorways and major roads. It provides information on shipping routes, distances in miles and kilometres, plan of London, services, sporting and tourist attractions and an index of places.

Country Maps

The Michelin Tourist and Motoring **Atlas** – Great Britain & Ireland (Scale 1 : 300 000 – 1cm = 3km – 1in : 4.75 miles) covers the whole of the United Kingdom and the Republic of Ireland. It provides information on route planning, distances in miles and kilometres, over 60 town plans, services, sporting and tourist attractions and an index of places.

Internet

Users can access personalised route plans, Michelin mapping on line, addresses of hotels and restaurants featured in The Red Guides and practical and tourist information through the internet:

www.ViaMichelin.com

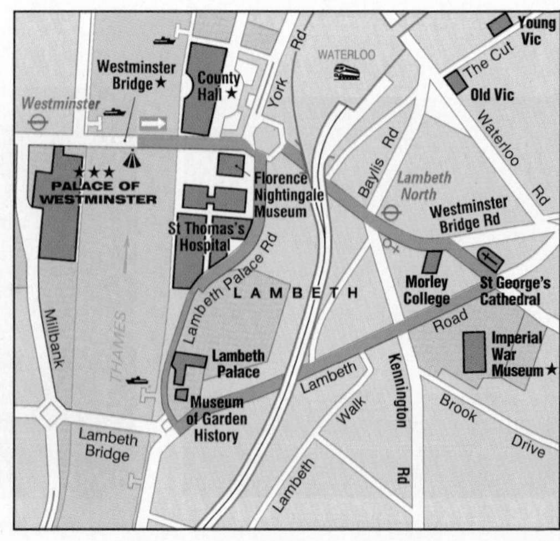

List of maps and plans

A map reference to the Map of Principal Sights and to the Map of Outer London is given for each chapter in the Sights section of this guide.

Local maps

Plan of museums and monuments

Key

Selected monuments and sights

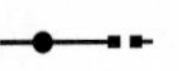 Tour - Departure point

Catholic church

Protestant church, other temple

Synagogue - Mosque

Building

Statue, small building

Calvary, wayside cross

Fountain

Rampart - Tower - Gate

Château, castle, historic house

Ruins

Dam

Factory, power plant

Fort

Cave

Prehistoric site

Viewing table

Viewpoint

Other place of interest

Sports and recreation

Racecourse

Skating rink

Outdoor, indoor swimming pool

Marina, sailing centre

Trail refuge hut

Cable cars, gondolas

Funicular, rack railway

Tourist train

Recreation area, park

Theme, amusement park

Wildlife park, zoo

Gardens, park, arboretum

Bird sanctuary, aviary

Walking tour, footpath

Of special interest to children

Special symbols

M3 Motorway

A2 Primary route

London wall

City boundary

Pub

Underground station

Abbreviations

C County council offices

H Town hall

M Museum

POL. Police

T Theatre

U University

Highly recommended ★★★
Recommended ★★
Interesting ★

Additional symbols

	Tourist information
	Motorway or other primary route
	Junction: complete, limited
	Pedestrian street
	Unsuitable for traffic, street subject to restrictions
	Steps - Footpath
	Train station - Auto-train station
S.N.C.F.	Coach (bus) station
	Tram
	Metro, underground
	Park-and-Ride
	Access for the disabled
	Post office
	Telephone
	Covered market
	Barracks
	Drawbridge
	Quarry
	Mine
B F	Car ferry (river or lake)
	Ferry service: cars and passengers
	Foot passengers only
③	Access route number common to Michelin maps and town plans
Bert (R.)...	Main shopping street
AZ **B**	Map co-ordinates

Places to stay and places to eat

20 rm	Number of rooms.
£76/100	Price of single/double room including breakfast.
£4.50	Price of breakfast when not included in the room price.
100 beds £19	Number of beds (youth hostel, university residence) and price per person.
£10/26,50	Restaurant prices: minimum and maximum price for a full meal excluding beverages. In many cases the first price refers to a lunch menu. For informal eating places an average price may be given.
	Major credit cards not accepted.
P	Car park for customers.
	No-smoking rooms available. Restaurant partly or wholly reserved for non-smokers.
	Rooms with wheelchair access.

All prices are given in £ Sterling. Prices quoted include VAT unless otherwise specfied. Service charge may be expected.

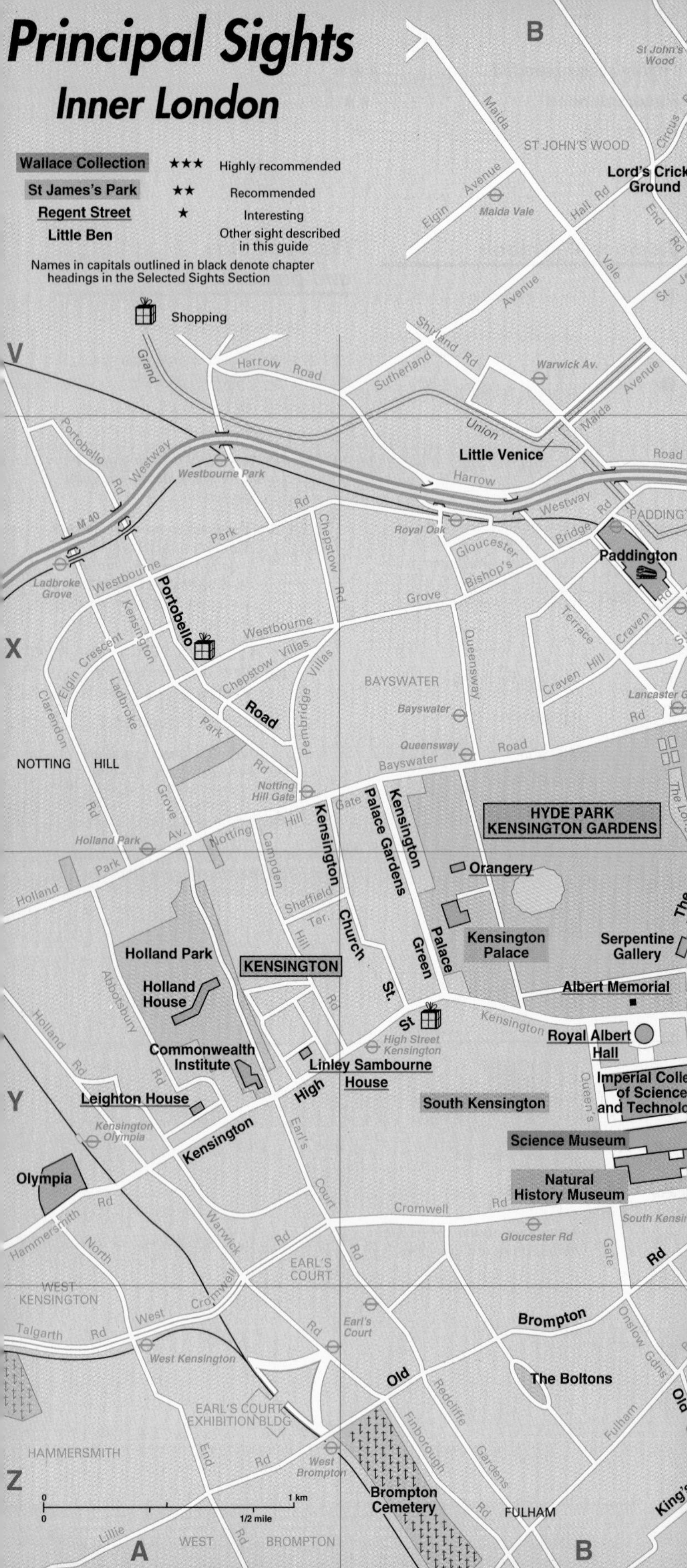

Principal Sights
Inner London
Wallace Collection ★★★ Highly recommended
St James's Park ★★ Recommended
Regent Street ★ Interesting
Little Ben Other sight described in this guide
Names in capitals outlined in black denote chapter headings in the Selected Sights Section
Shopping
A
B
V
X
Y
Z
ST JOHN'S WOOD
Maida Vale
Warwick Av.
Little Venice
Westbourne Park
Royal Oak
Paddington
Ladbroke Grove
Portobello
BAYSWATER
Bayswater
Queensway
Notting Hill Gate
NOTTING HILL
Holland Park
HYDE PARK
KENSINGTON GARDENS
Orangery
Kensington Palace
Serpentine Gallery
Albert Memorial
Royal Albert Hall
Holland Park
Holland House
KENSINGTON
Commonwealth Institute
Linley Sambourne House
High Street Kensington
Leighton House
South Kensington
Science Museum
Natural History Museum
Kensington Olympia
Olympia
Gloucester Rd
EARL'S COURT
WEST KENSINGTON
Earl's Court
West Kensington
The Boltons
EARL'S COURT EXHIBITION BLDG
HAMMERSMITH
West Brompton
Brompton Cemetery
FULHAM
WEST BROMPTON
1 km
1/2 mile

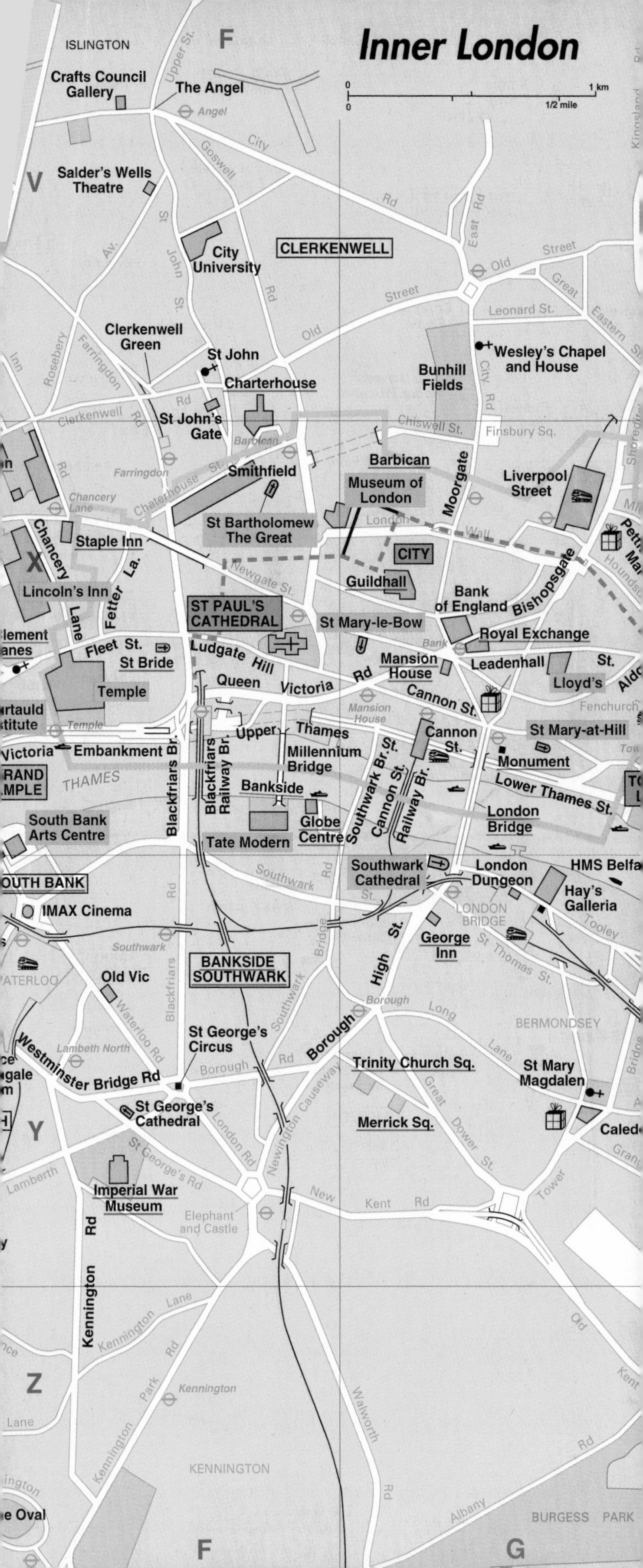

Inner London
0
1 km
0
1/2 mile
F
ISLINGTON
Crafts Council Gallery
The Angel
Angel
Upper St.
City
Goswell
Rd
V
Salder's Wells Theatre
City University
CLERKENWELL
St John St.
Rd
Old
Street
East Rd
Old
Street
Great
Eastern St.
Leonard St.
Av.
Rosebery
Farringdon
Inn
Clerkenwell Green
St John
Charterhouse
Bunhill Fields
Wesley's Chapel and House
City Rd
Clerkenwell
Rd
St John's Gate
Barbican
Chiswell St.
Finsbury Sq.
Farringdon
Smithfield
Barbican
Museum of London
Moorgate
Liverpool Street
Chancery Lane
Chaterhouse
St Bartholomew The Great
London
Wall
Chancery
Staple Inn
CITY
Bishopsgate
X
Lincoln's Inn
Fetter La.
Lane
Newgate St.
Guildhall
Bank of England
ST PAUL'S CATHEDRAL
St Mary-le-Bow
Royal Exchange
Fleet St.
St Bride
Ludgate Hill
Bank
Mansion House
Leadenhall
St.
Queen
Victoria
Rd
Cannon St.
Lloyd's
Temple
Mansion House
Fenchurch
Temple
Upper
Thames
Cannon St.
St Mary-at-Hill
Victoria
Embankment
Blackfriars Br.
Blackfriars Railway Br.
Millennium Bridge
Southwark Br. St.
Cannon St.
Railway Br.
Monument
THAMES
Bankside
Lower Thames St.
London Bridge
South Bank Arts Centre
Tate Modern
Globe Centre
Southwark
Rd
Southwark Cathedral
London Dungeon
HMS Belfa
Hay's Galleria
Tooley
OUTH BANK
IMAX Cinema
St.
LONDON BRIDGE
Rd
Bridge
High St.
George Inn
St Thomas St.
Southwark
Blackfriars
BANKSIDE SOUTHWARK
Old Vic
Waterloo Rd
Southwark
Borough
Long
Lane
BERMONDSEY
Westminster Bridge Rd
Lambeth North
St George's Circus
Borough
Rd
Borough
Trinity Church Sq.
St Mary Magdalen
St George's Cathedral
London Rd
Newington Causeway
Merrick Sq.
Great Dover St.
Y
St George's Rd
Lambeth
Imperial War Museum
Elephant and Castle
New
Kent
Rd
Tower
Kennington Rd
Kennington
Lane
Rd
Old
Kent
Z
Kennington
Park
Lane
Kennington
Walworth
Rd
KENNINGTON
Rd
Albany
BURGESS PARK
F
G

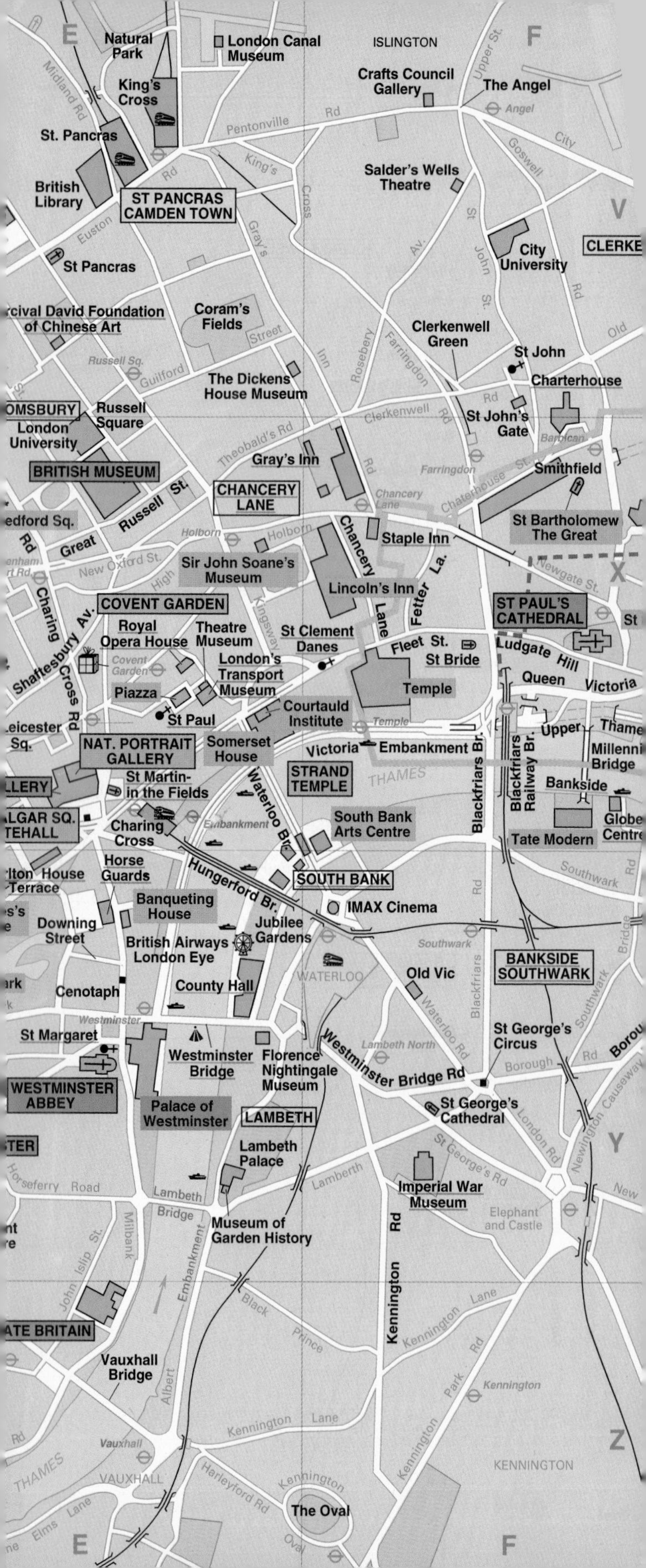

E
F
Natural Park
King's Cross
London Canal Museum
ISLINGTON
Crafts Council Gallery
The Angel
Angel
St. Pancras
Pentonville Rd
City
Goswell
King's Cross
Upper St.
Salder's Wells Theatre
British Library
ST PANCRAS CAMDEN TOWN
Euston Rd
Gray's
V
St Pancras
St John St.
City University
CLERKE
Av.
Rd
rcival David Foundation of Chinese Art
Coram's Fields
Street
Clerkenwell Green
Old
Russell Sq.
Guilford
Inn
Rosebery
Farringdon
St John
The Dickens House Museum
Charterhouse
OMSBURY
Russell Square
London University
Clerkenwell Rd
St John's Gate
Theobald's Rd
Barbican
BRITISH MUSEUM
Gray's Inn
Farringdon
Smithfield
Chancery Lane
Charterhouse St.
CHANCERY LANE
St Bartholomew The Great
edford Sq.
Russell St.
Holborn
Great
Chancery
Staple Inn
Rd
New Oxford St.
Sir John Soane's Museum
Newgate St.
X
High
Fetter La.
Charing
Lincoln's Inn
ST PAUL'S CATHEDRAL
St
COVENT GARDEN
Lane
Shaftesbury Av.
Royal Opera House
Theatre Museum
St Clement Danes
Fleet St.
St Bride
Ludgate Hill
Covent Garden
London's Transport Museum
Cross Rd
Queen Victoria
Piazza
Temple
Courtauld Institute
Upper Thame
St Paul
Temple
Leicester Sq.
NAT. PORTRAIT GALLERY
Somerset House
Victoria Embankment
Blackfriars Br.
Blackfriars Railway Br.
Millenni Bridge
THAMES
LLERY
St Martin-in the Fields
Waterloo Br.
STRAND TEMPLE
Bankside
Globe Centre
ALGAR SQ. TEHALL
Charing Cross
Embankment
South Bank Arts Centre
Tate Modern
rlton House Terrace
Horse Guards
Hungerford Br.
SOUTH BANK
Southwark
Banqueting House
IMAX Cinema
Rd
Downing Street
Jubilee Gardens
Southwark
British Airways London Eye
BANKSIDE SOUTHWARK
Bridge
WATERLOO
Old Vic
Cenotaph
County Hall
Southwark
Westminster
Waterloo Rd
Blackfriars
St Margaret
Westminster Bridge
Florence Nightingale Museum
Lambeth North
St George's Circus
Boro
Westminster Bridge Rd
Borough
Rd
WESTMINSTER ABBEY
Palace of Westminster
LAMBETH
St George's Cathedral
London Rd
Newington Causeway
TER
Lambeth Palace
St George's Rd
Y
Horseferry Road
Lambeth
Lambeth Bridge
Imperial War Museum
New
Elephant and Castle
Millbank
Museum of Garden History
Rd
Embankment
John Islip St.
Kennington
Lane
Black Prince
Kennington
ATE BRITAIN
Rd
Vauxhall Bridge
Albert
Park
Kennington
Kennington Lane
Rd
Z
Vauxhall
Kennington
KENNINGTON
THAMES
VAUXHALL
Harleyford Rd
Kennington
Lane
The Oval
Elms
Oval
E
F

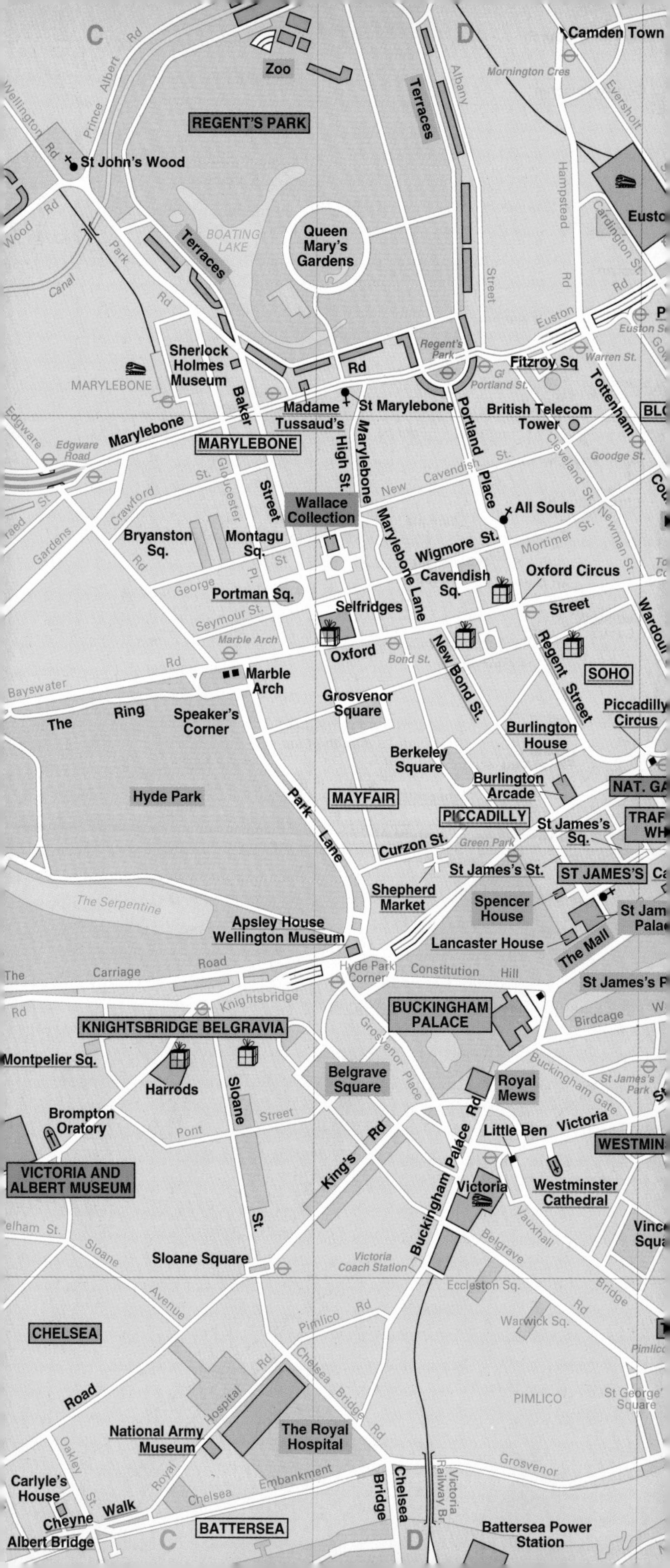

C
D
Camden Town
Zoo
Mornington Cres
Terraces
Albany
Eversholt
Prince Albert Rd
Wellington Rd
REGENT'S PARK
St John's Wood
Euston
Hampstead Rd
Cardington St.
Wood Rd
Park Rd
Canal
Queen Mary's Gardens
BOATING LAKE
Terraces
Street
Euston Rd
Euston Sq.
Regent's Park
Fitzroy Sq
Warren St.
Great Portland St.
Sherlock Holmes Museum
MARYLEBONE
Rd
Madame Tussaud's
St Marylebone
Portland Place
British Telecom Tower
Tottenham
Edgware Rd
Edgware Road
Marylebone
MARYLEBONE
Baker Street
Marylebone High St.
New Cavendish St.
Cleveland St.
Goodge St.
Gloucester Pl.
Crawford St.
Wallace Collection
All Souls
Newman St.
Gardens
Bryanston Sq.
Montagu Sq.
Marylebone Lane
Wigmore St.
Mortimer St.
George St.
Portman Sq.
Cavendish Sq.
Oxford Circus
Seymour St.
Selfridges
Street
Wardour
Marble Arch
Oxford
Bond St.
New Bond St.
Regent Street
Rd
Marble Arch
SOHO
Bayswater
Grosvenor Square
Piccadilly Circus
The Ring
Speaker's Corner
Burlington House
Berkeley Square
Burlington Arcade
NAT. GA
Hyde Park
Park Lane
MAYFAIR
PICCADILLY
St James's Sq.
Curzon St.
Green Park
St James's St.
ST JAMES'S
The Serpentine
Shepherd Market
Spencer House
St James's Palace
Apsley House Wellington Museum
Lancaster House
The Mall
The Carriage Road
Hyde Park Corner
Constitution Hill
St James's P
Rd
Knightsbridge
BUCKINGHAM PALACE
Birdcage
KNIGHTSBRIDGE BELGRAVIA
Montpelier Sq.
Grosvenor Place
Buckingham Gate
St James's Park
Harrods
Sloane Street
Belgrave Square
Royal Mews
Brompton Oratory
Pont Street
Little Ben
Victoria
WESTMIN
King's Rd
Buckingham Palace Rd
VICTORIA AND ALBERT MUSEUM
Victoria
Westminster Cathedral
St.
Pelham St.
Sloane Avenue
Vauxhall Bridge Rd
Belgrave
Sloane Square
Victoria Coach Station
Eccleston Sq.
Pimlico Rd
Warwick Sq.
CHELSEA
Pimlico
Rd
Chelsea Bridge Rd
Road
Hospital Rd
PIMLICO
St George's Square
National Army Museum
The Royal Hospital
Grosvenor
Oakley St.
Royal
Victoria Railway Br.
Carlyle's House
Chelsea Embankment
Bridge
Chelsea
Cheyne Walk
BATTERSEA
Battersea Power Station
Albert Bridge
C
D

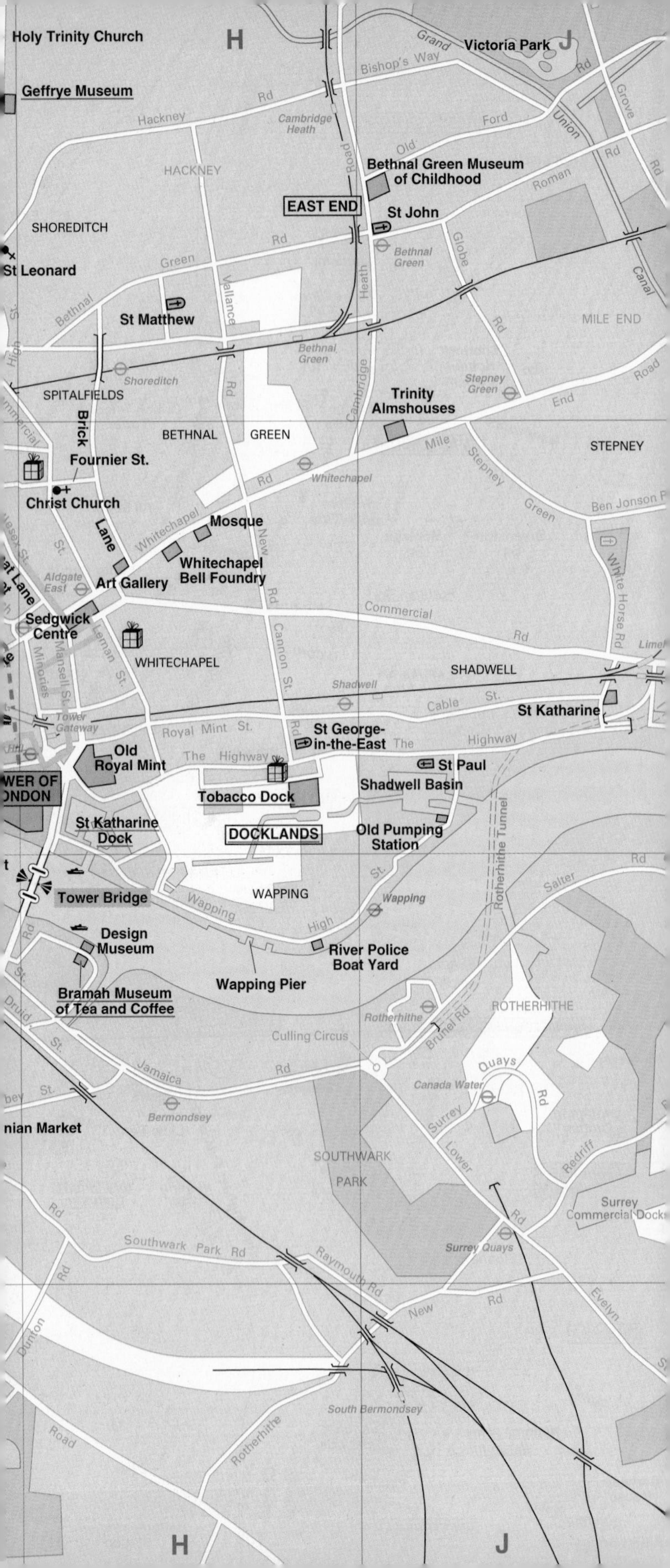
H
J
Holy Trinity Church
Geffrye Museum
Victoria Park
Bethnal Green Museum of Childhood
EAST END
St John
HACKNEY
SHOREDITCH
St Leonard
St Matthew
Cambridge Heath
Bethnal Green
Shoreditch
SPITALFIELDS
MILE END
Stepney Green
Trinity Almshouses
BETHNAL
GREEN
STEPNEY
Fournier St.
Christ Church
Whitechapel
Mosque
Whitechapel Bell Foundry
Aldgate East
Art Gallery
Sedgwick Centre
WHITECHAPEL
SHADWELL
Shadwell
Tower Gateway
St Katharine
Old Royal Mint
St George-in-the-East
St Paul
Shadwell Basin
Tobacco Dock
St Katharine Dock
DOCKLANDS
Old Pumping Station
Tower Bridge
WAPPING
Wapping
Design Museum
River Police Boat Yard
Wapping Pier
Bramah Museum of Tea and Coffee
Rotherhithe
ROTHERHITHE
Culling Circus
Canada Water
Bermondsey
SOUTHWARK
PARK
Surrey Commercial Docks
Surrey Quays
South Bermondsey
Hackney Rd
Bishop's Way
Grand Union
Old Ford Rd
Roman Rd
Grove Rd
Canal
Globe Rd
Cambridge Heath Road
Bethnal Green Rd
Vallance Rd
High St.
Brick Lane
Mile End Road
Stepney Green
Ben Jonson Rd
White Horse Rd
Whitechapel Rd
New Rd
Commercial Rd
Cannon St. Rd
Leman St.
Mansell St.
Minories
Cable St.
Royal Mint St.
The Highway
Rotherhithe Tunnel
Wapping High St.
Salter Rd
Brunel Rd
Druid St.
Jamaica Rd
Quays Rd
Surrey Lower Rd
Redriff Rd
Southwark Park Rd
Raymouth Rd
New Rd
Evelyn St.
Dunton Rd
Rotherhithe Rd
Road

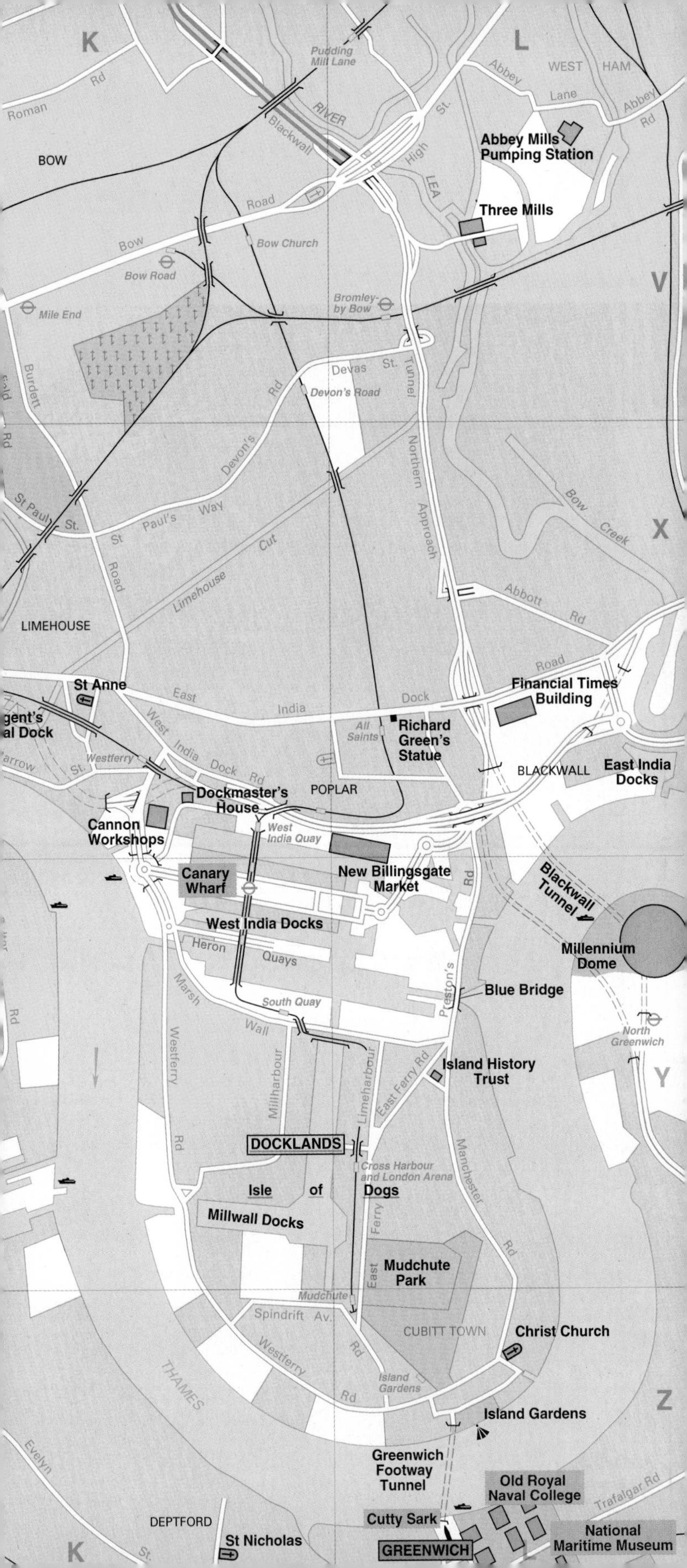

K
L
Pudding Mill Lane
WEST HAM
Abbey Lane
Abbey Rd
Roman Rd
RIVER
Blackwall
St.
High
BOW
Abbey Mills Pumping Station
LEA
Bow Road
Three Mills
Bow Church
Bow Road
V
Bromley-by Bow
Mile End
Devas St.
Tunnel
Burdett
Rd
Devon's Road
Northern Approach
Devon's
St Paul's Way
Bow Creek
X
St Paul St.
St Road
Limehouse Cut
Abbott Rd
LIMEHOUSE
Road
St Anne
East India Dock
Financial Times Building
Richard Green's Statue
All Saints
West India Dock Rd
Westferry
BLACKWALL
East India Docks
POPLAR
Dockmaster's House
Cannon Workshops
West India Quay
New Billingsgate Market
Canary Wharf
Rd
Blackwall Tunnel
West India Docks
Millennium Dome
Heron Quays
Marsh Wall
Blue Bridge
South Quay
Preston's
North Greenwich
Westferry Rd
Millharbour
Limeharbour
East Ferry Rd
Island History Trust
Y
DOCKLANDS
Cross Harbour and London Arena
Manchester Rd
Isle of Dogs
Millwall Docks
Ferry
East
Mudchute Park
Mudchute
Spindrift Av.
CUBITT TOWN
Christ Church
Westferry Rd
THAMES
Island Gardens
Z
Island Gardens
Evelyn
Greenwich Footway Tunnel
Old Royal Naval College
Trafalgar Rd
Cutty Sark
DEPTFORD
National Maritime Museum
St Nicholas
GREENWICH
K
St.

A traditional pub

Practical Points

Planning your Trip

Useful Addresses

The Internet is a useful source of information to enable you to make the most of your visit. You can contact Tourist Information Centres, consult programmes and brochures and make bookings on line.

Internet

London offers all kinds of entertainment and the following websites will put you in the mood and help you devise your programme:
For a visual aid to certain areas of the city: www.net-cities.com/virtual
Browse through the most popular London newspaper, the *Evening Standard*, for the latest news on the capital: www.thisislondon.com
Consult this site for up-to-date information on events in the capital: www.timeout.com
Comprehensive information on sightseeing, entertainment, services, shopping and many other topics is available on www.londontown.com
The complete guide to London's vibrant fringe arts and entertainment scene: www.theguide.net
London has a range of attractions and entertainment with free access: www.londonfreelist.com
This radio station is dedicated to London and broadcasts all the latest news and happenings in town: www.bbc.co.uk/londonlive

Tourist information centres abroad

The **British Tourist Authority (BTA)** provides assistance in planning a trip to London and an excellent range of brochures and maps. The addresses and telephone numbers of local Tourist Information Centres are given in the relevant chapters.

Australia: www.visitbritain.com/au Level 2, 15 Blue Street, North **Sydney**, NSW 2060. ☎ 2 9021 4400, 1200 85 85 89, Freephone 1300 858 589; Fax 2 9021 4499; visitbritainaus@bta.org.uk

Canada: www.visitbritain.com/ca 5915 Airport Road, Suite 120, Mississauga, **Toronto**, Ontario, L4V 1T1. ☎ 905 404 1720, Freephone 1888 VISIT UK; Fax 905 405 1835; britinfo@bta.org.uk

France: www.visitbritain.com/fr Maison de la Grande Bretagne, 22 avenue Franklin Roosevelt, 5th floor, F-75008 **Paris**. ☎ 01 58 36 50 50, 0825 83 82 81; Fax 01 58 36 50 51; Minitel: 3615 BRITISH; gbinfo@bta.org.uk

New Zealand: www.visitbritain.uk 17th floor, NZI House, 151 Queen Street, **Auckland 1**. ☎ 649 303 1 446; bta.nz@bta.org.uk

South Africa: www.visitbritain.com Lancaster Gate, Hyde Park Lane, Sandton 2196 (personal callers); PO Box 41896, Craighall 2024, **Johannesburg** (letters). ☎ (11) 325 0343; Fax (11) 325 0344; johannesburg@bta.org.uk

United States: www.travelbritain.org 625 North Michigan Avenue, Suite 1001, **Chicago**, Illinois 60611. ☎ 800 462 2748 (toll free); Fax 312 787 9641; travelinfo@bta.org.uk.
551 5th Avenue, Suite 701, **New York**, NY 10176-0799. ☎ 212 986 2266, 800 GO 2 BRITAIN (toll-free); travelinfo@bta.org.uk

Tourist Information Centres in London

The main information centres operated by the **London Tourist Board** are located as follows (others are listed under the chapter headings in the Selected Sights section):

Britain Visitor Centre – 1 Lower Regent Street, SW1Y 4NS. Open Mon-Fri, 9am-6.30pm, Sat-Sun, 10am-4pm; also Jul-Sep, Sat, 9am-5pm. ☎ 0906 866 3344 (info line 60p/min), 0870 240 4326 (London information pack); bvccustomerservices@bta.org.uk.

London Tourist Board – 1 Warwick Row, London SW1E 5ER: Written enquiries only or visit the website: www.visitlondon.com

City of London Information Centre – St Paul's Churchyard, EC4N 8BX. Open Easter-Sep, daily, 9.30am-5pm; Oct-Easter, Mon-Sat, 9.30am-5pm (12.30pm Sat). ☎ 020 7332 1456; Fax 020 7332 1457.

Victoria Station Forecourt – Open Mon-Sat, 8am-7pm (8pm May, 10pm Jun-Sep); Sun, 8am-6pm (7pm Jun-Sep).

Waterloo International Terminal Arrivals Hall – Open daily, 8.30am-10.30pm.

Telephone Guides - **London Line** is a recorded message service revised daily by the London Tourist Board *(60p per minute, plus any hotel/payphone surcharge)*.
Dial 09068 66 33 44 + 5 + one of the following numbers:
1 Changing of the Guard
2 Visitor Attractions
3 River Trips and Sightseeing
4 Accommodation
5 Theatres
6 Events
7 Children's London
8 Shopping and Eating out in London
9 Gay and Lesbian London

Kidsline answers individual queries about activities for children ☎ 020 7222 8070 *(During school holidays and half-term holidays: Mon-Fri 9am-4pm; otherwise Mon-Fri 4-6pm)*.

A **Weather Forecast** for Greater London is provided by **Weathercall** in association with the Meteorological Office on ☎ 09068 232 771.

Embassies and Consulates in London

Australian High Commission: Australia House, Strand, WC2B 4LA. ☎ 020 7379 4334; Fax 020 7240 5333; www.australia.org.uk

Canadian High Commission: Macdonald House, 1 Grosvenor Square, W1K 4AB. ☎ 020 7258 6600; Fax 020 7258 6333; ldn@dfait-maeci.gc.Ca; www.dfait-maeci.gc.ca/london/

Republic of Ireland: Embassy of Ireland, 17 Grosvenor Place, SW1X 7HR. ☎ 020 7245 2171; Fax 020 7245 6961; info@iveagh.irlgov.ie; www.irlgov.ie

New Zealand High Commission: 80 Haymarket SW1Y 4TQ. ☎ 020 7930 8422; Fax 020 7839 4580; email@newzealandhc.org.uk; www.nzhc.org.uk

South African High Commission: South Africa House, Trafalgar Square, WC2N 5DP. ☎ 020 7451 7299.

United States Embassy: 24-31 Grosvenor Square, W1A 1AE. ☎ 020 7499 9000; Passport affairs ☎ 020 7491 3506; www.usembassy.org.uk

Formalities

Documents

Passports – Despite the law, which came into force on 1 January 1993, authorising the free flow of goods and people within the European Union, it is nonetheless advisable for EU nationals to hold some means of identification, such as a **passport**. Non-EU nationals must be in possession of a valid national passport. Loss or theft should be reported to the appropriate embassy or consulate and to the local police.

Visas – A **visa** to visit the United Kingdom is not required by nationals of the member states of the European Union and of the Commonwealth (including Australia, Canada, New Zealand, and South Africa) and the USA. Nationals of other countries should check with the British Embassy and apply for a visa if necessary in good time.

Entry visas are required by Australian, New Zealand, Canadian and US nationals (for a stay exceeding three months).

Useful information for US nationals on obtaining a passport, visa requirements, customs regulations, medical care etc for international travel, is contained in the brochure *Safe Trip Abroad* (US$1.25), published by the government printing office; it can be ordered by telephone ☎ 1-202-512-1800 and ordered or consulted via the Internet on website www.access.gpo.gov.

American nationals may apply to National Passport Information Center 1 900 225 5674 http://travel.state.gov (download passport application).

Driving Licence – Nationals of EU countries require a valid **national driving licence**; nationals of non-EU countries require an international driving licence (obtainable in the USA from the American Automobile Association).

A US driving licence valid for 12 months; a permit (US$10) is available from the local branch of the American Automobile Association or from the National Auto Club, Touring Department, 188 The Embarcardero, Suite 300, San Francisco CA 94105.

For the vehicle it is necessary to have the **registration papers** (log-book) and a **nationality plate** of the approved size.

Vehicle Insurance – Insurance cover is compulsory; the **International Insurance Certificate** (Green Card), although no longer a legal requirement, is the most effective proof of insurance cover and is internationally recognised by the police and other authorities. Certain UK motoring organisations *(see below)* run accident insurance and breakdown service schemes for members. Europ-Assistance has special schemes for members. The American Automobile Association publishes a free brochure *Offices to Serve You Abroad* for its members.

Health

Visitors to Britain are entitled to treatment at the Accident and Emergency Departments of National Health Service hospitals. For an overnight or longer stay in hospital payment will probably be required. It is therefore advisable to take out adequate insurance cover before leaving home.

Visitors from EU countries should apply to their own National Social Security Offices for Form E111 which entitles them to medical treatment under an EU Reciprocal Medical Treatment arrangement.

It is important to take out medical insurance prior to departure as treatment in Great Britain may be extremely expensive.

Nationals of non-EU countries should take out comprehensive insurance. American Express offers a service, "Global Assist", for any medical, legal or personal emergency – call collect from anywhere ☎ 202 554 2639.

In case of an emergency, dial the free nationwide emergency number (999) and ask for Fire, Police or Ambulance.

To contact a doctor for **first aid, emergency medical advice** and **chemist's night service:** Doctor Call Out ☎ 07000 37 22 55 or Medicentre ☎ 0870 600 0870. Do not hesitate to ask for a photocopy of any prescription. This may be important if follow-on treatment is required back home.

Domestic animals

Domestic animals (dogs, cats) with vaccination documents are allowed into the country.

Customs regulations

Tax free allowances for various commodities are governed by EU legislation except in the Channel Islands and the Isle of Man which have different regulations. Details of these allowances and restrictions are available at most ports of entry to Great Britain.
The UK Customs Office produces a leaflet on customs regulations and the full range of "duty free" allowances;
In the United Kingdom a sales tax of 17.5 % (Value Added Tax) is added to almost all retail goods. Non-EU nationals may reclaim this tax from accumulated purchases when leaving the country; paperwork should be completed by the retailer at the time of purchase.
It is against the law to bring into the United Kingdom any drugs, firearms and ammunition, obscene material featuring children, counterfeit merchandise, unlicensed livestock (birds or animals), anything related to endangered species (furs, ivory, horn, leather) and certain plants (potatoes, bulbs, seeds, trees). It is also an offence to import duty-paid goods (to a maximum value of £145) from the EU other than for personal use.
HM Customs and Excise – www.hmce.gov.uk
London Contact Centre, Thomas Paine House, Angel Square, Torrance Street, London EC1V 1TA ☎ 0845 010 9000 (National Advice Helpline); 020 7620 1313 (HQ); 020 7928 3344 (switchboard); enquiries.lon@hmce.gsi.gov.uk.
A booklet *Know before you go* is published by the US Customs Service; its offices are listed in the phone book in the Federal Government section under the US Department of the Treasury or can be obtained by consulting website www.customs.ustreas.gov

Seasons

Climate

There is no season of the year when the weather is too inclement to permit visitors to enjoy the sights but the changeable British climate lives up to its reputation. In spring as the days grow longer and warmer, the light is glorious but showers are frequent. Summer is unpredictable with moderate temperatures and the fine weather may be late; in July and August there are occasional heat waves when the thermometer tops 30°C or the days may be cloudy and cool. Autumn can start dry and sunny with clear skies and beautiful sunsets; the air is crisp and invigorating. But as the days grow shorter the temperature may reach between 10-15°C. In winter it can remain fairly mild until Christmas; there may be cold snaps but the temperature rarely drops below freezing point; wind and dampness can make it feel very cold; it rarely snows in London.

Best time

London is a favourite destination as part of a tour of Britain or for short breaks throughout the year. Most sights are open, some with reduced opening times, in winter. The busiest periods are from Easter to September and when other European countries enjoy a public holiday. Young people often come for the weekend to enjoy the shopping, pubs, music venues and club scene.
Spring and autumn are the best seasons for visiting parks and gardens when the flowers are in bloom or the leaves are turning colour.
The summer season is marked by traditional events: the Grand National, Ascot Week, Henley Royal Regatta, Trooping the Colour and Royal Garden Parties.
Autumn and winter are the best time for visiting museums or for shopping as places are less crowded, except in the weeks before Christmas.
At Christmas baubles flash in the windows of Selfridges, Hamley's Toy Shop, Harrods and Harvey Nichols while the streets ring with the sound of carol singers and their charity collection boxes.
In addition to the usual school holidays in the spring and summer and at Christmas, there are mid-term breaks in February, May and October.

Public holidays

The following days are statutory or discretionary holidays, when banks, museums and other monuments may be closed or may vary their times of admission. It is also advisable to check boat, bus and railway timetables for changes in services. Most tourist sights are open on these days. Whitsun is seven weeks after Easter.

1 January .... New Year's Day
Friday before Easter Day.......... Good Friday
Monday after Easter Day .... Easter Monday
First Monday in May.... May Day Bank Holiday

Last Monday in May	Spring Bank Holiday
Last Monday in August	August Bank Holiday
25 December	Christmas Day
26 December	Boxing Day

TIME DIFFERENCE

In winter **standard time** throughout the British Isles is Greenwich Mean Time (GMT). In summer clocks are advanced by an hour to give **British Summer Time** (BST). The actual dates are announced annually but always occur at the weekend in March and October.
Time may be expressed according to the 24-hour clock or the 12-hour clock.

12.00	noon	19.00	7pm
13.00	1pm	20.00	8pm
14.00	2pm	21.00	9pm
15.00	3pm	22.00	10pm
16.00	4pm	23.00	11pm
17.00	5pm	24.00	midnight
18.00	6pm		

WHAT TO TAKE

At any time of year the wise traveller should carry light protection against rain (umbrella or hooded coat) in view of the fickle weather.
In summer it can be cool in the evening and it is advisable to bring some warmer clothes. Some visitors may find a hat useful as the sun can be quite hot. As the best way to visit London is on foot it is essential to wear comfortable shoes for sightseeing.

Budget

Compared to the rest of the country and other European cities London is acknowledged as being a very expensive city, in particular owing to the high cost of accommodation and transport.
For suggestions on ways of keeping the costs down refer to the chapter **Concessions**: transport and sightseeing passes, special deals on cinema and theatre tickets.
If you are on a tight budget it is possible to manage on a daily allowance of £120 by staying in a guest house in the "Budget" category (see **Where to Stay** section which also lists youth hostels, bed and breakfast agencies, university residences and camping sites for cheaper accommodation; this would bring the costs down to around £90); having a sandwich in a café or a light lunch in a pub (about £5) and eating in a pizzeria, tapas or noodle bar (£6-£10), a wine bar or a brasserie in the evening (£15).
The "Moderate" category is for those on an average budget. Allow £150-£200 daily including a room in a comfortable hotel, lunch in a pizzeria, wine bar or brasserie (£12-£15) and dinner in a medium-priced restaurant (£25).
If you choose to spend more (over £250 daily) you can select a hotel from the "Expensive" category (over £150) and enjoy gourmet restaurants.
Add £25 to these allowances to cover transport costs and admission charges.

Special Needs

Many of the sights described in this guide are accessible to disabled people. Sights marked with the symbols ♿ or (♿) have full or partial access for wheelchairs.
The *Michelin Red Guide Great Britain and Ireland* indicates hotels with facilities suitable for disabled people; it is advisable to book in advance.
Booklets for the disabled are published by organisations such as the British Tourist Authority, National Trust and the Department of Transport.
Many ticket offices, banks and other venues are fitted with hearing loops to assist those with a hearing impediment.
The Royal Association for Disability and Rehabilitation (RADAR) publishes an annual guide with detailed information on hotels and holiday centres as well as sections on transport, accommodation for children and activity holidays.
RADAR – www.radar.org.uk
12 City Forum, 250 City Road, London ECIV 8AF, ☎ 020 7250 3222;
Fax 020 7250 0212;
minicom 020 7250 4119;
radar@radar.org.uk
Artsline provides a disability access information service and publishes *Access in London* and other information on cinema, theatre and gallery access
Artsline – www.artsline.org.uk
54 Chalton Street, London NW1 1HS;
☎ 020 7388 2227; Fax 020 7383 2653;
minicom 020 7388 2227;
access@artsline.org.uk

TRANSPORT

Transport for London publishes information on low floor and wheel chair accessible bus routes and underground stations in London.
Access and Mobility, Transport for London, Windsor House, 42-50 Victoria Street, London SW1H 0TL.
☎ 020 7941 4600; Fax 020 7941 4605;
access&mobility@tfl.gov.uk;
www.transportforlondon.gov.uk
A Disabled Person's Railcard (£14) giving discounts on fares to the traveller and to a companion is available to UK residents who meet certain criteria.
Application form from rail stations or from:
Disabled Persons Railcard Office – www.disabledpersons-railcard.co.uk
P O Box 1YT, Newcastle upon Tyne NE99 1YT; ☎ 0191 269 0303 ;
0191 269 0304 (textphone)

Transport

Airlines and rail companies offer special rates outlined in **Concessions** *(p 42)*.

Getting there

By air

The various national and other independent airlines operate services to the five airports serving London – Heathrow, Gatwick, Luton, Stansted and London City.

Information, brochures and timetables are available from the airlines and from travel agents.

Enquiries on how to get to the airport may be directed through the London Tourist Board London Line service ☎ 09068 66 33 44; www.visitlondon.com

London Heathrow – Heathrow handles all major airline scheduled flights. It is situated 20 miles west of London off the A4 / M4 and equipped with short and long-term car parks at the airport.

Terminal 1	All domestic flights, European and long haul destinations
Terminal 2	Mainly European destination flights
Terminals 3 & 4	long-haul flights to America, Australia, New Zealand and the Far East

Airport Information – ☎ 08700 000 123

Heathrow – London

Tube / Underground services to Central London are provided by the Piccadilly Line between 5am and 12midnight *(see Underground map inside back cover)*. Average journey time from Heathrow to Piccadilly Circus: 50 minutes. Cost: £3.70 (single), £7.40 (return). At night the N87 bus shuttles between Heathrow and Trafalgar Square every 30min. London Transport Information ☎ 020 7222 1234.

The **Heathrow Express** (25min) provides a fast alternative rail link into Paddington Station. Express class £13 (single), £25 (return), First class £21, free for under-16s. www.heathrowexpress.co.uk; ☎ 0845 600 1515.

Airbus A2 services run every 20-30min to and from Heathrow Air Terminals and King's Cross via Holland Park, Notting Hill Gate, Bayswater Road, Lancaster Gate, Marble Arch, Baker Street, Great Portland Street, Euston Station, Russell Square. From Heathrow: 5.30-5.45am to 9.45-10.08pm; from King's Cross: 4am to 8pm. Tickets are purchased from the driver, the Tourist Information Centre at Victoria, Transport for London Information Centres and many hotels. ☎ 08705 747 777; www.nationalexpress.co.uk Approximate journey time 60/75 minutes. Cost £7 (single), £10 (return).

National Express also operate a coach service to and from Heathrow and London Victoria Coach Station every 30 minutes from 5.30am to 8.50pm. Approximate journey time: 60/75 minutes. Cost £7 (single), £10 (return).

Taxis are subject to road traffic conditions (40min on a good day to Marble Arch but it is best to allow an hour) at an approximate cost of £60. There are taxi desks and taxi ranks at all terminals. Services may be booked in advance on ☎ 020 8745 5325 (Black Taxis); 020 7286 0286 (Computer Cabs).

London Gatwick – 30 miles to the south down the M25/M23 (short and long-term car parks at the airport). Two, 'North' and 'South', terminals handle flights to destinations worldwide, charters and short-haul flights to the Channel Islands.

For general and flight enquiries ☎ 0870 000 2468

Gatwick – London

The Rail link **Gatwick Express** shuttles to and from Victoria Station (30min; 35min at night and on Sun). Departures every 15 minutes from 5am and hourly after midnight. Cost £11 (single), £21.50 (return). ☎ 0845 850 1530. www.gatwickexpress.co.uk

Frequent services are also offered to The City with Thameslink and Olympia with Connex. Gatwick Railway Station has more than 900 services daily to all parts of the UK. ☎ 08457 48 49 50 (enquiries); further information: www.baa.co.uk

Taxi services are provided by the airport's official concessionaire, Checker Cars in North and South Terminals. There is a quoted fare system and the cost of the journey is made known to customers in advance. Taxis can be pre-booked, and all fares can be paid in advance by cash or credit card or at the end of the journey by cash only: Checker Cars South Terminal ☎ 01293 502 808

Taxis are subject to traffic conditions. Allow 90min journey at an approximate cost of £80.

Airbus A5 and National Express Speedlink – www.nationalexpress.co.uk/

Buses operate daily between 4.15am and 9.15pm from Gatwick North and South Terminals to Victoria (90min) via Streatham High Road and Clapham Rd, Stockwell; and between 6am and 11pm

from London Victoria Coach Station to Gatwick North and South Terminals. £7 (single), £10 (return); concessions and discounts available.
☎ 08705 808 080 or 08705 747 777 (National Express/Flightline services)

City Airport (Docklands) – 2 miles from Canary Wharf; 6 miles from Bank of England; 8 miles from the West End. Services from European business centre destinations. 10min check-in time.
☎ 020 7646 0000; 020 7646 0088 (**general airport enquiries**); info@londoncityairport.com; www.londoncityairport.com

City Airport – London
Courtesy airport bus to Canning Town/or Canary Wharf (10min, Yellow Route) for transfer onto the DLR, and to Liverpool Street station (25min, Red Route) for services on the underground and mainline railway services to Cambridge. Reduced services at weekends. ☎ 020 7646 0000

Luton Airport – Located in Bedfordshire. ☎ (Luton) 01582 405 100; Fax 01582 395 313; info@london-luton.com; www.london-luton.com

Access – Thameslink trains or **Midland mainline** from St Pancras or King's Cross *(35min)* and airport bus *(5min)* or **Green Line bus 757** from Victoria Coach Station.

Stansted Airport – Located in Essex. ☎ (Bishop's Stortford) 08700 000 303
Access – Stansted Express from Liverpool Street Station to Stansted Airport (50min – ☎ 08457 818 919) and bus; www.baa.co.uk or **Airbus A6** to and from Victoria (100min – ☎ 08705 747 777).

Parking – There are short and long-term car parks at all airports with free shuttle buses to the terminals at regular intervals.

By Sea

There are numerous cross-Channel (passenger and car ferries, hovercraft) and other ferry or shipping services from the continent. For details apply to travel agencies or to the ferry companies.

Brittany Ferries – www.brittany-ferries.com
The Brittany Centre, Wharf Road, Portsmouth, Hants PO2 8RU.
☎ 08705 360 360 (from within the UK); Fax 08709 011 400;
Millbay Docks, Plymouth, Devon. PL1 3EW ☎ 08705 360 360

Hoverspeed – info@hoverspeed.co.uk; www.hoverspeed.co.uk
International Hoverport, Marine Parade, Dover, Kent CT17 9TG.
☎ 08705 240 241; Fax 01304 240 088

Irish Ferries – info@irishferries.com; www.irishferries.com
2-4 Merrion Row, Dublin 2.
☎ 0990 17 00 00; 08705 17 17 17; 01 638 3333 (reservations)
Corn Exchange Building, Fenwick Street, Liverpool L2 7TQ and Reliance House, Water St, Liverpool L2 8TP.
☎ 08705 17 17 17
Ferryport, Alexandra Road, Dublin 1;
☎ 00 353 1 661 0511;

P & O Ferries – www.poferries.com
Channel House, Channel View Road, Dover, Kent CT17 9TJ. ☎ 08705 202 020 (reservations); 08706 000 611 (information line); customer.services@Poferries.com

By Rail

A. Taverner/MICHELIN

Passengers milling about in Paddington Station

London has 13 main-line termini connected by the underground and in some cases by special inter-station single-decker buses. Tickets and information are available from the termini.
Information on fares and timetables, on special deals for unlimited travel or group travel in Europe, on rail services and on other concessionary tickets, including combined train and bus tickets, is available from National Rail Enquiries. *See also Concessions p 42.*
National Rail Enquiries – www.railtrack.co.uk; www.nationalrail.co.uk
Booking of train and other travel tickets including timetable information – www.totaljourney.com
☎ 08457 48 49 50 (National Rail Enquiries); 08457 11 41 41 (Network Rail)

Charing Cross – Connex and **South Central Trains** services to south-east England.

London Bridge – Connex, South Central Trains and **Thameslink** services to south central and south-east England.

Cannon Street – Connex services to south-east England.

Blackfriars – Connex, South Central Trains and **Thamselink** services to south central and south east England.

Fenchurch Street – c2c local commuter services to south Essex (Basildon, Southend).

Euston – Silverlink – local commuter services to the north of London including Watford, Hemel Hempstead, Northampton;

Virgin Trains – intercity services to the west Midlands; north Wales; northwest England; Scotland via the west coast; Northern Ireland; Republic of Ireland.

King's Cross – GNER – intercity services to east and north-east England; Scotland via the east coast. **West Anglia Great Northern** and **Thameslink** provide local commuter services to the north of London including St Albans, Bedford, Stevenage.

Liverpool Street – West Anglia Great Northern, Great Eastern and **Anglia Railways** operate local and intercity services to: Essex, East Anglia.

Marylebone – Chiltern Lines to Birmingham.

Paddington – First Great Western – intercity services to the west of England and south Wales. **Thames Trains** – local commuter services to the west of London including Maidenhead, Reading and the Thames Valley.

Heathrow Express – 15 minute service every 15 minutes to Heathrow Airport.

St Pancras – Midland Mainline intercity services to the Midlands including Luton, Bedford, Leicester and Sheffield.

Victoria – SouthCentral Trains, Gatwick Express and **Connex** services to Gatwick Airport and central southern England. The Orient Express also operates out of Victoria. ☎ 0207 834 2345.

London Tourist Board – *Victoria Station Forecourt. Open Mon-Sat, 8am-7pm (8pm May, 10pm Jun-Sept); Sun 8am-6pm (7pm Jun-Sept).*

Waterloo – South West Train – services to south western England and Windsor. ☎ 0207 928 5151.

Eurostar runs regular services to London (Waterloo International Station) from Paris (Gare du Nord ☎ 015 12 21 22; Minitel 3615 / 3616 SNCF) and Brussels (☎ 02 224 58 90).
EUROSTAR – www.eurostar.com ☎ 08705 186 186 (bookings); 0207 928 0660 (Special Services Unit)
Eurostar Enquiries, Customer Relations, Eurostar House, Waterloo Station. London SE1 8SE
Eurotunnel Customer Service – www.eurotunnel.com
St Martin's Lane, Cheriton, Folkestone CT19 4QD; ☎ 08705 353 535;
Fax 01303 288 784; 08000 969 992 (free 24hr information service).
Rail Passes – Check eligibility for the Network Card, Family, Young Persons (16-25 yrs), Senior Railcard (over 60s) and Disabled Persons schemes. **Note**: It is important for disabled travellers to check procedures and facilities before undertaking their journey ☎ 020 7918 3015.

By coach/bus

Express coach services covering all parts of the British Isles are operated by National Express in association with other bus operators. Details about international coach services to Great Britain are available from Eurolines. Most depart from Victoria Coach Station *(see Inner London Map page 7 DY)* (Gate 10) in Buckingham Palace Road (next to Victoria Railway Station) or from Marble Arch.
Special season ticket rates such as the National Express Familysaver coach cards and Tourist Trail passes, are available.

National Express –
www.nationalexpress.com
1 Hagley Road, Edgbaston, Birmingham B16 8TG ☎ 08705 808 080 (national call centre); ☎ 0121 625 1122;
Fax 0121 456 1397 (Head Office)

Eurolines –
welcome@eurolinesuk.com;
www.eurolines.co.uk
4 Cardiff Road, Luton, L41 1PP
☎ 0990 143 219; Fax 01582 400 694

City Link Oxford ☎ 01865 785 400;
Fax 01865 711 745;
info@oxfordbus.co.uk;
www.oxfordbus.co.uk

Greenline Coaches
☎ 0870 608 7261; Fax 0870 608 2608;
enquiries@greenline.co.uk;
www.greenline.co.uk

By car

The Michelin companion maps and plans for this guide are listed after the main contents page at the beginning of the guide. For useful information on essential documents see p 15, on Motoring see p 23. Most visitors travelling to London by car enter the country through the Channel ports (Dover, Folkestone, Newhaven, Portsmouth, Bournemouth, Weymouth and Plymouth), through the Welsh ports (Port Talbot, Pembroke Dock, Fishguard, Holyhead) or by the east coast ports (Harwich, Hull, Newcastle upon Tyne).
The main access roads to London are: from Dover and Folkestone M 20; from Newhaven M 23; from Portsmouth A 3; from Bournemouth A 31, M 3; from Weymouth A 35, A 31, M 3; from Plymouth A 38, A 30, A 303, M 3; from Plymouth A 38, A 30, A 303, M 3;
from Port Talbot M 4; from Pembroke Dock A 47, A 48, M 4; from Fishguard A 40, A 48, M 4; from Holyhead A 55, A 51, A 500, M 6, M 1;
from Harwich A 120, A 12; from Hull A 63, M 62, M 18, M 1; from Newcastle upon Tyne A 1, M 1.

Getting about

The following information lines are operated by London Tourist Board and Transport for London:
London Travel Check ☎ 020 7222 1200
London Travel Information ☎ 020 7222 1234; Minicom for deaf callers ☎ 020 7918 3015.

By bus and By underground/ tube train

London is a sprawling city but it has a comprehensive transport network which makes it easy to get around. It is better to travel outside the morning and evening rush hours *(Mon-Fri, 8am-9.30am and 5pm-6pm)* when busy Londoners travel to and from work. A full review is underway to improve public transport. The underground network has been extended to the east and south-east with eleven ultra-modern stations on the Jubilee Line (the designs have won wide acclaim), bus lanes have been introduced to reduce journey times and the Docklands Light Railway is a quick and comfortable way to travel to the east of the city and south of the river.

Transport for London – Customer Services – Windsor House, 42-50 Victoria Street, London SW1H 0BD. ☎ 020 7222 1234 (travel information); 020 7918 4300 (London bus information); 020 7649 9123 (textphone/minicom); Fax 020 7918 3134; enquiries@tfl.gov.uk; www.transportforlondon.gov.uk; www.journeyplanner.org

Buses – Bus-routes are displayed in bus shelters as well as inside the buses themselves; note that most bus-stop signs will bear the name of the stop, but if in doubt ask a passenger or the conductor. Reduced services on some routes operate through the night – special rates may apply.
White signs with the red logo indicate bus stops at which all listed buses must stop; red signs with the white logo are request stops at which passengers must wave to the bus to indicate that it should stop to pick up passengers. Night buses (prefixed with"N" or on a blue tile located on the bus stop) stop only if requested.
A simpler ticketing policy has been adopted: £2.50 one-day London-wide bus pass; £4.20 saver carnet of 6 tickets; £9.50 all zones 7 day pass. Children under the age of 11 years travel free on buses. In central London you must buy a ticket before you board. There are ticket machines at every bus stop within the pre-pay area.

London Buses – Further to the deregulation of the London Transport bus operator system and terrorist bomb in the City of London, bus routes have been subjected to change. With 17 000 vehicles on the road, however, buses provide an economical means of exploring the capital and admiring garden layouts and details of buildings above street level.
Classic routes include numbers **11** (King's Road, Palace of Westminster, Whitehall, Trafalgar Square, Fleet Street, St Paul's, Mansion House) and **15** (Paddington, Marble Arch, Oxford Street, Regent Street, Trafalgar Square, Strand, Fleet Street, St Paul's, Monument, Tower of London, Whitechapel).
Numbers **9** and **10** from Hammersmith go through Kensington and Knightsbridge to Hyde Park Corner; No 9 then runs to Piccadilly Circus and Trafalgar Square to the Strand and the Aldwych (for Covent Garden); No 10 continues along Park Lane to Marble Arch, Oxford St, Tottenham Court Rd to Euston and King's Cross.
No **8**, which starts in Victoria, travels along Park Lane to Marble Arch, Oxford St, past Bond St to Oxford Circus, Holborn and the City taking in Old Bailey, Guildhall, Liverpool St and Spitalfields to east London.
No **24** goes from Victoria to Hampstead via Westminster, Whitehall, Trafalgar Square, Leicester Square, along Charing Cross Rd, Tottenham Court Rd (for Bloomsbury) and through Camden to Hampstead Heath.
No **19** travels through Islington, Clerkenwell, Holborn and Bloomsbury, then along New Oxford St, Charing Cross Rd, Shaftesbury Ave and Piccadilly past Green Park and Hyde Park Corner, along Knightsbridge, Sloane St to King's Rd and then to Battersea.

R. Besse/MICHELIN

Doubledecker buses in Oxford Street

Underground – The London Underground network is divided into 6 zones with Zone 1 covering central London.
Single or return tickets can be purchased only at underground stations. They must be retained after passing through the electronic barrier as they are required to pass through a second barrier at the end of the

journey. Inspectors may also do spot checks so do not destroy or deface them. Single zone ticket extensions must be purchased before you travel. To calculate an estimated journey time, count three minutes between stations and an average of fifteen minutes to change lines. Trains run from Central London until 0.50am Mon-Fri and until midnight on Sun.

The Underground Map is located after the Index.

Docklands Light Railway (DLR) – The Docklands Light Railway consists of 5 lines: **line A** runs from Beckton; **line B** from Lewisham; **line C** from Stratford; **line D** from Tower Gateway; **line E** from Bank. Services are reduced at weekends.

Docklands Light Railway – www.dlr.co.uk
Castor Lane, Poplar, London E14 0DS
☎ 020 7918 4000 (Docklands Travel Hotline); Fax 020 7363 9532; cservice@dlr.co.uk

Ticket Purchase – Zoned tube tickets are sold singly at tube stations. Books of ten Underground tickets (carnet) valid for travel within Zone 1 may be purchased for £15 from Underground stations, TIC etc; they are also valid on the DLR but are not valid on buses or overground services (National Rail). All children under the age of 5 years travel free on the Underground, only two accompanied by an adult on the buses may travel free of charge. Passengers must have a valid ticket for their complete journey or they may be liable to pay on-the-spot penalties (£5 buses, £10 underground).

Travelcards – Multi-journey zoned passes are more economical for a stay in the capital valid for **One Day** or a 'season' (two-day **Weekend**, 7-day **Weekly**, 1 month, more than a month or 1 year).
A **Photocard** is required by adults and children using a Weekly Travelcard. It is also required by 14 and 15 year old children as a qualifier for the under 16 child fare One Day Travelcard and by youths applying for the 16-17 and student cards.
Family Travelcards are available for a group comprising two adults and one to four children for travel after 9.30am, Mon-Fri; all day, Sat-Sun and public holidays. Prices vary according to the number of zones covered by the ticket. These are available from Underground stations, National Rail stations and appointed newsagents.
One Day Travelcards may be used Mon-Fri from 9.30am to 4.30am (the following day), Sat-Sun and public holidays from any hour for travel on the Underground, Docklands Light Railway, National Rail overground trains and most London bus services (except night services), nearly everywhere within the designated 6 London zones. Adult £4.20 for zones 1 and 2, £5.30 for zones 1 to 6.
The **LT Card**, also valid for one day, is for use on the Underground, DLR and buses (no overground train services) only within the specified 6 London zones and not subject to any restriction during the morning rush-hour. Adult £5.30 for zones 1 and 2, £11 for zones 1 to 6.

By taxi

The traditional London cab is available at railway termini, Heathrow airport, taxi ranks and cruising the streets. An orange roof-light is displayed when the taxi is free to be hailed. They can usually be found in the vicinity of the green refuges – in Sloane Street, Pembridge Road, Bedford Square – which are run by a special charity catering exclusively to cab drivers.

Fares – Minimum charge £1.80. Special fares operate after midnight, at weekends and on public holidays. Gratuities are discretionary but 10% is usual.
Journeys beyond the limits of the Metropolitan Police District (MPD – an area broadly corresponding to but slightly less extensive than Greater London) are subject to negotiation. Taxis are not obliged to go outside the MPD nor more than 6 miles from the pick-up point within the MPD.
Enquiries may be directed to the Public Carriage Office, 15 Penton St, London N1 9PU. ☎ 020 7941 7800 – enquiries and complaints *(Mon-Fri, 9am-4pm)*; pco.tfl@gtnet.gov.uk; www.transportforlondon.gov.uk.

Unlicensed Taxis – Mini-cabs or other unlicensed car-services are not subject to the same stringent standards enforced on the distinctive London cabs; they will usually be open to negotiation about the price of long distance journeys but are to be used at the passenger's discretion.

Useful Numbers
Radio Taxis 020 7272 0272
Dial-A-Cab 020 7253 5000
Computer Cab 020 7286 0286

A black London cab

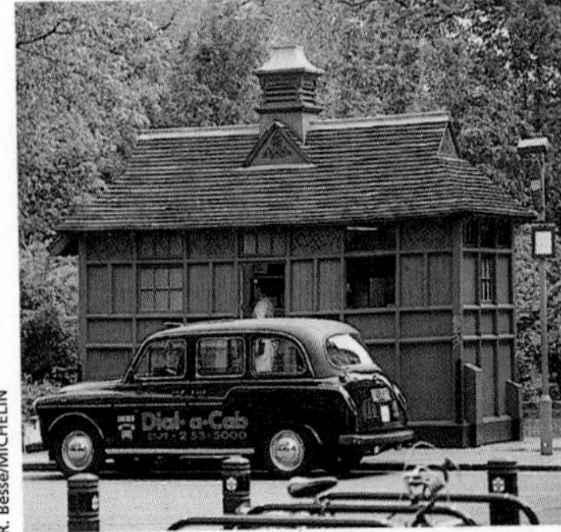

R. Besse/MICHELIN

By Boat

A novel way of getting about London is by river. To encourage Londoners to make more use of the river new piers have been built and regular commuter services have been introduced with hop-on hop-off fares and valid all-day tickets; travel card holders are entitled to a 33% discount off river service fares.

Ph. Gajic/MICHELIN

Commuting by boat

Transport for London publishes The **River Thames Boat Service Guide** booklet with timetables and fares. Some companies operate only weekdays and in summer, others all week and year round:

Chelsea Harbour, Cadogan Pier, Embankment. *Mon-Fri only (except public hols); £4 (single), £8 (round trip).* Riverside Launches ☎ 020 7352 5888

Savoy Pier, Blackfriars, Bankside, London Bridge City, St Katharine Dock, Canary Wharf, Greenland Pier, Masthouse Terrace: *Mon-Fri only (except public hols); £1.80-£3 (single), £2.40-£5 (round trip).* Thames Clippers ☎ 020 7977 6892; www.thamesclippers.com

Westminster to St Katharine Dock Hop-on Hop-off circular service: *daily; £3 one stop, £5.10 (single), £6.30 (round trip).* Crown River Cruises, ☎ 020 7936 2033

For leisure or luncheon/dinner cruises see Other Ways of Exploring London, By River Boat *(see p 53)*.

By bicycle

The London cycle network is well established in some parts of the city although cyclists may be deterred by the dense traffic in the city centre. A safety helmet and face mask are essential equipment; cyclists should exercise caution at all times and refrain from riding on the pavement. Bikes may be taken on the underground and on certain train lines: enquiries ☎ 0845 748 4950

On your Bike and *The Cyclists' Route Map* (£4.95 for both) are essential publications which include cycle routes and information on maintenance and security by The London Cycling Campaign, Unit 228, 30 Guildford St, SE1 0HS. ☎ 020 7928 7220; www.lcc.org.uk

Rental £12 first day, £6 subsequent days, £36 first week and £30 subsequent weeks. £12 3hr-bike tour Sat-Sun, 2pm. London Bicycle Tour Company, 1a Gabriel's Wharf, 56 Upper Ground SE1 9PP. ☎ 020 7928 6838; www.londonbicycle.com

Lost property

Do not despair, precious possessions are sometimes handed in.

For property lost in the **street** enquire at the local police station.

For property left on an underground train, London Bus or licensed taxi cabs enquire in person at the Transport for London Lost Property Office, 200 Baker Street, NW1 5RZ *(Mon-Fri, 9.30am-4pm)*; enquiry forms also available from any TFL bus garage or station.

☎ 020 7486 2496 (recorded).

Fax 020 7918 1028. ; lpo@tfl.gov.uk ; www.thl.gov.uk ☎ 020 7918 2000 (licensed taxi cabs only).

For property left on mainline railway **trains** enquire at station of arrival.

Motoring

If you are arriving by car it is advisable to find a place to stay on the outskirts and travel to the city centre by public transport to enjoy your visit as London traffic is so dense and parking is very expensive. Traffic in and around towns is heavy during the rush-hour (morning and evening). It is also very heavy on major roads at the weekend in summer, particularly bank holiday weekends.

Never leave anything of value in an unattended vehicle at any time.

Congestion charge

A £5 daily charge is levied on any vehicle (except motor cycles and exempt vehicles) entering the central zone Mon-Fri, 7am-6.30pm. Payment can be made in advance or on the day - £5 surcharge between 10pm and midnight - by post, on the internet, by telephone, at retail outlets or at certain carparks. There is an £80 penalty for non-payment, reduced to £40 for payment within 14 days. ☎ 04845 900 1234; enquiries@cc.london.com; www.cclondon.com

Highway code

The **minimum driving age** is 17 years old. Traffic drives **on the left** and overtakes on the right. Headlights must be used at night even in built-up areas and at other times when visibility is poor. Important **traffic signs** are shown at the end of the **Michelin Red Guide Great Britain and Ireland**, and in general correspond to international norms.

Seat Belts – In Britain the compulsory wearing of **seat belts** includes rear seat passengers when rear belts are fitted and all children under 14.

Speed Limits – Maximum speeds are –

70mph/112kph	motorways or dual carriageways
60mph/96kph	other roads
30mph/48kph	in towns and cities.

Bus Lanes: blue road signs indicate the hours between which certain lanes are reserved for buses and taxis. Most will bear a symbol permitting use by cyclists.

Pedestrian Crossings – Give way to pedestrians on zebra crossings and when traffic lights flash amber.

PARKING

Off-street parking is indicated by blue signs with white lettering (Parking or P); payment is made on leaving or in advance for a certain period. There are also parking meters, disc systems and paying parking zones; in the last case tickets must be obtained from ticket machines (small change necessary) and displayed inside the windscreen.
The usual restrictions are as follows:

Double red line
no stopping at any time (freeway)

Double yellow line
no parking at any time

Single yellow line
no parking for set periods as indicated on panel

Dotted yellow line
parking limited to certain times only

White zigzag lines at a zebra crossing
no stopping or parking at any time

Resident parking: Different boroughs operate varying restrictions and since enforcement has been granted to independent operators ticketing, clamping and removal are common.
In Covent Garden, for example, parking on a yellow line is permitted in some areas after 6.30pm and after 8.30pm in others.
Arrangements providing additional space for special occasions are announced by the police in the press; information also from the London Tourist Board.

PENALTIES

There are severe penalties for driving after drinking more than the legal limit of alcohol.
Roadside cameras may catch vehicles exceeding the speed limit.
Illegal parking is liable to fines and also in certain cases to the vehicle being clamped or towed away. The costs involved in retrieving the vehicle are very high. If your car has been clamped you will be given a notice of the payment centre to contact either by phone or in person and it may take some time to remove the clamp. If your car has been towed away you should contact the nearest police station or call the Trace Service hotline ☎ 020 7747 4747

ROAD SIGNS

Road signs have different coloured backgrounds as follows –

Blue	motorways
Green	major roads
White	local destinations
Brown	tourist signs

NATIONAL(REGIONAL) IDENTIFICATION LETTERS

In 2001 a new system was introduced into the UK. From March of that year the number plates on new vehicles had to conform to a standard typeface and size and a British Standard (with GB and EU symbols as permitted options). From September new plates started with a two-letter area code, a two-number age code and a three-letter random element at the end.

ROAD TOLLS

Tolls are rare; they are levied only on certain road tunnels (Dartford, Tyne), on the most recent bridges (Severn, Humber and Skye) and a few minor country bridges.

PETROL / GAS

In many service stations dual-pumps are the rule with **unleaded pumps** being identified by green pump handles or a green stripe.
Leaded two-star petrol is no longer available in Britain, only unleaded two-star.

MAPS AND PLANS

The companion maps and plans to be used with this guide are listed after the Contents Page at the beginning of the guide.

MOTORING ORGANISATIONS

The major motoring organisations in Great Britain are the Automobile Association and the Royal Automobile Club. Each provides services in varying degrees for non-resident members of affiliated clubs.

Automobile Association –
www.theaa.co.uk
Fanum House, Basingstoke, Hants, RG21 2EA ☎ 0870 600 0371 (information); 0870 243 2456 (textphone); customer.services@theAA.com;
☎ 09003 401 100 (traffic information and weather reports)

Royal Automobile Club –
www.rac.co.uk
RAC House, 1 Forest Road, Feltham, Middlesex TW13 7RR ☎ 020 8917 2500 (motoring services); 09068 347 333 (travel information), 0860 550 055 (international travel information); Fax 020 8917 2525

CAR HIRE

There are car rental agencies at airports, air terminals, railway stations and in all large towns throughout Great Britain. European

cars usually have manual transmission but automatic cars are available on demand.
An international driving licence is required for non-EU nationals. Most companies will not rent to those aged under 21 or 25. The following firms operate on a national basis. Before deciding to collect a car from the airport, check that parking facilities are available with the hotel.

Avis	0870 590 0500, 020 8848 8765; www.avis.com
Budget	08701 565 656, 01442 280 072; www.budget.co.uk
Europecar	0870 607 5000, 01923 811 000; www.europcar.co.uk
Hertz	0870 599 6699, 0870 844 8844, 020 8570 5000; www.hertz.com
National Car Rental	0870 600 6666, 0870 556 5656; www.nationalcar.co.uk

EasyCar offers very competitive rates available on line: www.easycar.co.uk

Where to Stay

Addresses listed in the Guide

Compared with other European cities, London is an expensive place to stay. Finding a suitable room in a metropolis with over 13 million visitors annually and an average hotel occupancy rate of 80%, often requires patience. Fortunately, the choice of accommodation is astounding – nearly 130 000 beds in London alone – and with proper preparation prior to your trip, you will undoubtedly find pleasant accommodation in your price range and in your favourite area. Bear in mind that advance reservation is a must in any season, especially during the school holidays (Christmas, Easter and June to September). Whether you are looking for a luxury hotel in Mayfair or a modest but pleasant family-run guesthouse away from the bustle of central London, you should find something to suit in the following listing of hotels, guesthouses, B&B's and youth accommodation that have been carefully chosen for their unique character, convenient location, quality of comfort and value for money. They are grouped in areas covering a number of districts that should be familiar to visitors.
Although all the places listed have been visited and selected with care, changes may have occurred since our last visit, so please send us your comments – favourable or not.

Selecting a district

As London is such a large conurbation, it is advisable to decide where to stay according to the size of your purse or what you plan to visit.
The most elegant central districts – Mayfair, St James, Strand – are home to world-renowned luxury hotels. In the fashionable Kensington, Notting Hill and Bayswater areas, many attractive 19C terrace houses have been converted into small, and often charming, moderate-to-expensive hotels. Centrally located Bloomsbury is packed with small, inexpensive-to-moderate family-run establishments often in former Georgian houses. Those travelling on a tight budget will find a large selection of small, no-frills hotels and B&B's in Earl's Court and Victoria. Considering the high costs of hotels in London, young travellers will be surprised at the choice of decent youth accommodation in the city's centre *(see below)*.
Lodging in Outer London is usually less expensive than in the centre. The Outer London hotels listed in this guide are located near tourist attractions.

Colourful houses in Notting Hill

A. Taverner/MICHELIN

For all budgets

Our selection is divided into three price brackets.
The **"Budget"** bracket – – comprises the best of the small, simple but well-maintained establishments charging £100 or less for a single room. Expect basic service and shared bathrooms for the least expensive room. The hotels of the Travelodge and Travel Inns chains *(see below)*, selected for their convenient locations, also fall into this category.
In the **"Moderate"** bracket – –, you can find singles from £100 to £160 in tastefully converted houses located in attractive neighbourhoods. We strongly recommend booking in advance as these small establishments usually have a faithful clientele and the few rooms at the lower rates are often booked.
In the **"Expensive"** bracket (over £160) – –, we recommend a limited number of centrally located upmarket establishments that guarantee a truly unforgettable London experience. Stylistically, these hotels run the gamut from traditional British to minimalist contemporary, and as to be expected, the rates reflect the outstanding quality of the comfort and service.
The two rates quoted for each establishment (for example £42/62) refer to the nightly rate of a single and a double (except for hostel rates, which are quoted per person) One person staying in a double room (indeed, singles in Central London are often pocket-size!) will generally be given a slight reduction on the double rate, except during great exhibitions or other major events. Additional charge for breakfast is noted when applicable. Service and the 17.5% Value Added Tax (VAT) are included in the quoted prices unless otherwise specified. It is always advisable to confirm all details, including the inclusion of VAT, breakfast and en suite facilities, before making the reservation. Bear in mind that many hotels offer special prices for short breaks – weekends or stays of at least three days. A credit card number (and possibly a fax for confirmation) will be requested for all reservations.
A note for light sleepers: traffic-clogged Central London is quite noisy by day and night. Inquire about noise levels and remember that in small hotels, rooms at the rear are often quieter.
Parking in Central London is expensive, frustrating and almost impossible. Simply put, it's best to leave the car at home.
A limited number of luxury hotels offer on-site parking, but expect to pay a hefty fee.

Breakfast – As well as the Continental-style light breakfast of coffee and bread and jam, most establishments offer the traditional cooked breakfast, which begins with porridge or cereal and fruit juice and ends with toast and marmalade. It is accompanied by tea or coffee. The main dish is usually eggs or fish.

Types of accommodation

The terms, "hotel", "guesthouse" and "Bed & Breakfast", are used very loosely to apply to a wide variety of accommodation, often according to the preference and whim of the proprietors. However, traditionally hotels tend to be medium to large establishments, with en suite rooms and a full-range of services. The term "guesthouse" connotes a smaller operation with fewer facilities and generally more appealing to visitors on holiday than on business. The distinction between hotel, guesthouses and **Bed-and-Breakfast** places is often fuzzy, but the traditional B&B is a family-run affair, offering one or two bedrooms at a moderate price. As individual capacity is low, this type of B&B is not given in our selection but information and addresses are available from the following agencies:

London Home-to-Home – 26 Ascott Avenue, London W5 5QB. ☎/Fax 020 8567 2998; stay@londonhometohome.com; www.londonhometohome.com

GB and France Bed and Breakfast – 94-96 Bell Street, Henley-on-Thames, Oxon RG9 1XS. ☎ 01491 578 803; Fax 01491 410 806; bookings@bedbreak .demon.co.uk; www.bedbreak.com

London Bed and Breakfast Agency Ltd – 71 Fellows Road, London NW3 3JY. ☎ 020 7586 2768; Fax 020 7586 6567; stay@londonbb.com; www.londonbb.com

Uptown Reservations – 41 Paradise Walk, London SW3 4JL. ☎ 020 7351 3445; Fax 020 7351 9383; inquiries@uptownres.co.uk; www.uptownres.co.uk

Youth accommodation

University Residences and Youth Hostels, as well as small hotels, guesthouses and B&B, accommodation in the budget price bracket are worthwhile options for young travellers. University Residences are often available during the vacations and offer good cheap places to stay in a central location (Bloomsbury). For a contemporary take on the youth hostel concept try The Generator *(see BLOOMSBURY)*. Some useful addresses:

Venuemasters, The Workstation, Paternoster Row, Sheffield S1 2BX. ☎ 0114 249 3090 ; info@venuemasters.co.uk; www.venuemasters.co.uk

Central Bureau for Educational Visits and Exchanges, Seymour Mews House, Seymour Mews, London W1H 9PE, ☎ 020 7486 5101

International Students House (ISH), 229 Great Portland Street, W1N 5HD. ☎ 020 7631 8300/8310 ; Fax 020 7631 8315

– for students (single, double and dormitory); accom@ish.org.uk; www.ish.org.uk

YMCA, National Council, 640 Forest Road, London E17 3DZ, ☎ 020 8520 5599; enquiries@ymca.org; www.ymca.org.uk; www.ymca.int/directory.htm

YWCA, National HQ, 52 Cornmarket Street, Oxford OX1 3EJ, ☎ 01865 304 2000; info@ywca-gb.org.uk; www.ywca-gb.org.uk

Holders of an International Youth Hostel Federation card should contact the **International Youth Hostel Federation** ☎ 01717 324 170. Otherwise the **Hostelling International / American Youth Hostel Association** in the US (☎ 202-783-6161) offers a publication *International Hostel Guide for Europe* (US$13.95) – also available to non-members.

Contact the **Youth Hostels Association**, Trevelyan House, Dimple Road, Matlock, Derbs DE4 3YH; ☎ 0870 870 8808; customerservices@yha.org.uk; www.yha.org.uk for information on youth hostels in the UK.

To book a room in one of the six Youth Hostels in London ☎ 020 7373 3400:

- 14 Noel Street, W1V 3PD, ☎ 020 7734 1618.
- 38 Bolton Gardens, SW5 0AQ, ☎ 020 7373 7083.
- Holland House, Holland Walk, Kensington, W8 7QU, ☎ 020 7937 0748.
- 36 Carter Lane, off St Pauls Churchyard, EC4V 5AB. ☎ 020 7236 4965.
- 4 Wellgarth Road, Hampstead Heath, NW11 7HR ☎ 020 8458 9054.
- Island Yard, 20 Salter Road, Rotherhithe, SE16 1PP. ☎ 020 7232 2114.

CAMPING SITES

There are several camp sites within reasonable distance of Central London; it is advisable to book in advance; prices vary according to the season:

Crystal Palace Caravan Club Site, Crystal Palace Parade, London SE19 1UF. 8mi/13km from Central London. Open all year. ☎ 020 8778 7155; Fax 020 8676 0980; www.caravanclub.co.uk

Lee Valley Camping and Caravan Park, Meridian Way, Edmonton, London N9 0AS. 10mi/16km from Central London. Open all year. ☎ 020 8803 6900; Fax 020 8884 4975; leisurecentre@leevalleypark.org.uk; www.leevalleypark.com

Abbey Wood, Federation Road, Abbey Wood, London SE2 0LS. 12mi/19km from Central London. Open all year. ☎ 020 8311 7708; Fax 020 8311 1465; www.caravanclub.co.uk

Riverside Mobile Home and Touring Park, Thorney Mill Road, West Drayton, Middlesex. 14mi/20km from Central London. Open all year. ☎ 01895 446 520.

CHAIN HOTELS IN AND AROUND LONDON

If you are willing to forego charm and personalised service and your budget is limited, a chain hotel might be a suitable alternative.

In Central London and on the outskirts the **Travel Inns** chain offers simple but comfortable hotels with rooms at a single rate of £44.95 – £82.95 (service, VAT inc); central booking: ☎ 0870 242 8000; www.travelinn.com: **Euston** *(see Bloomsbury)*, **County Hall** (Lambeth, *see South Bank*), **Tower Bridge** *(see Tower Bridge)*, **Putney** *(see Fulham-Putney)*, **Docklands, Beckton, Ilford** (E), **Kenton** (Harrow, NW), **Croydon** (S).

Travel Lodges offer similar facilities at a single rate of £44.95 – £79.95 (VAT inc); central booking ☎ 08700 850 950 (freephone); www.travellodge.co.uk: **Kings Cross** *(see St Pancras – Camden Town)*, **Battersea** (SW), **City of London (see City)**, **Docklands, Ilford** (E) **Park Royal** (W), **Kew Bridge** (W), **Wimbledon, Kingston** (SW).

Premier Lodge also offer suitable accommodation at a single rate of £56 – £72 (service, VAT inc); central booking ☎ 0870 010 203; www.premierlodge.com: **Southwark** *(see Bankside – Southwark)*, **Wembley** (NW), **Edgware** (NW), **Brentford** (W), **Twickenham** (SW).

Express at Holiday Inn offer comfortable rooms at moderate rates £49 – £110; central booking ☎ 0800 405 060; www.hiexpress.co.uk: **Victoria** *(see Westminster)*, **Southwark** *(see Bankside – Southwark)*, **Hammersmith** (W), **Wandsworth** (S), **Stratford, Royal Docks** (E), **Wimbledon** *(see Wimbledon)*.

HOTEL INFORMATION AND RESERVATION SERVICE

Among the numerous web sites worth consulting:

www.visitbritain.com – official web site of the British Travel Authority (BTA) with pages specially adapted according to visitors' country of origin

www.visitlondon.com – official web site of the LTB. Telephone booking service Mon-Fri 9.30am-6pm, ☎ 020 7932 2020 (£5 booking fee).

www.londontown.com offers hotel information and on-line reservations for moderate and luxury accommodation in London. Special discounted rates for selected hotels.

www.justbookit.com – **British Hotel Reservation Centre**, 13 Grosvenor Gardens, SW1W 0BD; ☎ 020 7828 2425; Fax 020 7828 6439; sales@bhrconline.com

And don't forget The Red Guide

If you are unable to find a suitable accommodation among the selected establishments described below, consult the Michelin Red Guide *London*, an extract from the annually revised Michelin Red Guide *Great Britain and Ireland*. This reputed guide lists over 250 hotels throughout Greater London.

Bloomsbury

The Generator – *Compton Pl, (off 37 Tavistock Pl), WC1H 9SD – Russell Square – 020 7388 7666 – Fax 020 7388 7644 – info@the-generator.co.uk – – 800 beds £13.50/53*. This immense industrial-complex-turned-youth-hostel with stylish graphics and neon and chrome decor comprises a games room, Internet space and a bustling bar open late. The spartan dormitories vary in size; the more you're willing to share with, the less you'll pay.

Cavendish Hotel – *75 Gower St, WC1E 6HJ – Goodge Street – 020 7636 9079 – Fax 020 7580 3609 – bookings@hotel.cavendish.com – 20 rm £38/66*. DH Lawrence once stayed at this Georgian house, run by the same family for over 40 years. Writers and artists from the nearby Slade art school can often be found musing in the small walled garden at the rear. Assorted period furniture adds to the charm.

Gresham Hotel – *36 Bloomsbury St, WC1B 3QJ – Tottenham Court Road – 020 7580 4232 – Fax 020 7436 6341 – info@greshamhotellondon.com – 42 rm £40/75*. Guests at this converted Georgian house will appreciate the competitive prices and its location near the tube station. Bedrooms are fairly spacious but not all are en suite; those at the rear are quieter. Breakfast is served in the glass-ceilinged basement room.

Crescent Hotel – *49-50 Cartwright Gdns, WC1H 9EL – Euston – 020 7387 1515 – Fax 020 7383 2054 – general.enquiries@crescenthoteloflondon.com – 27 rm £44/91*. This charming hotel occupying two Georgian houses in an attractive crescent has developed a loyal clientele over the years. Pleasant features include a cosy sitting room, the original cast-iron oven in the breakfast room and access to the large communal garden and its tennis courts.

Arosfa Hotel – *83 Gower St, WC1E 6HJ – Goodge Street – 020 7636 2115 – Fax 020 7636 2115 – – 16 rm £45/66*. A small family-run hotel in one of Bloomsbury's busiest thoroughfares, the Arosfa offers simple but impeccably clean accommodation at very reasonable rates. No en suite bedrooms. Ask for a quieter room overlooking the small rear garden.

Thanet Hotel – *8 Bedford Pl, WC1B 5JA – Russell Square – 020 7636 2869 – Fax 020 7323 6676 – thanethotel@aol.com – 16 rm £69/94*. Pretty hanging baskets adorn the Thanet's attractive façade in the middle of a Georgian terrace. The personable young owners make every effort to create a relaxing and friendly ambience. The British Museum is only a minute's walk away!

Jenkins Hotel – *45 Cartwright Gdns, WC1H 9EH – Euston – 020 7387 2067 – Fax 020 7383 3139 – reservations@jenkinshotel.demon.co.uk – – 14 rm £72/85*. This cosy hotel in an early-18C Georgian crescent is lovingly maintained by charming hosts who live here with their Labradors. Television fans may remember the house as the setting of a "Poirot" episode. Clean, well-kept and tastefully decorated bedrooms.

London Euston Travel Inn Capital – *141 Euston Rd, NW1 2AU – Euston Square – 020 7554 3400 – Fax 020 7554 3419 – – 220 rm £79.95*. Unbeatable value for central London; it may be a budget chain hotel but the rooms are spotless and spacious with well-lit en suite bathrooms. Rooms at the rear are quieter.

Blooms – *7 Montague St, WC1B 5BP – Russell Square – 020 7323 1717 – Fax 020 7636 6498 – blooms@mermaid.co.uk – 26 rm £135/225 – £10 – Rest £17.95/30.20*. Located in a well-preserved row of Georgian houses flanking the west side of the British Museum, Blooms will satisfy those in search of charm and intimacy. Individually designed "themed" rooms and a small garden in the rear.

Academy Hotel – *17-21 Gower St, WC1E 6HG – Goodge Street – 020 7631 4115 – Fax 020 7636 3442 – res_academy@theetongroup.com – Closed 24-26 Dec – – 49 rm £140/225*. With the British Museum as a neighbour, this "boutique" hotel is centrally located. The Georgian exterior belies the contemporary feel inside; bedrooms are stylish and comfortable and the basement bar and restaurant cool and sophisticated. Rooms at the back are quieter.

Charlotte Street – *15 Charlotte St, W1P 1HB – Tottenham Court Road, Goodge Street – 020 7806 2000 – Fax 020 7806 2002 – charlotte@firmdale.com – – 44 rm £217.30/346.60 – £17.50*. Upon entering the lobby, you'll feel the charm and tranquillity for which this contemporary English hotel is renowned. The individually appointed rooms have nice touches such as CD's and mobile phones. Visit the hotel's equally stylish bar and restaurant, Oscar. Well located on the fringes of Bloomsbury, very close to Oxford Street.

Chelsea, Earl's Court

Merlyn Court Hotel – *2 Barkston Gdns, SW5 0EN – Earl's Court – 020 7370 1640 – Fax 020 7370 4986 – london@merlyncourt.demon.co.uk – – 18 rm £35/70*. This friendly, family-run hotel overlooking a tranquil Edwardian square is just a short walk from Earl's Court underground station. Most of the simply furnished bedrooms have private facilities. Breakfast is provided in a cosy basement room, beside the traditional TV lounge.

Rushmore – *11 Trebovir Rd, Earl's Court, SW5 9LS – Earl's Court – 020 7370 3839 – Fax 020 7370 0274 – rushmore-reservations@london.com – – 22 rm £59/79*. This small hotel conveniently located close to Earl's Court tube has won a loyal following. Bedrooms are individually decorated and come in a variety of shapes and sizes. The piazza-styled conservatory breakfast room doubles as a bar.

Annandale House Hotel – *39 Sloane Gdns, SW1W 8EB – ⊖ Sloane Square – ☎ 020 7730 6291 – Fax 020 7730 2727 – info@annandale-hotel.co.uk – ⅔ – 15 rm £60/120 – ☕ £5.* Discreet Victorian terrace house ideally located for the fashionable Knightsbridge shops. Guests may use the secluded patio and a well-equipped kitchenette. Breakfast served in the spotless rooms. Discounted rates available for mid-week stays.

Willett Hotel – *32 Sloane Gdns, SW1W 8DJ – ⊖ Sloane Square – ☎ 020 7824 8415 – Fax 020 7970 1805 – reservations@eeh.co.uk – 19 rm £67/155 ☕ + VAT.* This friendly hotel is situated in a quiet retreat of Victorian terracotta terraces, yet only a short stroll from the bustle of the King's Road. Inside, stained glass, ornate chandeliers and a certain opulence remain. Modern brightly decorated rooms.

Amsterdam Hotel – *7-9 Trebovir Rd, Earl's Court, SW5 9LS – ⊖ Earl's Court – ☎ 020 7370 2814 – Fax 020 7244 7608 – reservations@amsterdam-hotel.com – ⅔ – 19 rm £68/88 – ☕ £2.75.* Just doors away from the Rushmore, this small hotel has bedrooms with vivid colour schemes and some with balconies. Several suites available. In good weather take advantage of the small garden off the basement breakfast room.

Henley House – *30 Barkston Gdns, Earl's Court, SW5 0EN – ⊖ Earl's Court – ☎ 020 7370 4111 – Fax 020 7370 0026 – reservations@henleyhousehotel.com – 21 rm £70/95 – ☕ £3.40.* Nestling in a pleasant redbrick square close to busy Earl's Court Road, this small friendly hotel will satisfy those in search of well-priced and reliable accommodation close to the museums of South Ken. Similar decor in all bedrooms. Breakfast served in the conservatory.

London Town Hotel – *15 Penywern Rd, Earl's Court, SW5 9TT – ⊖ Earl's Court – ☎ 020 7370 4356 – Fax 020 7370 7923 – londontownhotel@tiscali.co.uk – ⅔ – 30 rm £78/98 ☕.* Behind the porticoed Georgian exterior, you'll find a modern and commercial hotel. The cheerily decorated and thoughtfully equipped bedrooms are relatively spacious. Rooms to the rear, overlooking a small private garden, are quieter.

City

Travelodge – *1 Harrow Pl, E1 7DB – ⊖ Aldgate – ☎ 08700 850950 – Fax 020 7626 1105 – ⅔ ♿ – 142 rm £79.95.* Accommodation for the cost-conscious business traveller or families in the heart of the financial district. The en suite bedrooms of this chain hotel are all spacious, bright and modern. Extra sofa beds and ample workspace in all the rooms.

Clerkenwell, Islington

Jurys Inn London – *60 Pentonville Rd, Islington, N1 9LA – ⊖ Angel – ☎ 020 7282 5500 – Fax 020 7282 5511 – jurysinnlondon@jurysdoyle.com – ⅔ ♿ – 229 rm £99 – ☕ £10 – Rest £18.* Explore the fashionable shops of Islington, or make use of the easy access into the centre. All the bedrooms of this large hotel are uniform in style and comfort. A busy Irish pub on the premises.

The Rookery – *12 Peters Lane, Cowcross St, Islington, EC1M 6DS – ⊖ Farringdon – ☎ 020 7336 0931 – Fax 020 7336 0932 – reservations@rookery.co.uk – 32 rm £235/282 – ☕ £8.95.* This charming restored 18C house, with wood-panelling, period furniture and open fires, is located just a short distance from St Paul's. Bathrooms appointed with restored Victorian fittings, and the suite has a retracting roof over the bedroom.

Covent Garden, Soho, Chinatown

The Fielding – *4 Broad Court, Bow St, WC2B 5QZ – ⊖ Covent Garden – ☎ 020 7836 8305 – Fax 020 7497 0064 – reservations@the-fielding-hotel.co.uk – Closed 1 week at Christmas – 24 rm £76/130.* A hotel that enjoys an unrivalled location in a quiet pedestrian street in the very heart of Covent Garden. Bedrooms are compact but well kept. No breakfast, but there are dozens of cafes and restaurants nearby. A rare find for the area.

Hazlitt's – *6 Frith St, Soho, W1V 5TZ – ⊖ Tottenham Court Road – ☎ 020 7434 1771 – Fax 020 7439 1524 – reservations@hazlitts.co.uk – Closed 24-25 Dec – 22 rm £205.60/240.80 + VAT.* Virtually the only hotel in Soho. A row of three adjoining early-18C town houses, the former home of the eponymous essayist still attracts an assorted mix of well-heeled urban travellers. Individually decorated bedrooms, many with antique furniture and plenty of Victorian charm. Continental breakfast.

St Martins Lane – *45 St Martin's La, Covent Garden, WC2N 4HX – ⊖ Charing Cross – ☎ 020 7300 5500 – Fax 020 7300 5501 – sml@ianschragerhotels.com – ⅔ – 200 rm £276/305.50 – ☕ £20.* Bearing the distinctive signature of French lifestyle guru Philippe Starck, the St Martins Lane is widely considered the most spectacular of London's luxury designer hotels: from the starkly modern lobby to the state-of-the-art bedrooms and assorted bars and restaurants. The location could hardly be better.

Kensington, South Kensington, Notting Hill, Bayswater, Paddington

Portobello Gold Hotel – *95-97 Portobello Rd, W11 2QB – ⊖ Notting Hill – ☎ 020 7460 4900 – Fax 020 7229 2278 – enquiries@portobellogold.com – 6 rm £30/85 ☕ – Rest £14/19.* Located in the heart of one of London's most famous markets, this relaxed hotel-restaurant-pub offers good value in the chic Notting Hill area. Bill Clinton is among the celebrities who have popped in for a drink. Wireless internet access available throughout. The affable owner will even drive you in his 1952 Buick convertible for a fee.

Garden Court Hotel – *30-31 Kensington Gardens Sq, W2 4BG – ⊖ Bayswater – ☎ 020 7229 2553 – Fax 020 7727 2749 –*

info@gardencourthotel.co.uk – 32 rm £38/58 ☕. In the northwest corner of a lovely 19C garden square, stands the gleaming white façade of this friendly hotel. Family owned and run since 1954, the Garden Court features a cosy lounge and simply furnished rooms, half of which are en suite. Very good value for money.

Parkwood Hotel – *4 Stanhope Pl, W2 2HB – ⊖ Marble Arch – ☎ 020 7402 2241 – Fax 020 7402 1574 – www.parkwoodhotel.com – 14 rm £47/89* ☕. In a quiet residential street, this porticoed Georgian hotel is ideally situated for Oxford Street and Hyde Park. All the traditionally decorated and well-kept bedrooms, except one, have en suite bathrooms. Compact roof terrace on the 1st floor.

Pavilion Hotel – *34-36 Sussex Gdns, W2 1UL – ⊖ Paddington – ☎ 020 7262 0905 – Fax 020 7262 1324 – pavilionUK@aol.com – 29 rm £60/100* ☕. If you eschew the impersonal style of chain hotels, the Pavilion is the place is for you. The quirky Victorian house brims with pieces gleaned over the years from auctions and flea markets. Choose from various themed bedrooms ("Enter the Dragon", "Honky Tonk"...). Breakfast served in bedrooms; room service available.

Columbia Hotel – *95-99 Lancaster Gate, Bayswater, W2 3NS – ⊖ Lancaster Gate – ☎ 020 7402 0021 – Fax 020 7706 4691 – columbiahotel@btconnect.com – 103 rm £65/83* ☕ *– Rest £10/16.* This stately row of five 19C houses was occupied by the US Officers' Club until 1975. Although the decor of the bedrooms is unremarkable, half overlook lovely Kensington Gardens and many have balconies. The large lounge and bar have retained their high ceilings.

Gresham Hotel – *116 Sussex Gdns, Paddington, W2 1UA – ⊖ Paddington – ☎ 020 7402 2920 – Fax 020 7402 3137 – mail@rembec.com – 57 rm £70/95* ☕. Named after the founder of the Royal Exchange, the Gresham is a refurbished house with well-equipped bedrooms. The breakfast room is bright and spacious, and visitors can order refreshments at the small wooden-floored bar.

Byron Hotel – *36-38 Queensborough Terr, W2 3SH – ⊖ Bayswater – ☎ 020 7243 0987 – Fax 020 7792 1957 – byron@capricornhotels.co.uk – 44 rm £78/120* ☕. Reasonably priced accommodation in the heart of Bayswater, just steps away from Kensington Gardens. This unassuming hotel underwent refurbishment in the late 1990s. Bedrooms are bright and spacious and all have en suite showers.

Swiss House Hotel – *171 Old Brompton Rd, SW5 0AN – ⊖ Gloucester Road – ☎ 020 7373 2769 – Fax 020 7373 4983 – recep@swiss-hh.demon .co.uk – 15 rm £78/114 – ☕ £6.* Trailing ivy and flower boxes adorn the façade of this stately building. All bedrooms are en suite and decorated with antique pine furniture. The atmosphere is quite relaxed and the service is attentive and courteous.

Comfort Inn – *18-19 Craven Hill Gdns, Bayswater, W2 3EE – ⊖ Bayswater – ☎ 020 7262 6644 – Fax 020 7262 0673 – comfortinn_hydepark@compuserve.com – 67 rm £84/104 – ☕ £4.50.* A good option if you're more concerned with good value and central location than with charm. Convenient for Kensington Gardens and Hyde Park, this well-kept chain hotel has functional rooms and attractive prices for central London.

Abbey Court – *20 Pembridge Gdns, W2 4DU – ⊖ Notting Hill Gate – ☎ 020 7221 7518 – Fax 020 7792 0858 – info@abbeycourthotel.co.uk – 22 rm £99/135.* An ideal base for antique hunters roaming Portobello Road. The elegant five-story white town house has been converted into a charming hotel with that personal touch. Bedrooms are individually appointed, and the service is friendly. Take breakfast in the lovely conservatory.

Aster House – *3 Sumner Pl, SW7 3EE – ⊖ South Kensington – ☎ 020 7581 5888 – Fax 020 7584 4925 – asterhouse@btinternet .com – 14 rm £99/180* ☕. A true home-from-home experience. This pretty Victorian house is within easy walking distance of the Victoria & Albert Museum. Tranquil garden and airy conservatory accessible to guests.

Pembridge Court – *34 Pembridge Gdns, North Kensington, W2 4DX – ⊖ Notting Hill Gate – ☎ 020 7229 9977 – Fax 020 7727 4982 – reservations@pemct.co.uk – 20 rm £130/200* ☕. Close to Notting Hill tube, this 19C town house hotel has earned a good reputation among the fashionable and the famous who like staying in this chic district. Despite the hotel's popularity, the rates are not astronomical. A collection of framed antique clothing adorns the walls. Cosy sitting room and basement bar. Room service.

Portobello Hotel – *22 Stanley Gdns, North Kensington, W11 2NG – ⊖ Holland Park – ☎ 020 7727 2777 – Fax 020 7792 9641 – info@portobello-hotel.co.uk – Closed 22 Dec to 2 Jan – 24 rm £140/320 – ☕ £8.50 – Rest £21.* The quintessential Notting Hill hotel of charm. Fanciful elegance prevails throughout this gleaming white town house in a stately 19C terrace. Bedrooms are decorated with a theatrical flourish and no two are alike: circular beds, half-tester beds and free-standing Victorian bathtubs and rich fabrics...

Miller's Residence – *111A Westbourne Grove, Bayswater, W2 4UW – ⊖ Bayswater – ☎ 020 7243 1024 – Fax 020 7243 1064 – enquiries@millersuk.com – Closed 24-27 Dec – 8 rm £188/264.* Amid the shops of Bayswater, you'll find this quirky Victorian house. Laden with fine antiques and bric-a-brac, the hotel exudes a relaxed and informal atmosphere. Lavishly furnished bedrooms. Breakfast in the charming sitting room.

KNIGHTSBRIDGE, BELGRAVIA, WESTMINSTER, VICTORIA, PIMLICO

Melbourne House Hotel – *79 Belgrave Rd, Victoria, SW1V 2BG – ⊖ Pimlico – ☎ 020 7828 3516 – Fax 020*

7828 7120 – melbourne.househotel@virgin.net – ⊁ – 17 rm £30/75 ☕. A traditional family-run hotel located a short walk from Tate Britain. Most of the simple but immaculately kept bedrooms have en suite shower rooms. Reserve one of the rear facing rooms, they're quieter.

Luna Simone Hotel – *47-49 Belgrave Rd, SW1V 2BB – ⊖ Pimlico – ☎ 020 7834 5897 – Fax 020 7828 2474 – lunasimone@talk21.com – ⊁ – 35 rm £40/75* ☕. You'll receive a warm welcome in this family-run hotel with a sparkling porticoed façade. Refurbished in 2001, the house has modern and vibrantly decorated bedrooms with many thoughtful extras. Well-equipped computer room at residents' disposal.

Morgan House B & B – *120 Ebury St, SW1W 9QQ – ⊖ Victoria – ☎ 020 7730 2384 – Fax 020 7730 8442 – morganhouse@btclick.com – Open all year – 11 rm £46/86* ☕. A friendly guesthouse not far from Buckingham Palace and the shops in Knightsbridge. The listed Georgian house has individually decorated and well-equipped bedrooms; our favourite is room 8 on the top floor. En suite rooms available.

Woodville House B & B – *107 Ebury St, SW1W 9QU – ⊖ Victoria – ☎ 020 7730 1048 – Fax 020 7730 2574 – woodvillehouse@btclick.com – 12 rm £46/66* ☕. Guests at this intimate hotel in a listed Georgian property appreciate the comfortable bedrooms, the attractive south-facing patio, the well-stocked basement kitchenette and the amiable service. Three rear rooms equipped with air-conditioning.

James House B & B – *108 Ebury St, Victoria, SW1W 9QD – ⊖ Victoria – ☎ 020 7730 7338 – Fax 020 7730 7338 – jandchouse@aol.com – ⊁ – 9 rm £52/85* ☕. You'll be just a few minutes away from Victoria Station if you opt for this mid-terrace Georgian house. The traditionally furnished rooms are equipped with fans and breakfast is served in a bright conservatory overlooking a private patio.

Melita House Hotel – *35 Charlwood St, SW1V 2DU – ⊖ Pimlico – ☎ 020 7828 0471 – Fax 020 7932 0988 – reserve@melitahotel.com – ⊁ – 22 rm £60/100* ☕. In a fairly quiet residential street just off Belgrave Rd, Melita House sports attractive floral displays outside. Spacious and modern rooms have fridges, digital safes and modem points.

Cartref House – *129 Ebury St, SW1W 9QU – ⊖ Victoria – ☎ 020 7730 6176 – jandchouse@aol.com – ⊁ – 19 rm £62/85* ☕. This family-owned and operated B&B in a Georgian house is centrally located between Victoria Station and Sloane Square. A range of tastefully appointed and well-kept rooms to suit all budgets, including some on the ground floor. A strict non-smoking policy applies.

Sanctuary House Hotel & Pub – *33 Tothill St, Westminster, SW1H 9LA – ⊖ St James's Park – ☎ 020 7799 4044 – Fax 020 7799 3657 – sanctuary.house@fullers .co.uk – Closed 1 week Christmas – ⊁ ♿ – 34 rm £85/130 – ☕ £8.95 – Rest £9.95.* This restored Victorian hotel, above an authentic English pub, offers excellent value accommodation just a short walk from Big Ben and the London Eye. Bright and spacious rooms with air conditioning. Reduced rates may apply for Friday and Saturday nights.

The Diplomat – *2 Chesham St, Belgravia, SW1X 8DT – ⊖ Sloane Square – ☎ 020 7235 1544 – Fax 020 7259 6153 – diplomat.hotel@btinternet.co.uk – 26 rm £98/175* ☕. This reasonably priced hotel occupies an imposing late-19C corner house in the heart of Belgravia only a short walk from Knightsbridge. A fine sweeping staircase leads to the large and well-decorated rooms, all en suite except one.

Claverley Hotel – *13-14 Beaufort Gdns, SW3 1PS – ⊖ Knightsbridge – ☎ 020 7589 8541 – Fax 020 7584 3410 – reservations@claverleyhotel.co.uk – ⊁ – 30 rm £100/195* ☕. In a peaceful tree-lined cul-de-sac just a short stroll form Harrods, this hotel has a well-established reputation. The rooms are spacious and well-appointed, some even have four-poster beds. Prices vary greatly according to the rooms. Well-priced singles.

Knightsbridge Green – *159 Knightsbridge, SW1X 7PD – ⊖ Knightsbridge – ☎ 020 7584 6274 – Fax 020 7225 1635 – thekghotel@aol.com – ⊁ – 16 rm £110/145 – ☕ £10.50.* Discreet small hotel located in the heart of the famous shopping district. Additional features are the spacious rooms and reasonable rates for central London. Breakfast served in bedrooms. Suites also available.

Knightsbridge – *10 Beaufort Gdns, Knightsbridge, SW3 1PT – ⊖ Knightsbridge – ☎ 020 7584 6300 – Fax 020 7584 6355 – knightsbridge@firmdale.com £135/165.* A porticoed town house tucked away just behind Knightsbridge and close to the Victoria & Albert Museum. The rooms vary considerably in size but all are furnished with both mini-bars and safes. Enquire about reduced rates for long-term stays.

Cadogan – *75 Sloane St, SW1X 9SG – ⊖ Knightsbridge – ☎ 020 7235 7141 – Fax 020 7245 0994 – info@cadogan.com – ⊁ – 61 rm £164.50/282 – ☕ £16.50 – Rest £18.90/47.50 + VAT.* Over its long existence, this classic English hotel has welcomed such celebrities as Oscar Wilde and Lillie Langtry. The still-charming Cadogan remains a haven of peace just a short walk from Knightsbridge. The wood-panelled lounge is a favourite spot for afternoon tea.

Cliveden Town House – *26 Cadogan Gdns, Knightsbridge, SW3 2RP – ⊖ Sloane Square – ☎ 020 7730 6466 – Fax 020 7730 0236 – reservations@clivedentownhouse.co.uk – ⊁ – 31 rm £200/340 – ☕ £18.50 + VAT.* Country house living just minutes away from Harrods. This charming Victorian house is set in a smart residential street and many of the luxuriously appointed bedrooms overlook a tranquil communal garden. Room service.

The Goring – *15 Beeston Pl, Grosvenor Gdns, Victoria, SW1W 0JW – ⊖ Victoria – ☎ 020 7396 9000 – Fax 020 7834 4393 – reception@goringhotel.co.uk – 68 rm*

£235/287.80 – ☕ £17 – Rest £26.50/40 + VAT. Just around the corner from Buckingham Palace, this stunning landmark hotel opened in 1910 has remained in the Goring family for four generations. Elegance, charm and comfort in the best British tradition. The quietier rooms at the rear overlook a private garden.

The Berkeley – *Wilton Pl, Knightsbridge, SW1X 7RL – ⊖ Knightsbridge – ☎ 020 7235 6000 – Fax 020 7235 4330 – info@the-berkeley.co.uk – 186 rm £376/493 – ☕ £21.50 + VAT.* One side of this luxury hotel overlooks the park, the other a charming little church. The Berkeley's discreet charm is evident throughout: in the gilded and panelled drawing room, in the rooftop pool with its retracting roof, and in the opulently decorated bedrooms. Two restaurants, including La Tante Claire, one of London's finest dining rooms.

Marylebone, Regent's Park, Primrose Hill, St John's Wood

Blandford Hotel – *80 Chiltern St, W1U 5AF – ⊖ Baker Street – ☎ 020 7486 3103 – Fax 020 7487 2786 – blandfordhotel@dial .pipex.com – 33 rm £40/90 ☕.* In the vicinity of Madame Tussaud's and Regent's Park, this privately owned commercial hotel has a relaxed and friendly atmosphere. Refurbished and well-kept rooms are thoughtfully equipped. Car park adjacent.

Edward Lear Hotel – *28-30 Seymour St, Marylebone, W1H 5WD – ⊖ Marble Arch – ☎ 020 7402 5401 – Fax 020 7706 3766 – www.edlear.com – 31 rm £47.50/89 ☕.* This mid-terraced Georgian house was the former residence of the famous Victorian painter and limerick writer. Narrow staircases lead to brightly decorated rooms, four en suite. Quieter rooms overlook Quebec Mews. Complimentary Internet access in the cosy lounge.

Lincoln House – *33 Gloucester Pl, W1H 3PD – ⊖ Marble Arch – ☎ 020 7486 7630 – Fax 020 7486 0166 – reservations@lincoln-house-hotel.co.uk – 23 rm £59/89 ☕.* A friendly family-run hotel in a convenient location, housed in a late 18C townhouse. Breakfast is served in the pleasant basement room. The rooms at the back are quieter and those on the 1st floor are more spacious.

Hart House – *51 Gloucester Pl, Marylebone, W1U 8JF – ⊖ Marble Arch – ☎ 020 7935 2288 – Fax 020 7935 8516 – reservations@harthouse.co.uk – 15 rm £70/105 ☕.* In a very busy road just north of Portman Sq, this pretty Georgian house formerly provided refuge to French nobles fleeing the 1789 Revolution. It is now a well-maintained hotel where guests feel quite welcome. Rooms to the rear are quieter.

Americana Hotel – *172 Gloucester Pl, NW1 6DS – ⊖ Baker Street – ☎ 020 7723 1452 – Fax 020 7723 4641 – manager@americanahotel .demon.co.uk – 29 rm £73/92 ☕.* The hotel's Georgian façade is enlivened by attractive flower boxes. Although compact, the bedrooms are well-appointed and brightly coloured. Modern lounge with well-stocked honesty bar. Convenient for Lord's Cricket Ground.

Palace Hotel – *31 Great Cumberland Pl, Marylebone, W1H 7LF – ⊖ Marble Arch – ☎ 020 7262 5585 – Fax 020 7706 2427 – palacehotel@compuserve.com – 26 rm £80/120 – ☕ £5.* Within a stone's throw of Marble Arch and overlooking an attractive Georgian crescent, this hotel features striking polished wood, a sweeping staircase with handpainted walls and well-appointed modern rooms. Two apartments also available.

Durrants Hotel – *26-32 George St, Marylebone, W1H 5BJ – ⊖ Bond Street – ☎ 020 7935 8131 – Fax 020 7487 3510 – enquiries@durrantshotel.co.uk – 88 rm £92.50/165 – ☕ £13.50 – Rest £19.50/44.* Opened in 1790, this quintessentially English hotel with the grace and style of a bygone era is just around the corner from the Wallace Collection. Enjoy a classic afternoon tea in the charming fire-lit lounges or some traditional British fare in the cosy, wood-panelled dining room.

10 Manchester Street – *10 Manchester St, W1U 4DG – ⊖ Bond Street – ☎ 020 7486 6669 – Fax 020 7224 0348 – stay@10manchesterstreet.fsnet.co.uk – 37 rm 9 suites £120/150.* Behind the classic Victorian facade of this former nurses' home, is a relaxed and comfortable hotel, a short walk from the Wallace Collection and the famous department stores of Oxford Street.

Mayfair

Flemings – *Half Moon St, W1Y 7RA – ⊖ Green Park – ☎ 020 7499 2964 – Fax 020 7629 4063 – sales@flemings-mayfair.co.uk – 120 rm £199.25/233.80 – ☕ £18 – Rest £15/31.50.* The noted polymath Henry Wagner once resided at this address, just a minute's walk from Green Park. The Georgian architecture is complemented by the very traditional interior featuring oil paintings and antique English furniture.

The Metropolitan – *Old Park Lane, W1Y 4LB – ⊖ Green Park – ☎ 020 7447 1000 – Fax 020 7447 1100 – res@metropolitan.co.uk – 152 rm £293 – ☕ £18.* The ultra-minimalist design and hip reputation have made this the favoured haunt of assorted pop stars and other celebrities. The chic Met Bar (restaurant-bar reserved for residents and members) proves that hotel bars need not be dull. Rooms on the higher floors offer views of Hyde Park. Trendy restaurant Nobu (see Eating Out) also within the hotel.

Four Seasons – *Hamilton Pl, Park Lane, W1A 1AZ – ⊖ Green Park – ☎ 020 7499 0888 – Fax 020 7493 1895 – fsh.london@fourseasons.com – ♿ – 185 rm £346/423 – ☕ £21.* Just steps away from Hyde Park Corner, the Four Seasons draws international visitors who prefer their luxury to be more contemporary than traditional. Many of the bedrooms offer views of Hyde Park and some have their own conservatory. All the services expected of a first-class hotel in Mayfair.

Claridge's – *Brook St, W1A 2JQ – ⊖ Bond Street – ☎ 020 7629 8860 – Fax 020 7499 2210 – info@claridges.co.uk –*

♿ – 143 rm £370/493.50 – ☕ £22 – Rest £29.50/67. The hotel has enjoyed Royal patronage to such an extent that a telephone request to speak to the King once required the response 'Which one?'. Claridge's continues to epitomise English grandeur and is celebrated for its Art Deco design and sumptuous luxury.

Piccadilly, St James's

The Cavendish – *81 Jermyn St, SW1Y 6JF – ⊖ Piccadilly Circus – ☎ 020 7930 2111 – Fax 020 7839 2125 – cavendish.reservations@devere-hotels.com – 🚭 – 227 rm £235/265 – ☕ £16.95 – Rest £24.20/37.75.* Across the street from Fortnum & Mason, this large corporate hotel offers all the conveniences of a modern hotel including on-site parking. For great views, ask for a room on one of the top five floors.

The Stafford – *16-18 St James's Pl, SW1A 1NJ – ⊖ Green Park – ☎ 020 7493 0111 – Fax 020 7493 7121 – info@thestaffordhotel.co.uk – 75 rm £282/364.25 – ☕ £16.50 – Rest £23.50/53.* Tucked away in a residential street beside St James's Palace and Green Park, the genteel Stafford is one of London's quietest hotels. Rooms tastefully appointed with antiques. Have a drink in the famed "American bar" which has preserved the charm of a bygone era.

South Bank, Bankside, Southwark, Bermondsey, Waterloo

London County Hall Travel Inn Capital – *Belvedere Rd, Waterloo, SE1 7PB – ⊖ Waterloo – ☎ 020 7902 1600 – Fax 020 7902 1619 – 🚭 ♿ – 313 rm £79.95.* Difficult to find a hotel closer to the London Eye, which makes this budget hotel in central London the envy of more expensive hotels. Originally home to the Greater London Council, with the Houses of Parliament across the river, it offers spotless, uniformly fitted and affordable accommodation.

Outer London

North-west: Hampstead, Highgate, Swiss Cottage, Hendon

Mountview – *31 Mount View Rd, N44 SS – ⊖ Finsbury Park – ☎ 020 8340 9222 – Fax 020 8342 8494 – mountview@aol.com – 3 rm £40/70 ☕.* An attractively furnished Victorian house in a quiet, residential tree-lined street. Bedrooms are individually decorated; one still has the original fireplace and two overlook the secluded rear garden.

Hampstead Village Guesthouse – *2 Kemplay Rd, Hampstead, NW3 1SY – ⊖ Hampstead – ☎ 020 7435 8679 – Fax 020 7794 0254 – info@hampsteadguesthouse.com – 🚭 – 9 rm £48/120 – ☕ £7.* In a charming location, this Victorian house just a short walk from Hampstead Heath conjures up images of the writers and thinkers who have made their home in the area. Although not all rooms are en suite, they are all decorated with antiques and assorted knick-knacks.

Langorf – *20 Frognal, Hampstead, NW3 6AG – ⊖ Finchley Road – ☎ 020 7794 4483 – Fax 020 7435 9055 – langorf@aol.com – 31 rm £82/110 ☕.* Village life within the city. This converted Edwardian house is situated in a quiet residential area of charming Hampstead but with convenient transport links to central London. The bright breakfast room overlooks a peaceful walled garden. Spacious bedrooms.

North-east: East End, Hackney, Whitechapel

Express by Holiday Inn – *275 Old St, Hoxton, EC1V 9LN – ⊖ Old Street – ☎ 020 7300 4300 – Fax 020 7300 4400 – reservationsfc@holidayinnlondon.com – Restricted opening Christmas and New Year – 🚭 ♿ – 224 rm £110 – Rest £23.* When assorted artists began moving into warehouses in Hoxton, it wasn't long before the media started calling it the new Notting Hill. It still has some way to go but nonetheless provides easy access and this purpose-built hotel offers modern, affordable accommodation.

South-east: Greenwich, Blackheath

Express by Holiday Inn – *Bugsby Way, SE10 0GD – ⊖ Greenwich – ☎ 020 8269 5000 – Fax 020 8269 5069 – www.hiexpress.com – 70 £99/110 ☕.* Seven-storey modern hotel, just south of the Millennium Dome, with a panoramic view from all windows. Chinese restaurant at lower level.

South-south-west: Fulham, Putney, Wimbledon

London Putney Bridge Travel Inn Capital – *3 Putney Bridge Approach, Fulham, SW6 3JD – ⊖ Putney Bridge – ☎ 020 7471 8300 – Fax 020 7471 8315 – 🚭 ♿ – 154 rm £74.95.* One of the larger budget chain hotels. Converted from an office block on the north side of the bridge, it offers dependable and competitively priced accommodation. The bedrooms are spotless and well proportioned.

South-west: Richmond, Kew

Chase Lodge – *10 Park Rd, Hampton Wick, KT1 4AS – ⊖ Richmond – ☎ 020 8943 1862 – Fax 020 8943 9363 – info@chaselodgehotel.com – 13 rm £65/150 ☕ – Rest £14.13/23.87.* A warm welcome is guaranteed at this mid-terrace Victorian property located in an attractive residential road only a short distance from the Thames. Furnishings and decoration vary from room to room, but all rooms are comfortable.

Where to Eat

London has become a gourmet's paradise, and the capital now occupies a prominent role on the international culinary scene. The number and variety of of eating places reflect the multitude of current cooking styles ranging from traditional British (including fish and chips), to classic French, to the now-popular Mediterranean-style and world cuisine from far-flung places around the globe. Indeed, a tasty legacy of the British Empire's former worldwide ties is the abundance of dishes hailing from South Asia, Africa, the Caribbean and the Near and Far East.

The term "Modern British", coined in the late 1980s, is loosely applied to the wave of innovative cooking that borrows freely from various international sources, highlighting fresh home-grown products and eye-pleasing presentation. In the 1990s, the unofficial ambassador of British style, Sir Terence Conran, further enhanced London's culinary reputation by launching several spectacular "gastrodomes" (Bluebird in Chelsea, for example). In these sprawling "designer restaurants," eating becomes a multi-sensory experience, dazzling the eyes and ears as well as the taste buds.

Like the hotel listings, the restaurants recommended in this guide have been carefully selected for quality, atmosphere, location and value for money. The recommended restaurants presented in the listings below offer full meals for lunch and dinner. For more informal and inexpensive eating in the course of your visits throughout the city, consult the **Light Bite** and **Pub** listings within the Selected Sights section of the guide. We trust you will find places best suited to your specific tastes and budget. And remember to send us your comments...

For all budgets

Restaurants are divided into three price brackets. Prices refer to a full meal excluding beverages: Eateries in the **"Budget"** bracket – ⊜⊜ – are generally simple, unpretentious places where you can expect to spend no more than £20. The **"Moderate"** category – ⊜⊜⊜ – comprises restaurants slightly more formal where a meal will cost from £20 to £40.

The **"Expensive"** restaurants (over £40) – ⊜⊜⊜⊜ – are upmarket establishments with a high culinary standard and distinctive ambience.

(A tip: if you are tempted to try a noted pricey restaurant, but your budget is limited, consider the excellent value lunch menus proposed by many of these establishments.)

The two prices given for each restaurant represent a minimum and maximum price for a full meal excluding beverages. Note that in many cases, the minimum price refers to a menu served only at lunchtime during the week. Naturally, prices will vary depending on the number of courses and the beverages ordered. Wine can be an expensive item and consequently the cost of a meal will be substantially higher.

VAT and service (12.5%) are generally included in the bill. Tipping is optional, but it is very common to leave 10% when the service is particularly pleasing. Some restaurants will leave the total open on a credit card slip so that the customer can add a tip to the bill.

Restaurants are usually open in the evening from 6.30pm to 10pm (earlier and later if they are serving pre- and post-theatre meals) and also at lunchtime from noon to 2.15pm depending on the district. Many close one day a week.

It is always advisable to book in the evening, particularly at the weekend.

A formal evening meal – dinner – consists of three courses, but in many restaurants it is quite acceptable to eat only a starter and a main dish or a main dish and a sweet. Most restaurants will offer bottled water – still or sparkling – but tap water will be provided if requested.

Lighter Fare

Cafés and informal eating places and pubs *(see below)*, which keep flexible hours and can provide a light meal in the middle of the day, are listed under **Pubs** and **Light Bite** in the individual chapters in the Selected Sights section of the guide. An average meal in these places will cost under £15.

The following café/restaurant chains have numerous branches throughout Central London and provide consistent value: Pizza Express, Prêt-à-Manger, Café Uno, Café Rouge, Chez Gérard.

Afternoon Tea

Tearooms, cafés and hotels providing afternoon tea are listed in the individual chapters in the Selected Sights section of the guide. The traditional time for the celebrated institution of afternoon tea is 4 o'clock, but in most establishments, it is served between 3pm and 5pm.

Order a selection of sandwiches – cucumber is the traditional filling – or a cream tea (scones and jam and clotted cream) or crumpets or muffins with butter, cakes and fruit tarts. Choose from a variety of teas – Indian (Darjeeling) or China (green or perfumed like Lapsang Souchong or Earl Grey).

For the authentic atmosphere of an English tearoom try the Fountain Restaurant in Fortnum & Mason, the Ritz Hotel *(see PICCADILLY)*, Brown's Hotel, the Lanesborough Hotel at Hyde Park Corner *(see MAYFAIR)* as well as other well-known places such as the Dorchester Hotel *(see MAYFAIR)* (dress appropriately) and the Winter Garden in the Landmark London Hotel *(see MARYLEBONE)*. Less select but very good are the tearooms in the Richoux chain.

And don't forget The Red Guide

For a more extensive listing of recommended restaurants in the London area, consult the Michelin Red Guide *London*, an extract from the annually revised Michelin Red Guide *Great Britain and Ireland.* This respected gastronomical guide lists over 375 restaurants throughout Greater London.

Inner London

Abeno – *47 Museum St, WC1A 1LY – ⊖ Holborn – ☎ 020 7405 3211 – okonomi@abeno.co.uk – Closed 25-26 Dec and 1 Jan – £6.50/27.80.* As the address indicates, this original Japanese restaurant is not far from the British Museum. On your first visit, you must try the delicious house speciality: Okonomi-yaki, little pancakes cooked on a hotplate on your table. Up to you to select the size and filling.

North Sea Fish Restaurant – *7-8 Leigh St, WC1H 9EW – ⊖ Russell Square – ☎ 020 7387 5892 – Closed Sun – £8/45.* Drop into this friendly eatery for genuine fish and chips. Only ground nut or vegetable oil is used; egg and matzo coating also available. Jumbo sizes fried or grilled. Take-away service for those in a hurry.

Alfred – *245 Shaftesbury Ave, WC1E 6HG – ⊖ Tottenham Court Road – ☎ 020 7240 2566 – Closed 25-26 Dec, Sun, Sat lunch and Bank Hols – £13.90/25.45.* With generous views of the busy streets outside and a laid-back style, Alfred appeals to the sophisticated urbanite. It champions the cause of indigenous cooking by featuring specialities from around the British Isles.

Ristorante Paradiso – *35 Store St, WC1E 7BS – ⊖ Goodge Street – ☎ 020 7255 2554 – £15/18.* Founded in 1934, this pizzeria-ristorante with its typical decor of assorted bottles, pictures and black and white photos, has retained much of its original atmosphere. The competitively priced pasta dishes and pizzas are served by attentive Italian waiters.

Passione – *10 Charlotte St, W1P 1HE – ☎ 020 7636 2833 – Liz@passione.co.uk – Closed Christmas, Sat lunch, Sun and Bank Hols – £22.50/32.* Modern Italian cooking comes to Charlotte Street via this small but light and airy restaurant. The helpful service and the kitchen's lightness of touch usually guarantees a full house. Try the delicious risotto. Just minutes away from Oxford Street.

Chelsea, Earl's Court

itsu – *118 Draycott Ave, Chelsea, SW3 3AE – ⊖ South Kensington – ☎ 020 7590 2401 – cebs@netcomuk.co.uk – Bookings not accepted – £12/18.* Take your pick of the assorted European-style sushi as it passes before you on the slow-moving conveyor belt. Dishes are priced according to their colour, and the attentive staff is only a buzzer call away. Upstairs, a more formal area with a lively bar. Fashionable contemporary decor.

Racine – *239 Brompton Rd, SW3 2EP – ⊖ Knightsbridge – ☎ 020 7584 4477 – £15/28.75.* Dark leather banquettes, large mirrors and wood floors create the atmosphere of a genuine Parisian brasserie. Good value, well crafted, regional French fare.

MICHELIN

Bluebird – *350 King's Rd, SW3 5UU – ⊖ South Kensington – ☎ 020 7559 1000 – enquiries@bluebird-stove.co.uk – £15.75/47.25.* Walk around the successful Terence Conran "gastrodrome" comprising foodshop, flower market and café, before going upstairs to his lively, skylit restaurant and bar. Sample the modern British cuisine much of which is cooked in wood-fired ovens. Weekend brunch is very popular.

Chelsea Ram – *32 Burnaby St, Chelsea, SW10 0PL – ⊖ Fulham Broadway – ☎ 020 7351 4008 – pint@chelsearam.com – Closed 25, 26 and 31 Dec – Bookings not accepted – £15.85/22.85.* A short walk from the King's Road and Chelsea Harbour, this much-frequented pub is quite pleasant with its scrubbed pine table and walls packed with books and contemporary art. Ask for the daily specials. Modern British cooking.

Bibendum Oyster Bar – *81 Fulham Rd, South Kensington, SW3 6RD – ⊖ South Kensington – ☎ 020 7589 1480 – manager@bibendum.co.uk – Closed 1 week Christmas – £18/34.50.* The foyer of London's beloved Art Nouveau gem, Michelin House, provides the setting for an informal meal of light seafood and shellfish specialities. Like many other Conran eateries, the Oyster Bar is often packed.

⊖⊖⊖ **Gordon Ramsay** – *68-69 Royal Hospital Rd, Chelsea, SW3 4HP – ⊖ Sloane Square – ☎ 020 7352 4441 – Closed 1 week Christmas, Sat, Sun and Bank Hols – £35/65.* An outstanding gastronomic experience! Chef Gordon Ramsay's highly acclaimed dining room is quite sought after so book well in advance. Formal atmosphere and impeccable service...with prices to match. For a very special occasion.

City

⊖⊖ **London Winebars** – *44 Cannon St, EC4N 2JJ – ⊖ Mansion House – ☎ 020 7248 1700 – enquiries@thecolonies.co.uk – £3/12.50.* Those looking for a "City" experience can rub shoulders with stockbrokers beneath the TV screens of share prices at this modern restaurant. The menu is contemporary with lighter options in the ground-floor bar. Serving all day, from breakfast onwards.

⊖⊖ **Leadenhall Wine Bar** – *27 Leadenhall Market, EC3U 1LR – ⊖ Monument – ☎ 020 7623 1818 – Closed Sat and Sun – £14.* The striking Victorian architecture of Leadenhall Market provides the backdrop to this traditional wine bar. A slightly incongruous but nonetheless successful selection of Spanish tapas with seafood specialities and blackboard extras.

⊖⊖⊖ **1 Lombard Street (Brasserie)** – *1 Lombard St, EC2V 9AA – ⊖ Bank – ☎ 020 7929 6611 – Closed Sat, Sun and Bank Hols – £23.20/37.50.* A former banking hall provides the grand setting for this vibrant brasserie. Sample the modern European fare or just have a drink at the bar beneath the impressive cupola. A popular venue for City workers and often quite noisy. A more formal fine restaurant on the same premises.

Clerkenwell, Islington

⊖⊖ **Granita** – *127 Upper St, Islington, N1 1PQ – ⊖ Essex Road – ☎ 020 7226 3222 – www.granita.co.uk – Closed 2 weeks Aug, 1 week Easter, 10 days Christmas, Mon and lunch Tue – £12.50/29.50.* This smart restaurant earned a place in British political history when Tony Blair and Gordon Brown reputedly decided over dinner which of them would run for leader of the Labour Party. Boldly minimalist interior, young and energetic staff and contemporary cooking. Good value lunch menu.

⊖⊖ **St John's** – *91 Junction Rd, Islington, N19 5QU – ⊖ Archway – ☎ 020 7272 1587 – stjohnsarchway@virgin.net – £18/24.50.* This busy and refreshingly unpretentious restaurant is housed within a former 19C smokehouse. The bar is a popular afterwork meeting place for office workers while the menu specialises in offal and an original mix of traditional and rediscovered English dishes.

Covent Garden, Soho, Chinatown

⊖⊖ **Rock and Sole Plaice** – *47 Endell St, WC2H 9AJ – ⊖ Covent Garden – ☎ 020 7836 3785 – www.rockandsoleplaice.com – Closed bank hols – £7/20.* This informal fish and chips eatery, reputedly founded in 1871, has enough puns in its name to satisfy any tabloid editor and portions big enough to satisfy all appetites. The somewhat kitsch decor of aquatic murals of sharks and dolphins spills down to the basement dining room.

⊖⊖ **Porters** – *17 Henrietta St, WC2E 8QH – ⊖ Leicester Square – ☎ 020 7836 6466 – neil@porters.uk.com – Closed 25 Dec – £10/20.* This well-established restaurant is owned by the 7th Earl of Bradford. The menu specialises in traditional English dishes, and particularly homemade pies. Family friendly, with a separate children's menu; older guests can enjoy the adjacent bar.

⊖⊖ **Simpson's in the Strand** – *100 Strand, WC2R 0EW – ⊖ Charing Cross – ☎ 020 7836 9112 – simpsons@savoy-group.co.uk – £15/45.* An English institution since 1828. The "place" at which to dine on traditional "joints from the trollye". Well-priced set lunch and traditional breakfast.

⊖⊖ **Mon Plaisir** – *21 Monmouth St, Covent Garden, WC2H 9DD – ⊖ Covent Garden – ☎ 020 7836 7243 – eatafrog@mail.com – Closed 25 Dec, Sat lunch, Sun and Bank Hols – £15.95/36.50 + VAT.* Francophiles still flock to London's oldest French restaurant located within easy walking distance from the West End theatres. This family-run establishment, founded over 50 years ago, has four separate dining rooms all decorated differently but with a common Gallic touch. Expect all the usual favourites on the menu.

⊖⊖ **Smollensky's on the Strand** – *105 The Strand, WC2R 0AA – ⊖ Charing Cross – ☎ 020 7497 2101 – www.smollensky's.co.uk – £18/30.* If you have a craving for American food in central London, this large family-oriented basement restaurant will be your best bet. Ersatz Art Deco with booths and mirrors. Live jazz on Sundays. Good value for the area.

⊖⊖ **New World** – *1 Gerrard Pl, W1 – ⊖ Leicester Square – ☎ 020 7734 0677 – £19.90/35.* A favourite Dim Sum destination in the heart of Chinatown. Waitresses wheeling trolleys distribute assorted specialities and offer much-appreciated guidance to the uninitiated. Three vast floors appointed with typical oriental restaurant ornamentation.

⊖⊖ **Fung Shing** – *15 Lisle St, WC2H 7BE – ⊖ Leicester Square – ☎ 020 7437 1539 – www.fung.shing.com – Closed 24-26 Dec and lunch Bank Hols – £20/33.95.* A long-standing Soho favourite on the edge of Chinatown. Chatty and pleasant service. Lovers of Chinese food will find all the classics as well as more adventurous dishes.

⊖⊖⊖ **Ivy** – *1 West St, Covent Garden, WC2H 9NE – ⊖ Leicester Square – ☎ 020 7836 4751 – Closed dinner 24-26 and 31 Dec, 1 Jan and Aug Bank Hol – £23.25/61.50.* Once past the liveried doorman and waiting paparazzi, you'll find a decor of wood panelling and stained glass and an unpretentious menu. Ivy is one of London's most coveted "Theatreland" restaurants, so securing a table can be challenging. A veritable West End institution.

The Admiralty – *Somerset House, The Strand, WC2R 1LA – ⊖ Temple – ☎ 020 7845 4646 – Closed 25-26 Dec and Sunday evening – £25/33.* Interconnecting rooms with bold colours and informal service contrast with its setting within the restored Georgian splendour of Somerset House.

Rules – *35 Maiden Lane, Covent Garden, WC2E 7LB – ⊖ Covent Garden – ☎ 020 7836 5314 – info@rules.co.uk – Closed 4 days Christmas – £29.70/36.40.* Grouse, partridge, teal and woodcock are just some of the game on the menu at London's reputedly oldest restaurant, and all from its own estate! A fine collection of antique cartoons and drawings adorns the walls.

Kensington, South Kensington, Notting Hill, Bayswater, Paddington

Sausage & Mash Café – *268 Portobello Rd, Notting Hill, W10 5TY – ⊖ Ladbroke Grove – ☎ 020 8968 8898 – £6/10.* This unusual eatery under a bridge at the far end of the Portobello Road market is quite fun. Take a seat at the large pine tables shared with other patrons and choose from various types of homemade sausage and mashed potato. No one ever leaves hungry!

Timo – *343 Kensington High St, W8 6NW – ⊖ Kensington High St – ☎ 020 7603 3888 – Closed Christmas – £10/25.* Modern restaurant with unadorned lime green walls and comfortable seating in brown suede banquettes. Italian menus of contemporary dishes and daily changing specials.

Kam Tong – *59-63 Queensway, Bayswater, W2 4QH – ⊖ Bayswater – ☎ 020 7229 6065 – £12/25.* This long-established and smoothly run Chinese restaurant offers a less pricey menu than many in the area. A large brigade of bow-tied waiters stationed in the large dining room supervises the ever-popular Dim Sum (available throughout the day).

The Vale – *99 Chippenham Rd, Maida Vale, W9 2AB – ⊖ Maida Vale – ☎ 020 7266 0990 – Closed 1 week Christmas, last weekend Aug and lunch Sat and Sun – £12/25.* This former pub on the border of Maida Vale and Brent is a good place to sample modern British food with Mediterranean touches. Changing menu served in the bright and spacious conservatory or in the original bar. Another bar in the basement.

Café Med – *184a Kensington Park Rd, W11 2ES – ⊖ Ladbroke Grove – ☎ 020 7221 1150 – £15/80.* Those seeking a cosy yet stylish ambience need look no further than this bustling neighbourhood restaurant. The cavernous interior features exposed brick walls and a cast iron spiral staircase leading to a mezzanine floor. Grilled fare from salmon to ribs of beef.

Francofill – *1 Old Brompton Rd, South Kensington, SW7 3HZ – ⊖ South Kensington – ☎ 020 7584 0087 – www.francofill.com – £15/20.* Opposite South Kensington tube, this informal French restaurant serves traditional favourites from steak frites to snails. Appointed with pine tables and chairs, and photos of assorted French celebrities. Light snacks also available in the adjacent bar.

L'Accento – *16 Garway Rd, Bayswater, W2 4NH – ⊖ Bayswater – ☎ 020 7243 2201 – laccentorest@aol.com – £17/26.50.* Just off a garden square not far from Queensway shopping road, L'Accento is a favourite with aficianados of authentic Italian provincial cuisine. Delicious shellfish specialities. Choose from the lively front room or the rear conservatory with a removable roof.

Belvedere – *Holland House (off Abbotsbury Rd), Kensington, W8 6LU – ⊖ Kensington Olympia – ☎ 020 7602 1238 – sales@whitestarline.org.uk – £17.95/51.* On a summer's day secure a table on the balcony terrace at this 19C orangery in the middle of Holland Park. Large vases of flowers are spread generously over the two floors while the menu offers a modern take on some classic French and British dishes.

Malabar – *27 Uxbridge St, Kensington, W8 7TQ – ⊖ Notting Hill Gate – ☎ 020 7727 8800 – feedback@malabar-restaurant.co.uk – Closed last week Aug and 4 days Christmas – £18.55/25.40.* Lovers of Indian cooking flock to this restaurant conveniently located in a residential street just minutes from the Notting Hill Gate tube. Each of the three rooms has a different decor. Choose from an extensive range of good-value dishes, with a number of vegetarian options.

Jason's – *Blomfield Rd, Little Venice, Maida Vale, W9 2PD – ⊖ Warwick Avenue – ☎ 020 7286 6752 – enquiries@jasons.co.uk – Closed 25 Dec-2 Jan and Sun dinner – £18.95/28.90.* The extremely popular terrace is the perfect spot to watch the brightly painted barges chug gently down the Regent's Canal. On the menu: a mix of traditional and modern seafood dishes.

The Tenth – *2 -24 Kensington High St, Kensington, W8 4PT – ⊖ High Street Kensington – ☎ 020 7361 1910 – Closed Sun and lunch Sat – £21/40.50.* The name refers to the hotel's top floor where this stylish yet relaxed dining room is situated. Professional staff and contemporary menu. Spectacular views of Kensington Palace and Kensington Gardens. The lunch menu is a true bargain.

A pub lunch in Bayswater

A. Taverner/MICHELIN

Notting Grill – *123A Clarendon Rd, North Kensington, W11 4JG – ⊖ Ladbroke Grove – ☎ 020 7229 1500 – notting.grill@virgin.net – Closed 25-26 Dec, Sun dinner and Mon lunch – £26.50/39.* Mingle with the in-crowd at this typical Notting Hill hangout. With its bare brick walls and wooden tables, it has retained some reminders of the former pub that once stood here. Roof-top terrace. The kitchen uses organic produce and meat from rare breeds; steak a speciality.

Knightsbridge, Belgravia, Westminster, Victoria, Pimlico

Jenny Lo's Tea House – *14 Eccleston St, SW1W 9LT – ⊖ Victoria – ☎ 020 7259 0399 – Closed Sun and Bank Hols – From £5.* It's popular, authentically Chinese and the prices are right. The imaginative menu at this friendly "canteen" proudly informs clients that no MSG is added to the dishes. Come early to avoid the queues. Cash and cheques only.

Isola – *145 Knightsbridge, SW1X 7PA – ⊖ Knightsbridge – ☎ 020 7838 1044 – reception@isola-restaurant.co.uk – £15/41.50.* Take a drink in the bar or head downstairs for the Italian dishes, the impressive selection of Italian wines available by the glass and the lively atmosphere.

Christopher's – *Thistle Victoria, Buckingham Palace Rd, SW1W 0SJ – ⊖ Victoria – ☎ 020 7976 5522 – victoria@christophersgrill.com – £17/28.* This grand Victorian dining room received a modern facelift in 2000 and is now the impressive setting for a lively bar and restaurant serving the finest in classic and contemorary American cuisine. From burgers to lobster – an impressive and imaginative selection of meals and bar snacks served all day; eating at the bar is less expensive.

Oliveto – *49 Elizabeth St, SW1W 9PP – ⊖ Victoria – ☎ 020 7730 0074 – Closed bank hols – £17/30.* A bright and vibrant restaurant within easy reach of Victoria station. Extensive modern Italian menu with fabulous pizzas baked in wood-fired ovens. Efficient and friendly service. Advisable to book for lunch as it's quite popular with the local crowd.

Le Metro – *28 Basil St, Knightsbridge, SW3 1AS – ⊖ Knightsbridge – ☎ 020 7589 6286 – reservations@lhotel.co.uk – Closed 25 Dec and Bank Hols – £18/21.* Need a break from shopping? Try this modern basement bistro and café just round the corner from Harrods. Open throughout the day, a popular spot for a moderately priced light snack or a more substantial meal.

Swag and Tails – *10-11 Fairholt St, Knightsbridge, SW7 1EG – ⊖ Knightsbridge – ☎ 020 7584 6926 – swagandtails@mway.com – Closed 25-26 Dec, 1 Jan and Bank Hols – £18.45/26.70.* Tucked away in a side street close to Montpelier Sq and Harrods, the Swag and Tails is a handsome Victorian pub with a selection of daily specials and light snacks. Good service.

Zafferano – *15 Lowndes St, Belgravia, SW1X 9EY – ⊖ Knightsbridge – ☎ 020 7235 5800 – Booking essential – £24.50/37.50.* You may need to book about a month in advance to secure a table at one of London's finest Italian restaurants. You'll be tempted by robust dishes that reflect the season. Keep space for the wonderful tiramisu.

Marylebone, Regent's Park, Primrose Hill, St John's Wood

Café Bagatelle – *The Wallace Collection, Hertford House, Manchester Sq, W1M 6BN – ⊖ Bond Street – ☎ 020 7563 9505 – wallace@eliance.org.uk – Open Mon-Sat 10am (noon Sun) to 4.30pm and some bank hols – £10/30.* The glass-enclosed courtyard of Hertford House provides a stunning setting for this bright and relaxed restaurant amid bronze urns, a verdigris fountain and sculptures aplenty. The service is attentive, and the menu modern European. A popular spot for afternoon tea.

Chada Chada – *16-17 Picton Pl, Marylebone, W1M 5DE – ⊖ Bond Street – ☎ 020 7935 8212 – Closed Sun and Bank Hols – £12.50/26.95.* One of London's finest Thai restaurants and only a 2-minute walk from Oxford Street! Authentic and delicately spiced traditional Thai dishes as well as some innovative surprises. Good service. The small and intimate rooms fill up quickly.

The Queens – *49 Regent's Park Rd, Primrose Hill, NW1 8XD – ⊖ Chalk Farm – ☎ 020 7586 0408 – www.geronimo-inns.co.uk – £14/24.* One of the first "gastropubs" to hit the London scene, the Queens serves hearty traditional dishes listed on a blackboard menu. Try to grab a seat on the popular balcony overlooking Primrose Hill and the high street.

Black Truffle – *40 Chalcot Rd, Primrose Hill, NW1 8LS – ⊖ Chalk Farm – ☎ 020 7483 0077 – Closed 25 December, Sat lunch, Sun and Bank Hols – £15/25.* There was little doubt that the charm of Primrose Hill would lead sooner or later to the appearance of stylish new restaurants such as the Black Truffle. The chocolate brown tones and modern Italian cooking make a winning combination.

Odette's Wine Bar – *130 Regent's Park Rd, Primrose Hill, NW1 8XL – ⊖ Chalk Farm – ☎ 020 7586 5486 – Closed 1 week Christmas and Sun dinner – Booking essential – £15.50/23.* Very close to Primrose Hill, this inexpensive wine bar occupies the basement, below Odette's main restaurant. The menu is light and modern, and the walls are adorned with assorted photographs and pictures from the 1960s. The young staff provides chatty and attentive service. Well-priced lunch menu.

The Engineer – *65 Gloucester Ave, Primrose Hill, NW1 8JH – ⊖ Chalk Farm – ☎ 020 7722 0950 – info@the-eng.com – Closed 25-26 Dec and 1 Jan – £17.75/29.* Mingle with the locals in the busy front bar or dine by candlelight in one of the dining rooms. In summer, ask for a table on the attractive terrace. Unhurried service and an appealing modern menu.

The Salt House – *63 Abbey Rd, St John's Wood, NW8 0AE – St John's Wood – 020 7328 6626 – saltrestbar@aol.com – Closed Mon lunch – Booking essential – £18.65/22.40.* After paying homage to the Beatles at the nearby Abbey Road zebra crossing or taking in an exhibition at the Saatchi Gallery up the road, stop into this ever-busy gastropub for a sampling of modern British cooking. Choose between the comfortable lounge or the slightly more formal restaurant to the rear.

Union Café – *96 Marylebone Lane, Marylebone, W1M 5FP – Bond Street – 020 7486 4860 – unioncafe@winegallery.fsnet.co.uk – Closed Christmas, New Year, Sun and Bank Hols – £19/28.* This pleasant, luminous and laid-back restaurant is tucked away in a narrow lane near the Wallace Collection. Watch the chefs prepare your food in the open plan kitchen. Regularly changing menu of innovative Mediterranean cooking at reasonable prices.

Villandry – *170 Great Portland St, Marylebone, W1N 5TB – Great Portland Street – 020 7631 3131 – Closed 25 Dec, 1 Jan, Sun dinner and Bank Hols – £22/30.* Take a walk around the daytime deli brimming with epicurean delights before sampling the freshly prepared and tasty dishes in the restaurant to the rear. A relaxed and informal eatery with wooden tables and bare walls.

Ibla – *89 Marylebone High St, Marylebone, W1M 3DE – Baker Street – 020 7224 3799 – ibla@ibla.co.uk – Closed 1 week Christmas, Sun and Bank Hols – Booking recommended – £30/45.* Consider yourself fortunate to get a reservation at this increasingly popular Italian restaurant. The diverse menu combines gutsy traditional and modern dishes. For more intimacy, ask for a table in the room to the rear, as the bar area can be very noisy.

Mayfair

Momo – *25 Heddon St, W1B 4BX – Piccadilly Circus – 020 7434 4040 – momoresto@aol.com – Closed Christmas – £17/36.50.* Those wishing to mix with the "in" crowd should head for this colourful Moroccan restaurant. The decor of traditional rug, drapes and ornaments together with the entrancing Arabic music lend an air of authenticity. Staff will gladly guide the uninitiated through the menu.

Mirabelle – *56 Curzon St, W1J 8PA – Green Park – 020 7499 4636 – sales@whitestarline.org.uk – £19.95/53.50.* This legendary restaurant still oozes the glamour and style that made its reputation in the 1930s. Descend the staircase, stroll pass the elegant bar and into the superb dining room. Refined cuisine featuring both modern and classic dishes and a notable wine list. Reasonably priced lunch menu.

The Café at Sotheby's – *34-35 New Bond St, W1A 2AA – Bond Street – 020 7293 5077 – Open for lunch only. Closed 2 weeks Aug, 2 weeks Christmas, Sat and Sun – Booking essential – £21.50/29.50.* Now you can also eat in this prestigious auction house located in Mayfair's exclusive shopping district. In the simple room just off the main lobby, choose from a variety of light dishes. The aproned staff is pleasant.

Nobu – *19 Old Park Lane, W1Y 4LB – Green Park – 020 7447 4747 – confirmations@noburestaurants.com – Closed 25-26 Dec and Sat lunch – Booking essential – £24.50/85.* Fusion for the famous. At the Metropolitan's (see Where to Stay) ultra-trendy eatery, South America meets Japan to create highly original and extremely enjoyable cuisine which attracts a celebrity clientele. Stunning minimalist decor. Come with an open mind, a large wallet, and wear black.

Scotts – *20 Mount St, W1Y 6HE – Bond Street – 020 7629 5248 – bc@scottsrestaurant.co.uk – Closed 25 Dec – £25/59.* First opened in 1851 and a favourite haunt of Winston Churchill, Scotts was given a contemporary face lift in the late 1990s. The formal room on the upper floor specialises in oysters, Dover sole and modern fish dishes, while refreshing snacks are served in the piano bar downstairs.

Piccadilly, St James's

Alloro – Baretto – *19-20 Dover St, W1X 3PB – Green Park – 020 7495 4768 – www.atozrestaurants.com – Closed Sun and Sat lunch – £6/14.* Although more laid-back than its sister restaurant, Alloro's "small bar" offers authentic Italian fare in an elegant setting. On the short menu: fresh pasta dishes, soups and elaborate salads, traditional Italian charcuterie and cheeses. A lively bar in the evening.

Getti – *16-17 Jermyn St, SW1Y 6LT – Piccadilly Circus – 020 7734 7334 – Closed Sun – £15.50/18.50.* Among the handsome shops of London's most renowned tailors and shirtmakers, this pleasant modern Italian restaurant stands out. An extensive a la carte menu features both traditional and contemporary dishes. The "express menu" is good value.

Quaglino's – *16 Bury St, St James's, SW1Y 6AL – Green Park – 020 7930 6767 – www.conran.com – Closed 25 Dec – £16/35.* On the site of the original celebrated society restaurant, the present Quaglino's is a lively and buzzy brasserie that continues to draw a glamorous crowd. You might even spot a celebrity making an entrance on the impressive staircase. The seafood bar and the open plan kitchens give glimpses of the chefs at work.

China House – *160 Piccadilly, W1V 9DF – Green Park – 020 7499 6996 – sales@chinahouse.co.uk – £16.85/31.45.* Originally designed as a car show room in 1922, this elaborately decorated former banking hall provides a spectacular setting for a lively Chinese restaurant. To make your choice, just consult the placemat-menu.

Benihana – *37 Sackville St, W1X 2DQ – Piccadilly Circus – 020 7494 2525 – info@benihana.co.uk – Closed 25 Dec – £17/50.* It is worth coming here to marvel at the dexterity of the Japanese chefs as they chop, juggle and cook before their diners' eyes. Be prepared to chat with strangers as guests are seated in groups around the counters. Reasonably priced set lunch and dinner menus available; freshly prepared sushi to eat in or take away.

⊖⊖ **Just Oriental** – *19 King St, SW1A 1ER – ⊖ Green Park – ☎ 020 7930 9292 – bookings@juststjames.com – Closed Sat lunch and Sun – £17/22.* In the mood for Far Eastern fare? This brasserie-bar, in a contemporarily designed basement, features a menu running the gamut from Japanese to Mongolian specialities. Try the reasonably priced two-course midweek lunch menu. Lively cocktail bar scene throughout the evening.

⊖⊖ **Al Duca** – *4-5 Duke of York St, St James's, SW1Y 6LA – ⊖ Piccadilly Circus – ☎ 020 7839 3090 – info@alduca-restaurants.co.uk – Closed Sun – £19.50/23.* Considering its location in the heart of pricey St James's, this modern Italian restaurant offers good value. Friendly staff serves the hearty rustic cuisine, and the atmosphere is more relaxed than one would expect.

St Pancras, Camden Town

⊖⊖ **Camden Brasserie** – *9-11 Jamestown Rd, Camden, NW1 – ⊖ Camden Town – ☎ 020 7482 2114 – £15/20.* For over 20 years this popular brasserie has provided the perfect spot for a bite to eat after the hurly burly of the market. The specialities are grilled meats and fish, all served with large bowls of thin chips.

South Bank, Bankside, Southwark, Bermondsey, Waterloo

⊖⊖ **Studio 6** – *Gabriels Wharf, SE1 9PP – ⊖ Waterloo – ☎ 020 7928 6243 – www.studiosix.co.uk – £15/20.* Behind a modest façade among the riverside craft shops, is an informal, bustling brasserie with bar. T-shirt staff serves a European-influenced menu that changes daily.

⊖⊖ **Livebait** – *43 The Cut, Southwark, SE1 8LF – ⊖ Southwark – ☎ 020 7928 7211 – Closed Sun – £15.50/30.50.* With its characteristic wall tiles and booths, this popular seafood restaurant has something of a Victorian feel. Things get particularly lively with the steady flow of pre- and post-theatre crowds from the nearby Old Vic. Amateur chefs can glean a few trade secrets from the open-plan kitchen. Other central London locations: 175 Westbourne Grove (North Kensington) and 21 Wellington St (Covent Garden).

⊖⊖ **Cantina Vinopolis (Brasserie)** – *1 Bank End, Southwark, SE1 9BU – ⊖ Southwark – ☎ 020 7940 8333 – cantina@vinopolis.co.uk – Closed Sun dinner and Bank Hols – £15.75/32.50.* Calling all oenologists! These imposing Victorian railway arches, close to the Globe Theatre, now house a vaulted restaurant and an adjoining wine museum. The modern menu is sensibly priced, and a vast selection of wines is available by the glass.

⊖⊖ **The Fire Station** – *150 Waterloo Rd, Southbank, SE1 8SB – ⊖ Waterloo – ☎ 020 7620 2226 – firestation@wizardinns.co.uk – £18/25.* Located between the Old Vic and Waterloo Station, this 1910 fire station has been carefully refurbished to house a restaurant specialising in Mediterranean-style cuisine. Tiled floor, old church pews and an open kitchen contribute to the pleasant informal atmosphere.

⊖⊖ **Fish** – *Cathedral St, Borough Market, Southwark, SE1 9AL – ⊖ Southwark – ☎ 020 7407 3803 – info@fish.plc.uk – Closed 25 Dec, Sun dinner and Bank Hols – £20/25.* The nearby Old Borough Market and the surrounding streets hardly prepare you for this modern glass and metal structure. Inside, ordering can be fun: you choose the fish as well as the cooking method and accompanying sauce.

⊖⊖⊖ **Oxo Tower Brasserie** – *Barge House St (8th floor), Oxo Tower Wharf, Southwark, SE1 9PH – ⊖ Southwark – ☎ 020 7803 3888 – www.harveynichols.com – £21.50/31.50.* Sharing the 8th floor of a converted factory with the more formal restaurant, the brasserie offers the same spectacular view of the London skyline. Those facing inwards can watch the open-plan kitchen producing modern cooking with professional servers. Terrace dining in good weather.

⊖⊖⊖ **Blue Print Café** – *Butlers Wharf, Design Museum, Shad Thames, Bermondsey, SE1 2YD – ⊖ Bermondsey – ☎ 020 7378 7031 – www.conran.com – Closed Sun dinner – £22.50/42.* After visiting the Design Museum, secure a window table in this adjoining restaurant and enjoy the views of Tower Bridge and the Thames. Understated decor with black and white photographs on display. Informal and personable service and modern European menu.

Outer London

North-west: Hampstead, Highgate, Swiss Cottage, Hendon

The Magdala – *2A South Hill Park, NW3 2SB – ⊖ Belsize Park, Hampstead – ☎ 020 7435 2503 – Closed 25 Dec – £15.70/21.75.* A large pub on the edge of the Heath, ideally placed for walking off any lunchtime excess. Informal ground floor bar; first floor dining room. Traditional cuisine.

Base – *71 Hampstead High St, NW3 1QP – ☎ 020 7431 2224 – www.basefoods.com – £10.50/18.95.* In the middle of the high street, this informal restaurant features well-prepared Algerian and Moroccan specialities. If you drop in outside the normal serving hours, enjoy a mint tea in the all-day café in the front section of the narrow dining room.

North-east: East End, Hackney, Whitechapel

Cafe Spice Namaste – *16 Prescot St, Whitechapel, E1 8AZ – ⊖ Tower Hill – ☎ 020 7488 9242 – info@cafespice.co.uk – Closed Sun, Sat lunch and Bank Hols – £14.50/40.* Upon entering this Indian restaurant, you're greeted with a riot of colour, from the brightly painted walls to the flowing drapes. Friendly atmosphere and discreet, attentive service. The cooking is fragrant and competitively priced.

Café Naz – *45-48 Brick Lane, E1 6RF – ⊖ Aldgate East – ☎ 020 7247 0234 – Closed Sat lunch – £15.* Brick Lane is renowned for its Indian restaurants, and Café Naz is a more contemporary take on the theme. The menu has many Bangladeshi specialities. Service is prompt and efficient. A real "East-End" experience.

South-east: Greenwich, Blackheath

North Pole – *131 Greenwich High Rd, Greenwich, SE10 8JA – ⊖ New Cross – ☎ 020 8853 3020 – Closed 25 Dec and Mon lunch – £17.50/25.* After a short stroll from the centre of Greenwich, you'll arrive at this lively converted corner pub. The upstairs dining room has high ceilings, large windows and brightly coloured walls. Service is informal and obliging and the cooking should satisfy any appetite.

Chapter Two – *43-45 Montpelier Vale, Blackheath, SE3 0TJ – ⊖ New Cross – ☎ 020 8333 2666 – fiona.chapter2@talk21.com – ⅍ – £18.50/22.50.* Located at the upper end of the high street near the Heath, this contemporary neighbourhood restaurant, with its pine floors and primary colours, has a cool yet cosy feel. Well-prepared and well-priced modern European cuisine. Service is formal without being stuffy.

South: Battersea

Chada – *208-210 Battersea Park Rd, Battersea, SW11 4ND – ⊖ Pimlico – ☎ 020 7622 2209 – Closed Sun and Bank Hols – £13.30/27.75.* An exotic eating experience amid Thai ornaments and charming staff in traditional silk costumes. The extensive menu offers authentic and carefully prepared dishes from various parts of Thailand.

The Stepping Stone – *123 Queenstown Rd, SW8 3RH – ☎ 020 7622 0555 – thesteppingstone@aol.com – Closed 5 days Christmas, Sat lunch, Sun and Bank Hols – £18/30.* Big bold colours and thoughtful service make this pleasant contemporary restaurant a local favourite. Eclectic, modern menu. Small bar to the rear.

South-south-west: Fulham, Putney, Wimbledon

The Phoenix – *Pentlow St, Putney, SW15 1LY – ⊖ Putney Bridge – ☎ 020 8780 3131 – phoenix@sonny's.co.uk – Closed Bank Hols – £15/32.70.* Large French windows at this relaxed neighbourhood restaurant lead out onto a spacious terrace. The young staff provides considerate yet unfussy service, and the well-priced modern menu offers a good selection with some surprises.

Light House – *75-77 Ridgway, Wimbledon, SW19 4ST – ⊖ Wimbledon – ☎ 020 8944 6338 – lightrest@aol.com – Closed 1 week Christmas – £19/32.40.* Not far from Wimbledon tube, a former store selling lights has been nicely remodelled to accommodate a bright and modern neighbourhood restaurant with open kitchen. You'll appreciate the friendly and informal service and the changing menu featuring modern Italian and fusion dishes. Try the pizza and risotto specialities.

River Café – *Rainville Rd, Thames Wharf, Hammersmith, W6 9HA – ⊖ Hammersmith – ☎ 020 7386 4200 – info@rivercafe.co.uk – Closed Christmas-New Year, Easter, Sun dinner and Bank Hols – £38/55.50.* Owned and operated by food and lifestyle celebrities, Ruth Rogers and Rose Gray, this immensely successful restaurant in a converted warehouse has the feel of a canteen. Young staff, open kitchen and, best of all, first-rate Italian cuisine incorporating the best ingredients around.

South-west: Richmond, Kew

The Glasshouse – *14 Station Par, Kew, TW9 3PZ – ⊖ Kew Gardens – ☎ 020 8940 6777 – Closed 25 Dec, 1 Jan and Sun dinner – £19.50/30.* Beside Kew Gardens tube station and just a short walk from the botanical gardens, this luminous restaurant is recognisable by its large glass façade. Inside, the atmosphere, like the cooking, is contemporary, refined and very British. Attentive service.

Redmond's – *170 Upper Richmond Road West, East Sheen, SW14 8AW – ⊖ Kew Gardens – ☎ 020 8878 1922 – pippahayward@btconnect.com – Closed 4 days Christmas, Sat lunch, Sun dinner and Bank Hols except Good Friday – Booking recommended – £21/28.50.* Chef Redmond Hayward has a reputation for offering seasonal cooking, with game and fish signature dishes in this informal restaurant. The menu is trendily modern British, and the well-priced set menu offers good value.

Monsieur Max – *133 High St, Hampton Hill, TW12 1NJ – ⊖ Richmond (4mi/6.4km SW of tube station) – ☎ 020 8979 5546 – monsmax@aol.com – Closed Sat lunch – £25/37.50.* From Hampton Court, take a short taxi ride or build up a healthy appetite with a brisk walk along the Thames. Savour hearty traditional French dishes in a comfortable atmosphere. Don't miss the delicious rice pudding. Diners may bring their own wine (corkage charge applies).

Riva – *169 Church Rd, Barnes, SW13 9HR – ⊖ Hammersmith (1.5mi/2.4km S of tube station) – ☎ 020 8748 0434 – Closed last 2 weeks Aug, 1 week Christmas-New Year, 1 week Easter, Sat lunch and Bank Hols – £26/34.50.* Don't be fooled by the rather unassuming façade of this restaurant; Riva is one of London's finest exponents of rustic and authentic Italian cooking. Richmond Park and Kew Gardens are just a short taxi ride away.

Services

Concessions

Visitors wishing to keep costs down will find information on budget accommodation in the section Where to Stay which includes bed and breakfast establishments, guest houses and hotels as well as youth hostels and camping sites.
Several airlines offer budget fares to and from European destinations. Prices vary according to how far in advance the booking is made; there are also weekend rates and further advantages when booking on line:
EasyJet: www.easyjet.co.uk;
Virgin Express: www.virgin-express.com;
British Midland: www.britishmidland.com;
Ryan Air: www.ryanair.ie
A **Visitor Travelcard** for freedom of travel on the underground, most London buses, the Docklands Light Railway and most National Rail trains in the London area is very good value for sightseeing. The Visitor Card must be purchased from overseas agents. Enquire from your local travel agent. It comes with a free book of discount vouchers to be used on entry to tourist attractions and restaurants in London. Remember to take some passport-size photos with you if you want to purchase a public transport and museum pass on arrival.
Cinemas offer reduced rates for early afternoon performances. Theatre tickets are on offer at reduced prices for matinées and evening shows *(see Theatres)*.

Discounts for young people

Young people and students benefit from special rates on public transport and for a range of tourist attractions and other venues such as theatres and clubs. Children aged 5 to 15 years need proof of age when applying for a photocard. Accompanied children under 5 travel free on buses, underground and Docklands Light Railway. Children 14 and 15 years old with a Child Photocard qualify for child rate tickets. There are also Youth LT cards, Bus Passes and Underground only season tickets only for 16 to 17 year olds.
Students require an International Student Card to prove eligibility for reduced rates.

Discounts for senior citizens...

To qualify for reduced rates on public transport and museum, cinema and theatre admission charges visitors over 60 years must provide proof of age. It is always worth asking when no discount is listed.

Discounts for families...

Family Travelcards offering substantial discounts to families and groups of 1 or 2 adults travelling with up to 4 children are a great moneysaver and most sights offer special rates for a family group of 2 adults and 2 or more children.

Certain schemes are available for local visitors and to travellers from abroad.

English Heritage – Membership of this organisation provides free access to over 400 venues nationwide including the country houses of London (Kenwood, Chiswick House, Ranger's House). An **Overseas Visitor Pass** valid for 7 or 14 days at an initial cost of Adult £13 / £17, 2 Adults £24 / 32, Family (2A+2C) £29 / £37.
English Heritage, 23 Savile Row, London W1S 2ET ☎ 020 7973 3000; P O Box 569, Swindon SN2 2YR.
☎ 0870 333 1181 (customer services); Fax 01793 414 926; www.english-heritage.org.uk

London for Less – Valid for 4 persons over a period of 8 days, the card offers holders a variety of discounts on hotels, major attractions, restaurants, pubs, theatres, concerts, telephone calls and foreign currency exchanges.
A Smartsave discount card costs £12.95 for 4 persons for 8 days and is available through American distributors on ☎ 1 888 463 6753 or from Metropolis

International (UK) Ltd, 222 Kensal Road, W10 5BN. ☎ 020 8964 4242; Fax 020 8964 4141; www.for-less.com Payment may be transacted by credit card and arrangements made for the cards and information pack to be sent either to you at home prior to departure or to the first hotel ready for your arrival in London.Parallel schemes in operation for Bath, Edinburgh and York. The card is also available from all major book retailers, on-line booksellers and www.amazon.co.uk

London Pass – A visitors' smart card giving free access and fast track entry to over 60 attractions (and free public transport when purchased before arriving in London): museums, historic sites, guided tours, cinemas, cycling, ten-pin bowling and many other activities. Valid for 1 to 6 days: £27-£110 (adult), £18-£61 (child).
The card can be purchased on line or by phone or from London Transport Information Centres, London Tourist Information Centres, at Victoria Station, Liverpool Street Station and Heathrow Terminals Stations and other outlets.
London Pass – www.londonpass.com
P O Box 25, Melton Mowbray LE13 1ZG
☎ 0870 242 9988 (Mon-Fri, 9am-8pm, Sat, 10am-4pm); Fax 01664 480 257; info@londonpass.com

Regent Street Association

Christmas decorations in Regent Street

Practical Information

Emergencies

999 for all emergency services (no charge nationwide); ask for Fire, Police, Ambulance, Coastguard, Mountain Rescue or Cave Rescue.

Currency

The decimal system (100 pence = £1) is used throughout Great Britain; Scotland has different notes including £1 and £100 notes, which are valid outside Scotland; Isle of Man and the Channel Islands have different notes and coins, which are not valid elsewhere.

The common currency – in descending order of value – is £50, £20, £10 and £5 (notes); £2, £1, 50p, 20p, 10p, 5p (silver coins) and 2p and 1p (copper coins).

NOTES AND COINS

See Notes and Coins

Banks

OPENING HOURS

Banks are generally open from Mondays to Fridays, 9.30am to 3.30pm; some banks offer a limited service on Saturday mornings; all banks are closed on Sundays and bank holidays *(see below)*.
Exchange facilities outside these hours are available at airports, bureaux de change, travel agencies and hotels. Most banks have cash dispensers that accept international credit cards.

TRAVELLERS' CHEQUES

Some form of identification is necessary when cashing travellers cheques or Eurocheques in banks. Commission charges vary; hotels usually charge more than banks.

CREDIT CARDS

The main credit cards (American Express; Access/Eurocard/Mastercard; Diners Club; Visa/Barclaycard) are widely accepted in shops, hotels, restaurants and petrol stations. Most banks have cash dispensers which accept international credit cards.
In case of loss or theft, the loss should also be reported to the Police who will issue a crime number for use by the insurance or credit card company. Also phone the credit card company:

Amex	020 7222 9633
Access/Eurocard	01702 364 364
Barclay Card	01604 230 230

American Express Travel Services – www.americanexpress.co.uk
78 Brompton Road, London SW3 1ER.
☎ 020 7761 7905; Fax 020 7584 7480

Post

OPENING HOURS

Post Offices are generally open Mon-Fri, 9.30am-5.30pm and Sat mornings, 9.30am-12.30pm. Late collections are made from Leicester Square and throughout the night (and on Sun) at the principal sorting offices at Paddington, Nine Elms, Mount Pleasant, St Paul's.
Stamps are also available from many newsagents and tobacconists. Poste Restante items are held for 14 days; proof of identity is required. Airmail delivery usually takes 3 to 4 days in Europe and 4 to 7 days elsewhere in the world.
Within GB – *first class post 27p; second class post 19p*
Within EU – *letter (20g) 36p (additional charge for extra weight) postcard 36p*
Non-EU Europe – *letter (20g) 40p*

(additional charge for extra weight) postcard 40p
Elsewhere – *letter (20g) 66p (additional charge for extra weight); postcard 40p; aerogrammes 40-49p*

Telephone

Prepaid **British Telecom** phonecards, of varying value, are available from post offices and many newsagents; they can be used in booths with phonecard facilities for national and international calls. Some public telephones accept credit cards.
Rates vary: daytime, Mon-Fri, 8am-6pm; evening, Mon-Fri, before 8am and after 6pm; weekend, midnight Friday to midnight Sunday.
www.bt.com.phonenetuk
100 – *Operator*
118 500, 118 888 – *Directory Enquiries within the UK*
999 – *Emergency number (free nationwide); ask for Fire, Police, Ambulance, Coastguard, Mountain Rescue or Cave Rescue.*

International Calls – To make an international call dial 00 followed by the country code, followed by the area code (without the intitial 0) followed by the subscriber's number. The codes for direct dialling to other countries are printed at the front of telephone directories and in codebooks.
00 61 – *Australia*
00 1 – *Canada*
00 353 – *Republic of Ireland*
00 64 – *New Zealand*
00 44 – *United Kingdom*
00 1 – *United States of America*
155 – *International Operator*
153 – *International Directory Enquiries; there is a charge for this service*

Electricity

The electric current is 240 volts AC (50 HZ); 3-pin flat wall sockets are standard. An adaptor or multiple point plug is required for non-British appliances.

Newspapers and television

Time Out, published weekly (Thursdays) contains up to date information on venues and reviews for the theatre, cinemas, exhibitions, concerts, discos, restaurants, guided walks, cycle hire etc. Other listings appear in the **London Evening Standard** and the broadsheet newspapers. Information about local events is available from Town Halls and public libraries.

Shopping

The big stores and larger shops are open Mondays to Saturdays from 9am to 5.30pm or 6pm, Sundays from 10am or 11am to 4pm. Some are open late (8pm) one day a week – Wednesdays in Knightsbridge, Thursdays in Oxford Street and down Regent Street. Some supermarkets open round the clock and certain food (Indian or Arab) shops stay open until 10pm or later in Bayswater Road and Earl's Court Road.

Weights and measures

The official system is the metric system; however many people are more familiar with the imperial system.

Sightseeing

As admission times and charges are liable to alteration, the information printed in the guide – valid for 2003 – is for guidance only.

Special Needs – ♿ or (♿) mean full or partial access for wheelchairs. As the range of possible facilities is great (for impaired mobility, sight and hearing), readers are advised to telephone in advance to check what is available.
Dates – Dates given are inclusive. The term weekend means Saturday and Sunday (Sat-Sun). The term holidays means bank and public holidays, when shops, museums and other monuments may be closed or may vary their times of admission. The term school holidays refers to the breaks between terms at Christmas, Easter and during the summer months and also to the short mid-term breaks (one week), which are usually in February and October.

Admission Times – Ticket offices usually shut 30min before closing time; only exceptions are mentioned. Some places issue timed tickets owing to limited space and facilities.

Charge – The charge given is for an individual adult. Most places offer reductions for families, children, students, senior citizens (old-age pensioners) and the unemployed; it may be necessary to provide proof of identity and status. Large parties should apply in advance, as many places offer special rates for group bookings and some have special days for group visits.

Abbreviations –

EH =	English Heritage.
CADW =	Welsh Historic Monuments.
HS =	Historic Scotland.
NT =	The National Trust (for England, Wales and Northern Ireland).
NTS =	The National Trust for Scotland.
NTJ =	The National Trust for Jersey.
NTG =	The National Trust for Guernsey.

There are reciprocal arrangements among NT, NTS, NTJ, NTG and the Royal Oak Foundation in the USA.

NACF =	National Art Collections Fund.
RSPB =	Royal Society for the Protection of Birds.

Churches – Many churches are locked when not in use for services.

Ideas for Your Visit

Outlined below are some suggestions to help you plan your visit to London. There are day programmes for those on a weekend trip and we also make some suggestions for those on a longer visit to the capital. The section Themed Tours highlights aspects of the city for those with special interests.
Walks described in the Selected Sights section will give visitors with more time available interesting insights regarding the metropolis.

Weekend Breaks

Day 1: The highlights which should not be missed on a short visit are the romantic outlines of the **Houses of Parliament** and Big Ben in Westminster. From Westminster Bridge admire the **view** of the Thames with the busy river traffic, the spectacular London Eye on the south bank and St Paul's Cathedral in the distance. **Westminster Abbey** with its glorious monuments and historical associations is a must. Walk up Whitehall with its imposing buildings to **Trafalgar Square** with the lions guarding the towering Nelson's Column, a bustling piazza where visitors have their photos taken surrounded by fat pigeons. For a change of pace make for **Covent Garden** with its colourful markets and street entertainment to enjoy tea, window shopping and an evening drink.

Day 2: The **Tower of London** with its treasures exerts a great fascination. Aim to start as early as possible to avoid the crowds attracted by the Crown Jewels. The guided tour with the attendants attired in their finery highlights its long history. On a sunny day, walk under **Tower Bridge** and saunter around St Katharine Docks (picturesque marina with bars and restaurants) crossing to the south side of the River Thames to explore the Bermondsey riverside (Design Museum, Bramah Museum of Tea and Coffee) and **Bankside** which has a range of interesting attractions (HMS Belfast, London Dungeon, Hay's Galleria, Southwark Cathedral, Golden Hinde, Shakespeare's Globe, Tate Modern) and a vibrant atmosphere. There are good restaurants to sample and fine pubs for refreshment in the area.

Short Breaks

Option 1: Begin at the imposing **St Paul's Cathedral** which is an architectural marvel before exploring the **City** which is best visited during the week when there is much activity in the financial district. Visit the **Bank of England Museum** which explains the financial might of this City institution, wander through **Leadenhall Market** at lunchtime or have a break in the many historic pubs frequented by city workers before continuing to marvel at the modernistic Lloyds' Building. The **Guildhall** is at the heart of the administration of the city; the **Museum of London** presents fascinating aspects of the capital through the centuries. It is well worth visiting the **City Churches** with their attractive architectural features and treasures which reflect the spirit of an age. An excellent way to round off the day is to attend a concert or theatre performance at the prestigious **Barbican** centre.

Option 2: Located in **Bloomsbury,** once the heart of the literary set, is the prestigious **British Museum** where are exhibited treasures from around the world. Spend the afternoon and evening in bustling Soho. Leicester Square and Piccadilly are places to visit for pubs and restaurants as well as cinemas and theatres.

Option 3: A visit to the charming **Wallace Collection** may be followed by a shopping spree in bustling Oxford Street, exclusive Bond Street or elegant Regent Street which cater for all tastes.

Longer Breaks

Option 1: A day may easily be spent in the museums around **South Kensington.** Visitors interested in advances in science and technology will marvel at the exciting exhibits of the **Science Museum** while those passionate about the wonders of the natural world will find much of interest in the **Natural History Museum.** Or prepare to be entranced by the wonderful treasures of the **Victoria & Albert Museum.** Allow time to browse around the designer shops and stores in **Knightsbridge** and Sloane Street or the quirky shops in the King's Road, Chelsea. The area abounds in smart pubs and restaurants.

Option 2: To enjoy different perspectives of London take a round trip down river from Westminster to **Greenwich** famous for the National Maritime Museum, Queen's House, Old Observatory and Cutty Sark combined with a return through thriving **Docklands** (Canary Wharf) with its landmark buildings and new amenities by Docklands Light Railway to Tower Gateway *(see Getting About)* and the West End. Blackheath and Ranger's House are also of interest.

Option 3: Beyond the confines of Inner London there is **Kew** with the world famous gardens which are a delight in all seasons. The splendid ceremonial rooms of **Hampton Court** are complemented by the beautiful landscaped gardens. Consider returning down river by boat *(see Other Ways of Exploring the City)* to admire the upper reaches of the Thames. The more intimate **Ham House**, **Syon Park** and **Osterley Park** in the vicinity of the gardens are also well worth a visit.

Option 4: Spend part of the day in **Regent's Park** perhaps including a visit to the zoo or a short break from sightseeing in the delightful rose garden. You can also visit Lord's Cricket Museum nearby. For a different aspect of London make for Camden Town with its colourful markets, pubs and eateries or Little Venice by canal boat to take in the picturesque canal scenery.

Themed Tours – Most museums and art galleries organise guided tours and lectures. For information see the individual museum or gallery. Official 'Blue Badge' guides permitted to operate in London may be contacted through the Tourist Information offices; they may be hired for the day or for a series of visits. *See Other Ways of Exploring the City, Guided Walks.*

Lounging in Regent's Park

A. Taverner/MICHELIN

Notes and Coins

£50 note featuring
Sir John Houblon
(1632-1712),
Gatekeeper to the
Bank of England.

£20 note featuring
Michael Faraday (1791-1867),
physicist and inventor of the
Magneto Electric Spark
Apparatus.

£10 note featuring
Charles Dickens (1812-1870),
author of Pickwick Papers,
Oliver Twist, A Christmas
Carol etc.

£5 note featuring
George Stephenson (1781-1848),
engineer, inventor of the Rocket
Locomotive and builder of
the Stockton-Darlington Raiway.

All notes and coins bear an image of the sovereign on one side. A metal strip is threaded through the paper of the bank notes. The reverse side of the £1 coin features different symbols: Royal coat of arms and Three lions rampant (England), Thistle (Scotland), Prince of Wales feathers (Wales) among others.
The bank of Scotland issues £1 notes which are legal tender throughout the United Kingdom.

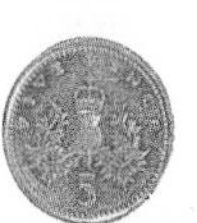

Conversion Tables

Weights and measures

1 kilogram (kg)	**2.2 pounds (lb)**	**2.2 pounds**
1 metric ton (tn)	**1.1 tons**	**1.1 tons**

to convert kilograms to pounds, multiply by 2.2

1 litre (l)	**2.1 pints (pt)**	**1.8 pints**
1 litre	**0.3 gallon (gal)**	**0.2 gallon**

to convert litres to gallons, multiply by 0.26 (US) or 0.22 (UK)

1 hectare (ha)	**2.5 acres**	**2.5 acres**
1 square kilometre (km²)	**0.4 square miles (sq mi)**	**0.4 square miles**

to convert hectares to acres, multiply by 2.4

1 centimetre (cm)	**0.4 inches (in)**	**0.4 inches**
1 metre (m)	**3.3 feet (ft) - 39.4 inches - 1.1 yards (yd)**	
1 kilometre (km)	**0.6 miles (mi)**	**0.6 miles**

to convert metres to feet, multiply by 3.28, kilometres to miles, multiply by 0.6

Clothing

Women			
Shoes	35	4	2½
	36	5	3½
	37	6	4½
	38	7	5½
	39	8	6½
	40	9	7½
	41	10	8½
Dresses & suits	36	4	8
	38	6	10
	40	8	12
	42	12	14
	44	14	16
	46	16	18
Blouses & sweaters	36	30	08
	38	32	10
	40	34	12
	42	36	14
	44	38	16
	46	40	18

			Men
40	7½	7	Shoes
41	8½	8	
42	9½	9	
43	10½	10	
44	11½	11	
45	12½	12	
46	13½	13	
46	36	36	Suits
48	38	38	
50	40	40	
52	42	42	
54	44	44	
56	46	48	
37	14½	14½	Shirts
38	15	15	
39	15½	15½	
40	15¾	15¾	
41	16	16	
42	16½	16½	

Sizes often vary depending on the designer. These equivalents are given for guidance only.

Speed

kph	10	30	50	70	80	90	100	110	120	130
mph	6	19	31	43	50	56	62	68	75	81

Temperature

Celsius (°C)	0°	5°	10°	15°	20°	25°	30°	40°	60°	80°	100°
Fahrenheit (°F)	32°	41°	50°	59°	68°	77°	86°	104°	140°	176°	212°

To convert Celsius into Fahrenheit, multiply °C by 9, divide by 5, and add 32.
To convert Fahrenheit into Celsius, subtract 32 from °F, multiply by 5, and divide by 9.

Special Interests

Art

London is well endowed with art venues. Besides the renowned National Museum, Tate Modern and Tate Britain which present European Art, there are several smaller galleries which hold many treasures, namely The Courtauld Galleries, Wallace Collection, Dulwich Picture Galleries. Maritime art is on view at the National Maritime Museum in Greenwich.
Splendid works of art belonging to the Royal Collections are on display in in royal palaces: Buckingham Palace, the Queen's Gallery, Kensington Palace, Hampton Court and Windsor.
Noble mansions such as Apsley House, Kenwood House, Ham House, Syon Park and Osterley Park also boast superb holdings of fine art.
Well presented temporary exhibitions devoted to major artists and schools are held at the Royal Academy in Piccadilly and the Hayward Gallery on the South Bank. The Whitechapel Art Gallery in the End, the Saatchi Gallery in St John's Wood, the Lux Gallery in Hoxton, the White Cube Gallery in Mayfair and Hoxton, and small specialist galleries present contemporary art. Check the press for fine exhibitions put on by art dealers in Mayfair, St James's and Knightsbridge.

Science

Besides the Science Museum, which covers all scientific fields and includes the Wellcome Wing devoted to contemporary science, technology and medicine, do not miss the Royal Observatory in Greenwich and the Planetarium. The Kew Bridge Steam Museum charts industrial advances and has huge machines on steam.

Bird's-Eye Views

A novel way of seeing the capital is from the **London Eye** on the South Bank: on a clear day the view extends to the distant suburbs. The viewing areas on the top floors of **Tate Modern** afford wonderful perspectives of the City of London with the majestic dome of St Paul's Cathedral in the foregound; there is a fine view up and down the Thames spanned by the elegant Millennium Bridge. The outlook from the dome of **St Paul's Cathedral** is spectacular. The view from the elevated walkway of **Tower Bridge** embraces the graceful Tower of London and Canary Wharf on the horizon. Although later structures hamper the view from **Monument** it is still worth climbing to the top. **Wellington Arch** at Hyde Park Corner, a busy hub, is the latest viewpoint dominating Buckingham Palace, Hyde Park and Knightsbridge. To enjoy an unusual view of the roof tops of neighbouring buildings, of Nelson's Column and of the vista down Whitehall go up to the top floor of the **National Portrait Gallery**. Visitors to **Kenwood** to the north should not miss the viewpoint in the grounds which pinpoints the distant landmarks of the capital.

Gardens

Gardens are a national passion and what better way of enjoying the great outdoors than to visit **Kew Gardens** which make a glorious show in all seasons (lilac, bluebells, azaleas, magnolias, cherry blossom in spring; rhododendrons and roses in summer; heathers in autumn-winter). The heady fragrances of the **Queen Mary's Rose Garden** in Regent's Park and of the rose garden in **Syon Park** are among the delights of summer in London. The fine gardens of **Buckingham Palace**, which were previously enjoyed only by privileged guests at royal garden parties, are now accessible as part of a visit when the palace is open to the public in summer. The Edwardian sunken garden and the Flower Walk are the glories of **Kensington Gardens**. The intricate Knot Garden, the Privy Garden and the Great Vine are special features of **Hampton Court** gardens. In spring the rhododendrons of **The Isabella Plantation** in Richmond Park gladden the eye. Further afield are the **Valley Gardens** with shrubs and trees and the landscaped **Savill Gardens** in Windsor.
Aromatic herb gardens are to be found at the **Museum of Garden History** in Lambeth, the Geffrye Museum in Shoreditch and at the **Chelsea Physic Garden**.

Royal London

From the earliest times the sovereigns have built their palaces in and around London. The **Tower of London** built after the Conquest is one of the earliest royal residences and the glittering Crown Jewels are one of its major attractions. All that remains of 11C Westminster Palace is the majestic **Westminster**

Hall. There are Tudor remnants of Whitehall Palace near Whitehall where Henry VIII held court. Also on the site is the harmonious **Banqueting House** with its wonderful interior décor. This building and the elegant **Queen's House** in Greenwich encapsulate the sophistication of the Stuarts.

St James's Palace is a splendid example of Tudor architecture. It is the London residence of members of the royal family. **Clarence House** nearby, formerly the home of Queen Elizabeth, the Queen Mother since the death of George VI in 1952, is now the residence of the Prince of Wales.

The red-brick **Kensington Palace** built in Jacobean style is associated with the reign of William III and Mary II; this is where several members of the present royal family have apartments.

The royal standard flies when the sovereign is in residence at **Buckingham Palace**. The palace is open to the public in season and the fascination of wandering through the State Rooms is irresistible. Do not miss the Changing of the Guard, or if you are lucky the elaborate pageantry of state occasions such as Trooping the Colour or the Opening of Parliament. To complete the picture it is well worth making pleasurable excursions to **Hampton Court** in its riverside setting and to the majestic **Windsor Castle** and the delightful town of Windsor.

Stately Homes

Several mansions in the vicinity of London retain the rural prospect enjoyed by their original owners. As they were built when the Thames was the main highway many have a riverside setting. **Chiswick House,** which was intended for entertaining, epitomises 18C refinement. **Syon Park**, an imposing mansion with royal associations, reflects the tastes of discerning patrons of the arts. **Osterley Park** is an elegant stately home with splendid furnishings in the Adam style (18C). The handsome 17C **Ham House** in the Jacobean style and the charming 18C **Marble Hill House** in Twickenham boast many treasures. **Kenwood House**, which was built as a country retreat in the 18C, stands in splendid grounds on Highgate Hill; it has been the setting for several award-winning films.

Military London

London boasts outstanding collections of arms and armour to satisfy the most demanding amateurs. The **Royal Armouries Collection** in the Tower of London is exceptionally fine. Find out about all aspects of warfare at the **Imperial War Museum.** The story of the British Army over five centuries is traced at the **National Army Museum** in Chelsea. Excellent displays are presented at the **Wallace Collection**, **Hampton Court** and the **Victoria and Albert Museum**. Thegrounds of the **Honourable Artillery Company HQ** in Clerkenwell were in use for military purposes as far back as the 16C. Be prepared for loud bangs at **Firepower!** the latest presentation of the Royal Artillery Company at Woolwich.

Literary London

A plethora of writers and dramatists have plied their trade in London and are household names in the history of the English language. The most illustrious are William Shakespeare and Ben Jonson whose fame is associated with The Globe and other theatres on Bankside. Geoffrey Chaucer is linked with Westminster Abbey; his pilgrims started from the inns of Southwark and made their way to Canterbury. The poet John Milton is recorded as living in the City in the 17C. The 17C diarist John Evelyn lived in Deptford near Greenwich. The great 18C scholar Dr Johnson compiled his Dictionary and drafted his essays while he lived off Fleet Street.

Several novels by Charles Dickens are set in Victorian London where he spent a difficult childhood. He lived in Bloomsbury with his family. The Bloomsbury Group, whose famous members included Virginia Woolf (she also resided in Richmond), EM Forster, Dora Carrington, Lytton Strachey and many others flourished around the leafy squares. Other celebrated figures are the poet Rupert Brooke, the novelist DH Lawrence and the philosopher Bertrand Russell.

Thomas Carlyle, Hilaire Belloc, Oscar Wilde and AA Milne resided in Chelsea, as did Mark Twain, Henry James and TS Eliot. Elizabeth Barrett and Robert Browning are associated with Marylebone which also lays claim to Sir Arthur Conan Doyle. Lord Byron won fame while living in St James's. Thomas Hardy and George Bernard Shaw were famous residents of the Adelphi, Strand. The leafy groves of Hampstead nurtured the poet John Keats, the novelist Agatha Christie and the writer Ian Fleming.

Cosmopolitan London

London has attracted people from the four corners of the earth who have integrated into the London social fabric.

African and Caribbean – The Afro-Caribbean communities which originally settled in Brixton and Notting Hill have since spread out all over the

Flamboyant costume at the Notting Hill Carnival

city, especially in northwest and south London. The Notting Hill Carnival is an international event. The vibrant markets in Brixton, Shepherd's Bush, north end of Portobello Road and Tooting are packed with exotic produce. The Africa Centre in King Street, Covent Garden provides a concert venue for music and entertainment and a craft shop. The arts of Africa are on display at the **British Museum** and at the **Horniman Museum** in Dulwich.

Jewish – London's Jewish community was well established at the time of the Norman conquest (1066) and after many travails throughout the ages, through hard work and perseverance has become an economic force.
The principal Jewish communities now reside in the north sector of London: Golders Green, Hendon, Brent, Barnet, Harrow and Redbridge.
The Jewish Museum *(see ST PANCRAS)* gives an introduction to the history and culture of London's Jewish community. For Jewish social history contact the museum's Finchley Road centre at 80 East End Road, London N3. Together, the two centres organise and promote walking tours, the Yiddish theatre and temporary exhibitions.

Indian and Pakistani – . Principal communities are located in the East End of London (Shoreditch and Whitechapel), Tooting, Shepherd's Bush, Southall and Ealing. Foodstuffs, fashion and crafts are available in London. The area around Brick Lane in the East End and Southall are notable for their restaurants.
The **Neasden Temple** *(Sri Swaminarayan Mandir, off the North Circular)* the first traditional Mandir temple in Europe opened in 1995. The temple has an excellent presentation of the Hindu religion.
There are displays of the most exquisite jewellery and artefacts at the **Victoria and Albert Museum** and an exhibition on Hinduism – daily life, sacred places and devotional practices in Southern India at the **Horniman Museum**.

Far Eastern – Chinese, Thai, Malaysian, Vietnamese and Filipino communities thrive in London. At the heart of the capital is Chinatown, an Oriental enclave which offers all kinds of services (legal advice, traditional medicine, supermarkets) and hosts the annual celebration of Chinese New Year. Limehouse in the East End is the area where the Chinese settled originally and there are many restaurants in Commercial Road.

Japanese expatriates, who live mostly in the affluent suburbs to the west and northwest, run their own schools and shops *(Oriental City, 399 Edgware Road, NW9)*. Japanese designer stores *(Muji)* are famous for simple forms, practical raw materials and plain colours.

The **Percival David Foundation** *(see BLOOMSBURY)* is dedicated to the promotion, appreciation and study of Chinese art and culture. Other important collections of Far Eastern art are on view at the **British Museum** and the **Victoria and Albert Museum** *(seeIndex)*. The Peace Pagoda in Battersea Park and a Thai temple in Wimbledon are distinctive landmarks.

Mediterranean – Soho and some areas of north London have been the preserve of Italian, Greek and Cypriot immigrants for decades. Spaniards and Portuguese have congregated around the top end of Portobello Road while Greek shopkeepers have been attracted to the vicinity of the **Greek Cathedral Aghia Sophia** *Moscow Road, W2*.

Middle Eastern – The Edgware Road and the Bayswater area, Shepherd's Market, Kensington High Street and Westbourne Grove are frequented by Turkish, Lebanese, Syrian, Iranian communities. The golden dome of the **Islamic Cultural Centre and London Central Mosque** *(146 Park Road, NW8)* dominates the skyline in Regent's Park and there are mosques in Whitechapel and other areas of the city. The Ismaili Centre in South Kensington promotes Islamic culture and rich collections of Islamic art are exhibited at the **British Museum** and the **Victoria and Albert Museum**.

Other Ways of Exploring the City

On Foot

Guided Walks – For information on guided walking tours consult the London Tourist Board, press listings, the company listed below or visit www.londontouristboard.com Guides include trained actors, historians, professional Blue Badge holders, botanists, authors etc. Themes available include: The City of London, Fleet Street, Legal London, Bloomsbury, Covent Garden Pubs, London theatres, Soho, the West End, Mayfair, Belgravia, Chelsea, Westminster, East End, Jewish East End, Docklands, Thames Pubs, Greenwich, Regent's Canal, Little Venice, Hampstead pubs, Royal London, Literary London, Shakespeare's London, Dickens' London, Sherlock Holmes' London, Beatles' London, the Swinging '60s...

Original London Walks – www.walks.com; P O Box 1708, London NW6 4LW ☎ 020 7624 3978, 020 7624 9255 (recorded information), 020 7624 WALK; Fax 020 7625 1932; london@walks.com

Mystery Walks – Jack the Ripper tour of the London's East End. ☎ 020 8558 9446

Guided Walks in London – 15 themed walks in interesting areas. ☎ 020 7243 1097

Clerkenwell and Islington Walks – Explore these districts to enjoy their historical associations. ☎ 020 7631 0659

City of London Walks – Exciting walks in the financial district. ☎ 020 7813 3874; 07076 441 569; cityoflondonwalks@blueyonder.co.uk; www.cityoflondonwalks.co.uk

Great London Treasure Hunt – Self-guided and guided tours to London's sights. ☎ 020 7928 2627; Fax 0870 137 4408; info@walkingtourslondon.com; www.walkingtoursinlondon.com

Walkways – Discover dramatic sights by following signed walks with viewpoints throughout the city: The *Financial Times* have sponsored a series of walks in **Docklands**: Isle of Dogs (1, 2, 3 & 4); Rotherhithe and Bermondsey (5 & 6); Wapping and Limehouse (7 & 8); Limehouse and Poplar (9).

Silver Jubilee Walkway – (10mi/16km in the heart of London)

LONDON'S BRIDGES

1 Kingston
2 Kingston Rlwy
3 Richmond
4 Richmond Rlwy
5 Twickenham
6 Richmond Footbridge
7 Kew
8 Kew Rlwy
9 Chiswick
10 Barnes Rlwy
11 Hammersmith
12 Putney
13 Fulham Rlwy
14 Wandsworth
15 Battersea Rlwy
16 Battersea
17 Albert
18 Chelsea
19 Victoria Rlwy
20 Vauxhall
21 Lambeth
22 Westminster
23 Hunderford Rlwy
24 Waterloo
25 Blackfriars
26 Blackfriars Rlwy
27 Millennium
28 Southwark
29 Cannon Street Rlwy
30 London
31 Tower

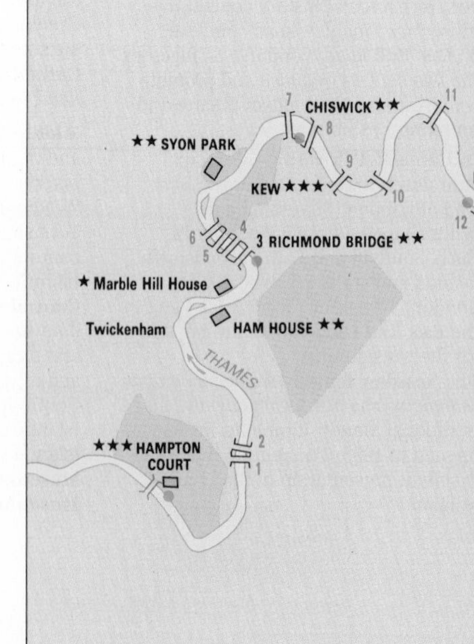

● Piers

A HMS Wellington
B HMS Belfast
D Cutty Sark

marked by special pavement markers and including two spurs to the Barbican and Bloomsbury and ten **viewpoints** with indicators identifying the neighbouring buildings: Leicester Square - Parliament Square - Lambeth Palace - Jubilee Gardens - National Theatre - Tate Modern - Southwark Cathedral - Hays Galleria - Tower Hill - Mansion House and Royal Exchange - Leicester Square. Maps can be bought *(charge)* from the London Tourist Board Information Centres.

Millennium Mile - A pleasant riverside walk along part of the Silver Jubilee Walkway starting from Westminster Bridge and continuing past the British Airways London Eye, Tate Modern and The Globe, London's latest landmarks, to London Bridge; the second part of the walk along the green path from Butler's Wharf takes in London Bridge City and goes inland to Southwark and Waterloo.

London Wall Walk - (under 2 m/2.8km long) marked by 21 panels and follows the line of the City wall between the Tower of London and the Museum of London.

The **Thames Towpath** - (180mi/228km) A National Trail marked by 1 200 acorn signposts, running upstream from the Thames Barrier to the Cotswolds; free leaflet available from the Countryside Commission, PO Box 124, Walgrave, Northampton NN6 9TL.

By River Boat

For information about Thames Cruises contact the **London Tourist Board London Line** ☎ 09068 66 33 44 (24hr recorded message) or the companies listed below.

Circular Cruises: Non-stop round trip featuring many of London's famous landmarks (taped commentary in seven languages): from **Waterloo Pier**, daily, every hour, 10.45am to 1.45pm and 3.45pm-5.45pm; from **Embankment Pier**, daily, every hour, 10.15am-12.15pm, 2.15pm, and every hour 6.30pm-8.30pm . £7.50. Show Travelcards for 33% discounts.
Catamaran Cruisers, Embankment Pier, Victoria Embankment, London WC2N 6NU ☎ 020 7987 1185; Fax 020 7839 1034; www.catamarancruisers.co.uk

Westminster Pier downstream:
to the **Tower** (25min) and **Greenwich**: Apr-Oct, daily, 10am to 5.35pm, every 20min; Nov-Mar, 10.30am to 3.45pm, every 45min; From £5.
City Cruises PLC, Cherry Gardens Pier, London SE16 4TU ☎ 020 7930 9033 or 020 7488 0344; www.citycruises.com
to **Greenwich** (45min) and **Thames Barrier**: daily 10am to 4pm/5pm every 30min in summer, 10.40am to 3.20pm every 40min in winter; £6.50 one way, £7.50 round trip. Sail and Rail tickets £8.80 allow passengers a single boat trip to/from Westminster and Greenwich in

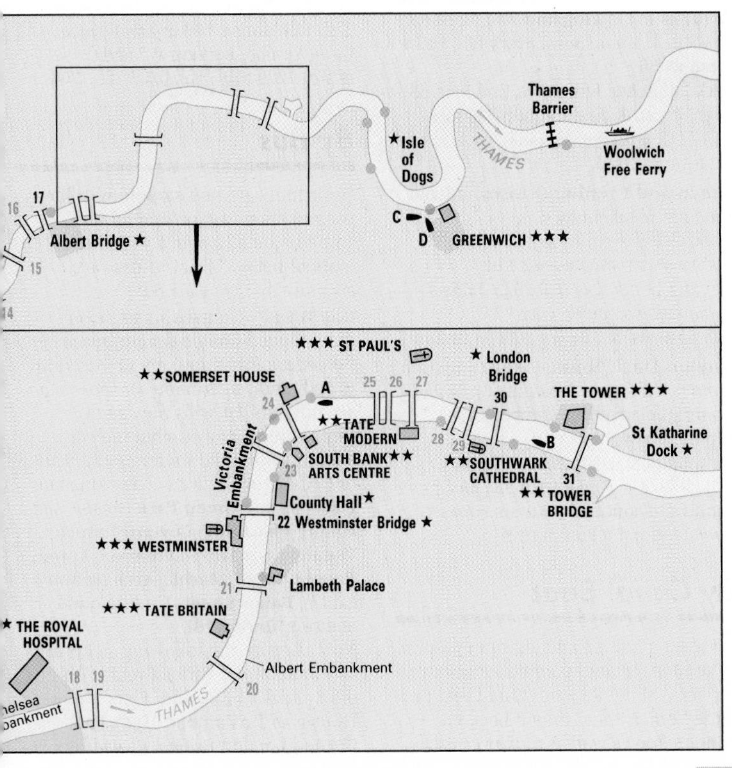

either direction plus unlimited travel on the Docklands Light Railway.
Westminster Passenger Service Association (WPSA), Westminster Pier, Victoria Embankment, London SW1A 2JH ☎ 020 7930 4097; www.wpsa.co.uk
Catamaran Cruisers, Charing Cross Pier, Victoria Embankment, Londn WC2N 6NU ☎ 020 7987 1185; Fax 020 7839 1034; www.catamarancruisers.co.uk
to **Kew** (90min) daily at 10.15am, 10.30am, 11am, 11.15am, noon, 2pm, 2.30pm. £7 (one way); £11 (round trip).
to **Hampton Court** (3hr 30min, calling at Richmond and Teddington Lock) daily at 10.30am, 11.15am, 12pm.
Thames River Services ☎ 020 7930 4097 ☎ 020 7930 4097 including Colliers Launches, 217 St Margaret's Road, East Twickenham TW1 1LU ☎ 020 8892 0741; www.collierslaunches.co.uk

Tower Bridge Pier:
to **Greenwich** (30min) and the **Thames Barrier** all year daily 11am to 4.30pm every 30min; £5.20.
to **Thames Barrier** (1hr) late May to Sep, Sun, 7pm ; £6.
Campion Launches, Greenwich Pier, King William Walk, London SE10 9NT ☎ 020 8305 0300

St Helena Pier, Richmond:
to **Hampton Court** (1hr 30min) Tue-Sun, 11am-4.15pm; return 11.15am, 2.35pm, 4.45pm. £5.50 (one-way), £7 (round trip).
to **Turks Pier**, **Kingston** mid-Apr-Sept, Tue-Sun 11am-6.15pm, every 60-75min. From £4.50.
Turk Launches Ltd, Town End Pier, 58 High Street, Kingston-upon-Thames KT1 1HR ☎ 020 8546 2434; www.turks.co.uk

Lunch and Evening Cruises – Music and/or a meal contact:
Woods River Cruises ☎ 020 7841 2711; www.woodsrivercruises.co.uk
Bateaux London ☎ 020 7925 2215; www.bateauxlondon.com
City Cruises ☎ 020 7740 0400 (at 7pm).

London Duck Tours – Departing from County Hall (near Westminster Bridge). An unique adventure on board an amphibious vehicle with a live commentary. Daily 10am-sunset. ☎ 020 7928 3132; Fax 020 928 2050; enquiries@londonducktours.com; www.londonducktours.com

By Canal Boat

Discover a hidden and charming aspect of London. Several companies operate services on the Regent's Canal between Little Venice and Camden Lock via London Zoo as well as dinner cruises.
There is a regular service operated by the **London Waterbus Company** (Operates Apr-Oct, daily, 10am-5pm, every hour; Nov-Mar, Sat-Sun, 10am-4pm (3pm Little Venice) every hour. £4.80 one way (50min), £6.20 round trip (110min) and from £12.70 including admission to London Zoo.
This company also organises special day trips from Camden Lock: east to Limehouse (£14); west to Brentford (£16.50). Booking essential for day trips.

London Waterbus Company – www.waterways.co.uk
Camden Lock Place, London NW1 8AF ☎ 020 7482 2550, 7482 2660 (information).

Jason's Trip – www.jasons.co.uk
Opposite 60 Blomfield Road, London W9 2PE ☎ 020 7286 3428; 020 7286 6752 (restaurant); enquiries@jasons.co.uk

Jenny Wren – www.walkersquay.com
250 Camden High Street, London NW1 7BX ☎ 020 7485 4433/6210; Fax 020 7485 9098

On the Water

For details on boating, canoeing, cycling and angling activities along the canals and the permits necessary (British Waterways boating license, National Rivers Authority, Thames Division, rod license) contact:
Lee & Stort Navigations, British Waterways, Enfield Lock, Ordnance Road, Enfield, Middx EN3 6JG. ☎ 01992 764 626; Fax 01992 788 226.
London Canals, British Waterways, The Toll House, Delamere Terrace, Little Venice, London W2 6ND. ☎ 020 7286 6101; Fax 020 7286 7306.

By Bus

Some tours are non-stop; some allow passengers to hop on and off and continue on a later bus with the original ticket. Ticket prices vary accordingly (from £11.50).
Bus Tours – Sightseeing tours on open-topped double-decker buses (weather permitting) are an excellent introduction to London for those who are not familiar with the capital. Departure points vary but include: **Victoria** (near the Underground Station or Grosvenor Gardens or Buckingham Palace Road); **Green Park** (by the Ritz Hotel); **Piccadilly**; **Coventry Street**; **Trafalgar Square**; **Haymarket**; **Lower Regent Street**; **Marble Arch** (subway exit 7); **Baker Street** (Underground Station); **Tower Hill**.
Note: Ensure the following sights are included on the various routes on offer: Bank of England, Fleet Street, Houses of Parliament, Hyde Park Corner, London Bridge, Piccadilly

Circus, St Paul's Cathedral, Strand, Tower Bridge, Tower of London, Trafalgar Square, Victoria Embankment, Westminster Abbey, Whitehall.

The Original London Tour – Hop-on-hop-off service, recorded commentary in 8 languages, 20 stops. Every 5-15min between 9am and 6-7pm (seasonal variations). £12.50, £7.50 (child). Starting points at Baker Street Underground, by Speaker's Corner at Marble Arch, Victoria Station, Piccadilly Underground station in Haymarket. ☎ 020 8877 1722; info@theoriginaltour.com; www.theoriginaltour.com

The Big Bus Experience – Hop-on-hop-off service, recorded commentary in 12 languages. Every 15min from 8.30am (seasonal variations). Free walking tours and river cruise included. ☎ 020 7233 9533; Fax 020 7828 0638; info@bigbus.co.uk; www.bigbus.co.uk

Evan Evans Tours also do Big Value Tours to Windsor, Oxford, Stonehenge and Bath. ☎ 020 7950 1777, Fax 020 7950 1771; reservations@evanevans.co.uk; www.evanevans.co.uk

Visitors Sightseeing Tours – Half-day and full day tours of London and tours outside London. ☎ 020 7636 7175; Fax 020 7636 3310; info@visitorsightseeing.co.uk; www.visitorsightseeing.co.uk

The London Experience – Contact Frames Rickards ☎ 020 7233 7030 ; Fax 020 7233 7039; reservations@framesrickards.co.uk; www.framesrickards.co.uk

By Taxi

London taxi drivers are renowned for their thorough "knowledge" of the streets of the capital and for their sense of humour. Besides themed tours of central London there are also visits to the "Villages of London": Hampstead, Richmond etc

A personal two hour tours day or night for up to 5 people in the comfort of a black cab costs £75 per taxi (8am-6pm); £85 per taxi (6pm-midnight). Half-day tours to Hampton Court and Windsor £130.

Black Taxi Tours of London
7 Durweston Mews, London W1U 6DF
☎ 020 7935 9363; Fax 020 7224 2823; info@blacktaxitours.co.uk; www.blacktaxitours.co.uk

On Two Wheels

Cycling and Rollerblading – Even the courier companies have resolved to beat the traffic by resorting to man-powered-wheels. Cycle routes run throughout the capital, across the Royal Parks (speed restrictions apply in Hyde Park) and along many bus routes. Special permission must be sought from London Canals / British Waterways for use of selected portions of the canal towpaths *(see above)*.

With the Children

Children's playgrounds in most parks are very popular and there are plenty of activities for children of all ages in London. Museums and galleries have special programmes to engage children's imagination. The wonderful exhibits of the **Natural History Museum** bring ecological and environmental issues to the fore. Children take part in experiments relating to scientific and technological advances which are entertainingly presented at the **Science Museum**. The mummies at the **British Museum** are particular favourites. Exciting maritime adventures are told at the **National Maritime Museum**. Experience the spartan conditions on board the clipper **Cutty Sark** and the **Golden Hinde** in contrast with the battleship **HMS Belfast** bristling with powerful guns. Visit **London Zoo** where you can watch the antics of the inmates and where you can adopt an animal. The **Planetarium** and the **Royal Observatory** at Greenwich have exciting presentations of the heavens.

The grisly exhibits of the **London Dungeon** and the **Chamber of Horrors** at Madame Tussaud's will bring a thrill to some while **Pollock's Toy Museum and Shop** and the **Bethnal Green Museum of Childhood** strike a nostalgic note. The delightful shows at the **Polka Theatre for Children** in Wimbledon and at the **Little Angel Theatre** in Islington will enchant the young ones; older children can take up **brass rubbing** at Westminster Abbey, in the crypt of St Martin in the Fields and at All Hallows by the Tower.

Going for a Drink

Public houses, more familiarly known as pubs, are the descendants of the inns and taverns of the Middle Ages; some were mere drinking shops with sawdust on the floor; others also served food. Their opening hours are usually Mon-Sat, 11am-11pm and Sun, noon-10.30pm. They play an important role in English social life; on any pretext people will go for a jar or a swift half at the local – at the end of the working day, on Sunday morning before the midday meal, to meet friends for a chat or a game of darts. If you are alone you may nurse your drink in a quiet corner listening to the hub-bub round you or strike up a conversation with the other drinkers at the bar.

Most pubs serve 'pub grub' – Shepherd's Pie (minced lamb with carrots covered with a layer of mashed potato), Lancashire Hot-pot (beef stew), Ploughman's Lunch (Cheddar or Stilton cheese with salad and pickles, bread and butter), pasta dishes, baked potatoes with fillings, fish or meat with chips, burgers, sandwiches; and various puddings. Numerous pubs noteworthy for their atmosphere or historic associations are listed in the Pubs section within the individual chapters in the Selected Sights section of the guide. The pubs given in our **Where to Eat** section have been chosen for their exceptionally good food. A few of the more traditional pubs are shown in red on the maps in the **Selected Sights** section.

Fine exterior of the Clachan pub

Ph. Gajic/MICHELIN

The traditional drink is beer, sold in pints and half pints, bottled or draught. A free house sells whatever selection of beers it chooses. If the house is tied it will sell the product of the brewery to which it belongs. Many pubs offer guest beers which change weekly. The most common types of beer are –

Pale ale – light and slightly bitter, pale in colour
Bitter beer – less sweet than Pale Ale, pale in colour
Stout – strong and nourishing, dark brown in colour
Porter – a variety of Stout but less strong
Lager – light an gazzy beer or the Continental type, served chilled
Ginger ale – ginger-flavoured drink

Wine bars are a more modern phenomenon; the accent is on wine rather than beer and they also serve food but there is no tradition of darts. Wine is sold by the glass or the bottle; other drinks available include port and sherry, brandy and whisky. As well as the cheaper blended whisky, try a glass of malt whisky, which has been maturing for up to 15 years in an old sherry cask and has a very smooth flavour.

Going out for the Evening

Besides enjoying the atmosphere of London pubs where people of all ages and walks of life congregate in the evening – West End pubs are particularly busy – or going out for a meal to sample the eclectic cuisine to be found in the city, visitors will find plenty of entertainment for their enjoyment.

Shows

London is the theatre and club capital of the world. The best source of information about where to go and what to see or hear are the daily newspapers – *Evening Standard* (particularly on Thursday when the cinema programmes change) – and the weekend newspapers – *The Times* (Sat), *The Independent* (Sat), *The Guardian* (Sun), *The Sunday Times*, *The Observer*, *The Independent on Sunday* – and specialist magazines such as *Time Out*.

Clubbing

The vibrant club scene is one of London's attractions, especially for energetic young people who love the latest music and dance crazes. Venues usually offer special rates in the early evening but the real action starts later and continues late into the night.
In 1990 all-night clubbing was legalised, however, licensing laws still apply so alcohol runs dry at 3am. Establishments without music-and-dance or club licences are prohibited from selling alcohol after 11pm.

Central London

Bar Rumba – *36 Shaftesbury Ave, Piccadilly, W1D 7ER – ⊖ Piccadilly – ☎ 020 7287 6933 – barrumba@thebreakfastgroup.co.uk – Open daily 6pm (8pm Sun; 9pm Mon and Sat) to 3pm or 4pm (1.30pm Sun (later preceding bank hols); 5am Sat) – £3-£12 depending on day and time.* In the heart of Soho, the Rumba is one of London's best clubs even if the size of the dance floor is far too small given the club's popularity. There's always a good atmosphere and the music varies from night to night, ranging from jazz, funk, house, drum n'bass to latino (salsa lessons).

Carwash – *256 Old St, W1F 8SN – ⊖ Barbican, Old Street – ☎ 0870 246 1966 – www.carwash.co.uk – Open Sat 10pm-3.30am – £15 on the door, £12 in advance.* Think of an Austin Powers movie, add a sound track of disco, funk and soul and the best party vibes for an award winning experience.

Cuba – *11-13 Kensington High St, W8 5NP – ⊖ High Street Kensington – ☎ 020 7938 4137 – cken@sfigroup.co.uk – Open Mon-Sat 5pm (noon Fri-Sat) to 2am – £3-£10.* Bar and restaurant on the ground floor; the small basement nightclub can get very crowded.

Embassy Bar – *119 Essex Rd, N1 2SN – ⊖ Angel – ☎ 020 7359 7882 – ollyembassy@hotmail.com – Open daily 5pm-11pm (1am Fri-Sat; 10.30pm Sun).* This club-bar situated just outside the centre of Islington is furnished with red and gold flock wallpaper and leather armchairs, giving it a glamorous retro feel. The always superb music varies with the days of the week, and the atmosphere is definitely one of the best in London.

Fabric – *12 Greenhill Rents, Clerkenwell, EC1M 6HJ – ⊖ Farringdon – ☎ 020 7336 8898 – info@fabriclondon.com – Open Fri 9.30pm-5am, Sat 10pm-7am, Sun 10pm-3am – £12-£15.* Opened in 1999, Fabric is a gigantic club capable of holding 2500 revellers in three originally decorated halls. The acoustics are exceptional and attract the top DJ's (Fat Boy Slim, the Chemical Brothers) and a mixed 20-30 year old crowd. The music is predominantly drum n' bass and techno-house.

Heaven – *The Arches, Villiers St, Strand, WC2N 6NG – ⊖ Charing Cross – ☎ 020 7930 2020 – info@heaven-london.com – Open Mon 10pm-3.30am, Wed and Fri 10.30pm-3am, Sat 10pm-5am – £2-£12.* This gay heaven is located under the railway arches. There are three dance-floors and three types of music from disco to techno and a stunning laser show. This place is buzzy and very popular, so get there early.

The End – *18 West Central St, WC1A 1JJ – ⊖ Holborn, Tottenham Court Road – ☎ 020 7419 9199 – info@the-end.co.uk – Open Mon 10pm-3am, Thu 10pm-4am, Fri 11pm-5am, Sat 10pm-6am, Sun 2pm-midnight.* 19C coaching inn converted into a nightclub with eye-catching metal and glass décor. The club has two large dance floors, and the favoured music is techno, drum n' bass and deep house. Livened by classy DJ's often sponsored by large record companies, the place is always packed and it is often necessary to queue for hours.

Turnmills – *63b Clerkenwell Rd, EC1M 5NP – ⊖ Farringdon – ☎ 020 7608 3220 – www.turnmills.co.uk/gaudi – Open Mon-Fri noon-2.30pm; Mon-Sat 7-10.30pm; Sun 1.30-7.30pm.* This club, which organises the wildest nights in the capital in a setting of vaulted cellars and alcoves, has been immensely successful. Friday is Gallery night and house music. On Saturday night newer techno reigns. The Gay Party Trade kicks off every Sunday morning at 5am and plays through to the early afternoon.

OUTER LONDON

Bug Bar, The Crypt-St Mathew's Church – *Brixton Hill, Brixton, SW2 1JF – ⊖ Brixton – ☎ 020 7738 3366 – info@bugbrixton.co.uk – Open Wed-Sat 7pm-1am (3am Sat), Sun 7pm-11pm – £3-£6.* Under the vaults of St Mathew's crypt, this is an intimate bar-club with comfy velvet sofas. The music (live or DJ) varies between soul, jazz, funk, blues and hip-hop. It draws a trendy crowd in the 20 to 35 year-old age group.

Le Palais – *242 Shepherds Bush Rd, Hammersmith, W6 7NL – ⊖ Hammersmith – ☎ 020 8600 2300 – www.ponana.co.uk – Open Tue (students only) 10pm-2am, Fri-Sat 10pm-3am – £5-£15.* Londoners have been coming here to dance since 1919. It now has a lively disco with flashing lights and wall videos.

Ministry of Sound – *103 Gaunt St, Elephant and Castle, SE1 6DP – ⊖ Southwark – ☎ 020 7378 6528 – info@ministryofsound.com – Open Fri 10.30pm-5am, Sat 11pm-8am – £12-£15.* London's best-known nightclub has become an institution in the capital and draws a mixed crowd of revellers (20-35 years old) every weekend. The sound is exceptional, the experience stunning, but behave yourself if you want to get through the door and above all be patient. The music is house, garage, techno.

The Fridge – *1 Town Hall Parade, Brixton Hill, Brixton, SW2 1RJ – ☎ 020 7326 5100 – info@fridge.co.uk – Open Sun-Thu 7pm-3am, Fri-Sat 10pm-6am – £2-£25.* This giant club (a converted cinema) with great mosaic decor can hold up to 1000 people. Gay night on Saturdays. The music is excellent: roots, funk, hip-hop during the week and trance and house at the weekend. Public: 20-30ish.

Theatre

Tickets may be purchased in person or from the theatre box office, by phone and credit card from the theatre or a ticket agency (booking fee) or in person from the Half-price Ticket Booth **(tkts)** in Leicester Square which sells tickets for the same day.

The major serious theatres in London are the **National** on the South Bank and the **Barbican** on the north side of the City. Experimental theatre starts in the provinces and on London's fringe circuit before moving to the West End for a season. During the summer, open air venues in Holland Park, Regent's Park and the Globe Theatre are an unusually historical and informal way to enjoy performances.

Most of the mid-range theatres are conveniently grouped together in the West End in and around Shaftesbury Avenue in Soho *(see district plan p 270)*, near a wide choice of restaurants, many of which are prepared for customers eating before or after a performance.

The theatres listed below are the most famous which feature long-running plays and musicals. For a complete listing of current shows, consult the publications mentioned above.

Adelphi – *The Strand, Strand, WC2E 7NA – ⊖ Charing Cross – ☎ 020 7344 0055 – £16-£41.* Several of Dickens' novels were adapted for the stage here soon after publication (1837-1845). This theatre is fondly remembered for some great musical productions (*Words and Music* by Noel Coward, *Me and My Girl, Sunset Boulevard*).

Apollo Victoria Theatre – *17 Wilton Rd, Victoria, SW1V 1LG – ⊖ Victoria – ☎ 0870 400 0650 – £10.75-£45.20.* This former cinema (built 1930)converted into a theatre in 1979, has played host to such famous performers as Shirley Bassey, Cliff Richards and Sammy Davis Jr. Among recent productions are Andrew Lloyd Webber's *Starlight Express* and *Bombay Dreams*.

Duke of York Theatre – *St Martin's Lane, WC2N 4BG – ⊖ Leicester Square – ☎ 020 7369 1791 – £9-£37.50.* Its name is synonymous with playwrights such as Shaw, Ibsen, Galsworthy; it was also the stage for Noel Coward's interpretation of the role of Slightly in James Barrie's *Peter Pan*, a play which is still popular (Noel Coward was both actor and playwright). The theatre is now the headquarters of the British comedians' syndicate.

Her Majesty's Theatre – *Haymarket, St James's, SW1Y 4QL – ⊖ Piccadilly Circus – ☎ 020 7494 5400 – www.rutheatres.com – £20-£42.50.* Designed in 1896 by architect C.J. Phills, the theatre seats 1200 people. The musical the *Phantom of the Opera* has been running here since 1986.

London Palladium Theatre – *8 Argyll St, Soho, W1F 7TF – ⊖ Oxford Circus – ☎ 020 7494 5020 – £11-£42.50.* A sumptuous theatre famous for variety shows and revivals of musical comedies (*Crazy for You*).

Open Air Theatre – *Inner Circle, Regent's Park, NW1 4NP – ⊖ Baker Street – ☎ 020 7486 2431 – www.open-air-theatre.org.uk – Performances Jun-Sep – £9-£26.* In summer the New Shakespeare Company, founded in 1932, stages productions here, including such favourites as *A Midsummer Night's Dream*. Bring warm clothing, a cushion, an umbrella and a picnic. Barbecue and cold buffet available. There is a bar in the pavilion, which also serves hot drinks.

Palace – *Shaftesbury Ave, Soho, W1D 8AY – ⊖ Leicester Square – ☎ 020 7434 0909 – £10-£42.50.* Opened as an opera house by Richard D'Oyly Carte, this grandiose building has retained its typically Victorian atmosphere. It is now a venue for large-scale musicals: *The Entertainer, Jesus Christ Superstar* and, more recently, an adaptation of Victor Hugo's *Les Misérables*.

Royal Court Theatre – *Sloane Sq, Chelsea, SW1W 8AS – ⊖ Sloane Square – ☎ 020 7565 5000 – info@royalcourttheatre.com – £5 Mon, 10p-£26 Tue-Sat.* The role of the Royal Court is to promote contemporary plays and new English and international talent. The theatre has been completely renovated.

Royal National Theatre – *South Bank, SE1 9PX – ⊖ Waterloo – ☎ 020 7452 3000 (ticket office) – info@nationaltheatre.org.uk – £10-£38 Olivier and Lyttelton; £10-£25*

Cottesloe. The National Theatre Company, founded by Sir Laurence Olivier in 1962, has been based since 1976 in this modern building, designed by Deny Lasdun, with three theatres : the Olivier, the Lyttelton and the Cottesloe. Some tickets are reserved for sale on the day of the performance. The doors open at 8pm for most performances. Daily backstage guided tour.

Royal Shakespeare Company at the Barbican – *Barbican Centre, Silk St, EC2Y 8DS – ⊖ Barbican – ☎ 020 7638 8891 – info@rsc.org.uk – Box office: Open daily 9am-8pm – £5-£35*. This arts complex, designed by Chamberlin, Powell and Bon, is a five-floor development housing a concert hall, a cinema, exhibition areas and restaurants.

Shakespeare's Globe – *21 New Globe Walk, Bankside, SE1 9DT – ⊖ Blackfriars, Cannon St, Southwark, Waterloo – ☎ 020 7902 1400 – www.shakespeares-globe.org – Box Office: Open Mon-Sat 10am-6pm; performances May-Sep – £5-£29*. This impressive white building with a thatched roof, on the south bank of the Thames, is identical to the original Elizabethan theatre, which was brought down by the 17C censure of the Church. It is both a museum and a functioning theatre but, as it is open to the elements, plays are put on only in the summer.

The Dominion – *268-269 Tottenham Court Rd, W1T 0AG – ⊖ Tottenham Court Road – ☎ 0870 607 7401 – £12.50-£50*. Built as a concert hall in a former leprosarium and brewery, the Dominion is famous for its musicals, in particular *Grease*.

The Lyceum Theatre – *21 Wellington St, Covent Garden, WC2E 7RQ – ⊖ Covent Garden – ☎ 0870 243 9000 (24hr) – www.disney.com – £17.50-£42.50*. The fourth theatre to be built on the site, the Lyceum resembles a Roman temple. Reopened in 1904, it was long a venue for ballets, musicals, and classical plays. Today the theatre produces mega-musicals like the *The Lion King*.

The New Ambassadors Theatre – *West St, Soho, WC2H 9ND – ⊖ Leicester Square – ☎ 020 7369 1721 – www.theambassadors.com – £7.50-£30*. This theatre, designed in 1913 by W.G.R. Spargue, played host to the West-End debuts of Vivien Leigh and Ivor Novello. Agatha Christie's *The Mousetrap*, a play that St Martin's Theatre kept running for twenty years was premiered here in 1952. *Dangerous Liaisons* by Christopher Hampton experienced similar success.

The New London – *167 Drury Lane, Covent Garden, WC2B 5PW – ⊖ Covent Garden – ☎ 020 7405 0072 – £20-£40*. Built on the site of the Elizabethan-era Winter Garden Theatre, the New London has been the setting for Andrew Lloyd Webber's musical, *Cats*, since 1980.

The Old Vic – *103 The Cut, Lambeth, SE1 8NB – ⊖ Waterloo – ☎ 020 7369 1722 (box office) – www.oldvictheatre.com – Pit Bar: Open daytime and evening*. Former home of the National Theatre, the Old Vic opened in 1818 as the Coburg Theatre. Taken over by Emma Cons in 1880, it was renamed the Royal Victoria Music Hall and Coffee Tavern. After Emma Cons died, in 1912, the "Old Vic", as it became known, was taken up by her niece, Lilian Baylis, who staged concerts, opera and tragedy. Managed by Sir Peter Hall since 1996, it again stages major plays from the classical and contemporary repertoire.

The Theatre Royal – *Drury Lane, Covent Garden, WC2B 5JF – ☎ 020 7494 5000 – £10-£42.50*. There has been a theatre on this site since 1633. The present building was designed in 1812 by Benjamin Wyatt. Productions over the years have featured Nell Gwynne, Mrs Jordan, David Garrick, Edmund Keane and the famous clown Grimaldi. Nowadays, it is a venue for popular musicals (Oklahoma, My Fair Lady, Miss Saigon).

Wyndham's Theatre – *Charing Cross Rd, Soho, WC2H 0DA – ⊖ Leicester Square – ☎ 020 7369 1736 – wyndhamsboxoffice@theambassadors.com – Box office Mon 10am-6pm, Tue-Sat 10am-8pm, Sun 10am-7pm – £19-£40*. A magnificent late-Victorian theatre famous for "whodunits" and musical comedy (*Godspell* with David Essex and Jeremy Irons). One of the finest auditoriums in the West End.

Cabarets

Madame Jo Jo's – *8-10 Brewer St, Soho, W1R 3SP – ⊖ Piccadilly Circus – ☎ 020 7734 3040 – info@madamejojos.com – Open Mon-Sat 10pm-3.30am, Sun 2pm-midnight – £6-£8 (arrive before 11pm). £27 for Sat show (booking recommended)*. A warm-hearted cabaret for night owls, and a favourite haunt of drag queens. Sometimes a bit of a madhouse, the ambience changes from day to day.

Cinemas

Catching the latest film releases in a comfortable cinema is a great way to relax after a day's sightseeing or to while away the evening. The West End cinemas boast the latest technology for your enjoyment.

BFI London IMAX Cinema – *1 Charlie Chaplin Walk, South Bank, SE1 8XR – ⊖ Waterloo – ☎ 020 7902 1234 – imax.cinema@bfi.org.uk – £7.50-£11.50*. The London IMAX opened in May 1999. The special cinema shows 2D and 3D films on a 26m wide screen: from underwater action to Antarctic adventure and Walt Disney films.

National Film Theatre – *Belvedere Rd, South Bank, SE1 8XT – ⊖ Waterloo – ☎ 020 7928 3232 – www.bfi.org.uk/nft – £7.50*. The London Film Festival is held here every year in November.

Odeon Cinemas – *22-24 Leicester Sq, Soho, WC2H 7LQ – ⊖ Leicester Square – ☎ 0870 505 0007 – www.odeon.co.uk – Daily 11am-9pm – £7-£10.50*. London's biggest cinema (1943 seats), where the premiers of prestigious British and Hollywood films are shown.

Ritzy Cinema – *Brixton Oval, Coldharbour Lane, Brixton, SW2 1JG – ⊖ Brixton – ☎ 020 7733 2229 – www.picturehouses.co.uk – £7*. This handsome Edwardian cinema was built in 1911 and renovated in 1995. Classics and recent films are shown here, and English producers like Ken Loach are particularly fond of the Ritzy.

Opera and Ballet

The Theatre Royal Covent Garden, know affectionately as the "Garden", is the home of the Royal Opera and Royal Ballet. The Coliseum presents opera in the English language.

English National Opera – *London Coliseum, St. Martin's Lane, WC2N 4ES – ⊖ Leicester Square – ☎ 020 7632 8300 – box.office@eno.org – £3-£64.* This large Edwardian theatre was built in 1904 by Oswald Stoll to rival Drury Lane. The building is quite spectacular: marble pillars, terracotta façade and lavish interior (mosaic ceiling, wood panelling and huge portraits). Since 1968 it has been home to the English National Opera.

Royal Opera House – *Bow St, Covent Garden, WC2E 9DD – ⊖ Covent Garden – ☎ 020 7304 4000 – www.royaloperahouse.org – Box office: Open Mon-Sat 10am-8pm; backstage tours: Mon-Sat at 10.30am, 12.30 and 2.30pm; £7.* In December 1999 after extensive renovation, the opera house re-opened its doors to reveal its new splendour. Admire the imposing Bow Street façade and the adjacent Floral Hall, which is reminiscent of the glasshouses at Kew. This is one of the world's most prestigious opera houses. Tickets are quite expensive and difficult to obtain.

J. Malburet/MICHELIN

The half-price ticket booth, Leicester Square

Sadler's Wells Theatre – *Rosebery Ave, Islington, EC1R 4TN – ⊖ Angel – ☎ 020 7863 8000 – reception@sadlers-wells.com – Box office: Open Mon-Sat 9am-8.30pm – £7.50-£35.* The only theatre in London to present both classical ballet and contemporary dance (1600 seats).

Theatre Tickets

Tickets for West End theatres and musicals are booked-up by agents who may charge a 10% booking fee on re-sale. To avoid paying a surcharge, seats should be bought via the theatre box office direct, but be prepared for long-term availability. One way to beat the system is to opt for matinée performances, although star casts may be replaced by understudies.

Ticketmaster, 48 Leicester Sq. WC2H 7LR ☎ 020 7344 4444/7316 4709; www.ticketmaster.co.uk and **First Call Ticket Agency**, 68 Long Acre WC2E 9 JH ☎ 020 7420 0000; 0870 333 7770/840 1111/906 3838; www.firstcalltickets.com

Tkts (Half-Price Ticket Booth) – *Leicester Square ⊖ Leicester Square.* Run by the Society of London Theatres (SOLT), tkts is the only official Half-Price and Discount theatre booth in London. It offers a limited number of half-price tickets to most West End shows on the day of performance. Available on a first-come-first-served basis, cash/credit card payment only accepted plus service charge, no returns, maximum four tickets per application. Open Mon-Sat, 10am-7pm; Sun for matinées only noon-3.30pm. For more information contact SOLT, 32 Rose Street WC2.E 9ET ☎ 020 7557 6700; Fax 020 7557 6799; www.officiallondontheatre.co.uk

Artsline, 54 Charlton St NW1 1HS ☎ 020 7388 2227 is a free advice service to assist people with disabilities in accessing arts and entertainment in the capital.

Classical Music

London offers a great range of classical music performed by world-class artists and orchestras under the baton of celebrated conductors. Westminster Abbey, Westminster Cathedral and St Paul's Cathedral all boast superb choirs.

City churches that organise lunchtime concerts include St Bride's, St Anne and St Agnes, St Lawrence Jewry, St Margaret Lothbury, St Martin-within-Ludgate, St Mary le Bow, St Michael's Cornhill, St Olave Hart Street.

Barbican Hall – *Silk St, City, EC2Y 8DS – ⊖ Barbican – ☎ 020 7638 8891 – tickets@barbican.org.uk – Box office daily 9am-8pm – £5-£35.* Home to the London Symphony Orchestra (founded in 1904), the Barbican is also used by touring orchestras.

Royal Festival Hall – *Belvedere Rd, South Bank, SE1 8XX – ⊖ Waterloo – ☎ 020 7960 4242 (box office) – boxoffice@rfh.org.uk – Open daily (except 25 Dec and 1 Jan) 10am-10.30pm.* The Royal Festival Hall, built in 1951 as part of the Festival of Britain celebrations, is the home of the London Philharmonic Orchestra. Programmes range from large-scale classical orchestral concerts, ballet, films and staged performances of opera, to the London Jazz Festival. The two smaller venues, Queen Elizabeth Hall and Purcell Room, host contemporary dance, music theatre, chamber music, solo recitals, world music, poetry events and live art.

St James's Church Concerts – *197 Piccadilly, St James's, W1J 9LL – ⊖ Piccadilly Circus – ☎ 020 7381 0441 – sjp.concerts@virgin.net – £8-£15.* Lunchtime recitals (no charge) and evening concerts of mainly classical music.

St John's, Smith Square – *Smith Sq, Westminster, SW1P 3HA – ⊖ Westminster – ☎ 020 7222 1061 – www.sjss.org.uk – Ticket office: Open Mon-Fri 10am-5pm; also evenings for concerts – £5-£30.* This church, a Grade I listed building, is the setting for the annual Lufthansa Festival of baroque music. There are regularly scheduled lunchtime concerts (Mon 1pm); chamber and vocal music events take place in the evenings at 7.30pm.

St Martin-in-the-Fields – *Trafalgar Sq, WC2N 4JJ – ⊖ Trafalgar Square – ☎ 020 7839 8362 – boxoffice@smitf.co.uk – Evening concerts: Thur-Sat at 7.30pm; tickets available by telephone or from the Crypt box office (Mon-Sat 10am-5pm) – £6-£18.* Candle-lit evening concerts in this famous church; also lunchtime concerts by talented young performers.

The Royal Albert Hall – *Kensington Gore, South Kensington, SW7 2AP – ⊖ South Kensington – ☎ 020 7589 8212 (box office) – sales@royalalberthall.com – Box office: Open daily 9am-9pm; hall 45min and restaurants 2hr before performance. Tours daily from Spring 2004. Access for the handicapped 020 7838 3110.* Home to the famous Promenade Concerts, held from mid-July to mid-September, and to the Royal Philharmonic Orchestra (founded in 1946 by Sir Thomas Beecham), the Royal Albert Hall also hosts a wide range of other events from Classical to rock, pop, jazz, tennis, opera, ballet, Cirque du soleil.

Wigmore Hall – *36 Wigmore St, Marylebone, W1U 2BP – ⊖ Bond Street, Oxford Circus – ☎ 020 7935 2141 – Box office: Open Mon-Sat 10am-8.30pm, Sun 10.20am-8pm (5pm Nov to mid-Mar); concerts Mon-Sat at 7.30pm, Mon at 1pm, Sun at 11.30am and 4pm (Nov to mid-Mar) or 7pm (mid-Mar to Oct) – From £6.* A lovely intimate hall, ideal for solo recitals and small chamber orchestras. Fine acoustics. The Sunday morning coffee-concerts are an institution.

Rock, Roots and Jazz

As the scene fluidly changes from acid to funk, Brit-pop, soul, salsa, techno, garage and new trends are constantly evolving, it is advisable to check the fixtures listed in the press (**Time Out, What's On** or **Evening Standard Hot Tickets**).

CENTRAL LONDON

Africa Centre – *38 King St, Covent Garden, WC2E 8JT – ⊖ Covent Garden – ☎ 020 7836 1973 – africacentre@gn.apc.org – Open Mon-Fri 9.30am-5.30am; Music Fri 10.30pm-3am – £10-£75.* Opened in the early 60s, the Africa Centre is billed as "The heart of Africa in the heart of London". Famous African Groups perform live on Fridays.

Cecil Sharp House – *2 Regent's Park Rd, Camden, NW1 7AY – ⊖ Camden Town – ☎ 020 7485 2206 – efdss@efdss.org – Open Tue and Thu-Sat 7.30pm-11pm – £2.50-£7.* Folk music, singing and dancing.

Dover Street Restaurant and Bar – *8-10 Dover St, W1S 4LQ – ⊖ Green Park – ☎ 020 7629 9813 – doverstrst@aol.com – Open Mon-Sat 10.30pm-3am.* Jazz bar-restaurant with live music and dancing every night from 10.30pm. It's a posh bar, so smart dress is par for the course. Cover charge for those not dining.

Jazz Café – *3-5 Parkway, Camden, NW1 7PG – ⊖ Camden Town – ☎ 020 7916 6060 – www.jazzcafe.co.uk – Open Sun-Thu 7pm-1am, Fri-Sat 7pm-2am, also Sun noon-4pm – £8-£45.* Jazz, soul, Latin American and African rap music every evening in this intimate, 2-storey club. Some of the greatest jazzmen have played here.

London Astoria – *157 Charing Cross Rd, Soho, WC2H 0EL – ⊖ Tottenham Court Road – ☎ 020 7344 0044 – management@londonastoria.co.uk – Box office: Open 10am-6pm; performances Mon-Thu 7pm-11pm, Fri 11pm-3.30am, Sat 10pm-6am.* Mixture of styles, large stage.

Pizza Express Jazz Club – *10 Dean St, Soho, W1V 5RL – ⊖ Tottenham Court Road – ☎ 020 7439 8722 – jazz@pizzaexpress.co.uk – Open daily 7.45pm-midnight – £15-£20.* Excellent modern jazz every evening in the basement.

Pizza on the Park – *11-13 Knightsbridge, Knightsbridge, SW1X 7LY – ⊖ Hyde Park Corner – ☎ 020 7235 5550 – Box office: Open 10am-5pm; performances: Mon-Fri 8.30am-midnight, Sat-Sun 9.30am-midnight (music daily from 9.15pm); advance booking advised. – £10-£20.* Situated in a renovated underground station, this basement venue features jazz nightly from 9.15pm.

Ronnie Scott's – *47 Frith St, Soho, W1D 4HT – ⊖ Leicester Square – ☎ 020 7439 0747 – ronniescotts@ronniescotts.co.uk – Open Mon-Sat 8.30pm-3am; music from 9.30pm – £15-£25.* Legendary Soho jazz club, outstanding music and atmosphere. Best to book in advance.

Shepherd's Bush Empire – *Shepherd's Bush Green, W12 8TT – ⊖ Shepherd's Bush – ☎ 0870 771 2000; 020 8354 3300 – mail@shepherds-bush-empire.co.uk – Box office: Open Mon-Sat noon-5pm – £10-£30.* Designed by Frank Matcham for Oswald Stoll in the early 20C, "The Empire" was bought by the BBC in 1953 and has played a major role in the history of television. Today it's a concert hall with excellent acoustics, welcoming the best rock, folk and jazz artists of the moment.

100 Club – *100 Oxford St, W1D 1LL – ⊖ Oxford Circus – ☎ 020 7636 0933 – info@the100club.co.uk – Open Mon-Thu 7.30/8pm-11pm/midnight (3am Fri, 1am Sat) – £5-£12.* This basement venue, where the Sex Pistols made their debut, now highlights jazz, modern jazz, blues and swing.

606 Club – *90 Lots Rd, Chelsea, SW10 0QD – ⊖ Earl's Court – ☎ 020 7352 5953 – jazz@606club.co.uk – Open daily 7.30/8pm-midnight/2am; closed 24 Dec to 1 Jan – Music cover charge £6-£8.* Book for dinner to hear top British jazz musicians play at this atmospheric basement venue.

OUTER LONDON

Brixton Academy – *211 Stockwell Rd, Brixton, SW9 9SL – ⊖ Brixton – ☎ 020 7771 3000 – post@brixton-academy.co.uk – Open for performances 7-11pm (later on club nights) – £10-£40.* Immense hall with stunning Art Deco interior, considered by many to be London's best concert hall. Many greats started out here, including the Rolling Stones, David Bowie, Jamiroquai and UB40. Standing and seating capacity of 4700.

Carling Apollo Hammersmith – *Queen Caroline St, Hammersmith, W6 9QH – ⊖ Hammersmith – ☎ 0870 606 3400; 020*

8748 8660 – www.cclive.co.uk – £15-£50. The place for concerts of popular music and to see some of the big stars.

Forum – *9-17 Highgate Rd, Camden, NW5 1JY – ⊖ Kentish Town – ☎ 020 7284 1001; 0870 906 3777 (ticket line) – www.meanfiddler.com – Open daily 7-11pm (2am Fri-Sat) – £5-£15.* Opened in 1934 as a movie house, this Art-Deco building became a concert hall in 1986. With a capacity of 2000 people, the biggest bands love its intimate charm. A long list of artists have performed here including Oasis, Iggy Pop and Macy Gray.

Union Chapel – *Compton Terrace, Islington, N1 2UN – ⊖ Highbury – ☎ 0870 120 1249; 020 7226 1686 – arts@unionchapel.org.uk – £3-£13.* A rock concert in a church! Using the church as a concert hall was the only way to save Union Chapel from demolition. All varieties of music are performed here, including rock, folk, Latino, jazz and blues and organ concerts.

Shopping

Shopping is a favourite activity most people are happy to indulge in. London shops offer the widest range of goods to satisfy the most demanding shopper. For opening times see p 00 and for sizes see conversion tables p 00.

The main shopping centres, together with large stores like IKEA, Toys R Us, etc are located on the outskirts of London in easy reach of the North (Brent Cross) and South Circulars (Croydon), Lakeside (Thurrock), Bluewater (Dartford). The main shops are featured in the Sell Out column in **Time Out**.

What to Buy Locally

The winter sales at Christmas and New Year and the summer sales in June and July are a popular time for shopping, as prices are reduced on a great range of goods.

Great Britain is a good place to buy clothes. There is a wide choice of woollen articles in cashmere or lambswool, particularly in Scotland. Classic styles are sold by well-known names such as Jaeger, Burberry, Marks and Spencer, John Lewis, Debenhams and House of Fraser. Made-to-measure clothing for men is available in London in Savile Row (tailors) and Jermyn Street (shirt-makers).

Shops specialising in reasonably priced ready to wear clothing often appeal to a young clientele given to the international fashion scene. For trendy shops offering styles from established and offbeat designers visit the King's Road in Chelsea, Carnaby in Soho and the area around Covent Garden. The craft studios at Oxo Tower on the South Bank and in Camden Lock Market are places to explore for a special gift.

The best makes of porcelain – Wedgwood, Royal Worcester, Royal Doulton – are available in London and elsewhere; seconds can be bought at the factory.

Food (smoked salmon, Stilton cheese, pickles, marmalade) and drink (tea, gin and whisky) are also favourite items.

Department Stores ans Shops

The Classics

Harrods – *87-135 Brompton Rd, Knightsbridge, SW1X 7XL – ⊖ Knightsbridge – ☎ 020 7730 1234 – www.harrods.com – Open Mon-Sat 10am-7pm; closed Sun except Jan and Jul sales and Nov to 24 Dec; closed 25-26 Dec, 1 Jan.* Harrods boasts that it can supply anything, even a pedigree dog. The food halls are particularly impressive (do not miss the displays of fish and cheese). The butcher will even sell you alligator or ostrich steaks. There is also a hairdresser's, a beauty parlour and a travel agency, and a shipping service. A world of elegance and comfort, to be visited as you would a museum.

E. Mathis/HARRODS

The ornate Harrods Meat Hall

Harvey Nichols – *109-125 Knightsbridge, SW1X 7RJ – ⊖ Knightsbridge – ☎ 020 7235 5000 – contact.us@harveynichols.co.uk – Open Mon-Sat 10am-8pm (7pm Sat), Sun noon-6pm.* This store regularly arouses curiosity with its unusual and daring window displays. There is a good range of fashion clothing, especially in smaller sizes, an excellent choice of hats (for Ascot!) and some fine jewellery (tempting Christian Lacroix trinkets and modern silver work).

John Lewis – *278-306 Oxford St, W1A 1EX – ⊖ Oxford Circus – ☎ 020 7629 7711 – jl_oxford_street@johnlewis.co.uk – Open Mon-Wed, Fri 9.30am-7.10pm, Thu 10am-8.10pm, Sat 9am-7pm.* Suppliers of school uniforms and other functional clothing, household fittings, linen and stationery. This store has everything you need for everyday, practical purposes and special occasions: invisible thread, matching lampshades and gloves for Ascot or garden parties.

Liberty – *210-220 Regent St, W1R 6AH – ⊖ Oxford Circus – ☎ 020 7734 1234 – londonstorecustomerservices@liberty.co.uk – Open Mon-Thu 10am-6.30pm (8pm Thu; 7pm Fri-Sat), Sun noon-6pm.* This intimate department store has a character all its own, owing to its roots in the East End of London: Liberty-brand and Indian silks, Chinese ceramics, contemporary glassware and designer clothes. The beautiful half-timbered Tudor façade was built in 1924 using traditional techniques.

Selfridges – *400 Oxford St, W1A 1AB – ⊖ Bond Street – ☎ 0870 837 7377 – www.selfridges.co.uk – Open Mon-Sat 10am (10.30am Sat) to 8pm, Sun noon-6pm.* This well-known department store sells everything from lingerie to household articles (kitchen and garden), beauty products and stationery. Highly regarded food hall as well.

HIGH STREET CHAINS

French Connection – *249-251 Regent St, W1R 7AD – ⊖ Oxford Circus – ☎ 020 7493 3124 – www.frenchconnection.com – Open Mon-Sat 10am-7pm (8pm Thu), Sun noon-6pm.* Trendy chain of stores selling moderately priced women's fashion and accessories.

H & M – *261-271 Regent St, W1B 2ES – ⊖ Oxford Circus – ☎ 020 7493 4004 – www.hm.com – Open Mon-Wed, Fri-Sat 10am-8pm, Thu 10am-9pm, Sun noon-6pm.* Trendy Swedish chain of stores selling moderately priced men's and women's fashion and accessories.

Karen Millen – *262-4 Regent St, W1R 5AD – ⊖ Oxford Circus – ☎ 020 7287 6158 – www.karenmillen.com – Open Mon-Sat 10am-7pm (8pm Thu), Sun noon-6pm.* This chain offers very feminine and sophisticated fashion and accessories at affordable prices. Evening wear as well.

Next – *201-203 Oxford St, W1D 2LD – ⊖ Oxford Circus – ☎ 020 7434 0477 – www.next.co.uk – Open Mon-Fri 10am-8pm (9pm Thu), Sat 9.30am-8pm, Sun noon-6pm.* Chain of shops selling relatively classic men's and women's items at modest prices, which also has a special "small-sizes" section.

Oasis Stores – *13 James St, WC2E 8BT – ⊖ Covent Garden – ☎ 020 7240 7445 – www.oasis-stores.com – Open Mon-Sat 10am-7pm (8pm Thu), Sun noon-6pm.* Trendy chain of stores selling moderately priced womens' fashion and accessories.

ART AND ANTIQUES

London has always had a buoyant trade in art and antiques. Fairs are held regularly in London hotels that attract dealers from the provinces: details available from the **Antiques Trade Gazette** which comes out on Tuesdays. For details of larger, international fairs, contact the **British Antique Dealers Association**, 20 Rutland Gate, SW7. ☎ 020 7589 4128.

Bonhams – *Montpelier St, SW7 1HH – ⊖ Knightsbridge – ☎ 020 7393 3900 – info@bonhams.com.* Founded in 1793, Bonhams merged with Brooks in September 2000 and are now the top vintage car valuers in Britain. Bonhams have also become the fourth biggest valuers in the world with expertise in 25 fields, ranging from wine to teddy bears, and including carpets, paintings and jewellery.

Christies – *85 Old Brompton Rd, South Kensington, SW7 3LD – ⊖ South Kensington – ☎ 020 7930 6074 – info@christies.com – Open Mon-Fri 9am-5pm (viewing and auctions at other times).* This internationally renowned institution, founded by James Christie in London in 1766, built up its reputation by promoting young artists such as Gainsborough but also by organising the major auctions of the 18 and 19C. The most spectacular auction remains the sale of 198 paintings by Sir Robert Walpole to Catherine the Great, now in the Hermitage museum. More recently, the *Dr. Gachet portrait* by Van Gogh sold for £49.1 million. Christies now has offices in 15 countries and operates in almost 80 fields.

Sotheby's – *34-35 New Bond St, Mayfair, W1A 2AA – ⊖ Bond Street – ☎ 020 7293 5000 – www.sothebys.com – Open Mon-Fri 9am-5pm (4.30pm viewing).* Sotheby's started out in 1744 as a book valuers. When it moved to its prestigious premises in New Bond Street, the establishment diversified into selling drawings and paintings. The sale of the Goldschmidt collection in 1958 marked a turning point, as did the concurrent opening of the New York office. Particularly memorable was the sale of the Duchess of Windsor's jewellery. Sotheby's, resolutely forward thinking, launched internet auctioning in 1999.

MARKETS

Browsing among market stalls holds a fascination for lovers of antiques hoping to find some desirable object. The stall holders are often amateurs but a real find is rare. The earlier you arrive the greater the choice. Flower stalls are a common sight in the streets of central London: in front of the Danish Embassy in Sloane St. **Gilding the Lily** at South Kensington Underground Station and **Wild at Heart** at 222 Westbourne Grove have wonderful displays. Fruit and vegetable markets are always a delight. Camden Town markets specialise in clothing.

ANTIQUES AND BRIC-À-BRAC

Alfie's Antiques Market – *13-25 Church St, NW8 8DT – ⊖ Edgware Road – ☎ 020 7723 6066 – alfies@clara.net – Open Tue-Sat 10am-6pm.* Don't be put off by its slightly scruffy appearance; this market sells everything but it is good to know what you are looking for.

Antiquarius – *131-141 King's Rd, Chelsea, SW3 5EB – ⊖ Sloane Square – ☎ 020 7351 5353 – Open Mon-Sat 10am-6pm.* 120 stalls, selling Art Deco items, buttons, textiles, silver, glassware, jewellery, and trade versions of fashion accessories.

Bermondsey (New Caledonian) Market – *Bermondsey St, Southwark, SE1 3UN – ⊖ Bermondsey – ☎ 020 7351 5353 – Open Fri 4am-2pm.* The market was revived on this site in 1950. Trade in copper and silverware, Victorian jewellery, furniture and other objets d'art begins by torchlight in the early hours; by 9am some dealers have already done their business and despatched their purchases to the continent.

Camden Passage Antiques Market – *Pierrepont Arcade, Camden Passage, Islington, N1 8EF – ⊖ Angel – ☎ 020 7359 0190 – murdochkdr@aol.com – www.camdenpassageislington.co.uk – Market days Wednesday and Saturday; some shops open daily.* The name is misleading as this small passage, opened in the 60s, is actually in Islington and not Camden. The antiques market (oriental art, Art Nouveau, Art Deco, silverware.....approximately 250 dealers) is open on Wednesdays and Saturdays; Thursday is for books.

Charing Cross Collectors Market – *Villiers St, WC2 – ⊖ Embankment – Open Sat 8.30am-3.30pm; closed 25-26 Dec and 1 Jan.* Beneath the Embankment tube station. Coins, medals and badges.

Covent Garden Market – *41 The Market, Covent Garden, WC2E 8RF – ⊖ Covent Garden – ☎ 020 7836 9136 – info@coventgardenmarket.co.uk – Open daily 8.30am-7.30pm.* In the 17C Inigo Jones created the Piazza to create a trading space for the original market, established by monks before the Reformation, which transferred to Nine Elms in 1974. The current market buildings, designed by Charles Fowler, were added in 1832. The flower market, haunted by the memory of Eliza Doolittle, is now occupied by shops, cafés, restaurants and wine bars. The Antiques market features coins, glasses, old tools and silverware.

Gray's Antiques Market – *58 Davies St, W1K 5AB – ⊖ Bond Street – ☎ 020 7629 7034 – grays@clara.net – Open Mon-Fri 10am-6pm.* The market occupies a split site incorporating 1-7 Davies Mews. The main hall has 170 permanent stands and London's biggest collection of antique jewellery.

Greenwich Antiques Market – *Greenwich High Rd, SE10 – ⊖ Greenwich rail – Open Sat-Sun 9am-5pm.* In this flea market expect to find international crafts rather than real antiques but the atmosphere here is pleasant, more family-oriented and less crowded than that of Camden Market.

Petticoat Lane Market – *Middlesex St, Wentworth St, EC1 – ⊖ Liverpool Street – Open Sun 9am-2pm (Wentworth Street also open Mon-Fri 10am-2.30pm).* A daily flea market, just down the road from its original 17C location, best visited on Sundays.

Portobello Road – *Portobello Rd, Notting Hill, W11 1AN – ⊖ Notting Hill Gate – ☎ 020 7727 7684 – www.portobelloroad.co.uk.* Browse for antiquities, Victoriana, later silver, chinaware, stamps, small items.

Spitalfields Market – *Brushfield St, Commercial St, E1 – ⊖ Liverpool Street – Open daily 10-5pm.* This large historic hall is home to a craft market. Saturdays the second-hand stalls expose their wares, but on Sundays the organic market takes over. The atmosphere is pleasant and there are many cafés and restaurants to choose from.

R. Besse/MICHELIN

Saturday morning, Portobello Road

FOOD AND FLOWERS

Berwick Street – *Berwick St, Soho, W1 – ⊖ Piccadilly Circus.* Berwick Street is frequented by many nearby restaurateurs. First just a fruit and veg market, it now has fish counters, flower stalls and an excellent baker. Atmosphere of bygone times.

Borough Market – *Stoney St, Borough High St, Southwark, SE1 1TL – ⊖ London Bridge – ☎ 020 7407 1002 – info@boroughmarket.org.uk – Open Fri noon-6pm, Sat 9am-4pm.* This is probably the oldest food market in London with archives dating back to 1014. It is known as "the London larder" and reputed for its organic products. Although reserved mainly for professionals, it is open to the public on Fridays and Saturdays.

Brixton Market – *Atlantic Rd, SW9 – ⊖ Brixton – Open Mon-Sat 8am-6pm (3pm Wed).* One of the South London's best markets for fresh food. Many exotic products.

Columbia Road Market – *Columbia Rd, Bethnal Green, E2 – ⊖ Buses 26, 48, 55 – ☎ 01268 281 403 – columbia_flower_market@blueyonder.co.uk – Open Sun 8am-2pm; closed 25 Dec.* The Columbia Road flower market east of the City is a victim of its success but as well as the flowers there are second-hand stores and also a good bakery. The street has a country atmosphere which gives it a charm all of its own. Come to the market when the flowers are cut-price and the gardeners are at lunch.

Leadenhall Market – *Whittington Ave, EC3 – ⊖ Monument – Open Mon-Fri 7am-4pm.* Especially impressive is the huge Hall of Glass designed by Victorian architect Sir Horace

Jones (Smithfields Market, Billingsgate Market). Apart from the poultry and fish market, there is just a small group of shops but an extremely good selection.

CLOTHING

Brick Lane Market – *Brick Lane, E1 – ⊖ Aldgate East – Open Sun 8am-1pm.* A vast hotchpotch of bric-a-brac and fabrics. Leather and new clothing is sold in the shops at the north end of Brick Lane.

Camden Lock Market – *Chalk Farm Rd, NW1 – ⊖ Camden Town – Open daily 10am-6pm.* Arts and crafts, designer and vintage clothes, jewellery and a wide range of goods are on sale.

Camden Market – *Camden High St, Corner of Camden High St and Buck St, NW1 – ⊖ Camden Town – Open daily 10am-6pm.* A real treasure trove for bargain leather goods and clothing, with 200 odd stands. New Dr Martens at old prices.

Camden Stables Market – *Chalk Farm Rd, Camden, NW1 8AH – ⊖ Camden Town – ☎ 020 7485 5511 – Open 10am-6pm.* The centre of the alternative fashion scene with a total of 350 shops.

Leather Lane Market – *Leather Lane, Chancery Lane, EC1 – ⊖ Chancery Lane – Open Mon-Fri 10.30am-2pm.* The market, dotted with cafés, is always full of bargains. Fashionable clothes for men and women (including sportswear), a tailor and, of course, all sorts of leatherwear: shirts, skirts, shoes and bags.

Fashion

Alexander McQueen *see MAYFAIR*
Burberry *see MAYFAIR*
Dr Martens Dept Store *see COVENT GARDEN*
French Connection *see LOND Shop – Dept Stores*
Gieves & Hawkes *see MAYFAIR*
H & M *see LOND Shop – Dept Stores*
Hilditch & Key *see ST JAMES'S*
John Lobb *see ST JAMES'S*
Karen Millen *see LOND Shop – Dept Stores*
Koh Samui *see COVENT GARDEN*
Manolo Blahnik *see CHELSEA*
Mulberry *see MAYFAIR*
N Peal & Co.Ltd *see PICCADILLY*
Next *see LOND Shop – Dept Stores*
Oasis Stores *see LOND Shop – Dept Stores*
Paul Smith *see COVENT GARDEN*
Philip Treacy *see KNIGHTSBRIDGE – BELGRAVIA*
Top Shop *see SOHO*
Vivienne Westwood *see MAYFAIR*

Books and Music

Borders Books & Music *see SOHO*
Foyles *see SOHO*
Hatchards Booksellers *see PICCADILLY*
HMV *see MAYFAIR*
Intoxica! *see KENSINGTON*
Ray's Jazz Shop *see SOHO*
Tower Records *see PICCADILLY*
Travel Bookshop *see KENSINGTON*
Virgin Megastore *see SOHO*
Waterstone's Booksellers *see PICCADILLY*
Zwemmer *see SOHO*

Food & Drink

Algerian Coffee Stores *see SOHO*
Berry Bros & Rudd *see ST JAMES'S*
Bluebird *see CHELSEA*
Milroy's of Soho *see SOHO*
Monmouth Coffee House *see COVENT GARDEN*
Neal's Yard Dairy *see COVENT GARDEN*
Paxton & Whitfield *see ST JAMES'S*
R Twining & Co *see COVENT GARDEN*

Other shops

The Conran Shop, Michelin House *see KENSINGTON*
General Trading Company *see CHELSEA*
Hamley's *see SOHO*
Neal's Yard Remedies *see COVENT GARDEN*
Penhaligon's *see COVENT GARDEN*
Wild at Heart *see KENSINGTON*

R. Besse/MICHELIN

A colourful display, Wild at Heart

Sports

Sports fixtures are popular events which arouse strong emotions. Dedicated fans follow the fortunes of their favourite teams throughout the sporting season.
The football season runs from the end of August to the end of May culminating in the FA Cup Final. London boasts a number of Premier League and First Division teams.

Cricket is a British gentlemen's sport that was exported to the Colonies so that it might encourage team spirit, discipline and sportsmanship. Test matches are followed with great interest in countries which were part of the British Empire. Tennis Championships are among the highlights of summer. Rugby matches, especially the Five Nations Cup, are special events.

All England Lawn Tennis Club – *Church Rd, Wimbledon, SW19 5AE* – ⊖ *Wimbledon* – ☎ *020 8944 1066* – *internet@aeltc.com.* The All-England Championships, first held in 1877, are open to all amateur and professional players. They are usually held at the end on June on the courts of the All-England Lawn Tennis and Croquet Club. The Centre Court, visible from the museum, is reserved exclusively for this great event. The Number One Court is also used on other special occasions, such as Davis Cup matches.

Arsenal Stadium – *Avenell Rd, Islington, N5 1BU* – ⊖ *Arsenal* – ☎ *020 7226 0304* – *www.arsenal.com* – *Tickets £16.50-32.* The Arsenal players are known as the "Gunners" because of the club's association with the former royal armaments factory.

Chelsea FC -Stamford Bridge – *Fulham Rd, Fulham-Chelsea, SW6 1HS* – ⊖ *Fulham Broadway* – ☎ *020 7385 5545* – *www.chelseafc.co.uk* – *£25-£33.* You must book well in advance to support one of London's most famous football clubs located in the centre of Fulham.

Guards Polo Club – *Smith's lawn, Windsor Great Park, Englefield Green, TW20 0HP* – ⊖ *Egham* – ☎ *01784 434 212* – *administration@guardspoloclub.com* – *£10-£20.* Matches played every Saturday and Sunday at 3pm. The Cartier International tournament is held here in July. The Ladies' National Polo Championship is held at Ascot Park (Sunningdale) in early July.

Lord's Cricket Ground – *St John's Wood Rd, NW8 8QN* – ⊖ *St John's Wood* – ☎ *020 7289 1066* – *www.lords.org.* London's main cricket ground. Headquarters of several autonomous bodies: the International Cricket Council, which supervises the game at international level; the Marylebone Cricket Club (MCC), founded in 1787, which set up the Test and County Cricket Board to administer international matches and the county game in the United Kingdom; and the Middlesex County Cricket Club, founded in 1877.

Foster'Oval – *Kennington Oval, Kennington, SE11 5SS* – ⊖ *Oval* – ☎ *020 7582 6660* – *www.surreyccc.co.uk.* The Oval, London's second cricket ground, is home to the Surrey County Cricket Club.

Twickenham – *Rugby Rd, TW1 1DZ* – ⊖ *Twickenham rail* – ☎ *020 8892 2000* – *www.rfu.com/twickenham.* Britain's finest rugby ground and the headquarters of the Rugby Football Union is at Twickenham, in West London. Major international matches are played on its hallowed turf, including home games in the Five Nations Tournament. The old wooden benches and stands have been replaced by modern seating for 75,000 spectators. The Museum of Rugby features the "Twickenham Experience": a guided tour of 14 exhibition rooms and the 50-year-old baths.

Harlequins Stoop Memorial Ground – *Langhorn Drive, Twickenham/ Richmond, TW2 7SX* – ⊖ *Twickenham rail* – ☎ *020 8410 6000* – *www.quins.co.uk.* Rugby

Walthamstow Stadium – *300 Chingford Rd, Walthamstow, E4 8SJ* – ⊖ *Walthamstow Central* – ☎ *020 8498 3300* – *mail@wsgreyhound.co.uk* – *Open Tue, Thu-Sat at 7.30pm* – *£5.* Famous greyhound racetrack.

Wimbledon Stadium – *Plough Lane, SW17 0BL* – ⊖ *Tooting Broadway, Wimbledon* – ☎ *020 8946 8000* – *wmraceoffice@gralimited.co.uk* – *£2.50-5.* Famous greyhound racetrack.

A Test Match at Lord's Cricket Ground

A. Taverner/MICHELIN

Books, Videos, CDs etc

Reference

AZ London Street Atlas
Survey of London John Stow 1603 (1980)
The Faber Book of London A N Wilson 1993
Georgian London John Summerson 1945 (1991)
In Search of London H V Morton 1951 (1988)
Docklands, Phaidon Architecture Guide Stephanie Williams 1990 (1993)
The Blue Plaque Guide to London Caroline Dakers 1982
Notting Hill and Holland Park Past Barbara Denny 1993
The London Market Guide Metro Publications 1994
Access in London Couch Forrester and Irwin 1996
Artists' Houses in London 1794-1914 Giles Walkley 1996
Impressionist London Eric Shanes
The Aesthetic Movement Lionel Lambourne
Kew, the History of the Royal Botanic Gardens Ray Desmond 1995
Curious London Robin Cross
London – A Guide to Recent Architecture Samantha Hardingham
A History of London Stephen Inwood 1998
Writing London Julian Woolfreys 1998
A Literary Guide to London Ed Glinert 1998

Biography

The Compleat Angler Izaak Walton 1653
The Shorter Pepys Robert Latham 1985
Diary John Evelyn 1818
All Done from Memory Osbert Lancaster 1963
Down and Out in Paris and London George Orwell 1933 (1982)
84 Charing Cross Road Helene Hanff 1978
In Camden Town David Thompson 1983
Three Men in a Boat Jerome K Jerome 1889
Six Wives of Henry VIII Antonia Fraser
Mrs Jordan's Profession Claire Tomalin 1995
William Morris Fiona MacCarthy 1995
Longitude Dava Sobel 1996
London The Biography Peter Ackroyd 2000

Fiction

The History of Pendennis W M Thackeray 1849/50
Our Mutual Friend Charles Dickens 1864/5
Picture of Dorian Gray Oscar Wilde 1891
The Adventures of Sherlock Holmes Arthur Conan Doyle 1892 (1993)
The Golden Bowl Henry James 1904 (1983)
Jeeves Omnibus P G Wodehouse
Mrs Dalloway Virginia Woolf 1925 (1972)
The Girl of Slender Means Muriel Spark 1963
The London Embassy Paul Theroux 1984
Hawksmoor Peter Ackroyd 1985 (1988)
Taste for Death P D James 1986
London Fields Martin Amis 1989 (1990)
The Secret Agent Joseph Conrad 1907 (1983)
The Buddha of Suburbia Hanif Kureishi 1990
Journal of the Plague Year Daniel Defoe 1722 (1992)
Liza of Lambeth W Somerset Maugham 1897
The Collected Stories of Muriel Spark 1994

Cinema and Television

1926 - The Lodger: A Story Of The London Fog tells the story of the unsolved Whitechapel Murders of 1888; directed by Alfred Hitchcock.
1928 - Pandora's Box (Die Büchse der Pandora) was a German film based on the evil story of Jack the Ripper; filmed in Germany; directed by G W Pabst.
1929 - Blackmail, directed by Alfred Hitchcock is considered as the first British talkie. **High Treason** creates a futurist vision of London in the 1940s; directed by M Elvey.
1941 - Dr Jekyll And Mr Hyde is evocatively set by Hollywood in London; directed by Victor Fleming.
1942 - Mrs Miniver, with Walter Pidgeon and Greer Garson, filmed in America, portrays London during the war; directed by William Wyler.
1945 - Pursuit to Algiers is an early tale involving Sherlock Holmes and Dr Watson, recreated by Hollywood. **Brief Encounter**, directed by David Lean, used the same sets at the Denham Studios as **Perfect Strangers**.
1946 - Great Expectations was carefully filmed in London after the war under the directorship of David Lean.
1948 - Oliver Twist with stage sets recreated by David Lean from Gustave Doré's illustrations to *London* (1870).
1949 - Stagefright with Marlene Dietrich singing *La Vie En Rose*, Michael Wilding and Jane Wyman set in London, directed by Hitchcock. **Passport to Pimlico** filmed in fact in Lambeth; directed by H Cornelius.
1953 - Genevieve is the name of a 1906 Darracq car that takes part in the famous London to Brighton veteran car run - made by Ealing Studios; directed by H Cornelius.
1955 - The Lady Killers set in Barnsbury, captures the Copenhagen Tunnels outside King's Cross on celluloid. **1984**, the first adaptation of Orwell's novel was partly filmed by London Wall under the directorship of M Anderson. **Witness for the Prosecution**, another Hitchcock was set amongst the legal fraternity in and around the Royal Courts of Justice.
1964 - Mary Poppins, that archetypal British nanny envisaged by the Americans resides with her wards in St John's Wood; directed by R Stevenson. **My Fair Lady**, made by the Warner Studios in California, recreates an evocative if sentimental interpretation of the London class divisions, with Audrey Hepburn and Rex Harrison, costumes by Cecil Beaton after Bernard Shaw's *Pygmalion*; directed by George Cukor. **A Hard Day's Night** boosted sales of Beatles records; directed by Richard Lester.
1965 - Blow-Up set in the 1960s, a photographer on a fashion shoot accidentally witnesses a murder with David Hemmings, Vanessa Redgrave and Sarah Miles - the quintessential London movie; directed by Antonioni (featuring Maryon Park, Woolwich).
1966 - Alfie tracks Jack-the-lad, south-London-born Michael Caine and the easy life; directed by Lewis Gilbert.
1971 - A Clockwork Orange, Stanley Kubrick's banned cult film is about the terrors of anarchy, sequences filmed at Thamesmead.
1973 - The Optimists of Nine Elms shows Peter Sellers in the role of an old street busker; directed by Anthony Simmons.
1979 - The Long Good Friday charts the decline of the Docklands; directed by John Mackenzie.
1980 - The Elephant Man is a provocative story set in Victorian England, directed by David Lynch, starring John Hurt, Anthony Hopkins, Anne Bancroft and John Gielgud.
1981 - The French Lieutenant's Woman, with several scenes shot in Shad Thames; directed by Karel Reisz.
1985 - My Beautiful Launderette explores racial tensions in south London; directed by Stephen Frears.
1986 - Sid and Nancy exposes the true spirit of Punk with Sid Vicious played by Gary Oldman; directed by Alex Cox.
1987 - Hope and Glory, John Boorman's London in the Blitz. **Full Metal Jacket** about the war in Vietnam was in fact made by Stanley Kubrick in London's Royal Docks.
1988 - A Fish called Wanda starring John Cleese, Kevin Kline, Jamie Lee Curtis in and around London Town and Docklands; directed by Charles Crichton. **Buster** tells the story of the Great Train Robber "Buster" Edwards who once sold flowers under the arches in Waterloo, acted by Phil Collins; directed by David Green.
1992 - Chaplin recreates the life of Charlie Chaplin in south London in the 1880s, directed by Richard Attenborough.
1994 - Madness of King George, Nigel Hawthorne in Alan Bennett's play about the mad monarch. Supported by Helen Mirren; directed by Nicholas Mytner.
1995 - Richard III, with a star-studded cast led by Ian McKellen exploits several famous London landmarks (Battersea and Bankside Power Stations, St Pancras).
1999 - Notting Hill, a romantic comedy with Julia Roberts and Hugh Grant set around Portobello Road; directed by Roger Mitchell.

Events and Festivals

Listed below are some of the most popular annual events. For specific dates and full details consult the national press and Tourist Information Centres.

January
Boat Show at Earls Court Exhibition Centre (*First Thursday*)
Start of Five-Nation Rugby Triple Crown at Twickenham
Charles I Commemoration held in Trafalgar Square

February
Chinese New Year in Soho
Clowns' Service at Holy Trinity, Dalston *(First Sunday)*

March
Chelsea Antiques Fair, Old Town Hall, Chelsea
Head of the River Race from Mortlake to Putney (420 crews leaving at 10 second intervals)
Oxford and Cambridge Boat Race from Putney to Mortlake

Easter
Service and distribution of Hot Cross buns at St Bartholomew-the-Great *(Good Friday)*
Carnival Parade in Battersea Park *(Easter Sunday)*
London Harness Horse Parade in Battersea Park *(Easter Monday)*
Kite Festival on Blackheath *(Easter weekend)*

April
RHS Spring Flower Show at Westminster
London Marathon from Docklands to Westminster

May
Royal Windsor Horse Show held in Home Park, Windsor
Chelsea Flower Show at the Royal Hospital, Chelsea
F A Cup Final
Chelsea Pensioners' Oak Apple Day Parade at the Royal Hospital, Chelsea *(29 May)*

June
Beating Retreat at Horse Guards Parade, Whitehall
Trooping the Colour at Horse Guards Parade *(Queen's Birthday)*
Hampton Court Music Festival at Hampton Court Palace
Spitalfields Annual Music Festival
Regent's Park Open Air Theatre Season
Stella Artois Grass Court (Tennis) Championships held at Queen's Club
Antique Fairs at Grosvenor House, Piccadilly and Olympia Exhibition Halls
Ascot Racing Week
British Polo Open Championships at Cowdray Park
Royal Academy Summer Exhibition at Burlington House, Piccadilly
All England Lawn Tennis Championships at Wimbledon *(2 weeks)*
Cricket Test Matches at Lord's and The Oval
Kite Festival on Blackheath *(last Sunday)*

July
Hampton Court Palace Flower Show
Royal Tournament at Earls Court
Sir Henry Wood's Promenade Concerts at the Royal Albert Hall *(8 weeks)*
Glyndebourne Opera Festival at Glyndebourne in Sussex
The City Festival is celebrated in the City Churches and Halls Swan Upping on the River Thames
Doggett's Coat and Badge Race rowed by 6 new freemen of the Watermen and Lightermen's Company from London Bridge to Chelsea Bridge
Opera and ballet at the Holland Park Outdoor Theatre

August
RHS Summer Flower Show in Westminster
Hampstead Heath Fair *(Bank Holiday Weekend)*
Notting Hill Carnival in Ladbroke Grove *(Bank Holiday Weekend)*

September
NatWest Trophy Final at Lord's Cricket Ground
Chelsea Antiques Fair held at Chelsea Town Hall *(First Saturday)*

October
Pearly Harvest Festival service for the Pearly Kings and Queens at St Martin-in-the-Fields *(First Sunday, afternoon)*
Goldsmith's Show, Goldsmiths Hall *(First week)*
Chelsea Crafts Fair held at Chelsea Town Hall *(two consecutive one-week shows)*
Opening of the Michaelmas Law Term: Procession of Judges in full robes carrying nosegays to Westminster Abbey

November
London to Brighton Veteran Car Run departing from Hyde Park Corner *(First Sunday)*
London Film Festival organised by the National Film Theatre *(three weeks)*
Lord Mayor's Show held in the City *(Saturday nearest to the 9th)*
Remembrance Sunday Cenotaph, Whitehall *(11am service; Sunday nearest 11 November)*
State Opening of Parliament by the Queen at Westminster
Regent Street Christmas lights are switched on

December
Lighting of the Norwegian Christmas Tree in Trafalgar Square
Carol Services throughout the capital's churches

A. Taverner/MICHELIN

An elegant scene on Ladies' Day at Ascot

The Gates of Buckingham palace

A. Taverner/MICHELIN

Insights and Images

Old Father Thames

Ph. Ed. Pritchard/FOTOGRAM-STONE

Aerial view of the Thames and the City

The banks of the Thames ring with gaiety as the river is once again an integral part of London life. Crowds drawn to the major riverside attractions marking the beginning of the third millennium admire the splendid views of the London skyline and enjoy the pleasure of ambling along the embankment as the tide ebbs and flows. New piers and pedestrian bridges and landscaped areas add to the vitality of the riverside.

Take a river boat to beat the traffic or to make a leisurely excursion or relax at the numerous venues ranging from trendy pubs and restaurants, fashionable designer shops to celebrated museums and world class theatres and concert halls. At night enjoy an entertaining evening aboard cruisers offering supper, music and dancing and gaze at the illuminated landmarks along the waterway. Some of the ships moored along the river banks are entertainment venues while others are museums of great historical interest.

From the King's Reach bend (at Waterloo Bridge) the view embraces two traditional monuments: to the east is the imposing dome of St Paul's Cathedral and to the west the multi-turreted Houses of Parliament. Across the water, adding a note of fantasy to the south bank rises a giant Ferris wheel, which affords a unique panorama of London extending to the far horizon.

Events and Celebrations

Events on the Thames feature prominently in the social calendar. Tradition is kept alive with The Doggett Coat and Badge Race rowed by six new freemen of the Watermen and Lightermen's Company and with the Swan Upping Ceremony at Teddington Lock when the beaks of the swans are marked by the guilds which own them – those owned by the Crown are left unmarked; both events are held in July. Sporting challenges such as the Oxford and Cambridge Boat Race (Easter), the Head of the River Race from Mortlake to Putney and the Great River Race from Ham House to Greenwich attract the crowds. Regattas are held up and down the river during the summer; the highlight of the season is the Henley Regatta (40mi/64km upstream). The Greenwich and Docklands Festival features events on or by the Thames; the exotic Dragon Boat Races are a Chinese tradition introduced in London in recent years. For special celebrations spectacular fireworks displays on the river light up the night sky.

A Changing Scene

In its upper reaches in Berkshire and the Cotswolds, the Thames, the major river in England (215mi/346km long), meanders gently through typically English countryside of low hills, woods, meadows, country houses, pretty villages and small towns. Oarsmen train in rowing skiffs and marinas provide moorings for private craft. Numerous locks add to the fun of a leisurely outing on the river with majestic swans and other waterfowl gliding by.

By the time the river reaches London it is a broad tidal waterway bustling with activity; barges ply their trade and modern craft offer daytime excursions

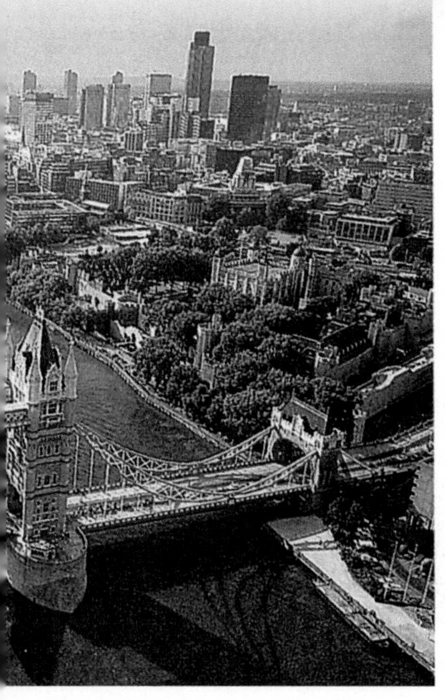

downstream to the Tower, Greenwich and the Thames Barrier or upstream to Kew and Hampton Court or evening cruises with entertainment. At low tide the muddy banks are also frequented by archaeologists and treasure seekers under the auspices of the Society of Mudlarks and Antiquarians and the Port of London Authority in search of precious artefacts, lost or discarded objects, old ship timbers and other salvage items. The Thames Barrier, an impressive engineering feat, was built to contain the high tides surging upstream at the equinox which can cause severe flooding in low-lying areas of London, especially as the land mass is tilting slowly to the south-east. The marshlands of the estuary are a haven for wintering birds, waterfowl and endangered species and have a unique charm.

Old and new now coexist as modern developments rise side by side with the old docks and warehouses. The cowls of the Thames Barrier dominate the scene at Woolwich and imaginative conversions of wharves (Butler's, Chelsea) and power stations (Bankside, Battersea, Lots Road) have turned these relics of the industrial era into the latest landmarks. Picturesque houseboats, formerly the homes of watermen and river pilots, provide desirable accommodation for the bohemian set.

Main Thoroughfare of London

Throughout the centuries the kings and nobles of England built palaces along the river from Greenwich to Hampton. Many of these grand buildings have been destroyed: Greenwich Palace, Rosary Palace (Bermondsey), Baynard, Bridewell and Mountfichet Castles (Blackfriars), Somerset House, Savoy Palace, York House (Strand), Whitehall Palace and Richmond Palace, but Ham House, Hampton Court and Syon Park still grace the banks of the Thames. Until the late 17C the Thames was the capital's main highway; the royal household, the City Corporation and the city livery companies had their own barges; ordinary citizens hired the services of the watermen who plied for hire at the many landing stages, called Stairs; cargo ships and men o'war added to the congestion. Old engravings show craft of every size thronging the Thames in those days. The watergates at Somerset House and at the south end of Buckingham Street as well as a quay and steps at Whitehall are reminders of the wider course of the river before the embankments were built.

The first regular steamer services began in 1816 and by mid-century were carrying several million people. On weekdays the boats were crowded with workers going into the docks and boatyards, the arsenal and south bank factories; fares were a penny from one pier to the next. At other times they carried families and friends for an evening trip or for an excursion, often to the estuary and seaside towns of Herne Bay, Margate and Ramsgate.

Pool of London

London grew to importance as a port, owing to its location on the Thames. From the 16C to the mid 20C the commercial prosperity of the city derived from the wharves and docks in the Pool of London and the shipbuilding yards downstream. The yards at Deptford founded by Henry VIII in 1513 grew rapidly and are associated with many historical events. Peter the Great of Russia visited Deptford to learn the art of shipbuilding. Here Drake was knighted aboard the *Golden Hinde* by Elizabeth I after his heroic voyage round the world. Many ships of the fleet which defeated the Spanish Armada were built at Deptford.

Merchantmen unable to sail under London Bridge or to approach the wharves across the mudflats, moored in midstream and depended on a vast fleet of lighters (3 500) for loading and unloading. This system provided many opportunities for pilfering by river pirates, night plunderers, scuffle hunters and mudlarks.

Dolphin Lamppost

Commercial Docks

The first enclosed commercial dock, designed to cut down the opportunities for theft, was built early in the 19C. By the end of the century, through the amalgamation of earlier smaller enterprises, there were four systems of enclosed docks extending over 3 000 acres/1 214ha with 36mi/58km of quays and 665 acres/270ha of dock basins: London Docks (1864), Surrey Commercial Docks (1864), East and West India Docks (1838), Royal Docks (1855-80). During the Second World War the docks suffered severely from bombing.

By the 1960s closure threatened because of the transfer of cargo handling to specialised riverside wharves and the dock at Tilbury.

During the 1990s, some of the surviving docks have provided good facilities for various water sporting activities. The City Airport at the Royal Docks is a daring and flourishing venture. Plans for Europe's largest aquarium are also afoot.

Water Supply

In the Middle Ages water supplies came from the Thames, its tributaries and from wells (Clerkenwell, Sadler's Wells, Muswell Hill). After 1285 conduits of leather or hollow tree trunks were provided by the City fathers to bring water from the Tyburn, Westbourne and Lea to lead cisterns in the City where it was collected by householders and by water carriers, who later formed a guild. During the next 300 years these provisions were augmented by private enterprise. Six tidal water-wheels were licensed under the northern arches of London Bridge between 1582 and 1822. The first pump driven by horses was set up in Upper Thames Street in 1594. The most elaborate undertaking, however, was the cutting (1609-13) of the New River.

The Industrial Revolution brought steam pumping, tried unsuccessfully in 1712 and gradually introduced from 1750 with cast-iron pipes: wooden mains could not sustain the higher pumping pressures. The widespread introduction of the water closet after 1820 resulted in sewage being discharged into the streams and rivers, polluting the water supply and bringing epidemics of typhoid and cholera (1832 and 1848). In 1858 the Thames was so foul that sheets soaked in disinfectant were hung at the windows of Parliament to keep out the stench.

Filtration (1829), the requirement to draw water from the non-tidal river above Teddington (1856) and chlorination (1916) made London's water safe to drink.

Today, supply is maintained by reservoirs situated on the periphery of London at Datchet (8 300 million gallons/37 700 million litres), Staines, Chingford and Walthamstow. In 1974 the Thames Water Authority was constituted to take over from the Metropolitan Water Board (1903). It levied its own rate and was responsible for the management of the Thames throughout its length and for London's water supply, sewage disposal and pollution control. Since 1989/90 the National Rivers Authority (Thames Region) has been responsible for flood defence and pollution control. By the 1980s pollution of the tideway was greatly reduced and many fish were descending the stream and re-entering the estuary. Licences for eel fishing are in demand and salmon have returned in quantity after an absence of more than 150 years; they were once so cheap and plentiful that apprentices complained of having to eat them every day.

Thames Tributaries

Most now flow underground in pipes although some have been dammed to form lakes. There is little except the occasional street name to recall the course of these lost waterways. Among the northern tributaries are (from east to west) the Lea; Walbrook (short) from north side of the City; the Fleet (two branches) from Hampstead and Highgate; Tyburn via Marylebone to Westminster (traced by Marylebone Lane); Westbourne via Paddington and Kensington to enter at Pimlico; Stamford Brook which enters at Hammersmith; River Brent which enters at Kew. Among the southern tributaries are (from east to west): the Ravensbourne which enters at Deptford Creek; Effra River which enters in Brixton; Falcon Brook which enters in Battersea; River Wandle which enters at Wandsworth.

River Crossings

London grew around a fishing village at Southwark and the only crossing was by a wooden bridge built by the Romans *(see THE CITY, London Bridge)*, subsequently replaced by a bridge cluttered with buildings. After the Norman Conquest (1066)

Sightseeing on the river

Richmond Bridge was the first to span the river (1139) upstream; this was followed by Putney Bridge (1729) and Westminster Bridge (1750). As the flow of the river was impeded by the bridges the Thames froze over in hard winters and great Frost Fairs were held. Tower Bridge (19C) with its high-level walkway and hydraulic lifts is a major landmark. Albert Bridge festooned by lights at night was at the cutting edge of 19C progress with its cantilever suspension structure. The tallest liners can pass under the Queen Elizabeth II Bridge (1991) at Dartford, the largest suspension bridge in Europe. The building of the Rotherhithe Tunnel (Rotherhithe – Wapping), the first underwater tunnel by Marc Brunel (1824-43), and the foot tunnel (1902, Greenwich – Isle of Dogs) by his son, Isambard K Brunel, with its two distinctive cupolas, introduced innovative engineering techniques which have been refined for the construction of the Channel Tunnel. The original Hungerford bridge was built by Brunel; two modernistic structures for pedestrians are elegant new features. The advanced design of the pedestrian Millennium Bridge which seems to float on the water evolved from the inspired collaboration of the architect Sir Norman Foster, the engineers Ove Arup and the sculptor Anthony Caro.

A Recurring Theme

The Thames has been a source of inspiration to major artists and writers. The celebrated views by Canaletto are of great topographical and historical interest. Monet and Turner were enthralled by the play of light on the water and their innovative style heralded Impressionism. The great bend of the Thames framed by idyllic scenery at Richmond was captured with great artistry by Reynolds and Turner. Whistler's paintings of Battersea Bridge entitled *Nocturne* are evocative works. The river is an idealised or a realistic backdrop in many literary works: the plays of Shakespeare and Ben Jonson, the musings of John Evelyn, Samuel Pepys, Samuel Johnson and James Boswell, the poetry of Edmund Spenser, William Blake and TS Eliot, and the novels of Charles Dickens, Jerome K Jerome, Joseph Conrad and Virginia Woolf.

For information on boat services see PRACTICAL POINTS.

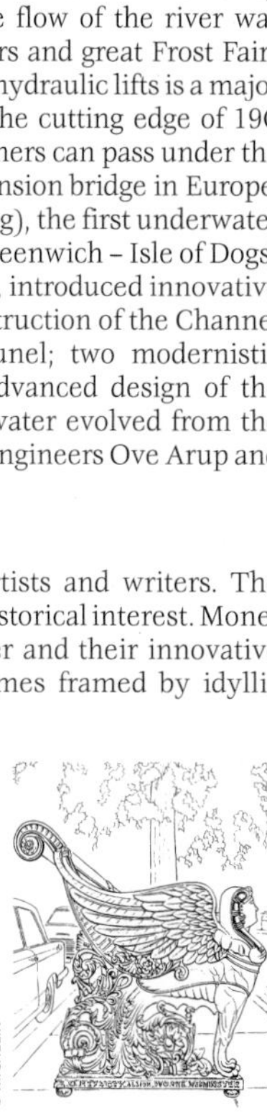

Victoria Embankment bench

Music and Theatre

Curtain up in Theatreland

It is acknowledged that the best way to capture the spirit of a place is to take part in its cultural activities. London has a proud reputation as an eclectic capital for the performing arts and Londoners have open minds and show a refreshing willingness to share new experiences.
The profusion of venues and the range and quality of the offerings attest to the vibrancy of the musical and theatrical scene. The diversity of this multicultural city is a further asset to which artists from all over the world also make a contribution.

A Musical Mosaic

London is one of the concert, opera and pop capitals of the world. Tradition and modernity are often juxtaposed to reflect diverse cultural influences at play; nowadays pop musicians and classical orchestras collaborate with great success. This significant development is a consequence of the fusion of genres, as audiences show a willingness to experiment with new musical forms. It is not unusual to mark events of national interest in a musical idiom fusing the popular and traditional styles. Opera performances are held in more accessible venues such as the arena at the Royal Albert Hall and the piazza in Covent Garden. Happy crowds enjoy The Proms in Hyde Park and the open-air concerts at Holland Park, Crystal Palace and Kenwood. Pop stars are equally at home at the Royal Albert Hall, the Wembley Arena and the London Arena in Docklands; the Royal Festival Hall and the Barbican host jazz and folk concerts.

The Swinging Capital

London's dizzying musical atmosphere is characterised by four prestigious orchestras, two celebrated opera companies, a multitude of pop groups, and a wide range of musical entertainment on offer in the capital: from buskers on the pavement to lunchtime church concerts and from polished orchestral performances to professionally staged rock shows and techno raves. Jazz music has achieved high status. The creative energy of the music scene which fosters inventive new styles shows no signs of abating.

A Formidable Tradition

The light airs of Tudor England (eg *Greensleeves* attributed to Henry VIII) developed into rounds, canons and finally a golden age (1588-1630) of madrigals. Much instrumental dance music was written with variations to display the performer's virtuosity; **John Dowland** excelled at solo songs accompanied by lute and viol. At the same time **Thomas Tallis** and **William Byrd** were composing religious music for the organ and voice in masses and anthems, set to the Latin and English liturgy; only in Elizabeth's reign did a distinctive Anglican style emerge.
In the latter half of the 17C composers extended their range with *Te Deums* and secular airs, songs and incidental music for the theatre. **Henry Purcell** (1659-96),

who dominated his own and subsequent generations, produced the first full-length opera *(Dido and Aeneas)* in 1689. Italian opera then became popular and was firmly established with *Rinaldo* (1711) by **Handel** who had arrived in England that year.
Handel resided at 25 Brooke Street, Mayfair until his death in 1759, and he produced operas based on mythological subjects which were satirised by John Gay in *The Beggar's Opera* (1728), occasional pieces such as the *Fireworks* and *Water Music* and a great succession of oratorios about religious heroes: *Esther, Messiah.*
Mozart visited England as a prodigy of eight in 1764 (composing his first symphony while residing at 180 Ebury Street; his name is perpetuated in Mozart Terrace in Pimlico), **Haydn** in the 1790s when he was the greatest musical figure in Europe. **Mendelssohn** came early in the 19C, although the *Scottish Symphony* and incidental music to *A Midsummer Night's Dream* were not completed until some 20 years later.

The Modern Age

English music entered an entirely new phase at the end of the 19C when it began to become widely popular. The Savoy operas – libretto by WS **Gilbert** and music by Sir Arthur **Sullivan** (1875-99) appealed to a wide audience. As radio became widespread in the 1930s, the BBC began to broadcast the **Promenade Concerts** which had been inaugurated in 1895 by the conductor, Henry Wood in the Queen's Hall. The programmes, organised by the BBC, include orchestral works and opera by classical and modern composers, performed by national and visiting musicians and conductors. Since 1941 these concerts have been held in the Albert Hall. The promenaders make a spirited contribution to the Last Night, when traditional pieces are played (including Elgar's *Pomp and Circumstance*).
The opening of the 20C also saw the appearance of a host of new British composers: Edward **Elgar** (*Enigma Variations* 1899, *Dream of Gerontius* 1900), Delius, **Vaughan Williams** (nine symphonies) and Gustav **Holst** (*The Planets* 1914-16). They were joined in the 1920s by Bax, Bliss and William Walton (*Belshazzar's Feast* 1931).
After the war they were reinforced by Michael **Tippett** (*A Child of Our Time* 1941, *The Midsummer Marriage* 1955) and Benjamin **Britten** who produced a magnificent series of works – *Peter Grimes* 1945, *Albert Herring, Let's Make an Opera, Billy Budd, Midsummer Night's Dream The War Requiem* and the operetta *Paul Bunyan.*
The second half of the 20C has seen the establishment of permanent centres of opera at Covent Garden and the London Coliseum, the construction of concert halls on the South Bank and at the Barbican and the birth of numerous provincial (summer) festivals.

Coda

The rich legacy of the music hall tradition and the fantastic success of contemporary musicals, which are explored below, are evidence of the happy fusion of two genres. Jazz music, which took over from the big dance bands, has a solid following and jazz clubs are flourishing with a high calibre of performers such as the saxophonist Courtney Pine. The Britpop music scene has never been so dynamic with a proliferation of new styles, the thundering rhythmic output of famous rock and dance venues and nightclubs, the chart-topping pop stars and bands and the independent groups performing in pubs and clubs.
A feast of music may be enjoyed as prestigious orchestras and celebrated artists make regular appearances at famous concert halls, opera houses, cathedrals and churches throughout London. Besides the classical repertoire, there is a drive to introduce music by modern composers exploring new idioms to a wide public.

The London Stage

From West End theatres and the subsidised theatres of the South Bank an Barbican to fringe venues and smoke-filled pubs in Battersea, Islington and Car the choice of theatrical entertainment is vast and the power of greasepaint and fa reigns supreme.

The success of the London stage has been built on a unique tradition which more than five centuries. Talented playwrights and actors have helped to est: the reputation of British theatre worldwide and plays and shows regularly tra to other countries. The capital is also receptive to foreign influences and play, to visiting artists in the field of the performing arts. New talent is applaud enthusiastic and knowledgeable audiences.

Today high standards and international reputations are maintained by the Shakespeare Company, the Royal National Theatre and successful musical w such as Andrew Lloyd Webber. Experimental theatre starts in the provinces a London's fringe circuit before moving to the West End for a season. Durin summer, open-air venues in Holland Park, Regent's Park and the Globe The are an unusually historical and informal way to enjoy performances.

A Rich Theatrical History

During the Middle Ages plays were performed outside the city boundaries as the City of London authorities were steadfast in refusing to allow theatrical performances within their jurisdiction. The first regular "public" performances were held in Clerkenwell and Shoreditch, where **James Burbage** founded the first English playhouse, and then moved south of the river to Southwark.

Meanwhile the courts of Henry VIII and Elizabeth I at Nonsuch Palace and Hampton Court attracted contemporary dramatists and entertainers for private functions. Masques were light amateur dramatic compositions enacted in elaborate costume and set to music often to celebrate a particular occasion. The legal fraternity also provided facilities for the performance of plays, masques and revels; in the late 16C *The Comedy of Errors* was staged in Gray's Inn and *Twelfth Night* was played beneath the hammerbeam roof of the Middle Temple Hall.

The true theatrical tradition as we know it today, however, is descended from the popular genre whose most famous exponents through the ages include **William Shakespeare** (1564-1616), **Christopher Marlowe** (1564-93), Ben Jonson (1572/3-1637), Wycherley, Congreve, Sheridan, Oscar Wilde...

From Restoration Comedy to Music Hall

The boisterous social climate of the Restoration is reflected in the witty comedy of manners of William **Congreve** (*The Way of the World* and *Love for Love*) with intricate plots and aristocratic characters. The most famous of the performers was Nell Gwynne, a royal favourite. The Theatres Royal of Drury Lane, Haymarket and Covent Garden opened under royal patronage in that period. The 18C was an era of great acting talent such as David Garrick, the Kembles, Sarah Siddons and Dorothea Jordan. *The School for Scandal* by **Sheridan** was a triumph. In the 19C the stage was dominated by Henry Irving, Ellen Terry and the great Shakespearean actor Edmund Kean.

In the Victorian era the growth of the urban population brought about new forms of entertainment: melodrama reflecting the popular taste for spectacle and sentimentality and music hall combining song and ribald comedy. The popularity of the latter genre – the star was the glamorous singer Marie Lloyd – led to bigger and grander theatres, known as Palaces of Variety, such as the London Palladium. The Hackney Empire, Collins Music Hall in Islington and Wilton's Music Hall in Wapping are rare survivals. Variety gave way to French-style revue combining songs and sketches. Its undisputed masters were Ivor Novello and Noel Coward who epitomised the glamour and sophistication of the period.

A Wave of Innovation

Farce and "kitchen sink drama" were both new vogues introduced by the English Stage Company at the Royal Court Theatre which opened in 1870. Coined as the "bad boy of West End theatre", this famous institution introduced the Arthur Pinero farces and was the launch pad for GB Shaw (1904-09) and John Osborne (*Look Back*

© B. Cooper/The Royal Ballet

The Royal Ballet – Daphnis and Chloë

in Anger 1956) and Arnold Wesker among others who dealt with current social and political issues. The innovative style of Harold Pinter, his sparse use of language and challenging political themes were in tune with the mood of the time.

The National Theatre Company was established to stage original works which might not be produced in the West End owing to commercial pressures. The Old Vic under Lilian Baylis had set the scene. Famous performers include many of the greatest: Sir Laurence Olivier, Sir John Gielgud, Sir Ralph Richardson, Sir Paul Scofield, Dame Peggy Ashcroft, Dame Maggie Smith and Dame Judy Dench have won acclaim internationally. The playwrights David Hare, Alan Ayckbourn, David Storey, Edward Bond, Michael Frayn and Tom Stoppard have achieved pre-eminence.

The Fringe

Alternative theatre dealing with experimental or controversial themes is performed in pubs, converted churches and small venues such as the King's Head (Islington), the Bush (Shepherd's Bush), the Gate (Notting Hill), the Battersea Arts Centre. The Donmar and the Almeida are reputed for staging intelligent and provocative plays and for attracting famous names. The fringe is the proving ground of many leading writers, directors and actors.

Stand-up comedy comes into its own at The Comedy Store, Jongleurs and a host of other venues. There is an atmosphere of fun and the shows are usually of a good quality with young hopefuls trying their luck and established comics running through new routines.

The British Musical

From the late 1960s musicals achieved huge popularity, dominated by the talented and prolific Andrew Lloyd-Webber who initially collaborated with Tim Rice (*Joseph and His Amazing Technicolour Dreamcoat*, *Jesus Christ Superstar* and *Evita*) and the producer Cameron Mackintosh (*Cats*). The shows, where the story is partly told in song instead of the spoken word, set the trend for spectacular staging, strong but simple melody and large casts. *Oh Calcutta!* was a more risqué production. Other thrilling shows such as *Oklahoma, My Fair Lady, Les Misérables, Phantom of the Opera* and *Miss Saigon* have enjoyed long runs in the West End. Recent revivals have included *Grease, Saturday Night Fever* and *The King and I*. A profitable outcome is that the successful shows are staged in cities worldwide and have won a huge following. *The Lion King* combines animation, music and song in a novel way. In a different style American musicals with their high-octane pace and slick choreography also feature on the London scene.

Verse and Prose

London has provided the setting for numerous works of fiction and has prompted strong emotions which have been translated into poetical expression. Diaries and letters bring London scenes to life through anecdote, observation and recollection.

© R.M.N.

William Shakespeare, a celebrated dramatist

A Captivating City

Not all have felt with William Dunbar "London thou art the flower of cities all" nor even with Dr Johnson that "there is in London all that life can afford" but at some point in their careers many writers lived in London. While some have detested the capital and some indulged in a love-hate relationship, others have known that for them it was the only place in the world to live. In consequence English literature from detective stories to diaries, from novels to biographies and histories, is permeated with scenes of London. The development first of radio, then of television and faster travel, has made it possible for late-20C and 21C writers to live and work outside the capital.

Despite their numbers there has been no regular forum for writers down the years: groups have shifted from the pubs near Blackfriars Theatre to those on Bankside and down the Borough High Street close to the Globe; to Highgate, to Chelsea and, for a charmed circle, to Bloomsbury; at the turn of the century a group around **Oscar Wilde**, which included Aubrey Beardsley and Max Beerbohm, and artists of the day met at the Café Royal. Since many writers have begun or earned a living as journalists, the first regular haunts were the coffee houses around Fleet Street; Addison and Steel frequented the George and Vulture, then doing greater business in tea, chocolate and coffee than in ale, and subsequently Button's at both of which they wrote copy for the *Tatler* and *Spectator*; **Dr Johnson** called at many coffee houses and taverns but nearest his own house was The Cheshire Cheese where, tradition has it, many of the great conversations took place.

Verse

Geoffrey Chaucer (1340-1400) was a courtier and diplomat; he drew on the rich tradition of contemporary French, Latin and Italian literature to recount his *Canterbury Tales* about pilgrims journeying between Southwark and Canterbury. The Elizabethan Age is encapsulated in Sir Edmund Spenser's *Faerie Queene,* a long poem populated with personifications of Justice, Temperance, Holiness, Chastity etc conceived as a glorious allegory of his times. Artists were seduced by "conceits": an intricately contrived sonnet as technically brilliant as a painted miniature. Skilled use of alliteration, assonance, rhythm and rhyme are inherited by the two great masters of theatre **Christopher Marlowe** (1564-93) and **William Shakespeare** (1564-1616), who used free verse enriched with powerful imagery and varied syntax.

Fashion in courtly poetry dwindled so it was not until **John Milton** (1608-74) emerged that the poetic genre heralded the Age of the Enlightenment. Intellectually provocative, modelled on Classical prototypes, Milton carefully expressed his Puritan

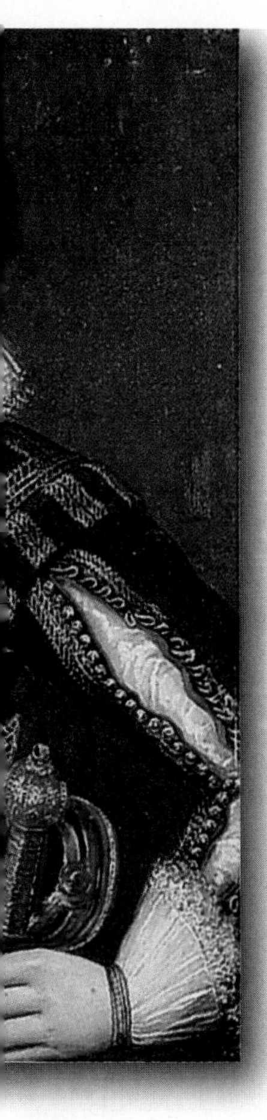

anti-Royalist politics in prose and his views on the Fall of Man in verse *(Paradise Lost, Comus, Lycidas).* The first Poet Laureate, **John Dryden** (1631-1700) recorded contemporary events in his poetry, criticism, drama and translations: his verse is often judged "occasional" in subject-matter, but clear and precise in style – heralding the rational climate of the period of **Alexander Pope**, **Jonathan Swift** *(Gulliver's Travels)* and **Samuel Johnson** (compiler of the first Dictionary 1755).

Such **Romantic** poets as Blake, Burns, Wordsworth and Coleridge are great and distinctive figures but like the Brontës, Hardy and Eliot wrote largely outside the London scene, turning instead to spirituality, Scottish patriotism, and Nature for inspiration. The quintessence of the movement exists in the tragically short life and inspired output of **John Keats** (1795-1821) who came to London to study medicine. The key to his spirit is provided by his own poetry: "A thing of beauty is a joy for ever." His verse is sensuous, rich in allusion and imagery, varied in form (sonnet, ode), spontaneous and yet meditative in expression. **William Wordsworth** mused on Westminster Bridge but lived in the Lake District; **Lord Byron** enjoyed high society.

For the Victorians, Imagination must reign over Reason – the Poet Laureate (1850-92) **Tennyson** *(Morte d'Arthur)* specialised in mellifluous poetry, **Browning** in more disjointed, exclamatory verse, and **Arnold** in descriptions of the moral dilemmas of life deprived of religious faith. Just as in Elizabethan times, Pre-Raphaelite poets such as **DG Rossetti**, his sister Christina, William Morris and **Swinburne** echo values explored by a movement in painting – imagery is pictorial, subject matter is drawn from the timeless if archaic myths and legends, form modelled on the ancient ballads.

The **Aesthetes** of the 1890s, originators of the *Yellow Book* including **Oscar Wilde** (1854-1900), **Beerbohm** and **Beardsley** among others, were greatly impressed by the philosophical writings of Henri Bergson (1859-1941) and affected by Huysmans' Symbolist novel *A Rebours (Against the Grain* alluded to in Wilde's *Picture of Dorian Gray).* The counter-reaction this provoked was a move towards realism: Kipling drew on popular music-hall song for his endearing verse full of colloquial language, natural rhythm and vitality, a marked contrast to that of **WB Yeats** (1865-1939). The Georgian poets including **TS Eliot** *(Waste Land, Old Possum's Book of Practical Cats, Murder in the Cathedral),* DH Lawrence and Walter de la Mare, defined the transition to Modernism: their work is haunted by the devastating effect of war – poignantly captured by the War Poets (Sassoon, Owen and Brooke), some of whom later rekindled their spirit of hope and celebration at having been spared. Verse form is carefully explored and blank verse is found to be the more flexible.

The 1930s era of depre ssion is recorded by **WH Auden**, **Cecil Day Lewis**, **Louis MacNeice** and **Stephen Spender**: contemporaries at Oxford, their verse is direct in appeal, colloquial in language and anti-establishment in politics. Metre and imagery are used with skill to enforce the topical concerns that characterise the period, so different in emphasis from the preoccupations of **Dylan Thomas** (1914-53) who explores childhood and innocence and **Ted Hughes** (1930-98) who describes the inherent violence of Nature.

Light Verse

Truly English in quality is the light, humorous and entertaining light verse. Many of the major writers dabbled in it, but it is the likes of **Edward Lear** (1812-88 – *Book of Nonsense*) and **Lewis Carroll** (1832-98 – *Alice in Wonderland*) that have been the most enduring masters of nonsense and limerick. **Hilaire Belloc** (1870-1953 – *Cautionary Tales*) and AA Milne (1882-1956 – *Winnie the Pooh*) contributed their verse to *Punch* magazine – a venue that in the pictorial arts had already long perfected the parallel genre of caricature and cartoon.

The Novel

"The object of a novel should be to instruct in morals while it amuses" observed **Anthony Trollope**. The first of a line of great novelists is **Daniel Defoe** (c 1661-1731), former political pamphleteer and author of *Robinson Crusoe,* and *Moll Flanders,* who managed to describe ordinary middle-class characters in credible plots. Following Defoe comes **Samuel Richardson** (1689-1761), originator of the epistolary novel with *Pamela* and *Clarissa* which explore human thought and emotion, and the popular playwright before he became a novelist, **Henry Fielding** (1701-54). *Tom Jones* is the history of a man of unknown birth who goes to London to seek his fortune: moralistic in tone, characterisation at times verges on caricature. At the turn of the century Oliver Goldsmith, Fanny Burney, Sir Horace Walpole found fame with single works prompting an interest in the Picturesque with the Gothic novel full of mystery and terror – a tradition which was to inspire Mary Shelley's *Frankenstein* (1818).

The Romantic movement is dominated by the prolific **Sir Walter Scott** (1771-1832), a specialist of the historical novel where high-born and more lowly characters seem powerless pawns before external political predicaments *(Waverley, Rob Roy, Ivanhoe).*

Charles Dickens, a social commentator

By contrast, **Jane Austen** (1775-1817) drew her six novels from personal experience - notably in matters of love and marriage; she writes with wry humour and sensitivity which give her novels an enduring popularity.

The Victorian chapter is dominated by **Charles Dickens** (1812-70), who animates his great catalogue of novels, set in and around London, with colourful characterisation, inventive plots, humour and pathos *(Pickwick Papers, Oliver Twist, Nicholas Nickleby, A Christmas Carol, David Copperfield, Bleak House, Little Dorrit, Great Expectations...)*. Published as serials, his stories quickly found a large audience and stirred contemporary Humanists to reform social conditions for children, the poor and the deprived. **Thackeray** (1811-63) sets his *Vanity Fair* in Regency England, reproaching hypocrisy and double standards.

HG Wells (1866-1946) drew on his studies at London University to create scientific romances that lead the way for the science fiction of John Wyndham (1903-69).

Travel and free thought are the principal themes of a new phase in literature: **EM Forster** (1879-1970) explores the frailty of human nature; **Virginia Woolf** (1882-1941) saw herself as a rational and enlightened thinker, an artist retaliating against the narrow-mindedness of Victorian London; she is certainly one of the most discerning and psychological novelists. **Evelyn Waugh** (1903-66) depicts social circumstances with wit, black comedy and farce that develop to realism in the face of the threat of war - a realism that pervades the work of **George Orwell** (1903-50) and his haunting images in *1984* of a spiritless, futuristic age.

The 20C was marked by various versatile personalities living and working in London, who transpose their experiences of the provinces and travel abroad into their novels: Graham Greene, Kingsley Amis, Muriel Spark, Doris Lessing, Iris Murdoch, Anthony Burgess....The Waterstone's Guide to London Writing is a comprehensive survey of books set in the city.

Language

The English language is a mighty river, fed and enriched by streams of words from many tongues; it owes its rich vocabulary to the many peoples who have settled in Great Britain or with whom the British have come into contact through overseas exploration and conquest. In 1600 there were about 2 million English speakers. The number is now nearer 400 million, including not only the population of countries such as Australia and New Zealand, Canada and the United States of America, but also of those where English is the only common and therefore the official second language.

Old English, a Germanic dialect spoken in AD 400 from Jutland to northern France, was established in Britain by AD 800 and by the 16C had taken on the syntax and grammar of modern English. Although Norman French was made the official language after the Norman Conquest, Anglo-Saxon eventually gained precedence and Norman French survives in a few formal expressions used in law and royal protocol.

English is a very flexible language which has readily absorbed a considerable inheritance from Celtic, Roman, Anglo-Saxon, Viking and Norman-French origins. Although the spoken language owes most to Anglo-Saxon, the written language shows the influence of Latin, which for many centuries formed the major study of the educated classes.

Immigration over the past hundred years or so has brought many other languages used by sizeable communities in Britain. The largest immigrant communities in Britain today are from Europe – mainly Germany, Italy, Poland, Spain and Cyprus – and from the Caribbean Islands, Africa, Hong Kong, India and Pakistan. Generations born here are often bilingual, speaking the mother tongue of their community and current English with the local accent.

Painting

The National Gallery
Mr and Mrs Andrews *by Thomas Gainsborough*

Prestigious museums, established galleries, artist-run and alternative spaces exhibiting the works of famous masters as well as the creative outpourings of modern artists attract much public interest. Innovative, often controversial, idioms which recognise no limitations to artistic inspiration, and original presentations foster new insights into the art of painting.

Patronage

The Tudor Era

The Renaissance master **Hans Holbein the Younger** (1497/8-1543) first came to London in 1526 with an introduction to Archbishop Warham and **Sir Thomas More** from the Humanist scholar **Erasmus**; his return in 1532 was largely prompted by the unsettled religious climate at home in Germany caused by the Reformation. His great draughtsmanship, penetrating eye and delicate colour suggest the artist's concern for capturing an accurate resemblance of physique and personality – formal portraits show the master keen to emphasise the exquisite detail of a jewel, brooch, brocade, silken velvet, fur or other such mark denoting status *(The Ambassadors* 1533, NG) – much in the manner of the 15C Flemish master **Jan van Eyck** (*Arnolfini Mariage* NG). Holbein joined the court of Henry VIII as a goldsmith's designer and decorator; he was subsequently sent abroad by the king charged with painting prospective brides (*Duchess of Milan* NG). **Hans Eworth** who came from Antwerp in 1549, fused his own style (*Sir John Luttrell*, Courtauld Collection) with that of Holbein, in order to be promoted to court painter by Mary I, and influenced the likes of British-born **Nicholas Hilliard** (c 1547-1619) who rose to become the most eminent Elizabethan portraitist in about 1570. Having been apprenticed to a goldsmith, Hilliard's jewel-like precise style was eminently suited to miniature painting (works in the Wallace Collection, V&A and Tate Britain). His greatest disciple and later rival was **Isaac Oliver** (d 1617).

The Stuarts

A move away from the Elizabethan "costume-pieces" came with a change in royal dynasties from the Tudor to the Stuart and a shift in artistic awareness: Thomas Howard, Earl of Arundel, Charles I and George Villiers, Duke of Buckingham emerge as three great patrons of the age: they sponsored the architect Inigo Jones, and the painters Paul van Somer, Daniel Mytens and Cornelius Johnson before the arrival of Van Dyck in England (1632). Prince Charles' interest was sparked off by the power of paintings by such masters as Titian, Velazquez, Rubens – an experience that resulted in the king acquiring the great Mantua collection that included Mantegna's *Triumphs of Caesar* (at Hampton Court).

Religious troubles continued to provoke restlessness on the Continent, and artists were obliged to seek patrons where they could. **Van Somer** settled in London in 1616 and quickly found favour at the court (*Queen Anne of Denmark*, 1617, Royal Collection). **Daniel Mytens** came to England c 1618 from The Hague bringing a new sense of confidence both in his bold style of painting and the stances given to his subjects; he was appointed Painter to Charles I in 1625. London-born **Cornelius Johnson** (1593-1661), a master of technique, painted in an honest, naturalistic way, setting his bust portraits in an oval like an intimate cameo. He, together with Mytens, was superseded in popularity by **Sir Anthony van Dyck** (1599-1641) whose full length official portraits project an air of gracious ease and elegance, synonymous with the restoration of peace after the Civil Wars. Van Dyck's Baroque compositions are a symphony of colour and texture – shimmering silk set against a matt complexion, heavily draped curtains contrast with

solid objects that might represent a distinctive attribute pertinent to the sitter (a sword for military might). His portraits of the English royal family set a benchmark for future generations perpetuated through Dobson, Lely, Reynolds, Gainsborough, Romney, Lawrence... (*Charles I in Three Positions* Royal Collection, *Charles I on Horseback* NG).

"The most excellent painter England hath yet bred", **William Dobson** (1610-46), was born in London and grew up to become a staunch Cavalier (Royalist). His portraiture in a robust, natural style influenced by Italian art is less refined than that of Van Dyck whom he succeeded as court painter: for his portrait of *Endymion Porter* (Tate Britain) he adopts Titian's pose for the Roman Emperor Vespasian and the attributes denote the sitter's patronage of the arts.

Sir Peter Lely (1618-1680) was born in Germany of Dutch parentage. His early works (1640s) in England are narrative religious pieces. At the Restoration he succeeded Van Dyck as Principal Painter to Charles II (1661). His studio produced stylised portraits celebrating the image of languorous Beauty (*Windsor Beauties* at Hampton Court) or the masculine Admiralty (*Flagmen* at Greenwich): one honouring virtue, the other victory in the Second Dutch War. His "history" pictures satisfied a less prudish market depicting the same modish voluptuous ladies (*Sleeping Nymphs* at Dulwich) in more sensual poses.

The reign of James II saw the appointment of a new Principal Painter, **Sir Godfrey Kneller** (1646/9-1723). Official portraits in the style of Lely are dignified if not beautiful in the Classical sense; well executed, they conform to a taste for formality and noble bearing (42 portraits known as the Kit-Cat series showing the head and one hand, *see NATIONAL PORTRAIT GALLERY*). Demand for portraits in the 18C was such that large numbers of assistants were trained and employed in an organised studio which was to provide a prototype for the institution of a Royal Academy in 1711.

Decorative Schemes – In 1635 **Peter Paul Rubens** (1577-1640) completed the ceiling of the Banqueting House in Whitehall: this was a complex allegorical painting commissioned by Charles I. He evolved his highly energetic Baroque style from studying works by Titian, Raphael, Velazquez and epitomised the best of contemporary Continental art: the impact on the English court of this bold political celebration of Charles's kingship should not be underestimated, nor should his influence on subsequent court painters be dismissed.

Lesser decorative schemes for stairways and panelled ceilings were undertaken by foreign artists, paid by the square foot: **Antonio Verrio**, a Neapolitan, is registered in the service of the Crown from 1676 until 1688 at Windsor, St James's Palace and Whitehall; he returned to Windsor and Hampton Court where he died in 1705. **Louis Laguerre** was trained in the French Classical tradition before coming to England at the behest of the Duke of Montagu, who was building Montagu House in Bloomsbury. **Pellegrini**, a follower of Ricci, was invited to England by the Earl of Manchester; he later became a founding member of the Royal Academy. The Venetian **Sebastiano Ricci** was responsible for the dome painting at Chelsea Hospital and a pair of large mythological paintings that hang in Burlington House. The great skill of these craftsmen and their ability to suggest luminosity and movement on a grand scale have secured their reputation. **Sir James Thornhill** (1675/6-1734), the British Baroque master of decorative painting, followed their example when engaged on such important commissions as the Painted Hall at Greenwich, the Prince's Apartments at Hampton Court and the dome of St Paul's Cathedral. Taste veered away from French art only when the Neoclassical designer **William Kent** clinched the commission to decorate Kensington Palace.

Landscape – **William van de Velde** was an official war artist employed by the Dutch navy to document battles against the British fleet. Works at the National Maritime Museum Collection, Greenwich confirm his ability to record precise detail – a quality that no doubt endeared him to the British authorities who persuaded him to switch sides and work for them; in 1674 he and his son William were given a studio in the Queen's House at Greenwich. Of the two, however, it is the younger William who left the more lasting impression on the evolution of British marine painting; he painted tranquil

Miss Jane Bowles *by J Reynolds*

topographical riverside views as well as warships at sea. Other Dutch painters specialised in recording such social events as hunting scenes and the construction of major buildings; this generated a taste in sporting pictures, decorative still-life paintings with game and flowers, topographical landscapes: genres which were to flourish throughout the 18C.

18C

The Age of Enlightenment promoted connoisseurship in the Italian art of the Renaissance and Classical art from Antiquity either from travel to the continent to study the styles at first hand or from drawings, engravings and folios; another, less intellectual but no less accomplished influence, came from Versailles in the form of a highly decorative French Baroque. Taste was a matter for stimulating debate much as were the politics of the day; preference for a particular style, therefore, varied from patron to patron.

William Hogarth (1697-1764). Apprenticed as an engraver, Hogarth struggled to earn respect and recognition for his work: despite striving to establish what he called "high art" or "history" painting, it was his "conversation" pieces like *The Beggar's Opera* that made him popular. In his treatise *The Analysis of Beauty* (1753) he upholds the importance of a national style at a time when foreign artists were achieving greater success; he propounded theories on naturalism, observing that figures conform to standard expressions, gestures and stances appropriate to age; he advocated the use of the serpentine line as a basis of artistic harmony and beauty in composition (inscribed on his palette in his self-portrait in Tate Britain).
Perhaps Hogarth's greatest follower was **Thomas Rowlandson** (1756-1827), a fine caricaturist and supreme draughtsman; he produced pictures drawn from low-life and populist subjects. His talent is Rococo in its freshness, although the humour and wit are undoubtedly English.

George Lambert (1700-65) is widely regarded as "the father of British oil landscape", although his pictures were often executed in collaboration with a figure painter (Hogarth) or a marine painter (Scott) who painted details into his landscapes as required.

Richard Wilson (c 1713-82) was given a classical education by his father. When he arrived in London in the 1740s he came as a portrait painter although early landscapes survive from 1746 (Coram Foundling Hospital Collection). In 1750 he is recorded working in and around Rome, forging a new style in the tradition of **Claude** and Vernet illustrating idyllic landscapes composed of clumped trees and buildings which might be linked with serpentine paths or rivers and populated with figures (usually drawn from Classical literature or mythology). On his return to England, the Roman Campania gently gave way to views of his own green and pleasant land.

Sir Joshua Reynolds (1723-92), a key figure in the development of British painting, was the son of an educated Devon family, a respected figure associated with the circles of Dr Johnson, David Garrick, Goldsmith and Burke. He drew inspiration from Van Dyck and the Old Master paintings known in England by engravings (Rembrandt self-portrait) or from posing his sitters according to Classical statues from Antiquity (Apollo Belvedere). The years 1752-54 he spent in Rome and was able to study the intellectual basis of High Renaissance Art. Returning to London via Venice, he resolved to merge the taste for the Italian "Grand Style" with the demand for "face-painting" at home.
In 1768 he was rewarded with the Presidency of the new Royal Academy and during his tenure outlined the way a British School of History might be forged. He advocated devoted study to the understanding of the Rules of Art and the analysis of the ideas of predecessors in arriving at modern composition. His history portraits endorsed his theories (*Three Ladies Adorning a Term of Hymen – The Montgomery Sisters* in Tate Britain) and provoked a shift in fashion towards simple neo-Classical "nightdresses" rather than billowing gowns of damask.

At his death the position of Painter to the King was taken by **Sir Thomas Lawrence** (1769-1830). Lawrence was commissioned by the Prince Regent, later George IV, to paint portraits of all the leading men who had opposed Napoleon; a large collection of sovereigns and statesmen now hangs in Windsor Castle.

Thomas Gainsborough (1727-88) developed his own very natural style of portraiture, while painting landscapes and "fancy pictures" for his personal pleasure. After residing several years in Suffolk, he moved to Ipswich, to Bath (1759) and then to London (1774) in the wake of Fashionable Society. In Bath his portraits become more assured, full-length, life-size and set in arcadian gardens. His landscapes meanwhile echo the Dutch style of Hobbema and Ruisdael. The rich palette used for his wooded country scenes is evidently drawn from Rubens: these small pictures seem to exude naturalism although the composition is carefully contrived. Gainsborough's textured rendering of foliage heralds Constable, while his skilled technique in capturing haze and flickering light foreshadows Turner.

George Stubbs (1724-1806) began as a portrait painter while studying anatomy in York. He visited Rome in 1754 in order to prove that the study of art was secondary to the observation of Nature; there he witnessed a horse being devoured by a lion, a scene that was to provide inspiration for later works. On his return to England, true to the spirit of the Age of the Enlightenment, he applied himself to the study of the skeleton and musculature of the horse by minute observation, dissection and from Renaissance drawings with a view to publishing his *Anatomy of a Horse* in 1766. Stubbs painted in oils but preferred to use enamels because of their assured durability, even if the medium demanded an exacting and meticulous technique.

19C

By the turn of the 18C/19C American independence had been recognised, the Parliamentary union of Great Britain and Ireland had been agreed (1800), in 1802 the Treaty of Amiens sealed a (temporary) end to war with France and in 1807 slavery was abolished throughout the British colonies: the age of reform and development had begun.

John Constable (1776-1834) developed his personal style and technique from observation and experimentation: his landscapes suggest topographical accuracy (*Salisbury Cathedral, Hampstead Heath*) when in fact realism has been compromised for the sake of art: trees, perspective or other such elements are contrived to improve the overall composition, which in turn is unified by *chiaroscuro* (patches of light and shade). Constable refused to depend upon formal patronage and therefore was able to explore a new relationship between man and the landscape, contradicting the 18C view of Nature as a force to appease and tame rather than accept and admire for its own sake. He considered how to convey the atmosphere of a pastoral landscape (*The Haywain,* National Gallery) by comparison with the fear and dread of a storm at sea; it is interesting to note how, from 1828, after the death of his wife Maria, Constable seems to betray a fascination for sombre skies and disturbed seas almost as if in protest against the forces of Nature. In this way Constable conveyed in landscape as much drama as any grand gesture or emotion in "high art". He arrived at his theories by sketching from nature – in oil, a medium which took time to dry and therefore intensified his awareness of fleeting effects of light, ephemeral phenomena like rainbows and transient cloud patterns and formations. As his work met with little success, he resolved to compete in terms of size and embarked upon a series of "six-footers" (*Flatford Mill* in Tate Bitain) for which he was forced to make scale sketches. In 1816 he settled permanently in London, spending the summer months in Hampstead and capturing scenes of kite flying high on the Heath.

In 1824 he was awarded gold medals for two pictures exhibited at the Paris Salon (*The Haywain* NG; *View on the Stour*), which provoked great interest from the members of the Barbizon School of outdoor painters and artists associated with the Romantic Movement, notably Delacroix.

Watercolour is a medium which found particular favour with English artists who found it a suggestive means of capturing changing qualities of light or the distance through rolling green fields to a far horizon and blue sky; for travellers on the Grand Tour it provided an efficient way of recording atmospheric details to complement topographical pencil drawings or thumb nail sketches (hence **John Ruskin's** near-obsessional realism). Unlike Continental predecessors, the English artists used opaque white paper which, if left blank, provided bright highlights. The leading watercolourists include Paul Sandby (1725-1809), JR Cozens (1752-97), JMW Turner (*see below*) and **Thomas Girtin** (1775-1802).

Drawings and Illustration – Romantic poetry and sensitivity to the forces of Nature were popularised by translations of foreign literature: Goethe, Voltaire, Rousseau, Baudelaire, Poe, while Beethoven and Wagner worked similar themes into music. In art, **Henry Fuseli** (1741-1825) explored the realms of the imagination, dreams and nightmares, full of drama and extravagant movement, stylised form in vivid if horrifying detail *(Lady Macbeth Seizing the Daggers)*: in 1787 he met the visionary poet **William Blake** (1757-1827), whose spirit contradicts the Age of Reason and heralds the advent of Romanticism. A large collection of Blake's works on paper is to be found at Tate Britain.

Joseph Mallord William Turner (1775-1851) showed precocious talent at painting topographical watercolours: by 1790 his work was hanging at the RA; six years later his *Fishermen at Sea* demonstrated his ability to handle oil and to show man in a natural world that was full of light, moving water and changing sky. Subsequent paintings confirmed his preoccupation with the same themes: *Snowstorm, Shipwreck* 1805; *Snowstorm, Hannibal and his Army crossing the Alps*. Meanwhile he continued to produce atmospheric studies of landscape (*London from Greenwich* 1809).

He went to France and Switzerland and made several trips to Italy (1819-40) visually cataloguing his impressions as he went. His sketchbooks contain evocative studies of climate, as Turner managed to suggest reflected sunlight, its blinding brilliance, its translucence and somehow its transience *(Norham Castle, Sunrise)*. In 1842 his Romantic predisposition to experience "atmosphere" at first hand before rendering it in paint was pushed to extremes: the drama captured in *Steamboat off a Harbour's Mouth* resulted from the artist insisting on being strapped to the mast of a ship pitching at sea in squally weather...

Turner also studied the work of Claude, the first artist really to attempt to paint the sun at dusk setting over rippling water *(see National Gallery)*.

Pre-Raphaelite Brotherhood – The initials PRB began to suffix Rossetti's signature in 1849 following discussions between the coterie of RA School artists **WH Hunt** (1827-1910), **DG Rossetti** (1828-82) and his brother William, **JE Millais** (1829-96), Collinson, the sculptor Woolner and Stephens. The Pre-Raphaelites considered the 15C Renaissance paintings by Raphael to be too sophisticated and over-praised: they therefore sought to develop a style which might have predated Raphael, insisting on serious subject matter, elaborate symbolism charged with poetic allusion, strong colour heightened by outdoor natural light and meticulous detail; they applied their paint to wet, white sized canvas. The key to their success came with Ruskin's defence of their art before harsh criticism from Charles Dickens (especially directed at Millais' *Christ in the House of his Parents,* better known as *The Carpenter's Shop,* Tate Britain). During the early 1850s, the group was dissolved: Millais to aspire to President of the Royal Academy, Rossetti to associate with William Morris and Burne-Jones, and Hunt to travel to Egypt, Palestine and the Holy Land in search of topographical settings for his Biblical subjects (one version of *The Light of the World* hangs in St Paul's Cathedral).

Associated in style but independent of the Brotherhood is Sir **Edward Burne-Jones** (1833-98), a fine technician with an excellent sense of style and visual appeal honed by travels in Italy with Ruskin for whom he executed studies of Tintoretto (1862); the influences of Mantegna and Botticelli are also apparent in his flat and linear designs for tapestries and stained-glass windows. In a similar vein and as accomplished are the members of the **Aesthetic Movement** *(see Inner London: TATE BRITAIN)* whose age was immortalised in **Oscar Wilde**'s *Portrait of Dorian Gray* and in the works of Frederic, Lord Leighton (1830-96), Albert Moore (1841-1893) and Whistler.

Foreign Artists – The American **JA McNeill Whistler** (1834-1903) trained as a Navy cartographer, hence his etching skills, before going to Paris to study painting. In 1859 he moved to London and earned notoriety for falling out with a patron over the so-called Peacock Room decor (now in the Freer Gallery, Washington), and later with Ruskin who accused the painter of "flinging a pot of paint in the public's face" when he exhibited *Nocturne in Black and Gold* (now in Detroit). Having been influenced by Courbet, Fantin-Latour, Degas and Manet during his life in Paris, Whistler introduced new perspectives to Victorian England, notably in the form of Japanese art.

JS Sargent (1856-1925) was both talented and prolific: born of American expatriate parents in Italy, Sargent settled in London to paint his vivid portraits and capture the elegance of Edwardian High Society with all its brilliance and sparkle.

French Impressionism came to England in the form of a large exhibition put on in London in 1883: the Impressionists used pure pigments to capture the effects of bright sunlight on coloured forms; vibrancy was achieved by contrasting complementary shades (green with red, magenta with yellow, orange with blue); texture and movement were suggested by bold brushstrokes. Simple family scenes, informal portraiture and landscape provided them with engaging subject matter. The portrayal of circus performers and cabaret entertainers for what they are was explored by Degas, Seurat and Toulouse-Lautrec; in turn they provided subjects for Walter Sickert and Aubrey Beardsley.

Rebellion – In 1886 the New English Art Club was founded to provide a platform for artists ostracised by the Royal Academy: Philip Wilson **Steer** (1860-1942) and **Walter Sickert** (1860-1942) went on to set up an alternative exhibition entitled London Impressionists, at the Goupil Gallery.

20C

In 1910 the critic and painter **Roger Fry** organised a major show of modern French art: "Manet and the Post-Impressionists" comprised 21 works by Cézanne, 37 by Gauguin, 20 by Van Gogh and others by Manet, Matisse and Picasso. In 1912 he organised another exhibition dedicated to Cubist art and large compositions by Matisse: "Second Post-Impressionist Exhibition".

Augustus John's reputation as a leader in modern British art hinged on *The Smiling Woman,* a portrait of his mistress exhibited in 1909: a famous series of contemporary luminaries followed.

Sickert conforms with the philosophy of Impressionism which he assimilated while living in Paris. In 1905 he moved back to London and founded the Fitzroy Street Group in 1907. Three years later he produced a series of works depicting the Old Bedford Music Hall, painting its performers, stage and audience with sympathy *(Ennui, La Hollandaise)*; in 1911 he founded the **Camden Town Group** which attracted Robert Bevan, Spencer Gore, Harold Gilman, Charles Ginner. Bold colour, strong outlines and broad brushstrokes were dedicated to depicting the urban landscape.

The **Bloomsbury Group** collected together writers and artists: the biographer Lytton Strachey, the economist Maynard Keynes, the novelist Virginia Woolf, her publisher husband Leonard Woolf, Clive Bell, Henry Tonks, Marc Gertler and the members of the **Omega Workshop**. Vanessa Bell, Roger Fry and Duncan Grant all used bright colour to delineate bold form in the manner of Matisse; by 1914 they were experimenting with abstraction.

The **Vorticists**, led by Wyndham Lewis and acclaimed by Ezra Pound, responded to Cubism and the dynamics of Futurism in painting and sculpture – Jessica Desmorr, Epstein, Gaudier-Brzeska were later joined in spirit by David Bomberg. Strong axes, parallel lines, harsh angles, stepped geometric forms, lurid colours proliferate, mesmerising the eye.

Pure Abstraction inspired **Nicholson**, Moore, Hepworth and Nash who explored form in relation to landscape: they considered the impact of Stonehenge, rounded pebbles so suggestive of the power and expanse of the ocean, reinforcing the image of Britain as an island... In 1936 the International Surrealist Exhibition was held in London, a high point in London's avant-garde artistic circles which at that time also included Ivon Hitchens.

Among post-war artists are Graham Sutherland, painter of religious themes, landscapes and portraits as well as scenes of urban devastation, and **Sir Stanley Spencer** whose visionary Biblical scenes are set in familiar surroundings and who explored eroticism as a means of exorcising the violence of war. Peter Blake, David Hockney and Bridget Riley were the exuberant exponents of **Pop Art** while the disturbing portraits and figures of Francis Bacon and Lucian Freud evoke a darker outlook.

Tate Modern, Whitchapel Gallery, Saatchi Gallery put on shows by artists such as Gilbert and George, Paula Rego, Beryl Cooke, Julian Opie, Damien Hirst, Tracy Emin, Rachel Whiteread, exploring new idioms – collages, installations, conceptual and performance art which challenge preconceptions and at times provoke strong reactions.

The success of the Young British Artists group is measured by the popularity of the White Cube Gallery, Jerwood Space, Lux Gallery, the Wapping Project and the South London Gallery, as well as alternative and artist-run spaces exhibiting contemporary art. Exhibitions such as "Freeze" and "Sensations" attract much media interest and are successful in attracting a young public.

Decorative Arts

As a rich trading centre London has always attracted talented craftsmen to satisfy the demands of wealthy patrons. Elegant furnishings and decorative features in a distinctive English style grace mansions and town houses. London is recognised for modern design.

Stuart

Furniture

Chippendale

Antique English furniture has long enjoyed favour. Distinctive types have evolved to suit changes in lifestyle and tastes in dress. Influences have been exerted by waves of craftsmen seeking refuge from Holland or France, and by the arrival of foreign pieces from Japan, China, India or other far corners of the Empire. The most complete display is to be found in the Victoria and Albert Museum, while most of the large houses provide period contexts in which original fixtures, fittings and furnishings may be appreciated (Ham, Osterley, Kenwood, Fenton). The height of English furniture-making came in the 18C when the greatest transformation occurred: oak was replaced by imported mahogany and later by tropical satinwood, before a return was made to native walnut. These new woods were embellished not only with carving but also with enrichments of brass in the form of inlays and gilded mounts, hardwood veneers and marquetry.

A handful of names dominates English furniture of the period. **Thomas Chippendale** (1718-79), was the son of a carpenter. He married and settled in St Martin's Lane and is recorded as importing uncompleted furniture from France which his workshops then finished off (1769). His reputation as the pre-eminent cabinetmaker of his day, famed for a classical sureness of style, was secured by his publication of *The Gentleman and Cabinet Maker's Director* (1754). It illustrated a comprehensive range of household furniture, predominantly Rococo in style, cataloguing impossible concepts alongside prototypes poached from Continental and rivals' pattern books. Perhaps the most original Chippendale designs were made for the great Neoclassical houses designed or remodelled by Robert Adam and his contemporaries, by the second Thomas Chippendale (1749-1822) who went on to produce an anglicised version of Louis XVI and archetypal Regency furniture. **John Linnell** (1729-96) also inherited his father's business. He began as a carver but soon expanded his workshops in Berkeley Square to include cabinet-making and upholstery. His reputation was secured by his association with William Kent, Robert Adam and Henry Holland (mirrors and chairs). The partnership of **William Vile** (1700-67) and **John Cobb** (1751-1778) produced the most outstanding pieces, certainly better crafted than Chippendale if less original. Vile was a favourite of the Prince of Wales, who on becoming George III appointed him cabinetmaker to the Royal Household.

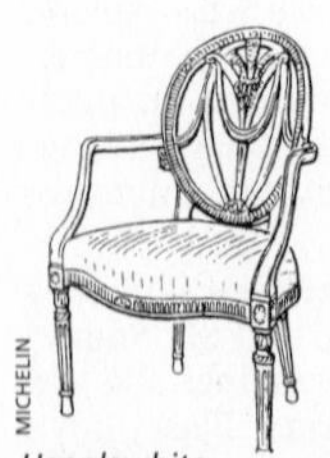

Hepplewhite

George Hepplewhite (d 1786) achieved widespread recognition two years after his death when *The Cabinet Maker and Upholsterer's Guide* was published. This codified 300 designs suited to Neoclassical interiors: best epitomising, some say, the application of Adam's principles of uniting elegance with utility. As intended, it became the standard handbook for country gentlemen commissioning furniture from artisans. Hepplewhite pieces are therefore considered as country furniture, simple, rational, extremely elegant and stylish. Typical features include bow-fronted and serpentine chests of drawers, oval, heart-shaped and shield-back chairs usually with straight or tapered legs; Prince of Wales' feathers and wheat-ear central splats are also characteristic.

Elizabethan *Regency*

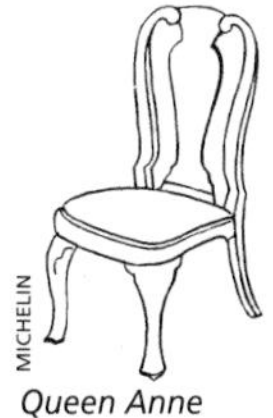

Queen Anne

Post-Hepplewhite but pre-Regency comes **Thomas Sheraton** (1751-1806) whose rectilinear designs dominate the 1790s, a perfect foil to Adam's delicate, intricate yet restrained interior stuccowork. His designs are recorded in *The Cabinet-Maker and Upholsterer's Drawing-Book* (1791-94), addressed primarily to the trade, and subsequently in two further less successful publications. He particularly exploits and celebrates the grain and textures of wood with contrasting inlays, relief panels and highly polished surfaces. Inspiration is drawn from Louis XVI furniture, notably for such subjects as small, rather feminine work tables, beautiful sideboards, secretaires and full-height bookcases. He also produced many "harlequin" or dual purpose items such as library tables containing hidden stepladders.

The Goliath of Victorian taste is undoubtedly **William Morris** (1834-96) whose firm of Art Decorators at Merton Abbey supplied the full gamut of furnishings: furniture – mostly designed by Philip Webb, textiles, wallpapers, carpets, curtains, tapestries often in collaboration with Burne-Jones, tiles, candlesticks and brassware. Many designs were collated by Morris himself who drew his inspiration from historic patterns found in churches, paintings or book illumination and natural forms. Some Arts and Crafts work, which was based on craftsmanship and pre-industrial techniques, is on show at the William Morris Gallery *(see index)*.

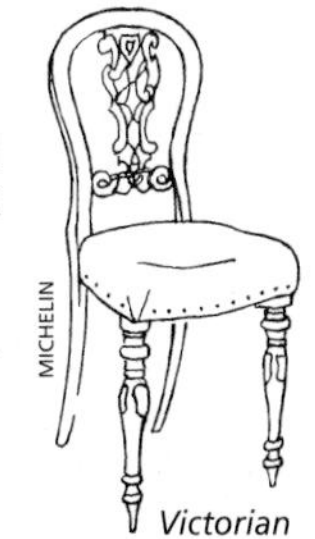

Victorian

In the following generation, Sir Ambrose Heal (1872-1959) became known for simple solid oak furniture, sometimes inlaid with pewter and ebony, often associated with Charles Voysey. His niche market was supplying middle-class homes with inexpensive alternatives to flimsy reproduction or expensive Arts and Crafts furniture – a niche-market now supplied by Conran and Habitat.

Ceramics

Tin-glazed Earthenware

The **Lambeth Potteries**, founded c 1601, are most often associated with a characteristic dark blue earthenware with a raised white ornamentation thereafter known as **Lambeth delft**; during the 18C decoration was influenced by chinoiseries – a European interpretation of Chinese designs.

The leading factory throughout the early 17C was the **Southwark Potteries**, founded by a Dutchman Christian Wilhelm in 1618. In 1628 he secured a 14-year monopoly for producing blue and white pieces fashioned in imitation of Chinese Ming, pre-empting the fashion for delft in the 1660s. On the whole the painting is judged heavy-handed.

The National Trust

Etruscan décor at Osterley Park by R Adam

Porcelain

The **Bow Factory** (identified by a variety of marks – incised, impressed or painted in underglazed blue and/or red), together with that at Chelsea were the first porcelain factories in England. Its early history is uncertain; it was founded by an Irish painter, Thomas Frye, with a glass merchant, Edward Heylyn, in the East End (Stratford Langthorne). In 1744 it registered a patent for wares crafted from a white clay (unaker) imported from America. Records show **soft-paste porcelain** being made by 1748 when Frye also patented the use of bone ash to make **bone-china** – a softer material than hard-paste, cheaper to manufacture and more durable than soft-paste. The height of production (1750-59) seems to come just prior to Frye's retirement. Early pieces include plain white figures, while receptacles appear to have been decorated with sprigs of flowers and foliage or painted in underglazed blue or enamelled with colour (Kakiemon quail pattern) or transfers. In 1775 the factory was bought by William Duesbury and amalgamated with the Derby factory.

The earliest pieces identified with the **Chelsea Factory** (incised with a triangle) are marked and dated 1745, most modelled on shapes then current for silver plate. The name "soft-paste" derives from the texture and translucence of the material, similar to white glass, as demonstrated to the Royal Society in 1742 by one Thomas Briand. After the first manager Charles Gouyon departed, the concern was headed by Nicholas Sprimont, a silversmith of Flemish Huguenot origin (raised anchor period 1749-52 followed by the red anchor period 1752-58. The factory closed in 1757/8 before reopening with the gold anchor mark 1758-69). From 1750-70 the factory enjoyed great commercial prosperity, owing to the high technical quality of the product and the adoption of new colours, including a red tint known as claret: influence shifts from Meissen prototypes – attractive, animated figures, Sir Hans Sloane's botanical specimen plants – to a taste for French Sèvres. Despite the flavour of Continental Rococo, the highly varied Chelsea wares (vegetable tureens, fruit containers, vases, chandeliers, figurines, busts, flasks etc) are somehow very English, their style of painted decoration being highly naturalistic.

In 1770 the factory came under the ownership of William Duesbury and in 1784 the Chelsea business was moved to Derby (marked with an anchor, and the letter D during the Chelsea-Derby period 1770-84). For definitions of ceramic types *see VICTORIA AND ALBERT MUSEUM*.

Metalwork

Gold and Silver

English gold and silversmiths were already known for their work in the Middle Ages and by 1180 they had formed a guild in London. In the Elizabethan period the pieces produced showed a bold and elegant line which gave way to greater austerity in the reign of James I. Pewter, considered as poor man's silver, followed the same trend. The 17C was an extravagant period for London silver which was particularly influenced by Dutch Baroque. Under Charles II the French style predominated as highly skilled Huguenots (Protestant Calvinists) were expelled from France following the Revocation of the Edict of Nantes (18 October 1685).

Under Queen Anne, in the early 18C, Dutch silver design ceded to more sophisticatedly ornate designs – cut card work, strap design, cast ornaments with scrolls, escutcheons, boss beading, repoussé and chasing. The rocaille style of Paul de Lamerie (1688-1741) was followed by more sober designs produced by William Kent (1684-1748) and others working within the delicate Adam style.

Important collections of silver plate (functional receptacles made of metal: tableware, church vessels, commemorative pieces etc.) are on view at the Tower of London, the Victoria and Albert Museum, Apsley House, the Courtauld Institute of Art, Bank of

England, the National Maritime Museum in Greenwich and the various military museums. Significant private collections, to which public access is restricted, survive at the Mansion House and in the halls of the City guild and livery companies (Drapers, Fishmongers, Tallow Chandlers, Skinners, Haberdashers, Goldsmiths, Ironmongers, Barber-Surgeons, Cutlers).

Iron

London offers many fine examples of decorative gates, railings, balconies and balustrades ranging from the work of masters such as **Jean Tijou** (active 1689-1712) at Hampton Court to the modern design of the Queen Elizabeth Gates in Hyde Park. Many City churches contain elaborate wrought-iron **sword rests** which date from the Elizabethan period (16C) when it was customary to provide a pew for the Lord Mayor of London in his own parish church furnished with a sword rest where he could deposit the Sword of State during the service.

In the 19C, design and iron casting complemented each other in the production of **street furniture**: the Egyptian-inspired bench ends along the Victoria Embankment by Cleopatra's Needle; the cannon ball and barrel bollards marking the Clink in Southwark; the beautiful dolphin lamp standards of 1870 which line the Albert Embankment; the pair of George III lamp-posts in Marlborough Road in St James's. The gold-crowned bracket lanterns at St James's Palace, made of wrought rather than cast metal, are of earlier date.

J. Malburet/MICHELIN

Sword rest in St Magnus the Martyr

The first **pillar boxes** in London, 15 years after the introduction of the penny post in 1840, were erected in Fleet Street, the Strand, Pall Mall, Piccadilly, Grosvenor Place and Rutland Gate; they were rectangular with a solid round ball crowning the pyramidal roof. Subsequent hexagonal, circular, fluted, conical designs followed, flat-roofed, crowned or plain, most emblazoned with the royal cipher. A few hexagonal boxes (1866-79) survive, as do some from the 1880s "anonymous" series which the Post Office forgot to mark with its name. Pillar boxes were promoted by the writer Anthony Trollope, who was a Post Office official, and were first painted red in 1874.

Brass

From the Middle Ages until the 17C **brass tomb plates** were very popular, and a variety are still to be found in several London churches. The design was engraved with a triangular-headed graving tool and the groove was sometimes filled with enamel, or black or coloured wax. A study of these brasses shows how fashions in dress changed over the centuries. The oldest show warriors clothed in chain mail from head to foot, armed with a heavy sword and shield; next come knights in armour wearing a helmet. From 1463 the footwear has rounded toes in accordance with an Act of Parliament prohibiting the toes of shoes to be more than 2in/5cm in length. The appearance of wives of such nobles range from the veiled simplicity of the 14C, via the rich dress and complicated headdress of the 15C, the plainer style of the Tudor period, to the ribbons and embroidery of Elizabeth's reign. In the 16C the brasses of the great churchmen were removed. In their place were rich merchants, with short hair and clean-shaven in the 15C and bearded in the Elizabethan period. **Brass-rubbing** is organised at All Hallows-by-the-Tower, St Martin-in-the-Fields and Westminster Abbey.

The long-standing tradition and patronage of fine craftsmanship and design in London is maintained today by the **Chelsea Craft Fair** and the **Goldsmith's** show at the Guildhall where international buyers come to explore ideas that will launch new trends worldwide *(see PRACTICAL POINTS – Events and Festivals)*.

The Changing Face of London

K. Brett/MICHELIN

Cumberland Terrace, Regent's Park

As London reinvents itself to suit the demands of the time, the architecture of the capital reflects its dynamic character. Tradition is an inherent part of the modern environment and a walk around London reveals an abundance of cultural landmarks. The extension of the city to the east and commissions for major buildings have provided architects with an opportunity to show a renewed sense of flair and innovation as old buildings are put to new uses and new architectural concepts are brought into play.

London through the Ages

Roman City Wall and Gates

None of the city gates has survived but their existence is recalled in the names of the modern streets or neighbouring churches: Ludgate, Newgate, Aldersgate, Cripplegate, Moorgate, Bishopsgate, Aldgate.

The wall was built by the Romans c AD 200. From the 12C to the 17C large sections were rebuilt or repaired. Demolition began in the 18C and by the 19C most of the wall had disappeared. The line of the old wall can be traced by excavated outcrops, usually consisting of an upper area of medieval construction resting on a Roman base (Barbican, St Alphage Church, All Hallows Church, Sir John Cass College and the Tower of London). The street known as London Wall more or less follows the line of the Roman Wall between Aldersgate and Bishopsgate; Houndsditch marks the course of the old ditch outside the wall.

The **London Wall Walk** *(just under 2mi/3km; about 2 hr)* between the Museum of London and the Tower of London is well mapped out with 21 descriptive panels.

Materials

A variety of materials are used in various forms of construction. Timber for a long time was the cheapest option. Stone, quarried in Kent or imported from Normandy was brought upriver to the Tower of London; Portland stone was first brought to London for St Paul's Cathedral (17C); Yorkshire stone for the Houses of Parliament (1835-60). Bricks were made locally in Kensington and Islington. In the City roofs were for the most part thatched until the 15C or 16C and were not uniformly tiled or slated until after the Great Fire (1666).

The Norman Conquest

Edward the Confessor grew up in exile in Normandy before assuming the throne of England (1042-66), it was therefore natural for him to model his designs for Westminster Abbey on the Abbey at Jumièges as a symbol of the Church Militant. The best examples of Norman architecture are to be found at St Bartholomew-the-Great, St John's Chapel in the Tower of London and the extant parts of Westminster Abbey rebuilt by Edward the Confessor before the arrival of William the Conqueror. The boldness of design and sheer scale of the Norman style are reflected in the White Tower built by William I, and in Westminster Hall – the largest to be built north of the Alps (240ft/73m long), which was constructed by William Rufus and given its great hammerbeam roof by Richard II.

The Tudor and Jacobean Eras

The greatest examples in the public domain are St James's Palace and Hampton Court, which have the typical multi-storey gateway. At Hampton Court are preserved decorative chimney-stacks, internal courtyards and the great hall with its hammerbeam roof. The first such roof and the most impressive (spanning 70ft/21m) is that in the hall of the Palace of Westminster, while other examples survive in the Middle Temple Hall (Elizabethan), Charterhouse and Eltham Palace (c 1479); decorative pendants used at Hampton Court also survive at Crosby Hall in Chelsea. Tudor brickwork with diaper patterning is visible at Charterhouse and Fulham Palace.

The Gothic Style

Gothic arrived in England from the continent in the 12C with the expansion of the Benedictine and, in the north, of the Cistercian Orders. It remained the predominant style for 400 years, evolving in three main phases.

Early English emerges as a distinctive style at Salisbury and is confirmed at Westminster (1220) where the fabric of the building was essentially conceived as a framework for traceried windows. When in 1245 Henry III assumed the financial burden for remodelling the Westminster church to his taste, the king assumed the role of pre-eminent patron of architecture in the country – an example continued until the reign of Henry VIII. While in the country the clergy relied upon local materials and building expertise which forged insular regional styles, the king, in London, could select the best craftsmen from home and abroad. The result is an English interpretation of French Gothic: Westminster never aspired to heights reached at Amiens or Beauvais, but was consolidated nonetheless with flying buttresses (cloister side of the nave). The elevation consisted of a high arcade, narrow triforium and tall clerestory with rose windows. However, what is distinctively English is the window tracery, so delicate and fluid as no longer to be considered stone masonry as such; the use of polished stone column shafts; the overall richness of applied decoration and the use of iron tie-rods as an alternative to flying buttresses; shallow doorways are adopted instead of deeply recessed porches and a centrally planned vaulted chapter-house is contrived as a function room for cathedral canons and clergy.

Decorated emerges in the late 13C and may be distinguished by the decorative richness and wealth of design in geometrical and later curvilinear tracery; from the 1290s, lierne vaulting becomes widespread. In essence, a spirit of experimentation and variety of approach pervade this transitional phase.

Perpendicular, which overlapped with the previous style for 50 years, inspired architects, on occasion, to abandon the quadrangular in favour of the polygonal, thereby giving greater visual play to the windows and the illusion of a more coherent space. In some cases this led to the use of timber rather than stone for roofing. At St Stephen's, begun by Edward I, structural and decorative elements become homogenous. Unfortunately, the Royal chapel was destroyed in 1834, as was the chapter-house of Old St Paul's built in the 1330s. Relying therefore on the contemporary building of Gloucester Cathedral choir, the new style may be identified by the use of panels of decoration to articulate structure – the effect is one of order and clarity. These visual patterns, repeated in three dimensions, heralded fan vaulting. During the 15C financial and human resources were drained by the Hundred Years War and the Wars of the Roses: when peace was restored by Edward IV, the Crown returned to being the leading patron leaving us the three Royal chapels in south-east England: St George's, Windsor (1474 crossing and aisles); King's College, Cambridge (1446, 1508-15) and Henry VII's Chapel, Westminster Abbey (1503-19).

Otherwise, this Perpendicular phase was the great age for secular building and for parish churches. Alas many of the London churches were damaged by the Reformation and/or destroyed in the City by the Great Fire (1666). Over the 45 years that followed, St Paul's Cathedral and 51 of the City's parish churches were rebuilt to designs by Sir Christopher **Wren** (1632-1723), marking an end to the evolution of Gothic architecture and the dawn of a different Continental influence.

Early Classicism or Palladianism

The turning point in the evolution of English architecture comes in the mid 16C when the Duke of Northumberland sent a certain John Shute to Italy "to confer with the doings of the skilful masters in architecture." His findings, together with Serlio's *Regole generali di architettura*, were superficially assimilated into decorative designs applied to rambling Elizabethan country houses.

At the turn of the century, **Inigo Jones** (1573-1652) emerges as the first British architect with a definable personality: this was moulded not only by his education according to the Renaissance Humanist ideal but also by his comprehensive understanding of Italian architecture, contained in Palladio's *I Quattro Libri dell'Architettura* published in Venice in 1570, and from personal experience gleaned on visits made to Venice (1601 and 1605), Padua and Rome (1613). Important projects to survive undertaken for the Crown by Jones include the Banqueting House completed in 1622 *(see WHITEHALL)* and the Queen's House *(see GREENWICH)*.

Classical Baroque and the Classical Revival (17C-18C)

In the wake of Jones comes **Sir Christopher Wren** who is perhaps one of the three or four greatest Englishmen: the dome of St Paul's is a masterpiece. Wren left England only once for Paris in 1665 where he met Bernini the famous Baroque sculptor, architect and designer from Rome. On his return to London, Wren drew up a series of designs for the rebuilding of the Old St Paul's inspired by Lemercier's dome at the Church of the Sorbonne. These were accepted on 27 August 1666: a week before the Great Fire destroyed the old Gothic cathedral. His plans to rebuild the City on a grid of long straight streets punctuated with open piazzas and such focal points of interest as the Cathedral and the Exchange were impractical, impossible even given the complex system of freehold land holdings. In the event houses and shops were rebuilt at their owners' expense: public buildings were paid for by the City and the Livery Companies; the churches were financed out of the proceeds from a tax on coal.

The City Churches – Although only a few of the parish churches were drawn in detail by Wren, most were planned by the Royal Surveyor, and later supplied with steeples. Each church is distinctive in appearance and suitably adapted to suit the new Anglican liturgy. The most complete Wren churches to survive include St Bride's, St Mary le Bow, St Stephen Walbrook, St Vedast, St Clement Danes and St James's on Piccadilly.

St Paul's Cathedral – What is remarkable is that Wren lived long enough to see the completion of his masterpiece (1675-1710). Its rich variety of detail and carefully contrived combination of elements have long provided later generations of architects with inspiration and solutions to design problems.

Wren also worked on Hampton Court Palace (south and east wings), the Chelsea Hospital and the Greenwich Hospital, where he was certainly assisted by Hawksmoor and Sir John Vanbrugh (1664-1726) – both use Classical elements with boldness and imagination to dramatic effect.

The Clerk of Works who followed Wren, **Nicholas Hawksmoor** (1661-1736) developed his own form of English Mannerism (St Mary Woolnoth in the City; St Alfege in Greenwich; St Anne's, Limehouse; St George-in-the-East, Stepney; St George, Bloomsbury; west towers of Westminster Abbey).

Neoclassicism

The rise of a new aristocracy together with the Duke of Marlborough's great military victories provided new opportunities for patronage and travel to the Continent. During the first decades of the 18C, **Colen Campbell** (d 1729) published *Vitruvius Britannicus*, a compilation of British buildings in the Antique manner – a veritable manifesto for Palladianism; the other two mainstays of the movement were **Lord Burlington** (1694-1753) and **William Kent** (1685-1748), who together went on to forge a powerful partnership that provided architectural designs, interior decoration and layouts for extensive gardens-cum-parks in the manner of Palladio's Brenta villas (Chiswick House).

The man who bridges the gap between Wren and the new surge of Palladianism is **James Gibbs** (1682-1754), the architect of St Martin-in-the-Fields. Gibbs was a great follower of Wren – his St Mary-le-Strand is a stylistic and physical neighbour of Wren's St Clement Danes up the Strand.

Ph. Gajic/MICHELIN

Palladian elegance at Chiswick House

Georgian Elegance

The next generation of eclectic designers working in the Classical vein is dominated by two rivals: **Sir William Chambers RA** (1723-96) an upholder of tradition, and the more innovative **Robert Adam** (1728-92).

Chambers travelled to the Far East and after publishing a book about his observations on China, he was asked to remodel Kew Gardens and embellish them with exotic temples and a pagoda. He gained particular favour with George III which allowed him to exercise his taste and judgement in such important commissions as Somerset House *(see STRAND)*.

Adam also travelled extensively, to France, Italy and Dalmatia to explore the Classical style and to draw inspiration direct from the example of Antique domestic architecture. In interior decoration he borrowed extensively from descriptions of Pompeii and Herculaneum which had recently been discovered, and from artefacts excavated from Palmyra and Greece, most especially from Greek vase painting – he developed a light touch and delicacy that, having found favour at Osterley Park and Syon House, was quickly assimilated into 18C aesthetic movements. Few Adam town houses survive intact: Home House at 20 Portman Square, the south and east sides of Fitzroy Square, single houses in St James's Square *(no 20)*, Chandos Street and behind the Adelphi.

English Neoclassicism evolved into an informal reinterpretation of the Antique: in its purest form it is limited to architecture, its spirit however affected all the decorative and applied arts. Multi-disciplined designers like Adam and Chambers were content to accommodate other revivalist styles in the form of follies, bowers and bandstands. Gothick which was promoted by Walpole's Gothick novels was limited to private houses (Strawberry Hill); chinoiserie to garden pagodas (Kew); Rococo to follies or pleasure gardens (Vauxhall); the Picturesque contrived to imitate untamed Nature, as depicted in painting – dead trees were planted and "ruins" were artificially assembled in gardens.

By the late Georgian period architects had begun to adapt freely the principles of the Classical style as is evident in **John Nash's** All Souls, Portland Place (1822-24).

The Regency Period (1811-30)

The key figure of this phase is probably **Henry Holland** (1745-1806) who designed Brooks's Club in St James's. The main thread of the Regency style came from pre-Revolution France, copied from picture books and interpreted by Continental craftsmen.

The period up to the death of George IV is dominated by three men. **Sir John Soane** (1753-1837), a professional and eclectic architect whose principal legacy was the Bank of England, now largely destroyed. **John Nash**, favourite architect of George IV, responsible for laying out Regent Street, the terraces of elegant residences for Members of Parliament surrounding Regent's Park (1810-11), for designing the grand Carlton House Terrace, Buckingham Palace (although much changed), for the Brighton Pavilion and various country houses. **Thomas Cubitt**, quality builder and property developer, worked from George Basevi's designs to create Belgrave Square and other large sections of Belgravia (1825), Pelham Crescent (1820-30); other squares, crescents and streets stretch from Putney and Clapham to Islington, Kensington to the Isle of Dogs.

Dutch gables in Cadogan Square

The Victorian Age (19C)

Social changes resulted from greater affluence and industrial expansion. A population explosion provoked a huge demand for urban housing that in turn necessitated a change in building practices that saw the demise of the individual craftsman. Materials began to be industrially manufactured (iron in the late 18C, plate glass in the mid 19C, by the 1840s whole buildings were being pre-fabricated, concrete was being tested in the 1860s) and transported cheaply by rail. The main phases may be identified as **Early Victorian**, characterised by earnest historicism and the use of plainish materials, **High Victorian** (1850s-1870s) which reacted against archaeological correctness with strong colour, contrasting materials, and strong sculptural effects, and **Late Victorian** which reverts to smooth contours and soft textures, intricate decoration and delicate colour.

A key figure who straddles all three phases was **Sir George Gilbert Scott** (1811-78). Not only did he restore buildings (notably Westminster Abbey in 1849) he applied his confident Gothic style as easily to religious buildings (St Mary Abbotts, Kensington) as to secular developments: St Pancras Station and Hotel, Albert Memorial, Broad Sanctuary west of Westminster Abbey; the new government buildings in Whitehall are forged in a rather staid, unimaginative Renaissance style. His grandson **Sir Giles Gilbert Scott** (1880-1960) proves himself to be a far more sensitive and inspired product of the Late Victorian age, bequeathing such individual landmarks of the post-industrial age as Battersea Power Station (1932-4), Waterloo Bridge (1939-45) and Bankside Power Station.

Functional cast-iron building became an art in itself (Palm House at Kew, Paxton's Crystal Palace, Lewis Cubitt's King's Cross Station 1852, Brunel's Paddington Station 1850), while in other domains, fashions for eclecticism and revivalist movements continued: turrets, gables, pointed windows and stained glass proliferated in the neo-Gothic architect-designed estates and the anonymous streets of the expanding suburbs.

Red-brick developments were instituted by the London County Council who drew inspiration from **Philip Webb** for Bethnal Green and Millbank. Another successful exponent of this practical, unfussy style was **Richard Norman Shaw** (1831-1912) who designed Lowther Lodge in Kensington (1873 now the Geographical Society), Swan House in Chelsea (1876) and four houses in Cadogan Square (*60a, 62, 68* and *72*) which inspired the 20C nickname "Pont Street Dutch." At Bedford Park near Turnham Green, Norman Shaw designed various functional two to three storey houses each with its own garden in the red-brick Queen Anne style with tile-hanging, rough-cast rendering and white woodwork, along with a church, shop and inn. The interior decoration and furnishings were left to the firm of the socialist **William Morris** (1834-96) and as such soon became identified with the **Arts and Crafts Movement**. Against the tide of mass production, came a revival of craftsmanship in architectural sculpture, stained glass, practical hand-made furniture, block-printed fabrics and wallpapers. While **Alfred Waterhouse** (1830-1905) designed the Natural History Museum combining naturalistic observation with fantastic imaginary beasts applied to some great Germanic Romanesque fabric, De Morgan tiles and Morris screens spurned the development of Art Nouveau.

Ecclesiastical Building – A surge in church building was provoked by demand to serve the new suburbs. Perpendicular spires spiked the sky as a new interest in Gothic architecture culminated in the new designs for the Palace of Westminster. The detailed designs of George Gilbert Scott and Augustus Pugin included every element accurately and skilfully executed. As in the 18C, fads and fashions proliferated prompting a revivalist taste for neo-Norman, neo-Early Christian and, in the mid century, for neo-Italian Romanesque.

20C Post-war Period

The International Style formulated by the Belgian **Henry van der Velde** (1863-1957) and the German **Peter Behrens** (1868-1940) – both painters turned designer and architect – were followed by **Walter Gropius** (1883-1969) in wanting to deny the impact of historical antecedents and any recognisable association of style with function (cast-iron construction being synonymous with railway stations and tropical palm houses). They nevertheless advocated quality in building and practical functionality – factories and power stations should not be dressed to look like schools or cathedrals. Meanwhile, steel-frame construction (Ritz Hotel 1904) and the use of concrete led to ever shorter building time-frames.

Churches – Not until the 1920s was the neo-Gothic tradition broken when Edward Maufe provoked a change of direction by building truly modern churches: St Columba's in Pont Street, St John's in Peckham, and beyond London the new cathedrals of Coventry, Guildford, Bristol RC and Liverpool RC.

R. Besse/MICHELIN

Residential Developments – Distinctive modern housing is rare: 64-66 Old Church Street in Chelsea (c 1934) by the International Modernist Mendelsohn and Chernayeff, the Sun House in Hampstead (1935) by **Maxwell Fry**, Highpoint One and Two in Highgate (1936-38) by the reclusive Berthold **Lubetkin** and Tecton, **Goldfinger's** custom-built 2 Willow Road and Cheltenham Estate (Kensal Rise). Lillington Gardens, Pimlico (1960s) and Aberdeen Park in Islington (1980s) by Darbourne and Darke show that council housing need not be unattractive.

R. Besse/MICHELIN

Today, important contemporary developments abound on the South Bank, in the City, Docklands, around Heathrow, Gatwick and Stansted airports, while imaginative conversions proliferate along the Thames and within London's mainline railway stations and disused markets (Billingsgate, Spitalfields) and power stations (Bankside, Lots Road). Notable landmarks on London's skyline include Centre Point, the South Bank Complex, Barbican, Telecom Tower, Richard Rogers's Lloyd's Building, Tower 42, Chelsea Harbour, Vauxhall Cross, and 1 Canada Square – known simply as Canary Wharf. The Millennium Dome in Greenwich and the new offices of the Mayor of London in Bermondsey add a futuristic note to the riverside. The distinctive Swiss Re building designed by Sir Norman Foster (2002) continues the trend for eco-friendly buildings.

Technical Architectural Terms

Ambulatory: continuation of the aisles around the east end sanctuary.
Apsidal or radiating chapel: apsed chapel radiating from the ambulatory or sanctuary.
Archivolt: continuous architrave moulding on the face of the arch, following its contour.
Axial or **Lady Chapel**: chapel radiating or extending from the sanctuary dedicated to the Virgin Mary.
Barrel vaulting: most basic form of tunnel vaulting, continuous rounded or pointed profile.
Basket arch: depressed arch common to late-medieval and Renaissance architecture.
Blind arcading: decorative frieze of small, interlacing, arches and intervening pilaster strips; typical of Romanesque architecture in Lombardy and West Country Transitional.
Buttress: a structural member placed along the exterior wall to reinforce and counter side thrust of a vault.
Capital: head or crowning feature of a column. In Classical architecture there are four orders: Doric, Ionic (with volutes), Corinthian (leaf decoration) and Composite (Ionic and Corinthian). Other forms include a Cushion capital (Romanesque cut from a cube) and a Crocket capital (decorated with stylised Gothic leaves terminating in volutes).
Caryatid: female figure used as a column (atlantes are male caryatids).
Clerestory: upper section of the elevation containing large windows.
Coffering: vault or ceiling decoration consisting of sunken panels.
Corbel: projecting block (stone) that supports a beam or other horizontal member.
Exedra: niche, usually semicircular, with a bench around the wall.
Flamboyant: latest phase (15C) of French Gothic architecture; name taken from the undulating (flame-like) lines of the window tracery.
Flying buttress: buttress of masonry decorated with pinnacles.
Foliated scrolls: sculptural or painted ornamentation depicting foliage, often in a frieze.
Fresco: mural paintings executed on wet plaster.
Gable: triangular part of an end wall carrying a sloping roof; the term is also applied to the steeply pitched ornamental pediments of Gothic architecture.
Gargoyle: waterspout projecting from the parapet often ornamented with a grotesque figure, animal or human.
Groined vault: produced by the intersection of two perpendicular tunnel vaults of identical shape.
Keystone: central stone of an arch or a rib, sometimes fashioned as a boss.
Lierne: a tertiary rib, one that neither springs from the main springers nor passes through the central boss.
Lintel, transom: horizontal beam or stone bridging an opening of a door, window.
Mullion: a vertical post dividing a window.
Pediment: low pitched gable over a portico, usually triangular, in Classical architecture.
Peristyle: a range of columns surrounding or engaged to the façade of a building.
Pier: solid masonry structural support as distinct from a column.
Pilaster: engaged (attached) rectangular column.
Pinnacle: small turret-like decorative feature crowning spires, buttresses.
Piscina: basin for washing the sacred vessels.
Quadripartite vaulting: one bay subdivided into four quarters or cells.
Rib vault: framework of diagonal arched ribs carrying the cells.
Rood screen: carved screen separating the chancel from the nave; rood was the Saxon word for a cross or crucifix and this might be flanked by figures of the Virgin and John the Baptist.
Rustication: large blocks of masonry often separated by deep joints and given bold textures (rock-faced, diamond-pointed...); commonly employed during the Renaissance.
Semicircular arch: round-headed arch.
Term: sculpted ornament consisting of a carved bust tapering to a square base pillar.
Tracery: intersecting stone ribwork in the upper part of a window.
Transept: transverse section of a cross-shaped church bisecting the nave.
Transverse arch: separates one bay from another, running perpendicular to the nave axis.
Triforium: arcaded wall passage running the length of the nave above the arcade and below the clerestory.
Triptych: three panels hinged together, chiefly used as an altarpiece.
Voussoir: wedge-shaped blocks of masonry making an arch or vault.

Sculpture

The quick pace of change in popular culture has a powerful impact on all forms of art. Sculpture is no longer restricted to traditional materials and a young generation of artists has the freedom to experiment with new forms which elicit a mixed public response. As more public spaces are created in the city, monumental sculpture becomes an interesting feature of the cityscape.

In sculpture the evolution from Gothic tomb effigies to modern abstract form begins with William **Torel**, citizen and goldsmith of London, who modelled Henry III and Eleanor of Castile (1291-92), and the visiting (1511-20) early Renaissance Florentine **Torrigiano**, who cast the gilt bronze figures of Henry VII (in the V & A), his queen, Elizabeth, and mother, Margaret, Duchess of Richmond. After the Reformation, contact with Italy was suspended, dominant influences are therefore imported from France and Flanders.

Henry Moore Sculptures in London

West Wind 1928/9 (St James's Park Underground) was Moore's first open air sculpture and his first public commission: the relief, reflecting Moore's empathy for Mexican sculpture, is to be contrasted with Epstein's *Night* over the doorway. In *Three Standing Figures* 1947/8 (west end of the lake in Battersea Park) Moore explores spatial unity of the three-dimensional group. *Time-Life Screen* 1952/3 (New Bond St, inset on the second floor of the former Time-Life Building). The 11ft/3.3m bronze *Upright Motives 1, 2 and 7* 1955/6 (Battersea Park) show Moore working on a grand scale specifically for the outdoors, conscious that surface detailing will evolve with weathering. *Two Piece Reclining Figure No 1* 1959 (Chelsea School of Art, Manresa Road). *Knife Edge Two Piece* 1962/5 (Abingdon Gardens, opposite Rodin's *Burghers of Calais*). *Locking Piece* 1963/4 (Millbank) was inspired by two pebbles. *Two Piece Reclining Figure No 5* 1963/4 (Kenwood House). *Circular Altar* 1972 (St Stephen Walbrook, City). *Large Spindle Piece* 1974 (Spring Gardens). *The Arch* 1979/80 (Kensington Gardens). *Mother and Child: Hood* 1983 (St Paul's Cathedral).

Actual portraiture appears in the 17C in the works of, among others, Nicholas Stone (John Donne), the French Huguenot **Le Sueur** (bronzes of Charles I and James I) and **Grinling Gibbons** (statues of Charles II and James II). Gibbons is better known and celebrated as a woodcarver of genius and great delicacy, who often signed his work with a peapod.

In the 18C, as a Classical style began to appeal to graduates of the Grand Tour, the Flemings, Michael Rysbrack and Peter Scheemakers, the Frenchman François **Roubiliac**, the Englishmen John Bacon, John **Flaxman** and Nollekens executed hundreds of figures, many with considerable strength of character, until the genre became stylised and empty in the 19C. Many examples of their work are to be found in the nave and north transept of Westminster Abbey.

Vigour began to return in the 20C in portraiture and religious sculptures with works by Jacob **Epstein**, in human, near abstract and abstract themes by Henry **Moore**, and pure abstract by Barbara **Hepworth**. In the 1930s after Dada and Surrealism had swept through Paris touching all forms of artistic consciousness, a number of painters, sculptors and architects emigrated, several moving to Hampstead which hosted a new move towards pure abstraction: Roland Penrose, Lee Miller, Henry Moore, Barbara Hepworth, Ben Nicholson.

Some fine contemporary sculpture adorns the open spaces created by modern town planning: the *Horses of Helios,* the Sun God, with the three Graces above, by Rudi Weller (corner of the Haymarket and Piccadilly Circus); *Boy with a Dolphin* in bronze by David Wynne (north end of Albert Bridge in Chelsea and outside the Tower Hotel in Wapping); *Fulcrum* by Richard Serra (Broadgate); a *Dancer* (Bow Street opposite the Royal Opera House); *Horse* by Shirley Pace (The Circle, Bermondsey); *The Navigators* by David Kemp (Hays Galleria, Southwark). Modern works temporarily displayed next to traditional statues in Trafalgar Square: *Ecce Homo* By Mark Wallinger, *Regardless of History* by Bill Woodrow and *Plinth (Untitled)* by Rachel Whiteread, have aroused much public interest. The sleek lines of the Millennium Bridge, built with the collaboration of the architect Sir Norman Foster, the sculptor Sir Anthony Caro and the engineering firm Ove Arup, break new ground as an engineering masterpiece and an artistic achievement.

Historical Perspective

Victoria, Queen and Er

For an appreciation of London's heritage, which reflects various influences throughout the centuries, important historical dates and events need to be placed in context. The city reveals its rich tapestry to visitors prepared to devote some time and effort to this end.

AD

- **43** – Roman Londinium founded.
- **61** – Revolt against the Romans by Boadicea; Londinium sacked.
- **2C** – Roman wall constructed.
- **5C** – Londinium evacuated by the Romans.
- **8C-10C** – Viking raids and barbarian invasions.

Saxon Dynasty

- **1015** – Edmund Ironside elected king by the assembly *(gemut)* of London; died the same year; succeeded by **Canute**.
- **1042-66** – Reign of **Edward the Confessor**.
- **1065** – Westminster Abbey founded.
- **1066** – Norman invasion.

Norman Dynasty

- **1066** – Coronation of William I. Royal charter granted to the City.
- **1066-87** – Reign of William I **(William the Conqueror)**.
- **1067-97** – Construction of the Tower of London.
- **1087-1100** – Reign of William II (Rufus).
- **1087** – Construction of Westminster Hall.
- **1100-35** – Reign of Henry I; Royal charter granted to the City.
- **1135-54** – Reign of Stephen.
- **1136** – St Paul's Cathedral and many wooden houses destroyed by fire.

Plantagenet Dynasty

- **1154-89** – Reign of Henry II.
- **1157** – Arrival of Hanseatic merchants in the City of London.
- **1189-99** – Reign of Richard I (the Lionheart).
- **1192** – Election of Henry Fitzailwin as first Mayor of the City.
- **1199-1216** – Reign of John (Lackland); Royal charter granted to the City.
- **1209** – Construction of the first stone bridge (London Bridge) replacing the Roman bridge.
- **1216** – *Magna Carta* signed at Runnymede.
- **1216-72** – Reign of Henry III.
- **1224** – Law courts established at Westminster.
- **1290** – Jews banished from the City of London.
- **1272-1377** – Reigns of Edward I (1272-1307), Edward II (1307-27) and Edward III (1327-77).
- **1349** – Black Death: population of London reduced by half to 30 000.
- **1377-99** – Reign of Richard II.
- **1381** – The Peasants' Revolt led by Wat Tyler *(see index)*.

House of Lancaster

• **1399-1461** – Reigns of Henry IV (1399-1413), Henry V (1413-22) and Henry VI (1422-61).
• **1450** – Rebellion of the men of Kent headed by Jack Cade; they occupied London for three days.
• **1453** – Wars of the Roses between Lancaster and York; Henry VI imprisoned in the Tower of London.

House of York

• **1461-83** – Reign of Edward IV.
• **1476** – First English printing press set up at Westminster by William Caxton.
• **1483** – Edward IV's sons assassinated (The Little Princes in the Tower).
• **1483-85** – Reigns of Edward V (1483) and Richard III (1483-85).

House of Tudor

• **1485-1509** – Reign of Henry VII.
• **1497** – Rebellion of the Cornishmen under Audley.
• **1499** – Perkin Warbeck, Pretender to the throne, hanged at Tyburn.
• **1509-47** – Reign of Henry VIII.
• **1530** – Construction of St James's Palace.
• **1536** – Execution of Anne Boleyn, second wife of Henry VIII.
• **1536-39** – **Reformation**: Papal authority rejected by the English Church; suppression of the monasteries.
• **1547-58** – Reigns of Edward VI (1547-53) and Mary I (Bloody Mary) (1553-58).
• **1555** – Execution at Smithfield of 300 Protestants. Founding of the Muscovy Company.
• **1558** – Population 100 000.
• **1558-1603** – Reign of Elizabeth I (Good Queen Bess, the Virgin Queen).
• **1567** – First Exchange established in the City.
• **1581** – Founding of the Turkey (later Levant) Company.
• **1599** – Inauguration of the Globe Theatre in Southwark.
• **1600** – Charter of incorporation granted to the East India Company.

House of Stuart

• **1603-25** – Reign of James I (James VI of Scotland).
• **1603** – Population 200 000.
• **1605** – The **Gunpowder Plot** was hatched by a group of Roman Catholics seeking religious toleration. The plot failed and Parliament declared 5 November a day of public thanksgiving.
• **1615** – Inigo Jones appointed Surveyor of the King's Works.
• **1616** – Queen's House at Greenwich, the first Classical building in England, designed by Inigo Jones.
• **1625-49** – Reign of Charles I.
• **1635** – Covent Garden Piazza built.
• **1642** – Beginning of the **Civil War**: Charles I opposed by Parliament; Royalists confronted at Turnham Green by City trainbands (citizen militia); Charles I deterred from attacking London.
• **1649 – Execution of Charles I** on Tuesday 30 January 1649 outside the Banqueting Hall in Whitehall.
• **1649-60 – Commonwealth**.
• **1653** – Cromwell appointed Protector of the Commonwealth.
• **1660 – Restoration**.
• **1660-85** – Reign of Charles II (the Merry Monarch, the Black Boy).
• **1660** – Royal warrants granted permitting theatres in Covent Garden.

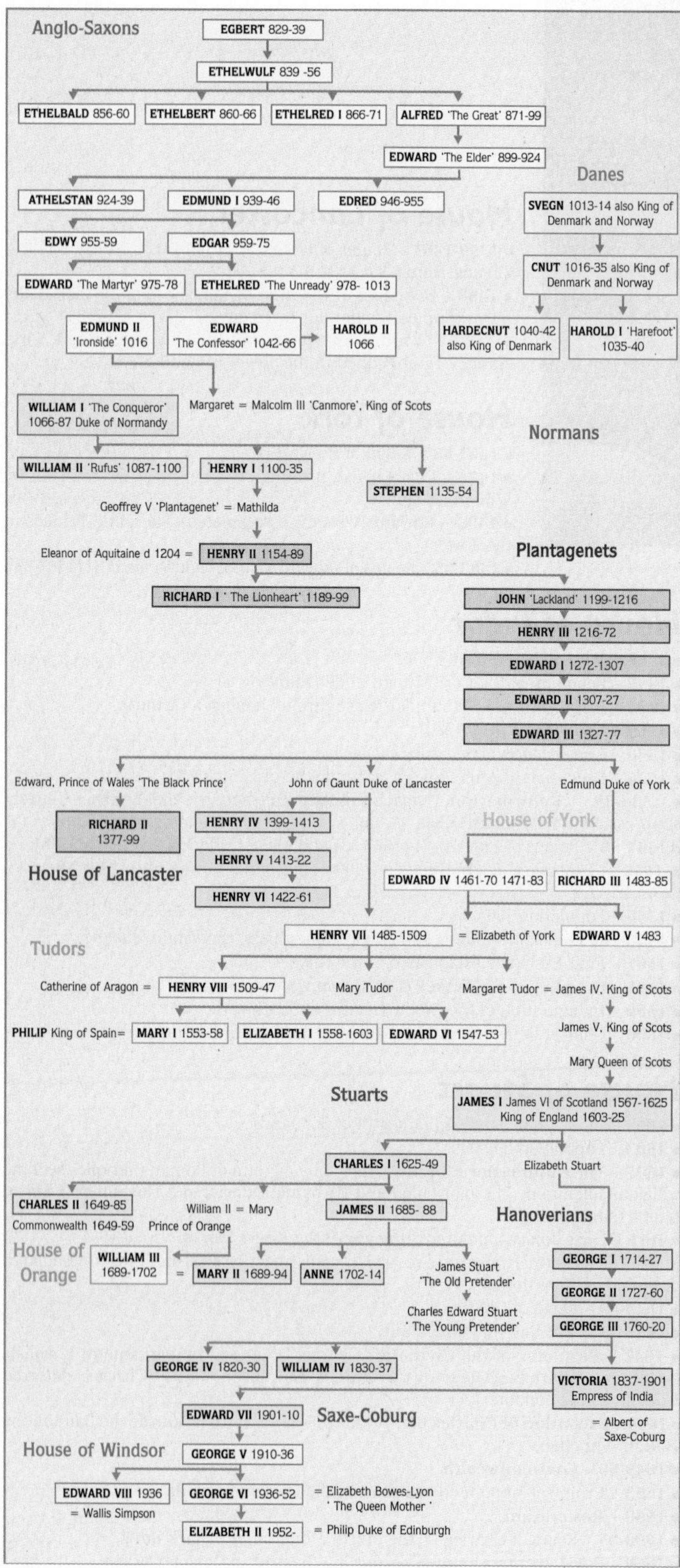

Anglo-Saxons
EGBERT 829-39
ETHELWULF 839 -56
ETHELBALD 856-60
ETHELBERT 860-66
ETHELRED I 866-71
ALFRED 'The Great' 871-99
EDWARD 'The Elder' 899-924
ATHELSTAN 924-39
EDMUND I 939-46
EDRED 946-955
EDWY 955-59
EDGAR 959-75
EDWARD 'The Martyr' 975-78
ETHELRED 'The Unready' 978- 1013
EDMUND II 'Ironside' 1016
EDWARD 'The Confessor' 1042-66
HAROLD II 1066
Danes
SVEGN 1013-14 also King of Denmark and Norway
CNUT 1016-35 also King of Denmark and Norway
HARDECNUT 1040-42 also King of Denmark
HAROLD I 'Harefoot' 1035-40
WILLIAM I 'The Conqueror' 1066-87 Duke of Normandy
Margaret = Malcolm III 'Canmore', King of Scots
Normans
WILLIAM II 'Rufus' 1087-1100
HENRY I 1100-35
STEPHEN 1135-54
Geoffrey V 'Plantagenet' = Mathilda
Eleanor of Aquitaine d 1204 =
HENRY II 1154-89
Plantagenets
RICHARD I ' The Lionheart' 1189-99
JOHN 'Lackland' 1199-1216
HENRY III 1216-72
EDWARD I 1272-1307
EDWARD II 1307-27
EDWARD III 1327-77
Edward, Prince of Wales 'The Black Prince'
John of Gaunt Duke of Lancaster
Edmund Duke of York
RICHARD II 1377-99
HENRY IV 1399-1413
HENRY V 1413-22
HENRY VI 1422-61
House of Lancaster
House of York
EDWARD IV 1461-70 1471-83
RICHARD III 1483-85
HENRY VII 1485-1509
= Elizabeth of York
EDWARD V 1483
Tudors
Catherine of Aragon =
HENRY VIII 1509-47
Mary Tudor
Margaret Tudor = James IV, King of Scots
PHILIP King of Spain=
MARY I 1553-58
ELIZABETH I 1558-1603
EDWARD VI 1547-53
James V, King of Scots
Mary Queen of Scots
Stuarts
JAMES I James VI of Scotland 1567-1625 King of England 1603-25
CHARLES I 1625-49
Elizabeth Stuart
CHARLES II 1649-85
Commonwealth 1649-59
William II = Mary Prince of Orange
JAMES II 1685- 88
Hanoverians
House of Orange
WILLIAM III 1689-1702
=
MARY II 1689-94
ANNE 1702-14
James Stuart 'The Old Pretender'
Charles Edward Stuart ' The Young Pretender'
GEORGE I 1714-27
GEORGE II 1727-60
GEORGE III 1760-20
GEORGE IV 1820-30
WILLIAM IV 1830-37
VICTORIA 1837-1901 Empress of India
= Albert of Saxe-Coburg
EDWARD VII 1901-10
Saxe-Coburg
House of Windsor
GEORGE V 1910-36
EDWARD VIII 1936
= Wallis Simpson
GEORGE VI 1936-52
= Elizabeth Bowes-Lyon ' The Queen Mother '
ELIZABETH II 1952-
= Philip Duke of Edinburgh

• **1661** – Design of Bloomsbury Square, the first London square.
• **1665** – **Great Plague**: records give the total mortality as 75 000 out of a population of 460 000, rapidly spreading through London from St Giles-in-the-Fields and causing the most deaths in the poorest, most over-crowded districts on the outskirts of the City (Stepney, Shoreditch, Clerkenwell, Cripplegate and Westminster). In June 1665 the king and the Court left London, only to return the following February; Parliament met briefly in Oxford. A vivid account of events is given by Daniel Defoe in his *Journal of the Plague Year (1722)*.
• **1666** – Publication of the first London newspaper.
• **1666** – **The Great Fire of London** was the worst in the history of the capital; it lasted four days (2 to 5 September) and destroyed four-fifths of the City: St Paul's Cathedral, the majority of the 87 parish churches, most of the civic buildings and 13 000 houses.
• **1666-1723** – Reconstruction of St Paul's Cathedral and the City churches by Sir Christopher Wren.
• **1670** – Founding of the Hudson Bay Company.
• **1682** – The Royal Hospital in Chelsea is founded for veteran soldiers.
• **1685-88** – Reign of James II.
• **1685** – Arrival of Huguenot refugees from France following the Revocation of the Edict of Nantes.
• **1688** – **Glorious Revolution**: flight into exile of James II; crown offered to William of Orange.
• **1689-1702** – Reigns of William III and Mary II until her death in 1694 and then of William alone.
• **1694** – Founding of the Bank of England.
• **1700** – Population 670 000.
• **1702** – Publication of the *Daily Courant* newspaper.
• **1702-14** – Reign of Queen Anne.

House of Hanover

• **1714-60** – Reigns of George I (1714-27) and George II (1727-60).
• **1750** – Construction of Westminster Bridge.
• **1753** – British Museum established.
• **1756-63** – Seven Years War.
• **1760-1820** – Reign of George III.
• **1775-83** – American War of Independence.
• **1780** – Gordon Riots against Roman Catholics.
• **1801** – First census: population 1 100 000.
• **1811-20** – Reign of the future George IV as Prince Regent.
• **1812** – Regent Street created by John Nash.
• **1820-30** – Reign of George IV.
• **1824** – Opening of the National Gallery.
• **1828** – Founding of University College, "that Godless institution in Gower Street".
• **1830-37** – Reign of William IV.
• **1831** – Founding of King's College.
• **1832** – Reform Bill.
• **1836** – **University of London** incorporated by charter as an examining body.
• **1835-60** – Reconstruction of the Palace of Westminster (Houses of Parliament).
• **1837-1901** – Reign of Queen Victoria.
• **1851** – Great Exhibition in Hyde Park. Population 2 700 000.
• **1852** – Founding of the Victoria and Albert Museum.
• **1856-1909** – Building of the South Kensington museums.
• **1860** – Horse-drawn trams introduced.
• **1863** – First underground railway excavated.
• **1894** – Opening of Tower Bridge.
• **1897** – First omnibuses (buses) introduced.

House of Windsor *(Saxe-Coburg until 1917)*

- **1901-10** – Reign of Edward VII.
- **1901** – Population 6 600 000.
- **1909** – Establishment of the **Port of London Authority** (PLO) to manage the docks.
- **1910-36** – Reign of George V.
- **1914-18** – Zeppelin raids on London.
- **1933** – Establishment of London Transport to coordinate public transport: underground, bus and railway.
- **1936** – Accession and abdication of Edward VIII.
- **1936-52** – Reign of George VI.
- **1938** – Establishment of the **Green Belt**.
- **1939** – Population 8 610 000.
- **1940-41** – **London Blitz** (aerial bombardment of London) during the Battle of Britain began in 1940 after the British retreat from Dunkerque (Dunkirk). The first heavy raids on London by the German Air Force (Luftwaffe) began on 7 September; for 57 consecutive nights 163 bombers per night flew over London dropping heavy explosive or incendiary bombs. Only adverse weather conditions brought respite.
- **1951** – The **Festival of Britain**, an echo of the Great Exhibition of 1851, was promoted as a "tonic to the nation" to bring colour, light and fun to the postwar scene.
- **1952** – Elizabeth II is crowned Queen.
- **1958** – First women peers introduced to the House of Lords. Gatwick Airport opened.
- **1966** – Founding of the City University.
- **1971** – 15 February: introduction of decimal coinage.
- **1975** – Population 7 million.
- **1976** – Opening of the National Theatre.
- **1979** – Margaret Thatcher elected the first woman Prime Minister.
- **1981** – **London Docklands Development Corporation** (LDDC) set up to regenerate the redundant London Docks. First London Marathon run. Violent confrontations in London betweeen Punks and National Front. Marriage of Prince Charles to Lady Diana Spencer at St Paul's Cathedral.
- **1982** – Barbican Centre opened in the City of London; Thames Barrier raised.
- **1986** – Deregulation of trading on the Stock Exchange. Abolition of the Greater London Council.
- **1988** – Jets begin landing at City Airport.
- **1995** – 50th Anniversary of Victory in Europe. Launch of the National Lottery.
- **1996** – The Queen celebrates her 70th birthday.

After 700 years the Stone of Scone is returned to Scotland.

- **1997** – Inauguration of the British Library, St Pancras.

1-6 September: London mourns Diana, Princess of Wales.

- **1998** – Referendum in favour of an elected mayor of London. Elections to be held in 2000.

Opening of Globe Theatre.

- **1999-2000** – London gains new landmarks to mark the third Millennium: Dome (Greenwich), Jubilee Line extension, Millennium Bridge and Tate Modern (Bankside), British Airways London Eye (South Bank).
- **2000** – Election of Mayor of London.

Urban Development

Site – London straddles the estuary of the largest river in Great Britain, in the south-east corner of the country, near the Channel ports and links with the Continent.
Although the Romans established their capital first at St Albans (Verulamium) and then at Colchester (Camulodunum), they recognised the importance of the site of London as a bridgehead and trading port.
By the 13C, however, the **City of London** had become a rich port and the **capital** of the kingdom. The **double centre** of London – a unique feature – was created by **Edward the Confessor** who, on being elected king by the people of the City of London, went upstream to **Westminster**; here he rebuilt the abbey and constructed a royal palace; since then the monarch and parliament have been separate from the business community in the City.

hysical Expansion – After Boadicea's attack in AD 61 the Romans encircled the ity with a defence wall. In the Dark Ages assaults came chiefly from invaders sailing priver and the wall fell into decay. It was rebuilt in the Middle Ages largely on the riginal foundations with an extension to the west; ruined sections are visible at ondon Wall and by the Tower.

n 1643, during the Civil War, earthworks were thrown up: on the north bank from Vapping via Spitalfields and St Giles-in-the-Fields to Westminster and on the south ank from Rotherhithe to Lambeth. At no time did any of these barriers prevent the xpansion of London; in 1598 Stow was describing "the suburbs without the walls." ueen Elizabeth, in whose reign the population doubled, passed the first of many cts prohibiting the erection of any new houses within 3mi/5km of the City Gates. he reason for the royal alarm was twofold; it was feared that the newcomers, poor ountry people, might easily be led into rebellion and that water supplies, sewerage nd burial grounds were inadequate. These and later decrees were, however, largely gnored or circumvented.

rom the 16C, fashionable society migrated westwards resulting in the development f the **West End** with its life of elegance and leisure. By contrast successive waves f immigrants from home and abroad tended to settle east of the City in dockland vhich by the 19C was known as the **East End**.

ire of London – The Great Fire (1666), which burned for four days, destroyed four fths of the buildings within the City walls. The city was rebuilt more or less according o the old street plan but the Act for Rebuilding the City of London of 1667 stipulated hat all future structures, houses included, should be of brick and thus reduce the isk of fire.

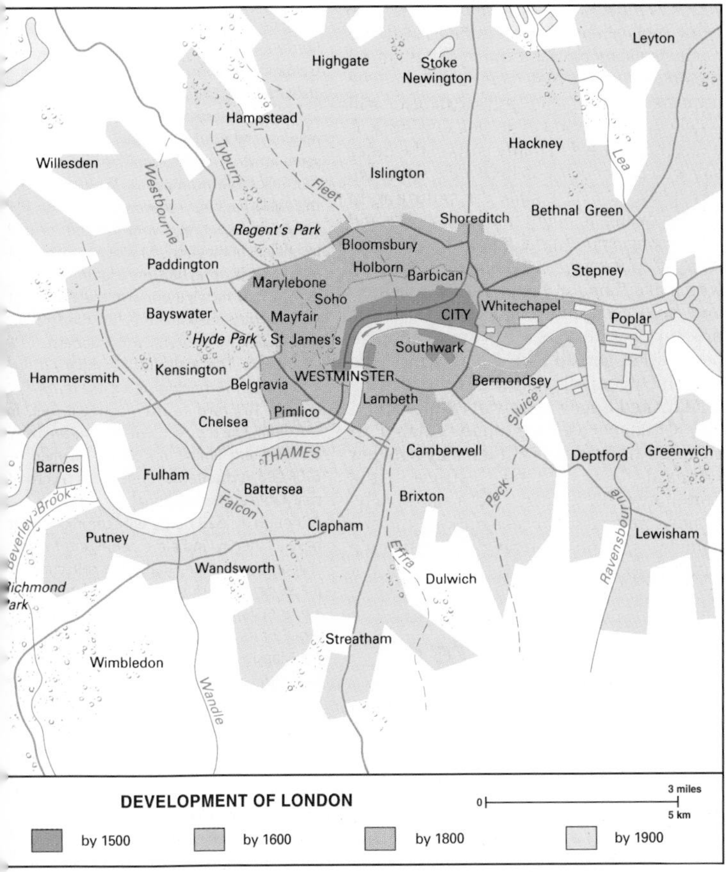

DEVELOPMENT OF LONDON

0 — 3 miles / 5 km

by 1500 | by 1600 | by 1800 | by 1900

Eleven out of 87 City churches survived undamaged and it was decided to rebui only 51 on former sites, often amalgamating several parishes. Money for rebuildir the churches was granted under acts of parliament which increased the dues on co entering the Port of London. The prisons, numerous and insanitary, corrupt ar cruel, were also rapidly rebuilt.

Industrial Revolution – As the London merchants established trading posts abroa great changes were simultaneously evolving at home as a result of the Industri Revolution. By the mid 18C people hitherto employed in agriculture were movir into London and the towns of the North and Midlands to work in the new factorie textiles and other products poured out on to the home and export markets.
Improved methods of transport were developed for the carriage of goods and ra materials: **canals** were excavated; Turnpike Trusts were established which by th mid 19C had constructed 20 000mi/32 180km of good **turnpike roads** and near 8 000 toll gates (including one in Dulwich, at Marble Arch, Hyde Park Corner **railways** were constructed. All roads and railways, both literally and metaphoricall converged on London. Easier travel led to the development of the **London Seaso** as men coming to London on business brought their wives and particularly the grown-up daughters who required husbands.

London Today – At the dawn of the 21C London is still evolving. The double centr remains the City of London for business and Westminster for politics. To the outwar eye the villages may have coalesced into a great urban sprawl but they are claime with local pride by their residents. During the Second World War, the City and the Ea End suffered greatly from bombing but, as in previous periods, new amenities in tune with the age have risen from the ruins. The docks, which stimulated the growth of the city, are being replaced by modern industries driven by the latest technology and by the financial sector expanding east from the City. The improvement of the infrastructure will accelerate this trend. The housing stock is being modernised in many parts of the inner city which is once again becoming attractive as a place to live; people are returning in droves owing to high transport costs and traffic congestion into London.
It is, of course, the inhabitants of London who make "London town": Londoners born and bred, adopted Londoners from the provinces, refugees from political persecution abroad (14C-17C Flemish and French Huguenots, political theorists such as Marx and Engels, post-war ex-monarchs, 20C Chileans and Ugandan Asians) or economic immigrants attracted by a higher standard of living (from the Commonwealth), men and women who achieve international recognition, and the nameless millions who ply their daily trade with wit and humour.

City Livery Companies and Ancient City Guild Halls

There are in existence 100 guilds of which 12 make up the so-called Greater Companies: Mercers, Grocers, Drapers, Fishmongers, Goldsmiths, Skinners, Merchant Taylors, Haberdashers, Salters, Ironmongers, Vintners Clothworkers. Most are successors of mediev religious fraternities, craft or social guilds, some of which adopted uniforms and were thus styled livery companies. The number of their halls has been reduced to 25 by the Great Fire, local fires, changes of fortune and incendiary bombs – the Master Mariners hav adopted a floating hall, the frigate *HMS Wellington,* which is moored in the Thames o the Victoria Embankment below the Strand. New guilds are created by the modern professions. The Worshipful Company of Information Technologists, whose ranks number 100, held its first meeting in 1992 ir Guildhall. The requirements for a new livery company are a minimum of 100 freemen, £100 000 in charitable funds and a record of charitable and educational good works. Although in 1523 Henry VIII "commanded t have all money and plate belonging to any Hall or Crypt", many halls have collections o pieces dating back to the 15C which they either managed to hide from the king or repurchased. Notable collections reside at the Mansion House; Clothworkers' Hall *(Mincing Lane);* Founders' Hall; Fishmongers Hall; Tallow Chandlers' Hall *(Dowgate Hill);* Skinners' Hall *(Dowgate Hill)*; Innholders' Hall *(College Street)* – salts and spoons; Vintners' Hall *(Upper Thames Street)*; Mercers' Hall *(Ironmonger Lane);* Haberdashers' Hall *(Staining Lane)*; Ironmongers' Hall *(Aldersgate Street)*; Barber-Surgeons' Hall *(Monkwell Square)*.

The City – Centre of Trade and Commerce

The City of London and its port developed in parallel until the latter half of the 20C when the port shifted downriver to Tilbury.

Roman Londinium – When the Romans invaded Britain, a Celtic fishing village had already existed since the 5C BC on the north

bank of the Thames by a gravel strand which was the first ford and later the first bridging point across the river. The Romans built on the twin hills above the river crossing; the community grew into a major town with a permanent stone bridge over the Thames and defended by walls. Archaeological remains of a basilica and forum (60 acres/24ha) extend between Cornhill, Leadenhall Street and Fenchurch Street; a large amphitheatre stretches under the Guildhall; important villas built of Kentish stone with mosaic floors have been found below Poultry; to the west was the Temple of Mithras *(see CITY – 4)*; to the south on the Thames foreshore stood the governor's palace. Much of Roman London was destroyed by fire in AD 125, and occupation finally gave way in the mid 5C.

Medieval City – Trade continued throughout the Dark Ages, despite the siege and fire of Germanic and Danish invasions. Although there is no mention of London for scores of pages in the *Anglo-Saxon Chronicle,* in the 8C it was recognised as the "mart of many nations by land and sea." Under Alfred for a brief period the kingdom was united and London was constituted a major city but an attempt to establish the metropolitan see in London was unsuccessful.

Slowly the **City** developed into an ordered and rich community: in 1016 the assembly *(gemut)* of London elected Edmund Ironside as King. When his successor, Canute, exacted tribute, the citizens contributed £ 10 500, an eighth of the total paid by the whole of England.

Two months after the Battle of Hastings (1066), the citizens of London submitted to William I, who built the Tower of London, Baynard's Castle and Mountfichet Castle on the river east and west of the City, less to defend it against future invaders than to deter the citizens from reconsidering their submission. The City requested and obtained a **Charter**, the first of several to be granted by the monarch, whereby government, law and dues devolved directly upon the citizens themselves. In 1215 under King John Londoners were empowered to elect annually their own mayor (elsewhere a royal appointee) who had only to submit himself formally at Westminster for royal approval; this was the origin of the Lord Mayor's Show *(see CITY – Mansion House)*.

The City merchants grew rich; they loaned or gave money to Edward III and Henry V for wars on the Continent and, apart from the risings of Wat Tyler in 1381 and Jack Cade *(see index)* in 1450, kept clear of strife, even during the Wars of the Roses. Indeed, the City never encroached on Westminster; with a few notable exceptions, citizens held no office under the Crown or Parliament. Many of the merchants, insurance brokers and bankers who later took over from the commodity dealers, were related to landed families; younger sons, such as Richard Whittington (d 1423), and the Hanseatics, who had arrived by 1157, were sent to seek their fortune in the City: they traded in everything and anything particularly wool and cloth, building great timber-framed and gabled mansions and buying country estates in the West End and the outskirts of London.

Religious Houses – Many monasteries and magnificent churches were erected in the City of London by the religious orders. The Dominicans, who arrived in England in 1221 constructed Blackfriars in 1276; the Franciscans (1224) began Greyfriars Church in Newgate in 1306; the Carmelites (1241) had a house off Fleet Street; the Austin friars (1253) settled near Moorgate; St John's Priory, the London Charterhouse and Rahere's priory with St Bartholomew's medical school were established on the north side of the City. At the **Dissolution of the Monasteries** (1539) Henry VIII seized their riches, destroyed the buildings and nominated himself as refounder of the hospitals – St Bartholomew's and Bedlam; this did not spoil his relations with the City, which became the home of the royal wardrobe. Under Edward VI St Paul's Cathedral, one of the great Gothic cathedrals of Europe, was stripped of its holy statues and remaining riches.

Elizabethan London – Queen Elizabeth tried vainly to curb the growth of suburbs outside the walls. James I, however, subsidised the New River scheme which brought fresh water to the street standards. Charles I was always forcing loans, applying restrictions to trade and requiring gifts, ship money and tonnage. The Jews, who had been banished in the late 13C, returned in strength under Cromwell during the Commonwealth (1649-60).

In the 16C, during the Age of Enlightenment, the city began to develop from a community of merchants, bankers and craftsmen, into a forum for men of letters and the arts.

Overseas Ventures – In the age of exploration the City raised loans and fitted out and financed merchant venturers. The Elizabethan navigators were knighted by Queen Elizabeth but the funds for the voyages of Drake, Frobisher, Hawkins and Raleigh were raised by the City. The aim of the adventurers was to make their fortune, of the City to establish trading posts. The result was a worldwide empire.

In 1600, under a charter of incorporation, Queen Elizabeth I granted a monopoly of trade between England and India to a new undertaking, the **East India Company**; by the 18C the larger part of India was being ruled by the company; after the Indian Mutiny (1858) administration passed to the Crown. The founding in 1670 of the **Hudson Bay Company**, with a monopoly that lasted until 1859 in the fur trade with the North American Indians, led to British rule in Canada. The head offices of all such companies were in the City.

Victorian Improvements – In the 19C as more bridges were built and traffic increased, new wide streets were created to relieve congestion: King William Street (1829-35) as a direct route from the Bank of England to the new London Bridge; Queen Victoria Street (1867-71), the first street to be lit by electricity.

21C City Corporation – The City is governed by the Corporation of London, which acts through the Court of Common Council. The latter, numbering 25 Aldermen and 159 Councilmen, who represent the different wards, is presided over by the Lord Mayor and meets in Guildhall. It has its own police force. Territorial boundaries are marked by the winged dragon of St George and street signs bear the City coat of arms.

Financial Centre – In the 1950s the importance of the Port of London faded: her smog-inducing industries were relocated and the demands for warehousing and docking dwindled. Instead efforts were concentrated on the service industries: company administration, banking, commerce, insurance.

Success, affluence and tradition pervade the streets of the City where dark-suited employees of international corporations, private institutions and merchant banks jostle with traders from the **LME** (London Metal Exchange Ltd for base metals – the precious metals silver, gold and platinum are traded directly) and **LTOM** (London Traded Option Market for share and stock options). London, strategically placed between Tokyo and New York attracts the lion's share of the world's business turnover conducted during European trading hours. Another important institution is BIFEX which trades in freight-forward cargo and container ship-space. This business thrives in part because of London's pre-eminent insurance and underwriting business.

In the past 50 years, the City has changed beyond recognition as a result of the "Big Bang" reforms of the 1980s (computerised share dealing, monitoring of transactions and investment business by government-appointed regulators, removal of restrictions on foreign ownership); the rise and fall of Lloyd's of London; Black Monday (the collapse of the London Stock Exchange in 1987) and other financial crises; the collapse of venerable banking institutions; foreign takeovers; and Bank of England independence. In view of these developments there is a determination to reassert the City's pre-eminence by forging new alliances in Europe.

Westminster – Centre of Government

Imperial State Crown

The Realm – Great Britain is composed of England, Wales, Scotland, the Channel Islands and the Isle of Man. The United Kingdom which is ruled from London's Palace of Westminster however, comprises England, Wales, Scotland and Northern Ireland but does not include the Channel Islands and Isle of Man which have their own parliaments and are attached directly to the Crown. Major recent constitutional reforms include devolution of some powers to a Scottish Parliament and to a Welsh Assembly.

Monarchy – The United Kingdom is a constitutional Monarchy, a form of government in which supreme power is vested in the **Sovereign** (king or queen): in law the Sovereign is the head of the **executive** (government elected by a majority, headed by a Prime Minister and implemented by civil servants),

D.R.

an integral part of the **legislature** (the Houses of Commons and Lords responsible for deciding upon matters of law), head of the **judiciary** (Criminal and Crown Courts of law), commander-in-chief of the armed forces, temporal head of the Church of England and symbolic Head of the Commonwealth. In practice the role is strictly a formal one, reigning supreme but acting on the advice of government ministers. During the reign of Queen Victoria (1837-1901), the monarch's right in relation to ministers was defined as "the right to be consulted, to encourage and to warn".

Parliament – The United Kingdom has no written constitution as such, but several important statutes underpin the institution and conventions of government: the **Magna Carta** (1215) sealed the king's promise to refrain from imposing feudal tax save by the consent of the Common Council of the Realm and instituted a fundamental human right: "To no man will we deny or delay right or justice"; **the Petition of Right Act** (1628) confirmed that no tax should be levied by the king without the consent of Parliament and that no person be imprisoned or detained without lawful cause; the **Bill of Rights** (1689) ensured ultimate supremacy of Parliament; the Act of Settlement (1701) established the independence of the law courts and regulated the succession to the Crown of England; the **Race Relations Act** (1968) aimed to prohibit prejudice on account of race, colour or ethnic origin; the **Representation of the People Act** (1969) gave the vote to all persons over the age of 18 listed on the electoral register save acting members of the House of Lords and those incapacitated through insanity or imprisonment.

The supreme legislature is Parliament, consisting of two bodies: the House of Commons and the House of Lords within the Palace of Westminster *(see WESTMINSTER)*. In the Middle Ages, the king would meet with his lords; the common people were rarely summoned and had no regular meeting place until 16C. Regular Parliament meetings were assured after the Bloodless or Glorious Revolution (1688) when Parliament repealed James II's rule by "divine right" and appointed William III and Mary II; both houses were dominated by "landed gentry" until the 19C (MPs were paid a salary from 1911).

Much of the traditional London pageantry and ceremony has its origins in royal protocol, military routine or the customs of the City of London.

House of Commons – Since the 17C two major parties have been predominant in Parliament (Her Majesty's Government and Her Majesty's Opposition) with Tories and Whigs, Conservatives and Liberals, Conservatives and Labour vying for power; representatives of other parties contribute to debates and may be lobbied for support by party whips to carry motions when opinion is equally divided.

Since 1992 the United Kingdom has been divided into 651 constituencies calculated to hold approximately 65 000 voters. A Member of Parliament is elected by a majority vote secured at a General Election to appoint a new government or at a by-election if the seat falls vacant in the interim. Government term is for a maximum of five years. The House is presided over by the Speaker, appointed at the beginning of each session. MPs sit on parallel benches: members of the government cabinet sit in the first row opposite the members of the shadow cabinet (frontbenchers) while members of their respective parties sit behind (backbenchers). Their combined function is to decide upon legislation: each act is subjected to two Readings, a Committee and a Report Stage and a Third Reading before going to "the Other House" and obtaining Royal Assent.

House of Lords – A major reform of the House of Lords is under way. The House of Lords Act 1999 removed the rights of most hereditary peers to sit and vote in the House. An amendment enabled 92 hereditary peers, **Lords Temporal**, to remain in the House until a Royal Commission reports on the role, functions and composition of the second chamber. **Life Peers** include the Lords of Appeal (Law Lords) and distinguished persons honoured for service to the Land (since 1958); the **Lords Spiritual** are the archbishops and bishops of the Church of England.

This body of the legislature made up of experienced professional men and women from all walks of life debates issues without the bias of party politics. It also acts as the highest court of appeal in the land, although only the Law Lords are involved in such proceedings. The main body of the legal establishment, the Royal Courts of Justice and Chambers reside between Westminster and the City, where the Strand gives way to Fleet Street.

Administration of London

Governing Bodies – Since the early Middle Ages the City has been administered by the Corporation of the City of London. After the Dissolution of the monasteries (1539) Westminster and Southwark, the other urban districts, were given into the care of newly appointed **parish vestries**, which differed in character and probity. Their powers overlapped and were insufficient to control, even where they thought it necessary, the speculators engaged in jerrybuilding in the centre and on the outskirts of the City. The builders erected tall houses with inadequate sanitation, which thus polluted the water supplies, and let off each room to one or often several families. Hogarth illustrated the scene in the 18C, Mayhew and Dickens described it in the press in the 19C. Conditions were not, of course, uniformly bad – the "good life" was led with considerable elegance in St James's and Whitehall, in Mayfair, Marylebone, Knightsbridge, Kensington and westwards beyond.

By the 19C reform began, spurred on by traffic congestion and the dangers of poor sanitation. In 1855 the Government established a central body, the **Metropolitan Board of Works**, with special responsibility for main sewerage. It was also to act as coordinator of the parish vestries (now elected), which were left in charge of local drainage, paving, lighting, and the maintenance of streets.

Slum clearance began as new roads were built to ease traffic congestion: Victoria Street, Northumberland Avenue, Trafalgar Square, Shaftesbury Avenue, Charing Cross Road, New Oxford Street, Queen Victoria Street and Southwark Street. Through its chief engineer, **Joseph Bazalgette**, the board reconstructed the drainage system for central London, removed the outflows into the Thames and, as part of the scheme, built the embankments – Victoria (1864-70), Albert (1866-69) and Chelsea (1871-74).

In 1888 the County of London was created with the **London County Council** (LCC) as the county authority with responsibility for an area equivalent to the present 12 inner London boroughs.

Further road building was continued in the 1920s and 1930s by the LCC, following bomb damage during the Second World War and the large-scale demolition of terrace housing in the 1960s. Municipal (council) housing is a 20C phenomenon; the first council flats were built under the LCC and its successor the GLC and the London boroughs.

In 1965, in the newly defined area of Greater London, the LCC was superseded by a regional authority, the **Greater London Council** (GLC). Greater London comprised the former County of London and former local authority areas surrounding London, in all a total of 610sq mi/1 579km, with a population of about 6.7 million.

Following the 1983 general election the structure of local government was reformed and the GLC and other metropolitan councils were abolished (1986). The GLC's functions were devolved largely to the borough councils and new statutory bodies were created to take over control of essential local services. For more than a decade London was without a voice, which brought about conflicts of interests and a lack of direction. A referendum in 1998 proved in favour of an elected mayor for London and following elections held in 2000, a Greater London Authority is now in place. It is made up of a mayor and the London Assembly and its main areas of responsibility are transport, policing, fire and emergency planning, economic development, planning, culture, environment and health.

Local Taxation – In 1601 a statute was passed requiring householders to pay **rates** to provide a dole for vagrants and the destitute, since the traditional almoners, the monastic foundations, had been suppressed by Henry VIII in 1539. For centuries the major part of the levy was employed for the relief of the poor; in 1813 out of £8.5 million raised nationally, £7 million went in relief and only £1.5 million on all other local necessities. The Greater London Authority is financed by a government grant and a proportion of the council tax.

Urban Improvements – The so-called **Improvement Acts of 1762** began the transformation of every street in the capital.

Paving became the responsibility of the parish vestries *(see above)* who found it in their interests to relay the streets which previously had been the responsibility of individual householders – each paving his frontage (or not) with stone or rubble at a level convenient to his house without regard to the general course.

The vestries replaced the deep central drains (kennels) with shallow underground sewers and lateral gutters. They provided scavengers and sweepers to clear the streets of night soil and garbage which were still thrown out of doors.

The same 1762 Acts also instituted **house numbering** and **street lighting**. Since 1416 householders had been required to burn a candle at night outside their doors; since 1716 those in the City had been ordered to burn lights on the 18 dark nights of each winter moon but snuffers and lampholders outside the 18C houses of St James's and Mayfair are a reminder of how pedestrians carried their own flaming torches and link boys walked ahead of sedans and carriages. Change began in 1738 when the vestries installed 15 000 oil-fed lamps with cotton wicks which burned from sunset to sunrise in such main thoroughfares as Oxford Street. In 1807, 13 gas lamp-posts were set up in Pall Mall. Seventy years later (1878) electricity was available and the first major street lighting project was inaugurated with the illumination of the Embankment.

The corollary to the 1762 Improvement Acts came with the passage of the **Clean Air Acts** (1956, 1962) controlling the burning of coal in furnaces and open grates, so banishing the notorious London pea-soup fogs.

Open Spaces – London is a very green city endowed with millions of trees, mostly cypresses , sycamores, ash, plane and cherry. **The Royal Parks** include St James's, Green Park, Hyde Park and Kensington Gardens at the very heart of inner London while Regent's Park, Greenwich Park, Richmond Park and Bushy Park extend beyond. There are some 3 500 acres/1 416ha of "common land" despite continual encroachment in the past by peasants, manorial farmers, larger landowners and, in the 19C, by land speculators, builders and local authorities constructing roads.

Only in the 1930s was a visionary solution proposed and enacted (1938); a **Green Belt** (840sq mi/2 179sq km) was designated to run through the home counties encircling London at a radius of 20-30mi/32-48km. Although in some sections the belt has disappeared completely, it has had some success in defining the limits of London and halting the metropolitan sprawl.

View of the City by night

Angus Taverner/MICHELIN

Selected Sights

Bankside – Southwark★

The Globe and Tate Modern, two potent symbols combining history and modernity, on Bankside, and the bustling London Bridge City and Hay's Galleria east of London Bridge, highlight the vitality of the borough of Southwark which extends south from the Thames to Crystal Palace. A multitude of attractions – theatres, museums, trendy bars, pubs and restaurants – and a relaxed atmosphere invite visitors to stroll at leisure and enjoy wonderful views of the river and of the City skyline dominated by the majestic dome of St Paul's on the north bank.

Location

Map p 13 (FGXY). Michelin Atlas London: pp 64-66. ⊖ Southwark, London Bridge, Blackfriars.

Bankside and Southwark extend from Blackfriars Bridge to Tower Bridge on the south bank of the Thames. Explore the last section of the Millennium Mile from Blackfriars, beyond Southwark Cathedral to Tower Bridge and Bermondsey *(allow 90min between Bankside and Rotherhithe).*

Adjacent Sights: SOUTH BANK; TOWER OF LONDON.

J. Malburet/MICHELIN

The imposing mass of Tate Modern flanked by the thatched circle of the Wooden "O"

Background

The Roman Invasion to the Dissolution of the Monasteries – The construction by the Romans of a bridge and the convergence at the bridgehead of roads from the south of England attracted settlers to the fishing village already established on one of the few sites relatively free from flooding on the low-lying marshlands of the Thames' south bank. By Anglo-Saxon times the bridge had become a defence against ship-borne invaders and the village, the *sud werk* or south work, against attacking land forces: **Olaf of Norway**'s rescue of Ethelred from the Danes is commemorated locally in Tooley Street (a corruption of St Olave's Street); the Conqueror fired Southwark before he took London by encirclement. In the *Domesday Book,* Southwark was described as having a strand where ships could tie up, a street, a herring fishery and a minster or priory. In 1540, at the Dissolution, the priory reverted to the crown; Henry acquired from Archbishop Cranmer the Great Liberty Manor, granted to Canterbury in the 12C (which extended from the Old Kent Road to the High Street). Among its tenants were the Bishops of Winchester, who erected a veritable palace, which they named **Winchester House,** and the notorious prison known as the Clink, and the Knights Templar whose 100 acres/247ha had by the 15C become the famous Paris Garden named after Robert de Paris, a 14C nobleman. The eastern strip belonged to Bermondsey Abbey.

The Dissolution to the 20C – Henry VIII rapidly sold off the monastery estates. The City increased its interests in Southwark but it never acquired jurisdiction over the Clink prison or Paris Garden which was a popular location for theatres. The area close to the river, largely owned by the City and known as the Borough of Southwark, which time has shortened to the **Borough,** became heavily industrialised, following the building of the bridges, the 19C expansion of the docks and the coming of the railway.

the end of the 19C the last of the isons had been demolished: the **ink,** instituted for miscreants thin the Liberty, in 1780; the **Mar- alsea,** where for three months in 24 Dickens' father had been :ked up for debt, in 1842; King's nch in 1860 and Horsemonger ne Jail in 1879.

1939-1945 came widespread vastation. Southwark is now, after tensive rebuilding, an amalgam of the ry old and the hi-tec, each area with particular characteristic even to eet furniture such as the bollards ade from sawn-off cannon with a nnon ball in the mouth, inscribed rdens of St Saviour's 1827, and Clink 12.

rough Market – The people of lworth, Newington and Camberwell ew and sold produce at the market first d on London Bridge, later in the High eet and finally on the present site; the rough Market, London's oldest (13C), s formally established in 1756 and the ofits go to rates relief. Southwark people re also fishermen and boatmen. lustries developed such as plaster and ortar making (pollution from the lime burners was being complained of to the King 1283), weaving, brewing (by refugees from the Low Countries), glassmaking and ather tanning.

THE PLAYGROUND OF LONDON

During the 16C hostelries, brothels (hence the existence of Love Lane), bear-baiting, cock-fighting and other such entertainments were set up in the area stretching westwards between the Liberty of the Clink situated by the **Clink Prison** and **Paris Garden,** named after Robert de Paris, a 14C nobleman.

In the 16C, permission was accorded by the authorities for two theatres to be set up in the old monastery cloisters north of the river in Blackfriars and the area became known as the playground of London.

The reign of the **Rose** (1587), the **Swan** (1595/6), the **Globe** (1599) and the **Hope** (1613) theatres was, however, brief: those that had not already reverted or become bull and bear baiting rings were closed finally under the Commonwealth by the Puritans in 1642.

For entertainment there were the midsummer Southwark Fair, the occasional **frost fairs** when the Thames froze over, the Elizabethan theatres, the brothels and taverns. Not all inns were licentious; many prospered as staging posts for the coaches going south and to the ports and as hostelries for travellers awaiting the morning opening of the bridge to enter the City.

Directory

LIGHT BITE

Wine Wharf – *Stoney St, Southwark, SE1 9AD – ⊖ London Bridge – ☎ 020 7940 3335 – brian@wineworth.co.uk – £10.* Convenient for the Globe Theatre, this wine bar is adjacent to the Vinopolis complex under converted railway arches. Atmospheric and relaxing, with exposed brick walls and comfortable leather sofas. Light menu from charcuterie to salads.

PUBS

George Inn – *77 Borough High St, Southwark, SE1 1NH – ⊖ London Bridge – ☎ 020 7407 2056 – george-southwark@laurelpubco.com – Open Mon-Sat 11am-11pm, Sun noon-10.30pm.* Part 17C galleried inn where plays by William Shakespeare are performed in summer in the cobbled yard *(see WALKING ABOUT).*

Horniman – *Hays Galleria, Tooley St, Bankside, SE1 2HD – ⊖ London Bridge – ☎ 020 7407 1991 – Open Mon-Sat 11am-11pm, Sat noon-11pm, Sun noon-10.30pm.* This smart pub is a good place for families at the weekend and in summer. Find a seat on the terrace and take in the fine views of London Bridge.

Kings Arms – *25 Roupell St, SE1 8TB – ⊖ London Bridge – ☎ 020 7207 0784 – Open Mon-Sat 11am-11pm, Sun noon-10.30pm. See WALKING ABOUT.*

The Anchor – *34 Park St, Bankside, SE1 9EF – ⊖ London Bridge – ☎ 020 7407 1577 – info@theanchorbankside.co.uk – Open Mon-Sat 11am-11pm, Sun noon-10.30pm; restaurant: Open Mon-Sat noon-3pm, Sun noon-3pm and 5-9.30pm.* At the foot of Southwark Bridge and near the Tate Modern, this large 18C tavern is associated in its history not only with the river and the prison (truncheons, manacles etc in one bar) but also with Shakespeare, Dr Johnson and his biographer Boswell, through their friends, the Thrales, who at one time owned it. It has a broad terrace and large patio overlooking The Thames. Smoky and noisy at busy times.

GOING OUT FOR A DRINK

Vinopolis – *1 Bank End, EC1 9BU – ⊖ London Bridge – ☎ 020 7940 8320, 0870 241 4040 – postmaster-wineworld@btinternet.com – Open daily noon-6pm (9pm Mon and Fri-Sat), last admission 2hr before closing; Dec and bank hols hours by phone – £11.50.* Presented in a large warehouse, an entertaining audio-visual exhibition allows visitors to wander through wine regions of the world and learn about wine-making. Winelovers can enjoy several tastings and then move on to the shop, wine bars and restaurants.

A SHAKESPEAREAN EXPERIENCE

The **Globe Theatre** proposes Elizabethan performances held during the afternoon or early evening much as in Shakespeare's day. For more details see 'Theatre' in *PRACTICAL POINTS* at the beginning of the guide.

Walking About

ALONG THE RIVERSIDE 1

⊖ Southwark, Blackfriars (on the other side of the bridge). From Blackfriars Bridge take Quee Walk past the Bankside Gallery and Tate Modern (for both, description in Worth a Visit).

Millennium Bridge

A remarkable architectural and technical achievement, the suspension bridge (320yds/338m long), built of stainless steel with curving stainless steel balustrades, forms "a blaze of light" spanning the Thames at night. After initial problems, it provides a pedestrian link to the north bank.

Old Houses

Turn right into **Cardinal Cap Alley.** On either side are two 18C private houses. The first (no 49), the oldest house on Bankside, was built on the site of the Cardinal's Hatte, a 16C stew, sor 50 years after the Great Fire (1666). The reference to Catherine of Aragon on t plaque is therefore questionable as is the tradition that Sir Christopher Wren liv there during the building of St Paul's Cathedral. The houses west of the alle slightly larger and more stylised are some 30 years later.

ENDOWMENTS

Alms houses and charities were founded by the Ci livery companies: the **Hopton Almshouse** *(Hopton Street)* consist of two-storey brick and til cottages, the main wing pedimented, built roun three sides of a garden in 1752; a terrace in **Nelso Square** survives from 1799 – now adjoined to pos war municipal accommodation, and the **Draper Almshouses,** two-storey cottages with neo-Goth windows from 1820.

International Shakespeare Globe Centre★

Bear Gardens. ♿ Open daily, May-Sep, 9am-noon (theatre tour every 30min); exhibiti noon-4pm; Oct-Apr, 10am-5pm (tours and exhibition). Closed 24-25 Dec. £8. Restaura and cafe. ☎ 020 7902 1500; Fax 020 7902 1515; www.shakespeares-globe.org

The idea for instigating a centre dedicated to encouraging the study and drama interpretation of Shakespeare's work came from the late American actor-direct Sam Wanamaker. Funding the realisation of such a dream has been arduous prompting many supporters to sponsor the project by paying for individual brick

Globe Theatre – The Wooden O (33ft/10m high, 100ft/30.5m in diameter a 300ft/91.5m in circumference) has been modelled on surviving documenta evidence provided by contemporary sketches of the original theatre, pulled down 1644, and from archaeological excavations of the original Globe founded by Cuthbe **Burbage** *(see EAST END – Shoreditch)* around the corner. Wherever possible simil materials (unseasoned oak, reed thatch) and building methods have been used recreate the half-covered theatre comprising an elevated stage, the open section f groundlings, surrounded on three sides by sheltered tiers of benches. To safegua authenticity, performances are held during the afternoon much as in Shakespeare day without the use of artificial stage lighting, and subject to fine weather!

Inigo Jones Theatre – Alongside the main thatched open-air theatre is this sma intimate playhouse built according to Jones' drawings, adapted today for priva concerts, poetry readings and workshop productions all year round.

Turn right into New Globe Walk and left into Park Street.

The Globe Education Centre underpins the spirit of the original enterprise whi was to promote the works of Shakespeare, to explore understanding, appreciati and practical interpretation of Elizabethan and Jacobean drama, and to stress t entertainment value of theatre for actors and audience alike. Other facilities inclu an undercroft **exhibition** area, a cinema and lecture hall, audio-visual archive a library.

The Rose Theatre Exhibition

56 Park Street. Guided tour for pre-booked groups only ☎ 020 7902 1500 (Shakespeare's Globe); admin-rose@theatre.org; www.rosetheatre.org.uk

An imaginative light and sound show brings to life the history of the Rose Theatre, the first theatre on Bankside. Excavations have revealed the remains of the building which are now covered by a pool of water because of lack of funds. It is planned to preserve the remains and put them on show in the future. The knowledge gained from the dig has proved invaluable for the building of the new Globe.

WILLIAM SHAKESPEARE (1564-1616)

England's greatest poet and playwright (38 play was born the son of a glover; he married Ann Hathaway in Stratford-upon-Avon before comin to London to find success and fame; he had thre children, and died on his 52nd birthday. H popularity is rooted in the rich use of colloqui language, humour that sometimes verges on th bawdy, and a timeless portrayal of human nature Although there are no autographed copies, a tot of 18 plays were printed in his own life time 36 followed in a folio, the first collected edition published in 1623. He also wrote 154 sonnets an four long poems.

Southwark Bridge

Rennie's bridge (1815-19), referred to by Dickens in *Little Dorrit* as the Cast Iron Bridge, was replaced in 1919 with the present three-arched iron structure by Ernest George.

Excavations in the Park Street area have revealed traces of a Roman warehouse. Cross the street to view the ground plan of the original Globe theatre clearly marked on the site of a former brewery. Continue to the end of the street and turn left back to the riverfront. **The Anchor** *(see Directory)*, is an historical tavern erected in 1770-75 on the site of earlier inns.

Continue past Clink Exibition (description in Worth a Visit).

Winchester Palace

At the heart of a large modern development stands the old ruin comprising the screen wall of the 12C **great hall** pierced by a graceful **rose window** (14C) of Reigate stone; three archways that once would have led to the servery and kitchens; excavation has revealed the cellars below. The existence of the palace is recalled in nearby Winchester Walk and Winchester Square.

The precinct of the Bishop of Winchester's Palace contained a prison for errant clergy and nuns, which lay below the water level at high tide. From the 15C it was known as the **Clink Prison,** from which derives the expression "to be in clink": between about 1630 until its closure in 1780 it was used for poor debtors.

St Mary Overie Dock

The full-scale galleon replica of Sir Francis Drake's **Golden Hinde** is made of African iroko hardwood and caulked with oakum in the traditional way; she was built in Appledore, Devon and launched on 5 April 1973 with a bottle of mead. When not away at sea (she has already undertaken several transatlantic journeys and at least one circumnavigation), the *Golden Hinde* may be boarded and a tour made with a member of her crew of her cabins and quarters, galley and hold. *Open daily, 10am-5pm/5.30pm; telephone ahead to confirm availability. Self-guided tour with leaflet: £2.75. Overnight stays, Pirate Parties for children, weddings, corporate functions. ☎ 08700 118 700 (bookings); 020 7403 0123; Fax 020 7407 5908; info@goldenhinde.co.uk; www.goldenhinde.co.uk*

A riverside **viewing panel** identifies the buildings on the north bank: the twin pavilions at the north end of **Cannon Street Railway Bridge** were built at the same time as the bridge (1866) by J W Barry and J Hawkshaw, and the (rebuilt) engine shed.

A Great Adventure

In 1577 Francis Drake (c 1540-96) set sail on the *Pelican* into the unknown: he returned three years later from the Pacific having laid claim to Nova Albion (California) and the Port of Sir Francis Drake (San Francisco) on the *Golden Hinde*, his ship having been renamed as she approached the Straights of Magellan. Drake chose the name after the symbol of a golden passant hind representing the armorial of the expedition's sponsor, Sir Christopher Hatton *(see INSIGHTS AND IMAGES – Historical Perspective, Elizabethan London)*. On arrival, the vessel was moored at Deptford *(see GREENWICH)* and visited by Queen Elizabeth I who took the opportunity to knight Drake there and then.

Southwark Cathedral** (St Saviour and St Mary Overie)

♿ *Open daily, 8am-6pm. Guide book. Donation £4. Audio tours £2.50. Exhibition. £3. Restaurant. cathedral@dswark.org.uk; www.dswark.org/cathedral*

The history of the site records a progress from Roman building to Saxon minster, from Augustinian priory (1106) to parish Church of St Saviour (1540) in the Winchester diocese and, finally, to Cathedral (1905). The name, according to the historian Stow, derived from the convent being endowed with "the profits of a cross-ferry" from which the church came to be known as "over the river" or St Mary Overie. The first sight of the present building is of a solid square central tower, 14C below, early 15C above, with paired lancets surmounted by a chequer pattern and pinnacles.

Interior – Immediately to the left is the Gothic arcading of the church rebuilt after a fire in 1206, for in addition to the succession of 'owners' who altered, embellished, restored or neglected the church, it suffered disastrous fires. Against the west wall at the end of the north aisle are 12 ceiling **bosses** rescued from the 15C wooden roof when it collapsed in 1830: the pelican, heraldic sunflowers and roses, malice, gluttony, falsehood, Judas being swallowed by the devil... Nearby stands a black marble stoup with a gilt cover set in a frame. The **nave** was rebuilt in neo-Gothic style in 1890-97 to harmonise with the 13C chancel. There are fragments of a Norman arch in the north wall. John Gower (1330-1408), poet and friend of Chaucer, with 'small forked beard, on his head a chaplet of four roses, a collar of Essex gold about his neck' lies, pillowed on his own works, beneath a canopy of red, green and gold. The **north transept**, with 13C Purbeck marble shafts set against 12C base walls, includes the allegorical Austin monument of 1633 showing a standing figure, Agriculture, between girls in large sun hats, fallen asleep in the harvest field; also the reclining figure, with gaunt face framed by a full wig, of the quack doctor, Lionel Lockyer (1672). Note also the Jacobean communion table with turned legs in groups of four in front and three behind, pulpit (1702) and wooden sword rest *(north transept end wall)*.

From the nave near the transept crossing where the great brass candelabrum of 1680 is suspended between the massive 13C piers which support the central tower, there is an uninterrupted view of the intimately proportioned, 13C chancel in true Early English style.

The **altar screen** (1520, the statues were added in 1905) appears in sumptuous Gothic glory, framed by the virtually unadorned arches to the chancel aisles, triforium and clerestory. Funeral pavement stones commemorate the burial in the church of Edmund (d 1607), brother of William Shakespeare, and the Jacobean dramatists, John Fletcher (d 1625) and Philip Massinger (d 1640).

Adjoining the asymmetrical, stilted arch which opens the north chancel aisle is the **Harvard Chapel**, dedicated to the founder of the Harvard University of America, **John Harvard** who was born in Borough High Street and baptised in the church in 1607 (emigrated 1638). Mementoes include the American-made window and a tablet to the Pilgrim Trust.

A colourful 17C wall monument, a 15C stone effigy of a shrouded corpse, a rare figure of a knight (against the wall), meticulously carved in oak (1280-1300) and a free standing monument to Richard Humble and his wives in full 17C finery are of interest. The sparsely adorned retrochoir, 13C and square ended, is divided into four equal chapels by piers; from 1540-1617 it served as tribunal, prison, billet, sty and bakery. Note the Nonesuch Chest (1588) of inlaid wood.

In the **south chancel aisle** near the altar is the free standing tomb of Lancelot Andrewes (d 1626), Bishop of Winchester, a figure in shallow ruff and ample deep blue robes, beneath a modern canopy, gilded and crested. In the **south transept** mainly 14C and early 15C, with early Perpendicular tracery (renewed) in the three light windows, the large window ornately 19C are, to the left, the red painted arms and hat of Cardinal Beaufort, 15C Bishop of Winchester, and on the right, a miniature recumbent effigy of William Emerson (d 1575), high above, a colourful half figure in gown and ruff, John Bingham (d 1625), saddler to Queen Elizabeth. Note the tessellated paving from a Roman villa at the chancel step.

Against the wall of the south aisle is a memorial to Shakespeare: a 1911 alabaster figure, reclining beneath a modern Shakespearean window.

Visitor Centre – *Access from the north aisle or from the north door into Lancelot's Link.* Discover the history of the cathedral through artefacts uncovered during recent excavations and using the latest technological aids: interactive cameras, touch-screen computers. A 360 degree view is reflected in a smooth dish. A 1C Roman road, vestiges of the Norman church, the medieval priory and 17C-18C pottery kilns can be viewed from the glazed link. Go up to the library to enjoy a fine view of the roof line.

Pass under London Bridge (description in The CITY).

London Bridge City

The sleek granite surfaces of **No 1 London Bridge** are in sharp contrast to **St Olaf House** (Hay's Wharf). The latter is built in Portland stone in Art Déco style; fine gilded faience relief panels designed by Frank Dobson provide a central motif on the Thames front, while on Tooley Street the bronze window casements would once have been gold-leafed (the coats of arms are those of the founders of Hay's Wharf partnership in 1862).

Hay's Galleria

The original Hay's Dock has been sealed over: the purpose-built Galleria now boasts a 90ft/27m high glass barrel vault. Pride of place is given to a monumental kinetic sculpture *The Navigators* by David Kemp, a somewhat nostalgic reminder of the clippers that once docked at Hay's Wharf. The buildings were converted from warehouses for tea, jute and spices and later adapted into major refrigerated units, and now house shops, bars and restaurants.

J. Malburet/MICHELIN

From riverside dock to modern mall – a lively scene at Hay's Galleria

The walk can continue along the riverside (Queen's Walk). Past *HMS. Belfast (description in Worth a Visit)*, opposite the Tower of London, on a large site where archaeological excavation has identified the precincts of **Edward II** 's 14C Rosary Palace, a landmark building, in the shape of a 10-storey glass dish, by **Sir Norman Foster** is under construction to house the office of the Mayor of London elected in 2000.

BOROUGH 2

Start from London Bridge Station.

Borough High Street

The Borough, kernel not only of Southwark but of London south of the Thames, rings with historic street and inn names though many of the old buildings have now gone. The street is slowly drawing a fashionable crowd as new attractions and restaurants open in the area.

Turn left into St Thomas Street. Continue past the Old Operating Theatre (description in Worth a Visit).

Guy's Hospital

The vast complex retains the iron railings, gateway and square forecourt of its foundation construction of 1725. The court is flanked by the original tile-roofed brick wings which lead back to the slightly later, Palladian style, centre range with a stone frontispiece decorated with allegorical figures by Bacon.

In the court stands a bronze statue by Scheemakers of Thomas Guy (1644-1724), son of a Southwark lighterman and coal dealer, who began as a bookseller (Bibles), gambled successfully on the South Sea Bubble and other enterprises and then became a munificent patron of medical institutions. In the chapel (centre of the west wing) is a full size memorial in high relief by John Bacon of Guy, portrayed before the 18C hospital into which a stretcher case is being borne. In the quadrangles to the rear are a statue of Lord Nuffield, a 20C philanthropist, and a mid-18C alcove from old London Bridge.

Return to the main road.

The Yards and the Inns of Southwark

Several narrow streets and yards off Borough High Street, south of St Thomas Street, mark the entrances to the old inns which were the overnight stop of people arriving too late at night to cross the bridge into the capital. These inns were also the starting point for coach services to the southern counties and the ports.

King's Head Yard [1]: the King's Head, known as the Pope's Head before the Reformation, now a 19C building, sports a robust, somewhat supercilious, coloured effigy of Henry VIII.

White Hart Yard [2]: the pub (no longer in existence) was the headquarters of Jack Cade in 1450 and where Mr Pickwick first met Sam Weller.

George Inn★ [3] – *See Directory.* The **George Inn,** when rebuilt in 1676 after a fire, had galleries on three sides, only part of the south range remains but this still possesses two upper galleries outside and panelled rooms inside. Shakespeare is performed in the cobbled yard in summer and open fires and traditional fare warm customers in winter. Note the Act of Parliament clock constructed in 1797 when a tax of five shillings (25 pence) made people sell their timepieces and rely on clocks in public places; the act was repealed within the year.

Talbot Yard [4]: recalled by **Chaucer** in the Prologue: "In Southwark at the Tabbard as I lay, At night was come into that hostelrie Wel nyne and twenty in a compagnye of sondrye folk... and pilgrims were they alle That toward Canterbury wolden ryde."

Queen's Head Yard [5]: site of the Queen's Head (demolished: 1900) sold by John Harvard before he set out for America; Newcomen Street: the **King's Arms** (1890) takes its name from the brightly painted lion and unicorn supporting the arms of George II (not George III as inscribed), a massive emblem which originally decorated the south gatehouse of old London Bridge *(see Directory)*.

A plaque at no **163** indicates the first site of **Marshalsea Prison** (1376 to 1811), the notorious penitentiary of which only one high wall remains on the later site *(no 211)*. No **116** marks the location of the 16C palace of the Duke of Suffolk who married a daughter of Henry VII.

St George the Martyr

(♿) Open Sun, 10am-4pm; Wed, noon-1.30pm; Thu (except holiday periods), 12.30-2pm. Guidebook. Induction loop. tonyslucas@btinternet.com; www.stgeorgethemartyr.co.uk

The stone spire and square tower of the 1736 church on a 12C site mark the end of the first section of the High Street. **Dickens** features the church in *Little Dorrit*, who is commemorated in the east window. The alms chest is a converted lead water cistern (1738), the pulpit the highest in London, the chandelier Georgian and the Te Deum ceiling unique, a replica of the late-19C Italian-style original, destroyed in the war, with cherubs breaking through a clouded sky accompanied by rays of glory.

Continue to the next crossroads and turn left into Trinity Street.

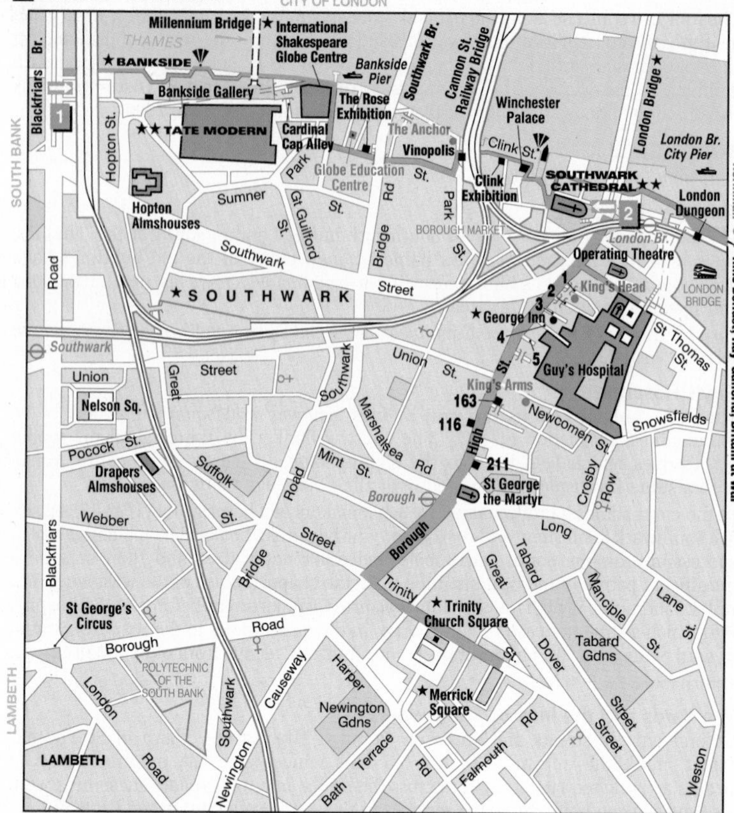

Trinity Church Square★

The early-19C square with its distinctive lamp standards is an unbroken quadrilateral of three-storey houses, punctuated by round-arched doorways and united above by a narrow white course and coping. The statue in the central garden is more than lifesize and is known as **King Alfred**; it is believed to be the oldest statue in London. The church (1824), which has a portico of colossal, fluted columns and a small openwork tower, was converted in 1975 into a studio for use by major orchestras.

Merrick Square★

The early-19C square with elegant lamp standards and modest houses is named after the merchant who left the property in 1661 to the Corporation of Trinity House.

Worth a Visit

Tate Modern★★

♿ Open daily, 10am (galleries 10.15am) to 5.50pm (10pm Fri-Sat); last admission 45min before closing. Closed 24-26 Dec. Parking for the disabled only; pre-booking essential. Restaurant and cafes. ☎ 020 7887 8000 (exhibitions), 020 7887 8008 (recorded information); 020 7887 8687 (minicom), 0870 166 8283 (ticketmaster); information@tate.org.uk; www.tate.org.uk

The former **Bankside Power Station,** a massive structure (1957-60), known to some as the "cathedral of the age of electricity" with its single chimney (325ft/99m) and Aztec-inspired stepped brickwork, was designed by Giles Gilbert Scott. The oil-fired power station which closed in 1981 has been imaginatively converted with the addition of a glass superstructure and large bay windows to house the Tate Gallery's collections of international **20C art**. The wealth of the Tate Modern Art Collection is largely due to the bequests made by Sir Roland Penrose, the one-time friend of Picasso and Ernst, and that of Edward James, a patron of Dali and Magritte. Works by 20C British artists are also on view at Tate Britain.

Gigantic sculptures by contemporary artists are set off by the vast spaces of the dramatic turbine hall (500ft/155m long and 115ft/35m high) where overhead cranes recall the building's industrial past; the amazing perspectives can best be appreciated from the upper galleries.

The radical decision to stage themed displays aims to trace the evolution of genres through the 20C to the present day, to explore various aspects of certain works and to place British art in the international context: Landscape, Matter,

Environment; Still Life, Object Real Life; Nude Action and Body; History, Memory, Society. Parallels are drawn between works of different periods, historical and stylistic associations are highlighted to challenge the viewer's perceptions of modern art.

Do not miss the panoramic **views★★★** *(from the top floor)* of the Thames and the city with St Paul's Cathedral as a counterpoint on the north bank which is linked to the museum by the striking **Millennium Bridge**.

As the exhibits are rotated according to the various themes the texts below trace the general evolution of genres for a better understanding of the displays.

France – Primitive Art inspired the amateur 'Sunday' painters Douanier **Rousseau** (1844-1910) and **Gauguin** (1848-1903) who stylised form, and used patches of flat colour for space within a composition, pattern to provide texture and relief. **The Nabis** group (1889-99) – from the Hebrew word for prophet – which included Edouard Vuillard, Bonnard, Maurice Denis and Maillol, rejected realism: "Remember that a picture .... is essentially a flat surface covered with colours assembled in a certain order".

Out of Impressionism was precipitated **Van Gogh** (1853-90) who used pure colour, painted out of doors and produced informal portraits of friends; his strong brushstroke and impasto technique betray a searing malaise with life. Only his early flower pieces show sensitivity to transient, ephemeral light.

The Neo-Impressionist **Georges Seurat** (1859-91) was fascinated by optics: as white light might refract the spectrum, so he might suggest luminosity by juxtaposing coloured dashes. His divisionism or pointillist technique is applied with scientific precision.

Henri Matisse (1869-1954) had a traditional artistic training first with Bouguereau and later with the Symbolist Gustave Moreau. Matisse was extremely versatile and prolific: he collaborated with the **Nabis** (Bonnard and Vuillard), the **Fauves** (Derain *Port of London* and Vlaminck), Cézanne, Signac, and Picasso. He travelled extensively and secured patronage from several collectors within his own lifetime.

Paul Cézanne (1839-1906) conceived landscape in terms of basic geometric volumes (cube, sphere, pyramid) existing in space in which perspective is determined by colour: green and blue for depth of field, warm golds and earthy ochres for foreground. His portraiture *(The Gardener)* and still-life paintings are also conceived as studies of mass, textured by pattern, moulded by shadow.

Pablo Picasso (1881-1973) draws on the Symbolist use of colour to suggest mood. Gouache, drawings and etchings dominate his Blue and Pink periods, echoing a transition from a desolate, poor and sad life to one shared with Fernande Olivier at the Bateau-Lavoir.

Picasso, Braque, Modigliani and Brancusi were all greatly impressed by stylised Iberian sculpture and Oceanic carvings then displayed at the ethnological museum in Paris *(see The Green Guide PARIS)*. From this powerful primitive artform, each explored the realms of eroticism or abstraction.

Cubism (1906-14) was the first truly abstract movement that evolved as a counter-reaction to the visual appeal of Impressionism and Fauvism: instead of flattening a three-dimensional object to a two-dimensional picture, Cubism attempted to capture the volume or essence of the subject (form, shape, texture, purpose) as a series of fractured details: as Picasso stated "A face consists of eyes, nose, ears, etc. You can put them anywhere in the picture, the face remains a face". In a *Clarinet and Bottle of Rum on a Mantelpiece,* **Braque** presents the instrument as something associated with music (represented by the word VALSE and symbols for the treble and bass clefs); later compositions evolve into collages. Fernand **Léger,** meanwhile, forged his own interpretation of the movement by integrating fragmented form, which he highlights with colour, with bits of black and white geometric patterning.

Dada and Surrealism – Dada (1915-22) came from Zurich: a deliberately nihilistic, anti-artform that was intended to shock and scandalise. Breton, Tzara, Duchamp *(Large Glass),* Arp and Picabia explored the fundamental nature of art by contradicting any established classification or justification with sharp wit and clever humour. Later, a more intellectual approach – prompted in part by the publication of Freud's theories – was pioneered by the Surrealist writers Apollinaire and Eluard who experimented with language, the realms of the subconscious, drug-induced dreams. They were joined in Paris by a second wave of foreign artists: Ernst *(Celebes),* De Chirico, Magritte *(The Reckless Sleeper),* Dali *(Metamorphosis of Narcissus, Lobster Telephone),* Miro, Penrose ...

Futurism – "A new art for a new century" was formulated by a group of Italians (Balla *Abstract Speed – the car has passed,* Boccioni *Unique Forms of Continuity in Space,* Carra, Severini *Suburban Train arriving in Paris*) to celebrate modern civilisation: the advent of electricity, mechanisation, the invention of the motor car, the glory of war... Tragically, several of the main protagonists died during the First World War, by which time the essence of the movement had fired the **Vorticists**.

Major movements and artists of the 20C

Shaded off colours indicate the origin and/or influence of a movement.

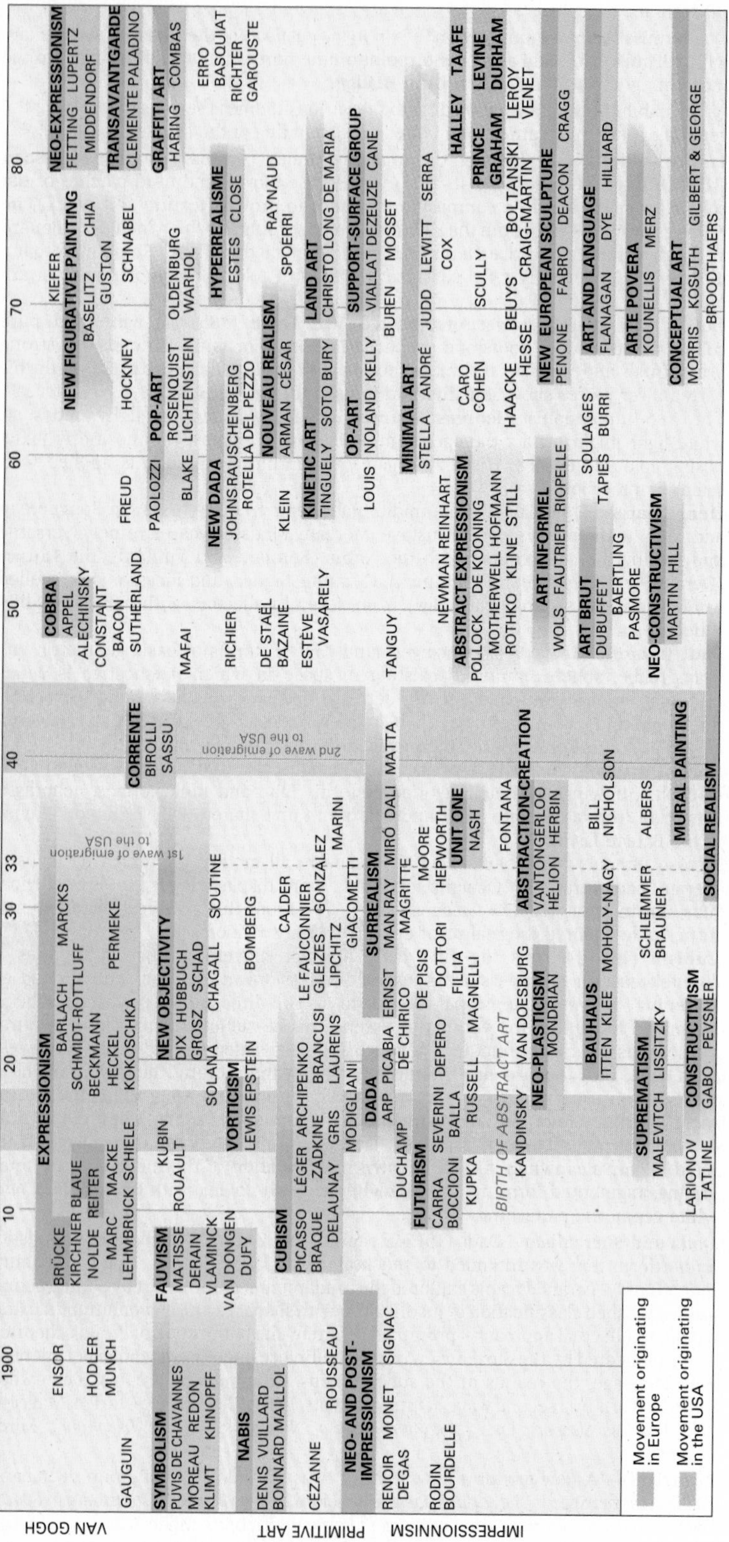

First World War
Second World War

1900 10 20 30 33 40 50 60 70 80

VAN GOGH
PRIMITIVE ART
IMPRESSIONISM

ENSOR
HODLER
MUNCH
GAUGUIN

EXPRESSIONISM
BRÜCKE
KIRCHNER BLAUE
NOLDE REITER
MARC MACKE
LEHMBRUCK SCHIELE
BARLACH MARCKS
SCHMIDT-ROTTLUFF
BECKMANN
HECKEL PERMEKE
KOKOSCHKA

1st wave of emigration to the USA

CORRENTE
BIROLLI
SASSU

COBRA
APPEL
ALECHINSKY
CONSTANT
BACON
SUTHERLAND
FREUD

HOCKNEY
KIEFER
NEW FIGURATIVE PAINTING
BASELITZ CHIA
GUSTON
SCHNABEL

NEO-EXPRESSIONISM
FETTING LUPERTZ
MIDDENDORF
TRANSAVANTGARDE
CLEMENTE PALADINO

SYMBOLISM
PUVIS DE CHAVANNES
MOREAU REDON
KLIMT KHNOPFF

FAUVISM
MATISSE
DERAIN
VLAMINCK
VAN DONGEN
DUFY
KUBIN
ROUAULT

NEW OBJECTIVITY
DIX HUBBUCH
GROSZ SCHAD
SOLANA CHAGALL SOUTINE

MAFAI

PAOLOZZI **POP-ART**
ROSENQUIST OLDENBURG
BLAKE LICHTENSTEIN WARHOL

GRAFFITI ART
HARING COMBAS
ERRO
BASQUIAT
RICHTER
GAROUSTE

NABIS
DENIS VUILLARD
BONNARD MAILLOL

VORTICISM
LEWIS EPSTEIN
BOMBERG

2nd wave of emigration to the USA

RICHIER

NEW DADA
JOHNS RAUSCHENBERG
ROTELLA DEL PEZZO

HYPERREALISME
ESTES CLOSE

CUBISM
PICASSO LÉGER ARCHIPENKO
BRAQUE ZADKINE BRANCUSI
DELAUNAY GRIS LAURENS
MODIGLIANI
CALDER
LE FAUCONNIER
GLEIZES GONZALEZ
LIPCHITZ MARINI
GIACOMETTI

DE STAËL
BAZAINE
ESTÈVE
VASARELY
KLEIN

NOUVEAU REALISM
ARMAN CÉSAR
RAYNAUD
SPOERRI

KINETIC ART
TINGUELY SOTO BURY

LAND ART
CHRISTO LONG DE MARIA

CÉZANNE
ROUSSEAU

NEO- AND POST-IMPRESSIONISM
RENOIR MONET SIGNAC
DEGAS

OP-ART
LOUIS NOLAND KELLY

SUPPORT-SURFACE GROUP
VIALLAT DEZEUZE CANE
BUREN MOSSET

DADA
ARP PICABIA
DUCHAMP

SURREALISM
ERNST MAN RAY MIRÓ DALI MATTA
DE CHIRICO MAGRITTE
TANGUY

MINIMAL ART
STELLA ANDRÉ JUDD LEWITT SERRA
COX

RODIN
BOURDELLE

FUTURISM
CARRA SEVERINI DEPERO
BOCCIONI BALLA
KUPKA RUSSELL MAGNELLI
DE PISIS
DOTTORI
FILLIA

MOORE
HEPWORTH
UNIT ONE
NASH

NEWMAN REINHART
ABSTRACT EXPRESSIONISM
POLLOCK DE KOONING
MOTHERWELL HOFMANN
ROTHKO KLINE STILL

CARO
COHEN
SCULLY

HALLEY TAAFE
PRINCE LEVINE
GRAHAM DURHAM

BIRTH OF ABSTRACT ART
KANDINSKY VAN DOESBURG
NEO-PLASTICISM
MONDRIAN

FONTANA
ABSTRACTION-CREATION
VANTONGERLOO
HÉLION HERBIN

HAACKE BEUYS BOLTANSKI LEROY
HESSE CRAIG-MARTIN VENET

ART INFORMEL
WOLS FAUTRIER RIOPELLE

NEW EUROPEAN SCULPTURE
PENONE FABRO DEACON CRAGG

BAUHAUS
ITTEN KLEE MOHOLY-NAGY
BILL
NICHOLSON

ART BRUT
DUBUFFET
BAERTLING
PASMORE
SOULAGES
TAPIES BURRI

ART AND LANGUAGE
FLANAGAN DYE HILLIARD

SUPREMATISM
MALEVITCH LISSITZKY
SCHLEMMER
BRAUNER
ALBERS

NEO-CONSTRUCTIVISM
MARTIN HILL

ARTE POVERA
KOUNELLIS MERZ

LARIONOV
TATLINE
CONSTRUCTIVISM
GABO PEVSNER

MURAL PAINTING
SOCIAL REALISM

CONCEPTUAL ART
MORRIS KOSUTH GILBERT & GEORGE
BROODTHAERS

Movement originating in Europe
Movement originating in the USA

erman Expressionism – In sympathy with ideas expressed by Gauguin, the xpressionists were happy to compromise naturalism by exaggerating form and olour if the end result had a more powerful impact (something Grünewald was ing in the first quarter of the 16C). **Die Brücke** (1905-13) meaning "The Bridge" nited Kirchner *(Bathers at Moritzburg)*, Heckel, Schmidt-Rotluff *(Dr Rosa Shapire)* d Bleyl in Dresden; soon it included Nolde *(The Sea B)* and Pechstein, the orwegian Edvard Munch *(The Sick Child)* and **Der Blaue Reiter** (The Blue Rider), group which was started in 1911 in Munich by Marc, Kandinski, Macke, ampendonk and Klee.

eorge Grosz *(Suicide)* admitted his "profound disgust for life" before the outbreak war, and his contempt was intensified by experience: familiar themes include ostitutes and bloated businessmen, death, an isolated church bathed in golden ght. **Max Beckmann** was scarred by the war; having served as a hospital orderly the Belgian Front, he was discharged in 1915 and evolved a new style of nnerving realism *(Carnival)*.

bstraction – If form is whittled to its purest outline and most perfect surface, then e subject has forsaken its personality and become abstract. In pursuing abstraction, n artist must necessarily pare away his character to explore his inner spirituality religion: Theosophy is the mystical rationale contained in Kandinsky's *Über das eistige in der Kunst* (Concerning the Spiritual in Art). **Suprematism** was pioneered Malevitch who rejected the "weight of the real world" in favour of a simple black uare, suspended in a void. **Constructivism** originated in Russia out of collages via liefs and mobiles into abstract compositions of diverse materials (wire, glass, metal, rspex in space). By 1921 the movement was dead, its exponents Taitlin, Pevsner nd Gabo (who moved to England in 1935-46) dispersed, its concepts transposed to chitecture and furniture design.

e Stijl was a Dutch magazine that promoted **Mondrian** (who was in London 38-40) and Neo-Plasticism. Born from a graphic medium, the greatest impact as delivered to poster art, packaging and commercial art, but it also left its mark n Gropius and the Bauhaus ideals.

ritish Abstraction – In Britain, an interest in abstraction can be dated to the rganisation of the conservative Seven and Five Society in 1919, which soon attracted **en Nicholson** (1924), **Barbara Hepworth** and **Henry Moore** (1932); it reformed 1926 as the Seven and Five Abstract Group and enlisted John Piper. **Paul Nash,** eanwhile started Unit One which also included Hepworth, Moore and Nicholson.

ealism and traditional values returned after the War, when it was recognised at art had splintered into fractured groups. **Stanley Spencer** excelled at figurave painting, **Lucian Freud** evolved his own searching realism from painting om life, the **Kitchen Sink** school emerged from the Royal College in the 1950s. ore violent and brash is the style fashioned by Dubuffet and Giacometti who receded the trio **Francis Bacon, Graham Sutherland** and **Henry Moore**, who ach individually reworked traditional subjects (Crucifixion; landscape at sunset; other and Child, reclining nude).

epercussions – The **Euston Road School** was founded in 1937 as a counteraction to the avant-garde, its prospectus stated: "In teaching, particular emphasis ill be laid on training the observation... No attempt, however, will be made to npose a style and students will be left with maximum freedom of expression." ondon provided a fertile source of subject-matter in which Coldstream, Graham ell, Rogers, Pasmore sensed the advent of the Depression. **Piper** and his wife lyfanwy Evans became exponents of a neo-Romanticism. A new look was cast at ne English landscape, its profiles, colours, heritage.

bstract Expressionism (1942-52) originated in New York, where Ernst, Masson, latta, Mondrian sought refuge during the war, with De Kooning (1904-97), Barnett ewman (1905-70), Pollock (1912-56), Rothko (1903-70) all exploring similar concepts different media and styles, often on a large scale: "The familiar identity of things as to be pulverised in order to destroy the finite associations with which our society ncreasingly enshrouds every aspect of our environment" (Rothko, 1947). A common ense of the collective unconscious was given in the ideas propounded by Jung, einforced by examples from primitive (American Indian, Mexican, Eskimo) art, urrealism, mythology, mysticism, the occult even...

p and Kinetic Art, which explores the distinction between reality, appearance nd the nature of illusion, was developed largely by the Hungarian Vasarely and ridget Riley.

op Art and New Realism is drawn as its title suggests from popular culture and raphic art. In the 1950s at the ICA, the likes of Paolozzi and Hamilton used collages f mundane objects to capture the spirit of the period. The second phase (1961) merged from the Royal College with Hockney, Peter Blake, Jones, Boshier, Phillips, aulfield: in America the movement was taken up by Lichtenstein, Oldenburg, Varhol, Jasper Johns...

Contemporary Figurative Art – Frank Auerback, Francis Bacon, Lucian Freu David Hockney, Howard Hodgkin, R B Kitaj, Leon Kossof, Uglow today continue historic British preoccupation for portraiture and the representation of contempora figures in their social context.

Bankside Gallery

(♿) Open Tue-Sun, 10am (11am Sat-Sun) to 5pm (8pm Tue). £3.50. ☎ 020 7928 752 Fax 020 7928 2820; info@banksidegallery.com; www.banksidegallery.com

The gallery, which opened in modern premises by the river in 1980, holds reg larly changing exhibitions under the aegis of the Royal Societies of Painters Water Colours (f 1804) and of Painter-Etchers and Engravers (f 1881).

Clink Exhibition

1 Clink Street. Open daily, 10am-9pm (6pm Oct-Mar). Closed 25-26 Dec. £4. Guided tou telephone for details. ☎ 020 7378 1558; Fax 020 7403 5813; www.clink.co.uk

Stairs lead down to a gloomy basement. The exhibition traces the history imprisonment and torture and of the Bankside brothels.

Old Operating Theatre, Museum and Herb Garret

9A St Thomas's St. Open daily, 10.30am-5pm. Closed mid-Dec to early-Jan. £4; gui book £2.50. ☎ 020 7955 4791; Fax 020 7378 8383; curator@thegarret.org.u www.thegarret.org.uk

The attic of St Thomas's Parish Church was already in use as a herb garr when, in 1821, it was converted into a women's operating theatre f St Thomas's Hospital *(see LAMBETH)* which moved to its present site near Wes minster Bridge in 1871. The theatre predates the advent of anaesthetics ar antiseptic surgery, the only one of the period to be preserved in London, la used in 1862. It is semicircular, about 40ft/13m across with a 14ft/4 amphitheatre ringed by five rows of "standings" for students. The operatir table is a sturdy wooden structure with upraised headpiece; below on the flo was a wooden box of sawdust which could 'be kicked by the surgeon's foot any place where most blood was running'. In the corner was a small wash-basi about the size of a large soup plate, in which surgeons washed their hands aft – sometimes even before – operating.

HMS Belfast

(♿) Open daily, 10am-6pm (5pm Nov-Feb); last admission 45min before closing. Clos 24-26 Dec. £5.80. Brochure (4 languages). Snack bar. ☎ 020 7940 6300; Fax 020 7403 071 www.iwm.org.uk

The cruiser saw service with the Arctic convoys and on D-Day. From the fla deck to the hull, it is painted in the original "Admiralty disruptive camouflag colours". Seven decks of the ship are on display; the Operations Room is broug to life with a surface action effect and the Forward Steering Position with soun and light displays; appropriate smells identify the bakery, the sick bay and th boiler rooms; the story of the North Atlantic Convoys in the Second World War told on film; the Falklands War exhibition retraces the campaign to recover th islands after the Argentine invasion in 1982.

London Dungeon

34 Tooley Street. ♿ Open daily, 10am (10.30am early-Nov to Easter) to 5.30pm (7.30p mid-Jul to Aug; 5pm early-Nov to Easter). Closed 25 Dec. £11.50. Leaflet (3 language Refreshments. ☎ 020 7403 7221; Fax 020 7378 1529; www.thedungeons.com

A gruesome and sombre parade of tableaux, complete with eerie sound effect relate scenes of death from disease (leprosy and plague), various methods of to ture and execution (hanging, guillotine – talking head narrating Anne Boleyn final demise), and early surgery. Separately narrated story of Jack the Ripper, th East End murderer *(optional)* complete with special effects. The exhibition make effective use of the space but is unsuitable for the squeamish and very youn children.

Winston Churchill's Britain at War

64 Tooley Street. (♿) Open daily, 10am-5.30pm (4.30pm Oct-Mar). Closed 24-26 De £6.50; £15 family. ☎ 020 7403 3171; Fax 020 7403 5104; britainatwar@dial.pipex.cor www.britainatwar.co.uk

An old London Underground lift provides Tardis-like time travel to an Unde ground station fitted with bunks, tables and chairs, a canteen and tea urn, WVS lending library and a video of scenes from the Second World War, regularl interrupted by the noise of an Underground train. The nostalgic exhibitio accompanied by rallying music, continues with displays of war-time fashior mementoes of rationing, air raids, an Anderson shelter and a refuge room, evac uation, women at work in factories and on the land, the life of Sir Winsto Churchill and an evocative reconstruction of simulated bomb damage after a air raid.

Fashion and Textile Museum

83 Bermondsey Street. ♿ Open Tue-Sun, 11am-5.45pm. Admission charge. ☎ 020 7403 0222, 020 7407 8664; Fax 020 7403 0555; www.ftmlondon.org

The focus of the museum is British and international fashion. It presents temporary exhibitions.

Bramah Museum of Tea and Coffee★

40 Southwark Street. ♿ Open daily, 10am-6pm. Closed 25-26 Dec. £4; £10 family. Tearoom. ☎/Fax 020 7403 5650; e.bramah@virgin.net; www.bramahmuseum.co.uk

The museum traces the fashion for tea and coffee drinking in England, the establishment of coffee houses and tea gardens in the 17C, the levy of taxes and the origins of the Boston Tea Party, smuggling and adulteration. A vast and varied collection of teapots includes ones shaped like the monkeys which were trained to pick tea and the largest teapot ever made.

Bloomsbury★

The once residential area comprises many 18C and 19C squares and is dominated by two major learned institutions, London University and the British Museum. Bloomsbury contains a concentration of medical institutions renowned for their expertise. The most famous is the Hospital for Sick Children (Great Ormond Street) founded only 20 years after the Coram Foundation for Children (1739).

Location

Map pp 11-12 (DEVX); Michelin Atlas London: pp 77-79, 94-95. ⊖ Tottenham Court Road; Goodge St, Russell Square. Bloomsbury is an area north of Covent Garden and Soho with Euston Rd as the boundary to the north.

Adjacent Sights: SOHO, REGENT'S PARK, MARYLEBONE, ST PANCRAS - CAMDEN TOWN.

Background

The Squares - The development of **Bloomsbury Square** in 1661 introduced a new concept in local planning. The 4th Earl of Southampton, descendant of the Lord Chancellor to whom **Henry VIII** had granted the feudal manor in 1545, erected houses for the well-to-do around three sides of a square, a mansion for himself on the fourth, northern, side and the innovation of a network of secondary service streets all around, with a market nearby, so ordering, in Evelyn's words, "a little town". He was successful: by 1667, when he died, he had a magnificent residence, the focus of fashion had transferred to his estate and he had made a fortune. His only daughter, Lady Rachel, married the future **1st Duke of Bedford**, uniting two great estates.

The other squares followed in the 19C: **Russell** in 1800, **Tavistock** in 1806-26, **Torrington** in 1825, **Woburn** in 1829, **Gordon**, originally by Thomas Cubitt *(see INSIGHTS AND IMAGES - The Changing Face of London)* in 1850.

Artistic Tradition - From the late 18C to the early 20C the Bloomsbury district was frequented by artists and writers: Richard Wilson and Constable (**no 76** Charlotte Street); Madox Brown and **Bernard Shaw**, **Whistler** and **Sickert** in **Fitzroy Square**; Verlaine and Rimbaud in Howland Street; Wyndham Lewis in Percy Street and David Garnet in Bedford Square.

Ph. Gajic/MICHELIN

Fanlights and wrought-iron balconies on the Georgian façades in Bedford Square

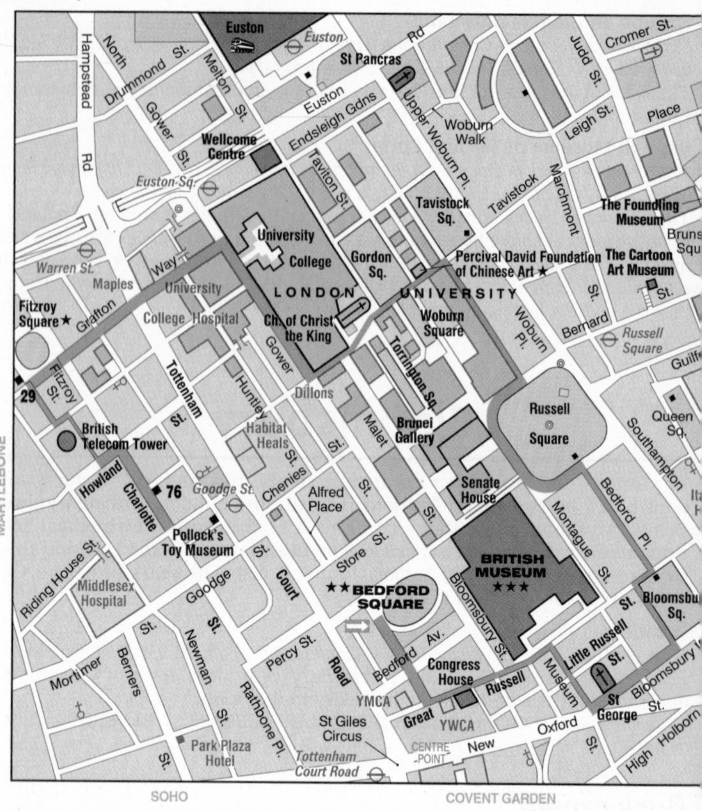

The most famous residents however, were the **Bloomsbury Group** (*see INSIGHTS AND IMAGES – Painting*) whose members included **Virginia Woolf**, who lived at **29 Fitzroy Square**, **Vanessa Bell, Roger Fry** the art critic who in 1910 organised the first Post-Impressionist Exhibition to be held in London, Clive Bell, EM Forster, Lytton Strachey – friend and mentor of Dora Carrington – Duncan Grant and Maynard Keynes, resident in Bedford Square. In the immediate vicinity of Gordon Square resided Rupert Brooke (war poet), DH Lawrence (novelist), **Bertrand Russell** (philosopher, social reformer, Nobel Prize for literature) and his mistress Lady Ottoline Morrell (influential patron of the arts). By the early 1930s their ideas and works, literary, critical and artistic, had become widely known and accepted, their influence absorbed into the artistic tradition.

Directory

Light Bite

October Gallery Café – *24 Lundonia House, Old Gloucester St, WC1N 3AL – ⊖ Holborn – ☎ 020 7242 7367 – octobergallery@compuserve.com – Closed Sat (café only), Sun, Mon and dinner – ✕ – £5/8.50.* This former Victorian school now houses an informal café and a small art gallery displaying works of contemporary artists. On the menu: home-cooked fare inspired by recipes from around the globe.

Coffee Gallery – *23 Museum St, WC1A 1JT – ⊖ Russell Street – ☎ 020 7436 0455 – Open Mon-Fri, 9.30am-6pm, Sat-Sun 10am6pm – ✕ – £8.* Take a break from the museum to enjoy a fresh sandwich, pastry or hot dish in this small friendly café, which serves organic and vegetarian food. The atmosphere is relaxed and pleasant, and the changing artwork on display is for sale. Internet access available.

Shopping

Contemporary Applied Arts – *2 Percy St, W1T 1DD – ⊖ Goodge St, Tottenham Court Rd – ☎ 020 7436 2344 – Open Mon-Sat 10.30pm-5.30pm.* Exhibitions and information on crafts and applied arts (pottery, studio ceramics, glass, wood, metal, jewellery, textiles and furniture).

Waterstones – *82 Gower St, WC1E 6EQ – ⊖ Goodge St, Euston Sq – ☎ 020 7636 1577 – Fax 020 7580 7680 – enquiries@gowerst.waterstone.co.uk – www.waterstones.co.uk – Open Mon-Sat 9.30am-8pm (7pm Sat), Sun noon-6pm.* Reputed bookshop, formerly Dillons, frequented by university students.

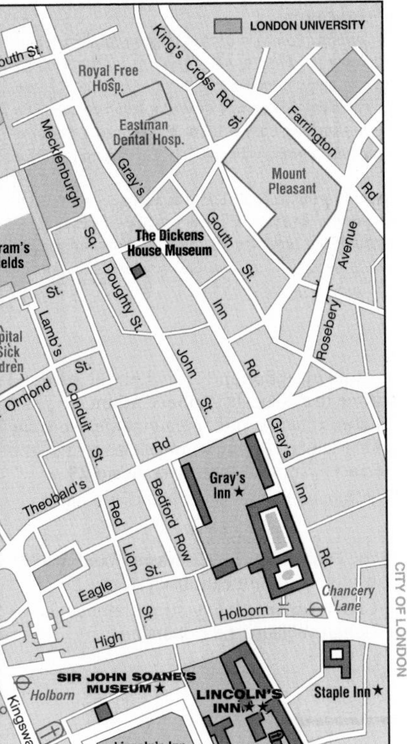

Walking About

Bedford Square★★

The most elegant of the squares, which is still complete, was developed in 1775 by Gertrude, widow of the 4th Duke of Bedford, to designs by Thomas Leverton. The three-storey brick terraces have rounded doorways, delicate fanlights and first floor balconies; the centre of each is relieved by a pedimented stucco centrepiece.

Proceed along Adeline Pl.

Great Russell Street

The west end of the street is marked by the YMCA, built in the 1970s, and the YWCA. The structural mass of **Congress House**, the TUC Headquarters, is lightened by a glass screen at ground level on the east side, giving a view of an inner court and hall, distinguished by a war memorial before a high green marble screen, carved on the spot from a block (weighing 10 tons) of Roman stone by Jacob Epstein (1958).

Cross Bloomsbury St and turn right opposite the British Museum (see BRITISH MUSEUM) into Museum St and left into Bloomsbury Way.

St George's Bloomsbury

Major restoration from May 1003 to Oct 2004. Open usually Tue and Thu, 10am-4/5pm, Wed and Fri, noon-2pm. Closed Bank Hols. ☎ 020 7405 3044

Hawksmoor's church (1716-31) makes the most of a difficult site, with a grand pedimented portico at the top of a flight of steps and a stepped stone tower surmounted by a spire. Topping the steeple, to the contemporary public's derision, is a classical statue of the unpopular George I. Inside, the problem of orientation on such a cramped site, resolved by Hawksmoor by hollowing out a small apse in the east wall, has since been settled by the transfer of the high gilded and inlaid reredos (1727) to the north wall. At the centre of the flat rectangular ceiling is a flower in richly gilded plaster and in the shell over the east niche another delicate gilded relief, both by the master plasterer, Isaac Mansfield.

Continue to Bloomsbury Sq and turn left.

Bloomsbury Square

None of the original houses has survived but in the south-west corner of the square are two mid-18C houses; the one with the cherub-decorated plaque was the residence of Isaac and Benjamin Disraeli from 1818 to 1826.

Walk down Bedford Pl and through Russell Sq and proceed to Tavistock St past the Percival David Foundation of Chinese Art (description in Worth a Visit).

Church of Christ the King

Gordon Sq. Open Mon-Fri, 8.30am-4.30pm.

The neo-Early English Gothic church, built in 1853 to cathedral proportions (the interior is 212ft/65m long), is now the University Church.

Continue to Gower St and turn right.

University College

The central range of this, the oldest of the university buildings, designed by William Wilkins, is marked by an imposing pedimented portico, behind which rises a high dome (1827-9); the interior gallery (first floor) is decorated with low-relief panels by John Flaxman. Guarding either side of the courtyard are a pair of miniature, domed, observatories. The college houses the **Flaxman Sculpture Galleries** and the fully-clothed body of Jeremy Bentham (1748-1832), inspiration of the college's founders.

Take Grafton Way.

London University

In 1828 a group of dissenters and radicals founded University College in London to give education in arts, sciences and medicine in a non-residential and non-sectarian milieu. It was referred to as "that Godless institution in Gower Street" by supporters of the Church of England, who reacted by founding King's College in the Strand in 1829 with a strong theological faculty. Neither college was allowed to grant degrees. The University of London was incorporated by charter as an examining body in 1836 and as a teaching body in 1900. It now comprises many colleges all over London and beyond with internal, external and part-time students.

London University moved from Piccadilly to Bloomsbury after the Second World War, although construction of the **Senate House**, a cold Portland stone building with a tall square tower (library) by Charles Holden, began in 1932. Colleges, faculties and new institutes are now housed throughout the immediate neighbourhood in old 18C-19C houses and in the ever-extending, heterogeneous complex of brick, stone, concrete, steel, mosaic and glass *(in pink on plan)*.

Fitzroy Square★

This square has changed in character since its inception in 1793 when the east and south sides were completed in Portland stone to designs by **Robert Adam**; 40 years later the square was completed but with stucco facing rather than stone. Note the giant columned centrepiece on the east side repeated in miniature at either end, and echoed in the centrepiece of the south terrace. Virginia Woolf lived at **no 29**.

Take Conway St SW of the square, turn right into Maple St and left into Cleveland St.

British Telecom Tower

The slim landmark, originally known as the Post Office Tower, was erected in 1965 to provide an unimpeded path for London's telecommunications system.

Turn left into Howland St and right into **Charlotte St**, a lively street famous for its restaurants. **No 76** was the residence of Richard Wilson and Constable.

Worth a Visit

Percival David Foundation of Chinese Art★

53 Gordon Sq. Open Mon-Fri, 10.30am-5pm. Reference Library (charge): 10.30am-1pm and 2-4.45pm. Closed Bank Hol Mon, Maundy Thu to Easter Mon, 2 weeks at Christmas and New Year. Guide book and information leaflet. Guided tour £4 per person (10 min - 20 max). ☎ 020 7387 3909; Fax 020 7383 5163; www.pdfmuseum.org.uk

The Foundation displays the world-famous collection of exquisite Chinese porcelain assembled between the wars by the late Sir Percival David, scholar and connoisseur of great distinction, together with the Elphinstone bequest. This specialist collection of the finest 14C to 18C porcelain figures and vessels reflects Chinese imperial taste notably from the Sung dynasty: plain, incised, monochrome, blue and white or bearing polychrome decoration. The pieces are selected for their classical shapes or delicate and refined decoration.

The Cartoon Art Museum

7 Brunswick Sq. Open Tue-Fri, 10am-5pm. Donation. Talks, lectures and events. Shop stocking cards and books. ☎ 020 7278 7172; Fax 020 7278 4234

Historic cartoons and caricatures not only chart developments and personalities through the ages but demonstrate a strong and determined sense of humour. The Cartoon Trust and its museum collect and exhibit humorous and satirical artworks, drawings, engravings, illustrations, advertisements, comic strips and animated films from the time of William Hogarth to the present. Evocative names include Mr Punch, Rupert Bear, The Beano, Dan Dare, Andy Capp, Bonzo the Dog, Captain Pugwash, Fred Bassett... Heath Robinson, HM Bateman, Giles, Calman, Garland...

The Dickens House Museum

48 Doughty Street. Open daily, 10am (11am Sun) to 5pm. Closed 25-26 Dec, 1 Jan. £4. Brochure and gallery cards (10 languages). ☎ 020 7405 2127; dhmuseum @rmplc.co.uk; www.dickensmuseum.com

Charles Dickens (1812-70)

Dickens drew generously on his fertile imagination as well as on his own experiences for his serialised novels: characters were modelled on friends, close relations and acquaintances made in connection with the theatre and the amateur dramatics he so enjoyed, and the philanthropic works he undertook. An early, happy childhood in Chatham was brought to an abrupt end when his father was sent to Marshalsea Prison for debts and he, aged 12, was put to work blacking shoes. As an office boy he studied shorthand and secured a place on the *Morning Chronicle* reporting on debates in the House of Commons. There he developed his acute sense of observation and sharp humour. Close associates and admirers included Thackeray, Wilkie Collins, Hans Christian Andersen... His wife, Catherine Hogarth (1815-79) was a promising young journalist when she married the rising novelist (1835). She bore him ten children (Dora died in 1851). She was persuaded to accept a deed of separation (1858) as Dickens was emotionally involved with Ellen Ternan, a beautiful young actress.

narles Dickens and his young family moved into the late-18C house, situated then a private road gated at either end and attended by burgundy-liveried porters, shortly ter his marriage to his "pet mouse" Catherine Hogarth. They were to live there for early three years from April 1837 to December 1839, during which time Kate's sister ary died in Dickens' arms, and he completed *Pickwick Papers,* wrote *Oliver Twist* and *icholas Nickleby* besides articles, essays, sketches and letters. The house, which ontains portraits and "knick-knacks", holds an interesting collection of letters and anuscripts, the early small paperback parts in which the novels were first issued, e prompt copies he used for his public readings and a large selection of original ustrations to his works.

he cluttered drawing-room, furnished with rosewood furniture and Hogarth ngravings has been meticulously decorated as in Dickens' time; in the basement e washroom and cellar capture a little more of the atmosphere of Dickensian ondon.

oram's Fields

uildford Street. A park reserved for children extends over part of the area once ccupied by the hospital buildings.

A Compassionate Man

n his sixties, **Thomas Coram**, a successful sea captain, trader and founder-trustee of the Colony of Georgia, was so distressed on his visits to London by the plight of abandoned infants and small children that he determined to better their lot. Campaigns, petitions to George II and determination won a charter of ncorporation in 1739; with wide support from the rich, the noble and the prominent, he raised enough money to purchase 56 acres of Lambs Conduit Fields – 20 for buildings and playing fields, the remainder to provide revenue for the hospital by development.

3y Coram's death at the age of 83 in 1751, the hospital was soundly established; hundreds of children had been saved. The patronage of artists, begun by Hogarth at the foundation, had already provided outstanding paintings and continued with gifts and donations by the least and the greatest such as **Handel**. Coram's tomb is in St Andrew's Church, Holborn *(see CHANCERY LANE)*.

In 1926 the children were moved to Berkhamsted, much of the land was sold and most of the buildings subsequently demolished. At a later date the Governors bought back the site of the present museum building) and adjoining Coram Children's Centre.

he Foundling Museum

0 Brunswick Sq. Closed for refurbishment until Summer 2004. ☎ *020 7841 3600; Fax 020 837 8084; janet@foundlingmuseum.org.uk*

bronze statue of Thomas Coram after Hogarth stands before the 1937 neo-Georgian building. The 18C hospital oak staircase (note the cartouches) climbs around an pen well, in which stands a jaunty peasant boy, hand on hip.

he Courtroom, exactly rebuilt with dark red walls setting off the moulded ceiling nd plaster enrichments, contains the mantelpiece with a relief of Charity Chilren given by Rysbrack, an oval mirror and eight contemporary views of London ospitals (Charterhouse is by Gainsborough). Other artefacts on display include oins and moving tokens left by destitute mothers with their children, rare letters nd autographs.

he Foundation has a fine collection of works of art by contemporary British artists, otably Hogarth *(Thomas Coram, March of the Guards to Finchley)*, Roubiliac *(bust of Iandel)*, full-length governors' portraits by Ramsay, Reynolds and Millais. Other lonations and bequests include part of a cartoon of the *Massacre of the Innocents* from he School of Raphael, the surprising *Worthies of Great Britain* by Northcote, a Georgian ilver gilt communion service, pewter porringers, Hogarth's punchbowl of Lambethlelftware, an organ keyboard presented by Handel and the 1739 royal charter.

ollock's Toy Museum and Shop

Scala Street. Open Mon-Sat, 10am-5pm. Closed Bank Hols. £3. Brochure (5 languages). ☎ *020 7636 3452; info@pollocksmuseum.co.uk; www.pollocksmuseum.co.uk; www.pollocksweb.co.uk*

Toy theatres, that 19C delight made from sheets described by Robert Louis Stevenson as "one penny plain and twopence coloured", can be seen amidst a nass of 19C and 20C toys: wax, tin, porcelain, peg and spoon dolls, teddy bears, carved wooden animals, optical toys, dolls' houses. Live toy theatre performances re given during the school holidays.

British Museum★★★

The British Museum is undoubtedly one of the finest institutions of th genre and its treasures represent a vast canvas of the history of civilisatio It is an uplifting experience to view the rare artefacts which reveal the i genuity of man and the cultural influences at play from early beginnin to the present day.

Location

Map p 12 (EX) and area map under BLOOMSBURY; Michelin Atlas London: p 7
⊖ Tottenham Court Road; Russell Square.

Background

Foundation – The final spur to found the British Museum was supplied in 1753 whe **Sir Hans Sloane**, physician, naturalist, traveller, bequeathed his collection to the natior Parliament already had stored in vaults in Westminster a priceless collection of mediev manuscripts acquired in 1700. Elsewhere there were manuscripts, charters and rol collected by the Earls of Oxford which were made available in 1753. In 1756 the ol Royal Library of 12 000 volumes, assembled since Tudor times, was officially presente to the museum by George II and deposited in the Westminster vaults in 1823.

A lottery was launched to raise money for a building worthy of such magnificer and extensive collections; £21 000 was spent on the purchase of Montagu Hous built in the late 17C; the building was altered and opened in 1759. Engravings sho a random display without labels: stuffed giraffes, portraits, fossils and manuscript books, dried plants, classical marble statues and coins, pots and Buddhas against background of heroic frescoes and plasterwork ceilings. Cobbett christened th institution "the old curiosity shop".

Collections – Presentations, bequests and special parliamentary purchases swelle the collections. Important acquisitions included: Thomason Tracts, pamphlet published during the Civil War and Commonwealth 1642-60 (presented by George II 1762); David Garrick Library (1 000 printed plays including First Folios, 1779); Si William Hamilton collection of antique vases (£8 400; 1772); Cracherode collectio of books, fine bindings, great master drawings, Greek and Roman coins (1799 Egyptian antiquities including the Rosetta Stone (under the Treaty of Alexandri 1802); Greek and Roman sculptures, bronzes and terracottas, the Townley Marble (1804, £20 000); sculptures from the Temple of Apollo at Bassae, 1815; sculptures fro the Parthenon, the Elgin Marbles (purchased 1816, £35 000)... Other significan purchases were transacted of manuscripts, minerals (Grenville), libraries (Hargrave legal), music collections (Burney), natural history collections, French Revolutio tracts and ephemera.

In 1823 George IV presented his father's library of 65 000 volumes, 19 000 pamphlets maps and charts; in 1824 came the Payne-Knight bequest of Classical antiquities bronzes and drawings; in 1827 the Banks bequest of books, botanical specimens an ethnography.

New light on the Classical splendour of the Great Court

> **CHANGES FOR THE THIRD MILLENNIUM**
> The Grand Rooms will be restored to their former glorious Regency decorative schemes; the King's Library will provide displays relating to the Age of Enlightenment and connoisseurship; Classical sculpture will be displayed in the Manuscripts Saloon. The North Library will provide an introduction to the **Ethnography Collections** with dependent galleries dedicated to the non-Western cultures of Africa, the Pacific, Asia, Near East and Europe *(completion date 2003)*.

Accommodation – In 1824 **Robert Smirke** was appointed to produce plans for a more permanent building, which would replace the decayed Montagu House. The new building with a Greek-inspired colonnaded façade was completed 20 years later. The Reading Room was added in 1857, the Edward VII Galleries in 1914, the Duveen Galleries in 1938. Further extensions were built in 1978 and 1991. Some departments were transferred to other sites: the natural history departments to South Kensington in 1880-83; the newspapers to Colindale in 1905 and the ethnographic collections to the Museum of Mankind *(see PICCADILLY)* in 1970. In 1973 the museum's library departments were vested in a separate authority and granted funds to have new premises built in St Pancras *(see ST PANCRAS – CAMDEN TOWN)*.
After the transfer of the library collections in 1998 and major rebuilding, the museum now boasts improved facilities with the creation of the spectacular Great Court and new galleries to reintegrate the ethnographic collections.

Highlights

♿ *Open daily, 10am-5.30pm (8.30pm Thu-Fri). Closed Good Friday, 24-26 Dec, 1 Jan. No charge to main galleries, variable rates for temporary exhibitions. Some rooms may be closed owing to lack of staff. Guided tour (90min); lectures, gallery talks and films. Guide (8 languages). Restaurant, café. Wheelchairs for hire. ☎ 020 7323 8299; 020 7637 7384 (recorded information for disabled visitors); 020 7323 8181 (bookings); Fax 020 7323 8616; information@thebritishmuseum.ac.uk; www.thebritishmuseum.ac.uk*

Great Court

The Great Court, which was designed by Sir Norman Foster and opened in 2000, is the hub of the museum. A stunning glass and steel roof spanning the space to the domed Round Reading Room, and thus creating the largest covered square in Europe, is an architectural marvel. Sculptures displayed in the public areas introduce the great civilisations.

Reading Room

The circular **Reading Room** (1857) was designed to occupy a gloomy courtyard at the centre of the building by the architect **Sydney Smirke** and Antonio Panizzi, a refugee Italian revolutionary, who was Principal Librarian (Director) in 1856. Panizzi was determined that the library should be open to "the poorest student" as well as to "men of letters". It accommodated 400 readers and 25 miles of shelving (1 300 000 books). Panizzi was also responsible for the compilation of the catalogue. The restored blue and gold decoration of the dome (140ft/43m in diameter and 106ft/32m in height) recreates the original setting.
The Reading Room is used for research as a hi-tech Information Centre and as a reference library for the museum's collections.

THE CLASSICAL COLLECTIONS

Start in Room 11 west of the main entrance.

Ancient Greece and Rome

The collections of Greek and Roman Antiquities range from the dawn of the Bronze Age (3200 BC) to the establishment of Christianity as the official religion of the Holy Roman Empire (Edict of Milan AD 313).

Prehistoric to Archaic Greece – *Rooms 11-14.* A distinctive civilisation flourished in the Cycladic Islands c 3200-2000 BC which is characterised by marble figurines usually found in graves. The pure lines of the stylised nude female forms with folded arms *(11)*, which may represent fertility goddesses, have influenced modern art. Finds also included pottery and stone vessels.
The influence of Minoan Crete spread throughout the Aegean in the Middle Bronze Age *(12)*. Fine pottery and bronzes were excavated from the palaces (c 1900 BC) at Knossos. A bronze group of an athlete leaping over a bull reveals an unusual ritual practice. The **Aegina Treasure** (c 1700-1500 BC) includes an elaborate gold pendant of a nature god and other ornaments. A fine example of the impressive remains of the warlike Mycenaeans who came to prominence in the Late Bronze Age (1500-1000 BC) is the **Treasury of Atreus**, a circular domed tomb with a decorated façade. Bronzes, jewellery, weapons and black-figured pottery *(13)* were traded in the Archaic period (1000-500 BC). Early Greek vases displayed narrative scenes drawn from mythology with geometric and oriental motifs, fantastic animals and realistic human figures. Red-figured vase painting *(14)* which originated in Athens depicted subjects from daily life and mythology.

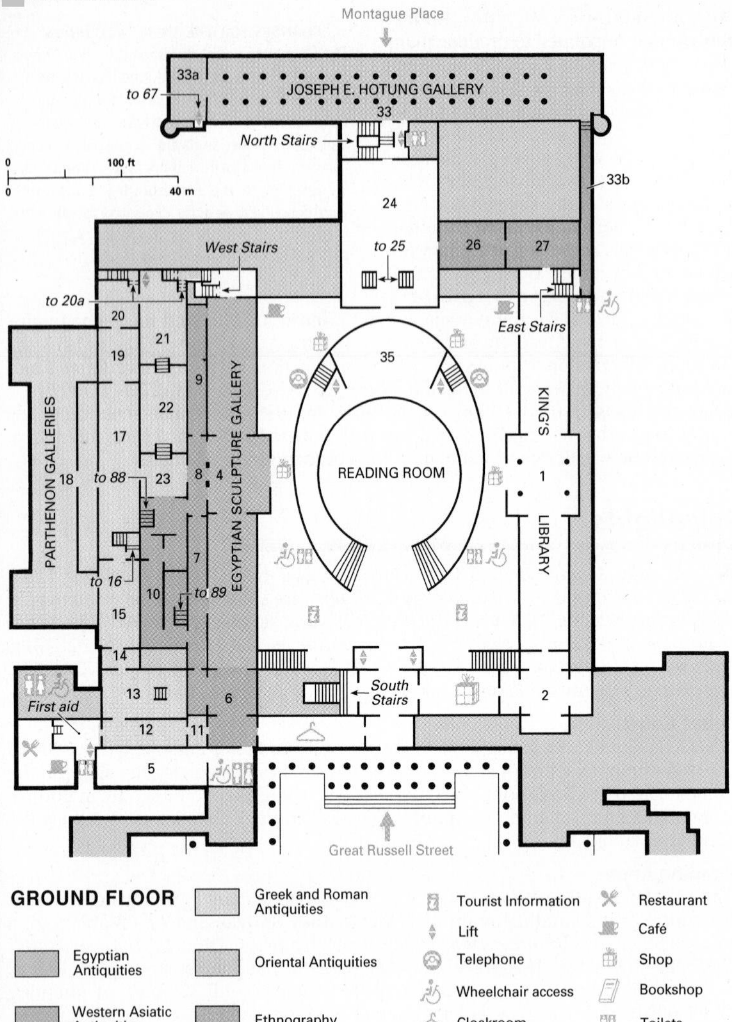

5C BC – *Rooms 15-20*. The Chatsworth Head (note the curly hair), youthful *Kouroi (14)* and the Strangford Apollo *(15)* are rare Classical statues. The stone reliefs of the Harpy Tomb *(15)* inspired from Ionian art predate the high-relief marble sculpture *(16)* from the Temple of Apollo at **Bassae**: lively battle of Centaurs and Lapiths, Greeks and Amazons (c 400 BC) and the reconstructed **Nereid Monument** (c 400 – *17*) at Xanthos in south-west Turkey with elegant statues of the breezes with clinging robes and majestic lion gate guardians. On the friezes are vivid battle scenes.

The Parthenon in Athens was built to the glory of the goddess Athena. The Parthenon Galleries *(18a, 18b, 18)* are dedicated to the famous **Parthenon (Elgin) Marbles**, the culmination of Hellenistic art from the 5C BC, which celebrate the Greek victory over Persia: battles of the Lapiths and Centaurs, pediment figures dressed in rippling robes. The computer-generated imaging of the frieze and a reconstruction of the northwest corner of the Parthenon bring the site to life. The **Caryatid Room** *(19)* displays sculptures from the Acropolis in Athens as well as pottery, terracottas, bronzes (430-400 BC).

4C BC – The **Payava Tomb** *(20)* from Xanthos (400-330 BC) on the Aegean coast of Turkey, decorated with scenes from the dead man's career, is typical of the local style of funerary monuments although Persia and Athens in turn controlled territories in Asia Minor. In contrast the **Mausoleum of Halicarnassus** *(21, 81)*, one of the Seven Wonders of the World, is of Greek design; it depicts courtly life with a colossal horse at the apex and a frieze of the furious battle of Greeks and Amazons. Another such monument is the Temple of Artemis at Ephesus with striking figured decoration on the columns *(21, 82)*.

Hellenistic art *(23)* is highly theatrical and stresses individual traits: a marble statue of **Demeter** from Cnidus with a calm and pensive expression is representa-

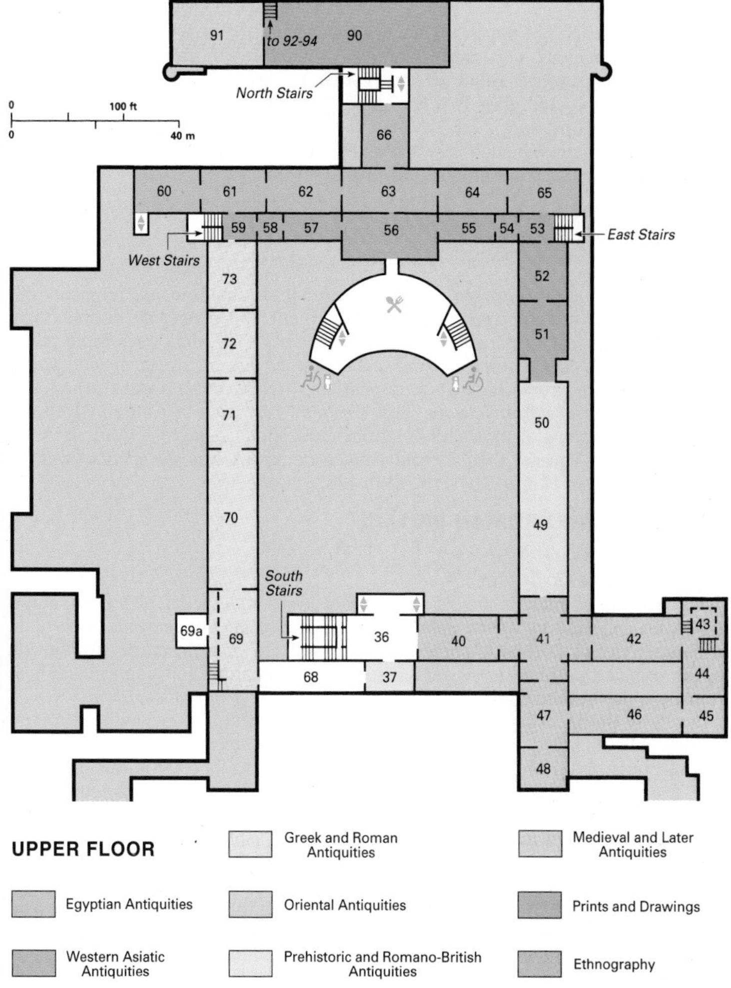

tive of the trend for free-standing sculpture by Greek masters; the life-like Tanagra figurines depict ordinary people; an ivory statuette of a hunchback and large bronze statues (Sophocles) are very realistic.

Take the West stairs up to the upper floor.

Greek Influences

Greek cities established colonies in southern Italy and Greek artistry is evident in the fine red-figured vases *(20a, 73)*, bronze figurines (fine bronze horseman c 550 BC, curious head of an athlete with a leather cap 300-200 BC) and funerary artefacts.

Cypriot Antiquities

A rich collection of artefacts *(72)* indicates that Cyprus had a prosperous civilisation which traded with Egypt and the Near East, Greece and Rome: vases with incised and painted decoration c 4500 BC-AD 300; terracotta figurine with earrings 1400-1200 BC; flat limestone statue 575-550 BC, fine jewellery 5C-4C BC.

Italy before the Roman Empire

The sophistication of the Etruscans *(71)* and other contemporary peoples is evident from the black lustrous ware known as "*bucchero*"; the ornate jewellery from the Tomb of a Taranto priestess c 350-340 BC; and a bronze cauldron and red figured cup from the Berone tomb 5C BC. A painted terracotta sarcophagus of a reclining female figure in flowing robes, bejewelled and holding a mirror, is a typical example of traditional funerary monuments. Hellenistic influence waned when the Etruscan city-states became allies of Rome before being assimilated into the Roman world by the 1C BC.

Portland Vase

Imperial Rome

Austere portraits *(70)* of patricians were intended to instil respect of authority. In the reign of Augustus, portraiture (statues, cameos, coins, mosaics) was used as propaganda: the bronze **Head of Augustus** (27 BC-AD 14) with staring eyes inlaid with marble and glass is remarkable. The **Portland Vase** is distinctive for its decorative technique.

Aspects of daily life *(69)* such as warfare, agriculture, commerce and religion are complemented by displays of glass, silver and jewellery.

COINS AND MEDALS

Up main stairs and through galleries 36 and 37.

Money

Coins and medals *(68)* provide valuable information about social, religious and political history; designs trace artistic development and images of rulers constitute a unique gallery of portraits. As prosperity grew base coins were replaced by precious metals. The comprehensive collection covers all areas of the world: cuneiform tablets from Ancient Mesopotamia, 7C BC coins from Turkey and China, treasure trove from Europe; paper money first used in China in 10C AD, paper denominations of international currencies, modern-day electronic transfer technology. The earliest English gold coin to be struck was the 'penny' minted during the reign of Henry III (1216-72) in 1257.

PREHISTORY AND ROMAN BRITAIN

Main stairs to upper level.

Stone Age to Celtic Britain

The evolution of man is traced from flints and implements *(37)* from major archaeological sites in Africa spanning 2 million years. Palaeolithic tools date human activity in Europe to some 700 000 years ago. A wide range of domestic objects indicate permanent settlements, crop cultivatation and domestication of animals in the Neolithic era.

In the Early Bronze Age the Beaker people produced fine pottery with geometric patterns and included rich grave goods in burials such as the **Folkton chalk "drums"** retrieved from a child's tomb in Yorkshire; the ribbed **Rillaton gold cup** from Cornwall. The reconstructed Barnack Barrow contained a large beaker, a dagger and other interesting artefacts. Gold ornaments from Ireland and Wales show original designs and exquisite craftsmanship. Displays of Bronze Age metalwork indicate trading patterns throughout Europe.

Celtic civilisation *(50)* flourished in the Iron Age: elegant bronze wine-flagons c 400 BC from Basse-Yutz, in France; splendid armour, mirrors and gold torcs. The dramatic Welwyn Garden City burial (1C BC), probably the tomb of a British chief, contained unique gaming pieces in glass. Swords, scabbards and shields (Witham, Battersea) were cast in rivers and lakes as offerings for the afterlife. The **Lindow Man** (1C AD), garotted and with his throat cut, preserved in a peat bog, is evidence of human sacrifices.

Roman Britain

(40) The Romans invaded Britain in AD 43 with the Emperors Claudius, Nero and Hadrian exerting the greatest influences. Treasures from Mildenhall, Thetford (gold jewellery, silver spoons), Lullingstone (wall paintings), Water Newton (silver vessels, votive offerings) provide a view of the lavish lifestyle enjoyed by the wealthier classes.

The Weston Gallery of Roman Britain *(49)* accommodates the largest permanent display of artefacts relating to Roman Britain, most notably the Mildenhall Treasure (fine silver dish and platters with dancing nymphs and gods and Bacchic motifs; artefacts with Christian symbols). To date the **Hoxne Hoard**, which comprises thousands of coins, jewellery and silver plate, acquired in 1994, is one of the finest treasure troves found in Britain (Suffolk). Other important displays include a building façade from Meonstoke in Hampshire and the Vindolanda writing tablets shedding a rare insight on Roman military life in the Border Country along Hadrian's Wall. The mosaic pavement from a Roman villa in Hinton St Mary shows the advance of Christian beliefs.

MEDIEVAL, RENAISSANCE AND MODERN COLLECTIONS

Up main stairs, through galleries 36 and 40.

The rich collections illustrate European art and archaeology and Christian and Jewish cultures from the Early Christian period to the modern age.

Foreign Influences

Among Anglo-Saxon and Norman antiquities (4C-11C) found in the British Isles *(41)* is the **Sutton Hoo Ship Burial** which shows the rich variety of artefacts retrieved from a royal tomb: fabulous gold jewellery, weapons and armour. A Viking hoard of silver was uncovered in Lancashire.

Religious and secular antiquities (9C-15C) from Western Europe and Byzantium *(42)* include icons, ivories, enamels, reliquaries, jewellery. The Franks Casket is carved with runic inscriptions, folk, historical and religious scenes. The mid-12C **Lewis Chessmen** are thought to be Scandinavian in origin. The hoard of 80 pieces carved from walrus ivory was found in 1831 buried in a sandbank on the Scottish Island of Lewis, in the Outer Hebrides. The fine carving of the **Lycurgus Cup** depicts a legendary king entwined in vine tendrils. A rare gittern (c 1300) is the only English medieval musical instrument in existence. Other outstanding exhibits include the **Paris Royal Gold Cup** (c 1380) decorated in *basse-taille* enamel; the early-15C Dunstable Swan Jewel, 15C Westminster Sword of State and the Savernake horn.

Lewis Chessman

The Ceramics Collection (7C-15C) *(43)* comprises fine examples of Early English tiles and pottery (13C-16C), Italian maiolica, Venetian glass, Dutch delft: Canynges pavement c 1461.

Clocks, watches, precision regulators (16C-20C) trace the evolution of mechanical timekeeping: the great astronomical **Strasbourg Clock** combining technical progress and decoration; the fascinating Prague-made **Ship Clock** (c 1585) with figures moving to music as the ship pitches and rolls, and a firing gun.

The splendid Waddesdon Bequest of Medieval and Renaissance treasures *(45)* includes a lovely reliquary for a thorn from Christ's crown made for the Duc de Berri (c 1400), jewellery and art objects of great craftsmanship.

Continental and British Applied Arts

A glittering array illustrates the craft of goldsmithing from the Renaissance to the end of the 18C: **Armada Service**; Wilding Bequest, **Lyte Jewel** (James I miniature); Limoges and Battersea enamels; 1554 iron shield, Royal seals; Huguenot silver. *(47)* 19C European ceramics (Wedgwood copy of the Portland Vase and jasperware) and glass: fabulous Hull Grundy Gift of jewellery, engraved gems and gold objects.

19C and 20C – *(48)* The Modern Gallery is dedicated to European and American decorative arts: examples of work by René Lalique, Christopher Dresser, CR Mackintosh, Henry van der Velde, Bauhaus.

EGYPTIAN ANTIQUITIES

Turn left from the main entrance and pass through the Asiatic galleries.

The superb collections illustrate the complex aspects of the glorious ancient Egyptian civilisation covering 6000 years of history and with particular emphasis on art, industry, religion and burial customs.

Egyptian Sculpture Gallery

The monumental sculptures *(4)* are of great historical interest. Kings were held as divine and they built great pyramids and temples as funerary monuments. Pride of place is given to the **Rosetta Stone** *(off the left wing)* which was the key to the decipherment of hieroglyphs. Painted limestone statues in a conventional pose (c 2400 BC) which were intended as abodes for the soul of the dead contrast with the realistic black granite statues of Sesostris III (1850 BC). The enigmatic expressions of the colossal statues of Amenophis III (c 1400 BC) and the head of a king or queen in green schist (c 1480 BC) are striking. The granite torsos of Ramesses II (c 1270 BC) exude power. Many deities are represented wholly or partially as animals such as the lion-headed figures of the goddess Sakhmet, the falcon-god Horus and the cow-headed Hathor. The granite lions from the reign of Amenophis III were temple door guardians. Obelisks, sarcophagi, votive offerings and inscribed stelae provide much interesting information.

Take the West stairs to the upper level.

An Important Find

The **Rosetta Stone** is part of a 6 foot block of black basalt found at Rashid or Rosetta in the Western Egyptian Delta region and retrieved by French soldiers on campaign there during the Napoleonic wars: with the Capitulation of Alexandria in 1801, the French were compelled to surrender the stone to the British: the stone went on show at the British Museum in 1802.

Its significance rests in the parallel transcriptions in Ancient Greek and two written forms of Egyptian of a decree passed on 27 March 196 BC: thereby Egyptologists were provided with the wherewithal to decipher pictorial hieroglyphs in use since the third millennium BC and the linguistics of Demotic texts formalised in 643 BC.

Egyptian Tombs *(first floor)*

The extraordinary fascination of funerary rituals remains undimmed. Mummies *(62, 63)* bandaged in cases and coffins, gilded and painted, include the preserved remains of humans, birds and animals, shedding light on the social rituals (amulets, clothing, hairstyles) and scientific advancements (artificial eyes) of the times. Tomb paintings and papyri are informative records. The Book of the Dead is a collection of spells to give the deceased safe passage through the Underworld to Heaven. Tombs also included artefacts associated with daily life: furniture, farming implements, turned stone vessels, musical instruments, furniture.

Galleries *(64-65)* dedicated to Early Egypt up to the Age of the Pyramids explore its relationship with neighbouring Africa (Nubia) and the introduction of Coptic Orthodox Christianity. "Ginger", a 5 000-year-old corpse that predates mummification practices, is surrounded by pots containing food and drink for the spirit's journey to Heaven. Cosmetic vessels and toilet articles reveal the interest of Ancient Egyptians in their appearance.

WESTERN ASIATIC ANTIQUITIES

Turn left from the main entrance.

The ancient lands of Mesopotamia and Asia Minor were the cradle of great cultures. From 3500 BC to the 7C AD successive empires controlled large territories from Egypt to Iran and from Anatolia into Arabia.

Assyrian Sculpture

Fabled kings built splendid palaces and temples lavishly decorated with statues and reliefs *(6-10, 88-89)*. Military campaigns are commemorated on carved slabs lining palace walls in the Assyrian capital cities of Nimrud, Khorsabad and Nineveh. Narrative scenes present a detailed contemporary picture: panels depicting the horses of Sennacherib; bas-reliefs of lion-hunts and banqueting scenes from Ashurbanipal's palace at Nineveh. Colossal stone statues of human-headed bulls and lions *(6)* guarded doorways to give magic protection to the king, and relief carvings *(10)* adorned the entrance of the Palace of Sargon at Khorsabad. The stone statue of Ashurbanipal II from Nimrud *(6)* shows the king in ritual dress and carrying a mace. A black obelisk (c 825 BC) depicts the victories of the king of Assyria and rulers paying tribute.

Take the East or West stairs for access to the north side of the first floor.

Palmyra and South Arabia

The prosperous city of Palmyra dominated the trading route between the Syrian coast and important Mesopotamian territories. Portrait heads from imposing tombs *(51)* are evocative contemporary images.

South Arabian territories (North and South Yemen) had their own alphabetic script which is inscribed on monuments, and a primitive style of sculpture illustrated by a bronze altar with bull's heads and sphinxes.

Ancient Iran

The rich artistic tradition of the Persian Empire is evident in metalwork and pottery *(52)*. The elaborate decoration of the **Luristan bronzes** c 1200 BC and a silver drinking horn with a griffin base is exceptional. The fabulous **Oxus Treasure** (5C-4C BC) attests to the wealth and sophistication of the Achaemenid court: gold armlet with winged and bird-headed creatures; chariot drawn by four horses. The Cyrus cylinder and reliefs (6C-5C BC) are important records from Persepolis, an imperial capital. Gold and silver ware (arms, vessels) from the Sassanian dynasty (3C-7C AD) show remarkable craftsmanship.

Ancient Turkey and Iraq

Antiquities (6000-536 BC) of Anatolia, notably of the Hittite and Urartian kingdoms *(53-54)* reveal Assyrian influence: bronzes from Urartu (9C-7C BC), Ararat (c 700 BC), Carchemish (10C-8C BC).

The collections relating to Early and Late Mesopotamia *(55-56)* illustrate the arts and daily life of the Sumerians and Babylonians. Cuneiform tablets from Nineveh *(56)* record events as well as information on all aspects of community life: The **Flood Tablet** tells a story from the Epic of Gilgamesh. The Chaldees treasure comprises jewellery, "lyres" and artefacts excavated from the Royal Cemetery at Ur (c 2600 BC). A curious Ram in a Thicket was probably used as a table support. The **Standard of Ur** bears mosaic scenes of war and peace.

The Ancient Levant

Rooms 57-59. Syrian civilisation flourished during the third and second millennium BC and exerted considerable political influence. An impressive statue of King Idrimi (16C BC) with eyes and eyebrows inlaid with black stone is in an austere and simplistic style.

Ancient Palestine was an important trading centre as evidenced by finds of pottery, fine jewellery, ivories, ossuaries, metalwork.

The Phoenicians established settlements throughout the Mediterranean as evidenced from stelae inscribed in Punic script They were renowned for their fine metalwork, jewellery and glass. A fine collection of ivories includes a delicately carved plaque of a Lion killing an African (8C BC).

ETHNOGRAPHIC COLLECTIONS

While work is being undertaken to create new galleries *(completion date 2003)*, temporary exhibitions will continue to feature a range of artefacts from the collections.

The **Wellcome Gallery of Ethnography**, the centrepiece of the Ethnography Galleries, will introduce cultural themes linking diverse societies explored in greater depth in specialised galleries.

Americas

Before the Spanish Conquest important civilisations in Mexico, Guatemala and adjacent countries were well organised and culturally sophisticated *(27)*. Elaborate jade and greenstone objects were highly prized by the Olmecs and the Mayas. The Maya pyramids decorated with superb stone sculpture and stuccowork (stelae, lintels, altars) date from the Classic period (c 4C-10C AD). The Huaxtec people (10C-15C AD) from the Gulf Coast and the Aztecs from central Mexico produced fine ceramics and sculpture. Masks, a knife, animal carvings and serpent ornaments in turquoise mosaic are outstanding.

Exhibits illustrate the life, customs and arts of the Native peoples of North America *(26)* – Inuit Indians and Eskimos, Cherokee, Iroquois, Navajo, and peoples from the pueblos of New Mexico. The simple materials (early Cherokee basket, gourd rattle) are indicative of a nomadic lifestyle: simple hunting and fishing equipment; feather ornaments, blankets, rugs; hides decorated with embroidery and painted designs.

Easter Island Statue

From the 17C onwards contacts were made with explorers and colonists. Masks, feast bowls and ceremonial weapons and clothing date from the late 18C.

In the east stairwell stands a **Canadian Totem pole**, 88 steps high.

Take the stairs down from Room 24 on the north side.

Africa

The galleries *(25)* explore the interaction of past and present African cultures to reflect the vitality and diversity of the continent ranging from North Africa to Madagascar. Highlights include the magnificent 16C Benin bronzes, a brass head, masks and carvings from Nigeria; Asante goldwork from Ghana, 16C Afro-Portuguese ivories. The styles of wood carvings are varied: masks of the Dogon of Mali, figure sculpture of the Bamana people, helmet masks from Sierra Leone. West Africa is represented by masks, textiles, pottery and domestic objects. Three kingly figures from Congo (Zaire) with emblems carved on the plinths date from the 18C; geometric patterns on decorative objects are distinctive. Beadwork is favoured by the peoples of Eastern and Southern Africa. Patterns and motifs distinguish textiles from the various regions. Textiles, charms and jewellery from Madagascar show influences from Asia and Africa.

PRINTS AND DRAWINGS

National Collection of Western Graphic Art

(90) Special exhibitions only are mounted from the extensive collection of drawings, watercolours, etchings, prints, engravings, lithographs from the 15C to modern times: works available include those by the likes of Pollaiuolo, Botticelli, Leonardo da Vinci, Bellini, Michelangelo, Tiepolo, Piranesi; Dürer, Hans Holbein, Bosch, Rubens, Rembrandt; Claude, Watteau, Ingres, Rousseau, Corot, Bonnard, Matisse, Picasso; Goya; Gainsborough, Turner, Blake, Henry Moore, Piper, Sutherland...

ORIENTAL ANTIQUITIES

Ground floor, by the Montague Place entrance.

Islamic Art

Antiquities from the Islamic collections *(34)* range from decorative pottery with geometric designs and arabesques, glass carved in relief and mosaic glass to inlaid and engraved metalwork: tiles from Isfahan (Iran), Iznik pottery from Turkey, lustreware from Spain, Egyptian enamelled glass mosque lamps, filigree and enamel jewellery. Among treasures from the Mughal Empire which combined Muslim and Hindu cultures are a large jade tortoise (17C), jade vessels, weapons with precious handles, and jewellery set with precious stones.

Take the North stairs to Level 5.

Korea

The Arts of Korea *(67)*, which testify to the creativity of its people, were strongly marked by the Chinese and Buddhist traditions: gold crown (Silla kingdom 5C-6C), Buddhist art (ceramics) and manuscripts (Amitabha Sutra) dating from 10C to 14C. From 15C onwards Confucianism influenced society: portraits of scholars and high-ranking men.

China, South and South-east Asia

The Joseph E Hotung Gallery *(33)* displays sculptures from the South and South-East Asia: arranged chronologically are Chinese bronzes, exquisite jades (from 3500 BC), ceramics that became mass-produced and diffused throughout Asia to the West. Stylistically, the early pieces show homogeneity from 200 BC when a centralised state had been forged by the first emperor (who built the Great Wall and was buried with the legendary terracotta army). A Tang period tomb group (8C AD) is complete with representation of horses traded along the Silk Route to Baghdad; silver that may have inspired forms used by potters. Imperial patronage flourished with an ever more sophisticated court culture until the 20C when it was shattered by Communism.

Buddhism, introduced from India, was quickly embraced by the leaders of the Chinese state but followers still incurred brutal persecution. Elsewhere: early Buddhist art from Gandhara (modern Pakistan) reflects the prolific generation of followers from the 5C BC. Pieces in the **Asahi Shimbun Gallery** *(33a)* are from the Great Buddhist Stupa at Amaravati in southeast India. In the main gallery, exquisite interpretations come from Nepal, Tibet and Sri Lanka. The **Hindu** god Shiva with his consort Parvati are accompanied by followers: Ganesh, Vishnu...

Take the North stairs to level 5.

Japan

This isolated country was slow to be affected by influences from Asian countries and Western civilisation. Buddhism was introduced in the mid-6C. Society was strictly regulated and its complexity is reflected in the arts. Fine laquerware, mother-of-pearl inlaid objects and porcelain with enamelled decoration were prized export goods. An interesting collection of netsuke – belt ornaments – *(92)* and the classic teawares associated with the famous tea ceremony ritual are on permanent display. The main Japanese gallery *(93)* and the Konica Gallery *(94)* exhibit variable arrangements of objects from the large Japanese collection.

Buckingham Palace★★

The ceremonial heart of London is a focal point for Londoners and visitors alike. State occasions are marked with the pomp and circumstance associated with the sovereign and people congregate at the palace when national events arouse strong emotions.

Location

Map p 11 (DEY); Michelin Atlas London: pp 44-45. ⊖ Green Park; St James's Park. South of the palace is Westminster with Trafalgar Sq to the north-east and St James's and Piccadilly to the north. Constitution Hill leads to Hyde Park and Knightsbridge to the west.

Adjacent Sights: ST JAMES'S, TRAFALGAR SQUARE – WHITEHALL; KNIGHTSBRIDGE – BELGRAVIA.

Background

Mulberry Garden to Royal Palace – In 1703 a piece of land at the west end of St James's Park, partly planted the previous century by **James I** as a mulberry garden, was granted by Queen Anne to John Sheffield, newly created Duke of Buckingham, who built a town residence of brick, named Buckingham House. In 1762 the property was purchased for £28 000 by **George III**, presented to his bride, Charlotte, and renamed Queen's House.

In 1825 **John Nash** was commissioned by **George IV** to turn the house into a palace. He enclosed the core of the old brick mansion in a cladding of Bath stone, added a grand entrance portico and a range of rooms along the west front overlooking the garden. The king died however in 1830 before the alterations were complete. The work was completed by Edward Blore in 1837, by which time William IV also had died. Three weeks after her accession **Victoria** took up residence and at last the royal standard flew on the **Marble Arch** which Nash had designed as a state entrance to the open forecourt.

Ten years later a new east range enclosed the courtyard linking the advanced north and south wings; it contains the famous balcony, where members of the Royal Family greet the crowds massed in the Mall on state occasions. Marble

Arch, being superfluous, was removed in 1851 to the north-east corner of Hyde Park. The private apartments of the Royal Family are in the north range.

St James's Park – Henry VIII acquired St James's Park in 1532 when he exchanged a building occupied by a community founded before the Conquest as a "spittle for mayden lepers" for land in Suffolk. According to the 16C antiquarian **Stow**, the king demolished the hospital and "built there a goodly manor, annexing thereunto a park, closed about with a wall of brick, now called St James's Park, serving indifferently to the said manor and to the manor or palace of White Hall". In Tudor times the park was stocked with deer.

James I established a menagerie of animals and exotic birds. **Charles II** aligned aviaries along what came to be called Birdcage Walk and had the park laid out according to the fashionable goosefoot *(patte d'oie)* design. The marshy ponds were systematised into an east-west canal from the west end of which extended two avenues – one along the line of the Mall towards the houses of Charing village.

In the 19C Nash designed a project for the park's improvement, with terraces as in Regent's Park; only **Carlton House Terrace** was built. Nash replaced the wall by iron railings and landscaped the park itself, planting trees and shrubs and transforming the long water into a lake with islands.

Highlights

Buckingham Palace**

Tour: 1 hour. ♿ *Open Aug to 28-Sep, daily, 9.30am-4.30pm (4.15pm last admission); timed ticket. £12. Brochure (6 languages).* ☎ *020 7321 2233; buckinghampalace @royalcollection.org.uk; www.royal.gov.uk*

The interior presents the suite of state rooms designed by John Nash, examples of the later Edwardian taste which replaced the polychrome decor of Victoria's reign, reminders of Britain's imperial past and treasures from the Royal Collection, many of which were originally acquired by George IV for **Carlton House**: magnificent and rare Sèvres porcelain, ornate 18C French clocks and furniture, royal portraits and chandeliers.

From the Ambassadors' Entrance pass into the courtyard dominated by the entrance portico; the pediment bears carvings of Britannia in her chariot. The Entrance Hall leads to the **Grand Staircase**, lit by a domed skylight of 80 etched panes. 18C Gobelins tapestries and magnificent chandeliers adorn the **Guard Room**. The **Green Drawing Room**, which has an extravagant coved white and gold plaster ceiling and a gilded frieze, contains two splendid 18C cabinets inlaid with panels of *pietre dure.* Red and gold predominate in the **Throne Room**; the ceiling is decorated with shields bearing the coats of arms of England, Scotland, Ireland and Hanover and a frieze depicts the Wars of the Roses. Winged genii holding garlands frame the canopy; the two chairs were used at the Coronation (1953) by the Queen and the Duke of Edinburgh.

In the **Picture Gallery** hang masterpieces from the Royal Collection: by Van Dyck *(Charles I)*, Rembrandt and Frans Hals (expressive portraits), Van de Velde (seascapes), Vermeer (*A Lady at the Virginals* – an intimate scene) and Rubens (remarkable pastoral and religious scenes) among other major artists.

On the west front are the state rooms: the **Dining Room**, resplendent in red and gold and adorned with royal portraits (*George IV* with his hand resting on the Commanders' Table – *see below,* which was commissioned by Napoleon in 1806 and presented to George IV by Louis XVIII in 1817). In the **Blue Drawing Room** Shakespeare, Milton and Spenser are commemorated in the ceiling arches. The

View of Buckingham Palace from the lake in St James's Park

A. Tavernier/MICHELIN

decor is articulated by 30 columns in imitation onyx topped by gilded Corinthian capitals. Here stands the **Commanders' Table**, decorated with the head of Alexander the Great surrounded by 12 commanders of Antiquity, in hard-paste Sèvres porcelain with gilt-bronze mounts. The gilded ceiling of the **Music Room** features the rose of England, the thistle of Scotland and the shamrock of Ireland with a border of fleur-de-lys; it is matched by a marquetry floor. In the ornate **White Drawing Room** the Corinthian pilasters, embellished with the Star and Garter, the gilt-bronze candelabras, a piano in a gilt case painted with figures and a roll-top desk by Riesener are of special interest.

Two graceful sculptures by Canova, *Mars and Venus* and *A Fountain Nymph* (by the Ministers' Stairs and Marble Hall), are noteworthy. The **Bow Room** is named after the Bow porcelain in the display cases rather than the bow window.

From the garden, where traditional garden parties are held in summer, there is a superb view of the west front of the palace. The lawns extend to the magnificent herbaceous borders and a lake.

Changing the Guard

The ceremony takes place in the forecourt when the sovereign is in residence and the Royal Standard flies over the palace. The guard is mounted by the five regiments of Foot of the Guards Division. Their uniform of dark blue trousers, scarlet tunic and great bearskin is distinguished by badges, buttons and insignia: the Grenadiers (f 1656) by a white plume and buttons evenly spaced; the Coldstreams (f 1650) by a scarlet plume and buttons in pairs; the Scots (f 1642) by no plume and buttons in threes; the Irish (f 1900) by a blue plume and buttons in fours; the Welsh (f 1915) by a green and white plume and buttons in fives.

Takes place usually May to early-Aug daily at 11.30am; otherwise alternate days at 11.30am. ☎ 020 7414 2497.

Royal Mews★★

Open Mar-Oct, daily, 11am-4pm (3.15pm last admission); Aug-Sep, daily, 10am-5pm (4.15pm last admission). £5. ☎ 020 7321 2233; buckinghampalace@royalcollection.org.uk; www.royal.gov.uk

Apart from the earlier Riding House (1764), the mews were built by Nash. A lion and unicorn gate leads to a Classical archway, topped by a small clock tower. The blocks around the square, tree-shaded courtyard house stables, harness rooms and coach houses, where the equipages vary in splendour from modest, covered two-wheelers to the open state landau, the Glass Coach in which royal brides and bridegrooms return from the church ceremony, the Irish Coach in which the Queen rides at the State Opening of Parliament and the gold State Coach (1762) which has been used at every coronation since 1820.

The frieze (6 panels, 129ft/39m long) depicts the Coronation procession of William IV and Queen Adelaide in 1831.

In the **Queen's Gallery** are mounted small temporary exhibitions of treasures drawn from the Royal collections (Holbein watercolours, Leonardo da Vinci drawings). The entrance hall is a modern addition in a sensitive style. *Open daily, 10am-5.30pm (4.30pm last admission). Timed ticket, £6.50. ☎ 020 7321 2233; buckinghampalace @royalcollection.org.uk; www.royal.gov.uk*

Wellington Barracks

On the south side of the parade ground stand the Wellington Barracks, built in 1833 by Sir Francis Smith and Philip Hardwick.

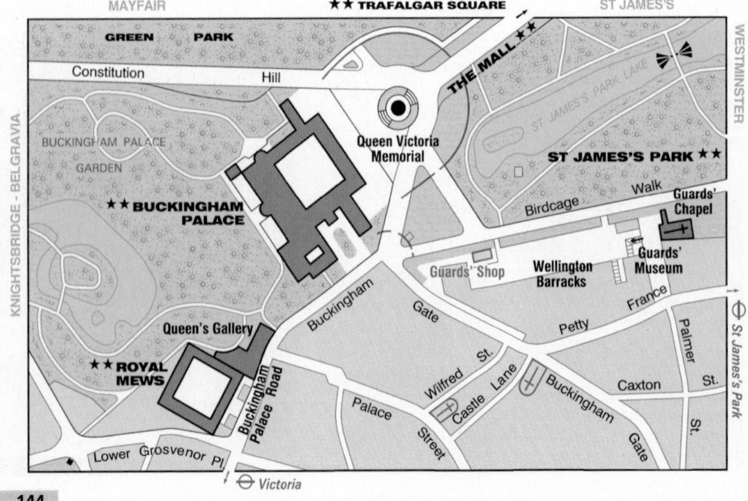

Guards' Museum – Dioramas, weapons, trophies, uniforms, memorabilia, documents and paintings tell the history of the Guards Regiments from their Civil War origins to the present day, of their military campaigns and their historic role in guarding the sovereign.

Guards' Chapel – The chapel dates from 1963. The lofty clean-lined interior is of white marble with clear glass lancet windows opposing brightly lit memorial chapels aligned in a cloister along the south wall. Above hang regimental colours. Note the engraved side chapel windows and the terracotta frieze in the Household Cavalry chapel. The screens in the choir arch and the dark apse, lined with mosaic, are all that remains of the 19C chapel, which was destroyed by a flying bomb in June 1944 killing over 120 people.

Museum and Chapel: ♿ Open (except some ceremonial days) early-Feb to late-Dec, daily, 10am-4pm; check by phone. £2. ☎ 020 7414 3271; Fax 020 7414 3411; www.army.mod.uk

Walking About

St James's Park★★

London's oldest park *(see above)* is known today for its brilliant flower borders and for the pelicans and wildfowl on the lake. It is an ideal place for a break from the busy pace of city life: take a stroll in the fresh air and watch the Guards march by on their way to Horse Guards; in summer relax on the grass, soak up the sun and enjoy rousing band music.

From the bridge there are **views** of Buckingham Palace and Whitehall.

PRIZED BIRDS

St James's Park pelicans have a long-standing history: the first one, from Astrakhan, was a gift to Charles II given by a Russian ambassador – it promptly flew off and was shot over Norfolk. Peter from Karachi stayed 54 years before emigrating, no one knows where. The present pair of *Pelecanus onocrotalus* were acquired from Prague Zoo.

The Mall★★

The Mall was first traced at the time of the Stuarts (17C). In 1910 it was transformed into a processional way by **Sir Aston Webb** who designed the **Queen Victoria Memorial**, a white marble monument comprising a seated figure of the Queen facing east and a gilded bronze victory at the summit. **George V** was the first monarch to ride along the Mall to his coronation.

At the far end, the thoroughfare stretches straight past a statue of Captain Cook, through Admiralty Arch to Trafalgar Square, while the processional route leads right to **Horse Guards** *(see TRAFALGAR SQUARE – WHITEHALL)*. The pebble and flint Citadel on the park side of Admiralty Arch served as the operational centre for **Churchill**, the cabinet and chiefs of staff from 1939 to 1945.

The north side is flanked by **Green Park** and **Carlton Terrace** *(see ST JAMES'S)*.

Colourful Pageantry

Ph. Gajic/MICHELIN

WHEN WE WERE VERY YOUNG

"'They're changing the guard
at Buckingham Palace -
Christopher Robin went down with Alice.
A face looked out but it wasn't the King's.
'He's much too busy a-signing things'
Says Alice"'

A A Milne

Chancery Lane★

The character of the area bounded by High Holborn and Fleet Street is defined by the ancient traditions of the Inns of Court. Take the time to wander through the hidden alleyways to discover the fascinating history that underlies modern sites and stresses continuity through the ages. Leafy squares provide a haven from the bustling crowds attending to business or visiting modern shopping centres.

Location

Map p 12 or 13 (EFX); Michelin Atlas London: p 79. ⊖ Holborn; Chancery Lane. This area is to the north of Fleet St and west of the City of London.

Adjacent Sights: BLOOMSBURY, CLERKENWELL, The CITY, STRAND – TEMPLE.

Background

During the Middle Ages, this area depended upon the manors of Holborn around the palace of the **Bishop of Ely**, flanked by a market and surrounded by open fields on which beasts grazed, archery was practised, duels were fought and washing laid out to dry. By the late 16C the four **Inns of Court** and dependent (now defunct) **Inns of Chancery** had been established for nearly 300 years as the country's great law societies. Litigation was a serious business; there were endless disputes on land entitlement and inheritance while actions for slurs and insults, real or imagined, were also a fashionable and obsessive pastime indulged in by many. They offered a lucrative field which was also a good stepping stone to high office; from the 16C there were some 2 000 students dining in the halls.

Chancery Lane runs along the border of the City, a mediator between the realms of government and commerce *(see INSIGHTS AND IMAGES – Historical Perspective)*.

Directory

Light Bite

Cafe at the Crypt – *St Etheldreda's Church, EC1N 6RY – ⊖ Chancery Lane – ☎ 020 7405 1061 – Open Mon-Fri noon-2.30pm.* A pleasant place for a break with freshly cooked food and light refreshments.

Pubs

Cittie of York – *22-23 High Holburn, Holburn, WC1V 6BS – ⊖ Chancery Lane – ☎ 020 7242 7670 – Open Mon-Sat 11.30am-11pm.* This inn dating from 1667 is a true delight. A pleasant room at the front and the nave of a church at the back with tall columns, pointed arches, confession boxes for repentance and a bar to seek sanctuary in.

The Seven Stars – *53 Carey St, WC2A 2JB – ⊖ Holborn – ☎ 020 7242 8521 – nathan.silver@ntlworld.com – Open Mon-Sat 11am-11pm; closed bank hols.* A really charming pub dating from 1602. Large lawyer, musician and student clientele.

Ye Olde Mitre – *1 Ely Court, Ely Place, EC1N 6SJ – ⊖ Chancery Lane, Farringdon – ☎ 020 7405 4751 – Open Mon-Fri 11am-11pm. Closed Bank Hol.* This historic 16C pub was once part of a bishop's residence. Surviving among modern buildings and large avenues in the very heart of London, this small picturesque establishment with irregular shaped rooms is well worth the visit.

Events and Festivals

The **Feast of St Etheldreda** is celebrated annually with a street fair, Strawberrie Fayre *(Saturday nearest to 23 June).*

Walking About

From Holborn Station walk down Kingsway and turn left after a church to Lincoln's Inn Fields.

Lincoln's Inn Fields

By 1650 a developer, who had purchased the common fields to the west of Lincoln's Inn 20 years before, had surrounded them on three sides with houses. Of that period, one, **Lindsey House**, remains, probably designed by Inigo Jones (since divided, nos 59-60, west side). The brickwork was originally all exposed, giving greater emphasis to the segmental pediment, the accented window and giant, wreathed pilasters. 18C houses in the square include the Palladian style nos 57-58 dating from 1730, no 66, **Powis House** of 1777, with a pediment marking the centre window. On the north side nos 1-2 are early 18C, 5-9 Georgian, and no 15 with an Ionic columned doorway, frieze and pediment, mid-18C.

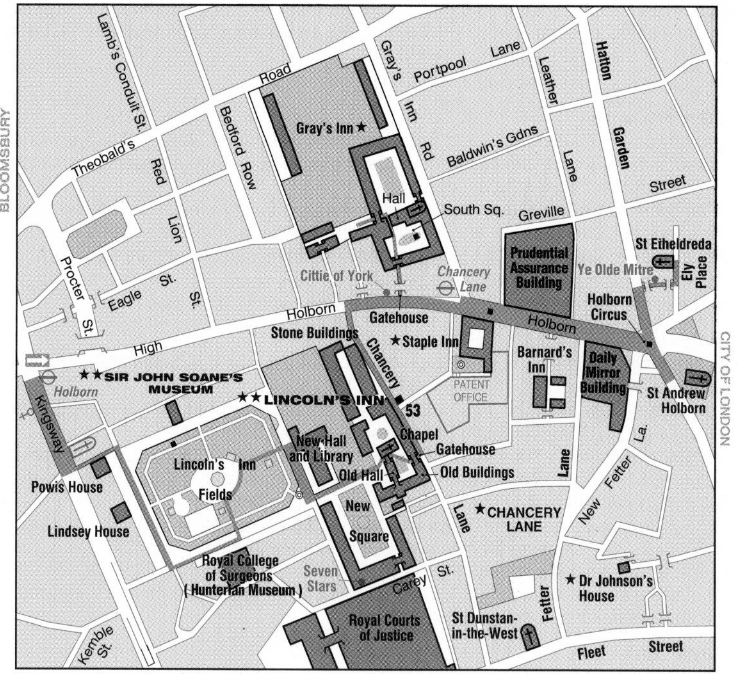

On the north side of the square is the unusual Sir John Soane's Museum *(description in Worth a Visit)*. The square's south side is occupied by official buildings: the neo-Jacobean Land Registry, neo-Georgian **Nuffield College of Surgical Sciences** (1956-58), 19C-20C **Royal College of Surgeons**, housing the **Hunterian Museum** dedicated to the study of pathology and anatomy. ♿ *Closed for refurbishment until end of 2004. Open previously Mon-Fri, 10am-5pm. ☎ 020 7869 6560; Fax 020 7869 6564; museums@rcseng.ac.uk; www.rcseng.ac.uk/museums*

The half-timbered building on the corner of Portsmouth Street is said to date back to the late 1500s and may be one of the oldest in London.

Walk through the square and turn right to the porter's lodge.

Lincoln's Inn★★

Grounds: Open Mon-Fri, 9am-5.30pm (5pm Fri). Closed Sat-Sun and Bank Hols. Chapel: Open Mon-Fri, noon-2.30pm. Old Hall, New Hall and Library: Guided tour (minimum 15; £2 per head) on written application to the Assistant Under Treasurer, Lincoln's Inn, London WC2A 3TL. ☎ 020 7405 1393; Fax 020 7831 1839; mail@lincolnsinn.org.uk; www.lincolnsinn.org.uk

The site belonged to the Dominicans until 1276, when they moved to Blackfriars, before being acquired by the Earl of Lincoln who built himself a large, walled mansion which he bequeathed as a residential college, or inn, for young lawyers.

Buildings – These are mainly of brick with some stone decoration and date from the late 15C. The self-contained collegiate plan of intercommunicating courts is entered through a main gateway and the surroundings are enhanced by beautiful gardens with an ornate Gothic toolshed.

By Lincoln's Inn Fields is **New Square**, built in 1680 with identical four-storey ranges with broken pediments above the doors and incorporating in the south range an archway to Carey Street, wide and ornate with differing pediments on either side.

The **Stone Buildings** date from 1775-80. The red-brick mid-19C **New Hall** and **Library** are diapered in the Tudor manner.

The **Old Hall**, with paired bay windows at either end, dates from 1490. Inside modern linenfold panelling complements an early-17C oak screen, which is notable especially for the busts carved on the end pilasters; the painting *St Paul before Felix* (1748) is by Hogarth.

The stone-faced **Chapel**, which is raised on an open undercroft, was rebuilt in 1619-23 and endowed later in the 19C with pinnacles and extensions at the west end. John Donne laid the first foundation stone and preached at the consecration. In the windows, benchers and treasurers since the Middle Ages are commemorated by their arms and names: Thomas More, Thomas Cromwell, Pitt, Walpole, Newman, Canning, Disraeli, Gladstone, Asquith...

The gabled brick buildings immediately south of the court, known as the **Old Buildings**, are Tudor in style (redone in 1609). The **gatehouse** on Chancery Lane, built of brick with square corner towers and a four-centred arch filled with the original massive oak doors, dates from 1518. Above the arch are the arms of Henry VIII, the Earl of Lincoln and Sir Thomas Lovell.

Pass through the gate and walk north along Chancery Lane.

Chancery Lane

The lane, which takes its name from the grant of land by **Henry III** to his Lord Chancellor, Bishop of Chichester in 1227 (hence Rolls Passage, Bishop's Court etc.), is now commercial as well as legal.

At no **53** the **London Silver Vaults** comprising some 40 rooms, entered through a strong-room door, present an almost blinding array of Georgian, Victorian and modern silver and silverplate. ♿ *Open Mon-Sat, 9am-5.30pm (1pm Sat). Closed Good Fri to Easter Mon and Bank Hols. Information Bureau.* ☎ 020 7242 3844

In High Holborn turn right, cross the road and pass under a wide arch.

Gray's Inn★

Gardens: Open Mon-Fri, noon-2.30pm. Closed Bank Holidays. Squares: Open Mon-Fri, 9am-5pm.

Gray's Inn dates from the 14C in its foundation and from the 16C in its buildings, many of which, however, have had to be renewed since the war.

The main entrance is through the **Gatehouse** of 1688. **South Square**, which, except for no 1 of 1685, has been entirely rebuilt, has at its centre an elegant bronze statue of **Sir Francis Bacon**, the Inn's most illustrious member.

The gardens, delighted in by **Pepys** and **Joseph Addison**, were considered by many, besides Charles Lamb, to be "the best gardens of the Inns of Court". The very fine wrought-iron garden gateway is early 18C.

The hall, which was burnt out, has been rebuilt in its 16C style with stepped gables at either end and late Perpendicular tracery.

Staple Inn★

Lying just inside the limits of the City, Staple Inn was one of the Inns of Chancery where law students spent their first year studying. Originally the home of wool merchants, it became a dependent of Gray's Inn.

Rare view of medieval London – half-timbered buildings, Staple Inn, Holborn

Ph. Gajic/MICHELIN

For the row of half-timbered houses to have survived on such a site since 1586-96, when they were built, seems incredible: true they have been restored (19C) and the backs rebuilt (1937) but their overall character remains, providing some insight into the appearance of the pre-Fire City. The west house of two gables is the taller with two floors overhanging; the east range has five gables each marked by an oriel and again two floors overhanging. An arched entrance at the centre leads to the Inn surrounding a central courtyard at the rear. The east and west red-brick ranges were erected in the 18C. Much of the rest has had to be rebuilt, including parts of the hall which dates from 1581 and possesses an original hammerbeam roof.

Barnard's Inn

Once an Inn of Chancery, it was rebuilt in the 19C; the Great Hall has 16C linenfold panelling and heraldic stained glass. It is now home to **Gresham College** *(see The CITY – Guildhall)*, an institution that dates back over 400 years.

Continue to Holborn Circus.

Holborn Circus is now punctuated by a traffic island with a statue of Prince Albert, mounted and with hat aloft.

The **Daily Mirror Building** is marked by a curtain wall of stone (170ft/52m high), elbowed by yet taller buildings of glass extending south between Fetter and New Fetter Lanes (1957-60). Still within the City boundary, on the site of Furnival's Inn, stands the **Prudential Assurance Building**, an all red building designed by Alfred Waterhouse at the turn of the century for the Pru.

St Andrew Holborn

Open Mon-Fri, 9am-5pm. ☎ 020 7583 7394; Fax 020 7583 3488; guildchurch @standrewholborn.org.uk

The City church escaped the Fire but was rebuilt nevertheless. Saxon, Norman and 15C churches all stood on the site; by the 17C, however, the medieval church had fallen into decay. Wren designed a long basilica of stone with windows in two tiers, a square tower with angle buttresses and a crowning balustrade.

The restored interior is once more panelled complete with pillars which support the gallery and continue as Corinthian columns to the green and gold ceiling, and a stained-glass lunette at the east end. At the west end, in a recess, is the tomb, delightful with its shy child, of **Thomas Coram** (d 1751), sea captain and parishioner *(see BLOOMSBURY, The Foundling Museum)*. The font (1804), the pulpit (1752), and the case and organ presented to Coram by **Handel** in 1750 are of interest.

Cross the circus.

Hatton Garden

Ely Place recalls the Bishop of Ely's town house in Holborn, alluded to by Richard, Duke of Gloucester: "My lord of Ely, when I was last in Holborn, I saw good strawberries in your garden there, I do beseech you send for some of them" (*Richard III*; 3 iv). From 1381 when the **Savoy Palace** was burnt down until his death in 1399, the house was the residence of **John of Gaunt**, who converted it into a minor palace, visited over the years by many monarchs.

In 1576 the property, which extended from Holborn to Hatton Wall and from Leather Lane *(daily market)* to **Saffron Hill**, was given at Queen Elizabeth's command to **Sir Christopher Hatton**, her "dancing Chancellor" for a yearly rent of 10 pounds, a red rose and 10 loads of hay. Hatton, whose portion included the famous garden, built a fine house and made such improvements that when he died in 1591 he was in debt to the crown for £40 000. The third Christopher Hatton, who followed **Charles II** into exile, sold the property to builders who erected slum tenements.

The property deteriorated, except when leased (1620-24) to the Spanish Ambassador as his residence. Under the Commonwealth, Ely Place became a prison and a military hospital (1643); a century later the property was purchased through the crown by a Mr Cole who demolished the hall and built the pleasant four-storey brick terrace, with pilastered straight hooded doorways, which still lines the east side of Ely Place.

The Garden, built up in the 1680s, is today the centre of diamond merchants and jewellery craftsmen. Half way down are the **London Diamond Club** *(no 87, west side)* – a white stucco house six bays wide with a triangular, pedimented door and, on the opposite side, a former church *(no 43)*, attributed to Wren, built in 1666 by Lord Hatton. In 1696 it became a Charity School and figures of 17C charity schoolchildren still flank the pedimented doorway.

Early history is recalled in the name of the **Mitre Tavern** *(see Directory)* in Ely Court, a narrow alley leading east from Hatton Garden.

St Etheldreda's

Open daily, 8am-6pm. ☎ 020 7405 1061; Fax 020 7405 7440; kitcunningham @stetheldreda.com

The church was built as a chapel attached to the Bishop of Ely's house; St Etheldreda was the founder of Ely Cathedral. By the early 17C the crypt had become "a public cellar to sell drink in". Mr Cole retained the church for his tenants but stripped it of such medieval furnishings as remained. In 1873 Ely Place again came up for auction and the church became the first pre-Reformation shrine in the country to be transferred to Roman Catholics. It is owned by the Rosminian Order. Subjected to neglect and wartime bombing, little of the 13C building remains but the outer walls and undercroft. New stained-glass windows depict the five English martyrs beneath Tyburn gallows and on the aisles the arms of the pre-Reformation bishops of Ely: note the four cardinals' hats. Against the east wall is a carved medieval wood reliquary. The **crypt** (which houses a café, *see Directory*) has bare masonry walls (8ft/2.5m thick), modern abstract single-colour windows, blackened medieval roof timbers, a floor of London paving stones. The six supporting roof columns were placed down the chamber's centre in the 19C.

Worth a Visit

Sir John Soane's Museum**

13 Lincoln's Inn Fields. ♿ Open Tue-Sat, 10am-5pm; first Tue of each month, 6pm-9pm. Closed Bank Hols, 24 Dec. Guided tour: Sat at 2.30pm (£3; no booking; 22 tickets given out from 2pm). Library and drawings collection available to scholars by appointment. ☎ 020 7405 2107; Fax 020 7831 3957; www.soane.org

In 1833 Soane obtained a private Act of Parliament to ensure the perpetuation of the museum after his death. A stipulation was that nothing should be altered in any way, so the house and collections are of interest not only in their own right but as an insight into the particular mind of a British connoisseur and collector of that period.

He acquired as his town house no 12 Lincoln's Inn Fields in 1792, no 13 in 1805 as his museum and in 1824 he built no 14.

Sir John Soane (1753-1837)

Born the son of a country builder, Soane made his way through his talent: he worked under **George Dance** Junior and **Henry Holland**; he won prizes and a travelling scholarship to Italy (1777-80) while at the Royal Academy where, in later years, he was Professor of Architecture. He held the important office of Surveyor to the Bank of England (1788-1833) for which he executed the most original designs ever made for a bank.

Interior – The rooms are small, passages narrow, the stairs not "grand" (note the wedge shape of the stairs in no 13 following the line of the house site), but recessed and angled mirrors, rooflights and windows on inner courts, ceilings slightly arched and decorated with only a narrow border or, as in the breakfast room of no 12, painted to resemble an arbour, give an illusion of space and perspective. Fragments, casts and models are displayed high and low throughout the galleries, while below ground are the Crypt, the Gothic Monk's Parlour and the Sepulchral Chamber containing the intricately incised sarcophagus of the Egyptian pharaoh Seti I (c 1392 BC), celebrated on its acquisition in 1824 by Soane with a 3-day reception.

On the first floor, past the Shakespeare recess on the stairs, in the drawing rooms and former offices are models, prints and architectural drawings (8 000 by Robert and James Adam, 12 000 by Soane), rare books and a collection of Napoleonic medals. The south drawing-room contains original furniture and a painting by Turner hanging in its original position opposite the fireplace.

The ground floor, with dining table and chairs, desk, leather chairs, the domed breakfast room, the portrait of Soane at 75 by Lawrence, is highly evocative. His **collection of pictures★★**, mostly assembled on folding planes in the picture room, includes drawings by Piranesi and 12 of **Hogarth**'s minutely observed paintings (from which the engravings were made) of the *Election* and the *Rake's Progress*. Elsewhere are paintings by **Canaletto**, **Reynolds** and **Turner**.

Chelsea★★

Chelsea is synonymous with a fashionable lifestyle but it boasts artistic associations which hold a fascination to this day. The lively atmosphere with a Bohemian flavour draws people seeking to be in the limelight and join in the trendy social scene. People-watching is an entertaining pastime and there are plenty of elegant boutiques, antique shops, cafés and restaurants to indulge one's fancy. Explore King's Road and the residential squares and walk along Chelsea Embankment for views of the Thames to appreciate the charm of the area.

Location

Map p 10 (BCZ); Michelin Atlas London: pp 8-9, 24-27. ⊖ Sloane Square. Chelsea extends on the north bank of the Thames from Chelsea Bridge to Chelsea and from Sloane Square to the junction of King's Rd and Fulham Rd.

Adjacent Sights: KNIGHTSBRIDGE – BELGRAVIA; KENSINGTON; FULHAM – PUTNEY; OUTER LONDON: BATTERSEA.

Background

The completion of the embankment in 1874 removed for ever the atmosphere of a riverside community: boats drawn up on the mud flats, trees shading the foreshore, people walking along a country road as painted by **Rowlandson** in 1789 *(Chelsea Reach)*, watched in his old age at sunset by Turner and luminously captured by **Whistler** *(Old Battersea Bridge)*.

Chelsea had royal connections but the only royal building to survive is the Royal Hospital. Architectural interest lies in the churches and also in the squares and terraces, attractive houses of all periods and 19C and 20C blocks of flats.

Henry VIII's Palace – The river still served as the main access when the king's riverside palace was built in 1537 near Albert Bridge; it was known as the New Manorhouse as there was an Old Manorhouse, demolished in 1704, on the site of Lawrence Street. The palace was a two-storey Tudor brick mansion including "three cellars, three halls, three parlours, three kitchens... a large staircase, three drawing rooms, seventeen chambers"; water was brought by conduit from Kensington.

Here resided Prince Edward, Princess Elizabeth and their cousin **Lady Jane Grey**, followed at the king's death by Catherine Parr (d 1548) and then by Anne of Cleves (d 1557). It was owned by the Cheynes in the 17C and then by **Sir Hans Sloane** *(see index)*, who retired to Chelsea with his two daughters and his collection from 1712 until his death in 1753 when the house was demolished.

Sir Thomas More – Henry VIII's Chancellor bought a parcel of land at the water's edge west of the church (approximately on the site of Beaufort Street). The house he built was large enough to contain his extensive family, portrayed vividly by **Holbein** on his first visit to England. One regular guest in the 12 years More lived in Chelsea, before sailing downriver to his execution in 1535, was **Erasmus**; another who came informally, appearing unannounced at the river gate, was **Henry VIII** himself.

A Fashionable Set – Chelsea has frequently been the setting for a new or revived fashion: the smart and cosmopolitan crowds in the Ranelagh and Cremorne Gardens, the exclusivity of the Pre-Raphaelites and the individuality of Oscar Wilde's green carnation. The opening of Bazaar in 1955 by the designer **Mary Quant** led to a radical change in dress with the launch of the mini skirt: in the 1960s Chelsea was the "navel of swinging London" and King's Road, a Mecca of the avant-garde. In 1971 **Vivienne Westwood** opened her clothes shop at 430 King's Road; it became the centre of Punk fashion. Today the King's Road has weathered into a convenient shopping area for local residents...

Chelsea Luminaries

A varied group of notable people has lived in Chelsea: the famous actresses Nell Gwynne, Dame Ellen Terry, Dame Sybil Thorndyke (who inspired GB Shaw to write *St Joan* for her); Sir Joseph Banks (botanist, explorer and President of the Royal Society); Sir John Fielding (a respected magistrate who was blind from birth), the engineers **Sir Marc Isambard Brunel** and his son Isambard Kingdom; Charles Kingsley (author of *The Water Babies*); Mrs Elizabeth Gaskell (novelist); the **Pre-Raphaelite** poets and painters **Dante Gabriel Rossetti**, his sister Christina, Burne-Jones, William and Jane Morris, Holman Hunt, Swinburne, Millais. Other artists include **William de Morgan**, Wilson Steer, Sargent, Augustus John, Orpen, Sickert. Mark Twain, **Henry James**, TS Eliot are among Chelsea Americans. Smollett lived in Lawrence Street, **Oscar Wilde** at 34 Tite Street, AA Milne at 13 Mallord Street (1919-42). There were also Hilaire Belloc, the Sitwells, Arnold Bennett...

Directory

Light Bite

Bluebird Café – *350 King's Rd, SW3 5UU – ⊖ South Kensington – ☎ 020 7559 1155 – www.conran.co.uk – Open Mon-Sat 8am-11pm, Sun 10am-6pm – £14.* This informal café is part of Conran's renowned "gastrodome", which also includes a food store, florists and a smart restaurant (see below and Where to Eat in the Practical Points section). Order a croissant, fresh juice or a light meal and a cocktail while watching the world go by in the fashionable King's Road.

Vingt Quatre – *325 Fulham Rd, SW10 9QL – ⊖ Gloucester Road – ☎ 020 7376 7224 – £17.* 24/7/52 is proudly displayed on the canopy as this 12C brasserie is open 24 hours a day, 7 days a week, 52 weeks a year. This lively and popular evening haunt provides an elaborate international café menu. Cover charge from 10.30pm to 7am.

Taking a Break

Babushka House – *354 King's Rd, SW3 5UZ – ☎ 020 7352 2828 – babushka_chelsea@styleinthecity.co.uk – Open Mon-Fri noon-11pm, Sat-Sun 11am-11pm (10.30pm Sun).* Vodka cocktail bar which is a mixture of 70's kitsch and 'noughties' cool. Relaxed during the day and very busy in the evening with the young Chelsea set.

Pubs

Chelsea Potter – *119 King's Rd, SW3 4PL – ⊖ Sloane Square – ☎ 020 7352 9479 – Open Mon-Sat 11am-11pm, Sun noon-10.30pm.* Ideally located in the heart of one of London's foremost shopping areas, this pub, with a tile decor, is authentic and unpretentious. Full of tourists by day, at night a young crowd takes over.

King's Head and Eight Bells – *50 Cheyne Walk, SW3 5LR – ⊖ Sloane Sqaure.* This pub, an attractive establishment with ornate mirrors, was probably frequented by the various artists (including Dylan Thomas) living locally; it is reputed to have been visited frequently by Charles II, in whose reign it was founded.

Phene Arms – *9 Phene St, SW3 5NY – ⊖ Sloane Square – ☎ 020 7352 3294 – Open Mon-Sat noon-11pm, Sun noon-10.30pm.* A quite friendly and authentic pub in Chelsea with a good selection of beer. It is quite small but the "beer garden" to the rear is open all year round.

The Builders Arms – *13 Britten St, SW3 3TY – ⊖ Sloane Square – ☎ 020 7349 9040 – Open Mon-Sun 11am-11pm (10.30pm Sun); closed 25 Dec and 1 Jan.* Comfortably elegant and smartly designed, this pub is located just a stone's throw from the King's Road. The atmosphere is laid-back, bustling and fun. Excellent well priced food.

Shopping

Bluebird – *350 Kings Rd, SW3 5UU – ⊖ Sloane Square – ☎ 020 7349 1650 – www.conran.co.uk – Open Mon-Sat 9am-8pm (9m Thu-Sat), Sun noon-6pm.* An old garage converted into a gastronomical paradise in 1997. It's an all-in-one bar, restaurant, food shop and flower shop according to Terence Conran's winning formula. High-quality products are sold here (fresh foods, oils, teas, wine...), the presentation is faultless but it comes at a price.

Bourbon-Hanby Antiques Centre – *151 Sydney St, SW3 6NT – ⊖ Sloane Square – ☎ 020 7352 2106 – i.barrett@btconnect.com – Open Mon-Sat 10am-6pm, Sun 11am-5pm; closed bank hols.* 28 exhibitors in a very beautiful Victorian building. Mostly 19C jewellery, furniture, paintings and textiles, chandeliers and lighting.

General Trading Company – *2 Symons St, SW3 2TJ – ⊖ Sloane Square – ☎ 020 7730 0411 – www.general-trading.co.uk – Open Mon-Sat 10am-6pm (7pm Wed).* This unique emporium specialises in home furniture and accessories in contemporary and various ethnic styles. A good selection of greetings cards, books, jewellery, and bags as well. Pleasant café.

Manolo Blahnik – *49-51 Old Church St, SW3 5BS – ⊖ Sloane Square – ☎ 020 7352 3863 or 8622 – Open Mon-Fri 10am-5.30pm, Sat 10.30am-5pm; closed bank hols.* The source of the most desirable shoes in London. Well-heeled women around the world appreciate the creative and ultra-feminine designs of Blahnik's entirely hand-sewn footwear. Men's shoes also available.

Events and Festivals

Chelsea Flower Show – *See PRACTICAL POINTS – Events and Festivals.* Held in May, it is one of the high points of the summer season. The splendid show displays flowers, plants and everything imaginable for a garden.

Walking About

Sloane Square

The square boasts three very different institutions: Peter Jones, the purveyor of household effects and domestic appliances, has been judged to have one of London's most successful shop exteriors (1936). It was here too that William Willett invented daylight saving or **summer time** (adopted 1916).

The **Royal Court Theatre** has twice, since it opened in 1870, launched a new vogue: in 1904-07 when Harley Granville Barker put on Arthur Pinero farces and plays by Bernard Shaw and Somerset Maugham, and in 1956-58 when the English Stage Co under George Devine presented John Osborne's *Look Back in Anger*. The theatre retains its pioneering role.

Walk up Sloane St.

Holy Trinity

Open Mon-Fri, 9am-6pm, Sat, 9.30am-6pm. Concerts. ☎ 020 7259 0240; Fax 020 7730 9287; bishop@holytrinitysloanestreet.org; www.holytrinitysloanestreet.org

The church was rebuilt in 1888 when the **Pre-Raphaelites** were at their height by a leading exponent of the **Arts and Crafts movement**, John Dando Sedding (1838-91). **Burne-Jones**, seeing it under construction, proposed the design with flowing tracery of the 48-panel east window with Apostles, Patriarchs, Kings, Prophets and Saints – St Bartholomew by **William Morris**. All decoration is of the period and harmonises with the High Altar marble crucifix and candlesticks, designed by the architect, who had met Morris when he was studying with GE Street. Note also the very fine metalwork inside: bronze panels in the choir stalls, the gilded organ case fashioned like a portcullis, decorative pulpit stair rail, golden lectern; and unusual railings outside on Sloane Street.

Return to Sloane Sq and walk past the Royal Court Theatre to the top of King's Rd.

King's Road

This used to be the route taken by **Charles II** when calling upon **Nell Gwynne** at her house in Fulham: between 1719 and 1830, the King's Road was closed to all but those holding a royal pass owing to its attraction to footpads. It is now famous for its shops selling fashion accessories and antiques, restaurants and pubs, while the small streets around are lined by traditional cottages once built for artisans.

Past the Guards' barracks turn left into Royal Avenue.

Between the King's Road and the Royal Hospital lies the playing field **Burton's Court**, flanked by **St Leonard's Terrace** – a most attractive mid-18C Georgian row *(nos 14-31)*. At the centre of the terrace is **Royal Avenue**, planted in 1692-94, which was planned to extend as far as Kensington Palace but was never completed; the houses on either side date from the early and mid 19C.

The Royal Hospital**

Open Mon-Sat, 10am-noon and 2-4pm; and Apr-Oct, Sun, 2-4pm. Grounds: Open usually daily, 10am-4pm. Leaflet (8 languages). ☎ 020 7881 5204; info@chelsea-pensioners.org.uk; www.chelsea-pensioners.org.uk

Chelsea Pensioners have been colourful members of the local community for over 300 years. The idea for a veterans' hostel would appear to have come to **Charles II**, who had re-established a standing army in 1661, from reports of the Invalides built by Louis XIV in Paris in 1670. The next 10 years are summarised in the Latin inscription in the Figure Court: "For the support and relief of maimed and superannuated soldiers, founded by Charles II, expanded by **James II** and completed by **King William** and **Queen Mary** 1692."

The architect Sir Christopher **Wren** provided a quadrangular plan with a main court open on the south to the grounds and the river. He added courts to east and west always leaving one side open. The main entrance is beneath the lantern-crowned Octagon Porch in the north range of the original **Figure Court**, so-called after the Classical statue of Charles II by **Grinling Gibbons** at the centre. The porch emerges on the south side beneath a portico of giant Tuscan pillars, which is flanked on either side by a colonnade of small paired Tuscan pillars. Along the entablature runs the historical Latin inscription *(see above)*.

Chapel and Great Hall – From the Octagon Porch steps rise on either side to the Chapel and Great Hall, both panelled beneath tall rounded windows. The Chapel has a barrel vault, decorated like the piers and with delicate plasterwork (Henry Margetts) and, at the end, a domed and painted apse by Ricci. The end wall of the Hall is decorated with an 18C mural of Charles II on horseback before the hospital. Here the Duke of Wellington lay in state in 1852.

Charles II in Classical dress in Figure Court, Royal Hospital

Council Chamber – The Chamber *(west wing)* was decorated by both Wren and Robert Adam; Van Dyck painted the portrait of Charles I and his family.

Museum – The exhibits include Wellington mementoes and illustrate the history of the hospital and its members.

Grounds – Since 1913 the **Chelsea Flower Show** *(see Directory)* has been held in the grounds by the **Royal Horticultural Society**.

Ranelagh Gardens – In 1805 the Hospital repurchased the land formerly occupied by the celebrated Ranelagh Gardens (1742-1805), which offered patrons *alfresco* meals, concerts and spectacles in the Rotunda, a building (150ft/46m in diameter) containing tiers of boxes.

Leave by Royal Hospital Rd to the west past the National Army Museum (description in Worth a Visit).

Chelsea Physic Garden

♿ *Open early-Apr to late-Oct, Wed, noon-5pm; Sun, 2-6pm. Chelsea Flower Show week: Open Mon-Fri, noon-5pm. £5. Guide book. No dogs. Plants for sale. Refreshments. ☎ 020 7352 5646; Fax 020 7376 3910; maureen@cpgarden.demon.uk; www.chelseaphysicgarden.co.uk*

The garden, frequented by such leading lights as Linnaeus who propounded early theories on genetics, was founded in 1673 by the Worshipful Society of Apothecaries of London on land leased from Sir Hans Sloane: in 1722 he granted the lease to the Society in perpetuity.

The record of the garden, overlooked at the centre by a statue of Sir Hans by Rysbrack, is remarkable: Georgia's cotton seeds came from the South Seas via the Physic Garden, India's tea from China, her quinine *(cinchona)* from South America, Malaya's rubber from South America...

The garden of wound medicine shows plants used for medical purposes by the Chinese, North American Indians, Maoris etc.

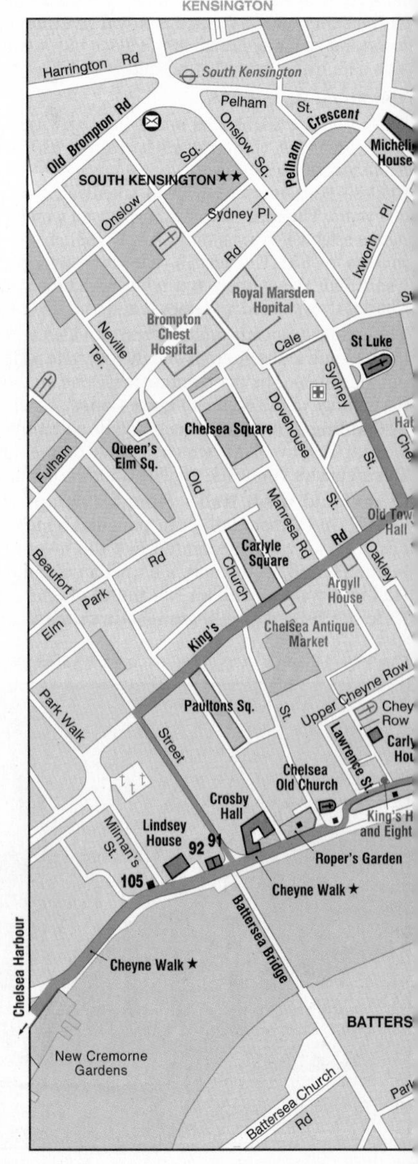

Cheyne Walk★

The terraces of brick houses standing back from the river front are rich with memories of artists, writers and royalty. Corinthian pilasters and an entablature mark the entrance to **no 4** where the painter Daniel Maclise lived and **George Eliot** spent her last weeks. Beautiful railings and fine urns distinguish **no 5**; **no 6** is remarkable for the Chinese-Chippendale gate and railings.

Verse from a popular song

"Though the philistines might jostle, you would rank as an apostle
In the high aesthetic band
If you swanned down Cheyne Walk with just a sunflower on a stalk
In your medieval hand."

The **Queen's House** *(no 16)* was the home of the poet and painter D G Rossetti where the Pre-Raphaelites used to meet. In the gardens opposite, facing onto the river stands a fountain bearing a portrait bust of Rossetti by Seddon. **No 18**, distinguished by its first floor railed balconies and parapet, was the popular Don Saltero's coffeehouse and museum. **Nos 19-26**, built between 1759 and 1765, occupy the site of Henry VIII's riverside palace *(see Background)*.

For Albert Bridge see Outer London – BATTERSEA. For Carlyle's House, 24 Cheyne Row, see Worth a Visit.

In **Lawrence Street** flourished the **Chelsea China Works** (1745-84) before being transferred to Derby *(see INSIGHTS AND IMAGES – Decorative Arts)*. Among the 18C houses to remain are the early Georgian Duke House and Monmouth House sharing a pedimented porch on carved brackets *(nos 23-24)*. The **King's Head and Eight Bells** dates back to the 17C *(see Directory)*.

> **Houseboats**
>
> Moored on the river are several permanent houseboats: larger and more spacious than a canal barge, these would once have accommodated watermen and river pilots. Today they provide homes for a more Bohemian set of Chelsea residents.

Chelsea Old Church

Open Tue-Fri, 2-5pm, Sun, 1.30-6pm. ☎ 020 7352 5627 (parish office), 7795 1019 (administrator); Fax 020 7795 0092; www.domini.org/chelsea-old-church

The church dates from pre-Norman, possibly Saxon times. By the 20C it consisted of a nave and tower of c 1670, 13C chancel and early-14C chapels of which the south one had been remodelled by **Sir Thomas More** in 1528. Following bomb damage, in the 1950s it was reconstructed on the old foundations, modelled on records provided by old prints and paintings. Many monuments were rescued from the rubble; the altar and rails are 17C, the small marble font dates from 1673; the **chained books**, presented by Sir Hans Sloane, are the only ones in a London church.

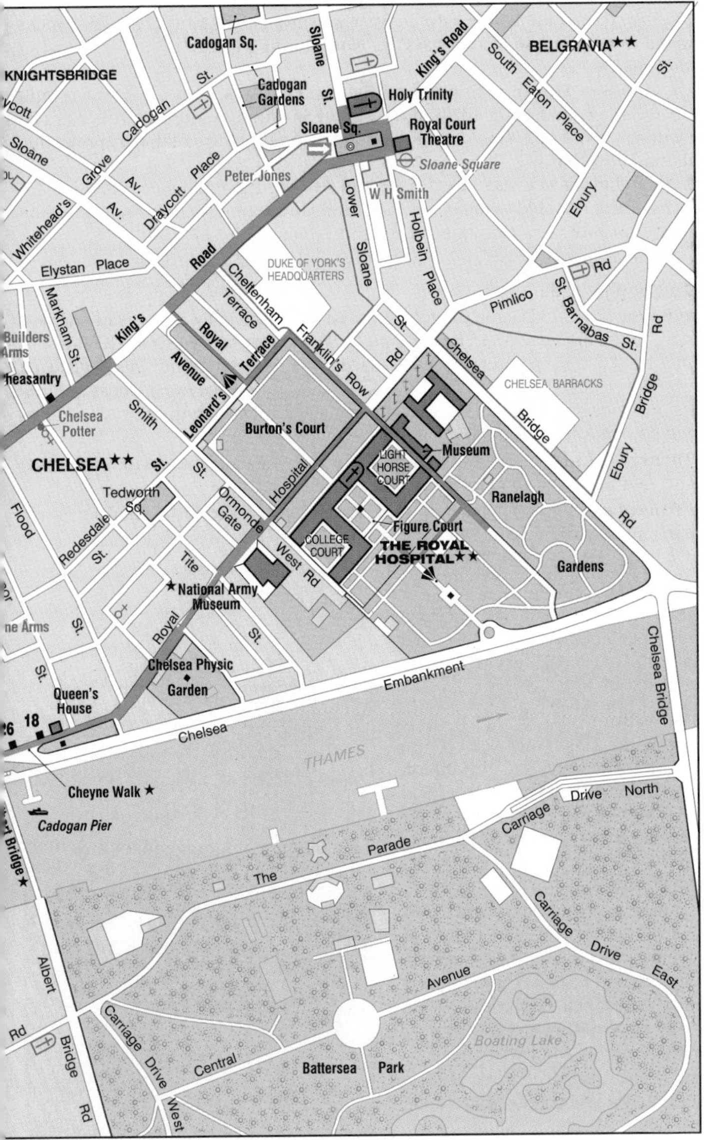

Among the monuments are the reclining figure of Lady Jane Cheyne (1699), Sarah Colville with aghast expression and upraised hands (1631; Lawrence Chapel), the massive Stanley monument of 1632 and, near the squint, the small alabaster group of Sir Thomas Lawrence, City goldsmith and merchant adventurer, at prayer with his wife and eight children. More's self-composed inscription stands against the south wall of the sanctuary by the arch with capitals dated 1528, designed by Holbein. The novelist Henry James is also buried here, while in the churchyard an urn marks the grave of Sir Hans Sloane and a **statue** of a seated black-robed figure with gilded face and hands commemorates Sir Thomas More, that "man of marvellous mirth and past-times and sometimes of as sad a gravity, (that) man for all seasons."

Roper's Garden

This walled garden, once part of More's orchard, is named after William Roper, his son-in-law. An upstanding stone relief of *A Woman Walking against the Wind* by **Jacob Epstein** commemorates the artist's years in Chelsea (1909-14).

Crosby Hall

The medieval great hall, which was transferred to Chelsea in 1910, was built between 1466 and 1475 in Bishopsgate as part of the residence of the 15C wool merchant, Sir John Crosby; the interior is panelled, has a painted hammerbeam roof and is lit by a three-tier oriel window.

From Cheyne Walk there is a fine view of Battersea Bridge *(see Outer London – BATTERSEA)*. **Nos 91-92** were built in 1771 and have several Venetian windows: no 91 *(entrance in Beaufort St)* has a modest but fine entrance and a first floor conservatory commanding a view of the river, and no 92 is contained between arches serving the front door and former passage. **Nos 93 and 94** date from 1777. Whistler resided at **no 96**.

The large **Lindsey House** with mansard roof-storey, dates from 1752. It was built for the 3rd Earl of Lindsey in 1674 on the site of Sir Thomas More's farm. The 17C Lindsey mansion of brick (since subdivided and painted), is articulated by projecting central and lateral bays.

Marc Brunel and his son, Isambard Kingdom Brunel, the engineers, who lived at no 98, are commemorated in the modern **Brunel House** on the corner *(no 105)*. Note the tall studio south-facing window on the third floor of no 109.

Option 1: Proceed along the embankment and Lots Rd to Chelsea Harbour.

104-120 Cheyne Walk

Hilaire Belloc (1873-1953), the Catholic essayist and historian was a versatile writer, author of *Cautionary Tales* and *The Bad Child's Book of Beasts*. **PW Steer** (1860-1942), the son of a portrait painter achieved particular recognition for his landscape paintings. He studied in Paris during the early 1880s but discovered Degas and the Impressionists only towards the end of the decade, after which time his Constable-like style becomes freer and more robust.

JMW Turner (1775-1851) spent his last years in near seclusion at no 119, while taste for his art dwindled and the Pre-Raphaelites found favour.

Sylvia Pankhurst, the second daughter of Emmeline, worked for women's suffrage and participated in organising the Women's Social and Political Union.

Chelsea Wharf

Old and new co-exist as modern developments encroach upon the old warehouses, London Transport Electric Power-substation and gasworks.

Chelsea Harbour

As recently as 1960, this was where barges would unload coal for the London Underground Power Station in Lots Road (now a residential development) – a far cry from the luxury, modern riverside development of today, highlighted by its Belvedere Tower.

The complex is organised around a 75-berth marina and it comprises a series of elegant and exclusive apartments, offices, a hotel, shops and restaurants: those that face onto the river enjoy fine views across the water to **St Mary's Church** *(see BATTERSEA)* on the south bank.

Option 2: From Cheyne Walk turn right into Beaufort St which leads back to King's Road and turn right.

Marina at Chelsea Harbour

Ph. Gajic/MICHELIN

Three squares, **Paultons** (1830-40), **Carlyle** (mid 19C) and **Chelsea** (18C-20C) illustrate the evolution of styles in residential development.

Continue to Chelsea Town Hall and take Sydney St opposite.

St Luke's

(♿) To view contact the Parish Office: Open Mon-Fri, 10am-12.30pm. ☎ 020 7351 7365; Fax 020 7349 0538; parishoffice@chelseaparish.demon.co.uk

The Bath stone church of 1820, an early example of the Gothic Revival, is tall and lanky both outside and in. The pinnacled and slimly buttressed west tower (242ft/74m) is pierced at the base to provide a porch which extends the full width of the west front.

Retrace your steps and continue east along King's Road.

Further along stands what was the **Pheasantry** *(no 152, now a restaurant)* which was erected in 1881 by the Jouberts to sell French wallpapers and furniture; alas, only the façade and portico survive. In 1916 the site was occupied by a Russian dance school attended among others by Margot Fonteyn. By 1932 it had been converted into a popular meeting-place frequented by Bohemian artists and left-wing politicians.

Worth a Visit

National Army Museum★

♿ Open daily, 10am-5.30pm. Closed Good Fri, May Day Hol, 24-26 Dec, 1 Jan. Lecture: Thu at 1pm; £2.50. ☎ 020 7730 0717; Fax 020 7823 6573; pr@national-army-museum.ac.uk; www.national-army-museum.ac.uk

The museum tells the story of the British Army over five centuries from the formation of the Yeomen of the Guard by Henry VII on Bosworth Field in 1485; it also covers the Indian Army, colonial forces and the rigours of UN peacekeeping today. The Story of the Army illustrates campaigns in every continent, the evolution from armour to khaki and tin helmets, with reconstructions, models, dramatic audio-visual displays (Battle of Waterloo) and dioramas. One gallery celebrates the "Forgotten Army", another the domestic life of the soldier. A considerable collection of weapons demonstrates the development of hand-held weapons from pikes and swords to revolvers and repeating rifles, pistols and machine guns. The Uniform gallery displays buckskin breeches, helmets, caps and hats. Notable medals, honours and decorations wrought in the finest coloured enamelwork and craftsmanship are also displayed. Other exhibits of interest include portraits by Reynolds, Romney, Gainsborough, Lawrence and others, and the skeleton of Napoleon's horse Marengo.

Carlyle's House

24 Cheyne Row. (NT) Open Apr-Oct, Wed-Sun and Bank Hol Mon, 2pm (11am Sat-Sun and Bank Hol Mon) to 5pm. £3.70. ☎ 020 7352 7087; Fax 020 7352 5108; carlyleshouse@ntrust.org.uk; www.nationaltrust.org.uk/carlyleshouse

The philosopher and man of letters Thomas Carlyle (1795-1881) lived in this modest Queen Anne brick house for 47 years – "as usual, never healthy, never absolutely ill, – protesting against 'things in general'...". He had the garret-room at the top of the house soundproofed in order to write his biography of Peter the Great. At such times he largely ignored his company-loving, but rather sickly, wife Jane Welsh who took to recording her miserable and lonely life in long letters to her family and a journal. On discovering these at her sudden death and the evidence of his wretched behaviour, Carlyle's final years were racked by guilt and shame.

The four-storeyed house is compact, uncluttered and yet filled with portraits of Thomas, his library, his manuscripts, artefacts, relics, Jane's blue and white china and simple furniture that reflect the couple's comfortable but unpretentious lifestyle. The "Sage of Chelsea" is commemorated in a statue by Boehm in Cheyne Walk gardens facing onto the river.

The City★★★

The City of London, also known as the Square Mile, is a compact area on the north bank of the Thames, now identified with finance and business *(see INSIGHTS AND IMAGES – Historical Perspective)* and therefore animated by a commuting workforce on weekdays and left silent and eerie at night to Barbican residents. As Docklands makes its mark as a potential rival in the world of finance the City continues to expand and reinvent itself as is evident from numerous high-rise buildings in modern architectural styles which punctuate the skyline.

The pace of City life is deemed to be particularly stressful and City people have a reputation for hard work but they also like to unwind and enjoy the fruits of their labour. There is a multitude of old pubs, smart wine bars, expensive restaurants and elegant shops teeming with business people. The arts also flourish at the Barbican Centre and small theatres such as the Bridewell.

Location

Map p 13 (FGHX); Michelin Atlas London: pp 64-66, 81-82.

City of London Information Centre, St Paul's Churchyard, EC4. Open May-Oct, daily, 9.30am-5pm; otherwise Mon-Sat, 9.30am-5pm (12.30pm Sat). ☎ 020 7332 1456; Fax 020 7332 1457.

The City of London extends north from the river between Blackfriars Bridge and the Tower of London as far as the Barbican. It is adjacent to the East End and Docklands.

Adjacent Sights: CHANCERY LANE; CLERKENWELL; DOCKLANDS; STRAND-TEMPLE; EAST END.

Background

Between and beneath the modern buildings are traces of Celtic and Roman settlements, sections of the city wall, medieval and Wren churches, rare and tiny gardens, Victorian market and office buildings. Here rather than elsewhere in London, vestiges of the old city, her trades and traditions survive as does the medieval network of narrow courts and alleys, yards and steps steeped in local history by association: Pope's Head Alley, Puddle Dock, Glasshouse Alley, Panyer Alley, Wardrobe Terrace, Seacole Lane, French Ordinary, Ave Maria Lane, Paternoster Row, Amen Court, Turnagain Lane...

Traditions – Of the many practices maintained: the royal carriage still halts at Temple Bar when the sovereign enters the City; annually the Prime Minister makes a major policy speech at the Lord Mayor's Banquet; visitors of state are invited to attend a banquet or ceremony in the City; on 20 June each year the guild of Watermen and Lightermen pays a "fine" of one red rose to the Lord Mayor imposed on Lady Knollys in 1381 for building a bridge across Seething Lane without permission...

City Churches

There have been churches in the Square Mile since Saxon times. By 1666, there were 100 of which 88 were destroyed by the **Great Fire** – 53 were rebuilt under the supervision of Wren, more were constructed by Hawksmoor.

The City churches are usually symmetrical and rectangular in plan, orientated as far as possible in the cramped and awkward sites available. The choir played a reduced part in the new Protestant Service which hinged rather on long sermons: large open galleries were therefore provided to accommodate extra seating, while side chapels, transepts and side aisles were eliminated. The prototype for these light, spacious and airy hall-churches derived partly from Dutch Calvinist models and partly from Jesuit churches where the altar was placed against the east wall. Exceptions are centrally planned as a cross in a square (St Martin Ludgate, St Anne and St Agnes, St Mary at Hill), as a vaulted octagon or a domed square (St Mary Abchurch) – perhaps the most original experiment is St Stephen Walbrook which achieves a truly Baroque spirit hitherto unknown in Puritan England.

By 1939 the construction of new roads in the 19C and 20C had reduced the number of City churches to 43 of which 32 were by Wren. Nearly all were damaged and several totally destroyed during the war, but as the floor plans survive, it was possible for some to be reconstructed. Today there are some 39 City Churches, 11 are pre-Fire and 23 by Wren; 6 of the 9 free-standing towers are by Wren. Twenty-four continue to be parish churches, 15 have become guild churches, some are both. Most city churches are open weekdays and hold midday services; many also organise recitals, debates and counselling.

For detailed information apply to the City Information Centre or enquire at the churches themselves. If you wish to provide voluntary help or contributions to the upkeep of these monuments, contact Friends of The City Churches, 68 Battersea High Street, London SW11 3HX.

Directory

Light Bite

Carluccios – *West Smithfield, EC1A 9JR – ⊖ Faringdon, St Pauls – ☎ 020 7329 5904 – smithfieldcarluccios@carluccios.com – £5/8.* A long counter links the delicatessen shop to the large restaurant in the rear. Modern decor and Italian cooking using fresh ingredients accompanied by Italian wines.

George and Vulture – *3 Castle Ct, EC3 – ⊖ Bank – ☎ 020 7626 9710 – Open noon-2.pm.* A picturesque establishment serving traditional food. For description see p 167.

La Grande Marque – *47 Ludgate Hill, EC4M 7JU – ⊖ St Paul's – ☎ 020 7329 6709 – www.lagrandemarque.com – Closed Sat and Sun – £6/14.* This converted bank retains considerable Victorian charm and stands in the shadow of St Paul's. Over 110 wines are offered, some by the glass, and you can order light snacks – from salads to assorted fresh sandwiches.

Le Coq D'Argent – *1 Poultry, EC2R 8EJ – ⊖ Bank – ☎ 020 7395 5000 – www.conran-restaurants.co.uk/restaurants/restaurants/coq/ – Open Mon-Fri 11.30am-11pm, Sat 6.30-11pm.* Situated in the centre of the City, this spectacular bar-restaurant is yet another brainchild of Terence Conran. Lovely roof terrace.

Simpson's Tavern – *Ball Court, 38 Cornhill, EC3V 9DR – ⊖ Bank – ☎ 020 7626 5750 – Open Mon-Fri 11.30am – 3pm. Bank tube.* An 18C eating-house with dark woodwork and polished brass.

Pubs

Black Friar – *174 Queen Victoria St, EC4V 4EG – ⊖ Blackfriars – ☎ 020 7236 5474 – Open Mon-Sat 11.30am-11pm, Sun noon-10.30pm.* Opposite the underground station stands London's only Art Nouveau pub. It was founded in 1875 and is dedicated to the black monks of the Dominican Priory which stood on the site between 1279 and 1539. Admire the stained-glass windows, paintings and bronze and copper sculptures. The pub was due to be demolished in the 1960s but the public, backed by some influential figures, successfully opposed the plans. Lively atmosphere.

Jamaica Wine House – *St Michael's Alley, off Cornhill, EC3 9DS – ⊖ Bank – ☎ 020 7626 9496 – Open Mon-Fri 11am-11pm.* This delightful watering hole with historical associations (once frequented by Charles Dickens' Mr Pickwick) is hidden in a small alley.

Lamb Tavern – *10-12 Leadenhall Market, EC3V 1LR – ⊖ Monument – ☎ 020 7626 2454 – Open Mon-Fri 11am-9pm.* The oldest pub in the centre of Leadenhall Market, Lamb Tavern has an exceptional interior of stunning marble pillars and a glass roof. The terrace is busy at lunchtime when the office workers pour in. The pub is also a popular haunt for film producers.

Williamson's Tavern – *1 Groveland Court, EC4M 9EH – ⊖ Mansion House – ☎ 020 7248 5750 – Open Mon-Fri 11am-11pm.* A traditional pub with a lively atmosphere.

Ye Old Wine Shades – *6 Martin Lane, EC4A 2BU – ⊖ Monument – ☎ 020 7626 6303 – www.elvino.co.uk – Open Mon-Fri 8.30am-10pm (9pm Mon); closed bank hols.* This delightful old pub (1663) is authentically furnished with dark wooden booths inside and is frequented by business people. It serves excellent wines accompanied in the evenings by a variety of hot and cold bar snacks; at lunchtime traditional dishes such as steak and kidney pie and fish and chips are served in the downstairs restaurant.

Events and Festivals

Lord Mayor's Show – Second Sun in Nov. A traditional procession of floats through the City to celebrate the swearing-in of the Lord Mayor of the City of London. See p 174.

Walking About

This chapter is divided into walks which take visitors through old alleyways, hidden gardens, city churches and the main points of interest to experience the fascination of this vital area. For each walk the Underground station nearest to the starting-point is given first and other stations along the way are also listed. We suggest visits during the week when the streets are lively and churches and pubs are open. Some churches are open only by appointment. If you are interested in a particular church it is best to check the opening times in advance.

The heart of the City and the national economy is that important institution: the Bank of England **(Bank)** and from here radiate the principal thoroughfares:

Throgmorton Street runs to Broadgate.

Threadneedle Street provides access to **Bishopsgate** and the north beyond the city wall.

Cornhill leads eastwards to Leadenhall Street and Aldgate.

Lombard Street runs east to **Fenchurch Street** and Aldgate.

To the south stands **Monument** and the river.

Mansion House is the official residence of the Lord Mayor.

Queen Victoria Street runs down to Blackfriars Bridge and St Bride's.

Cheapside goes to St Paul's Cathedral.

Due north of Bank sits the **Guildhall**.

Straddling the boundaries of the City of London are the areas **Barbican** and **Smithfield**.

If visiting the area for the first time: start at **St Paul's Cathedral** *(listed separately)* before popping into St Mary le Bow, walking down past the Bank of England, Mansion House and the Royal Exchange, and on to Leadenhall Market and the Lloyd's building.

J. Malburet/MICHELIN

At the heart of the City of London

This route will provide an impression of the City's principal institutions and her broad range of architectural styles.

Note: Most of the City institutions do not admit casual visitors off the street for security reasons.

BANK – BISHOPSGATE 1

⊖ *Bank: Lombard Street exit.*

Bank of England

Seven floors of offices are housed in the Bank, massive, blank and undistinguished, designed and erected by Sir Herbert Baker, an associate of Lutyens (1924-39) to replace an earlier building by **Sir John Soane**. The façade sculptures representing Britannia served by six bearers and guardians of wealth are by Sir Charles Wheeler.
On the corner of Princes Street and Lothbury stands the Temple, a circular domed pavilion encircled with fluted columns and urns, crowned by a statue of Ariel. Masks of Mercury and representations of his caduceus refer to the god's role as patron of bankers.
The Bank was incorporated under royal charter in 1694 with a capital of £1 200 000 to finance, in the modern way by raising loans and not by royal extortion as heretofore, the continuation of the wars against Louis XIV. It acquired its nickname a century later during the Napoleonic wars during a crisis when the institution was forced to suspend cash payments: Sheridan referred in the House to the "elderly lady in the City of great credit and long standing", Gillray drew a caricature which he captioned "The Old Lady of Threadneedle Street in Danger". The Bank has since weathered other crises, become a bankers' bank and in 1946 was nationalised. It supervises the note issue and national debt and acts as the central reserve. The Governor is appointed by the Crown.

Follow Princes Street and turn right into Throgmorton St to the rear of the building for the Bank of England Museum (description in Worth a Visit).

St Margaret Lothbury★

Open Mon-Fri, 7am-7pm. Closed Bank Hols. Organ recitals: Thur at 1.10pm. Guide book. ☎ 020 7606 8330; Fax 020 7606 1204; admin@stml.org.uk; www.stml.org.uk

While the derivations of Lothbury are speculative and various, the church's certain foundation dates back to the 12C. The present building was designed by Wren in 1686-1701. The square stone tower, topped by an iron railing, rises to a lead-covered cupola and a slender obelisk **spire★** balancing a gilded ball and vane.
The unequal parallelogram inside is divided by Corinthian columns into a nave and chancel and shorter south aisle. The **woodwork★** is especially remarkable: from a dark base of wall and column panelling and cut-down box pews, rise in clear silhouette an exquisitely carved **pulpit★** with massive sounding board, gay with dancing cherubs, and a reredos with balustered rails. A wonderful oak **screen★** dated c 1689 and one of only two to Wren's design, is divided into four paired arcs by two strand balusters; at the centre are pierced pilasters and above three broken pediments, the central one supported by a great carved eagle and filled above with a royal coat of arms. There are 18C sword rests and a bust of Sir Peter le Maire (d 1631) by H Le Sueur.

The south aisle with a dividing screen made from the altar rails of St Olave Jewry, has a reredos also from St Olave. The **font★** is attributed to Grinling Gibbons.

Stock Exchange

8 Throgmorton Street. Trading in stocks and shares originated in this country, in the 17C: first in the coffee-houses of **Change Alley** *(off Lombard St, see below)* where shopkeepers used to barter for goods, then in the Royal Exchange. The first stock exchange, as such, was inaugurated in 1773 in Threadneedle Street. In 1801 and 1971 ever larger buildings rose on the site. As transactions are now carried out electronically, away from the Exchange, the frenetic activity on the trading floor has been stilled.

Continue to Broad St.

At the junction, Austin Friars to the left leads to the modern Dutch Church, built on an ancient site. Proceed along Broad St past Tower 42, a tall glass tower, and take London Wall to the left.

All Hallows London Wall

Open Fri, 11am-3.30pm. Lunchtime talk (40min): 1.10pm last Fri of each month. ☎ 020 7496 1680; Fax 020 7496 1684

The Portland stone tower rises by stages from a pedimented doorway to an urn-quartered cornice, pilastered lantern cupola and final cross. The interior, lit by semicircular clerestory windows, has a particularly fine "snowflake" patterned barrel vault rising on fluted Ionic pilasters from a frieze, and a coffered apse.

Finsbury Circus

Mid-19C to 20C buildings surround the only bowling green in the City. The green is popular with office workers; visitors can rest their weary feet and have a snack at the café while watching the quaint game in summer.

Continue along Bloomfield St.

Broadgate

The redevelopment on a grand scale of the site of Broad Street Railway Station was begun in 1985 and consists of 39 buildings designed in a variety of architectural styles, grouped round squares and open spaces enhanced by fountains and dramatic modern sculpture on a monumental scale. At the centre is a circular Arena for open-air entertainment which turns into an ice rink in winter. Smart watering holes and restaurants attract City workers.

A lively scene at the Broadgate Arena

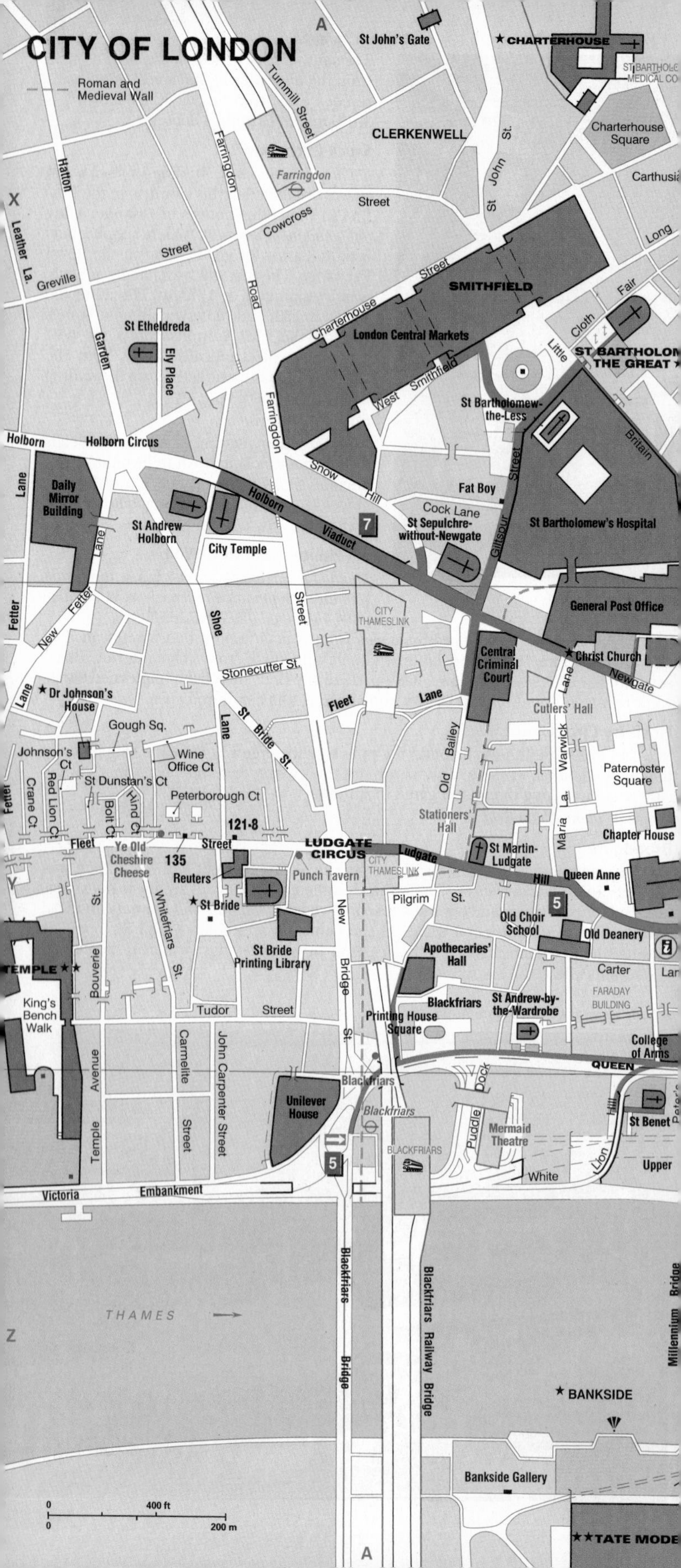

CITY OF LONDON
Roman and Medieval Wall
St John's Gate
CHARTERHOUSE
CLERKENWELL
Charterhouse Square
Farringdon
SMITHFIELD
London Central Markets
St Etheldreda
Holborn Circus
St Bartholomew-the-Less
ST BARTHOLOMEW THE GREAT
Daily Mirror Building
St Andrew Holborn
City Temple
Fat Boy
Cock Lane
St Sepulchre-without-Newgate
St Bartholomew's Hospital
General Post Office
CITY THAMESLINK
Central Criminal Court
Christ Church
Dr Johnson's House
Gough Sq.
Cutlers' Hall
Paternoster Square
Ye Old Cheshire Cheese
Reuters
Punch Tavern
LUDGATE CIRCUS
St Martin-Ludgate
Chapter House
Queen Anne
St Bride
St Bride Printing Library
Old Choir School
Old Deanery
Apothecaries' Hall
TEMPLE
King's Bench Walk
Blackfriars
St Andrew-by-the-Wardrobe
Printing House Square
FARADAY BUILDING
College of Arms
Unilever House
Mermaid Theatre
St Benet
BLACKFRIARS
Victoria Embankment
THAMES
Blackfriars Bridge
Blackfriars Railway Bridge
Millennium Bridge
BANKSIDE
Bankside Gallery
TATE MODE
400 ft
200 m

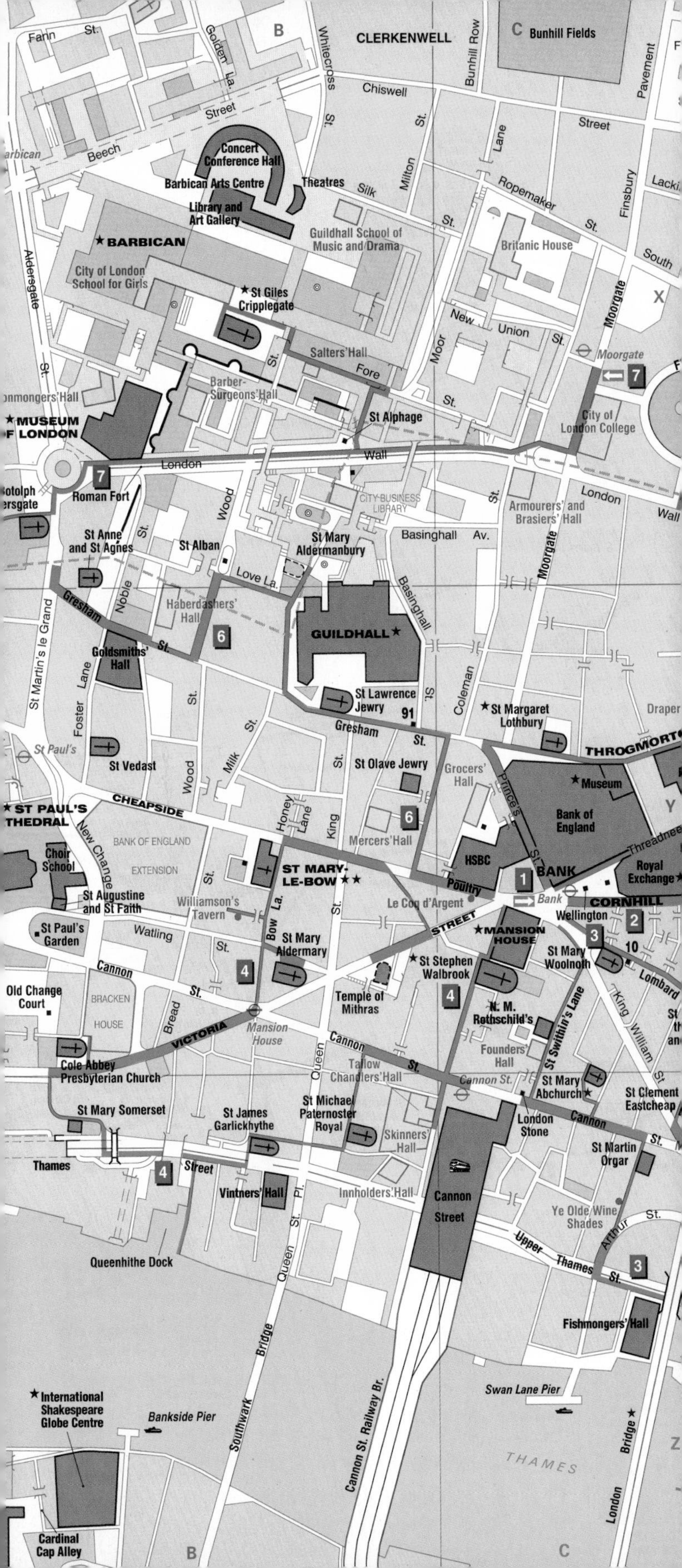

B
C
CLERKENWELL
Bunhill Fields
Fann St.
Golden La.
Whitecross St.
Bunhill Row
Pavement
Chiswell St.
Street
Beech Street
Concert Conference Hall
Barbican Arts Centre
Theatres
Silk St.
Milton St.
Lane
Ropemaker St.
Finsbury
Library and Art Gallery
★ BARBICAN
Guildhall School of Music and Drama
Britanic House
South
City of London School for Girls
★ St Giles Cripplegate
New Union St.
Moorgate
X
Aldersgate St.
Salters' Hall
Fore St.
Moor St.
Moorgate
7
Barber-Surgeons' Hall
St Alphage
City of London College
★ MUSEUM OF LONDON
London Wall
7
Roman Fort
Botolph Aldersgate
CITY BUSINESS LIBRARY
Armourers' and Brasiers' Hall
London Wall
St Anne and St Agnes
Wood St.
St Alban
St Mary Aldermanbury
Basinghall Av.
Love La.
Moorgate
Noble St.
Gresham St.
Haberdashers' Hall
Basinghall St.
6
GUILDHALL ★
St Martin's le Grand
Goldsmiths' Hall
Foster Lane
St Lawrence Jewry
Coleman St.
★ St Margaret Lothbury
Draper
91
Gresham St.
St Paul's
St Vedast
Milk St.
St Olave Jewry
Grocers' Hall
THROGMORTON
Wood St.
★ Museum
★ ST PAUL'S CATHEDRAL
CHEAPSIDE
Honey Lane
King St.
6
Prince's St.
Bank of England
Y
Threadneedle
Choir School
New Change
BANK OF ENGLAND EXTENSION
Mercers' Hall
HSBC
1
BANK
Royal Exchange
St Augustine and St Faith
Williamson's Tavern
ST MARY-LE-BOW ★★
Poultry
Bank
CORNHILL
Le Coq d'Argent
Wellington
2
St Paul's Garden
Watling St.
Bow La.
St Mary Aldermary
STREET
★ MANSION HOUSE
3
St Mary Woolnoth
10
4
Lombard
Cannon St.
★ St Stephen Walbrook
Old Change Court
BRACKEN HOUSE
Bread St.
Temple of Mithras
4
King William St.
N. M. Rothschild's
VICTORIA
Mansion House
Cannon St.
St Swithin's Lane
Founders' Hall
Cole Abbey Presbyterian Church
Queen St.
Tallow Chandlers' Hall
Cannon St.
St Mary Abchurch ★
St Clement Eastcheap
St Mary Somerset
St James Garlickhythe
St Michael Paternoster Royal
London Stone
Cannon St.
Skinners' Hall
St Martin Orgar
Thames
4
Street
Vintners' Hall
Innholders' Hall
Cannon Street
Queen St. Pl.
Ye Olde Wine Shades
Arthur St.
Upper Thames St.
3
Queenhithe Dock
Southwark Bridge
Fishmongers' Hall
Cannon St. Railway Br.
Swan Lane Pier
★ International Shakespeare Globe Centre
Bankside Pier
London Bridge ★
THAMES
Z
Cardinal Cap Alley
B
C

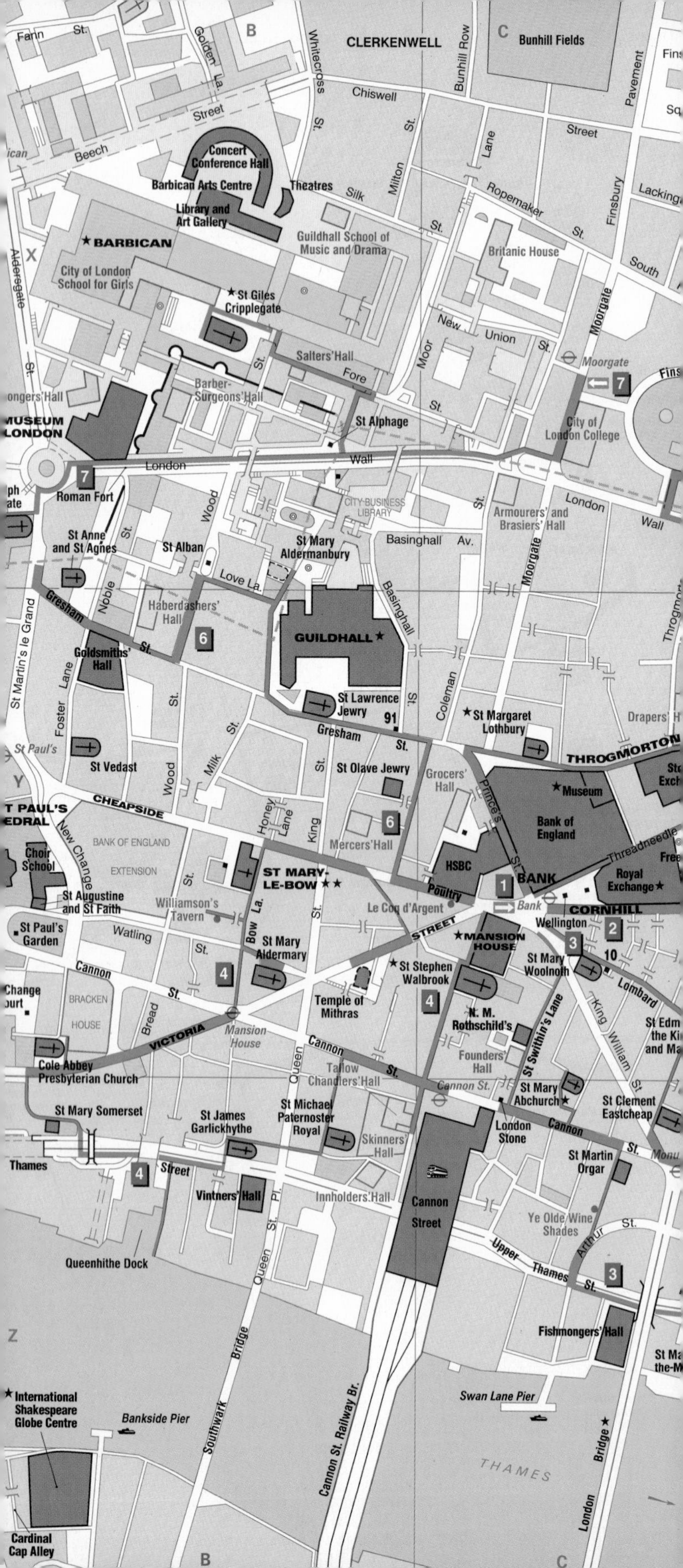
CLERKENWELL
Bunhill Fields
Barbican Arts Centre
Concert Conference Hall
Theatres
Library and Art Gallery
BARBICAN
City of London School for Girls
Guildhall School of Music and Drama
St Giles Cripplegate
Britanic House
Salters' Hall
Barber-Surgeons' Hall
MUSEUM LONDON
St Alphage
City of London College
Moorgate
London Wall
Roman Fort
St Anne and St Agnes
St Alban
St Mary Aldermanbury
CITY BUSINESS LIBRARY
Armourers' and Brasiers' Hall
Haberdashers' Hall
Goldsmiths' Hall
GUILDHALL
St Lawrence Jewry
St Margaret Lothbury
THROGMORTON
St Vedast
St Olave Jewry
Grocers' Hall
Museum
Bank of England
CHEAPSIDE
BANK OF ENGLAND EXTENSION
Mercers' Hall
HSBC
BANK
Royal Exchange
ST MARY-LE-BOW
Poultry
CORNHILL
Threadneedle
Choir School
St Augustine and St Faith
Williamson's Tavern
Le Coq d'Argent
Wellington
St Paul's Garden
St Mary Aldermary
MANSION HOUSE
St Mary Woolnoth
Lombard
St Stephen Walbrook
Temple of Mithras
BRACKEN HOUSE
N. M. Rothschild's
VICTORIA
Mansion House
Cannon St.
Founders' Hall
Tallow Chandlers' Hall
St Mary Abchurch
St Clement Eastcheap
Cole Abbey Presbyterian Church
St Mary Somerset
St James Garlickhythe
St Michael Paternoster Royal
Skinners' Hall
London Stone
St Martin Orgar
Thames Street
Vintners' Hall
Innholders' Hall
Cannon Street
Ye Olde Wine Shades
Upper Thames St.
Queenhithe Dock
Fishmongers' Hall
Swan Lane Pier
International Shakespeare Globe Centre
Bankside Pier
Southwark Bridge
Cannon St. Railway Br.
THAMES
London Bridge
Cardinal Cap Alley

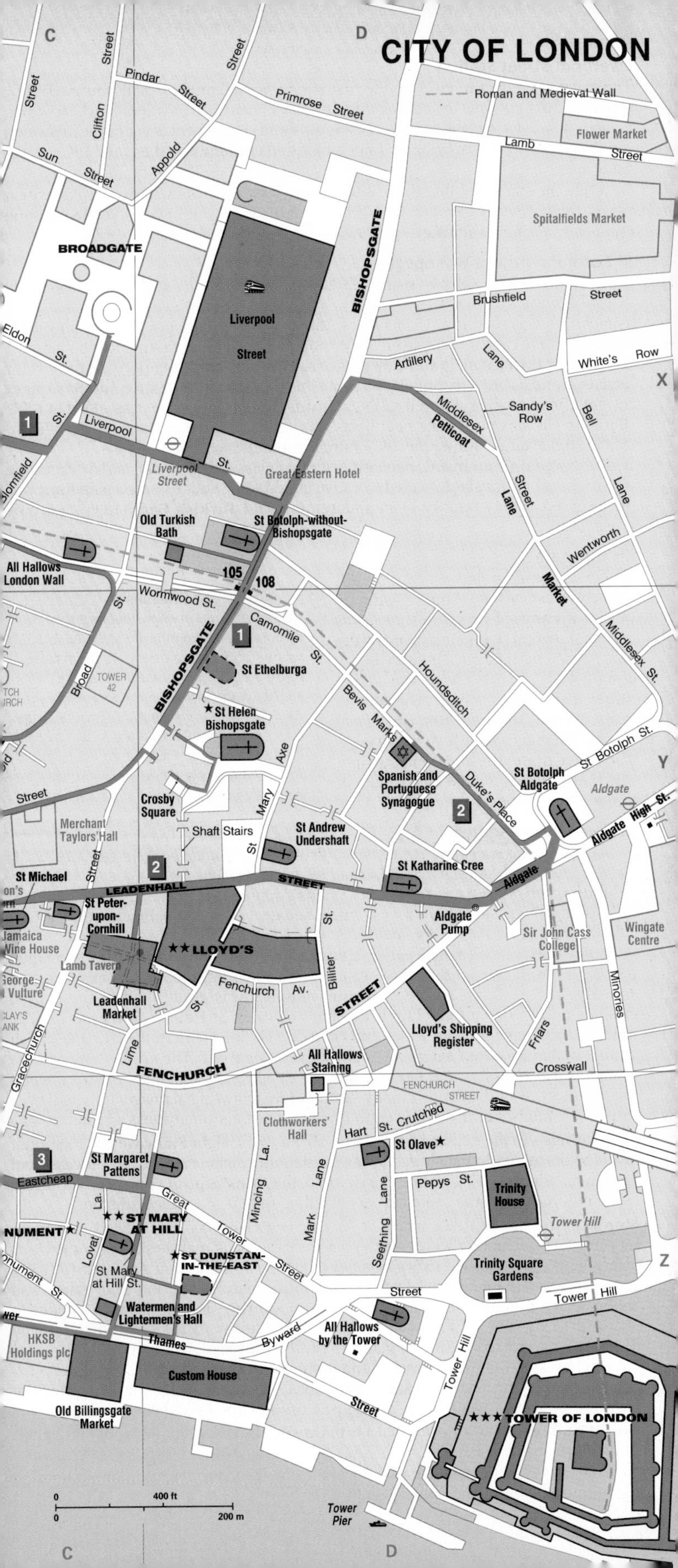

CITY OF LONDON
Roman and Medieval Wall
Liverpool Street
BISHOPSGATE
Spitalfields Market
Flower Market
BROADGATE
Great Eastern Hotel
Old Turkish Bath
St Botolph-without-Bishopsgate
All Hallows London Wall
St Ethelburga
St Helen Bishopsgate
Crosby Square
Shaft Stairs
St Andrew Undershaft
Spanish and Portuguese Synagogue
St Botolph Aldgate
St Katharine Cree
Merchant Taylors' Hall
St Michael
St Peter-upon-Cornhill
LEADENHALL STREET
★★LLOYD'S
Aldgate Pump
Sir John Cass College
Wingate Centre
Lamb Tavern
Leadenhall Market
Lloyd's Shipping Register
FENCHURCH STREET
All Hallows Staining
Clothworkers' Hall
St Olave★
Trinity House
Tower Hill
Trinity Square Gardens
St Margaret Pattens
★★ST MARY AT HILL
★ST DUNSTAN-IN-THE-EAST
Watermen and Lightermen's Hall
All Hallows by the Tower
HKSB Holdings plc
Custom House
Old Billingsgate Market
★★★TOWER OF LONDON
Tower Pier
400 ft
200 m

Liverpool Street Station

The station, erected in 1875 on the first site of Bethlehem Hospital (founded 1247, removed 1676) is vast: an iron Gothic cathedral, romantic or impractical according to taste. Take a look at the soaring arches; the delicate fretwork is very fine. Adjoining it is the renovated Great Eastern Hotel gabled and mullioned in the grand 19C railway tradition.

Opposite the station on Broadgate is Middlesex Street. The long narrow street, which marks the boundary between Spitalfields and the City, is known as **Petticoat Lane** and is famous for its **market** – *see PRACTICAL POINTS, Markets.*

St Botolph-without-Bishopsgate

Open Mon-Fri, 8am-5.30pm. ☎ *020 7588 3388, 020 7588 1053; Fax 020 7638 1256; botolph.bgate@carefree.net*

The church was rebuilt in 1725-29 on a 13C site. The square brick tower, unusually at the east end, rises directly from the Bishopsgate pavement to support a balustrade, clock tower, turret, cupola and crowning urn. The south front, overlooking the former burial ground, is brick trimmed with stone. Inside, giant Corinthian columns support the galleries and wide coffered ceiling; a drum-shaped glass dome was added in 1821; there are 19C box pews. The poet Keats was baptised in the existing font in 1795. Coade stone statues frame the 19C church hall at the west end.

In Bishopsgate Churchyard, beneath a stained-glass onion dome, stands an exotic one-roomed building faced with decorative glazed tiling and rosewood panelling; this once served as the entrance to an underground **Old Turkish Bath** (1895); it is now a restaurant.

Bishopsgate

The gate, said to have been rebuilt slightly west of the Roman gate by Bishop Erkenwald in Saxon times, was renewed several times, once even by the Hanseatic merchants, before being demolished in 1760. Note the gilded mitres from the old Bishop's Gate on the walls of **nos 105** and **108** *(first floor, Wormwood and Camomile St corners).*

The street, one of the longest in the City, was the principal road to East Anglia in Roman and medieval times.

St Ethelburga

The early-15C church which stood on this site until destroyed by a terrorist bomb on 24 April 1993, was the City's smallest church and one of the few medieval buildings to escape the Great Fire (1666) and survive the Second World War with only slight damage. The church accounts date from 1569. The church has been rebuilt to its original plan as three walls and much of the timber, stone mouldings and fittings have survived; it serves as a Centre for Reconciliation and Peace.

St Helen Bishopsgate★

♿ *Open Mon-Fri, 9am-5pm, via Church office entrance. Guide book.* ☎ *020 7283 2231; Fax 020 7626 8184; st-helens@st-helens.org.uk; www.st-helens.org.uk*

Behind a patch of grass and plane trees stands a double-fronted stone façade, beneath embattled gables, surmounted by a small, square 17C white belfry turret, lantern, ball and vane. *Entrance on the south side.*

St Helen's began as a small parish church which by 1150 extended in two equal rectangles from the present east wall to the south entrance (originally Norman arched). In the early 13C a Benedictine nunnery was established in the church grounds and a conventual church was built abutting St Helen's to the north. The nun's chapel was probably wider and considerably longer than the existing parish church which was then extended to give the double front. The arcade between the churches was rebuilt in the late 15C and the dividing screens were removed when the nunnery was dissolved (1538). Restoration following damage inflicted by a terrorist bomb has returned the church to pre-Reformation airiness and lightness.

Furnishings – In the middle of the north wall is a small **Night Staircase** of c 1500, built from the dormitory to the church for nuns attending night services, the **Processional Entrance**, originally 13C, and, at the east end, the **Nuns' Squint** (since 1525 arranged as a memorial). Note the canopied carved pulpit, the 17C doorcases and font.

Monuments★★ – In 1874 when St Martin Outwich was demolished, 18 major monuments and brasses were transferred here: the black marble slabbed tomb chest of Sir Thomas **Gresham** (d 1579); the memorial to Sir Julius Caesar Adelmare (d 1636), Privy Counsellor to James I has no effigy but a parchment and seal; railed and canopied is the marble effigy of Sir William Pickering, Elizabeth's Ambassador to Spain (d 1574); others include those of Sir John Crosby (d 1475) and his first wife (d 1460), owner of the great City mansion Crosby Hall *(see CHELSEA)*. There are also 15C-17C **brasses** rich in expression and costume detail *(north wall).*

Shakespeare (north wall) was assessed for local rates at £5 6s 8d in 1597 but left the parish, according to the record, having paid off only the 6s and 8d!

Crosby Square records the original site of **Crosby Hall** which now stands on Chelsea Embankment *(see CHELSEA).*

Turn left into **Threadneedle St** past the ornate façades of imposing buildings housing banks and the Merchant Taylors' Guild.

Royal Exchange★

The exchange was 'first built with brick at the sole charge of **Sir Thomas Gresham,** merchant, who laid the foundation 7 June 1566... On 27 January (1571) **Queen Elizabeth** came to view it and caused it to be proclaimed the Royal Exchange. But after being consumed by the dreadful Fire in 1666 it was rebuilt with Portland Stone by the City and Mercers' Company... **King Charles II** laying the first stone. It was again burned down in 1838 and a third, larger building constructed. The wide steps, monumental Corinthian portico and pediment with allegorical figures (10ft/3m tall), provide an impressive entrance to an edifice that was once the very hub of the City. Around and on the outside walls are 19C portrait statues: in front, an equestrian bronze statue of **Wellington** modelled from life and lacking stirrups (Chantrey); against the north wall, Whittington and Myddelton; at the rear, Gresham, whose emblem, a gilded bronze grasshopper, acts as a weathervane (further down Bishopsgate *[no 52]* a beaver weathervane distinguishes the former Hudson Bay House).

Freeman's Place – Behind the Exchange is a pedestrian area, with fountains at either end: bronze maiden beneath a pillared red granite canopy; mother and child by Georges Dalou (1879). The seated figure is **George Peabody** *(see index)*, the American philanthropist who founded the Peabody Trust to provide housing for the poor.

CORNHILL – ALDGATE 2

⊖ Bank: Lombard Street exit or start from ⊖ Aldgate and do the tour in reverse order.

Cornhill

This is one of the two hills upon which London was first built and is named after a medieval corn market. The junction of Cornhill with Leadenhall Street was once the most central point of London.

St Michael's

Open Mon-Fri, 8am-5.30pm. Organ recital: Mon (except Bank Hols) at 1pm; occasional Tue lectures. ☎ 020 7248 3826; citychurches@pmullen.freeserve.co.uk; www.st-michaels.org.uk

The tower (1718-24), was designed by **Hawksmoor** to replace the one that had survived the Fire but which had become unsafe. It rises by four stages to a series of pinnacles, braceleted by a balustrade. The neo-Gothic doorway, framed by small marble columns, and the carved stone covings and tympanum were designed by **Giles Gilbert Scott**, as part of a later remodelling (1857-60). Inside, Wren's vault rests on tall Tuscan columns (1670-77); the Venetian windows, the pulpit and lectern and the carved bench ends in the Wren tradition, all 19C, are noteworthy. The font dates from the 17C; the large wooden pelican from the 18C.

Explore the alleys south of St Michael's before returning to Cornhill.

Former Coffee Houses

The **Jamaica Wine House** *(see Directory)* dates from 1652 when, as the Pasqua Rosee Wine House, it was the first establishment licensed to sell coffee in London. Note the early percolator.

The **George and Vulture** *(see Directory)* has been twice destroyed by fire in its 600-year-old history. On the introduction of coffee in 1652 part of the then tavern became a chocolate, tea and coffeehouse.

Other Change Alley establishments besides the money-lenders have long gone, including Garraways which was the first to brew and sell tea, and Jonathan's, the haunt of financiers.

St Peter-upon-Cornhill

Entrance from St Peter's Alley. Open by appointment. ☎ 020 7283 2231 (St Helen's Bishopsgate Church Office)

St Peter's-upon-Cornhill claims to stand on the highest ground and on the oldest church site in the City.

The present building (1677-87) was designed by Wren. The obelisk **spire**, from which flies a vane in the form of a key (9ft long, 2 cwts in weight), is visible only from the churchyard *(south)* and Gracechurch Street *(east)*. It rests on a small green copper dome surmounting a square brick tower.

Inside, the basilica is lit by arched windows; square piers rise to tunnel vaulting, the arches articulated by a double plaster fillet that merges with the outline of the rood screen. The upper area is light and minimally decorated; the lower, to sill level, darkly panelled. The pews were all cut down in the 19C save two, retained for church wardens *(at the back)*. The oak **screen★**, one of only two to survive in Wren's churches *(see INSIGHTS AND IMAGES – The Changing Face of London)* is said to have been designed by the architect and his young daughter: it has strong central pillars rising high to support a lion and unicorn, the central arch bears the arms of Charles II. The organ gallery which is meant to have accommodated Mendelssohn on at least two occasions is original, as are the door-cases *(west end)*, sounding board with cherubs' heads, pulpit with domed panels and carved drops of fruit and leaves. The font dates from 1681.

Leadenhall Market

Gracechurch Street. Open weekdays.

Leadenhall, a bustling retail market specialising in game but also selling poultry, meat, fish, fruit, and cheese, is at its most spectacular at the start of the shooting season when the shop fronts are hung with grouse, partridge, pheasant... and at Christmas. The glass and ironwork market hall is an architectural delight. **Lamb Tavern** *(see Directory)* with its early-20C décor is frequented by market traders.

In Roman times the area boasted a forum with a basilica for public debate and a central market for trade; then when Whittington purchased and converted the manor there (hence Whittington Avenue), it returned, in part, to being a market under the Corporation (14C). The market takes its name from the house's lead-covered roof. Burned down in the Fire, the market buildings were re-erected then and again to their present form in 1881.

Ph. Gajic/MICHELIN

The Distinctive Architecture of The Lloyd's Building

Lloyd's★★

The trading activities of Lloyd's, the biggest insurance corporation in the world, which is said to cover everything except mortality, are conducted in a striking steel and glass building (1986) designed by **Sir Richard Rogers**, one of the architects of the Pompidou Centre in Paris.

The building is conceived as a great hollow space in which glass-walled galleries of offices are supported by eight colossal internal members. Six towers enclose a central atrium that rises 200ft/90m to a glass barrel vault. Great long escalators link the storeys with ground level where the business of brokering insurance is transacted in a bustling, noisy open-plan environment between underwriters at old-fashioned benches. More discreet means of accessing higher levels are provided by glass lifts that travel up the exterior of the building. Ventilation shafts, power ducting and water conduits are also streamlined along the outside of the construction.

Lloyd's Institutions

The **Lutine Bell** was retrieved from *HMS Lutine*, a captured French frigate which was sunk off the Netherlands in 1799 with gold and specie valued at nearly £1.5 million and insured by Lloyd's. Its bullion was partly salvaged in 1857-61. The bell is struck to mark the end of a crisis involving an overdue vessel: once for a loss, twice for a safe arrival.

A reminder of coffee house origins is provided by the **liveried doormen**, resplendent in red frock coats with black velvet collars and gilt-buckled top hats.

Lloyd's Register of Shipping *(71 Fenchurch St)* gives details of ownership, tonnage etc. **Lloyd's Shipping Index** is a daily publication which records the movements of some 20 000 vessels.

History – In 1691 Edward Lloyd, who owned a coffee house near the Tower, took over Pontaq's at 16 Lombard Street (plaque on Coutts' Bank), a French-owned eating house. Owing to its situation at the heart of the business world, under Lloyd the house became the meeting place favoured by merchants, shippers, bankers, underwriters, agents and newsmen. These he attracted by inaugurating the still current system of posting notices and lists of port agents, transport vessels, cargo shipments agents and other such shipping intelligence. Edward Lloyd died in 1713 (plaque in St Mary Woolnoth) and in 1769 his successors split; New Lloyd's moved into 5 Pope's Head Alley; the house in Lombard Street closed in 1785.

In 1774, Lloyd's transferred to more spacious quarters "over the northwest corner of the Royal Exchange" at Cornhill where it remained until 1928 when the first insurance offices opened in Lime Street.

Make a short detour to St Mary Axe.

St Andrew Undershaft

Open by appointment. ☎ 020 7283 2231 (St Helen's Bishopsgate Church Office); st.helens@st-helens.org.uk; www.st-helens.org.uk

The present 16C church, the third on the site, is named after the maypole shaft which stood in front of it until 1517 and, which after being laid up, was finally burnt in 1549. A replica stands further west *(Shaft Stairs)*.

A staircase turret breaks the square outline of the ancient stone tower, part of which is probably early 14C; the crenellated top is 19C.

The nave, now bare of pews, is divided from the aisles by five slender shafts and hollow columns which support a plain glass clerestory. Flat wooden roofs cover the aisles and nave, the latter punctuated by 130 carved and gilded 16C oak bosses. The west window depicting Tudor and Stuart sovereigns, the Renatus Harris organ, pulpit and font are all late 16C and 17C; the altar rails are by **Tijou** (1704).

Among St Andrew's **monuments★** are the **Datchelor family** *(see index)* memorial and, most famously, in a decorated alcove, **Nicholas Stone** 's half-length carved alabaster ruffed figure of **John Stow** (1525-1605), the antiquarian whose *Survey of London and Westminster*, published in 1598, remains a major source for every guide to London. The quill pen poised to "write something worth reading about" is renewed annually by the Lord Mayor.

Proceed along Leadenhall St past No 49 (Institute of London Underwriters) and No 56 (London Metal Exchange).

St Katharine Cree

Open daily except Sat, 10.30am-4pm. ☎ 020 7283 5733

The present compact, light and airy church is thought to be the third on the site which marked the corner boundary of the precincts of the Augustinian Priory of Holy Trinity, Christchurch, founded in 1108 by Matilda, Queen of Henry I, and dissolved in 1539.

The ragstone corner tower, lower section from late 15C and 16C above, rises to a parapet and small white-pillared turret. Note the two tiers of windows in the stone wall on Leadenhall Street, straight headed with centres raised to include three lights each. Inside the nave, giant Corinthian columns support a series of decorative round arches below the clerestory. High up, above the plain reredos, is a traceried rose window glazed with 17C glass; the central ridge of the lierne vault is decorated with a row of brightly coloured bosses bearing the badges of 17 City Companies. Note the early-17C alabaster font, 18C pulpit and altar table, and the Throgmorton effigy (1571) in the Laud Chapel.

Aldgate

The name derives from the Anglo-Saxon *aelgate* meaning free or open to all. The Romans built a gate here on the road to Colchester. In the 14C Chaucer leased the dwelling over the gate and in the 16C Mary Tudor rode through after being proclaimed queen. The gate was demolished in 1761. The **Aldgate Pump** still stands at the west end of the street.

St Botolph Aldgate

Open Mon-Fri, 10am-3pm. ☎ 020 7283 1670; brian.stbotolphsaldgate@eggconnect.com

The site on the outer side of the gate in the City Wall and beside a bridge spanning the moat (Houndsditch) had been occupied by a church for 1 000 years or more when **George Dance the Elder** came to rebuild it (1741-44). The stone steeple stands on a four-tier brick tower trimmed with stone quoins. Dance's interior was transfigured in 1889 by **JF Bentley** who redecorated the church, fronting the galleries with balusters, geometrically re-leading all but the east window, decorating the coved ceiling with a plasterwork frieze of standing angels and shields linked with leafy garlands. The domed font cover, rails and inlaid pulpit are all 19C.

In the forecourt of the Wingate Centre *(opposite Aldgate station)* stands a splendid bronze (1980) by K McCarter.

Walk up Duke's Place to Bevis Marks.

Bevis Marks

The street name is a corruption of Buries Marks, an abbreviation for the mark or site of the 12C mansion of the abbots of Bury St Edmunds. In the 16C the mansion was acquired by Thomas Heneage whose name is perpetuated in the nearby lane.

Spanish and Portuguese Synagogue

Open Sun and Mon-Wed, 11.30am-1pm; also late-Mar to late-Sep, Fri, 11.30am-1pm. £2. Guided tour: at noon. ☎ 020 7626 1274

The synagogue, a perfectly preserved vestige of the Old City, is the oldest in England (1701) and the only one in the City of London, succeeding one in Creechurch Lane *(plaque)* which was the first to open after the Jews had been invited to return by Cromwell in 1656.

Set back from the street, this building is plainly functional. Clear glass windows and dark oak furnishings are set off by the seven splendid brass chandeliers, one from Holland, which hang down low and which are lit for all Jewish festivals, weddings and other occasions. It is also notable for other surviving rich appointments: the Ark containing the handwritten Scrolls, the raised Tebah surrounded by twisted balusters. On the Fast of Ab (summer) the Haphtarah is read in medieval Spanish.

MONUMENT 3

⊖ Bank: Monument exit. Take King William St and Lombard St.

St Mary Woolnoth of the Nativity

Open Mon-Fri, 9.30am-4.30pm. Closed Bank Hols. ☎/Fax 020 7626 9701; admin @marywoolnoth.org

A Saxon church, possibly built on land given by Wulfnoth – hence the name – was rebuilt in stone by **William the Conqueror**. This medieval church was damaged in the Fire of London and replaced by the present English Baroque structure (1716-27) designed by **Nicholas Hawksmoor**.

The rusticated stone tower rises to Corinthian columns and twin turrets, linked and crowned by open balustrades. The west façade is surmounted by the unique broad belltower; Hawksmoor's treatment of the blank north wall on Lombard Street is one of the masterpieces of English architecture.

Inside, Hawksmoor planned the nave as a square within a square, with massive fluted Corinthian columns in threes marking each corner and supporting a heavily-ornamented cornice with semi-circular clerestory windows above. Also by Hawksmoor are the reredos with its twisted columns and the inlaid pulpit. On the right wall is a plaque commemorating Edward Lloyd (d 1713).

Lombard Street

The name derives from the late-13C Italian and Lombard merchants, money-changers and pawn-brokers who settled there. The street, now synonymous with City banking, is lined with 19C and 20C buildings; association dignifies it; the gilt, the brightly painted bank signs, overhanging the pavement, distinguish it. Beginning with Lloyd's horse of 1677 *(left)*, it continues with a grasshopper, 1563, formerly Martins, a cat and fiddle *(by Nicholas Lane)*, a crown and Charles II *(by Clements Lane)*, a tower and portcullis dating from 1820 *(by Birchin Lane)*, the anchor of the former Williams and Glyn's *(left)*, and at the end, a massive Barclays eagle in stone.

The Clearing House – *10 Lombard Street.* This institution has its origins in the 18C and grew out of the daily meeting in the streets of bank clerks, known as "clearers", to exchange and settle for cheques payable at their respective banks. From a post and one another's backs which they used as desks, the clearers migrated to a bay window, a room and finally a house, always in the same street. The first Clearing House was built on the site in 1833. The present building is post-war.

St Edmund the King and Martyr

Closed for renovation until Sep 2004. Open previously Mon-Fri, 10am-4pm. Closed Bank Hols. ☎/Fax 020 7626 9701

The distinctive black (lead-covered) octagonal lantern and stout **spire★** ending in a bulb and vane, rise from a square stone belfry. The corbelled parapet and inverted brackets at the tower base are decorated with flaming urns. The façade is outlined by quoins and a central pediment.

The interior was altered in the 19C but is remarkable for its woodwork: carved pulpit with drops and swags, urns on choir stalls, balustered railing round the font, panelling in the sanctuary framing the Ten Commandments and paintings of Moses and Aaron attributed to William Etty, RA. The east window was made in Munich c 1880 for St Paul's Cathedral but passed on to this church.

Walk down St Clements Lane.

St Clement Eastcheap

Open Mon-Fri, 9am-4pm. ☎ 020 7626 0220; nisuk@aol.com

The tower is built of brick with stone quoins and a balustrade.

The former St Clement's was the first City church to burn in the Great Fire; it cost £4 362 3s 4 ? d to rebuild to Wren's design (in which there is no right-angled corner!). The panelled interior is complemented with finely carved 17C door and organ cases (Purcell played on the organ) and a very fine **pulpit★★** surmounted by a massive sounding board, gay with dancing cherubs, flowered garlands and swags of fruit; the font cover bearing the Stuart arms and the sword rest are all contemporary. A gilded oval wreath adorns the flat ceiling while the ornate gilded altarpiece shows the Virgin and an angel with St Martin and St Clement.

St Clement claims to be the church of the old *Oranges and Lemons* rhyme: its parish East Cheap dates from the time of the Saxon market on the City's eastern hill, its association with oranges from the Middle Ages, when Spanish barges tied up at London Bridge to sell their oranges on the stone steps all within cry of the church *(see STRAND – TEMPLE, St Clement Danes)*.

Continue to the main crossroads and into Eastcheap; turn first left into Fish St Hill.

Monument★

Open daily, 9.30am-5pm. Closed 24-26 Dec, 1 Jan. £1.50. ☎ 020 7626 2717

The fluted Doric column of Portland stone, surmounted by a square viewing platform and gilded, flaming urn, was erected in 1671-77 in commemoration of the Great Fire. The hollow shaft stands 202ft/62m tall and 202ft/62m from the baker's in Pudding Lane where the Fire began, plumb on the route between London and

The Great Fire

The Monument was erected near to the point where it began in the king's baker's house in Pudding Lane near London Bridge; it ended at Pie Corner near Smithfield. The flames, fanned by a strong east wind, raged throughout Monday and during part of Tuesday; on Wednesday the fire slackened and on Thursday it was thought to be extinguished. When it burst out again that evening at the Temple, adjoining houses were demolished with gunpowder to prevent it spreading further. People escaped with what they could carry by boat or on foot to Moorfields or the hills of Hampstead and Highgate. The most vivid account is told in the Diary of **Samuel Pepys** (2 September 1666):

... So near the fire as we could for smoke; and all over the Thames, with one's face in the wind, you were almost burned with a shower of fire-drops... When we could endure it no more upon the water, we to a little ale-house on the Bankside... and there staid till dark almost, and saw the fire grow; and as it grew darker, appeared more and more; and in corners and upon steeples, and between churches and houses, as far as we could see up the hill of the City, in a most horrid, malicious, bloody flame, not like the fine flame of an ordinary fire... The churches, houses, and all on fire, and flaming at once; and a horrid noise the flames made, and the cracking of houses at their ruine. So home with a sad heart, and there to find every body discoursing and lamenting the fire...

Southwark until the construction of Blackfriars Bridge (1769). The relief of Charles II before the City under reconstruction (on the west face of the pedestal) is by Caius Cibber. A later inscription blaming the papists for the Fire was finally effaced in 1831.

The **view**★ from the platform (up 311 steps) is now largely obscured by the towering office blocks which also mask the column at ground level.

Return to Eastcheap.

St Margaret Pattens

Open Mon-Fri, 10.30am-4pm. Closed Bank Hols. ☎ 020 7623 6630

The site at the corner of Rood Lane was possibly already occupied by a wooden church in 1067. A square stone tower, ornamented by a pinnacled balustrade supports a hexagonal lead-covered and therefore black **spire**★ which sharpens to a needle point on which balances a gilded vane.

The church, as redesigned by Wren, is a plain oblong with a flat ceiling and round clerestory windows. The carved **woodwork**★ is outstanding: to the east, the reredos, 17C, gold lettered and framing a contemporary Italian painting, is carved with fruit, a peapod, flowers; in front, turned balusters support the communion rail; note a high boxed beadle's pew and below, a low "punishment bench" with ferocious devil's head, the choir stalls, a finely carved eagle lectern and the only two canopied pews in London.

"Pattens" was added to the dedication for distinction and, according to Stow, referred to the pattens, iron shod overshoes, sold in the abutting lane.

Walk down St Mary-at-Hill opposite.

A Quaint Verse

To remember the dates of the **Great Plague** and the **Great Fire of London** children once were taught:

"In sixteen hundred and sixty five,
scarce a soul was left alive.
In sixteen hundred and sixty six,
London burned like rotten sticks."

The Monument: engraving of 1680

St Mary-at-Hill★★

Entrance located between 6 and 7 St Mary-at-Hill. Open Mon-Fri, 11am-4pm. ☎ 020 7626 4184 (office)

A church is first mentioned on the site in 1177. The stock-brick tower dates from 1780.

The Wren **plan**★ (1670-76), almost square, is divided into 3 x 3 bays beneath a shallow central dome, supported on free-standing Corinthian columns; at each corner are plain square ceilings at cornice height.

The interior was damaged by fire in 1988 and not all the **woodwork** for which St Mary's was known was restored: note the font cover (late 17C); great oak reredos, communion table, altar rails (early 18C); organ gallery (musical trophies), lectern and turned balustrade, pulpit garlanded with fruit and flowers beneath a massive sounding board and approached by a beautiful curved staircase by **William Gibbs Rogers** (19C); box pews. Six gilded and enamelled wrought-iron sword rests added to the splendour of the interior.

St Dunstan-in-the-East★

A magnificent garden flourishes in the ruins of the church, dominated by the elegant Portland stone steeple which rests on a four-tier **tower★**, canted by flying buttresses with pinnacles, designed by Wren.

Thames Street

Probably in Roman times and certainly in the early Middle Ages, Thames Street ran the length of the river wall; by the 17C, it served as a route between the Wardrobe and the Tower, crossing the furriers' and vintners' quarters: it would have been lined by eight churches and provided rear access to castles and mansions, quays, warehouses and markets, whose main thoroughfare was the river. Today Upper and Lower Thames Street are separated by London Bridge.

Custom House

The house of rusticated stone and yellow stock brick, nearly 500ft/152m wide, dates from 1813-17; its central river front bay was added later by Robert Smirke (1825). Three storeys high, with five lanterns as sole decoration, it is the sixth to stand on this reach of the Thames.

Across Lower Thames and up St Mary-at-Hill on the left *(no 18)* is the small **Watermen and Lightermen's Hall** (1780) which belongs to an ancient City Guild dating back to Tudor times. Stand on the pavement opposite to catch a glimpse of the ornate ceiling.

Old Billingsgate Market

There was a market on the site from 1297 to 1982, when the wholesale fish market established as a free fish market in 1699 moved to new premises in the West India Docks on the Isle of Dogs. The market building, designed in 1876 by Sir Howard Jones, with Britannia presiding over two dolphins on its decorative roof, was converted into offices in 1990.

Between two elegant period buildings stands a striking blue mirrorglass construction *(10 Lower Thames St)*.

St Magnus the Martyr

Lower Thames Street. ♿ Open Sun (for services) and Tue-Fri, 10am-3pm. Brochures. Guide sheets. ☎ 020 7626 4481

The massive square stone **tower★**, decorated with a balustrade and urns, rises to an octagonal belfry, a leaded cupola, lantern, and obelisk spire surmounted by a golden vane. A clock (1709) projects over the churchyard.

From 1176 St Magnus stood, a stone sentinel on an ancient Roman wharf at the foot of London Bridge. Wren rebuilt it on the same site. When, c 1760, the houses and shops which lined the bridge were removed, Wren's building was curtailed to leave the tower as a church porch astride the bridge's east footpath. Its postern situation continued until 1831 when Rennie's bridge was constructed 100ft/30m upstream.

The interior, remodelled in the late 18C, has a barrel-vaulted nave, supported by fluted Ionic columns and punctuated by the deep recesses of the oval clerestory windows. Although much remains from the 17C, inscriptions on the west gallery explain the decoration: the church was "repaired and beautified" in 1886 and 1924. Note the iron **sword rest★** dated 1708, 16C-17C shrine (right of the altar), altarpiece and rails, font (1683) and pulpit.

London Bridge★

London Bridge was the only crossing over the lower Thames until 1750 when Westminster was constructed. The Romans probably built the first bridge on the single gravel spit which exists in the clay; the Saxons certainly erected a wooden structure which had to be repeatedly rebuilt against the ravages of floodwater, ice and fire. Between 1176 and 1209 a stone bridge (905ft/276m long and 40ft/12m wide) was constructed on 19 pointed arches rising from slender piles anchored onto wood and rubble piers. These so obstructed the flow of the river that water gushed through them as if forced through sluices; many refused to shoot the bridge in a boat, the principal transport of the day, so passengers would often disembark on one side only to re-board on the other. In winter, the reduced river flow meant that ice would form so that when at last the river froze over great **Frost Fairs** could be held (the most famous being between 1683 and 1684).

> **A Levy**
>
> The saying "London Bridge was built upon woolpacks" alludes to the fact that the new stone bridge was built with money raised from a tax on wool.

The bridge itself was lined with houses, shops, even a chapel; it was here that traitors' heads were exposed: Jack Cade (1450), Thomas More (1535).

In 1831 John Rennie constructed a robust granite bridge 60yds/55m upstream. In 1973 it was replaced by the existing sleek crossing, Rennie's bridge was sold for £1 million and removed to Arizona, USA.

On the west side of London Bridge sits **Fishmongers' Hall**, its fine features best seen from the river. This neo-Greek building (1831-34) enjoys a unique position; light reflected from the water enhances the Hall's rich interior gold leaf decoration (restored post war).

Cross to Arthur St and Martin Lane.

Ye Olde Wine Shades is a colourful double fronted pub (1663) with painted boards outside much like a 17C tavern *(see Directory)*. It claims to be the oldest wine house in London having originally been the bar attached to the Fishmongers' Hall, in whose shadow (immortalised in its name) it was to survive. Presently it is surrounded by the spiky marble and glass buildings of Minster Court.

The square brick and stucco tower (19C) marks the site of the medieval church of **St Martin Orgar.**

Proceed west along Cannon St and cross to the north side.

St Mary Abchurch★

Open Wed, noon-2pm.

The Fire consumed "a fair church", last of a line dating back to the 12C. The site was minute, some 80ft/24m square, and Wren decided to cover the new church with a painted **dome★**. Approximately 40ft/12m in diameter, it cannot be seen from outside and inside it rises from arches springing directly from the outer walls. There are no buttresses and only one interior column.

Tall carved pews line the north, south and west walls as in the original church – although the kennels reserved for the congregation's dogs have gone.

Receipts in the parish records show that many of the greatest craftsmen of the day worked on the furnishings: the font and stonework, Robert Bird's original gilded copper pelican weathervane (removed as unsafe in 1764) is over the west door, the pulpit with garlands and cherubs' heads, doorcases, font rails and cover, the lion and unicorn and royal arms. Authenticated by bills and a personal letter from **Grinling Gibbons** himself, is the **reredos★★**, massive in size, magnificent in detail and delicacy. Note the many rich monuments and urns.

The **tower and spire★** are on the same small scale as the church: red brick with stone quoins, surmounted by a cupola, lantern and slender lead spire.

On the opposite side of the street stands Cannon Street Station *(for description see walk no 4)*.

London Stone

A block of limestone *(set into the wall of 111 Cannon Street)*, "its origin and purpose are unknown", may have been a milestone or milliary or, according to legend, may be a fragment of an altar erected in 800BC by Trojan, the mythical founder of Britain.

St Swithin's Lane

The street is synonymous with the prestigious merchant bank NM Rothschild's. The clean lined building is post-war; the lane remains old and narrow, and is often blocked from end to end with waiting Rolls-Royces, Bentleys, Jaguars...

N M Rothschild and Sons Ltd

The merchant bank Rothschild's earned its status in this country when in its first years, under its London branch founder, Nathan Mayer Rothschild (1777-1836), it acquired at low cost the drafts issued by Wellington which the government was unable to meet, and renewed them; ultimately they were redeemed at par. NMR increased his fortune and the government appointed him chief negotiator of future Allied war loans!

His confidence in victory against Napoleon and in his own intelligence service again increased NMR's wealth, it is said, on the occasion of Waterloo, fought throughout Sunday 18 June: on the Monday, when only rumour was circulating, Nathan bought; the market rose; he sold; the market plunged; he bought again and made a fortune as his personal messenger arrived from the battle scene confirming victory; Wellington's despatches only arrived by messenger the following Wednesday and a report was published in *The Times* on Thursday (22nd). Other business included negotiating lucrative textile deals.

MANSION HOUSE 4

⊖ Bank: Lombard Street exit; Cannon Street; Mansion House

Mansion House★

The house dates only from 1739-52 – previously lord mayors remained in their own residences during the years of their mayoralty. The **Lord Mayor** is Chief Magistrate of the City and on the ground floor on the east side is a Court of Justice, with cells below, the only such appointments in a private residence in the kingdom.

Lord Mayor's Show

The show *(see Directory)* is the Lord Mayor's progress to his swearing-in before the Lord Chief Justice, an observance which dates back to the charter of 1215 which required that the mayor be presented to the monarch or his justices at the Palace of Westminster. The procession was, for centuries, partly undertaken over water when the mayor owned a civic barge (15C). In 1553 full pageantry became the order of the day with men parading their best liveries, trumpets sounding, masques and poems recited along the route. Today, with the judges removed from Westminster, the oath is taken at the Royal Courts of Justice in the Strand; the pageantry, after a decline in the 19C, has returned with floats and the new and old mayors progressing in the golden state and other horse-drawn coaches accompanied by outriders.
The spectacular show is followed on the Monday evening by the Lord Mayor's Banquet in Guildhall, which by tradition (although not invariably) begins with turtle soup, and at which the principal speakers are the new Lord Mayor and the Prime Minister.

George Dance the Elder designed a Palladian style mansion in Portland stone; modest staircases on either side at the front lead to a raised portico of six giant Corinthian columns, surmounted by a pediment decorated with an allegory of the splendour of London. *For the description of the interior, see Worth a Visit.*

Proceed along Walbrook Ct.

St Stephen Walbrook★

Open Mon-Fri, 10am-4pm (3pm Fri). Services: Thu at 12.45pm (Sung Eucharist – Monteverdi, Lassus, Byrd, Palestrina). Organ recital: Fri, 12.30-1.30pm, no charge. ☎ 020 7283 4444, 020 7626 8242 (Verger)

The **tower and steeple★** are square. The ragstone tower rises to a trim balustrade; the later steeple of Portland stone rises through eight similar stages to two balls and a vane. The characteristic dome, green turreted and also vaned can be seen at the rear.

The most striking feature is Wren's **dome★** which undoubtedly served as a model for St Paul's which it pre-dates: slightly off centre, the cupola rests on a ring of eight circular arches strategically placed within the asymmetrical square ground plan. The bays are delineated by free standing Corinthian columns grouped to produce unexpected perspectives within the characteristic dark oak panelling and carved lighter wood furnishings. Below the dome and raised on two communion steps sits **Henry Moore**'s monumental altar of golden travertine (1986).

K. Brett/MICHELIN

The ornate pulpit and cupola of St Stephen Walbrook

Cannon Street

In the Middle Ages Candelwriteystrete was the home of candle makers and wick chandlers – hence the presence on Dowgate Hill of the **Tallow Chandlers' Hall**, rebuilt in 1670-72 and Italianised in 1880, and **Skinners' Hall**, a late-18C building accommodating a fine staircase, aromatic sandalwood panelling dating from 1670, 18C plasterwork and a hall (1850) decorated by Frank Brangwyn (1904-10).

Cannon Street Station

The station stands on the site of two churches and the important medieval steelyard of the Hanseatic merchants. All that remains of the mid-Victorian station building are two monumental towers adorned with gilded weathervanes flanking the viaduct high above the river bank.

Continue along Cannon St west and turn left into College Hill.

St Michael Paternoster Royal

Open Mon-Fri, 9am-5pm. ☎ 020 7248 5202; Fax 020 7248 4761; general@missiontoseafarers.org; www.missiontoseafarers.org

The square stone tower rises to a balustrade quartered by urns. The **spire★**, added in 1715, takes the form of a three-tier octagonal lantern, marked at each angle by an Ionic column and urn; on high is a vaned spirelet.

The "fair parish church", as Stow described it, "new built by Richard Whittington", in place of the earliest known building of the mid 13C, was destroyed in the Fire; in July 1944 history was repeated.

The south wall with six rounded lights and a balustraded parapet is of stone, the east end of brick, stone trimmed. Above the door and windows are cherubs' head keystones. The pulpit, reredos and lectern are 17C. The red, gold, green windows include *(south-west corner)* young Dick Whittington with his cat. **Whittington** *(see walk no 7)*, who lived in an adjoining house, founded an almshouse, also adjoining, and on his death in 1423, was buried in the church.

St James Garlickhythe

Open usually Mon-Fri, 10am-4pm. Closed Bank Hol Mon. Services: Sun at 10.30am (Sung Eucharist), Wed at 1.15pm. ☎ 020 7248 7546

The square stone tower ends in a balustrade, quartered by pointed urns. The **spire★**, added in 1713, rises in a square three-tiered lantern, quartered by paired and advanced columns, crowned on high by a vaned spirelet.

Inside the tower, through the door decorated with a scallop shell – the emblem of St James of Compostella to whom the church is dedicated – two tablets summarise the later history of the church which dates back to the 10C-11C.

The church was built to a perfectly symmetrical plan, on an isolated site, and christened "Wren's Lantern" owing to its many windows. The woodwork is principally 17C: note the dowel peg for the preacher's wig. The marble font carved with cherubs' heads is late 17C. The ceiling is ornamented with gilded plasterwork. **Sword rests★**, complete with unicorn supporters, recall six medieval lord mayors and others.

On the other side of Upper Thames Street stands the **Vintners' Hall**; built in 1671, restored in 1948 and boasting a majestic hall with fine late-17C panelling.

Beyond, an unremarkable inlet is all that remains of **Queenhithe Dock**, once London's most important dock above London Bridge.

After the footbridge but before the tunnel, on the north side of Upper Thames Street stands all that survives of **St Mary Somerset**. The slim, square, white tower (1695), built by Wren and adorned with masks, rises from its garden setting to a parapet, quartered with square finials and obelisk pinnacles.

Walk up Lambeth Hill and cross Queen Victoria St (for description of the street see walk no 5).

Cole Abbey Presbyterian Church

Open by appointment. ☎ 020 7248 5213; www.london-freechurch.org.uk

The small square stone tower, marked by corner urns, supports an octagonal lead **spire★** which rises to **a gilded three-masted ship** weathervane.

The recorded history of the church, formerly known as St Nicolas Cole Abbey, goes back to 1144 but even **Stow** "could never learn the cause of the name and therefore let it passe". The church was burned out in 1666 and again in 1941. The stone exterior is pierced by tall rounded windows beneath corbelled hoods and circled by an open balustrade. Its woodwork is 17C.

At the crossroads, cross over to join Bow Lane.

Bow Lane

Stow tells how the area was once occupied by shoemakers and that the narrow and winding Bow Lane was previously known as Hosiers' Lane.

Turn right into Watling St past an old pub.

St Mary Aldermary

Open Mon-Fri, 11am-3pm. Leaflet. Guided tour by appointment Fri. www.stmaryaldermary.co.uk

Corner buttresses, robust pinnacles and gilded finials adorn the Gothic tower of St Mary, "the older Mary Church", older that is than the Norman St Mary-le-Bow. After the Great Fire, a benefactor appeared offering £5 000 to rebuild the church as it had been; Wren, therefore, built a Gothic church for £3 457!

Despite successive remodelling, the interior retains its fan vaulting and central rosettes, a **Grinling Gibbons** pulpit and rich west doorcase (with a peapod), a 1682 font and, against the third south pillar, an oak **sword rest** also of 1682 – one only of four in wood to survive and uniquely carved with fruit and flowers by Grinling Gibbons.

Return to Bow Lane.

Williamson's Tavern *(Groveland Court – see Directory)* is accommodated in a 17C house with a contemporary wrought-iron gate which once served as a Lord Mayor's residence (1666-1753).

St Mary-le-Bow★★

Open Mon-Fri, 7.30am-6pm (4pm Fri). Closed Bank Hols. Concerts: Thu in term time at 1.05pm. Brochure (2 languages). ☎ 020 7248 5139; Fax 020 7248 0509; administrator@bowbells.dircon.co.uk

The tower which advances into Cheapside contains the famous **Bow Bells** and supports Wren's most famous **spire★★** (1671-80) in which he used all five Classical orders and the bow (the mason's term for a stone arch). The weather **vane**, a winged dragon (8ft 10in/3m long) is poised at the top (239ft/73m) with a rope dancer riding on its back.

Completed in 1673 in Portland stone, the church was Wren's most expensive, costing over £8 000 and the steeple only slightly less. It was based on the Basilica of Constantine in Rome.

In May 1941 the church was bombed. The exterior was restored to Wren's design while the interior layout was redesigned. The unique carved rood is a gift from the people of Germany. The bronze sculpture was given by the Norwegians in memory of those who died in the Resistance. The twin pulpits are used for the famous dialogues where two public figures of opposing views debate moral points.

The Great Bell of Bow

In 1334 the Great Bell of Bow called people from bed at 5.45am and rang the curfew at 9pm; the practice continued for over 400 years ceasing only in 1874: this sound came to define the limits of the City, giving rise to the saying that "a true Londoner, a Cockney, must be born within the sound of Bow Bells". According to legend it was these bells that chimed out "Turn again Whittington, Lord Mayor of London". During the 1939-45 war the 12-bell chime was used as a recognition signal by the BBC and came to mean hope and freedom to millions all over the world thus deserving the title "the most famous peal in Christendom".

The Norman **crypt**, built in 1087 with rough ragstone walls on the ruins of a Saxon church, contains the original columns with cushion capitals supporting the bows (arches) from which the church takes its name. Also named after them is the Court of Arches, supreme judicial court of the Archbishop of Canterbury, which has met here since the 12C.

West of the church is a small garden in which stands a statue of Captain John Smith (1580-1631), a pioneer and settler of Jamestown in Virginia. A tablet commemorates the poet Milton.

Turn right into Cheapside (see ST PAUL'S), take Bucklersbury Passage and walk down Queen Victoria St.

Temple of Mithras

The stone temple with a double course of red tiles, 60ft long, 20ft wide, was erected on the bank of the Walbrook in the 2C AD when Roman legions were stationed in the City. All traces had long since vanished and even the Walbrook had altered course and level by 1954 when excavations revealed walls laid in the outline of a basilica divided into a narthex, nave and aisles separated by columns and a buttressed apse at the west end.

The head of the god Mithras in a Phrygian cap, those of Minerva and Serapis the Egyptian god of the Underworld with a corn measure on his head, together with other retrieved artefacts are now in the Museum of London *(description in Worth a Visit)*. The temple itself, removed to enable an office block to rise as planned, was then reconstructed in the forecourt.

The temple would have stood near the centre of the Roman city: to the south stood the governor's palace on the Thames foreshore, to the northwest was sited the basilica and forum which stretched some 60 acres from Cornhill and Leadenhall Street to Fenchurch Street.

BLACKFRIARS 5

⊖ *Blackfriars*

The name **Blackfriars** commemorates Blackfriars Monastery, dissolved in 1538, and abandoned until 1576 when a theatre was founded in the cloisters; here a professional children's company would rehearse before performing at court. Twenty years later **James Burbage** converted another part of the monastery into the Blackfriars Theatre for the performance of Shakespeare's later plays and those of Beaumont and Fletcher. The theatre, demolished in 1655, is commemorated in Playhouse Yard.

Blackfriars Bridges

James Cubitt's iron and stone road bridge (1899) replaced a previous 18C structure. The iron railway bridge (1896) with high parapet and coats of arms at each end, celebrates the prosperity enjoyed by the railways in the 19C.

A modern footbridge leads directly to the piazza of the Tate Modern on the south bank *(see Bankside – Southwark)*. The striking structure marks a technical achievement combining sculpture and architecture

Unilever House

The vast stone building (1931) with its rusticated ground floor, pillars, large sculptures and miles of corridors inside, stands on part of the site of **Bridewell Palace**, built by Henry VIII in 1522 and where he received Emperor Charles V, who elected to stay in Blackfriars Monastery on what was then the far bank of the Fleet. Edward VI gave the Bridewell to the City, which converted it into an orphanage (from where in 1619 two lots of one hundred orphans were sent across the Atlantic to populate the burgeoning State of Virginia), and after the Fire rebuilt it as a prison, soon notorious as one of London's most evil houses (demolished 1864).

The Black Friar, a wedge-shaped pub (1896), is fronted by a jolly fat friar *(see Directory)*.

Queen Victoria Street

The street, the first City street to be lit by electricity, was created in 1867-71 by cutting through a maze of alleys and buildings. Stretching from Bank to Blackfriars, it is lined with a number of widely contrasting ancient and modern institutions.

Printing House Square

The square acquired its name after the Fire, when, on the site of the **Norman Mountfichet Castle** and the later Blackfriars Playhouse, the King's Printer set up presses and began to publish acts, the King James Bible, proclamations and the *London Gazette* (1666 – as *Oxford Gazette* 1665). The name remained after the printer moved, in 1770, nearer to Fleet Street.

In 1784 John Walter purchased a house in the square and the following year began publication of the *Daily Universal Register*, altering its title on 1 January 1788 to ***The Times***. In 1964 a new slate and glass building was constructed for the broadsheet's offices with the old square as forecourt; 10 years later they moved to Gray's Inn Road before transferring (1986) to Wapping *(see Outer London: DOCKLANDS)*.

The square's history is related in full on a plaque situated on what is now the Continental Bank house.

Up Blackfriars Lane stands **Apothecaries' Hall** (1632, rebuilt c 1670): in the courtyard a pillared lamp stands over the old monastic well.

St Andrew-by-the-Wardrobe

Open usually Mon-Fri, 10am-4pm. Services: Tue at 12.30pm, Wed at 12.30pm, Thu at 6.15pm. ☎/Fax 020 7329 3632; acc@standrew.reewire.co.uk; www.standrew.reewire.co.uk

The church was known as St Andrew juxta Baynard Castle until the Great Wardrobe or royal storehouse, previously in the Tower, was erected on a site close by in 1361 *(plaque in Wardrobe Place)*. Church, Wardrobe, Castle and St Ann Blackfriars, were all destroyed in the Fire; only St Andrew was rebuilt. On 29/30 December 1940, fire again gutted the church leaving just the tower and outer walls. It was rebuilt in 1959-61. The galleried church has attractive vaulting and plaster work. The square red-brick tower is decorated with irregular stone quoins and a crowning balustrade.

Baynard Castle

In c 1100 a fort was built on the river bank, pendant to the Tower downstream, by one "Baynard that came with the Conqueror" according to Stow. When it burnt down in 1428 it was rebuilt by Duke Humphrey of Gloucester; it was here in 1460 that Richard of Gloucester heard that his plans to seize the crown were progressing *(Richard III, 3 vii)*. Henry VII reconstructed a more spacious palace in which Lady Jane Grey received the news that she was to be queen (1553). It finally disappeared in the Fire of 1666.

College of Arms

Open Mon-Fri, 10am-4pm. Closed Bank Hols, State and special occasions. Brochure. Shop. ☎ 020 7248 2762; Fax 020 7248 6448; enquiries@college-of-arms.gov.uk; www.college-of-arms.gov.uk

The college, overlooking a forecourt behind splendid wrought-iron gates, dates from 1671-88 when it was rebuilt after the Fire.

The compact red-brick building, formerly pedimented and now parapeted, was truncated when Queen Victoria Street was created. The interior woodwork, staircases, panelling, pilastered and garlanded screen is by William Emmett, a contemporary of Grinling Gibbons. The Earl Marshal's Court, the principal room, is panelled and furnished with a throne and a gallery.

The College is responsible for granting coats of arms and monitoring their application; it also organises State ceremonies and undertakes genealogical research.

Cross Queen Victoria St.

St Benet's Welsh Church

Open for services Sun at 11am and 2.30pm; also open by apppointment with the Churchwarden. ☎ 020 7489 8754 (church), ☎ 020 8399 6158 (Churchwarden)

At the time of the Great Fire, the church, which was already some six centuries old, stood directly behind Baynard Castle which fronted the river and, like the church, was totally destroyed. Wren designed a small brick church with a hipped roof, rounded windows with carved stone festoons and a general country, Dutch air: the castle was not rebuilt. The tower of a dark red brick is defined with white stone quoins and rises only two stages before being crowned by a small lead cupola, lantern and spire. The interior is lined with galleries, divided at the north-west corner by the tower and supported on panelled Corinthian columns which rise above the base of the galleries. Below all is of wood: the west doorcase decked with cherubs and royal arms, a balustered communion rail, ornate table and a high pedimented reredos with surmounting urns.

Walk up Peter's Hill, turn left past St Paul's Cathedral (see ST PAUL'S CATHEDRAL) to Ludgate Hill.

Ludgate Hill

A plaque on the south abutment of the 19C railway states "In a house near the site was published in 1702 the ***Daily Courant*** first London daily newspaper." Above the bridge stood Lud Gate, demolished in 1760: plaque on the wall of St Martin-within-Ludgate *(see below)*. It was the first curfew gate to be closed at night and was named after the legendary King Lud (66 BC), who is said to have built the first gate on the site. Statues from the 1586 gate were removed to St Dunstan-in-the-West *(see STRAND - TEMPLE)*.

St-Martin-within-Ludgate

Open Mon and Wed-Fri, 11am-4pm. Music recitals: Wed at 1.15pm. Brochure. ☎/Fax 020 7248 6054; stmartin_within_ludgate@hotmail.com

The church, which stood by the medieval **Lud Gate** and had its west wall just inside the Roman perimeter, is said to have been built first by King Cadwalla in the 7C; it was certainly rebuilt in 1439 before being burnt down in the Fire.

Wren cut off the hill frontage inside by means of stout pillars on which he rested a gallery and thick coffered arches. At ground level beneath the gallery the bays were filled with three doors, their **cases★** richly carved by **Grinling Gibbons**. The remaining area is laid out as a square within a square by means of four inner columns on which rest the groined vault formed by the intersection of barrel vaulting above the nave, chancel and transepts. The woodwork is 17C. The churchwardens' double chair dating from 1690 is unique.

From a lead-covered cupola and lantern, ringed by a balcony, rises a black needle **spire★**, the perfect foil to the green dome of St Paul's Cathedral.

Ludgate Circus

The circus, which was built in 1875 on the site of the Fleet Bridge to Ludgate Hill, includes a plaque (north-west angle) to Edgar Wallace (1875-1932), a Greenwich foundling who became a successful writer of crime novels.

GUILDHALL 6

⊖ Bank: Lombard Street exit; St Paul's

Poultry

The buildings (HSBC) on the north side were designed by Lutyens (1924-39) – high on the corners is a sculpture by Dick Reid of a fat boy driving a goose to the Stocks Market (1282-1737) which was once located nearby and was famous for its herbs and fresh fruit. Rent from the stalls was allocated to the maintenance of London Bridge.

Walk up Poultry and turn right into Old Jewry.

St Olave Jewry

The two-stage stone tower is topped by a beautiful **weathervane**, a three-master fully rigged, from St Mildred's Church, Bread Street. The church, rebuilt by Wren (1670-76), was destroyed in 1940.

Gresham Street

The street bears the name of Sir **Thomas Gresham** *(see above: Bank – Bishopsgate)*, who in his will founded **Gresham College** as a kind of free university in his mansion in Bishopsgate, Gresham House, which fronted on Old Broad Street. The house was demolished in 1768 and the institution re-established in 1843 at no 91 Gresham Street. The college, an independent institution supported by the corporation of London and the Mercers' Company, now occupies premises at **Barnard's Inn** *(see CHANCERY LANE)*.

The 1956 **Mercers' Hall** in Ironmonger Lane is situated on the site of the former St Thomas of Acon Hospital.

St Lawrence Jewry

Open Mon-Fri, 7.30am-2pm. Recitals: Mon at 1pm (piano); Tues at 1pm (organ); daily in Aug. Guide book. ☎ 020 7600 9478

The stone tower rises to a balustrade with corner obelisks which enclose a pedimented lantern set in line with Gresham Street but out of alignment with the base, which parallels the west wall. Above is a lead obelisk spire from which flies the original gridiron weathervane, now also incorporating a replica of the incendiary bomb which caused the almost total destruction of the church in 1940.

"St Lawrence, called in the Jury because of old time many Jews inhabited thereabout" was, according to Stow, a "fair and large" parish church. Built in 1196 and closely surrounded by houses, it perished completely in the Fire. Wren designed a building of modest outward appearance squaring up the interior by varying the thickness of the walls. The restored ceiling, coffered and decorated to Wren's original design with gilded plaster work, emphasises the rectangular plan. The brilliant windows by Christopher Webb contrast with the plain and unassuming modern woodwork. The modern church is the church of the City Corporation.

Past the Guildhall (description in Worth a Visit) turn right into Aldermanbury.

St Mary Aldermanbury

The 12C site is now a garden, with only bases of the perimeter walls and pillars outlining the bombed Wren church (1670). The stones were numbered and sent to Fulton, USA where the church has been rebuilt to its 17C plan.

Take Love Lane.

St Alban

All that remains of Wren's church (1697-98) is the pure Gothic tower with slim corner buttresses crowned by a balustrade and crocketed pinnacles, which rises like a white stone needle above the traffic.

Walk down Wood St back to Gresham St.

Goldsmiths' Hall in Foster Lane dates from 1835. It is endowed by an exceptional collection of gold and silver plate. Its Baroque interior provides a lavish setting for its annual jewellery exhibition.

St Anne and St Agnes

Open Sun, all day, Mon-Fri, 10am-6pm. Concerts: Mon (except Bank Hols and during Aug) and Fri at 1.10pm. ☎ 020 7606 4986; Fax 020 7600 8984; stanneluthch@lutheran.fsnet.co.uk; www.StAnnesLutheranChurch.org

The present Lutheran church, which was mentioned c 1200, was rebuilt by Wren (1676-87) to the ancient domed-cross plan within a square, and again after the Second World War. The exterior is of rose-red brick with round-headed windows under central pediments. The small, square, stuccoed-stone tower is surmounted by an even smaller square domed turret, flaunting a vane in the shape of the letter A.

For St Botolph Aldersgate – see Barbican below.

BEYOND THE CITY WALL 7

⊖ Moorgate; Barbican

Moorgate

The street is named after a gate cut in the City wall in 1415 (demolished in 1760) to provide access to Moorfields the open common on which people practised archery, dried clothes *(plaque on site of Tenter Street by Tenter House)*, flew kites; two and a half centuries later it was one of the main exits for thousands fleeing the Great Plague. The street is today overlooked by the modern office buildings and the City of **London College** which dates from the rebuilding of London Bridge in 1831.

Proceed along Moorgate to London Wall.

St Alphage

14C pointed stone arches in black flint walls mark the west tower of the chapel of Elsing Spital Priory dissolved by Henry VIII. (Revealed by 1940 bombs.)

St Giles Cripplegate★

♿ *Open Mon-Fri, 11am-4pm. Guided tour: Tue, 2-4pm. ☎ 020 7638 1997 (admin); lesley@stgilescripplegate.com; www.stgilescripplegate.com*

Dwarfed but in no way overpowered by the Barbican, St Giles' tower is built of stone and brick; corner pinnacles guard an open cupola merry-go-round-shaped turret which sports a weathervane. (Peal of 12 bells; chiming clock.)

During its 900-year history since 1090 when a Norman church was first erected on the site outside the City Wall beside the postern gate on to the moor, St Giles' has been scarred by regular acts of destruction and rebuilding – the most recent caused by bombing in 1940. A 15C arcade rises to a clerestory to divide the nave from the aisles. Few memorials, after so many vicissitudes, survive, although signatures recorded in the registers confirm associations with the poet **John Milton** (buried in the chancel, 1674; bust by John Bacon, 1793, south wall), the navigator **Martin Frobisher** (buried in south aisle, 1594), the author of the *Book of Martyrs* **John Foxe** (buried 1587), the mapmaker **John Speed** (buried 1629 below his monument on the south wall), **Oliver Cromwell** (married 22 August 1620), **Sir Thomas More**, **Ben Jonson**, **Shakespeare** (at the baptism of his nephew), Edward Alleyn, Prince Rupert, Holman Hunt, Sir Ebenezer Howard (pioneer of garden cities). Other notable fixtures include a fine sword rest, lectern and marble font, a display of ecclesiastical and secular silver, and, in the south-east corner of the chancel, a medieval sedilia and piscina.

Barbican★

The Barbican Project, a residential neighbourhood incorporating schools, shops, open spaces, a conference and arts centre, to be established in the City on the bombed sites of Cripplegate, was conceived in the aftermath of World War II; construction began in 1962. The first residential phase was completed in 1976 and the arts centre finally opened in 1982.

The rounded arch motif, used vertically in the arcades and on the roofline and horizontally round the stairwells, gives a sense of unity to the various elements: 40-storey tower blocks, crescents and mews linked by high and low level walkways and interspersed with gardens and sports areas. At the heart of this city within a city, beside the lake with its cascades and fountains, stands St Giles' Church *(see below)*, a vestige of Cripplegate and the only tangible link with the past.

Barbican Arts Centre – The complex, of which five out of ten storeys are below ground, contains a concert hall (the permanent home of the London Symphony Orchestra), two theatres, three cinemas, a library, art gallery, sculpture court (on the roof of the concert hall), exhibition halls, meeting rooms and restaurants. The soaring theatre fly-tower is disguised by a roof-top conservatory harbouring a green jungle of ficus, eucalyptus, ferns and cacti.
Also incorporated into the concrete maze is the **Guildhall School of Music and Drama** (1977) endowed with a canted façade.
Follow the signs to the Museum of London (description in Worth a Visit).

High-rise living in the Barbican

Ph. Gajic/MICHELIN

Aldersgate

The original gate was said to have been built by a Saxon named Aldred. As James I entered the capital at this point on his accession, the gate was rebuilt in 1617 in commemoration of his entry, but demolished in 1761.

St Botolph Aldersgate

Open: Sat nearest to 9 Nov (Lord Mayor's Show Day); open house weekend in Sep; groups by prior arrangement ☎ 020 8464 3058. ☎/Fax 020 7606 0684 (Churchwarden); DavidPowell@xalt.co.uk
The church (1788-91) is built of dark red-brown brick and is lit by conventional rounded windows. Its small square tower is topped by a cupola with a wooden turret and gilded vane. The building was "improved" in 1829 by the addition of a pedimented east end in stucco. The interior is mainly Georgian with elaborate rosettes in high relief on the white plaster ceiling, coffered apses and 19C glass; in the galleries are two ward rooms where the children sat during the services. One window commemorates John Wesley in Moorfields; the east "window" transparency depicting the *Agony in the Garden* is a painting on glass by James Pierson (1788). The inlaid pulpit stands on a carved palm tree.
Given its situation by a gate in the City Wall, the church is dedicated to the 7C Saxon saint and patron of travellers.
Take Little Britain, Bartholomew Close and an alleyway to St Bartholomew-the-Great.

St Bartholomew-the-Great★★

♿ *Open normally Tue-Fri, 8.30am-5pm (4pm in winter); Sat, 10.30am-1.30pm; Sun, 2pm-6pm. Donation £3. Guide book. ☎ 020 7606 5171; Fax 020 7600 6909; st.bartholomew@btinternet.com; www.greatstbarts.com*
St Bartholomew's was once a great, spacious church of which the present building was only the chancel. It was founded in 1123 by a one-time courtier, **Rahere**, following a pilgrimage to Rome: on land granted by **Henry I** he established both the hospital and an Augustinian priory of which he became the first prior. By 1143, when he died, the Norman chancel had been completed; nearly 400 years later the church was 280ft/85m long, the west door being where the gateway on to Little Britain now stands. In 1534 the priory was valued at £693 9s 10d. In 1539 **Henry VIII** dissolved the priory, demolished the church nave and ordained that the truncated building be used only as a parish church. The monarch's attorney-general, Sir Richard Rich, paid him £1 064 11s 3d for the property which the family retained for 300 years. In that time the church fell into disrepair: the Lady Chapel was "squatted in", became a printers' workshop (where in 1724 **Benjamin Franklin** was employed) and later a fringe factory; the north transept was turned into a forge (note the blackened walls) the remains of the cloister became a stable, a thick layer of earth covered the church floor, limewash obscured the walls and murals, a brick receptacle behind the altar, known as Purgatory, was filled with human bones...
Restoration, including the buying out of extraneous occupants, took from 1863 to 1910.

The Building – The gateway, a 13C arch and the original entrance to the nave, is surmounted by a late 16C half-timbered gatehouse (restored 1932). The path through the churchyard is at the level of the medieval church. The square brick castellated **tower**, with a small vaned turret, was erected in 1628 off-centre at the west end of the curtailed church. The porch, west front and other exterior flint and stone refacing date from 1839 (restoration by Sir Aston Webb).
The **choir★** is Norman. An arcade of circular arches springing from massive round piers and plainly scalloped capitals supports a relieving arch and a gallery of arched openings divided into groups of four by slender columns. The late Perpendicular style clerestory, rebuilt in 1405, has survived intact save for the insertion of an **oriel** window in the south gallery by Prior Bolton in 1520 stamped with his rebus: a bolt or arrow transfixing a tun or cask; from here, behind the leaded lights, he could follow the service. The Lady Chapel completed in 1336 was all but rebuilt in 1897 so only the end north and south windows are original. 15C oak doors (by the west door) lead to the east walk of the old cloister (c 1405, rebuilt early this century).
Rahere, the founder, lies on a 16C decorated tomb chest beneath a crested canopy, all fashioned some 350 years after his death. The **font**, used at Hogarth's baptism in 1697, dates from the early 15C and as such is one of the oldest in the City.

St Bartholomew-the-Less

Open daily, 8am-8pm.
The 12C hospital church *(for description of St Bartholomew's Hospital see Worth a Visit)* appears on mid-17C maps as a substantial building with a stalwart tower; by the 18C, however, it was so derelict as to need repair first by **George Dance the Younger** (1789) and again, in 1823, by **Philip Hardwick**. Monuments date back to the 14C (vestry pavements), while the more modern ones chiefly commemorate hospital personnel. The 15C square tower with a domed corner turret is visible from the market although the church stands within the walls of the hospital.
Cross the square.

Smithfield London Central Markets

Smithfield was opened as a wholesale and retail dead meat, poultry and provision market only in 1868. Previously the stock had come in live, driven into the City through Islington. The name, derived from "smooth field" is associated with a stock market in Saxon times and from the 12C with the summer Fair of St Bartholomew, held from 1614 all the year round and banned by the Victorians because of the riotous debauchery it provoked. The site was also used for executions until the gallows were moved to Tyburn, and for the burning of martyrs at the stake during Mary Tudor's time. After centuries of overcrowding on the site, chaos and congestion in the narrow streets, the livestock market was transferred in 1855 to the Caledonian Market, Islington. The listed buildings, erected in 1868 and since enlarged, are of red brick and stone with domed towers at either end; they extend over 8 acres/3ha, with 15 miles/24km of rails capable of hanging 60 000 sides of beef. An underground railway depot *(car park)* originally linked the market to the national railway network.The market closed in 1998 and the site has been redeveloped.
Return to Giltspur St and walk down.

Fat Boy

The gilded oak figure, said to mark where the **Great Fire** stopped, stands on a site then known as Pie Corner; hence the saying that the Fire began in Pudding Lane and ended at Pie Corner.

St Sepulchre-without-Newgate

Open Tue-Thu, noon (11am Wed) to 2pm (3pm Wed). Recitals: Wed at 1pm; organ recitals: 2nd and 4th Tue at 1pm; other times various programmes. ☎/Fax 020 7248 3826; citychurches@pmullen.freeserve.co.uk; st-sepulchre.org.uk
The **Church of the Holy Sepulchre** which stands "without the city wall" was of an earlier foundation, renamed at the time of the crusades after the Jerusalem church. The square stone tower (restored) surmounted by four heavy crocketed pinnacles dates from 1450 as does the fan-vaulted porch decorated with carved bosses. The bright interior is furnished with a contemporary pulpit, font and octagonal cover gay with cherubs' heads, and at the entrance, the beautiful font cover rescued by a postman from Christ Church *(see below)* in 1940. St Sepulchre is "the Musicians' Church", its choir central to the emergence of the Royal School of Church Music. Along the north side is the Musicians' Chapel which contains the ashes of **Sir Henry Wood** (1869-1944), and windows, chairs, kneelers dedicated to the memory of British musicians. The organ (1670) which has a superb case that includes the monogram of Charles II, is reputed to have been played by **Handel** and **Mendelssohn**; it was also where the young Henry Wood aged 14 officiated as assistant organist.
Other mementoes include a stone from the Church of the Holy Sepulchre in Jerusalem; sword rests; the hand bell rung outside condemned men's cells at midnight in the old Newgate Prison; a brass plate to **Captain John Smith** – sometime Governor of Virginia who died in 1631 and is buried in the church; the colours of the Royal Fusiliers City of London Regiment.

J.Malburet/MICHELIN

A shining symbol of Justice crowning the Old Bailey

Central Criminal Court, the Old Bailey

♿ *Open to the public when the Courts are sitting, Mon-Fri, approximately 10am-4.30pm with an adjournment for lunch. Bags, cameras, recording equipment, mobile telephones, food and drink prohibited.*

This is the third Criminal Court to occupy this site. The original trial halls, erected in 1539, were built to protect the judges from "much peril and danger" in the form of sickness and infestation so rife in the gaols – indeed they still carry posies from May to September traditionally to ward off gaol fever. The Common Council, therefore, passed a resolution "that a convenient place be made... upon the common ground of this City in the old bailey of London": the site chosen was located by New Gate, a gate in the wall built by the Romans for the main road west enlarged in the early Middle Ages, near which a City gaol had been constructed (1180) to relieve the ever overcrowded Fleet Prison. Remains of a triumphal arch c AD 200 marking the western entrance to the city have been excavated in Newgate Street.

The Building – The granite structure is dressed in Portland stone, its dramatic entrance emphasised with a broken pediment and allegories of Truth, Justice and the Recording Angel, while the Lady of Justice, a gold figure (12ft/3.5m tall) holding scales and a sword (3ft 3in/1m) stands high above perched on a green copper dome (1907). This dominant feature of the London skyline is cast in bronze and covered in gold leaf (regilded every five years and cleaned every August) – unusually she is neither blindfolded nor blind.

Inside all is marble, a grand staircase sweeping up to halls on two floors decked with painted murals; the four original courts are large. The complex also has 60 cells to accommodate prisoners brought daily from Brixton and Holloway.

Proceed along Newgate St.

General Post Office

Plaques on the turn of the 19C century building indicate the site of Greyfriars (f 1225) and Christ's Hospital which occupied the buildings from 1552 to 1902. Outside the main building stands the statue of Sir Rowland Hill, who in 1840 introduced the penny post, the uniform rate for a letter sent anywhere in the kingdom.

Christ Church★

The slender square stone tower rises by stages alternately solid and colonnaded, adorned by urns, to a slim decorated turret and vane. Christ Church was founded by Henry VIII on the site occupied by the Greyfriars monastery (1225-1538) possibly to serve Christ's Hospital, the second royal foundation nearby, also known as the Bluecoat School (1552-1902). The church, destroyed in the Fire and redesigned by Wren (1667-91) on sufficient scale to accommodate the boys, is now a garden. The tower houses an office.

Return to the crossroads and walk on.

Dick Whittington

Whittington was four times Lord Mayor; in 1397, 1397-8, 1406-7 and 1419-20; he died in 1423, a man in his early sixties. The 3rd son of a Gloucestershire squire, he came to London, entered the mercers' trade, married well and rose rapidly both in trade, from which he amassed a fortune, and in the Corporation where he progressed from ward member to Lord Mayor. He was not knighted though an important part of his contact with the Crown seems to have been the provision of considerable loans; according to legend he gave a banquet for Henry V at which he burned bonds discharged for the King worth £60 000.

His great wealth continued after his death, as in his lifetime, to be devoted to the public cause: permanent buildings for Leadenhall Market, the construction of Greyfriars Library, half the cost of founding the Guildhall Library, the foundation of a college and almshouses at St Michael Paternoster Royal...

Such great personality, wealth, benefactions, were embroidered into legend until in 1605 licence was granted for performances of a play (now lost), *The History of Richard Whittington, of his lowe byrth, his great fortune*; when an engraver, Renold Elstrack, about the same time portrayed him in classic pose with his hand upon a skull, popular protest was so loud that the engraver altered the plate replacing the skull with a cat which may have given rise to the legend of Dick Whittington and his cat, although an alternative source is a coal barge, known as a catte, since Whittington traded in coal.

Holborn Viaduct

The viaduct was built in 1863-69 to connect the City and West End; previously all traffic had to descend to the level of Farringdon Street and climb up again. The bridge is an example of Victorian cast iron work: strongly constructed and ornate with uplifting statues and lions.

Alongside the viaduct stands the **City Temple** marked by its high square and pillared tower surmounted by a square lantern, lead dome and cross. The history of the City Temple, the only English Free Church in the City, goes back to 1567 although occupation of the site on the viaduct dates only from 1874. The church is famous for its preachers. Wartime bombing gutted the sanctuary so that the building now presents the contrast of a Victorian/Palladian exterior and modern interior.

For Holborn see CHANCERY LANE.

Worth a Visit

Museum of London★★

♿ *Open daily, 10am (noon Sun) to 5.50pm (last admission 5.30pm). Closed 24-26 Dec, 1 Jan. ☎ 020 7600 3699; Fax 020 7600 1058; info@museumoflondon.org.uk; www.museumoflondon.org.uk*

The museum occupies the best of modern architectural style buildings, designed by Powell and Moya, faced with white tiles below and linked by a bridge to a purple brick rotunda set like an advanced bastion in the sea of Aldersgate traffic; in traditional City fashion it makes the best use of an awkward site shaped around Ironmongers' Hall with its 1924 Gothic stone porch.

By the main entrance of the museum in Nettleton Court stands a monumental bronze leaf as a memorial to the Methodist **John Wesley** *(see index)*.

The museum operates a team of archaeologists specialising in urban excavation; this allows sites to be dug with the cooperation of building developers – work is undertaken to restricted time-frames before great concrete foundations are irrevocably sunk through the layers of history. Over the long term, digs have revealed a broad range of artefacts which, classified and compared to other flora, fauna, bone, wood, ceramic, glass or metal finds, provide a reliable record of London and her inhabitants through the ages and ravages of war, fire, flood and plague...

Displays are organised into galleries of bays according to time and theme from prehistory to the present: exhibits include the best Roman wall painting in Britain and the sculptures from the Roman Temple of Mithras, medieval pilgrim badges, a model of the Rose Theatre based on evidence excavated by Museum of London archaeologists, the Cheapside Hoard of Jacobean jewellery, a diorama of the Great Fire, the doors from Newgate Gaol, 19C shops and interiors, the Lord Mayor's Coach, souvenirs of the women's suffrage movement, the 1930s lifts from Selfridge's department store and a revealing exposition on the Second World War. The development of domestic life and public utility services – gas, drainage, the Underground – are illustrated as well as political and fashionable London.

Roman Fort – This, the west gate of the Romans' north fort, including the outline of the guard turret, lies in a chamber off the west end of the underground car park.

Bank of England Museum★

♿ *Open Mon-Fri, 10am-5pm. Closed Bank Hols. Brochure (9 languages). ☎ 020 7601 5545, 7601 5491 (infoline); Fax 020 7601 5808; museum@bankofengland.co.uk; www.bankofengland.co.uk*

The museum, which traces the history of the bank, opens with a description of the history of the building in a reconstruction of Sir John Soane's Bank Stock Office. Chronological displays illustrate early banking using goldsmiths' notes; the Charter dated 27 July 1694; Letters Patent under the Great Seal of William and Mary; a £1 million note used for accounting purposes only; display of gold bars; paper money and forgeries; the gold standard; silver vessels; minted coins. Interactive touch screens explain modern banking while a modern dealing desk with telephone and screen provide an insight into money dealing.

Mansion House★

Guided tour for groups only (15-40min) Tue-Thu at 11am and 2pm on written application to the Principal Assistant-Diary, Mansion House, London EC4N 8BH. Closed Easter, Aug and Christmas. ☎ 020 7626 2500; Fax 020 7623 9524

The interior is designed as a suite of magnificent state rooms from the portico leading to the dining or Egyptian Hall. In the hall, giant Corinthian columns forming an ambulatory support the cornice on which the decorated ceiling rests; the walled niches are filled with Victorian statuary on subjects taken from English literature from Chaucer to Byron. The Ball Room is on the second floor

Plate and Insignia★★ – The Corporation plate, rich and varied, dates from the 17C. The insignia includes much older pieces: the Lord Mayor's **chain of office**, c 1535 with later additions, suspends from a collar of SS gold links, knots and enamelled

Tudor roses; a pendant known as the Diamond Jewel consists of an onyx piece, carved in 1802 with the City arms, and set in diamonds; the **Pearl Sword**, 16C and according to tradition presented by Queen Elizabeth at the opening of the Royal Exchange in 1571; the 17C **Sword of State** and the 18C **Great Mace** of silver gilt and 5ft 3ins/1.7m long.

Guildhall★

Open (civic functions permitting) May-Sep, daily, 10am-5pm; Oct-Apr, Mon-Sat, 10am-5pm. Closed Good Fri, Easter Mon, 25-26 Dec, 1 Jan. ☎ 020 7332 3063; Fax 020 7332 1996; julia.vonmatzenau@corpoflondon.gov.uk; www.cityoflondon.gov.uk

"This Guildhall", Stow quoted in 1598 "was begun to be built new in the year 1411;...the same was made of a little cottage, a large and great house... towards the charges whereof the (livery) companies gave large benevolences; also offences of men were pardoned for sums of money, extraordinary fees were raised, fines... during 7 years, with a continuation of 3 years more... Executors to Richard Whittington gave towards the paving of this great hall... with hard stone of Purbeck". All was complete by c 1440. The Great Fire left the outer walls and crypt standing. Rebuilding began immediately and in 1669 Pepys noted "I passed by Guildhall, which is almost finished."

In 1940 history repeated itself. Reconstruction was once more completed in 1954. In the course of recent building work, excavations have revealed the site of a Roman amphitheatre, traces of the medieval Jewish quarter and of the 15C Guildhall chapel.

The City was granted its first charter by **William the Conqueror** in 1067; the first **Mayor** was installed in a building, of which no trace remains, probably on the present site in 1193; for at least 850 years, therefore, Guildhall has been the seat of civic government.

Architecture – Guildhall's 18C façade, a mixture of Classical and Gothic motifs, extends across nine bays, rises to four storeys and culminates, on the four buttresses which divide the face into equal parts, in large and peculiar pinnacles. Crowning the central area are the City arms which are composed of the Cross of St George, the sword of the patron saint, St Paul, on a shield supported by winged griffins, probably incorporated in the 16C. The **porch**, at the centre, however, is still covered by two bays of medieval tierceron vaulting.

Inside, the **hall** also is in part medieval: the walls date back to the 15C and the chamber in which today's banquets are held is the same in dimension (152ft/46m x 49 ft/15m) as that in which Lady Jane Grey and others were tried. A cornice at clerestory level bears the arms of England, the City and the 12 Great Livery Companies whose banners hang in front; below, the bays between the piers contain memorial statues, notably (north wall) a seated bronze of **Churchill** by Oscar Nemon; Nelson; Wellington; Pitt the Elder by John Bacon. East of the entrance porch in the south wall, behind where the lord mayor sits at banquets, is a canopied oak buffet on which are displayed the City sword and mace and plate; to the west beneath the only remaining 15C window are the Imperial Standards of Length (1878) with the Metric measures (1973) on the right.

J. Malburet/MICHELIN

Gog and Magog

Guarding the Musicians' Gallery are the post-war replica giants (9ft 3ins/3m tall) carved in limewood by David Evans after the figures set up in Guildhall in 1708, themselves descendants of 15C and 16C midsummer pageant figures who were said to have originated in a legendary conflict between ancient Britons and Trojans in 1000 BC.

J. Malburet/MICHELIN

Crypt – *Guided tour. ☎ 020 7332 3063 (Mon-Fri – Assistant Remembrancer).*

The crypt comprises two parts: the western pre-15C section with its four pairs of stone columns was vaulted by Wren after the earlier hall above collapsed in the Fire. The 15C eastern section below the present Guildhall – the largest medieval crypt in London – survived both 17C and 20C fires: it remains notable for its size and the six blue Purbeck marble clustered piers supporting the vaulting.

Library – ♿ *Open Mon-Sat, 9.30am-5pm. Closed Bank Hols and Sat preceding Bank Hol Mon (print room closed Sat). ☎ 020 7332 1868/1870; printedbooks.guildhall@corpoflondon.gov.uk*

The library, founded c 1423, despoiled in the 16C and refounded in 1824, possesses a unique collection of maps, prints, drawings and manuscripts on the history and development of the City and London.

Clock Museum★ – *Open Mon-Fri, 9.30am (later on Mon) to 4.45pm. Closed Bank Hols. ☎ 020 7332 1868 (Guildhall Library)*
The 700 timepieces which make up the Museum of the Worshipful Company of Clockmakers range in size from long case (grandfather) clocks to minute watches, in date from the 15C to the 20C, in manufacture from all wood composition, in movement from perpetual motion (with a ball that rolls 2 522 mi/4 058km a year) and in esthetic appeal from a silver skull watch, said to have belonged to Mary Queen of Scots, to jewelled confections, enamelled, decorated, engraved, chased... The collection also includes two Harrison clocks *(see Outer London: GREENWICH – National Maritime Museum)*.

Guildhall Art Gallery – *Open Mon-Sat, 10am-5pm; Sun, noon-4pm. Closed 25-26 Dec, 1 Jan and special occasions. £2.50; no charge Fri all day and other days after 3.30pm. ☎ 020 7332 3700 (recorded information); Fax 020 7332 3342; guildhall.artgallery@corpoflondon.gov.uk; www.guildhall-art-gallery.org.uk*
In a fine modern building which replaces the original gallery (burned down in 1941) are displayed the art collection owned by the Corporation of London: portraits of dignitaries from 17C to 20C, 18C paintings, works by Victorian painters (Pre-Raphaelites) and other eminent artists.

St Bartholomew's Hospital
Guided tour (including St Bartholomew the Less, St Bartholomew the Great and Cloth Fair) Fri at 2pm. Closed Good Fri and 24 Dec. £4. ☎ 020 7837 0546 (City of London Guides Association)
The hospital, known as Barts, was founded by Rahere in 1123 as part of an Augustinian priory. Modern blocks now supplement the collegiate style buildings (1730-66) designed by James Gibbs. The north wing includes the great staircase decorated with vast murals by **Hogarth** (1734) and the Great Hall *(not open)*; displays of items (documents, charters, medical paraphernalia) relate the evolution of this historic institution.
The gatehouse from West Smithfield erected in 1702, contains an 18C statue of Henry VIII who dissolved the priory and gave the hospital to the City of London in 1546.

Clerkenwell

As the fashion for loft living took hold in the 1990s the secluded character of Clerkenwell underwent a radical change. Warehouses and commercial properties were transformed with glass frontages and the trendsetters moved in, soon followed by a range of select eating-places and a popular clubbing scene. However, for those in the know it has always been a desirable area owing to its air of faded gentility and to its convenient location on the edge of the City and a short hop from the West End.

Location
Map pp 13-14 (FGV); Michelin Atlas London: pp 80-81, 96. ⊖ *Barbican; Farringdon; Old Street.*
Clerkenwell is bounded by Bloomsbury, Islington and the City. As the sights are spread out it is best to start the first tour from Farringdon and the second from Old Street.
Adjacent Sights: BLOOMSBURY; EAST END; The CITY; CHANCERY LANE; ISLINGTON.

Background

Clerkenwell recalls in name the medieval parish clerks who each year performed plays outside the City at a local well-head *(viewed through a window at 14-16 Farringdon Lane)*.
Finsbury is named after the Fiennes family, the owners of the local manor (bury/burh/burg in Old English) who in the 14C gave **Moorfields**, an unprofitable marsh, to the people of London as an open space, the first so designated.
Some open land remains: Finsbury Square, Finsbury Circus, Bunhill Fields and the Honourable Artillery Company Fields *(see below)* but the outflow of artisans and cottage industry workers from the City, particularly after the **Plague** (1665) and Fire (1666), caused poor quality housing and tenements to be erected right up to the walls of the Charterhouse, St John's Priory, Bethlem *(in what is now City Road)* and the other hospitals in the district – the only one of which now extant is **Moorfields** Eye Hospital, founded in 1805.
The crowded days of home industry in the early 19C are recalled by the Eagle Pub *(see Directory) (Shepherdess Walk, City Road)* and the old rhyme:
Half a pound of twopenny rice, Half a pound of Treacle,...
Up and down the City Road, In and out the Eagle,
That's the way the money goes, Pop goes the Weasel.
Over the centuries, as Clerkenwell was outside the City wall, it became the home of groups holding nonconformist or radical beliefs such as Quakers, Chartists and other militant movements. It acquired a notorious reputation and was the scene of serious disturbances. St Peter's Church in Clerkenwell Road, colourful festivals and excellent Italian grocery stores recall the sizeable Italian quarter with street entertainers, ice-cream vendors and craftsmen which grew in the 19C and flourished until fairly recently.

National newspapers in the area are the **Morning Star** *(75 Farringdon Road)* in a plain building of concrete and brick by **E Goldfinger** (1949) and **The Guardian** *(119 Farringdon Road)*.

Water Supply – The New River undertaking *(see below)* originated in 1609 when **Sir Hugh Myddelton**, a City goldsmith and jeweller, put up the capital to construct a canal from springs in Hertfordshire to the City. The winding channel some 40mi/64km long took four years to dig and might well have ruined Myddelton but for the personal financial support of James I.

The New River Head was inaugurated in 1613 when water carried down from Clerkenwell to the City in wooden pipes. Individual subscribers were supplied with water on tap at 5s a quarter; the enterprise was a financial success and was sold for £5 million when taken over by the Metropolitan Water Board (1904-1974) which built its head office on the site of the New River Head so that the river is now only 24mi/38km long ending at Stoke Newington.

Directory

Pub

Eagle – *159 Farringdon Rd, EC1R 3AL – ⊖ Farringdon, Chancery Lane – ☎ 020 7837 1353 – Open Sun-Sat noon-11pm (5pm Sun); closed bank hols, 1 wk Christmas-New Year.* A large eagle stands sentinel over the green façade of one of London's first gastropubs. The regular clientele enjoys the simple cuisine and the place is often packed in the evenings.

Taking a Break

Smiths of Smithfield – *67-77 Charterhouse St, EC1M 6HJ – ⊖ Farringdon – ☎ 020 7236 6666 – www.smithsofsmithfield.co.uk – Open Mon-Sat 7am-midnight, Sun 11am-11pm.* The renovation of this gigantic former meat warehouse, opposite Smithfield Market, cost 3 million pounds. It has been an undisputed success since opening and the bar is often packed. You can enjoy a quiet brunch on Sundays though.

Walking About

CLERKENWELL ROAD TO ROSEBERY AVENUE

From Farringdon Station walk up Turnmill St and cross Clerkenwell Rd to Clerkenwell Green.

Clerkenwell Green

The rallying point in the 18C and 19C for work people protesting against the social and industrial injustices of the period is an appropriate site for the **Karl Marx Memorial Library**, an 18C house *(no 37a)*. Cheerful pavement cafés strike a more affluent note. Artists' studios around the Green mark the renewal of the craft tradition which flourished in the past.

Proceed east along Clerkenwell Rd past St John's Gate and Charterhouse (descriptions in Worth a Visit). Then continue north up St John's St to Rosebery Av.

City University

St John Street. Surrounded by the modern buildings of the City University is the original Northampton Institute (1894-96), designed by E Mountford in an eclectic baroque style.

Sadler's Wells Theatre

Rosebery Avenue. Music house at the centre of late-17C pleasure gardens and medicinal wells, mid-18C theatre, Shakespearean and classical drama centre under **Samuel Phelp** in the 1840s, music hall, derelict ruin: such was the site's history when **Lilian Baylis** took it over and had a new brick theatre built (1931). The theatre is named after a builder, Mr Sadler, whose workmen in 1683 rediscovered the medicinal wells. The well-appointed new building which dates from 1998 has given a new impetus to the theatre. *See PRACTICAL POINTS – Going out for the Evening, Opera and Ballet.*

New River Head

Thames Water Authority, Rosebery Avenue. The neo-Georgian building (now flats) contains a fireplace attributed to Grinling Gibbons and plaster ceilings c 1693.

Make a detour to Myddelton Sq.

The elegant terraces of **Myddelton Square** were built in the late 1700s on part of the New River Company's estate.

Mount Pleasant

The early-18C landmark, perhaps ironically named as it was the local rubbish dump, is now one of the main Post Office inland mail sorting offices and the centre of the Post Office railway. The line runs 70ft/21m below ground from Paddington to Liverpool Street and Whitechapel, carrying the mail in automatically controlled trucks along 2ft/0.6m gauge tracks.

Walk down Farringdon Rd past some good restaurants and busy pubs.

CITY ROAD

From Old St walk south past Companies House (55-71) towards Moorgate.

Wesley's House and Chapel

47 City Road. ♿ Open Mon-Sat, 10am-4pm; Sun, 12.30-2.00pm (11am service). Closed Bank Hols, 25-26 Dec. Audioguides, videoshow, brochures and guidebook. ☎ 020 7253 2262; Fax 020 7608 3825; curator@wesleyschapel.org.uk; www.wesleyschapel.org.uk

The charismatic Methodist minister **John Wesley**, who is buried in the churchyard, laid the foundation stone of the chapel in 1777. The oblong building of stock brick with a shallow apse, is notable inside for the tribune supported on seven jasper columns, presented by overseas Methodists in replacement of the pine dockyard masts (now in the vestibule) originally given by George III, and the white and gold ceiling by **Robert Adam**. Wesley's mahogany pulpit, formerly a two decker, 15ft/4.5m tall, stands at the centre.

A **Museum of Methodism** is housed in the crypt.

Next door, the preacher's house is rich in mementoes: his desk, study and conference chairs, clock, clothes, library, furniture and, in the tiny prayer room, table desk and kneeler.

Bunhill Fields

City Road. Long before 1549 when the first wagon load of bones was delivered for burial from the overflowing charnel house in St Paul's Churchyard, the field had been given the name Bone Hill. From 1665, when the City Corporation acquired it, to its closure in 1852, 120 000 were buried there including many non-conformists since the ground was never consecrated.

Among the tombs are those of: **William Blake** (1757-1827), **John Bunyan** (1628-88), **Daniel Defoe** (1661-1731), Susanna Wesley, mother of John and Charles (1669-1742)... In the adjoining Quaker yard is the grave of the founder of the Society of Friends, **George Fox** (1624-91).

Honourable Artillery Company HQ

Finsbury Barracks. The buildings on the historic Artillery Fields, designated for archery practice in Tudor times, date from 1735 and 1857.

Worth a Visit

Charterhouse*

Guided tour Apr-Aug, Wed pm. ☎ 020 7251 5002 (tour information). £5. Guide book. ☎ 020 7253 9503; Fax 020 7251 3929; tregistrar@aol.com

At every stage of its history – 14C priory, Tudor mansion, 17C hospital and boys' school, 20C residence for aged Brothers – the buildings of the Charterhouse have been replaced or altered in a variety of materials and architectural styles.

Between 1535 and 1537 the Prior and 15 monks of the 170-year-old Charterhouse were executed for refusing to recognise Henry VIII as head of the Church; he dissolved the community and removed treasure, timber, stone and glass for his own use. Within 10 years, the house began a new life as a Tudor mansion under the Norths and then passed to the Norfolks whom Elizabeth visited several times. In 1611 the house was sold to **Thomas Sutton** for £13 000 and letters patent were issued for the founding of a hospital for 80 old men and 40 boys. Sutton (d 1611) lies in an elaborate tomb by **Nicholas Stone** in the crypt under the chapel. In 1872 the school moved to Surrey.

The Tudor Great Hall of Charterhouse

K. Brett/MICHELIN

The Building – The 15C gateway, with its original massive gates, is built in flint and stone chequerwork like the precinct wall to the east. The superstructure and adjoining house, now the Master's lodging, are dated 1716. The graceful concave pyramidal roof opposite the gate covers the water conduit house of the monastery. On the north side of Master's Court the Tudor **Great Hall**, with hammerbeam roof and 16C screen and gallery remains intact. The carved stone fireplace was added in 1614. The Elizabethan **Great Chamber**, hung with Flemish tapestries, has a painted and gilded late-16C plaster ceiling, an ornate painted chimney-piece and leaded lights. The ante-room opens on to a terrace built in 1571 by Norfolk above the west walk of the Great Cloister.

In the tower, to which the belfry and cupola were added in 1614, is the treasury, vaulted in the Tudor period, with a squint looking down on the high altar of the original chapel where the tomb of the founder, Sir Walter Manny (d 1372), was discovered in 1947.

The present **chapel** was created in 1614 out of the monks' Chapter House with the addition of a north aisle and further enlarged to the north in 1824. The 17C screen, organ gallery, pew heads and pulpit are noteworthy.

St John's Gate

The Order of the Grand Priory in the British Realm, which developed from the First Crusade as a religious order to look after pilgrims visiting the Holy Land, became a military order during the 12C. It left the Holy Land on the fall of Acre in 1291, establishing itself first in Cyprus, then Rhodes (1310) and finally Malta (1530) where it became a sovereign power. Priories and commanderies were instituted in Europe, the **Grand Priory of England** being in Clerkenwell in 1144; to these were added the Templars' properties on their suppression in 1312. In 1540 **Henry VIII** dissolved the **Hospitallers** and in 1546 issued a warrant *(in the museum)* for the buildings to be dismantled (**Protector Somerset** later took the stone for his house in the Strand) but the gate survived. St John's was re-established as a Protestant Order by Royal Charter in 1888.

Gatehouse and Museum – ♿ *Open Mon-Sat, 10am-5pm (4pm Sat). Closed Sun and Bank Hol Sat-Mon. Guided tour (1hr) Tue, Fri, Sat at 11am and 2.30pm. Donation. ☎ 020 7324 4070; Fax 020 7336 0587; museum@nhq.sja.org.uk; www.sja.org.uk /history*
The 16C gatehouse, flanked by four-storey towers, was the Priory's south entrance. Wide, vaulted, with the Lamb of God, the arms of the order and of Prior Thomas Docwra, who built it, on the bosses, it contains the rooms which were occupied in the reigns of Elizabeth and James I by the Master of Revels, and in the 18C Edward Cave, publisher and printer of England's first literary periodical ***The Gentleman's Magazine*** (1733-81).

In the 20C Tudor-style Chapter Hall, where the Maltese banners hang in the lantern, in the Council Chamber and the Library are displayed pharmacy jars from the hospitals in Rhodes and Malta, silver filigree work and a rare collection of beaten silver Maltese glove trays, fine inlay work in wood and marble, two magnificent Chinese tobacco jars and the illuminated Rhodes Missal on which the knights took their vows. A rare 16C spiral staircase with wooden treads leads to a room displaying insignia, portrait medals and the Order's own coinage issued in Rhodes and Malta. The museum illustrates the life of the Order with items from its priories and commanderies and from its hospitals (including the Ophthalmic Hospital in Jerusalem). A gallery traces the history of the St John Ambulance Brigade from 1887: uniforms, medical instruments, first aid kits, medals...

St John's Church and Crypt – The Grand Priory Church of St John once extended further west into the square where setts in the road mark the site of the round nave. The 16C and 18C brick walls of the former choir are now hung with the chivalric banners of Commonwealth priories.

The crypt is 12C, the only original Priory building to survive. Beneath the low ribbed vaulting, against the north wall, lie the rich alabaster forms of a Spanish grandee and the cadaverous effigy of the last Prior before the Dissolution.

Covent Garden★★

Lively crowds enjoy the animation of the central piazza until a late hour with street entertainers, and quality craft and antique markets. The refurbishment of the opera house and its new facilities have given a new cachet to Covent Garden which recalls its heyday in the 19C.
Today, a general air of prosperity and success pervades Covent Garden: old warehouses have carefully been adapted to accommodate enticing small shops and boutiques selling off-the-peg designer clothing to young people, while long-established businesses continue to thrive (*The Lady Magazine*, Moss Bros, the map specialists Stamfords). Street cafés cater to the browsers by day and smart restaurants to the theatregoers by night.

Location

Map p 12 (EX); Michelin Atlas London: pp 2-3. ⊖ Covent Garden; Leicester Sq; Charing Cross. Covent Garden is the area delimited by Strand, Kingsway, Charing Cross Rd and New Oxford St.
Adjacent Sights: STRAND – TEMPLE; SOHO; BLOOMSBURY.

J. Malburet/MICHELIN

The Classical elegance of the Opera House beside the wrought-iron tracery of the spectacular Floral Hall

Background

In the Middle Ages, St Giles consisted of a leper colony established outside the town limits by Queen Matilda in 1117 (dissolved 16C) and Covent Garden was a 40 acre/16ha walled property belonging to the Benedictines of Westminster. Henry's dissolution of the monastery at Westminster and confiscation of the garden was followed in 1552 by the first of the royal warrants which were to shape the area to its present form, thereby establishing several important traditions and much of its character.
Edward VI granted the land to the long-serving Tudor diplomat and soldier, John Russell, later **1st Earl of Bedford**. The 4th Earl, on payment of £2 000 – **Charles I** was ever impecunious – obtained a licence in 1631 to erect buildings "fitt for the habitacions of Gentlemen and men of ability" subject only to the approval of the King's Surveyor, Inigo Jones.
When the theatres, hitherto principally in Southwark, which had been closed during the Commonwealth, reopened after the Restoration (1660), **Charles II** – a lover of the theatre and its actresses – permitted women to tread the boards for the first time and granted two royal warrants for theatres. The first resulted in the **Theatre Royal, Drury Lane** (1663), the second in the **Theatre Royal, Covent Garden** (1732) which opened with Congreve's *Way of the World*. The theatrical tradition of Covent Garden was so well established that, when the monopoly of the two royal theatres was broken by the Theatre Regulation Act in 1843, some 40 new theatres mushroomed within as many years; in 1987 the Theatre Museum opened.

Coffee houses

The fashion for coffee houses was introduced to London during the Commonwealth (1652). Originally they served as meeting places in the City for the exchange of business intelligence. By 1715 there were over 500 not only in the City but also in Covent Garden and the Strand, St James's, Mayfair and Westminster. Customers of like interests would gather regularly, even daily, in the same houses or call at several houses at different times to pick up messages and even letters or to read the news sheets, which at first circulated from one house to another, and the later newspapers (***Daily Courant***, 1702) which were available to customers for the price of a single cup of hot chocolate or coffee. At the end of the 18C the City coffee houses reverted to being pubs and the West End houses disappeared, except **Boodle's** and **White's** which became clubs. Of the 17C and 18C coffee houses for which Covent Garden was as famous as the City, none remain: **Will's**, frequented by "all the wits in town" according to Pepys used to stand at no 1 Bow Street, **Button's** in Russell Street, the **Bedford**, the **Piazza**...

Directory

Light Bite

The Opera Terrace at Chez Gerard – *The Piazza, WC2E 8RF – ⊖ Covent Garden – ☎ 020 7379 0666 – £6/12.* After finding the entrance on the east corner of the Central Market, you'll be rewarded with a tranquil vantage point from which to survey the buskers and general activity of Covent Garden below. A good selection of light meals is provided, with unhurried service.

Wagamama – *1 Tavistock St, WC2E 7PG – ⊖ Covent Garden – ☎ 020 7836 3330 – coventgarden@wagamama.com – – £7/12.* Finding quick and inexpensive food around the Piazza can be difficult. Step down into this minimalist basement and feast on healthy Japanese-style dishes. The reasonable prices make this quite popular with Londoners and tourists.

World Food Café – *14 Neals Yard, WC2H 9DP – ⊖ Covent Garden – ☎ 020 7379 0298 – www.worldfoodcafe.com – Open Mon-Sat 11.30am-4.30pm (5pm Sat) – £10/16.* Overlooking quaint and eco-friendly Neal's Yard, this 1st floor vegetarian restaurant is known for its hearty recipes from exotic lands around the globe, particularly Asia and Africa. Shared pine tables around a central kitchen counter. If you are pressed for time, pick up a healthy snack at one of the ground floor outlets.

Pub

The Lamb & Flag – *33 Rose St, WC2E 9EB – ⊖ Covent Garden, Leicester Square – ☎ 020 7497 9504 – Open Mon-Sat 11am-11pm (10.45pm Fri-Sat), Sun noon-10.30pm; closed 25-26 Dec, 1 Jan.* This pub, nestling in a tiny alley, is the oldest and perhaps the most pleasant in the area. It opened in 1623 as the Cooper's Arms and became known unofficially as the Bucket of Blood from 1679, after an incident involving John Dryden who was attacked outside while on his way home to Long Acre. Good selection of beers. Our favourite pub around Covent Garden, it is best enjoyed during off-peak hours.

Taking a Break

Café Baroque – *33 Southampton St, WC2E 7HE – ⊖ Covent Garden – ☎ 020 7379 7585 – Open Mon-Sun noon-midnight (11.30pm last orders).* This wine bar with a 1900 feel is a peaceful haven in an otherwise lively area. White walls and tablecloths, soft lighting and a good selection of French wines.

Shopping

Birkenstock – *37 Neal St, WC2 – ⊖ Covent Garden – ☎ 020 7240 2783 – info@birkenstock.co.uk – Open Mon-Sat 10am-6pm (7pm Thu-Fri, 6.30pm Sat), Sun noon-5.30pm.* Small but very popular shop selling over 100 different styles, colours and textures of comfortable good quality footwear developed by Birkenstock, a family of German origin, who designed the first flexible arch support which mirrors the shape of the foot.

Carluccio's – *28a Neal St, WC2H 9PS – ⊖ Covent Garden – ☎ 020 7240 1487 – www.carluccios.com – Open Mon-Fri 11am-7pm, Sat 10am-7pm, Sun noon-6pm.* This top-notch delicatessen sells Italy's finest culinary delights including bread, pasta, olive oil.

Jones – *13 Floral St, WC2E 9DH – ⊖ Covent Garden – ☎ 020 7240 8312 – info@jones-clothing.co.uk – Open Mon-Fri 10am-6.30pm, Sun 1-5pm.* In this spacious boutique in Floral Street, Jones offers an unrivalled choice of men's fashion featuring labels by the best stylists of the moment – Martin Margiela, Vries van Noten and Rogan.

Jubilee Market – *1-4 King St, WC2E 8HN – ⊖ Covent Garden.* Stall holders sell antiques (Mon), general goods (Tue-Fri) and hand-made crafts (Sat-Sun).

Koh Samui – *65-67 Monmouth St, WC2H 9DG – ⊖ Covent Garden, Leicester Square – ☎ 020 7240 4280 – Open Mon-Sat 10am (10.30am Tue-Fri, 11am Sun) to 6.30pm (6pm Sun, 7pm Thu); closed 25 Dec and 1 Jan.* The only boutique devoted exclusively to the creations of young up-and-coming English and European fashion designers. Wide selection.

Monmouth Coffee House – *27 Monmouth St, WC2H 9DD – ⊖ Covent Garden – ☎ 020 7379 3516, 020 7645 3562 – coffee@monmouthcoffee.co.uk – Open Mon-Sat 9am-6.30pm.* A small shop operated by true coffee connoisseurs who will give you excellent advice. The range of coffees changes regularly, and you can sample them on the spot.

Neal's Yard Dairy – *17 Shorts Gardens, WC2H 9AT – ⊖ Covent Garden – ☎ 020 7240 5700 – Open Mon-Wed 11am-6.30pm, Fri-Sat 10am-6.30pm; closed Sun.* This popular cheese merchant sells products of the British Isles only. The house classics: Montgomery's Cheddar, Colston Bassett Stilton and Cashel Blue (a creamy Irish cheese).

Neal's Yard Remedies – *15 Neal's Yard, WC2H 9DP – ⊖ Covent Garden – ☎ 020 7379 7222 – cservices@nealsyardremedies.com – Open Mon-Sat 10am-7pm (6pm Mon, 8pm Thu), Sun and bank hols 11am-6pm; closed 25-26 Dec.* Established in 1981 by Romy Fraser

Browsing in Covent Garden Market

B. Pérousse/MICHELIN

and identifiable by its dark blue packaging, this popular brand of beauty care products and cosmetics prides itself on using only natural ingredients. Here you will find aniseed toothpaste, rosemary shampoo and all you need to make your own beauty products. Advice given by a herbalist and homeopath; 9 therapy rooms.

Paul Smith – *40-44 Floral St, WC2E 9DG – ⊖ Covent Garden – ☎ 020 7836 7828 – www.paulsmith.co.uk – Open Mon-Sat 10.30am-6.30pm (7pm Thu).* Ever-inventive fashion for men, women and children, designed by the man who revolutionised the British fashion world. Fans should also drop into Smith's unusual Notting Hill boutique (122 Kensington Park Rd) set up in a former house and designed as an exhibition hall.

Penhaligon's – *41 Wellington St, WC2E 7BN – ⊖ Covent Garden – ☎ 020 7836 2150 – ByRequest@penhaligons.com – Open daily 10am (noon Sun) to 6pm (7pm Thu).* Perfume supplier to the aristocracy since 1870, Penhaligon counts many prominent members of the Royal Family among its clients. Favourite scents are "Hammam Bouquet", still made according to the original 1872 composition, or "Blenheim Bouquet", which Churchill loved. For women "Cornubia" with woody and spicy fragrances or spring scented "Bluebell".

Entertainment

Opera Nights in the Piazza – In summer operas are broadcast on giant screens to enthusiastic crowds. It is a great opportunity to hear world class singers in major productions in a congenial atmosphere. Enquiries from box office and in the press.

Covent Garden Festival – *Covent Garden, WC2 – ☎ 020 7379 0870 – Mid-May to early June.* Events in St Paul's Church, Freemasons Hall and Peacock Theatre.

Walking About

Start from the Piazza.

The Piazza★★

The 1631 licence gave **Inigo Jones** the opportunity to design London's first square which he modelled after those he had seen in Italy: approach roads bisected the north and east sides interrupting the terraces of three-storey brick houses rising tall above a stone colonnade; behind the covered walkway nestled shops and coffee houses. On the south side, meanwhile, ran the garden wall of the Earl's new town house which fronted on the more fashionable Strand. By 1681, the area was populated with brothels, so when fashion departed, Bedford House was demolished (1700) and the area was developed. Today the piazza is a meeting place for Londoners and visitors alike for relaxation and entertainment.

A. Taverner/MICHELIN

Street artists entertaining the crowds in Covent Garden Piazza

Covent Garden Market

The market was set up by the monks before the Reformation and persisted throughout the development of the Piazza; it was regularised by Letters Patent in 1670 and reconstituted in 1830 when royal permission was granted for special buildings to be erected. The **Central Market Buildings**, consisting of three parallel units running off a north-south colonnade, were designed by **Charles Fowler** (1832) and linked by glass canopies in 1872.

By the turn of the 19C/20C, the market not only filled the Piazza but spilled into the neighbouring streets. Throughout the day, from midnight to noon, the district was brilliant with flowers and fruit, crowded with vendors, porters and buyers who frequented the area's open pubs and blocked the thoroughfares with lorries. In November 1974 the market and its characteristic reek of old cabbage moved to **Nine Elms** *(see Outer London: BATTERSEA)*, leaving Eliza Doolittle's flower market to franchised shops, canopied cafés, vaulted pubs and wine bars.

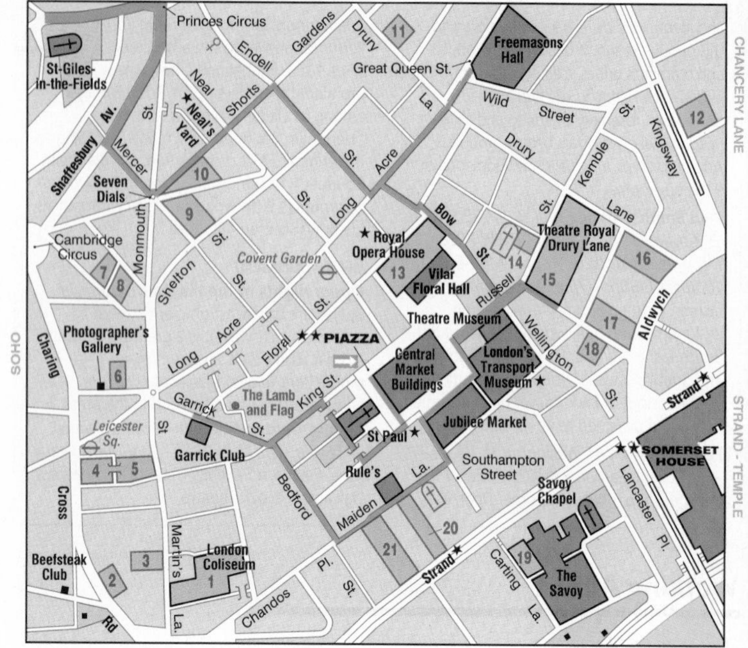

THEATERS

Adelphi	21	Cambridge	9	Royal Opera Covent Garden	13
Albery	5	Donmar Warehouse	10	Royalty	12
Aldwych	16	Duchess	18	St Martin's	8
Ambassadors	7	Duke of York's	3	Savoy	19
Arts Theatre	6	Fortune	14	Strand	17
		Garrick	2	Theatre Royal Drury Lane	15
		London Coliseum	1	Vaudeville	20
		New London	11	Wyndham's	4

St Paul's Church★

Entrance from Bedford Street. A church was planned for the west side of the Piazza but the Earl was unwilling to afford anything "much better than a barn" so Jones, declaring he should have "the handsomest barn in England", designed the church with classical simplicity in red brick (the easterly stone facing was a later addition) covered with a pitched roof. Almost ever since the church was completed (1633) it has been closely associated with the world of entertainment: actors, artists, musicians and craftsmen – a wreath of limewood, carved by Grinling Gibbons for St Paul's Cathedral, now decorates the west screen (beside the door).

Overlooking the square is the famous Tuscan portico from which on 9 May 1662 **Pepys** watched the first ever **Punch and Judy** show in England; much later **Shaw** set the opening scene of ***Pygmalion*** there. Today, it provides a dramatic backdrop to jousting acrobats, mime artists and colourful clowns happy to perform to the passing public.

Leave by the alley giving onto King St.

Pubs and Clubs

The quarter's oldest tavern is the **Lamb and Flag** *(see Directory).* Two traditional clubs still flourish: the **Garrick** (founded in 1831) has since 1864 occupied its purpose-built premises in the new street which the club requested should be named after the actor *(no 15);* on the walls hang an unrivalled collection of theatrical portraits that may be glimpsed from the street on a summer's evening; the **Beefsteak** *(9 Irving Street)* is a dining club that dates from 1876 and which has always drawn its members from the worlds of politics, the theatre and literature.

Walk back to Bedford St and turn left into Maiden Lane.

Rule's

34-35 Maiden Lane. London's oldest restaurant and oyster bar was established in 1798 by Benjamin Rule and his sons, "who rush wildly about with dozens of oysters and pewters of stout". *See PRACTICAL POINTS, Where to Eat.*

Continue to Southampton St and turn left and right past the Jubilee Market. Descriptions of London's Transport Museum and Theatre Museum in Worth a Visit. Proceed along Russell St before returning to Bow St.

Theatre Royal, Drury Lane

The present Georgian theatre is the fourth on the site, one of London's largest (2 283 seats) and beautiful inside with symmetrical staircases, rising beneath the domed entrance to a circular balcony.

Killigrew's company, known as the King's Servants, opened in 1663 in the first theatre which was frequently patronised by Charles II who met "pretty witty Nell" (Nell Gwynne) there in 1665. After being burnt down, the theatre was replaced in 1674 by one designed by **Wren** which knew a golden age under **Garrick** (who was manager from 1747 to 1776 and lived at 27 Southampton Street), the Kembles and **Sarah Siddons** and was replaced in 1794 by a third building which opened under **Sheridan's** management with his new play *The School for Scandal.* Fire again destroyed the theatre, and the present house, to designs by **Wyatt**, was erected in 1812. Kean, Macready, Phelps, **Irving**, Ellen Terry, Forbes Robertson played there; **Ivor Novello**'s dancing operettas filled the stage; *My Fair Lady* entranced there...

The **Baddeley Cake** is a Lane tradition even older than the ghost; it is provided from money left by an 18C actor, Robert Baddeley, and is cut on stage after the performance on Twelfth Night. The ghost emerges from the left circle wall (where a corpse and dagger were found bricked up in the 19C) to cross the auditorium and disappear.

Bow Street

The street is 'so called as running in the shape of Bent Bow' according to John Strype, the early-18C mapmaker. By the mid 18C, when **Henry Fielding**, novelist, dramatist and magistrate and his half-brother, John, the **Blind Beak**, moved into a house opposite the Opera House the street had become the haunt of footpads. At once the Fieldings began their crusade for penal and police reform which included the organisation in 1753 of the **Bow Street Runners**. The present building on the site of their house dates from 1881; it was the only police station in the country to be identified by white lights instead of the customary blue, because the blue reminded Queen Victoria of the death of her husband, the Prince Consort. In 1992 the police moved to new premises at Charing Cross.

Royal Opera House★

Charles II's patent was eventually secured by **John Rich** whose earlier presentation in 1728 of **John Gay**'s ***The Beggar's Opera*** "had the effect, as was ludicrously said, of making Gay rich and Rich gay" (Samuel Johnson). He leased a site, erected a playhouse and in December 1732 opened his Theatre Royal, Covent Garden, with Congreve's *Way of the World* which he followed with a revival of *The Beggar's Opera.* A second theatre, designed by Robert Smirke, after the first had burned down, opened in 1809 with a double bill lasting nearly four hours, presenting Kemble and Mrs Siddons in *Macbeth* plus a musical entertainment. After a second fire in 1856 the present house was built, with a first floor portico and Classical pediment facing Bow Street, thus leaving room to the south for EM Barry's green-painted glass and iron structure, known as the **Floral Hall** which was used for promenade concerts and balls. When the theatre fell into financial straits the hall was leased to the market in 1887 and for nearly 100 years served as an annexe to the fruit and vegetable, not the flower, market. Inside the theatre, decoration has always been white and gold with deep crimson and rose hangings; the blue dome is also a dominant feature. From the first there was a Crush Room.

Extensions to the west (in the 1858 style) house new dressing rooms and rehearsal facilities. A second phase of improvements provides the opera house with an exquisitely restored auditorium with raised seating, improved sightlines and air conditioning, modern facilities for storing and shifting scenery and for staging big productions. The iron and glass Vilar Floral Hall is used to great effect as the main foyer with escalators rising to the mezzanine galleries which accommodate bars and restaurant – panoramic **views** of the piazza from the loggias. There are also airy rehearsal studios for the ballet company and ample space for the costume departments under the eaves.

The **Sadler's Wells Ballet** transferred to the house in 1946 and in 1956 it was granted a charter by the Queen to become **The Royal Ballet**.

At the top of Bow St turn right into Long Acre and walk down to Great Queen St.

Royal Masonic Institution

The Masons occupy the greater part of the street which includes 18C houses *(nos 27-29)* and the **Freemasons Hall** (1927-33).

Walk back and turn right into Endell St to Shorts Gardens and turn left.

Neal's Yard★

The picturesque yard, complete with period hoists, dovecote, trees in tubs and geranium-filled window-boxes has attracted eco-friendly shopkeepers: vegetarian food bars, organic produce and essential remedies; other specialist shops are to be found in Neal Street.

Seven Dials

Seven Dials derives its name from a 40ft/12m Doric column, adorned with a sundial on each face, erected at the centre of seven radiating streets when the area, a notorious slum, was rehabilitated in the early 1690s by Thomas Neale. It was pulled down by a mob in 1773 on a rumour that treasure was buried underneath it. Crime was rife in the area in the 18C-19C. A replica of the pillar has been erected on the original site.
Walk down Monmouth St, down Shaftesbury Ave to Princes Circus and left into St Giles High St.

St Giles-in-the-Fields

Open Mon-Fri, 9am-4pm and for services. ☎ 020 7240 2532; verger.giles@btopenworld.com; www.giles-in-the-fields.org
The church, which is of ancient foundation and was on the edge of Westminster, served a poor and dismal area frequented by a transient population. It was rebuilt in 1734 by Flitcroft after the styles of Wren and James Gibbs; the steeple rising directly from the façade echoes St Martin-in-the-Fields. The pulpit in the north aisle was used for almost 50 years by John and **Charles Wesley** when it was in their "West Street Chapel".

Worth a Visit

London's Transport Museum★

♿ *Open daily, 10am (11am Fri) to 6pm; 5.15pm last admission. Closed 24-26 Dec. £5.95. Interactive display (5 languages); fun bus for under-5s; kid-zones for children 7-12yrs. Café. Shop. ☎ 020 7565 7299 (24hr information); 020 7379 6344; Fax 020 7565 7254; contact@ltmuseum.co.uk; www.ltmuseum.co.uk*
The Transport Museum documents 200 years of history and technology. The collection was formed in the 1920s and 1930s by the London General Omnibus Company and was moved in 1980 into part of the old flower market. Extensive refurbishment has provided 2 additional floors of steel and glass that complement the fabric of the original cast iron structure. Fourteen permanent displays show the development of one of the world's earliest and largest networks, and its impact on London from trams and trolleybuses, the advent of the motor bus and its extended use into the suburbs, the first underground – its design, form and function, and finally the development of driverless LRT (Light Rapid Transit) used by the Docklands Light Railway.
Real vehicles and fixtures withdrawn from service include the Shillibeer Horse Omnibus (1829-34), Type B Bus (1910-27), Metropolitan Railway Class A Locomotive (1866), ticket machines, signalling equipment, power generator control panels, etc. Technical information, such as manufacturing specifications, is available from touchscreen terminals; historical data is presented by video projections of newsreel, documentary and archive photographs. Interactive learning is encouraged for all ages with bus interiors and driver's cabs to be explored, scale models of steam/electric engines to be activated.
The **Harry Beck Gallery** – named after the engineer draftsman who adapted geographical conventions to design the first schematic map of the underground (1931) based on an electrical circuit diagram – displays London Transport maps. The **Ashfield Gallery**, named after the American pioneer of reliable cheap transport for the working middle classes, holds temporary exhibitions on secondary issues associated with the service (immigrant workforce, town-planning consequences, patron of poster art and poetry).
The **Frank Pick Gallery** exhibits selections by theme or series, of posters commissioned by London Transport from an archive of 5 000 or more, reflecting changes in fashion and taste, commemorating great events or achievements, sport or general interest. Works by important British artists include Graham Sutherland and Paul Nash. Pick (1878-1941) joined London Underground Electric Railway in 1906 and rose to become vice-chairman (1933-40). His vision transformed London Transport into a modern system, instigating a corporate image that has endured – fanatical about design, he advocated the universal application of particular typefaces for all printed documentation and station signage.

Theatre Museum

♿ *Open Tue-Sat, 10am-6pm. Closed 24-26Dec. Visitor notes (6 languages). Guided tour, make-up demonstrations, costume workshops: daily. ☎ 020 7943 4700; Fax 020 7493 4777; tmenquiries@vam.ac.uk; www.theatremuseum.org*
The Theatre Museum of the Victoria and Albert Museum opened in April 1987 in the old flower market. On the ground floor a large mural, a golden angel blowing a horn, ornate theatre boxes and an old box office set the theatrical theme. Its rich collections relate to all aspects of the performing arts: opera, ballet, Edwardian melodrama, pantomimes, circus, toy theatre and plays, popular music, music hall and puppetry, and include designs, archives, portraits, drawings, photographs and a wealth of other material. A gallery houses a semi-permanent display of the story of the performing arts. Two other galleries are devoted to temporary exhibitions. There are also a Paintings Gallery and a theatre for special events.

Hyde Park – Kensington Gardens★★

The green expanses of Hyde Park and Kensington Gardens at the heart of London which offer many attractions in all seasons give the capital a special charm. Every day, people flock to the parks to walk their dogs, jog, ride, go boating, swim (even if it means breaking the ice on Christmas morning), rollerblade, sail model boats, feed the pigeons, play bicycle polo, rounders, tennis or bowls... Concerts and celebrations in the park also attract the crowds.

Location

Map pp 10-11 (A-DXY); Michelin Atlas London: pp 55-59. ⊖ Marble Arch; Hyde Park Corner; Lancaster Gate; Queensway, Bayswater. Park Lane, Knightsbridge, Kensington Rd and Bayswater Rd mark the boundaries of the two parks. This chapter is divided into two walks: one starting from either Hyde Park Corner or Marble Arch and the other from Kensington Palace.

Adjacent Sights: KENSINGTON; KNIGHTSBRIDGE - BELGRAVIA; MAYFAIR; MARYLEBONE.

Background

In Saxon times the acres were part of the Manor of Eia which, until "resumed by the King" in 1536, belonged to **Westminster Abbey**. **Henry VIII** enclosed the area and having stocked it with deer kept it as a royal chase. In the 16C and later the park was used for military manoeuvres and encampments. In 1637 it was opened as a public park and the crowds came to watch horse racing and other sports only to be debarred when it was sold by the Commonwealth to a private buyer who, to Pepys' indignation, charged for admission. At the Restoration the contract of sale was cancelled and the park again became public.

The activities of those who frequented and made use of the park were even more diverse in the 18C and 19C than now: the last formal royal hunt was held in 1768; pits were dug to supply clay for bricks to build the new houses of Marylebone and Mayfair; gunpowder magazines and arms depots were sited in isolated parts; soldiers were executed against the wall in the north-east corner; at the same time it was a fashionable carriage and riding promenade first round the road known as the Tour and then **the Ring** (originally a small inner circle) or along the Row **(Rotten Row)**. It was a convenient place for duels and a common spot for footpads.

F. Vidal/MICHELIN

A glittering memorial to a visionary prince

Directory

Entertainment

Bayswater Road Art Exhibition – *Bayswater Rd, W2 – ⊖ Lancaster Gate, Queensway – ☎ 020 7641 6000 – info@bayswater-road-artists.com – Sun 10am-6pm or dusk.* An open-air exhibition of pictures and crafts offered for sale by aspiring artists.

Serpentine Gallery – *Kensington Gdns, W2 – ⊖ Gloucester Road, Knightsbridge – ☎ 020 7298 1515 – www.serpentinegallery.org – Open daily 10am-6pm (10pm Fri).* Exhibitions of modern art.

Shopping

Whiteleys Shopping Centre – *Queensway, W2 4YN – ☎ 020 7229 8844 – Open Mon-Sat 10am-8pm, Sun noon-6pm.* Formerly a fancy drapery shop and a grand department store, is now a modern shopping mall with smart boutiques, food outlets and a cinema multiplex.

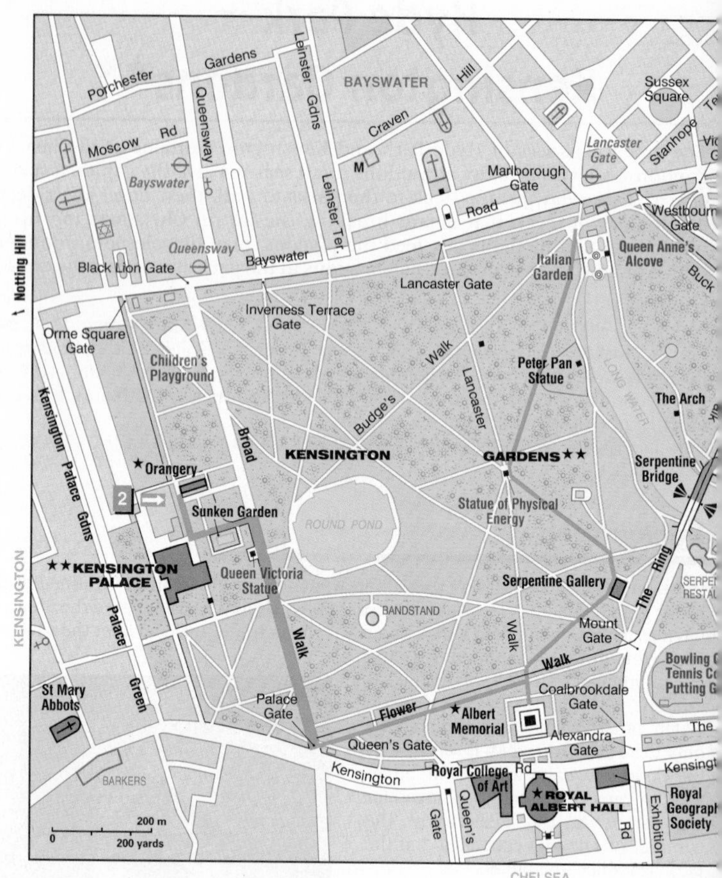

Great Exhibition – The most extraordinary event to take place in the park was the Great Exhibition, which was conceived and planned by Prince Albert. The huge exhibition was housed in the **Crystal Palace**, a vast iron and glass structure designed by Joseph Paxton. The palace was capable of rapid erection owing to the use of prefabricated unit parts and tall enough to enclose the giant elms on the site.

Queen Victoria, Wellington and some 6 030 195 others visited the exhibition which aimed to demonstrate man's inventiveness and 19C British achievement in particular; it made a net profit of just under £200 000. The profit was used to establish the museums in South Kensington *(see KENSINGTON)*. The Crystal Palace *(see Outer London: DULWICH)* was dismantled and re-erected at Sydenham where it was destroyed by fire in 1936.

Walking About

Hyde Park 1

It was **Pitt the Elder** in the 17C who aptly called the former deer park "the lungs of London". The park is put to many uses: as a place of relaxation and free speech, a rallying ground for parades and royal salutes, since 1800 a burial ground for pet dogs (at the Victoria Gate).

Marble Arch

At the north-east corner stands a fine triumphal arch of Italian (Seravezza) white marble with three closely patterned bronze gates. Modelled on the Arch of Constantine in Rome by **John Nash** (1827), it was intended to stand before Buckingham Palace, a monument to celebrate the end of the Napoleonic wars but the central archway was not wide enough to accommodate the Gold Stage Coach: when Queen Victoria needed to enlarge the palace, the arch was dismantled (1837) and in 1851 was rebuilt where the **Tyburn gallows** had stood until 1783 when hangings were removed to Newgate. Two narrow spiral staircases at either end access a broad central room with in-built furniture.

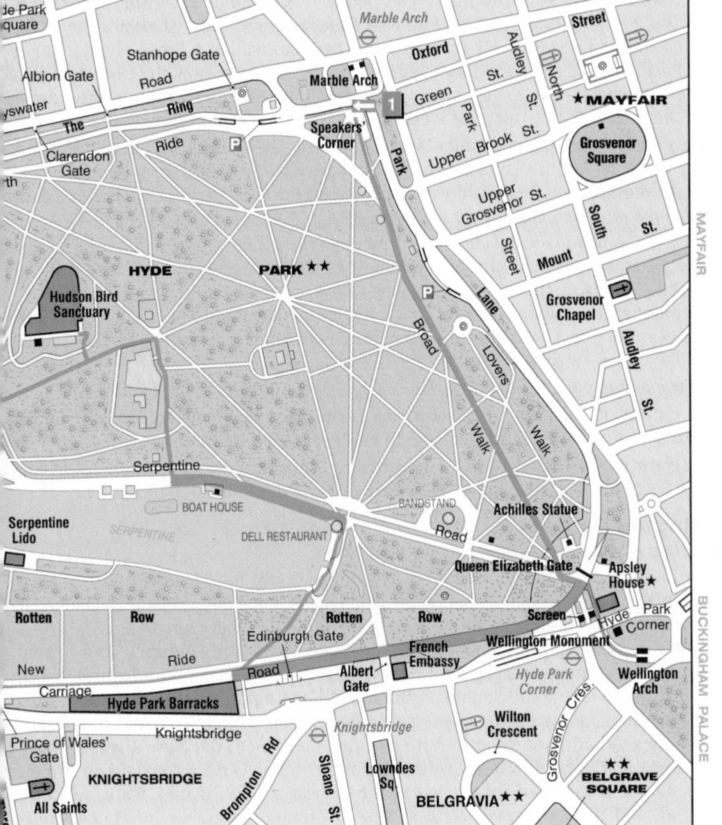

Speakers' Corner is a relatively modern feature of the park; not until 1872 did the government recognise the need for a place of public assembly and free speech. Anyone may mount their soap box and address the crowds irrespective of creed (Darwinians or Hebrew scholars), colour or persuasion (Communists or Nationalists) as long as the speaker does not blaspheme or incite a breach of the peace.

Walk down Broad Walk.

At the bottom end of Park Lane stands the **Queen Elizabeth Gate**, erected in 1993 in celebration of Queen Elizabeth, the Queen Mother's 93rd birthday. The two sets of gates, designed by Giuseppe Lund, provide a cast-iron screen for the central lion and unicorn panels sculpted by David Wynne.

Inside the park is **Richard Westmacott**'s so-called **Achilles** statue (18ft/5.5m), cast from captured cannon and modelled on an Antique horse tamer on the Quirinal Hill in Rome – it is said to have embarrassed the women who presented it to Wellington by its nakedness. Opposite is Byron meditating on a rock, in his own words "a worst bust".

Hyde Park Corner

The south-east corner of the park was transformed in 1825-28 by the erection of a triple arched **screen**, crowned by a sculptured frieze, and a **triumphal arch** surmounted by a colossal equestrian statue of the Duke of Wellington, intended by Decimus Burton to mark the royal route from the palace to the park. In 1883 the arch was moved to its present position, the statue was transferred to Aldershot and replaced by a quadriga (1912).

Take the underpass to the central reservation.

Wellington Arch – *Open Wed-Sun and Bank Hol Mon, 10am-6pm (5pm Oct; 4pm Nov-Mar). Closed 24-26 Dec, 1 Jan. £2.50.* ☎ *020 7930 2726; www.english-heritage.org.uk*

Tyburn Gallows

The gallows, first a tree, then a gibbet, was finally replaced by an iron triangle for multiple executions. From the Tower or Newgate the condemned were drawn through the streets on hurdles to be hanged (and sometimes drawn and quartered too) before the great crowds who gathered to hear the last words, see the spectacle and enjoy the side shows. Popular victims were toasted in gin or beer as they passed. A stone in the park railings in the Bayswater Road marks the site.

Hemmed in by the busy traffic, the arch has been restored to its former glory. The present **Wellington Monument**, placed before the entrance to Apsley House *(see PICCADILLY)*, is by Boehm (1834-90); cast from captured guns, it shows the Duke mounted on his horse Copenhagen, guarded by a Grenadier, a Royal Highlander, a Welsh Fusilier and an Inniskilling Dragoon. An exhibition relates the history of this historic landmark. Go up to the viewing platforms to enjoy splendid views of the parks and of the towers of the Palace of Westminster with the London Eye on the horizon.

With his back to Park Lane stands *David leaning on Goliath's sword* (1925; Derwent Wood), while facing the Lanesborough Hotel *(see KNIGHTSBRIDGE- BELGRAVIA)* stands the memorial of the Machine Gun Corps and the Royal Artillery War Memorial.

Return to the park and proceed along Carriage Rd.

From Carriage Road (south side) walk down to Albert Gate, the site of a bridge over the Westbourne. The twin houses flanking the gate were built in 1852 for a railway baron called Hudson; the house on the east side is occupied by the **French Embassy**. Further along, the angular dark red brick building is **Sir Basil Spence's Hyde Park Barracks** and stables (1970-71). From here the Guardsmen ride down to Horse Guards' when the Queen returns to London.

Walk through the park past a restaurant, along Serpentine Rd and up a path.

At the centre of the park is the **Hudson Bird Sanctuary**, marked by the **Jacob Epstein** sculpture *Rima* (1925), where over 90 species have been recorded.

The **Serpentine Bridge** (1826-28), designed by John Rennie, spans the Long Water and the Serpentine. It also links Hyde Park to Kensington Gardens.

Kensington Gardens 2

Description of Kensington Palace in Worth a Visit

The gardens, originally 20 acres/8ha and extended finally to 275/110ha, were at their prime under Queen Mary, Queen Anne and Queen Caroline, consort of George II and the Royal Gardeners, **Henry Wise** (portrait in Kensington Palace) and his successor in 1728, Charles Bridgman. The original style of geometric and formal wilderness was transformed in the 18C when an octagonal basin, the **Round Pond**, was constructed facing the State Apartments of Kensington Palace *(see below)*. With the pond as focal point, borders were planted around it with flowers and small trees and avenues radiating north and south-east and due east to the New River, now the Serpentine and the Long Water terminating in the Italian Garden and Queen Anne's Alcove. Other features of the period which persist are the **Broad Walk**, recently replanted, and the **Orangery**★ with a massive stone centrepiece by **Hawksmoor** (1705). Later additions are the Edwardian **sunken garden** in which pleached limes surround brilliant flower beds and a long canal, the statue of **Peter Pan** (1912) to the west and **The Arch** sculpted by **Henry Moore** in 1979 from Roman Travertine to the east by the Long Water and the **Flower Walk** north of the Albert Memorial.

Take the Broad Walk and continue along the Flower Walk.

Albert Memorial★

Proverbial as the epitome of mid-Victorian taste and sentiment, the memorial which stands at the summit of four wide flights of granite steps, was designed by **Sir George Gilbert Scott** (1872) as a neo-Gothic spire (175ft/53m), ornamented with mosaics, pinnacles and a cross. A gilded figure (14ft/4m) of the Prince Consort sits at the

Boating on the Serpentine View east towards the towers of Westminster

A. Taverner/MICHELIN

centre surrounded by allegorical statues. Around the podium runs a frieze of 169 named architects, artists, composers, poets. *For details of Royal Albert Hall and surrounding buildings across Kensington Road, turn to KENSINGTON.*

Follow the path to the Gallery.

Serpentine Gallery

♿ *Open for bookshop daily, 10am-6pm; also for temporary exhibitions. Gallery talks: Sat, at 3pm. ☎ 020 7402 6075; Fax 020 7402 4103; info@serpentinegallery.org; www.serpentinegallery.org*

This small compact pavilion, shaded by great trees, was formerly a fashionable tea house. It holds exhibitions of modern art.

Take a diagonal path to view the Statue of Physical Energy and branch right past Peter Pan to the Italian Garden.

Separating the gardens from the Bayswater Road are the railings where artists exhibit their works which are very popular with tourists.

To the north, the residential Bayswater area with its original layout of crescents, squares and terraces retains period terraced houses in Hyde Park Gate, with shallow bow-windows in Gloucester Terrace.

The delicate wrought-iron screen against the red-brick façade of Kensington Palace

Worth a Visit

Kensington Palace★★

♿ *Open daily, 10am-6pm (5pm Nov-Feb); last admission 1hr before closing. Closed 24-26 Dec. Guided tour. £10; £30 family; joint ticket with other Royal Palaces. No photography. Disabled visitors should telephone in advance. ☎ 020 7937 9561; www.hrp.org.uk*

"The house is very noble, tho not greate, the Gardens about it very delicious." Since its purchase in 1689 by **William III**, Kensington Palace has passed through three phases: under the House of Orange it was the monarch's private residence with **Wren** as principal architect; under the early Hanoverians it was designated as a royal palace with **William Kent** in charge of alterations; since 1760 it has been a residence for members of the royal family, notably the late **Diana**, Princess of Wales.

"Kensington is ready" wrote Queen Mary to her husband, William, in July 1690 and, disliking Whitehall, she moved in. The house grew from an early-17C Jacobean house, rebuilt in 1661, to a rambling mansion around three courts by the early 18C. Throughout Wren kept to a style befitting a modest house in red brick beneath slate roofs.

Decoration was limited to the finely carved William and Mary monogram in the hood above the entrance to the Queen's Staircase and the royal arms on the pediment of the turreted clock tower. When **Hawksmoor**, working for Wren in 1695-96, designed the south front, the only embellishment was a central attic screen topped by Portland stone vases. Subsequent external modifications were of a minor character: a Georgian doorway giving access to the Queen's Staircase, a portico on the west front.

The **State Apartments** are approached up the Queens' Staircase designed by Wren (1691).

The Queen's Apartments – The **gallery** (84ft/26m long) is rich in carving, with cornice and door heads by **William Emmett** and sumptuous surrounds to the gilt Vauxhall mirrors above the fireplace in the gallery by Grinling Gibbons in 1691. Portraits in the rooms are personal: *Peter the Great* in armour by Kneller in commemoration of his visit in 1698, *William III* as King and Prince of Orange, *Queen Mary* by Wissing, *Anne Hyde* by Lely and in the adjoining closet, *Queen Anne* and *William, Duke of Gloucester* by Kneller. In the **Drawing Room** Kneller painted *Queen Anne* in profile and the first Royal Gardener, *Henry Wise*. The furniture includes an 18C mahogany cabinet (gallery), a late-17C inlaid cabinet, 17C-18C Oriental porcelain and a fine Thomas Tompion barometer of c 1695 (drawing room). In the bedroom are a state bed of James II and an ornate, mid-17C, Boulle writing cabinet.

The King's Apartments – The lofty rooms designed by Colen Campbell in 1718-20 for George I, bear William Kent's strong decorative imprint. The **Privy Chamber**, above busts of 17C-18C scientists and David Garrick, Oriental porcelain and Mortlake tapestries, has an allegorical ceiling of George I as Mars; the **Presence Chamber**, a red and blue on white ceiling with arabesque decoration by Kent (1724). Remaining from the 17C are the cornice and the Grinling Gibbons pearwood overmantel.

Royal Ceremony

The **Court Dress Collection** traces the evolution of court dress from the 18C to the 20C. Dictated by protocol, elegant dresses and accessories (Orders of Chivalry), court suits and ceremonial uniforms resplendent with gold and silver, lace and embroidery, worn at levées and at court are presented in contemporary settings. More contemporary exhibits include pieces from the Queen's wardrobe, largely designed by the late Sir Norman Hartnell to suit the sovereign's various State functions.

The **King's Grand Staircase**, built by Wren in 1689, was altered first in 1692-93 when the **Tijou** iron balustrade was incorporated and again in 1696 for George I by Kent who covered walls and ceiling with *trompe-l'œil* paintings including a dome and gallery of contemporary courtiers. **The King's Gallery** was intended as the setting for the greatest pictures in the royal collection and decoration was, therefore, limited to an elaborately carved cornice, enriched window surrounds and the practical and ornamental wind-dial (1624) connected from its position over the fireplace to a vane on the roof. The ceiling by Kent depicts scenes from the story of Ulysses. The gallery is hung with 17C paintings from the Royal collection.

Although the 19C **Victorian Rooms** were redecorated by Queen Mary, all else belonged to and epitomises **Queen Victoria** and her family: furniture, wallpaper, ornaments, portraits, photographs, toys and doll's house... The **Council Chamber** at the far end of the east front, contains mementoes of the 1851 Exhibition, including the famous picture of the opening crowds in the Crystal Palace, a garish jewel casket with inlaid portraits of the royal family and a massive carved Indian ivory throne and footstool. Only the ceiling of arabesques, figures and medallions remains of Kent's Baroque decoration in the **King's Drawing Room**. The musical clock (1730) depicts four famous figures (Alexander, Cyrus, Ninos, Augustus). In the **Cupola Room**, high and square with a vault patterned in blue and gold, where Queen Victoria was baptised, are trophies and gilded Classical statues and busts divided by fluted pilasters and a colossal marble chimney-piece.

The Red Saloon in which Queen Victoria held her Accession Privy Council in 1837 and the room in which she is said to have been born in 1819 are also on view.

Kensington★★

The Royal Borough of Kensington takes great pride in its aristocratic connections. In the elegant residential streets are spacious, white-stuccoed houses with all the trappings of affluence. It is also famous for its world-class museums and its fashionable amenities which are highly popular attractions. Notting Hill to the east is famous for its market (Portobello Road).

Location

Map p 10 (ABXY); Michelin Atlas London: pp 38-40, 24-25, 54-55. ⊖ High Street Kensington; South Kensington; Notting Hill Gate; Holland Park. Kensington and South Kensington are to the south and west of Kensington Gardens. The neighbouring districts are Knightsbridge and Chelsea. To the north lie the trendy residential area of Notting Hill and Portobello Road.

Adjacent Sights: HYDE PARK – KENSINGTON GARDENS; CHELSEA; KNIGHTSBRIDGE – BELGRAVIA.

Background

The village of Kensington was for centuries manorial, with a few large houses at the centre of fields. It increased slowly from small houses lining the main road to squares and tributary streets as estates and separate parcels of land were sold.

Among the famous mansions were Nottingham House – later Kensington Palace, Campden House, Notting Hill House later Aubrey House, Holland Park House and, on the site of the Albert Hall, Gore House, the home of **William Wilberforce** until 1823 and for 12 years from 1836 the residence of "the gorgeous" Lady Blessington whose circle included Wellington, Brougham, Landseer, Tom Moore, Bulwer-Lytton, Thackeray, Dickens, Louis Napoleon and other such poets, novelists, artists, journalists, French exiles...

Directory

Light Bite

Tom's – *226 Westbourne Grove, Notting Hill, W11 2RH – ⊖ Notting Hill – ☎ 020 7221 8818 – tomsdeli@easynet.co.uk – – £8/12.* The eponymous owner, son of Terence Conran, has his father's eye for style and design. Half-deli, half-café with framed vintage posters and an impressive cake display. Popular spot with the fashionable Notting Hill crowd.

The Orangery – *Kensington Palace Gdns, W8 3UY – ⊖ Kensington High Street – ☎ 020 7938 1406 – orangery@digbytrout.co.uk – Closed dinner – – £14/20.* This delightful orangery, built for Queen Anne in 1704 in the grounds of Kensington Palace, affords charming views of the gardens and park through the vast windows. It is the ideal spot for morning coffee, a light lunch or afternoon tea. Perfect for a summer's day.

Pubs

Churchill Arms – *119 Kensington Church St, W8 7LN – ⊖ Notting Hill Gate – ☎ 020 7727 4242 – Open Mon-Sat 11am-11pm, Sun noon-10.30pm.* An eclectic collection of wicker baskets, photographs, butterflies, tankards and Churchill memorabilia adorn the ceiling and walls of this large cosy pub. Thai cuisine is served under the veranda in a jungle setting.

Ladbroke Arms – *54 Ladbroke Rd, W11 3NW – ⊖ Holland Park, Notting Hill Gate – ☎ 020 7727 6648 – enquiries@ladbrokearms.com – Open Mon-Sat 11am-11pm, Sun noon-10.30pm.* A country style pub with a meticulous decor in the middle of the residential district of Notting Hill. Large terrace for the summer.

Scarsdale Arms – *23A Edwardes Sq, W8 6HE – ⊖ Kensington High Street – ☎ 020 7937 1811 – Open noon-11pm (10.30pm Sun).* An attractive Victorian pub in a leafy square, ornate decor and simple food, fine ales and decent wines.

The Cow – *89 Westbourne Park Rd, Notting Hill, W2 5QH – ⊖ Royal Oak, Westbourne Park – ☎ 020 7221 0021 – thecow@thecow.freeserve.co.uk – Open daily noon-11pm (10.30pm Sun).* A popular Notting Hill pub, serving oysters and Guinness as well as other seafood and beer. The small space is often packed. Excellent drinks.

The Westbourne – *101 Westbourne Park Villas, Notting Hill, W2 5ED – ⊖ Royal Oak, Notting Hill Gate – ☎ 020 7221 1332 – odaniaud@aol.com – Open noon (11am Sat, 5pm Mon) to 11pm, Sun noon-10.30pm; closed 25 Dec-1 Jan.* Well renovated, with large windows and sun-drenched terrace, the Westbourne is a most popular pub with the locals who also enjoy its cuisine.

Taking a Break

Julie's Wine Bar – *137 Portland Rd, Notting Hill, W11 4LW – ⊖ Holland Park – ☎ 020 7727 7985 – info@juliesrestaurant.com – Open daily 10am-11.30pm (1.30am restaurant).* This bar offers an intimate, oriental setting and a good selection of European and New World wines. When the weather is good you can enjoy the terrace which opens onto a small charming square away fom the noise.

Portobello Gold – *95-97 Portobello Rd, W11 2QB – ⊖ Notting Hill Gate – ☎ 020 7460 4906 – mike@portobellogold.com – Open daily 10am-midnight (noon Sun); closed 25 Dec to 1 Jan.* More of a pub than a bar, it's a popular spot with net surfers. Computers on the ground floor.

Shopping

Intoxica! – *231 Portobello Rd, Notting Hill, W11 1LT – ⊖ Ladbroke Grove – ☎ 020 7229 8010 – ijntoxica@intoxica.co.uk – Open Mon-Sat 10.30am-6.30pm, Sun noon-5pm; closed 25-26 Dec, 1 Jan.* Considered London's best second-hand record store, Intoxica! specialises in music of the 1960s and 1970s.

Kensington High Street – *Kensington High St, WC2 – ⊖ High Street Kensington.* A street of boutiques and department stores. Take a stroll under the arcades of Hyper Hyper, where the work of young fashion designers is displayed, or through the labyrinth of Kensington Market, across the street, to view a host of exotic and trendy clothes.

The Conran Shop, Michelin House – *81 Fulham Rd, South Kensington, SW3 6RD – ⊖ South Kensington – ☎ 020 7589 7401 – www.conran.com – Open daily 10am (noon Sun) to 6pm (6.30pm Sat, 7pm Thu).* Smart decoration shop offering a large selection of furniture and stylish accessories for the home and garden. Situated in the old Michelin offices; the shop's famous trend-setting owner, Terence Conran, has wisely preserved the superb Art Nouveau stained-glass windows depicting, "Bibendum" (aka the Michelin Man), which make this one of the most distinctive London shopfronts.

Travel Bookshop – *13 Blenheim Crescent, Notting Hill, W11 2EE – ⊖ Ladbroke Grove – ☎ 020 7229 5260 –*

Michelin House in Art Nouveau style

K. Brett/MICHELIN

post@thetravelbookshop.co.uk – Open Mon-Sat 10am-6pm; Sun sometimes noon-5pm. Catapulted into international celebrity by the film "Notting Hill", this bookshop, in a street with numerous specialist bookshops, offers a fine selection of maps and guidebooks, but don't expect to see Hugh Grant.

Wild at Heart – *222 Westbourne Grove, The Turquoise Island, Notting Hill, W11 2RH – ⊖ Notting Hill Gate, Westbourne Park – ☎ 020 7229 1174 – flowers@wildatheart.com – Open Mon-Sat 8.30am-7pm.* Nikki Tibbles had the unlikely idea of opening her first flower store in the old public lavatories. Since then she has teamed up with Terence Conran and regularly arranges for large fashion shows.

CARNIVAL

Notting Hill Carnival – Revellers throng the streets on the last weekend in August. The fantastic costumes and floats are a riot of colour. Hip music (calypso, soca, reggae, jerk, mas and steel bands) played live or blaring on massive sound systems. There are costumed parades, floats, friendly policemen, food and drink galore. The Children's Carnival is on Sunday and the Adults' Carnival taking place on Monday.

MARKET

Portobello Road – Browse for antiquities, Victoriana, later silver, chinaware, stamps, small items. *See PRACTICAL POINTS – Shopping.*

Statue of Prince Albert commanding the southern approach to the Royal Albert Hall

J. Malburet/MICHELIN

A Visionary Enterprise – When the **Great Exhibition** held in 1851 in Hyde Park was over, **Prince Albert**, its initiator, proposed that the financial profit, nearly £200 000, be spent in establishing a great educational centre in South Kensington by buying land on which have become established the world famous museums and colleges to be found there today. In the event 86 acres/35hectares were bought and there began a sequence of construction which has given the area a distinct identity.

Walking About

KENSINGTON VILLAGE 1

Kensington High Street

In 1846 when **Thackeray** and his daughters moved into a house in Young Street, the eldest described Kensington High Street as "a noble highway, skirted by beautiful old houses with scrolled iron gates", while Thackeray himself noted that there were "omnibuses every two minutes." Within a few years the population was to multiply from 70 to 120 000; shops spread along both sides of the High Street.

Down Young Street is **Kensington Square**, one of the oldest in London with houses dating from the 17C-19C, as varied in design as the people who have lived in it: Sir Hubert Parry *(no 17)*, John Stuart Mill *(no 18)*, Mrs Patrick Campbell *(no 33)*. The two oldest houses are nos 11 and 12 in the south-east corner; a cartouche over the door mentions previous owners: the Duchess Mazarin (Henrietta Mancini, niece of the Cardinal) 1692-98, Archbishop Herring 1737 and Talleyrand 1792-94.

Over British Home Stores (BHS) is the **Roof Garden** *(no 99 Kensington High Street; entrance in Derry Street)*, laid out in the 1930s in three sections: Spanish, Tudor and a water garden whose fountain is fed by an Artesian well. ♿ *Open (private functions permitting) daily, 11am-5pm by appointment. ☎ 020 7937 7994; Fax 020 7938 2774; www.roofgardens.com*

Kensington Church Street

Commercial and residential developments stretch right across the Campden House estate. On the corner with the High Street an unusual vaulted cloister leads to the parish church of **St Mary Abbots**, built in 19C Early English style, with a towering spire (278ft/85m high), although the dedication goes back to the 11C.

In the churchyard sits the tomb of Elizabeth Johnston, modelled by John Soane in 1784 on the oval sarcophagus of Cecilia Metella.

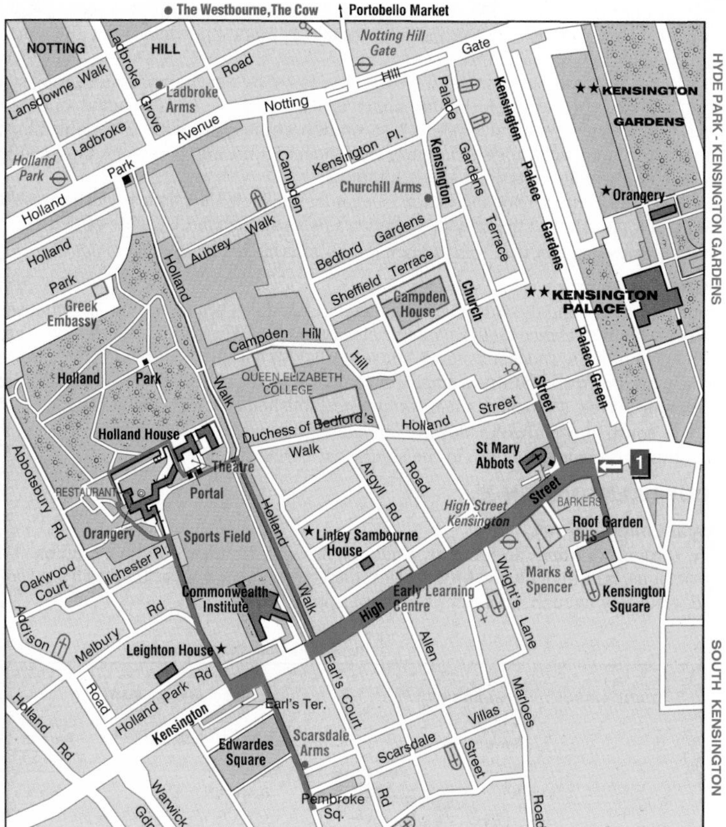

Commonwealth Institute

Kensington High Street. The unique tent-shaped building, with its four peaked, green copper roofs supported on glass curtain walls, was opened by the Queen in 1962 to replace the former Imperial Institute, opened in 1893 by Queen Victoria, of which only the imposing Queen's Tower *(see below)* survives.

This modern complex equipped with three floors of gallery space and an area for live theatrical, dance performances is dedicated to celebrating the different cultures of the 50 Commonwealth countries.

Take Holland Walk.

Holland Park

Park: Open daily, 8am-8pm (dusk in winter). Open-Air Theatre: Open Jun-Aug. Brochures. Café. Sports facilities (golf range, tennis courts, cricketpitch and nets, football pitch). ☎ 020 7471 9813 (enquiries); ☎ 020 7602 7856 (theatre); ☎ 020 7602 2226 (sports bookings). Fax 020 7602 6130; leisureservices@rbkc.gov.uk

It is 100-200 years since Holland House was in its heyday and approaching 400 since the City merchant and courtier Sir Walter Cope built the first large house in the scattered village of Kensington. The mansion, characterised by Dutch gables, and known until 1624 as Cope's Castle, was lavishly furnished, equipped with a library and soon became a place of entertainment for king and court. Advanced wings on either side of the central range were added by Cope's daughter whose husband, in 1624 was made Earl Holland in recognition of soldierly and other such services. The tradition of hospitality was maintained in the 2nd Earl's time and extended when his widow married **Joseph Addison**.

In the mid 18C Holland House was acquired by the politician Henry Fox, who was also created Baron Holland. He was rich, a spendthrift and corrupt; he knew everyone, entertained lavishly and fathered a second son, **Charles James Fox** who continued to frequent the house when it passed to his nephew, 3rd Baron Holland, politician, writer, literary patron and the last great host of Holland House. Among those who dined and visited frequently were the Prince Regent, Sheridan, Wilberforce, William Lamb – the future Lord Melbourne, Byron, Talleyrand, Louis Napoleon, Macaulay (whose own house, Holly Lodge, stood on the site now occupied by Queen Elizabeth College), William IV, and almost the last visitor, Prince Albert;

little wonder that Sydney Smith in a bread and butter letter to his hostess had once written "I do not believe all Europe can produce as much knowledge, wit and worth as passes in and out of your door."

Today, the restored east wing and George VI Hostel by Sir Hugh Casson serve as a youth hostel. In summer the forecourt is canopied to accommodate open-air performances of opera and dance. A restaurant occupies part of the 17C stable block converted to a conservatory in the early 19C; the Ice House and Orangery, meanwhile are used for private functions and exhibitions.

The woodland has been re-established and the gardens replanted after long neglect; peacocks flaunt their plumages in the gardens and water tinkles through the Japanese garden.

Continue down Ilchester Place and Melbury Rd, cross the high street and walk to Edwardes Sq.

Edwardes Square

Tucked away behind the Odeon Cinema, and the uniform brick range of large houses known as Earl's Terrace (1800-10) is this elegant square. The east and west ranges are composed of more modest 3-storey houses (1811-20) complete with balcony, garden and square ironwork, built as a single undertaking. In the southeast corner stands the **Scarsdale Arms**, a flowered Victorian pub "established in 1837" *(see Directory)*.

To the south is **Pembroke Square**, lined on three sides with Georgian ranges, matching iron balconies and, in the south-east corner, its pub.

SOUTH KENSINGTON 2

Royal College of Art

The Darwin Building, designed by Cadbury-Brown with eight floors of studios and workshops, is built of purple-brown brick, dark concrete and glass. It dates from 1961 and, uniquely in such a district, is without applied adornment.

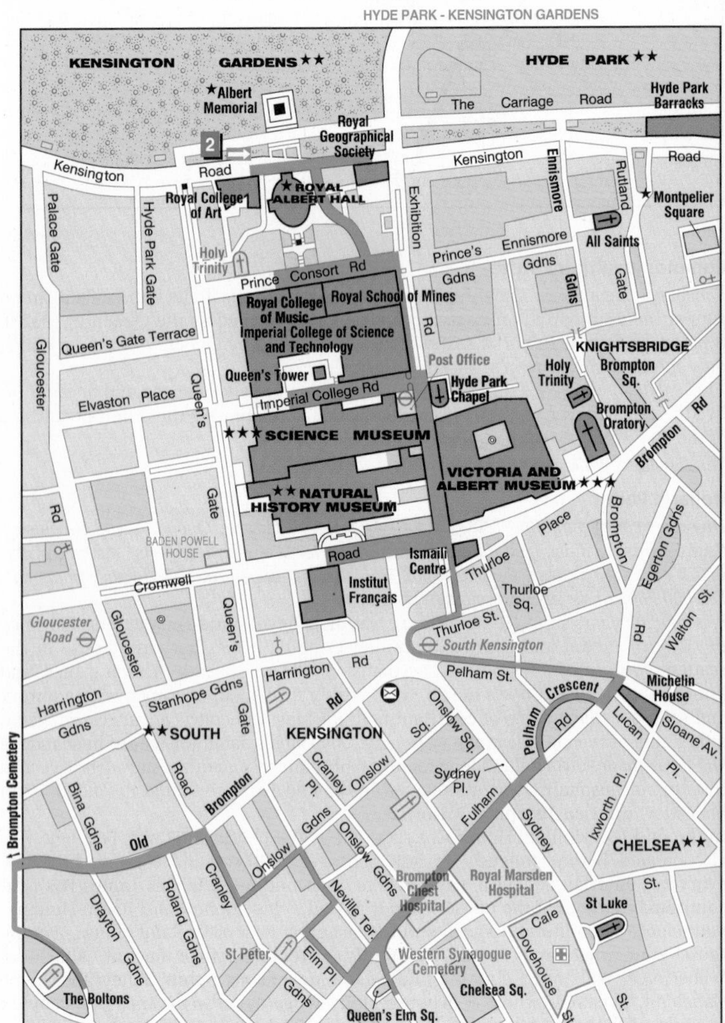

A. Taverner/MICHELIN

Graceful symbols of the Arts and Sciences in the decorative frieze on the Royal Albert Hall

The Royal College evolved from a fusion of the Government School of Design and the National Art Training School (1896). In its time it has nurtured many eminent artists, architects, sculptors, craftsmen, industrial and fashion designers.
In sharp contrast, the small building four floors tall, three bays widealongside is the former home of the **Royal College of Organists**. Designed by Royal Engineer, Lt HH Cole (1875), it is almost obscured by its ornate decoration (FW Moody) of chocolate brown panels patterned in cream, a frieze of putti carrying musical instruments, garlands incorporating the VR monogram around the door.

Royal Albert Hall★

The round hall was designed by another RE, Captain Fowke: almost 1/4 mile in circumference, built of red brick with a shallow glass and iron dome, it is the foil in shape and ornament to the Albert Memorial *(see HYDE PARK – KENSINGTON GARDENS)* opposite since its only decoration is an upper frieze of figures illustrating the Arts and Sciences. Reunions, pop and jazz sessions, exhibitions, boxing, political meetings, conferences and concerts, particularly the eight-week summer series of **Promenade Concerts**, fill the hall with up to 7 000 people at a time. The refurbishment of the interior and of the South Steps and the replanting of the gardens are part of a restoration scheme to create a grand south entrance and to transform the hall for the 21C.

Behind the Albert Hall stands a monument to Prince Albert, a driving force behind the 1851 Great Exhibition; the square chimney is a ventilation shaft for an electricity substation.

The **Royal Geographical Society** was founded in 1830. Statues of explorers Shackleton and Livingstone adorn the outer wall of the many-gabled house, which was designed in 1874 by **Richard Norman Shaw**. The Map Room contains 30 000 old and historic maps beside the largest modern private collection in Europe. ♿ *Map Room and Library: Closed until 2004. Open previously Mon-Fri, 11am-5pm. Picture Library: Mon-Fri, 10am-5pm by appointment. ☎ 020 7591 3060; Fax 020 7591 3061; picture@rgs.org; www.rgs.org/picturelibarary*

Take Exhibition Rd south.

Royal College of Music

The college dates from 1893; Sir Arthur Blumfield designed, in dark red brick and grey slate, stepped and decorated gables between pavilion roofed towers, and finally quartered his construction with pepper-pot turrets after the French style. Inside are the **Department of Portraits** and the highly prized **Museum of Instruments**, including the Donaldson, Tagore, Hipkins, Ridley and Hartley Collections, Handel spinet and Haydn clavichord. *Open in term time, Wed, 2-4.30pm. Closed all Jan. £1.20 ☎ 020 7591 4346; Fax 020 7589 7740; museum@rcm.ac.uk; www.rcm.ac.uk*

Imperial College of Science and Technology

The schools which go to make up Imperial College extend from either side of the Royal College of Music in Prince Consort Road south to the Science Museum, apart from the small enclaves occupied by Holy Trinity Church (1909 replacement of a chapel of 1609), the Edwardian Post Office Building and the Underground exit. With the exception of the neo-Georgian 1909-13 **Royal School of Mines**, of stone with an apsed entrance flanked by giant sculptures, the buildings date from the mid 50s. They are vast, clean lined, in single, right-angled and hollow square ranges, surrounding interconnected quadrangles. From one of the quadrangles, guarded at its foot by a pair of lions, rises the old **Queen's Tower** (280ft/85m high), brick and stone below, green copper and gold turreted at the summit, last relic of Colcutt's Imperial Institute (1887-93), erected following the Colonial Exhibition of 1886. Opposite, the glass-fronted Sir Alexander Fleming building with a stepped double-glazed roof designed by **Sir Norman Foster** combines architectural flair and high technology.

Hyde Park Chapel

Exhibition Road. The stylish Mormon chapel dates from 1960 and is surmounted by a needle spire of gilded bricks.

Continue down the road lined by the Science Museum, the Natural History Museum (descriptions under Worth a Visit below) and the Victoria and Albert Museum (see separate listing) and cross Cromwell Rd.

Ismaili Centre

This distinctive modern building faced in grey-blue marble and adorned with slim windows serves as a religious and cultural centre for Ismailis.

Walk a short distance along Cromwell Rd.

Institut Français

The institute buildings, although in *Art Nouveau* style, date only from 1938. It is a cultural and educational centre founded in 1910. Many of the students enrolled in the Institut and the nearby Lycée are English.

Retrace your steps and turn right into Cromwell Pl to Thurloe St and past the station take Pelham St to the left.

Michelin House

The 1910 purpose-built building, the first in Britain to be constructed with a reinforced-concrete frame, is the former UK headquarters of the Michelin Tyre PLC. Its original *Art Nouveau* **decoration★** has been lovingly restored and the tiled tyre-fitting bays preserved despite considerable internal restructuring (60 steel pillars have been inserted from the open ground floor to support a fourth floor). It is now a shop *(see Directory)*.

Pelham Crescent (mid 19C), which is probably by Basevi, extends in an elegant curve around a private square.

Proceed along Fulham Rd and past two major hospitals.

The Tudor style architecture of **Queen's Elm Square** reflects the tradition that **Elizabeth I** sheltered here under an elm tree during a storm.

Cross Fulham Rd and continue a short distance to Elm Pl on the right.

There are 19C artisan cottages in Elm Place and its immediate vicinity, still surrounded by small gardens brilliant with flowers throughout the summer.

Turn right towards Neville Terr past a pleasant pub and bear left towards Onslow Gdns.

Onslow Gardens are a typical mid-19C development of tall cream stuccoed houses with advanced pillared porches.

Cranley Gdns leads to Old Brompton Rd; turn left.

Bolton Pl, on the left, leads to **The Boltons** where fine white-stuccoed houses are laid out in a mandorla crescent.

Proceed along Old Brompton Rd.

Brompton Cemetery (entrance from Old Brompton Rd) is a vast 19C necropolis containing neo-Gothic, Egyptian and Baroque style tombs.Worth a Visit

MUSEUMS

Science Museum★★★

♿ *Open daily, 10am-6pm. Closed 24-26 Dec. Brochure (6 languages). Bookshop. Restaurant; picnic area.* ☎ *0870 870 4868; sciencemuseum@nmsi.ac.uk; www.sciencemuseum.org.uk*

The spirit of the Science Museum is to encourage initiative and reception in learning and education by presentation, exploration and explanation. There are innumerable objects displayed and constantly updated relevant and topical 'Science Boxes'.

This factory-laboratory of man's continuing invention extends over 7 acres/3 hectares on seven floors. Some of the exhibits listed below may have been moved to a different location. There are countless working models and interactive computer terminals with handles to turn and buttons to press, while assistants are on hand throughout the galleries to advise and inform.

Basement: Children of varying ages enjoy the interactive exhibits of **The Garden**, **Things** and **Launch Pad** which aim to encourage play, exploration and education while the ingenious displays of **The Secret Life of the Home** place domestic technology in an original light.

Ground Floor: The **Synopsis Gallery** *(stairs up to mezzanine)* presents a fascinating review of the contents of the museum illustrating the extraordinary technological advances which have shaped modern life. Look out for Arkwright's water frame, Davy's safety lamps and a reconstruction of James Watt's workshop.

Power (East Hall) celebrates the mighty machines of the Industrial Revolution: Boulton and Watt rotative steam engine (1788); Trevithick high pressure engine and boiler (c 1806); Harle Skye red mill engine (1903); and the development of gas, oil, and air engines. A new version of Foucault's pendulum demonstrates the rotation of the earth. Rockets, satellites and space exploration are the exciting themes of **Space**

with the Apollo lunar lander among the prized exhibits. In **Making the Modern World** diverse exhibits such as *Puffing Billy* (1813); 1905 Rolls Royce; Stephenson's *Rocket* (1829); Rover safety cycle; Crick and Watson's DNA spiral and the Apollo 10 command module mark the development of the modern industrial world.

First Floor – Challenge of Materials *(east gallery)* explains the various processes and uses of metals, plastics and glass. A spectacular glass bridge spans the gallery and a Mondeo car features the latest bodywork. Original artefacts, pictures and interactive exhibits – Marconi beam transmitter; electric telegraph (1846); ship's radio cabin (1910) – illustrate the development of **Telecommunications** and the advanced technologies in use. A drilling rig dominates **Gas** which explores production, exploration, extraction, distribution and use. A combine harvester contrasts with the early machines (Bells' reaper, 1826) that have profoundly changed the world of **Agriculture**. Next are galleries devoted to **Surveying**, **Time Measurement** and **Weather** displaying a range of instruments and equipment (Ramsden's theodolite, Wells Cathedral clock; Coster clock (c 1658), barographs; anemometers etc). **Food for Thought** examines nutrition, diet, additives: Sainsbury store (1920s), energy bike, weight/height chart.

> **PLANNING YOUR VISIT**
>
> **Highlights** – For a quick tour consider visiting the sections entitled Power; Space, Making the Modern World; Optics; The Science and Art of Medicine (Sir Henry Wellcome collection); Flight; Chemical Industry; Food for Thought; Antenna; Digitopolis.
>
> **Children** – For the very young, recommended sections include those entitled Launch Pad *(basement)*, Pattern Pod, Space, Antenna *(Ground floor)*; Digitopolis, Food for Thought *(First floor)*; Flight and Flight Lab *(Third floor)*; Glimpses of Medical History *(Fourth floor)*.
>
> **Interactive learning** – Demonstrations are given in Food for Thought, Launch Pad and Flight Lab sections: enquire at the information desk for times.
>
> **Overcrowding** – To save popular galleries from becoming overrun with parties of school children, a system of timed-ticketing has been implemented. Ask at the information desk for details.
>
> **Science Museum Library** – A reference library is available for study and research, located within the precincts of Imperial College; enquire at the Visitor Information Desk or call ☎ 020 7938 8234.
>
> **Books** – The museum boasts a large and well-stocked bookshop with technical manuals, documentation, teaching packs and souvenirs. General information ☎ 020 7942 4455 or 4454; Educational group visits ☎ 020 7942 4777. Touch-screen Information terminals around the museum display details of exhibitions, events and visitor facilities in six languages, as well as floor plans.

Second Floor – Chemistry of Everyday Life *(east gallery)* features the wonders of science: pioneering research, chromatography tables, a 'Forest of Rods' (3D electron-density map). **Printing and Papermaking** presents the development of printing from clay tablets to the modern press: 18C printing shop. National standard measures used around the world are displayed in **Weighing and Measuring** and the making of light – oil lamps, Lacemakers' condenser, Edison's early lamps, fluorescent lighting – is explained in **Lighting**. The awesome history of **Nuclear Physics and Power** is told through models and equipment including Thomson's electron tube (1837) and an advanced gas-cooled reactor. **Chemical Industry** highlights novel products and concerns relating to uses in daily life. In **Computing and Mathematics** are Babbage's Difference Engine No 2 and Pilot Ace computer (1950), the forerunners of the modern computer. A splendid collection of model ships, navigation equipment and exhibits (*HMS Prince*; Gyro compasses; radars; turbines, paddle wheels; diving bell; aqualung) is displayed in **Ships**, **Marine Engineering**, **Docks and Diving**.

Third Floor – Early instruments explain the principles of **Heat and Temperature** measurement *(east gallery)*: Joule's apparatus is a prized exhibit. **Optics** illustrates the nature of light: Dorset lighthouse optic, shadow wall, holograms, lasers; and **Photography and Cinematography** presents the inventions of Daguerre, Fox Talbot, Muybridge and Edison and high-speed cinematography. George IV's collection of scientific apparatus (Hauksbee's air pump; Adam's silver microscope) forms the nucleus of **Science in the 18C**. **Geophysics and Oceanography** studies the earth's gravity and magnetism and investigates lightning and atmospheric electricity: Boys' gravitational apparatus, Kelvin's tide predictor, seismographs, instruments for exploring the oceans and seabed. Nearby is the **Rosse Mirror,** the largest telescope metal mirror ever made. A computer simulation enables visitors to compile a mix in **On Air**, a radio and sound studio. Learn about the principles of flight in **Flight Lab**: computer games, wind tunnels, demonstrations, motionride simulator. The progress of aviation is traced in **Flight** which displays a collection of aircraft and aero engines: balloons; Wright brothers' plane; Hawker P1127 jump jet; Whittle's jet engine.

Fourth Floor – The Wellcome Museum of the History of Medicine: **Glimpses of History** provides a graphic historical record from the Neolithic Age to the modern age: medicine man, Egyptian mummy, Mr Gibson's pharmacy, Lister's ward (1868), open heart surgery (1980). A social and scientific history of medicine through many cultures around the world is presented in **The Science and Art of Medicine**: 17C Chinese acupuncture figure; drug jar (1641); 16C Genoese medicine chest; Jenner memorabilia; Laennec stethoscope; Pasteur's equipment. **Veterinary History** illustrates the treatment of animals: anatomical model of a horse.

Wellcome Wing – This modern annexe is devoted to innovative displays on contemporary science, technology and medicine with visitors invited to make a contribution. **Antenna** *(ground floor)* features current scientific information while **Talking Points** with images from the worlds of art, sport and medicine aims to make modern science more accessible. An IMAX film theatre presents spectacular shows. **Virtual Voyages** with amazing special effects is a thrilling experience. Human identity and the effects of biomedical sciences are the themes explored in **Who am I?** *(first floor)*: DNA evidence, physical and psychological characteristics, biomedical research. The interactive **Digitopolis** *(second floor)* studies the impact of digital technology: images and sounds, artificial intelligence, future issues. Take part in thought-provoking games on various themes relating to technological developments in **In Future** *(third floor)*.

Natural History Museum★★

♿ *Open daily, 10am (11am Sun) to 5.50pm (5.30pm last admission). Map and guide. Changing programme of special events. Book shop. Restaurant, café, coffee bar, snack bar and picnic area. ☎ 020 7942 5000, ☎ 020 7942 5011 (information); www.nhm.ac.uk*

The main building (1873-80) expresses the solemn reverence and sense of mission in public education in the 19C. Alfred Waterhouse, the architect, took as his model 11C to 12C Rhineland Romanesque cathedral architecture producing a vast symmetrical building (657ft from end pavilion to end pavilion with central twin towers (190ft/58m high) above a rounded, recessed entrance, ornate with decorated covings and pillars. The fabric is buff and pale slate-blue terracotta blocks. The decoration includes lifelike mouldings of animals, birds, fishes: living organisms in the western half of the building; extinct specimens in the eastern half. Since 1989 the museum has incorporated the **Geological Museum**, which was established in an adjoining building in 1935.

K. Brett/MICHELIN

The ornate entrance of the Natural History Museum

The museum has accumulated about 68 million specimens; the collections continue to grow by some 350 000 specimens a year, mostly insects. Such increase would not have surprised **Hans Sloane** *(see index)* whose own collection, begun with plant specimens from Jamaica, had outgrown his house, the house next door and the accommodation at Chelsea Manor, when he bequeathed it to the nation.

The **Walter Rothschild Zoological Museum, Tring**, which was bequeathed to the nation in 1938 by Baron Rothschild *(see index)*, also houses mammals, insects and the major bird collections.

Note: numbers in italics given here refer to gallery numbers.

Life Galleries – *Ground Floor*. The display in the **dinosaur gallery** *(21)* traces the development and extinction of these creatures: an elevated walkway provides a close view of skeletons suspended from the ceiling; tableau of three smaller reptiles killing and eating a larger (blood and sound effects). In **Human Biology** *(22)* the displays explain the working of the human brain, hormones, reproduction, the development of a baby, memory, vision, colours and language. The gallery on **marine invertebrates** *(23)* displays corals, urchins, crabs, starfish, sponges, molluscs, squid and shells. A blue whale suspended from the ceiling dominates the gallery on **mammals** *(24)*; the relationship between four-footed mammals and their

An Imaginative Display

The **Ecology Gallery** has been carefully designed to complement the nature of the displays therein. Opti-white glass is illuminated by coloured lights to suggest fire, water and sheer ice. Clear strips seem to have been rubbed as if from a frosted window. Raised walkways are made from different materials to illustrate earth's different elements.

environment is explained through audio-visual programmes *(3min)*, films, sounds, written panels, illustrations and stuffed originals; whales and their relatives are described in the gallery (upstairs). **Creepy Crawlies** *(33)* illustrates the nature and diversity of arthropods, how and where they live and their relationships with man. **Fish, Amphibians and Reptiles** *(12)* includes snakes, tortoises, terrapins, turtles, lizards, crocodilians, coral reef fish etc. The **Ecology Gallery** *(32)* traces the impact of man's activities on our living planet through spectator participation. The **Bird Gallery** *(40)* displays birds from all over the world.

First Floor – The **Origin of Species** *(105)*, Darwin's theory of evolution by natural selection, is elucidated in the west gallery; the adjoining balcony is devoted to primates. The east balcony traces **our place in evolution** *(101)*. The east gallery displays **minerals, rocks and meteorites** *(102 and 103)* in show cases.

Second Floor – At the top of the stairs is a slice through the trunk of a Giant Sequoia *(201)* felled in 1892 in San Francisco.

Earth Galleries – Enter into the secret of the planet: a gallery of gods stands for the timeless mysteries associated with our world. **Visions of Earth** features displays of gleaming gems, minerals and fossils set against etched slate walls; an escalator lends a sense of journeying from the molten magma core to the tallest mountains, as it rises to the first floor where, with sound effects, flashing lights and vibrations, **the power within** is outlined in terms of earthquakes and dramatic volcanic activity.

The restless surface comprises an excellent explanation of erosion. The various changes in the earth's surface caused by water (tidal waves, flood, avalanche, landslide) and wind (hurricanes, tornadoes, sandblasting) are provocatively presented. **From the beginning** traces the history of the earth from the Big Bang through rocks and fossils of extinct species and predicts its future. A glittering array of precious stones is the highlight of **Earth's treasury** presenting rock and mineral specimens. Exploration and sustainable use of mineral and energy resources, man's demands on the environment are the themes explored in **Earth today and tomorrow**. The diversity of British geology is featured in **Earth lab**.

Darwin Centre – The high-tech design features an inflatable 'caterpillar' roof and a solar wall. The centre aims to make the amazing diversity of its reserve collections as well as the fascinating research carried out by scientists more accessible to the public.

HOUSES

Linley Sambourne House★

18 Stafford Terrace. Guided tour Sat-Sun, at 10am (conventional guide), 11am, 1pm, 2.15pm and 3.30pm (costumed actor). £6. ☎ 020 7602 3316; LinleySambourneHouse@rbkc.gov.uk; www.rbkc.gov.uk/linleysambournehouse

Edward Linley Sambourne, a leading *Punch* cartoonist and book illustrator, moved into this later Victorian town house on its completion in 1874. The original wall decoration by William Morris *(see index)* and the furniture, listed in an inventory dated 1877, have survived largely unaltered.

Cartoons by Sambourne and his contemporaries line the stairs; pictures occupy every inch of spare wall space in the crowded rooms. The fan *(principal bedroom)* signed by Millais, Frith, Alma-Tadema and Watts testifies to the family's artistic connections; the back bedroom typifies Edwardian bachelorhood. The stained-glass panels were designed by Sambourne.

Note the enclosed window boxes like mini-greenhouses, the aquarium on the landing, the ventilators incorporated in the ceiling roses, the bell pulls and speaking tubes complete with whistles.

The exotic decoration of the Arab Hall, Leighton House

Ph. Gajic/MICHELIN

Leighton House★

12 Holland Park Road. Open Wed-Mon, 11am-5.30pm. Closed Sep-Apr, Bank Hols; also 25-26 Dec, 1 Jan. Guided tour Wed and Thu at 2.30pm, £3. Brochure (7 languages). Concerts, lectures and exhibitions. Photography by appointment. ☎ 020 7602 3316; Fax 020 7371 2467; leightonhousemuseum@rbkc.gov.uk; www.rbkc.gov.uk

The Orientalist **Lord Leighton** (1830-96), President of the Royal Academy, Victorian painter supreme, "high priest of the cult of eclectic beauty" as he has been described, remains most originally reflected in the house which he built for himself in 1866. True to High Victorian fashions in art the house is furnished and appointed to the highest standards: domestic rooms upstairs contrast with the rooms for entertaining on the ground floor. The **Arab Hall** is covered with exotic panels of glazed tiles imported from the Middle East (13C, 16C and 17C tiles from Rhodes, Damascus and Cairo), some bearing formal floral arrangements, others Arab inscriptions from the Koran set below an elaborate frieze of fabulous animals, mythological birds and stylised flora designed by **William de Morgan** *(see BATTERSEA - De Morgan Foundation)*. A mosaic floor spreads around a bubbling, cool fountain inspired by Leighton's own travels and those of such friends as the flamboyant Sir Richard Burton (translator of *The Arabian Nights, The Kama Sutra, The Perfumed Garden*). The dining room painted in deep red is particularly stunning in the early spring, its interior contrasting brilliantly with the view of new green grass and fresh bluebells... Upstairs, the walls are hung with pictures by Leighton, Burne-Jones, Millais and their contemporaries.

NOTTING HILL AREA

To the north of Kensington is **Notting Hill**, a fashionable residential area that boasts London's oldest working cinema.

Portobello Road*

The winding road, once a cart-track through the fields from the Notting Hill turnpike, is now a smart area with all amenities. It comes unhurriedly to life on Saturdays as a motley crowd arrives to search the market stalls *(see PRACTICAL POINTS - Shopping)*. It is the venue for the Notting Hill Carnival in August *(see Directory)*.

Knightsbridge - Belgravia**

Knightsbridge and Belgravia are the most exclusive residential districts in the capital and the fashionable emporia and designer shops along Brompton Road, Sloane Street and Beauchamp Place which cater for the pampered lifestyle of the rich and famous are temples of delight. It is a pleasurable pastime to mingle with the leisured classes and to admire the stylish displays. The area also boasts some of the finest hotels and restaurants.

Location

Map p 10 (CDY); Michelin Atlas London: pp 41-44. ⊖ Knightsbridge, Hyde Park Corner, South Kensington. This area is bounded by the green expanses of Hyde Park to the north and the museum district of South Kensington is accessible to the west. Buckingham Palace to the east sets the scene.
Adjacent Sights: PICCADILLY; BUCKINGHAM PALACE; HYDE PARK – KENSINGTON GARDENS; KENSINGTON; CHELSEA; WESTMINSTER.

Background

Until the end of the 18C **Knightsbridge** was an unkempt village beside a stone bridge across the **Westbourne River** (marked by Albert Gate). As it lay outside London and on a major highway it soon accommodated spitals, cattle markets and slaughterhouses, taverns, footpads and highway robbers, and pleasure gardens.
In 1813 Benjamin **Harvey** opened a linen draper's (Harvey Nichols), in 1849 Henry **Harrod** took over a small grocer's shop. These stores, which over the years have become household names for luxury shopping and superlative service and still set standards to this day, attract an elegant and wealthy clientele.

It was probably **George IV** 's decision to transform Buckingham House into Buckingham Palace which provided the impetus for the development of **Belgravia** (150 acres/61 hectares), part of the Grosvenor estate. Until 1821 it consisted of the Five Fields and market gardens, bordered along Upper Grosvenor Place by houses and stables and St George's Hospital *(see below)*. The site was prepared with soil excavated from St Katharine Docks *(see Outer London: DOCKLANDS)*. It was developed to the basic terrace design of the architect, **George Basevi,** varied by the addition of combinations of a restricted number of related forms of ornament to afford a strong overall family resemblance. The builder was **Thomas Cubitt** *(see index)*. By 1827 **Wilton Crescent, Belgrave Square** *(see below)*, Eaton Place and **Eaton Square** had been erected. Cubitt and Basevi were probably responsible for the adjoining square and streets extending far south into Pimlico: Eccleston (formerly New) Square, Warwick Square, Upper Belgrave Street, Belgrave Place and Chester Square.

Directory

Light Bite

Wagamama – *At Harvey Nichols, Knightsbridge, SW1X 7RJ – ⊖ Knightsbridge – ☎ 020 7201 8000 – knightsbridge@wagamama.com – ⚔ – £7/12.* Wagamama presence in this chic department store is proof of the mini-chain's popularity among Londoners. The winning formula: minimalist decor, long refectory tables, carefully prepared and healthy Japanese dishes and reasonable prices. Generally crowded.

The Knightsbridge Café – *5-6 William St, Knightsbridge, SW1X 9HL – ⊖ Knightsbridge – ☎ 020 7235 4040 – knightsbridgecafe@hotmail.com – Open for breakfast, lunch and dinner – £9.* Just a credit card's throw from Knightsbridge's designer shops, a café with smart modern decor, slick and eager-to-please service and a wide range of salads, sandwiches and pastries. Attractive pavement terrace.

Harrods – *Brompton Rd, Knightsbridge, SW1X 7XL – ⊖ Knightsbridge – ☎ 020 7730 1234 – www.harrods.com – Open Mon-Sat 10am-7pm. – £14.* London's most famous emporium presents an array of restaurants and cafés to suit all palates. In the dazzling Art Nouveau food hall are a rotisserie, oyster bar, seafood grill and deli. For a traditional tea, make for the 4th-floor Georgian Restaurant. The Green Man Pub offers a traditional pub lunch and a pint of Harrods Ace.

Harvey Nichols – The Café – *109-125 Knightsbridge, SW1X 7RJ – ☎ 0207823 1839 – Open Mon-Sat 10am-10.30pm, Sun 11am-6pm – £7/15.* The well-heeled Knightsbridge shoppers enjoy the informal atmosphere of this airy, clean-lined café-bar. There is also a smart restaurant.

Pubs

Grenadier – *18 Wilton Row, Belgravia, SW1X 7NR – ⊖ Knightsbridge, Hyde Park Corner – ☎ 020 7235 3074 – Open Mon-Sat noon-11pm (10.30pm Sun).* This area has been haunted since one of the Duke of Wellington's officers was mysteriously murdered here when the pub was used as a mess. According to the landlord, the officer's ghost is now a good friend, who may be seen wandering around the pub and down the alley (one of London's most picturesque). The ghost has an excellent home as the pub is friendly and cosy. Up-market clientele. Good selection of whiskies. Restaurant service.

The Bunch of Grapes – *207 Brompton Rd, Knightsbridge, SW3 1LA – ⊖ Knightsbridge – ☎ 020 7589 4944 – Open Mon-Sat 11am-11pm (9.45pm for food), Sun noon-10.30pm (8.45pm for food).* This Victorian pub has many of the hallmarks – a mahogany interior, engraved glass sides and a wrought-iron balcony. Its location near Harrods makes it a popular tourist spot. Restaurant on the upper level.

The Nag's Head – *53 Kinnerton St, Knightsbridge, SW1X 8ED – ⊖ Knightsbridge, Hyde Park Corner – ☎ 020 7235 1135 – Open daily 11am (noon Sun) to 11pm (10.30pm Sun).* A country setting just five minutes from Harrods. Follow the picturesque road, which appears to be a dead-end, to this friendly pub. At the counter you can order homemade sausages before chatting with the landlord or a guest by the fireplace. As friendly a welcome as you'll receive anywhere in London.

Taking a Break

EasyEverything – *9-13 Wilton Rd, Near Victoria Station, SW1V 1LL – ⊖ Victoria – ☎ 020 7233 8456 – www.easyeverything.com – Open daily until late – £1/ 30 min.* EasyEverything, opened in 1999, is London's largest cybercafé (330 terminals). Prices vary according to the time of the day. In addition to this one located close to Victoria Station, there are nine other cybercafés in London belonging to the same chain.

Library – Lanesborough Hotel – *1 Lanesborough Place, Hyde Park Corner, SW1X 7TA – ⊖ Hyde Park Corner – ☎ 020 7259 5599 – scalabrese@lanesborough.com – Open Mon-Sat 11am-1am, Sun noon-10.30pm.* This hotel, which serves the best martinis in town thanks to Salvatore's expertise, has a refined atmosphere. Large sofas and fashionable clientele.

Shopping

Philip Treacy – *69 Elizabeth St, Belgravia, SW1W 9PJ – ⊖ Sloane Square – ☎ 020 7730 3992, 020 7824 8787 – sales@philiptreacy.co.uk – Open Mon-Fri 10am-6pm, Sat 11am-5pm – From £65.* This hat master is always in the public eye, at Ascot and in lifestyle and fashion magazines. He makes all sorts of headwear from the classic to the extravagant, from Navy blue to fuchsia. His creations are also distributed by Harrods, Harvey Nichols, Liberty and Selfridges.

Beauchamp Place, Halkin Arcade, Brompton Rd, Sloane St are lined with elegant specialist shops where it is pleasant to browse for distinctive items.

Walking About

Start from Hyde Park Corner. For Apsley House see PICCADILLY.

Lanesborough Hotel

The handsome building (1827-29) has a central porch with square columns facing east, flanked by two wings. It was designed by **William Wilkins** to house St George's Hospital, which was founded in 1719 in Lanesborough House in Westminster and moved to Tooting in 1980.

Walk down Knightsbridge and turn left into Wilton Place.

Wilton Crescent

The diameter and inner perimeter are lined by stuccoed terraces. The 17C brick terraces of Wilton Place predate by a century St Paul's Church, which was erected in Perpendicular style by Thomas Cundy in 1843 on the site of a Guards' barracks, still recalled in local street and pub names.

Make a short detour to Wilton Row to visit the Grenadier pub (see Directory), then return to Belgrave Sq.

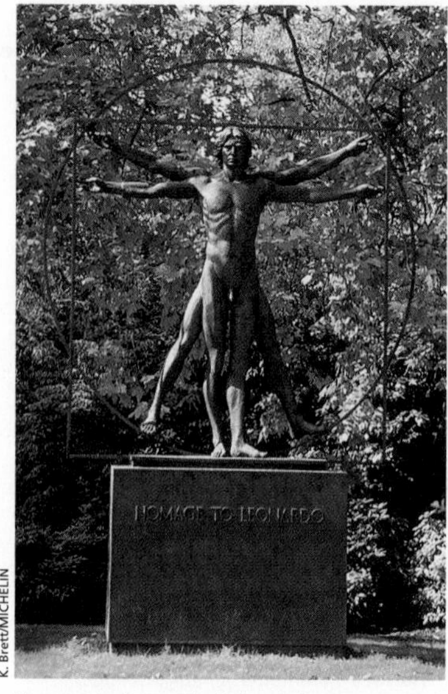

Homage to Leonardo, *Belgrave Square*

Belgrave Square★★

The square (10 acres/4 hectares) is bordered by twinned, but not identical, ranges consisting of a uniform three storeys, cornice and upper floor, all in white stucco. The centres and ends are in the Corinthian style with urns and balustrades, pillared porches and an attic screen decorated with statues. Three of the corners are canted allowing two roads to enter on either side of a detached house also facing the square. The ironwork matches the fence enclosing the central garden; a bronze statue of Simon Bolivar stands in a bay at the south-east corner. Seaford House *(opposite)* was the residence from 1841 to 1870 of the statesman, Lord John Russell.

Continue down Upper Belgrave St.

St Peter's

The church was erected in 1827 in the Classical style, as part of the original development project; owing to its position parallel with Eaton Square there is no vista of the elegant portico. The interior was refurbished after a fire in 1988.

Proceed along Eaton Sq and Belgrave Pl north then turn left into Chesham Pl, through Belgrave Mews to Halkin Place and West Halkin St.

Pantechnicon

The august Doric-columned warehouse dates from 1830. There were also stables and wine vaults. On either side and in West Halkin Street and Halkin Arcade are a number of small shops dealing in luxury goods.

Make for Lowndes St west and walk up Lowndes St.

Lowndes Square

The smart square is the centrepiece of the Lowndes estate; it was developed separately in mid 19C with houses by Cubitt and was largely rebuilt in the 20C.

Walk back and into Cadogan Pl and then past the square.

Sloane Street

The street, first developed in 1773 to link Knightsbridge to Chelsea and the river, has been rebuilt piecemeal. The **Danish Embassy** (1976-77) was designed by Ove Arup. The area west of Sloane Street was developed late in the 18C and is known as **Hans Town**. The tall red brick buildings, purpose-built to provide London lodgings, belong for the most part to the Cadogan Estate.

Turn right into Pont St.

On the right is Hans Pl, a pleasant residential area.

St Columba's

♿ *Open Mon-Fri, 9.30am-5pm. ☎ 020 7584 2321; Fax 020 7584 5446; office@stcolumbas.org.uk; www.stcolumbas.org.uk*

The London Church of Scotland (1950-55) was designed by **Edward Maufe;** its square stone tower capped by a green cupola stands on the axis of Pont Street.

In the late 19C the area around **Cadogan Square** and Cadogan Gardens was rebuilt in unfading red brick, nicknamed "Pont Street Dutch."

*Turn right into Walton St and then left into Hans Rd.*Harrods

Since 1905 the shop, which claims to sell everything, has been housed in the familiar terracotta building with towers and cupolas; the lofty **food halls** are decorated with *Art Nouveau* wall tiles *(see PRAVTICAL POINTS, Shopping)*.

Cross Brompton Rd and follow the itinerary outlined to explore the charming streets and squares. Description of Brompton Oratory and Holy Trinity Church at the end.

Brompton Road

The triangle between Kensington Road and Brompton Road developed as a residential district in typical Georgian fashion around a series of squares: **Trevor Square** (1818), **Brompton Square** (1826), **Montpelier Square** ★ (1837); the houses have trim stucco ground floors and basements with brick upper storeys, neat windows and doors and slender balconies. Linking the squares are narrow streets, mews and closes lined by one-up one-down colour-washed cottages with handkerchief-sized front gardens (Rutland Street). **Ennismore Gardens,** although only slightly later in date, is mid-Victorian in style, its stucco ranges having square pillared porches; **All Saints,** also built at that time in the Early English style, is now a Russian Orthodox Church.

Oratory of St Philip Neri (Brompton Oratory)

♿ *Open daily, 6.30am-8pm. ☎ 020 7808 0900; Fax 020 7584 1095; www.brompton-oratory.org.uk*

The main body of the church was designed (1881) by Herbert Gribble in the Italian Baroque style in Portland stone, the dome and lantern, meanwhile, was planned by George Sherrin (1895-96) so as to span the exceptionally wide and lofty nave. The 18C Italian Baroque statues of the Twelve Apostles by Giuseppe Mazzuoli (1644-1725) used to stand in Siena Cathedral. The Baroque pulpit and much of the mosaic decoration are by Commendatore Formilli. The inlaid wooden floor and carved choir stalls inlaid with ivory date from the previous church. In St Wilfrid's Chapel is a photographic replica of the original triptych by Rex Whistler depicting Thomas More and John Fisher; the altar is early 18C Flemish Baroque.

A monument by Chavalliaud to Cardinal Newman, who preached at the official opening in 1884, stands in the forecourt.

Hidden behind Brompton Parish Church is the attractive **Holy Trinity Church**garden; the building dates from 1827 and the chancel by Blomfield from 1879.

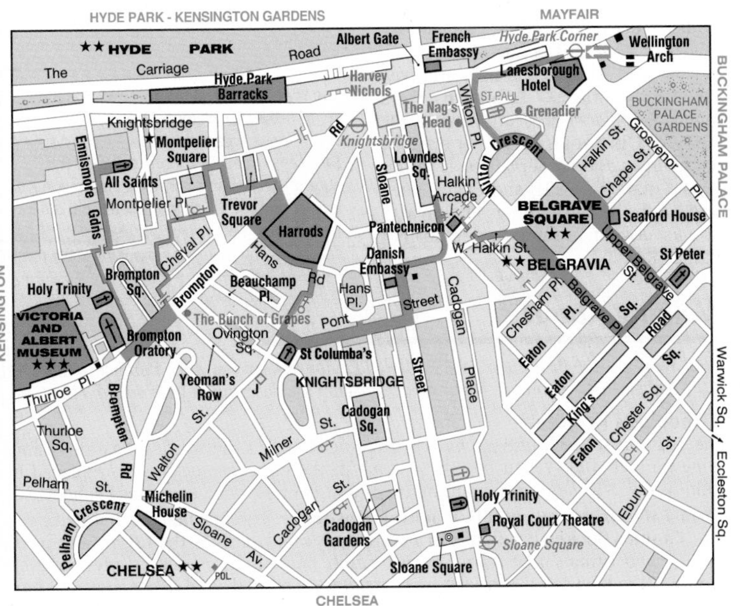

Lambeth

At the start of the third millennium the property boom has made the south bank very desirable and as young professionals move in, the signs of change are evident all over the district. With its convenient location, a world class museum and the Eurostar rail terminus at Waterloo, the future is bright as the regeneration of the south bank progresses apace.

Location

Map p 12 (EFY); Michelin Atlas London: pp 47, 30-31. ⊖ Lambeth North. This built-up area wedged between Southwark and Battersea is the gateway to the southern suburbs and to Kent and Surrey.

Adjacent Sights: SOUTH BANK; BANKSIDE – SOUTHWARK; BATTERSEA.

Background

In the Middle Ages the public horse-ferry from Westminster landed at Lambeth and it was here, close but not too close to the crown, that the Archbishop of Canterbury obtained a parcel of land on which he built himself a London seat, first known as Lambeth House, then **Lambeth Palace** (description in *Walking About*).

In the mid 18C the building of Westminster Bridge and of new roads brought about industrial development such as timber yards, vinegar and dye works, soap and tallow manufacturing, potteries and lime kilns, and the Coade Stone factory. The population increased and in the early 19C there arose prisons, welfare institutions and asylums. There were also louche taverns and pleasure gardens which gave the area a dubious reputation. In the late 19C and early 20C St Thomas's Hospital and the Imperial War Museum were established and changed the character of this proletarian area.

To the south the streets of Kennington are lined with elegant Georgian houses and terraces and Victorian houses and bay-windowed cottages. **Lambeth Walk** *(north side of Black Prince Rd)*, formerly the centre of Old Lambeth, is now lined by grass verges and modern flats; it recalls the old market (1860s) and the cockney gusto of the war-time song. **The Oval**, a famous cricket ground, was a former market garden.

Pub

The Waterloo Fire Station – *150 Waterloo Rd, SE1 8SB – ⊖ Waterloo – ☎ 020 7620 2226 – www.wizardinns.co.uk – Open Mon-Sat 11am-11pm, Sun noon-10.30pm.* This huge scarlet pub in a converted fire station is a local institution, which is absolutely packed in the evening. It offers a good selection of beers and wines and there is a restaurant at the rear.

Walking About

From Westminster Bridge (see WESTMINSTER for description) take Lambeth Palace Rd to the right. For the Florence Nightingale Museum see description in Worth a Visit.

St Thomas's Hospital

The red and white buildings have scarcely changed in outward appearance since being built in 1868-71. In the 1970s some of the eastern blocks were replaced by buildings of 7-14 storeys containing treatment centres, clinics, medical school...

From 13C Infirmary to 20C Teaching Hospital – The hospital, at first dedicated to St **Thomas Becket**, originated in an infirmary set up early in the 13C in Southwark by the Augustinians of St Mary Overie Church, possibly immediately after the great fire of 1212. By 1228 the priory quarters were too small and a hospital was built opposite on a site which eventually extended the length of St Thomas Street. It was endowed by **Dick Whittington** *(see index)* with a laying-in ward for unmarried mothers. In the 16C, although St Thomas's was caring for the sick, the orphaned and the indigent, it was forfeited, as a conventual establishment, to Henry VIII and closed, only to be rescued in 1552 by the City which purchased it for £647 4s, and rededicated it to Thomas the Apostle (Thomas Becket having been decanonised).

The story since is one of expansion, of removal to Lambeth in the 19C, of research and development, of the foundation of the Nightingale Fund Training School for Nurses, of 10 aerial attacks between September 1940 and July 1944 when at least one operating theatre was always open...

Lambeth Palace

From outside the high crenellated wall one can glimpse the mellow red-brick building, begun in the early 13C, the Lollards' Tower (1434-35) and the Great Hall with hammerbeam roof. The magnificent gateway dates from 1490. Archbishop's Park to the north east, formerly part of the palace grounds, provides a good view of the medieval palace.

Walk past the Museum of Garden History and turn left into Lambeth Rd passing the Imperial War Museum (descriptions in Worth a Visit).

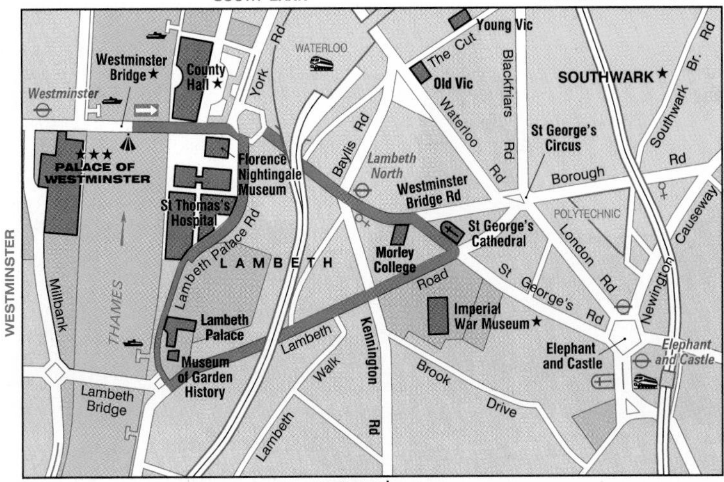

St George's Roman Catholic Cathedral

(♿) Open daily, 7.30am-7pm. Guided tour by appointment. Brochure. ☎ 020 7928 5256; Fax 020 7202 2189; info@southwark-rc-cathedral.org.uk; www.southwark-rc-cathedral.org.uk

St George's, one of the first major Roman Catholic churches to be built in England after the Reformation, was opened in 1848. It was designed by **AW Pugin** (1812-52), the impassioned advocate of the Gothic Revival (of the late-13C and early-14C English architectural style), who ended his days in the Bedlam hospital opposite, now the Imperial War Museum. The cathedral, destroyed by incendiary bombs during the War, was rebuilt and reopened in 1958. Pugin's vision was never realised, so the stock brick exterior is characterised by a massive stump, the foundation of what was to have been a soaring spire.

Interior – The new cathedral with an added clerestory is much lighter than the old: fluted columns of white Painswick stone support high pointed arches; plain glass lights the aisles, the only elaborate windows being those at the east and west ends which form jewelled pendants with rich red and deep blue glass. The new building's sole ornate feature is the high altar with its carved and gilded reredos. Statues are modern in uncoloured stone, memorials few but include the canopied figure of Cardinal Manning.

St George's Circus

The circus, now a forlorn roundabout, was laid out in 1769 by act of parliament as London's first designed traffic junction with an obelisk to **Brass Crosby** marking the central island. Five, now six, roads converged at the centre of St George's Fields, long an open area crossed by rough roads where rebels had assembled (the Gordon Rioters), cattle grazed, a windmill turned, preachers roused crowds.

Westminster Bridge Road

Along the road which was developed in 1750 when the bridge was built stands **Morley College** *(no 61)*, erected in 1920 when the college removed from the Old Vic, and rebuilt in 1958 to designs by **Edward Maufe**. Near the crossroads is a distinctive landmark in the white spire encircled by red brick bands of Christchurch, built in 1874 with funds from the USA.

Waterloo International Terminal

Almost in honour of the great Victorian engineer Isambard Kingdom Brunel, the new 'Gateway to Europe' was conceived by **Nicholas Grimshaw** primarily as a simple, functional train shed spanning five new railway tracks laid by British Rail for the high-speed Eurostar trains. Below ground level, built over the Underground tunnels, sits a great car park which in turn provides support for a two-storey viaduct bearing the unusually long platforms. A glass canopy, comprising standard-size glass sheets sealed with concertina-designed joints, slinkily snakes its way over the curving tracks.

Worth a Visit

Imperial War Museum★

♿ Open daily, 10am-6pm. Closed 24-26 Dec. Parking for the disabled. Leaflet (3 languages). Café. ☎ 7416 5320 (enquiries), 0900 1600 140 (recorded information), 020 7416 5252 (info for disabled); Fax 020 7416 5374; mail@iwm.org.uk; www.iwm.org.uk

The museum covers all aspects of warfare, military and civil, allied and enemy, involving Britain and the Commonwealth since 1914.

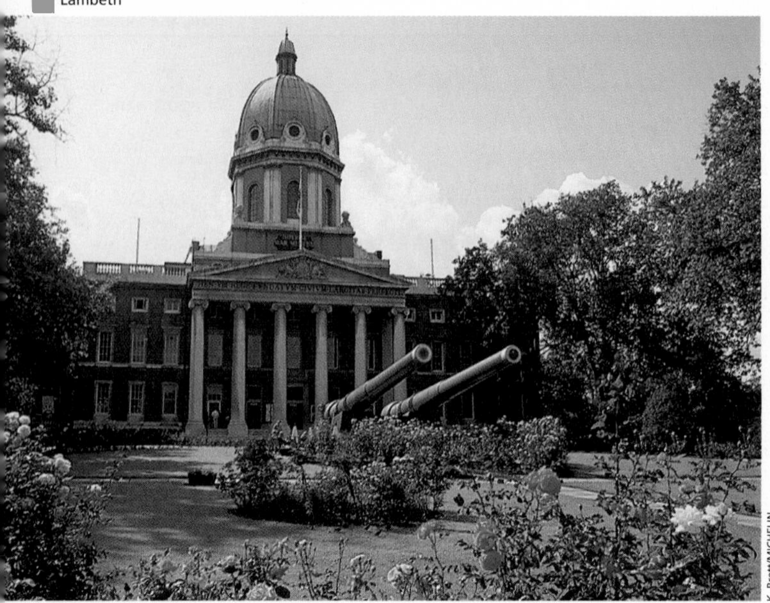

The majestic Imperial War Museum

History – The museum of what Churchill termed the Age of Violence stands on the site of a 19C madhouse. It was founded in 1917, opened in 1920 at the Crystal Palace, transferred in 1924 to South Kensington and in 1936 to the present building. This, to which the dome and giant columned portico were added by Sydney Smirke in 1846, originally comprised the present central area (900ft/274m wide) and extensive patients' wings since it was designed in 1812-15 to serve as the new **Bethlem Royal Hospital** or Bedlam, as it was known, which dated back to the founding of the Priory of St Mary of Bethlehem in Bishopsgate in 1247. In 1547 this had been seized by **Henry VIII** but then handed over to the City Corporation as a hospital for lunatics. It was transferred in 1676 to **Moorfields** where the inmates afforded a public spectacle. A century and a half later came the move to Southwark and in 1930 the final remove to Beckenham.

The white obelisk milestone, originally at St George's Circus, commemorates **Brass Crosby**, Lord Mayor of London in 1771, who refused to convict a printer for publishing parliamentary debates. The authorities thereupon imprisoned the mayor in the Tower but he was freed by the populace, and press reporting of Commons' proceedings was inaugurated.

The Exhibits – The museum in no sense glorifies war but honours those who served. Two British 15in naval guns command the main gate. A wide range of weapons and equipment is on display: armoured vehicles, field guns and small arms, together with models, decorations and uniforms. Among the more notable exhibits are a Mark V Tank, "Ole Bill" (most famous of the London "B" type buses which carried troops to the Western Front in the First World War); a Spitfire; the smallest craft used in the Dunkirk evacuation in May 1940; Churchill Mark VIII infantry tank; the M3A3 Grant tank used by Montgomery during the Battle of El Alamein; the Trench Experience; the Blitz Experience *(10min)*; the Jericho Operation simulating an RAF flight over France in 1944 to release captured Resistance fighters; the VC and GC Room. Historic documents include the typewritten sheet of foolscap which was the Instrument of Surrender of German armed forces in north-west Europe signed, complete with the corrected date, 4 May 1945. There are numerous mementoes of famous men and women, many unknown until all too often a final act of bravery or skill brought posthumous award. The **Holocaust Exhibition** is a sober testimony to this sombre page of history: original artefacts, documents and moving audio-visual presentations.

Paintings and sculptures from the museum's collection of 10 000 works of art reflect particularly the individual's lot in war: Orpen, Augustus John, Paul Nash, Piper, Moore, Stanley Spencer, Sutherland, Topolski painted food queues, people sleeping in tube shelters, the wounded, service life, boredom...

Florence Nightingale Museum

2 Lambeth Palace Road. ♿ Open Mon-Fri, 10am-5pm, Sat-Sun and Bank Hol Mon, 11.30am-4.30pm; last admission 1hr before closing time. Closed Good Fri, Easter Sun, 24 Dec to 2 Jan. £4.80. Film (20min). Refreshments. ☎ 020 7620 0374; Fax 020 7928 1760; info@florence-nightingale.co.uk; www.florence-nightingale.co.uk

The work of Florence Nightingale (1820-1910), nicknamed the "Lady of the Lamp" by the British soldiers she nursed during the Crimean War (1854-56) has become

legendary in pioneering healthcare. Photographs and written panels are supplemented by various personal exhibits: souvenirs of her girlhood and family; case notes, a prescription book, her medicine chest; a Scutari lamp and relics from the battlefields; Crimean medals and commemorative pottery; copies of her many publications on nursing and the organisation and design of hospitals; a nurse's uniform (1880); honours and gifts she received.

Museum of Garden History

(♿) Open Feb to mid-Dec, daily, 10.30am-5pm. Exhibitions, lectures, courses, outings. Donation £2.50. Refreshments. ☎ *020 7401 8865; Fax 020 7401 8869; info@museumgardenhistory.org.uk; www.museumgardenhistory.org*

The museum was founded by the **Tradescant Trust** (1977) in the redundant church of St Mary-at-Lambeth, which contains the graves of the two John Tradescants, father and son, who planted the first physic garden in 1628 at their house in Lambeth and were gardeners to the first Lord Salisbury and Charles I.

The centrepiece in the churchyard is a garden, including a knot garden, created with 17C plants. There is an exhibition of historic garden tools. Lawrence Lee designed the window depicting Adam and Eve and the Tradescants.

At their house they also exhibited a collection of "all things strange and rare" which later, under their neighbour, Elias Ashmole, formed the nucleus of the Ashmolean Museum in Oxford. Admiral Bligh of the *Bounty*, who lived at 100 Lambeth Road, is buried in the churchyard and commemorated in the church.

Marylebone★

The appeal of Marylebone is in the contrast between the intense activity along Oxford Street, the longest commercial street in the world, and the calm atmosphere of the dignified squares lined with attractive buildings. Famous department stores, elegant outlets along Wigmore Street and tiny shops in quaint alleyways make for a shopper's paradise. However Marylebone has a complex identity. There are splendid 18C mansions built for high society; one now houses a famous museum (The Wallace Collection) and another is used as an exclusive club (Stratford House). Harley Street is famous as a centre of medical expertise, and cultural interest is provided by Broadcasting House, the home of the BBC, and the Wigmore Hall.

Location

Map p 11 (CDVX); Michelin Atlas London: pp 74-75. ⊖ Baker St, Regent's Park, Bond Street. The main thoroughfares criss-crossing this area are Oxford Street, Portland Place and Regent St, Baker Street and Marylebone Road. On the northern edge is leafy Regent's Park.

Adjacent Sights: MAYFAIR; REGENT'S PARK; BLOOMSBURY; SOHO.

Background

The only remaining traces of St Marylebone village are Marylebone High Street and its continuation south, Marylebone Lane, which followed the winding course of the Tyburn River. The land belonged to Barking Abbey until the Reformation when it was confiscated by **Henry VIII**, who enclosed the land which lay north-east of the village, to form a royal park. He built a hunting lodge, the Manor House (demolished 1791), which he and **Elizabeth I** used for entertaining important guests.

In 1611 the southern part of the royal lands was sold off by James I. In 1650 part was laid out as the **Marylebone Gardens** where patrons could wander under the trees or take tea and bread and butter in pleasant arbours; the gardens closed in 1778.

On old maps **Oxford Street** appears variously as Tyburn Road, Uxbridge Road and Oxford Road. A turnpike just before the junction with Park Lane marked the western limit of what soon became London's prime shopping street.

18C Development – Early in the 18C Edward Harley, 2nd Earl of Oxford, who had inherited the land sold by **James I**, began to develop Cavendish Square. By the end of the century St Marylebone village and the surrounding waste land was covered by the most complete grid layout of streets in any area of London;

ELEMENTARY MY DEAR WATSON!

Baker Street, the wide thoroughfare, was 100 years old when **Conan Doyle** invented **221B** as the address of his famous detective **Sherlock Holmes**; 85 was then the highest number as the street was in two sections. Hansom cabs, gas lamps and fog have gone but 221B now exists since the street was renumbered in 1930.

Star-gazing at the domed Planetarium and at Madame Tussaud's Waxworks

J. Malburet/MICHELIN

each street is named after a member of the Earl's family or their titles or estates. Between Oxford Street and Regent's Park the only streets not to conform to the rectangular theme, are Marylebone Lane and Marylebone High Street.

In 1756 Marylebone Road and its eastward extension then known as the New Road was created to link the City directly to Paddington and west London.

Directory

Light Bite

De Gustibus – *53 Blandford St, W1H 3AF – ⊖ Bond Street – ☎ 02 07486 6608 – www.degustibus.co.uk – Open Mon-Fri 8.30am-4.00pm –* ⊭ *– £7.* Awarded by the British Baking Industry for two consecutive years, this renowned shop boasts an extensive range of freshly baked breads with Mediterranean-influenced fillings which change daily and other enticing snack food. Eat in the brightly decorated cafe, on the pavement terrace or take away.

Carluccio's – *3-5 Barrett St, St Christopher Pl, W1U 1AY – ⊖ Bond Street – ☎ 020 7935 5927 – www.carluccios.com – £10.* Lovers of Mediterranean savours will adore this popular modern Italian deli and restaurant in a bustling square just behind Oxford St. Full menu with good selection of classic antipasti and pastas and other traditional dishes. Owner also runs the well-known restaurant and deli on Neal St. *(see COVENT GARDEN).*

The Sea Shell – *49-51 Lisson Grove, NW1 6UH – ⊖ Marylebone – ☎ 020 7224 9000 – zen18154@zen.co.uk – Closed Sun – £13.50/19.50.* Venture beyond the lively, marble-tiled take-away section and take a seat in this popular fish and chip restaurant. Extensive selection of traditional and more adventurous seafood dishes. Try the Dover Sole. Carnivores are also well catered for.

Pub

The O'Conor Don – *88 Marylebone Lane, W1U 2PY – ⊖ Bond Street – ☎ 020 7935 9311 – info@oconordon.com – Open Mon-Fri 11am-11pm; closed bank hols and 25 Dec – 1 Jan.* An authentic Irish pub operated by true Irish people. Head upstairs to the eating area to try the famous Irish stew.

Taking a Break

The Landmark London – *222 Marylebone Rd, NW1 6JQ – ⊖ Marylebone – ☎ 020 7631 8000 – www.landmarklondon.co.uk – Open for tea daily 3pm-6pm, for brunch Sun 11.45am-3pm.* At this traditional British hotel, you can take tea beneath the glass roof in the very impressive winter garden. On Sundays brunch is served to the beat of a jazz orchestra.

Walking About

NORTH OF OXFORD ST 1

Start from Baker St station. Walk up Baker St if you wish to visit Sherlock Holmes Museum (description in Worth a Visit). Continue past the Planetarium and Madame Tussaud's (also in Worth a Visit).

Marylebone Road

The road is now a six-lane highway, bordered by several buildings of interest. On the north side is the **Royal Academy of Music** accommodated in an attractive building (1911) in red brick and stone, ornamented with reclining figures in the large segmental pediment.

Cross the road to Marylebone High St.

St Marylebone

♿ *Leaflet (6 languages). ☎ 020 7935 7315; Fax 020 7486 5493; office@stmarylebone.org; www.stmarylebone.org*

The church by **Thomas Hardwick** was completed in 1817, a large balustraded building with a three-stage tower ending in gilded caryatids upholding the cupola. The pedimented Corinthian portico was added by Nash to provide an appropriate close to the view from Regent's Park down the axis of York Gate. It was here that **Robert Browning** illicitly married the poet Elizabeth Barrett (1846).

A sculptured panel showing characters from the six principal works written by **Charles Dickens** commemorates the novelist who lived in a house on the site.

Walk on, then turn right into George St and left into Spanish Pl.

Manchester Square

The last of the three principal squares dates from 1776 when the 4th Duke of Manchester acquired the land after the death of Queen Anne brought an abrupt end to plans for an elegant square to be completed in her honour. Manchester Square, which is attractive with late Georgian houses, developed to the south of the house during the next 12 years. The house served as residence to the Spanish ambassador, who built the Roman Catholic Chapel of St James's in the adjoining street, henceforth known as **Spanish Place**, and then his French counterparts (Talleyrand and Guizot among others). In 1872 the house was bought by **Richard Wallace**, **Marquess of Hertford**, who renamed it **Hertford House** and entirely remodelled it to display the **Wallace Collection** *(description in Worth a Visit)*.

Return to George St and walk on, across Baker St and Gloucester Place.

The Squares★

In **Gloucester Place** there are attractive small doorways, ironwork balconies and railings. **Montagu Square**, which dates from the early 19C, is notable for its houses with shallow ground-floor bow windows – at no 39 lived the novelist **Anthony Trollope** (1873-80) – while the early-19C **Bryanston Square** is graced with long stucco terraces.

Take Greater Cumberland Pl, turn left into Upper Berkeley St.

At the northwest corner of **Portman Square**★ there remain two of the finest houses (**nos 20-21**) that ever graced the square. No 20 by **Robert Adam** was built and furnished in 1772-77 for Elizabeth, Countess of Hume.

Turn right into Baker St, cross and take Wigmore St as far as Wimpole St.

Wigmore Hall

The concert hall, famed for its intimate atmosphere conducive to chamber music and solo recitals borrows its name from the street.

Wimpole Street

No 64 is the home of the **British Dental Association** . Before her marriage to **Robert Browning** in the Church of St Marylebone in 1876, **Elizabeth Barrett** lived at no 50, which was demolished when the street was largely rebuilt at the turn of the century. At no 80 died the novelist Wilkie Collins (1889).

Turn right into Henrietta Pl.

St Peter's

Vere Street. Open Mon-Fri, 9.30am-5pm. Guide book. ☎ 020 7399 9555; Fax 020 7399 9556; mail@licc.org.uk; www.licc.org.uk

Originally designed as a chapel of ease to serve the residents of Cavendish Square, this attractive small dark brick building (1721-24) has quoins emphasising the angles, square turret and open belfry.

The unexpectedly spacious interior includes galleries supported on giant Corinthian columns with massive entablatures. Designed by the architect **James Gibbs**, St Peter's may have been an experimental model for St Martin-in-the-Fields *(see TRAFALGAR SQUARE)*. Having collaborated with Gibbs in the painting of '*The Pool of Bethesda* and *The Good Samaritan* in Bart's Great Hall, **Hogarth** used St Peter's to set the marriage scene in *The Rake's Progress*. The quite lovely stained-glass windows were designed by Edward Coley Burne-Jones and made by William Morris & Co at their Queen's Square premises.

Take Marylebone Lane to Oxford St, and walk west towards Selfridges.

Stratford Place

This quiet cul-de-sac recalls the early 18C; the north end is closed by **Stratford House** (now the **Oriental Club**), an imposing mansion designed in 1773 by R Edwin in the Palladian style.

St Christopher's Place

The narrow pedestrian passage with flower baskets has been restored to its Victorian appearance and is well known for its outdoor cafés and its small specialist shops.

SOUTH OF PORTLAND PLACE 2

Start from Regent's Park station.

Portland Place

In the 18C the street was a fashionable promenade; the north end was closed by gates; both sides were lined by houses designed by Robert and **James Adam**; its width was dictated by the façade of Foley House at the south end.

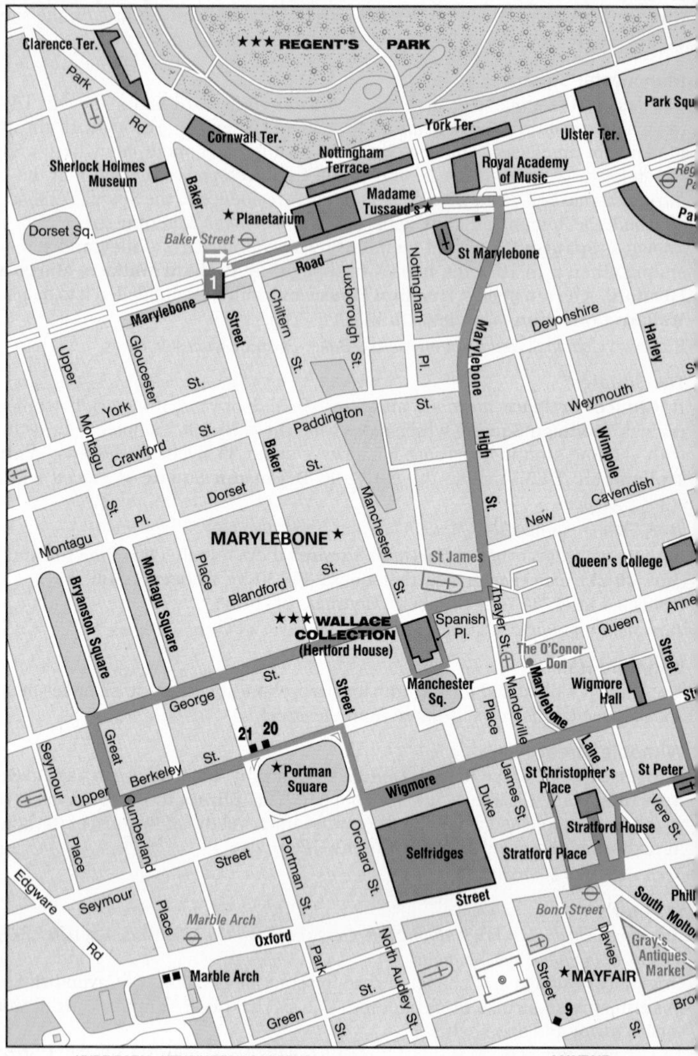

At either end are statues of Lord Lister (1827-1912), the founder of antiseptic surgery who lived in Park Crescent, and Quintin Hogg, who founded the Regent Street Polytechnic in 1882. Only one (**no 46**) of the Adam houses has survived. The tall stone corner building *(no 66)*, adorned with reliefs on the façade and on the pillars, was erected in 1934 to celebrate the centenary of the **Royal Institute of British Architects** (RIBA). In 1864 Foley House was replaced by the **Langham Hotel**, a high Victorian building with a pavilion roof. The distinctive curved front of **Broadcasting House**, home to BBC Radio, was designed by G Val Myer in 1931.

All Souls

(♿ lift) Open Mon-Fri, 9.30am-6pm (8pm occasionally); Sun, 8am-8.30pm. ☎ 020 7580 3522; Fax 020 7436 3019; vestry@allsouls.org; www.allsouls.org

The church was designed by **John Nash** as a pivot between Portland Place and Regent Street. Its unique feature, a circular portico of tall Ionic pillars, surmounted by a ring of columns supporting a fluted spire, was designed to look the same from whatever angle it was approached. The church, Nash's only important church, is a traditional, galleried hall-church, built of Bath stone. The unusual inverted arches of the foundations were revealed in 1976, when the undercroft was excavated and the floor raised 18in/46cm.

Take Portland Pl by the Langham Hotel.

Chandos Street

The street is named after the Duke of Chandos, who proposed to build a palatial residence but was hard hit when the South Sea Bubble burst in 1720.

At the north end, facing south, is the perfectly proportioned **Chandos House** (1771),

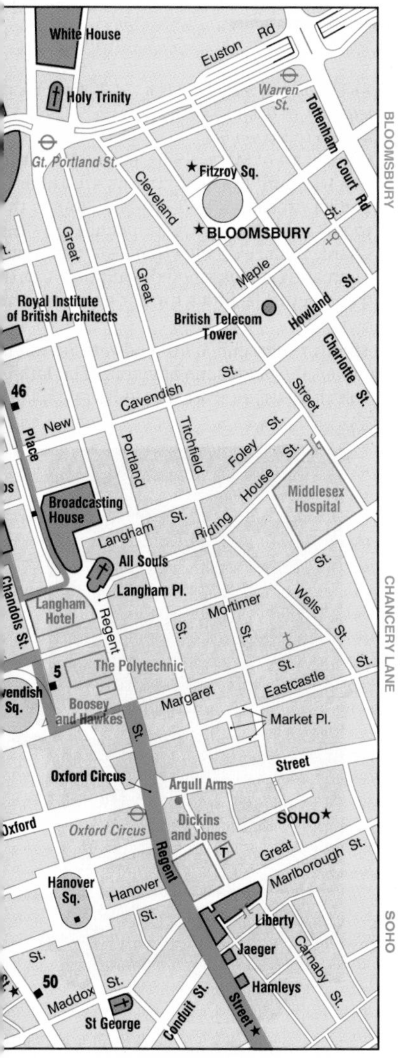

now occupied by the **Royal Society of Medicine**, designed by **Robert Adam** and resembling one of his own immaculate drawings. It is built of Portland stone, is four bays wide and three floors high; the only embellishments are a narrow frieze above the second floor, the square porch and the 18C iron railings, complete with lamp holders and snuffers.

Turn left into Queen Anne St and into Harley St south.

Harley Street

It seems that every door, three steps up from the pavement, is emblazoned with the brass plates of medical consultants. The street is an architectural mixture, dating from the original Georgian, through the terracotta, brick and stone of the mid 19C to the present. Florence Nightingale lived at no 47. The Tuscan pillared stucco portico *(nos 43-49)* is the entrance to **Queen's College**, the oldest English school for girls, which was founded in 1848 initially to provide a proper training for governesses and counted Miss Beale and Miss Buss among its early pupils.

Before it was monopolised by the medical profession operating their private surgeries, Harley Street was home to many eminent figures, notably **Wellington** *(11)*, **Turner** *(64)*, **Gladstone** and **Allan Ramsay**.

Cavendish Square

On the north side of the square (1717) stands a pair of stone-faced Palladian houses of the 1770s *(opposite John Lewis)*: these are now linked by a bridge designed by Louis Osman (1914-96) against which stands a moving composition of the *Madonna and Child* by **Jacob Epstein** (1950) cast in lead to prevent staining. There are late-18C and 19C houses, much altered, along the east side; no 5 was the home of Nelson in 1787 and of Quintin Hogg (d 1903), founder of the Regent Street Polytechnic.

The square was designed as a focal point north of Oxford Street with dependent residential and service streets and a local market; Market Place still exists on the east side of Oxford Circus. Where John Lewis, the department store now stands used to be the house where Lord Byron was born (1788).

Go round the north and east sides of the square, left into Margaret St and down Regent St.

Oxford Circus

Oxford Street stretches west to Marble Arch and Hyde Park beyond. Its status as a shopping street was confirmed when Gordon Selfridge erected his vast and imposing shop in 1908; colossal Ionic columns soared up through three floors to an attic and balustrade; a canopy protected the entrance and the windows displayed goods in a new way. The other major shops are John Lewis, House of Fraser, Debenhams and Marks and Spencer.

Eastwards this major thoroughfare becomes New Oxford Street and stretches to Bloomsbury.

Regent Street Polytechnic

On 20 February 1896 the first public demonstration of the Lumière Brothers' Cinématographe was made at the Regent St Poly at 9 Regent's Street, now part of the University of Westminster. Due to the apparent lack of interest, the showing of the most popular films, *The Arrival of a Train* and *Baby's Breakfast Time*, were soon moved from the Great Hall to the Marlborough Hall. On 9 March screenings were transferred to the Empire in Leicester Square – which continues to this day to premiere films.

Worth a Visit

Wallace Collection★★★

♿ *Open daily, 10am (noon Sun) to 5pm. Closed Good Fri, May Day Hol, 24-26 Dec, 1 Jan. Guided tour (1hr). Leaflet. Guide book (3 languages).* ☎ *020 7563 9500; Fax 020 7224 2155; admin@thewallacecollection.org; www.thewallacecollection.org*

On the north side of Manchester Square at the heart of Marylebone, stands **Hertford House**, formerly Manchester House, which was built (1776-88) by the 4th Duke of Manchester. The house was let to the Spanish Embassy (1791-95) and later to the French Embassy (1834-51). From 1872 to 1875 the house was remodelled by the architect Thomas Ambler to house Richard Wallace's collection. An ingenious remodelling of the courtyard (1999-2000) creating a glass-roofed Sculpture Court, galleries exhibiting the reserve collection and better facilities further enhances the appeal of this charming museum.

Noble patronage – The Marquesses of Hertford are descended from Edward Seymour, **Duke of Somerset** and Lord Protector, brother of Queen Jane Seymour. The family art collection was started by the 1st Marquess (1719-94) Ambassador to Paris and Lord Lieutenant of Ireland, increased by the 2nd Marquess (1743-1822) Ambassador to Berlin and Vienna and further enlarged by the 3rd Marquess (1777-1842): he purchased 17C Dutch paintings, 18C French furniture and Sèvres porcelain while acting as a saleroom agent for the Prince of Wales.

A magnificent 18C French Cabinet by AC Boulle

It was transformed into one of the world's finest collections of 18C French art by the reclusive **4th Marquess of Hertford** (1800-70) who lived most of his life in Paris. His taste was traditional; he collected old masters, tapestries, and accumulated the most comprehensive collection of Sèvres porcelain (1752-94) and the finest French furniture of the 17C and 18C from the workshops of the master cabinet makers: **Boulle** (1642-1732), **Cressent** (1685-1768) and **Riesener** (1734-1806). He declared "I only like pleasing paintings" and bought extensively the 18C French painters, Watteau, Boucher and Fragonard.

Richard Wallace, the 4th Marquess' natural son (1818-90), founder of the Hertford British Hospital in Paris and provider of the drinking fountains still known by his name (one in the forecourt), moved the collection to Britain for safety from the Commune uprisings and made substantial additions, specialising in the decorative arts. The collection was bequeathed to the nation by his widow Lady Wallace (1897) on condition that the government provide premises in central London for the collection and that objects never be loaned or sold. Hertford House was therefore purchased from the Wallace family heir and transformed into a museum (1900).

Entrance Hall – *The Arab Tent* (1866) by Landseer is the collection's most expensive work, having been purchased from Edward VII for £7 800.

Gallery 2 – The Billiard Room is presently furnished with Louis XIV (1643-1715) and Régence (1715-23) period furniture: Portrait of Louis XIV and his Bourbon family; inlaid coffers on stands (c 1820); wardrobe and inkstand by Boulle.

Gallery 3 – The former dining room displays the fine and applied arts of the **Louis XV** (1723-74) and **Louis XVI** (1774-92) periods: fabulous crystal chandelier and wall-sconces; paintings by the master of still-life **Oudry** and the portraitist of elegant society **Nattier**; lovely **Carlin secretaire** (1776) and *table à pupitre* (1783) veneered in tulip wood with inset porcelain plaques painted with exquisite floral arrangements.

Gallery 4 – The Back State Room is decorated in the Louis XV Rococo style: Georges Jacob chairs, covered in Beauvais tapestry; fine chandelier; magnificent Sèvres porcelain; four overdoor animal pictures by Oudry.

The Collection

For a full tour allow about 4 hours. For those with less time available most medieval and Renaissance pieces, and the armouries collection are displayed on the ground floor; Old Master pictures are hung in Gallery 22; finest 18C French furniture, porcelain and paintings in Galleries 4, 16, 24 and 25.

The central face of the astronomical clock shows the passage of the sun through the zodiac constellations, the age, longitude and phases of the moon and the time anywhere in the northern hemisphere; the two lower faces show the rising and setting of the sun (left) and moon (right).

Gallery 5 – The Front State Room is hung with English 18C and 19C portraits by Reynolds, Hoppner *(George IV as Prince of Wales)*, Lawrence *(Countess of Blessington)*. The striking *bleu céleste* Sèvres wine and ice-cream coolers are from an 800-piece dinner service (1778-79) made for Empress Catherine II of Russia.

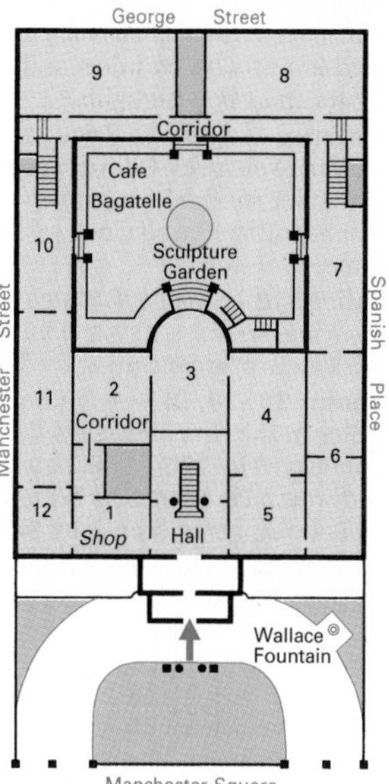

Galleries 6 and 7 – The Canaletto and Sixteenth Century room contains medieval, Renaissance and Baroque works of art and curiosities: *Eleonora di Toledo* after Bronzino (1503-72); 15C and 16C Italian and Northern School sculpted figures (bronze, boxwood, ivory); wax miniatures *(case 2)*; fragments of 14C and 15C illuminated manuscripts *(case 3)*; Limoges enamels; chased silver plate; Venetian glass and Syrian mosque lamp (c 1350).

The former Smoking Room was, until 1937, decorated throughout with Iznik-style Minton tiles. Cases enclose rare medals of Gianfrancesco Gonzaga **(Pisanello)**, Sigismondo Malatesta, Desiderius Erasmus **(Massys)** and Emperor Charles V **(Dürer)**; Renaissance jewellery including early pieces set with faceted gems and a lovely French girdle enamelled with hunting scenes; ceramics by Bernard **Palissy** (1510-90), **Hispano-Moresque pieces**, Italian **maiolica** and lustreware. Note also the fabulous horse trophy and elegant silver ewer.

Galleries 8, 9, 10 – Displays of European weapons and arms capturing the spirit of a lost age are arranged chronologically – *Gallery 10: Medieval and Renaissance; Gallery 9: Renaissance; Gallery 8: 16C-19C.* Remarkable items include "dress" and ceremonial cast and decorated swords; firearms, inlaid crossbows, chased steel armour and shields, engraved helmets, horse armour and red velvet trappings.

Gallery 11 – Oriental arms with hilts carved of jade and set with gemstones, armour and works of art; 19C French Orientalist paintings echoing a taste for North Africa and the Middle East prompted by Napoleonic campaigns there.

Gallery 12 – The former Housekeeper's Room is dedicated to English and French paintings of the 1820s and 1830s, notably by **Richard Parkes Bonnington** (1801/2-28): shimmering landscapes, Romantic history pictures.

Stairs – The Louis XV wrought-iron and brass **balustrade** is chased and decorated with interlaced Ls and sunflowers, made (1719-20) for the proposed Banque Royale in Paris; it was adapted by Wallace to the present marble staircase.

The walls are hung with large decorative **canvases** by Boucher: *The Rising* and *The Setting of the Sun*, and *An Autumn* and *A Summer Pastoral* illustrating theatrical scenes.

Gallery 13 – In Lady Wallace's boudoir hang paintings reflecting the 18C cult of sensibility: sentimental genre pictures by **Greuze** (*The Inconsolable Widow, The Broken Mirror* and *Innocence*) and fancy pictures by **Reynolds** *(Miss Jane Bowles, The Strawberry Girl)*. Empress Josephine's work table by Weisweiler is inset with Wedgwood plaques.

Corridor – A collection of exquisite gold **snuffboxes★** painted with enamels or lacquered, and set with precious stones, Sèvres porcelain, mother-of-pearl and tortoiseshell is remarkable.

Louis XV perpetual almanack in four sections (1741-2) and an ornate 18C silver writing, breakfast and toilet service are also noteworthy.

Gallery 14 – The study accommodates splendid marquetry furniture by **Boulle** (wardrobe with ormolu groups of *Apollo and Daphne* (left) and *The Flaying of Marsyas* (right); toilet mirror and writing table; pedestal clock mounted with four figures representing the four continents, and Dutch paintings.

Six Plaques Mounted in a Coffer, French, 18C

Gallery 15 – The Oval Drawing-Room retains its original fireplace. Besides the 18C paintings (Mme Vigée-Lebrun's *The Comte d'Espagnac or Boy in a red coat,* Fragonard's charming *A Boy as Pierrot* – maybe the painter's son), it is ornamented with two marble busts by **Houdon** and furnished with a roll-top desk by **Reisener**, elegant chairs and fine wall-lights.

Galleries 16 and 17 – The Large and Small Drawing Rooms are hung with sparkling views of Venice by **Guardi** and **Canaletto**. Sèvres soft-paste porcelain (rare inkstand and toilet service) ornaments the Louis XV furniture. Note the pier glass (16) and the magnificent wall clock (17) by **Cressent** (1685-1768), with Love triumphing over Time.

Gallery 18 – Small 17C Dutch and Flemish easel pictures deck the walls of the East Drawing Room: striking floral piece painted from life by Van Huysun. Note the intricate workmanship at the back of the Boulle toilet mirror.

Rooms 19, 20, 21 – A Boulle kneehole desk complements the pair of Boulle side tables in the first of these galleries built to accommodate Richard Wallace's oriental armoury. The 17C Dutch paintings include landscapes by **Ruisdael**; idyllic marine and waterside scenes by Willem **van de Velde** the younger and **Cuyp**; oil sketches by Rubens; genre scenes by **Steen**.

Gallery 22 – The large purpose-built Gallery is hung with the larger 17C pictures and Old Master paintings in the collection: **Titian**'s *Perseus and Andromeda*; *The Holy Family, The Rainbow Landscape* and *Christ's Charge to Peter* (note the interplay of block colour and facial types contrasting youth with age) by **Rubens**; Philippe de Champaigne's *Annunciation, Adoration of the Shepherds, Marriage of the Virgin*; religious paintings by **Murillo**; *A Dance to the Music of Time* by Poussin is a dramatic landscape inspired by Ovid; portraits by **Velazquez** *(A Lady with a Fan, Don Balthasar Carlos)*, **Rembrandt** *(The artist's son Titus)*, **Van Dyck** (formal portraits of his friend *Philippe le Roy* and his wife *Marie de Raet*), **Gainsborough** (*Miss Haverfield* a small girl in a large ribboned hat and red slippers; *Mrs Robinson Perdita*, 1781); **Lawrence** (*George IV* by a Boulle table and ormolu inkstand); **Reynolds** (*Nelly O'Brien, Perdita, Mrs Carnac*): the most popular painting is **The Laughing Cavalier** by Frans Hals.

A Moralising Tale

A Dance to the Music of Time was painted for Giulio Rospigliosi, a learned patron of Poussin who later was elected Pope Clement X. It represents the perpetual cycle of the human condition: Poverty (crowned with leaves) holds hands with Labour who rises to Riches and Pleasure, only to indulge in excess and luxury that will lead back to Poverty. Seated putti watch bubbles and an hour glass that allude to the brevity of life as the winged figure of Father Time plays upon his harp. In the heavens, Apollo represents the inevitable change of day into night, while the two-faced stone herm of Janus on the right looks perpetually back to youth and forwards to old age.

Gallery 23 – 19C French painting and miniatures: Romantic history pictures *(Execution of the Doge Marino Faliero* by Delacroix); genre scenes from recent history by Meissonier, Vernet and Isabey who specialised in miniatures of Napoleon, Empress Josephine, the Empire court and the Bourbon monarchy (central cases).

Gallery 24 – The former dressing room of Sir Richard and Lady Wallace is furnished with fine 18C French furniture: combined toilet and writing table by **Oeben**; chest of drawers with dragon mounts; two drop-front secretaires by **Reisener**.

Rococo landscapes painted by **Watteau** include *A Lady at her Toilet, The Music Party, Fête in a Park, The Music Lesson, Gilles and his family*; Lancret: *La Belle Grecque; Mlle Camargo dancing*; by **Fragonard**: *Souvenir, The Swing.* **Miniatures** include a portrait of **Holbein** by Lucas Horenbout.

Gallery 25 – Lady Wallace's Bedroom is appropriately decorated in a feminine 18C style with elegant perfume burners, the glorious Avignon clock and delicate paintings by François **Boucher** (1703-70): *Mme de Pompadour; The Judgement of Paris.*

Madame Tussaud's Waxworks★

♿ *book in advance. Open daily, 9am (9.30am Sat-Sun) to 5.30pm (last admission). Closed 25 Dec. £18.95 (£16.95 afater 2pm); also valid for the Planetarium. Brochure (5 languages).* ☎ *0870 400 3000 (recorded information), 020 7487 0200; Fax 020 7465 0862; www.madame-tussauds.com*

Marie Grosholtz (1761-1850) acquired her modelling skills and much of her business through Philippe Curtius (1737-94), a doctor and talented modeller who mixed with the French aristocracy (Louis XV's mistress Mme du Barry is portrayed as *Sleeping Beauty*) and contemporary leading lights including the philosopher Voltaire and American statesman Benjamin Franklin. For nine years she was employed at Versailles supervising the artistic training of the young royal family – for which she was incarcerated and prepared for execution by the guillotine. Released, she was forced to return to work, surviving the terror of the French Revolution by taking death masks of its victims many of whom she had known personally: Louis XVI, Marie-Antoinette... In 1802, she decided to emigrate with her two children to England:

for 33 years the family toured the country before at last she settled on premises in the Baker Street Bazaar. The last figure to be modelled by the old lady is that of a small, bespectacled, but evidently highly alert, person at the age of 81, in fact a self-portrait. The waxworks moved to their present site in 1884.

Figures are arranged in separate rooms on various floors. **The Garden Party** and **Hollywood Legends and Superstars** exhibitions, which are regularly updated to reflect changing times, allow visitors to mingle and be photographed with contemporary rich and famous personalities drawn from the "show-biz" worlds of entertainment and sport (music, TV, film, tennis, football, cricket) – the likes of Michael Jackson, Madonna, Superman, James Bond... the list is endless.

Royal, historical and political dignitaries are assembled in the **Grand Hall**: Henry VIII and his wives; the Royal Families of Europe; past and present Prime Ministers and foreign statesmen.

Downstairs, the **Chamber of Horrors** which may be by-passed by the very young and faint-hearted, presents a series of tableaux illustrating various methods of execution (Joan of Arc burning at the stake), famous murderers and serial killers.

The **Spirit of London** is a dark ride *(5min)* in a simulated London taxi cab on a whirlwind tour of the history of London: from the reign of Elizabeth I, through the Plague and the Fire, the reign of Queen Victoria, the Second World War to the present day.

Planetarium★ – ♿ *book in advance. Open daily, 9.30am (sometimes 12.30pm) to 5pm (last show). Closed 25 Dec. £2.40; joint ticket with Madame Tussaud's Exhibition £18.95 (£16.95 after 2pm). ☎ 0870 400 3000 (recorded information), 020 7487 0200; Fax 020 7465 0862; www.madame-tussauds.com*

Access: by bus 2, 13, 18, 27, 30, 74, 82, 113, 159, 176, 274; ⊖ Baker Street

Three floors of information – Launch Zone, Planet Zone, Space Zone, and the latest hi-tech Digistar II projector are today accommodated in the old cinema that was bombed during the Blitz. Information panels, complemented by computers, video and interactive displays, chart developments in the science of astronomy and elucidate such cosmic phenomena as galaxies, suns, planets, stars, comets, Big Bang and black holes.

The show "Cosmic Perceptions" *(30min)* is projected into the planetarium dome. Dramatic animation effectively transports visitors through time from Stonehenge to the space probe, via observations and discoveries made by Ptolemy, Copernicus, Galileo, Newton, Hubble, Einstein and Hawking...

Sherlock Holmes Museum

Open daily, 9.30am-6pm. £6. Brochure (7 languages). ☎ 020 7935 8866; Fax 020 7738 1269; info@sherlock-holmes.co.uk; www.sherlock-holmes.co.uk

The interior of the narrow town house, which was built in 1815 and registered as a lodging house from 1860 to 1934, has been arranged as described in the novels by Sir Arthur **Conan Doyle.** In the study are the familiar pipes and deerstalker hat, a Persian slipper, a violin and bow, magnifying glass, telescope and binoculars, chemical apparatus and back numbers of *The Times*. Visitors may browse among the photographs, newspapers, literature and paintings of the period exhibited in Dr Watson's room.

Mayfair★

Mayfair is synonymous with elegance and luxury; through the middle runs Bond Street agleam with handsome shop-windows full of rare and exquisite goods. There are luxurious hotels along Park Lane which overlook the green expanses of Hyde Park. Although there are modern office buildings and the Georgian mansions are now mostly offices and embassies, the area retains its prestige with numerous art galleries, auction houses, casinos, boutiques and restaurants frequented by glamorous society people. The Royal Academy and the Royal Institution are renowned institutions.

Location

Map p 11 (DXY); Michelin Atlas London: pp 59-60. ⊖ Bond Street; Green Park; also Piccadilly Circus; Oxford Circus; Marble Arch; Hyde Park Corner. Mayfair is bounded by four important thoroughfares: Oxford Street to the north, Regent Street to the east, Piccadilly to the south and Park Lane to the west; and bordered by two vast parks, Green Park and Hyde Park.

Adjacent Sights: MARYLEBONE; ST JAMES'S; PICCADILLY; SOHO; KNIGHTSBRIDGE - BELGRAVIA.

Background

The name Mayfair, immortalised by Waddington's board game Monopoly, is derived from the cattle and general fair which was held annually in May; this became so unruly and the neighbourhood so notorious that it was officially closed in 1706. In 1735 the architect, Edward Shepherd took a 999-year lease on the site and opened a food market for the sale of fish, fowl, herbs and vegetables. Around the square and dependent streets he erected small houses, a practice followed by his heirs, so creating Shepherd Market. Large squares were the centrepiece of vast estates; elegant streets lined with Georgian mansions and brick houses found favour with fashionable society. Some developments included a parish church. Entertainment on a grand scale was lavished on brilliant and talented visitors.

Artisans' mews houses and stables have now been converted into desirable residences. Development elsewhere arose as a rich overspill from the City.

Directory

Pubs

The Guinea – *30 Bruton Place, W1J 6NR – ⊖ Bond Street, Green Park – ☎ 020 7409 1728 – guinea@youngs.co.uk – Open Mon-Fri 11am-11pm, Sat 6.30pm-11pm; closed bank hols and 24 Dec – 2 Jan.* A small very welcoming pub with an old-fashioned charm, often used as a waiting room for the Guinea Grill restaurant in the back room.

Ye Grapes – *16 Shepherd Market, W1Y 7HU – ⊖ Green Park, Hyde Park Corner – ☎ 020 7499 1563 – Open Mon-Sat 11am-11pm, Sun noon-10.30pm.* Located in the mews of Shepherd Market at the centre of Mayfair, this is a friendly pub which draws a mixed crowd. The weekends are always lively, and it is not uncommon to have to take your pint into street with you. In summer it is very busy during the week.

Taking a Break

Browns Hotel – *33-34 Albermarle St, W1S 4BP – ⊖ Green Park – ☎ 020 7493 6020 – tea@brownshotel.com – Open daily 3pm (2.30pm Sat-Sun) to 5.45pm – Tea £25.* Elegant and slightly old-fashioned tearoom. Enjoy the calm setting and tasty sandwiches.

The Lanesborough – *Hyde Park Corner, SW1X 7TA – ⊖ Hyde Park Corner – ☎ 020 7259 5599 – reservations@lanesborough.co.uk – Open daily 3.30pm (4pm Sun) to 6pm – Tea £24.50-£32.* Taking afternoon tea in the winter garden of this luxury hotel by the plants and fountain is a must for all lovers of tradition. Specialities include homemade lemon-curd and marmalades.

Intercafé at Debenhams – *334-348 Oxford St, WC1 1JG – ⊖ Bond Street – ☎ 020 7580 3000 – www.intercafe.co.uk – Open Mon, Tue 9.30am-7pm, Wed 10am-8pm, Thu 9.30am-9pm, Sat 9am-8pm, Sun Noon-6pm – £2/ demi-heure.* Situated within Debenhams department store, this small modern Internet café has a knowledgeable and helpful staff. Scanner available.

Taking a break in Shepherd Market

J. Malburet/MICHELIN

Going out for the Evening

Windows – London Hilton – *22 Park Lane, W1K 1BE – ⊖ Hyde Park Corner – ☎ 020 7493 8000 – www.hilton.co.uk – Open daily noon (5.30pm Sat) to 2am (3am Fri-Sat; 10.30pm Sun).* One of the few London bars located high in the sky, this one is on the 28th floor of the Hilton. The décor is relatively cool but it's worth a visit for the view over Hyde Park in the day and the lights of Knightsbridge at night.

Shopping

Alexander McQueen – *47 Conduit St, W1S 2YJ – ⊖ Piccadilly Circus – ☎ 020 7734 2340 – www.alexandermcqueen.co.uk – Open Mon-Sat 10.30am-6.30pm (7pm Thu).* Nicknamed the "enfant terrible" of the fashion world, the former Givenchy designer has just opened a chic, minimalist boutique with all the hallmarks of an art gallery.

Bond Street – *Bond St, W1.* The boutiques of international fashion designers (Maud Frizon, Stephan Kélian, Kenzo, Prada, Ungaro, Steiger, Yves Saint-Laurent, Rive Gauche, Chanel, Ferré, Joseph, Dior, Céline, Browns, Cartier, Hermès, Louis Vuitton) are concentrated in this area, not far from the Emporio Armani and Harvey Nichols.

Burberry – *21-23 New Bond St, W1S 2RD – ⊖ Bond Street, Oxford Circus – ☎ 020 7839 5222 – www.burberry.com – Open Mon-Sat 10am-7pm, Sun noon-6pm.* In 1997, the somewhat stodgy English brand asked the former president of Saks in New York to give a boost to business. Rose Marie Bravo appointed the talented young designer Roberto Menechetti to the job of rejuvenating the brand's image.

Gieves & Hawkes – *1 Savile Row, W1S 3JR – ⊖ Piccadilly Circus – ☎ 020 7434 2001 – www.gievesand hawkes.com – Open Mon-Thu 9.30am-6.30pm, Fri 9am-6pm, Sat 10am-6pm.* On London's premier street for gentlemen's tailoring, Gieves & Hawkes is the most famous outfitter of them all. Under the leadership of a former designer for Calvin Klein, the brand has expanded its range and now offers the British classics as well as less formal fashion.

HMV – *150 Oxford St, W1D 1DJ – ⊖ Oxford Circus – ☎ 020 7631 3423 – www.hmv.co.uk – Open Mon-Sat 9am (9.30am Tue) to 8pm (9pm Thu), Sun noon-6pm.* Large record shop with an impressive DVD and game console section upstairs.

Mulberry – *41-42 New Bond St, W1S 2RY – ⊖ Bond Street – ☎ 020 7491 3900 – www.mulberry.com – Open Mon-Sat 10am-6pm (7pm Thu).* Established only 30 years ago, this trendy establishment is a leading exponent of contemporary English chic. A large range of leather clothes carries the famous mulberry tree label. Also handbags, wallets and attractive organiser products.

Vivienne Westwood – *6 Davies St, W1K 3DW – ⊖ Bond Street – ☎ 020 7629 3757 – www.viviennewestwood.com – Open Mon-Sat 10am-6pm (7pm Thu).* The lady known as "Queen Viv'", who brought respectability to punk, still shows off her tremendous talent and extravagance. Her couture headquarters is on Davies Street, while her prêt-à-porter boutique is on Conduit Street. Worth seeing, just for the sheer pleasure of the spectacle and all the colour.

South Molton Street – An attractive pedestrian precinct with pavement cafés, restaurants and small fashion boutiques.

Cork Street – The galleries offer the best in modern art.

Savile Row – The home of tailoring businesses since the 19C.

Walking About

Start in Park Lane.

Park Lane

Once a winding road on the edge of Hyde Park, Park Lane is now an eight-lane highway. At the north end a few individual houses with graceful curved balconies have survived; elsewhere the town residences of local estate owners have been replaced by hotels: **Grosvenor House** (1930) replaced the early-19C mansion of the Duke of Westminster; the **Dorchester** (1930) replaced the mid-19C Dorchester House; the **London Hilton** (1960s) replaced a short terrace; the Londonderry stands on the site of Londonderry House (1765); the **Inn on the Park** and the **Intercontinental** *(Hamilton Place)* occupy the site of the Earl of Northbrook's residence.

Walk down Curzon St.

Curzon Street

This street is different again, being part residential and part commercial. There are 18C houses along the south side at the Park Lane end. **Disraeli** died in 1881 at no **19**.

Crewe House

No 15. The house standing back behind gates and lawns is the only surviving example of a type familiar in engravings as an 18C gentleman's London mansion. Sometime residence of the Marquess of Crewe (d 1945), the house was built in 1730 by **Edward Shepherd** and subsequently enlarged and altered to its present seven bays with large bow-fronted wings at either end. The entirely white stucco is relieved and ornamented by the curves of Venetian windows, a pillared, square porch and above, a triangular pediment.

Shepherd Market★

A maze of lanes, alleyways and paved courts linked by archways forms the market which contains Victorian and Edwardian pubs and houses with small, inserted shop fronts which serve as pavement cafés and antique shops. It retains a village atmosphere.

Return to Curzon St, walk up and turn right into Chesterfield St to Charles St.

Charles Street

The street contains several 18C houses, some refaced or remodelled in the 19C, such as the **English Speaking Union** (no **37**); it ends in a confusion of backs and fronts and a small 19C-20C pub in a cobbled yard.

Berkeley Square

Berkeley Wood is recalled by the plane trees which date from 1789. Berkeley House, erected in 1664 overlooking Piccadilly, was replaced in 1733 by Devonshire House which was demolished this century. The square was laid out in 1737. On its west side survive a few 18C houses with ironwork balconies, lamp holders at the steps to each house and torch snuffers: the façade to no **52** is in Charles Street; no **50,** a four-floor brick and stucco house is occupied by Maggs, the antiquarian book and map specialists; no **47** was rebuilt in 1891; stone-faced and pedimented nos **46** and **45** have balustraded balconies at the first floor windows; **Clive of India** lived at no 45.

Turn left into Hill St and right into Farm St.

The **Church of the Immaculate Conception**, the 1844-49 church of the Jesuit community, has a particularly fine high altar designed by **Pugin**. *Open daily, 7am-6.30pm.* ☎ *020 7493 7811; Fax 020 7495 6685*

Continue along South St and take South Audley St on the right and make a detour to Mount St

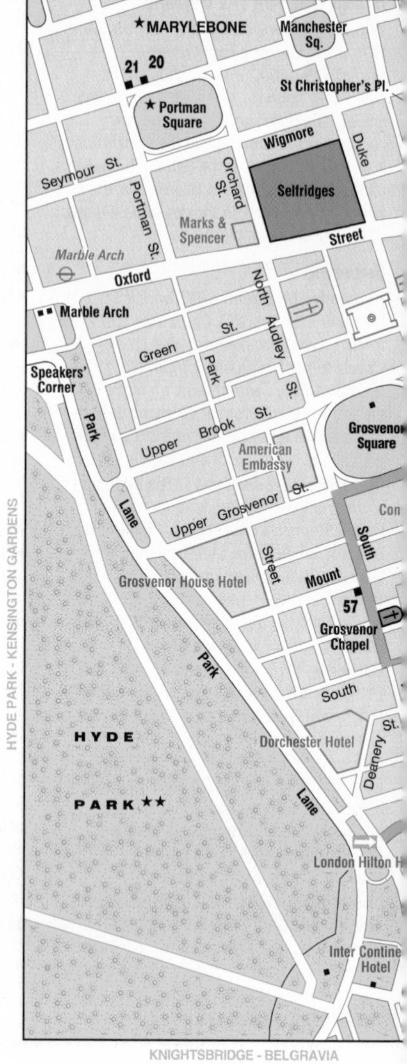

South Audley Street

The **Grosvenor Chapel** (1739) has a distinctive Tuscan portico, square quoined tower and octagonal turret. The garden was part of Berkeley Wood before becoming the burial ground for St George's Hanover Square *(see below). Open Mon-Fri, 9.30am-1pm.* ☎ *020 7499 1684; info@grosvenorchapel.force9.co.uk; www.grosvenorchapel.org.uk*

Purdeys, the gun and riflemakers at no **57** established in 1881, bears the richly-coloured royal coat of arms above the door.

Mount Street

A leisurely air pervades this street which veers round to the north-west corner of Berkeley Square past the **Connaught** (that epitome of late 19C luxury hotel building) to Park Lane. It is lined by tall, irregularly gabled terracotta brick houses of 1888, 1893... At street level, window after window displays choice objects: antique furniture, Lalique glass, porcelain, pictures, Oriental screens... and then comes a butcher's shop faced internally with turn of the century tiles.

During the Civil War the parliamentarians raised defensive earthworks here; hence the name and the topography.

Grosvenor Square

The square (1725), one of London's largest (6 acres/2.4ha), might be said to have been effectively redesigned in the 20C. Even the garden, originally circular with a central statue of George I, is now square with a memorial to **Franklin Roosevelt** on

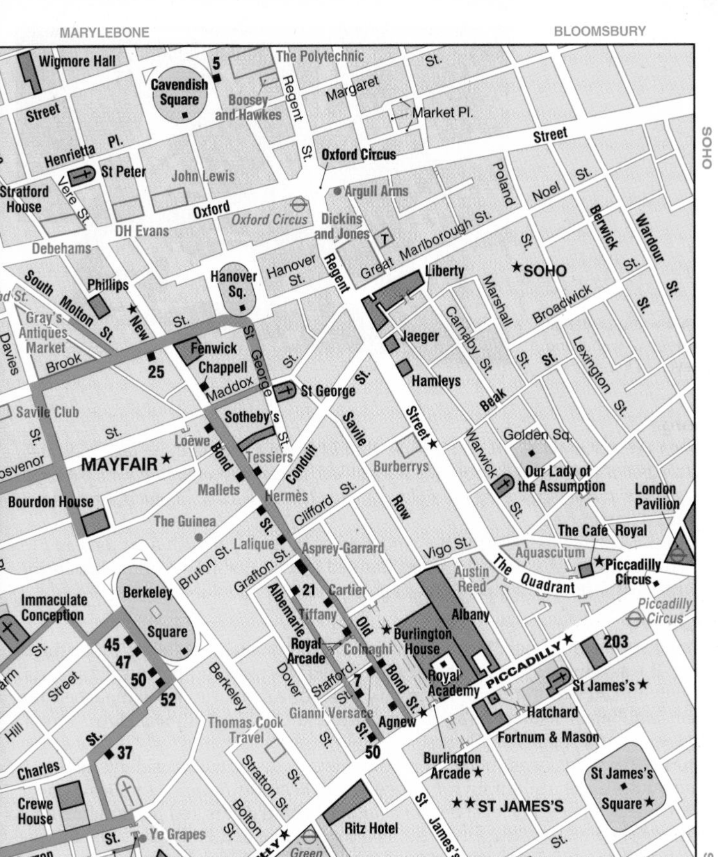

the north side and a monument to the RAF American squadrons. The first American resident *(at no 9)* was **John Adams**, the first Minister to Britain and later President. Today the neo-Georgian buildings to north, east and south are almost all US State Department offices while the entire west side, since 1961, has been filled with the embassy designed by **Eero Saarinen**.

Follow Grosvenor St and turn left.

Davies Street

Davies Street runs north from Berkeley Square to Oxford Street. At no 2 stands **Bourdon House**, a small square brick house (now Mallett's antique dealers) which was built in 1723-25 as a manor house amid fields and orchards. It boasts a fine 18C interior.

Turn right into Brook St past Gray's Antique Market and South Molton St and across Bond St.

Hanover Square

A bronze statue of William Pitt graces the spacious square, which was laid out in about 1715 as part of a large estate which included a parish church.

Walk down St George St, then take Maddox St.

Handel in Mayfair

George Frederick Handel (1685-1759) came to England in 1711 in the wake of George IV *(see INSIGHTS AND IMAGES – Music)*; his Italian operas were received with great acclaim. Over a period of 18 years he wrote nearly 30 such operas and, as popularity for this genre waned, he turned to composing oratorios with as much success, setting works by Milton and Congreve – adapted by Pope and Dryden. Handel lived at **25 Brook Street** for 36 years. It was here that he composed *Messiah.* He was a practising Christian and a regular attender at St George's. The **Handel House Museum** comprises his home and the adjoining house (no 23) with restored Georgian interiors and displays of fine and decorative arts. (♿) *Open Tue-Sat, 10am-6pm (8pm Thu); Sat and Bank Hol Mon, 12pm-6pm. £4.50. Audio-tour. ☎ 020 7495 1685; Fax 020 7495 1759; mail@handelhouse.org; www.handelhouse.org*

A friendly exchange between Churchill and Roosevelt in Bond Street

A. Taverner/MICHELIN

St George's

Open Mon-Fri, 8.30am-3.30pm. Guide book. Handel Festival: Apr-May. ☎ 020 7629 0874; Fax 020 7629 0874; ☎ 020 8244 3561 (booking office); verger@stgeorgeshanoversquare.org; www.stgeorgeshanoversquare.org; info@london-handelfestival, com; lhandelf@cwcom.net; www.london-handel.com

The church (1721-24) is a distinctive landmark with its tower with a lantern and its portico projecting across the pavement flanked by two cast-iron game dogs. Inside all is white with the detail picked out in gold.

Bond Street*

Bisecting Mayfair from north to south is Bond Street, which existed in Tudor times as a lane. It was named after Sir Thomas Bond who was treasurer to Henrietta Maria. Having given £20 000 to the impecunious Duke of Albemarle, he demolished the mansion and began redeveloping the area around Old Bond Street, Dover Street, Stafford Street and Albemarle Street.

New Bond Street was constructed in 1720 and soon boasted such residents as (Lord) Nelson and Emma Hamilton, Byron, Boswell and Beau Brummell – the *Beau Monde* that were happy to employ local bespoke tailors, haberdashers and perfumers. Bond Street therefore predates Sloane Avenue as the street that retails elegance, the unique and the luxurious. It is lined with specialist shops offering handmade leather goods and luggage (Hermes, Louis Vuitton, Loewe, Gucci), stationery (Smythsons), perfume and toiletries (Fenwick), antique furniture and fine art (Bond Street Antique Centre, Wildenstein, Partridge, Fine Art Society, Mallett ...). From the realms of haute couture the register lists such international names as Betty Barclay, Cerruti, Louis Féraud, Guy Laroche, Lanvin, Ballantyne, Max Mara, Valentino, Céline, Yves St Laurent, Salvatore Ferragamo...

At no 63 is the department store **Fenwick**; no 50, the musical store **Chappell's**; no 35, **Sotheby's** who began in 1744 as book auctioneers produced a turnover of £826 in the first year and are now the biggest firm of art auctioneers in the world – their notable rivals, **Bonhams** (formerly Phillips' at **7** Blenheim Street) are also located nearby – their first big sale on 9 February 1798 consisted in auctioning Marie Antoinette's pictures; no 143 has an early-19C chemist's shop-front and interior; the fine art dealers Partridge (no **144**), Mallett's (no **141**), the Fine Art Society (no **148**). Beyond the bronze group of Churchill and Roosevelt extends **Old Bond Street***, lined with well-established institutions specialising in fine porcelain, jewellery and watches (**Cartier, Tiffany, Boucheron –** *no 180*, Bentley & Co – *no 8*, George Jensen, **Asprey & Garrard** – *nos 43, 165...*), Antiques and fine art (Agnew – *no 43*, Marlborough Fine Art – *no 39*, Colnaghi – *no 14*).

Take Royal Arcade.

Several 18C houses survive in **Albemarle Street**: no 7 and no 21 are occupied by the **Royal Institution** (f 1799) and the **Michael Faraday Laboratory and Museum**, respectively. *Open Mon-Fri, 9am-6pm. £1. Guided tour by appointment with The Royal Institution of Great Britain, 21 Albemarle Street, London W1S 4BS; £5. ☎ 020 7409 2992; Fax 020 7629 3569; ril@ri.ac.uk; www.ri.ac.uk*

No 50 is home to the veteran publisher, John Murray.

Michael Faraday (1791-1867)

Faraday was apprenticed to Sir Humphry Davy at the Royal Institution, succeeding him as professor of chemistry. It is in the field of electromagnetism, however, that he is particularly revered, having set himself the objective of ascertaining the links between the forces of light, heat, electricity and magnetism: theories that were to lead to the advent of the electric motor, the transformer and the dynamo, so crucial to the development of physics and electronics. Other areas of research include the properties of fuel, notably the isolation of benzene. He was also responsible for inaugurating the tradition of Christmas Lectures held at the Royal Institution for young audiences.

National Gallery★★★

The focal point of Trafalgar Square is the popular National Gallery, one of the highlights of the capital; stand on the portico to enjoy a particularly fine perspective of the square and down Whitehall. The collection is one of the finest in the world and represents the best in all European schools. To many devotees the gallery is a place to visit time and time again. After a visit to the gallery, it is a short walk to the cinemas, theatres and other entertainment venues of the West End.

Location

Map p 12 (EX) and area map under TRAFALGAR SQUARE – WHITEHALL; Michelin Atlas London: p 2. ⊖ *Charing Cross.* Several main thoroughfares converge in Trafalgar Square. The gallery is well served by public transport and is conveniently situated near Leicester Square, Piccadilly Circus and Covent Garden.

Adjacent Sights: TRAFALGAR SQUARE – WHITEHALL; ST JAMES'S; STRAND – TEMPLE; COVENT GARDEN.

Background

Origin – The collection was founded, after more than a century of discussion, by parliamentary purchase in 1824. The nucleus was not the spoils of monarchy as so many of the older European collections were, but 38 pictures assembled by **John Julius Angerstein** (1735-1823), City merchant, banker, owner of a mansion in Greenwich, a town house at 100 Pall Mall and friend of **Sir Thomas Lawrence** whose portrait of him can be seen in the main vestibule. £57 000 was given for the pictures: Titian's *Venus and Adonis,* Rubens' *Rape of the Sabine Women,* Rembrandt's *Woman taken in Adultery* and *Adoration of the Shepherds,* five paintings by Claude, Hogarth's *Marriage à la Mode* series and Reynolds' *Lord Heathfield.* These remained in Pall Mall, where 24 000 people came to view them in the first seven months.

Move to Trafalgar Square – Only in 1838, fifteen years after Angerstein's death, was the new gallery completed in Trafalgar Square on the site of the Royal Mews. At first it was shared with the Royal Academy before the latter's removal to Burlington House. The gallery was intended to provide an architectural climax to the square; it succeeded better, however, in its internal arrangement than in its monumentality of which the most spectacular feature in the long, disproportionately low and subdivided front relieved by a small dome and turrets, is the great pedimented portico composed of Corinthian columns, similar to those of the recently demolished **Carlton House**. The Carlton House columns had been frugally preserved by the authorities who, however, had not noticed their friable condition so that no economy was effected since, the design having been approved, more solid ones had to be made. In subsequent years various alterations and extensions were made to **William Wilkins**' original building to afford additional space not only for the permanent collection but also for occasional special exhibitions based on the gallery's pictures supplemented by private and international loans, complemented by furniture, sculpture and fine art from other museums.

During the Second World War the collection was evacuated to Wales but every month one painting was brought to London and exhibited to long queues of art lovers.

Sainsbury Wing – After much public discussion of content and architectural style during the 1980s, the Sainsbury Wing, designed by R Venturi to

Planning your visit

Rambling through a large museum is both exhilarating and exhausting. If you are pressed for time, choose a favourite period in history, locate it on the gallery floor plan and explore the art of the times. Because individual pieces in the collection are occasionally rehung it is impossible to pin-point particular masterpieces. Browsing, however, will allow you to discover unfamiliar images and perhaps provide you with new 'favourites'.

Gallery Floor plan – Free of charge, this is available from the entrance foyers.

Books – The NG has an extensive bookshop selling general and specialist publications on the fine arts, cards, slides and posters.

Gallery Soundtrack – Soundtrack is a random-access audio CD-Rom guide to the NG main collection providing pertinent information on over 1 000 paintings. A shorter tour of 30 highlights is also available in several languages.

Micro Gallery – This is a computerised information system containing background information on every painting in the NG Collection: 12 workstations access this visual encyclopedia free of charge.

Popular Exhibitions – For the important temporary exhibitions in the Sainsbury Wing Basement, it is sometimes necessary to control the number of visitors with timed tickets.

Special Note – The NG stays open until 9pm on Wednesday evenings.

complement the existing building, was opened in 1991. Its five floors provide additional permanent and temporary exhibition galleries, a theatre and cinema, a computer information room, shop, restaurant and cloakroom facilities. With the improved design of lighting and ventilation systems, the Sainsbury Wing accommodates the earliest and most fragile paintings of the collection, although the numbering of the galleries continues that already in use in the main building.

Collection – There are now more than 2 000 paintings in the collection hung in chronological order; they represent the jewels in the public domain from early to High Renaissance Italian paintings, early Netherlandish, German, Flemish, Dutch, French, Spanish pictures and the masterpieces of the English 18C. A fuller representation of the British School of Painting, together with 20C art is in the Tate Gallery.

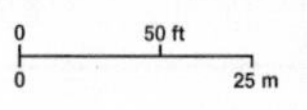

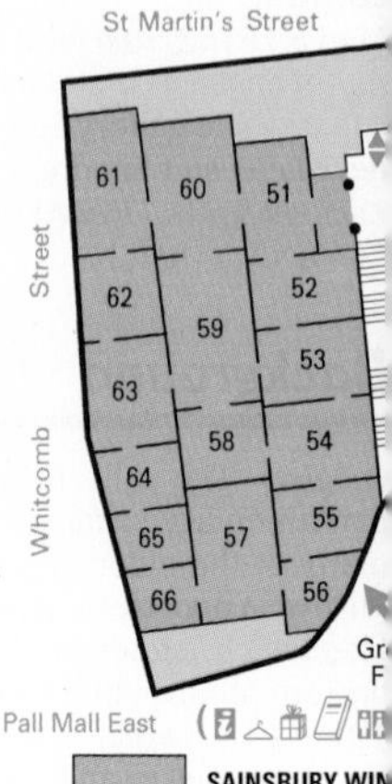

Highlights

♿ *Open daily, 10am-6pm (9pm Wed). Closed 24-26 Dec, 1 Jan. No charge to main galleries. Micro Gallery: Open daily, 10am-5.30pm (8.30pm Wed). Guided tour (1hr): daily at 11.30am and 2.30pm (also 6.30pm Wed); meet at Sainsbury Wing Information Desk. Gallery Guide Soundtrack for hire (6 languages). Welcome sheet (6 languages). Restaurant, café. No photography.* ☎ *020 7747 2885; Fax: 020 7747 2423; information@ng-london.org.uk; www.nationalgallery.org.uk*

PAINTING FROM 1260 TO 1510 *Sainsbury Wing*

Italian School

The earliest identifiable master, **Giotto (51)** is considered as the forefather of Renaissance painting. **Leonardo**'s fragile preparatory 'cartoon' of *The Virgin and Child with St Anne and John the Baptist* is spectacular, representing two ageless images of motherhood with their young sons. *The Virgin on the Rocks* is similarly enigmatic and engaging: *sfumato* light picks out the figures from the dark background of craggy rocks and identifiable plants.

Before 1400 (52): Three-panelled triptych; gold backgrounds, Byzantine features, graceful lines, incised patterns heighten the jewel-like quality of these small devotional pieces. **Duccio**'s green underpainting that once would have given the Virgin an ivory glow now strangely tinges the fleshtones. Gradually perspective is used to suggest space, figures are given bulk and volume with shadows and enveloping draperies.

After 1400: Narrative is introduced: a figure is painted several times embarking on a journey or enacting several consecutive incidents on the same journey. The **Wilton Diptych** (c 1395) could be French or English **(53)**.

The Florentine **Masaccio (54)** explores space and volume, using light to cast shadows and mould three-dimensional form: *Virgin and Child*. Realism is infused into the work of the Sienese **Sassetta**, but an air of gentleness still animates his figures and colours are delicately subdued: *Story of St Francis*.

Uccello (55) exploits strong lines and colour to define perspective: *The Battle of San Romano*. Pisanello is a master of detail: armour is carefully drawn, animals and plants are sensitively arranged in a pictorial world where visions and miracles are completely credible: *Vision of St Eustace*.

Haunting realism and solemn stillness pervade the works of Campin, **Van Eyck** and Van der Weyden **(56)**, painstakingly painted in some cases as a document, witnessed by the artist: *Virgin and Child before a Firescreen, Arnolfini Portrait, The Magdalene Reading*.

Brittle textures, complex imagery and restlessness are characteristic of works of the Venetian Crivelli and of **Tura**, the Master of Ferrara: *The Annunciation with St Emidius St Jerome* **(57)**.

A Florentine artist of the early Renaissance, **Botticelli (58)** was the supreme master of line: *Portrait of a Young Man, Venus and Mars, Mystic Nativity*. **(59)** Note Pollaiuolo's complementary arrangement of nude figures in *Martyrdom of St Sebastian*.

Master of the Umbrian School, Perugino **(60)** learned the art of colour from Piero della Francesca and taught **Raphael** to endow his figures with grace and poise: *The Virgin and Child with Saints*. Raphael's style radically altered when he went to Rome, evolving into what is considered as the epitome of the High Renaissance: strong portrait of his patron *Pope Julius II*.

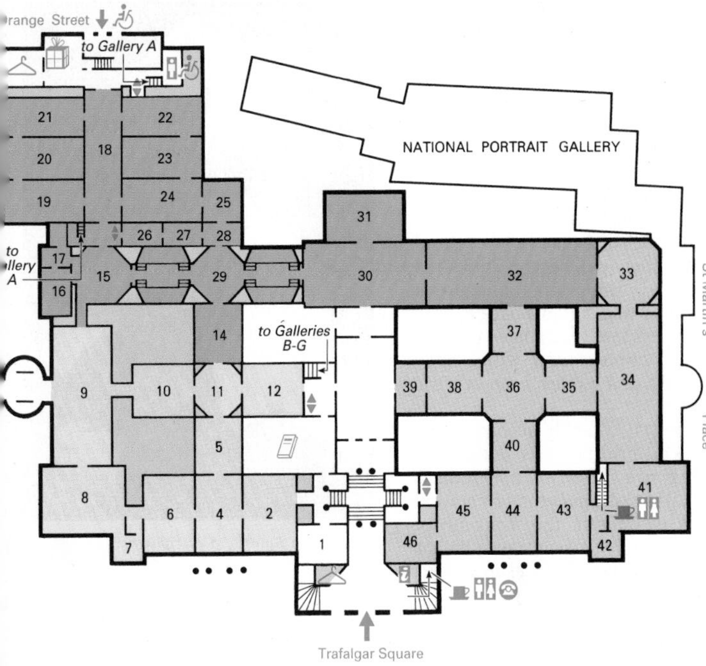

WEST WING	NORTH WING	EAST WING
PAINTING FROM 1510 TO 1600	PAINTING FROM 1600 TO 1700	PAINTING FROM 1700 TO 1900

Lift — Telephone — Toilets — Wheelchair access

Café — Shop — Bookshop

Mantegna studied the arts of Antiquity; strong use of line and uncompromising realism: *Agony in the Garden*. **Bellini** perfected the use of oil paint, using it to capture rich tones of colour and contrasted light: *Madonna and Child* **(61)**.

Northern Schools

Development of landscape painting, as imaginary or topographical views stretch beyond the reality of a religious figure or portrait. In France, patronage of noble courts betrays an early interest in fashion. Introduction of oil painting into Italy. Netherlands and France **(62)**; Germany **(63)**: **Dürer**. Netherlands and Italy **(64)**.

Antonello's *Portrait of a Man* and *Doge Leonardo Loredan* by Bellini **(65)** are glorious examples of portraiture influenced by the unforgiving realism of Northern painting and of the early use of oil painting in Italy..

Piero della Francesca (66) achieved perfect balance with calculated symmetry and perspective in *The Baptism of Christ. St Michael, The Nativity*.

PAINTING FROM 1510 TO 1600 *West Wing*

The formality of the High Renaissance is gone: playful gestures and softness (*Madonna of the Basket* by Correggio, *Madonna and Child with Saints* by Parmigianino) *(2)* hint at the advent of Mannerism, which eventually degenerates into elongated forms and contorted positions.

As Humanism reached the north which was already troubled by the Reformation, different genres develop: piercing realism fashions portraiture; fervent spirituality pervades religious subjects; mysticism shapes landscape and idealised mannerism figurative subjects **(4)**: *The Ambassadors* **(Holbein)**, *Cupid complaining to Venus* (Cranach), *Christ taking leave of His Mother* (Altdorfer).

Accomplished artists – Dosso, Garofalo; Lotto, Moretto, Moroni **(5; 6)** – demonstrate their equal abilities in portraiture and religious and mythological subjects in an age of relative ease in Italy.

Grand gesture and bold use of paint is typical of the Venetian **Tintoretto (7)**: *St George and the Dragon*. Obvious influences absorbed by **El Greco** who was born in Crete, trained in Venice and settled in Spain, are evident in his paintings: *Agony in the Garden*.

Powerfully distinctive styles reflect the current tastes in Rome: **Michelangelo**'s monumental but uncompleted *Entombment*; Sebastiano's crowded *Raising of Lazarus* echoing gestures from other works; Bronzino's enigmatic, almost awesome *Allegory with Venus and Cupid* **(8)**.

The transfer of patronage to Venice following the Sack of Rome (1507). Bold compositions, luminous use of colour on a grand scale, celebration of texture characterise the works of Titian; Veronese; Tintoretto **(9)**: *Bacchus and Ariadne, The Vendramin Family*.

Large decorative pieces were often painted as panels for a sumptuous palace or dimly-lit church. The characteristics of the **Venetian School (10)** include perceptive informal portraiture; important allegorical iconography relevant to a patron, with complex perspective arranged to suit a particular context and which may appear odd in a picture seen at close quarters.

Lady with a Squirrel, *Hans Holbein*

Veronese (11), a highly accomplished artist, was prolific. His decorative schemes are often conceived as theatrical backdrops to the celebration of mass in church, the welcome of dignitaries to a palace entrance hall or an exuberant banquet in a sumptuous dining room: *Allegory of Love, The Family of Darius before Alexander*.

Portraiture verging on caricature as Gossaert and **Brueghel (12)**, these perceptive portrayers of personality, exaggerate features and facial expression: *An Elderly Couple, Christ Mocked*.

In the **Domenichino** frescoes **(13)** note the sensitive and decorative rendering of landscape, contrived by the artist as an organised series of elements. The apparent subdued colour is appropriate to the medium which involves paint being applied to and absorbed by wet plaster: *Apollo pursuing Daphne*.

PAINTING FROM 1600 TO 1700 *North Wing*

Ter Bruggen **(14)** visited Rome whence he brought back a style resembling that of Caravaggio, heightened by candlelight: *The Concert*. **Hals** revels in painting formal portraits and happy lowly people or 'genre' subjects; brilliant technique animates the surface of his paintings: *A Boy with a Skull*.

Works by **Claude** and **Turner** are exhibited together **(15)**. This unusual association is a special concession made for Turner who bequeathed many paintings to the Nation with the specification that his *Sun Rising through Vapour or Fishermen cleaning and selling fish* and *Dido building Carthage or The Rise of the Carthaginian Empire* should be hung with *Seaport with the Embarkation of the Queen of Sheba* and *The Mill: Landscape with the Marriage of Isaac and Rebekah* by Claude. Turner greatly admired Claude and his audacious depiction of the sun (as the source of pure light it had hitherto not been painted as a ball of colour).

Vermeer and De Hooch **(16)** specialise in tranquil domestic scenes bathed in a balmy winter light: *A Young Woman at a Virginal, A Woman and her Maid in a Courtyard*.

(17, 18) Dou collaborated with Rembrandt *(Tobit)*, specialising later in elaborately wrought small scenes from everyday life. The **Hoogstraten Peepshow** is a curiosity.

Claude (19) painted pastoral landscapes and peaceful coastal scenes at sunset, giving them mythological subjects almost in order to raise the status of landscape to History painting, a genre much sought after by wealthy patrons in and around Rome for their country villas and *castelli*.

Poussin (20) spent many years in Rome. In 1629-30 he suffered from a grave illness which radically altered his style: he abandoned the showy Baroque in favour of a more intellectual, Classical style inspired by the poets of Antiquity (Tasso). He constructed his compositions with the help of a miniature stage set in which wax figures could be placed. Notable patrons secured in France included Cardinal Richelieu: *The Adoration of the Golden Calf, Cephalus and Aurora*. The gallery also has works by Champaigne, an early colleague of Poussin, who was an accomplished portraitist: *Cardinal Richelieu*.

French School and Painting in Paris (21, 22): the climate of the Age of Reason in France allowed for a broad range of subject matter and styles that would appeal to the Crown, the Church and the wealthy nobility.

The main patrons of painting in Holland were wealthy merchants and traders: for them the landscape of their homeland bathed in different light and subject to seasonal changes in the weather was enough material for paintings. The **Dutch School (23, 24)** includes Avercamp, Van Goyen and **Ruysdael** who depict various aspects of the landscape.

Luminosity is perhaps the characteristic quality of the landscape painted by Cuyp and Both **(25)**; incidental scenes full of warm light, shaded by feathery foliage.

People are the main subject of **Rembrandt**'s paintings **(26, 27)**: *Belshazzar's Feast, Saskia, A Woman bathing in a Stream, Margaretha de Geer, Self-portrait. A Boy with a Skull* by **Hals** is full of vitality.

Whereas Rembrandt was Dutch, **Rubens (28)**, diplomat as well as artist, was Flemish: the alliance of the Low Countries with Spain and therefore with the Court of Naples and Venice permitted the latter to live at, travel to and visit other Royal courts, assimilating influences and inspiration for his painting along the way. Rubens demonstrates his skill in all genres: *Portrait of Susanna Lunden ("Le Chapeau de Paille"), Peace and War, Judgement of Paris, Autumn Landscape*.

The political climate in Spain, however, was far from exuberant or liberal: only the most uncontroversial subjects were permitted. Notable masters of the **Spanish School (29)** include **Velazquez** who evolves a strong portrait style under Royal patronage: *Kitchen Scene with Christ in the House of Martha and Mary, The Toilet of Venus (The Rokeby Venus), Philip IV of Spain in Brown and Silver.* **Murillo** uses delicate colours in his gentle, religious, devotional pieces: *The Two Trinities (The Pedroso Murillo)*. Zurbaran's pictures are edged with realism.

Van Dyck (30) is the supreme master of portraiture in a grand confident style: *Equestrian Portrait of Charles I, The Balbi Children*.

Intense drama animates pictures painted at the height of the action, often with intense emotion by Carracci, Caravaggio, Guercino **(32)**. **Caravaggio** intensifies the theatricality with the use of strong highlights and dark shadows known as *chiaroscuro: The Dead Christ Mourned, The Supper at Emmaus, The dead Christ mourned by Two Angels*.

PAINTING FROM 1700 TO 1900 *East Wing*

Small pictures were in demand for more intimate interiors **(33)**. **Chardin**'s paintings stand out as simple domestic scenes often with a moralising overtone: *The House of Cards*. **Fragonard** caters to the contemporary taste for the Rococo: delicate, pretty pictures, beautifully painted; similar works were crafted by Boucher and Lancret.

Two mainstays of the **British School** at its height: portraiture and landscape *(34)* – *(see INSIGHTS AND IMAGES – Painting)* as exemplified by *Anne, Countess of Albemarle* **(Reynolds)**; *The Morning Walk* **(Gainsborough)**; *The Fighting Temeraire; Rain, Steam and Speed* **(Turner)**; *The Haywain* **(Constable)**.

Small scale "Fancy" pictures were a more lowly artform **(35)**: Hogarth's narrative cycles, sporting and animal pictures and picturesque landscapes of the highest quality. *The Marriage Contract* **(Hogarth)**; *Wooded Landscapes*; *The Melbourne and Milbanke Families* **(Stubbs)**.

18C British portraiture **(36)** by the likes of Sir Thomas Lawrence and Allan Ramsay includes formal portraits of the extensive Royal family, successful naval and military leaders, statesmen, members of the Royal Society and their consorts.

Solimena **(37)** was described in 1733 as "by universal consent the greatest painter in the world"; he forged his style from that of several Baroque artists (including Luca Giordano) to paint gentle figures in soft colours, often in religious contexts.

Canaletto (38), the Venetian master of sparkling topographical landscape painting, was especially popular with English travellers on the Grand Tour of Italy.

"Marriage A-la-Mode: The Marriage Settlement", *William Hogarth*

Guardi and **Goya (39)** were two quite distinctive masters responding to the different types of patronage available in Venice and Spain. Guardi's paintings are full of atmosphere while Goya's portraits are character studies.
Gloriously bright decorative paintings on a large scale by Tiepolo **(40)** include *An Allegory of Venus and Time.*
Neo-Classicism came into favour with the rise of Napoleon as a counter-reaction to the Rococo of the Ancien Régime. **David (41)** is a master of draughtsmanship; **Ingres** follows closely, producing clear and penetrating portraiture: *Mme Moitessier.* **Delacroix**, together with Gericault, was sparked rather by colour and atmosphere, the glories of Napoleon's campaigns in North Africa, the relationship of a man with his horse. Beautiful flower paintings by Fantin-Latour.
The Barbizon School practised landscape painting out of doors. Corot **(42)** captures the different tonality of sunlight on the landscape; figures are usually incidental.
In Germany, the power and magic of Wagner's Romanticism is transposed into paint as exemplified by *A Winter Scene* by Friedrich.
Topographical views of landscape and informal figure compositions are the trademarks of **Impressionism (43)**, a new and exciting movement in art. The transient quality of light is carefully explored and captured in intimate family scenes *(Boating on the Seine)* by the likes of Pissarro, Renoir, Monet and Manet, or in a celebration of modern industrialisation – street lighting in *The Boulevard Montmartre at Night,* trains in *The Gare St Lazare...*
Van Gogh, Cézanne, Seurat **(44)** present highly individual artistic styles: different subject matter, different techniques are used to apply the paint, different reactions to the social climate of the age. *Van Gogh's Chair; Sunflowers; Bathers; Bathers at Asnières.* Another distinctive figure is **Henri Rousseau** *(Tiger in a Tropical Storm).*
Cézanne, Picasso and **Matisse (45, 46)** stand as the heroes of modern painting. Not only do they explore colour, form, space and composition, they experiment with the relationship between the two-dimensional picture plane and the three-dimensional space within.

National Portrait Gallery★★

The fascination of gazing at portraits of the great and the good who have wielded power and influence or made a significant contribution in various fields of endeavour throughout the centuries, is irresistible as a panorama of British history unfolds. Wander through the gallery at leisure; enjoy a meal in the roof-top restaurant which gives a panoramic view, and browse through the collection on-line using state-of-the-art technology.

Location

Map p 12 (EX) and area map under TRAFALGAR SQUARE – WHITEHALL; Michelin Atlas London: p 62. ⊖ Leicester Square, Charing Cross. The gallery, which is adjacent to the National Gallery, is within a stone's throw of the diverse attractions of Leicester Square and Covent Garden.
Adjacent Sights: TRAFALGAR SQUARE – WHITEHALL; ST JAMES'S; STRAND – TEMPLE; COVENT GARDEN.

Background

Portraiture forms an important part of the British School of painting having evolved as a genre to satisfy different patrons through the ages. Sitters are portrayed as active within or aspiring to various social classes and provide a colourful insight into the spirit of each historical period. The key to this collection is therefore as a social history of each age.
The National Collection – Founded in 1856, the collection moved to its present late 19C Italian-Renaissance gallery behind the National Gallery in 1896. Today, the policy of commissioning and collecting works by contemporary artists continues with over 5 000 personalities portrayed in various media representing the young and the old, the rich and poor, the famous and the unknown, from times past and present.
The permanent collection is presented in chronological order. The Balcony Gallery presents distinguished contemporary figures and the IT Gallery, which offers state-of-the-art facilities, makes the gallery's collections accessible to all.
Some of the works listed below may have been moved to a different location. Numbers in brackets refer to rooms.

Highlights

♿ *Open daily, 10am-6pm (9pm Thu-Fri). Closed Good Fri, 24-26 Dec, 1 Jan. No charge except for special exhibitions. CD-Rom sound guide (4 languages). Gallery Restaurant, café. ☎ 020 7306 0055, 020 7312 2463 (infoline); Fax 020 7306 0056; www.npg.org.uk Take the escalator to the second floor.*

FROM THE MEDIEVAL AND TUDOR PERIODS TO THE REGENCY

Second Floor

The clean architectural lines of the **Tudor Galleries** *(1-3)* in the Ondaatje Wing are a perfect setting for the Tudor portraits. As in architecture *(see INSIGHTS AND IMAGES – The Changing Face of London)* the king and his court were the most obvious patrons of portraiture, eager to define their status as handsome, powerful and wealthy monarchs: **Edward IV**; **Richard III**; **Henry VII** (1457-1509) is painted four years before his death by the Flemish artist Michel Sittow; Holbein's fragment of a larger sketch, intended as a mural for Whitehall Palace, shows **Henry VIII** (1491-1547) and his wives: Catherine of Aragon (first); Anne Boleyn (second); Catherine Parr (sixth and last); the distorted portrait of **Edward VI** painted by William Scrots (1546) can be viewed in correct perspective.

16C – The statesman and Humanist author **Sir Thomas More** (1478-1535) is portrayed with his family by Rowland Lockey: he was executed for opposing Henry VIII's self-appointment as Head of the Church. Famous Tudor personalities include **Thomas Cranmer** (1489-1556), the author of the English Bible and Book of Common Prayer and ardent supporter of the Reformation, he served as archbishop of Canterbury both under Henry VIII and **Edward VI**; he was burnt at the stake unable to recant his Protestant faith. Roman Catholic **Mary Tudor**, Mary I (1516-58) reversed the religious changes instituted by her father Henry VIII and brother Edward VI and sent 300 Protestants to death – including her half-sister Lady Jane Grey (1537-54), before marrying Philip of Spain.

A long gallery **(2)** in the Tudor tradition displays portraits of the Elizabethan age. **Elizabeth I** (1533-1603) is painted aged 42 and in old age (1592) by Gheeraerts. She was a stable and intelligent monarch who saw the Spanish defeated, the New World revealed, the Church of England established and a flowering of literature, and liked to be portrayed as such as in the 'Ditchley' portrait. **Mary Stuart**, Queen of Scots (1542-87) was deemed to be a threat in her claim to the English throne; she was imprisoned and executed by Elizabeth I.

Sir Walter Raleigh (1552-1618), pictured with his son Walter, was an adventurer and favourite at the court of Elizabeth I. In a rare painting attributed to John Taylor, **William Shakespeare** (1564-1616) appears at the apogee of his career. A showcase of **miniatures★ (3)** illustrates the exquisite art of Hans Eworth, Nicholas Hilliard and Isaac Oliver; they were designed as powerful tokens of love and political loyalty – Elizabeth I (1572) and her favourites, Robert Dudley (1576), Sir Francis Drake (1581) and Sir Walter Raleigh (c 1585), Robert Devereux (1596) and Anne of Denmark (1589), wife of James I and their son Henry, Prince of Wales.

The Jacobean Court (4): The son of Mary Stuart, **James I** (1566-1625) acceded to the throne of Scotland in 1567 before being crowned King of England in 1603 following the death of Elizabeth I: his portrait is by Daniel Mytens (1621), that of his wife Anne of Denmark, is attributed to Marcus Gheeraerts the Younger (c 1612); their daughter and son-in-law Elizabeth and Frederick of Bohemia are painted by Honthorst (1653). **Charles I** (1600-49), King of England, Scotland and Ireland attracted to his court **(5)** the diplomat and painter P P Rubens (*Thomas Howard, Earl of Arundel* – 1629) and Sir Anthony van Dyck (*Henrietta Maria,* painted in 1635, was the daughter of Henri IV and Marie de Medici of France and wife of Charles I).

During the Civil Wars **Oliver Cromwell** (1599-1658) fought against the king under the Earl of Essex; he promoted the king's trial and subsequent execution (1649), and was appointed Protector of the Commonwealth of England, Scotland and Ireland in 1653.

An electrotype metal statue commemorates the philosopher **Francis Bacon** (1561-1626) who contradicted Aristotle's deduction logic (presupposing certain basic truths) with inductive reasoning based on observation; he also upheld the practice of debate and his writings underpin the objectives behind the foundation of the Royal Society *(see index)*.

17C Arts and Sciences (6): the London-born poet **John Milton** (1608-74) was a supporter of Cromwell and ardent advocator for a free press. This is also the age of the poet John Donne, the dramatist Ben Jonson, the philosopher Thomas Hobbes and the diarist John Evelyn (note his effeminate hands).

The showcase of delicate miniatures demonstrates the continued prestige of the genre: Cromwell (1649) is painted by Samuel Cooper who painted his subjects by candlelight to accentuate the contours; Charles I (1628) is portrayed by Honthorst and (1631) by Daniel Mytens; his children Charles II aged 9, James II aged 6 and Mary in a blue dress are by Cornelius Johnson.

Charles II and James II (7): Charles II (1630-85) is portrayed by Thomas Hawker in old age with mace and garter at his knee – although the hands are those of a younger man. He was a shrewd and realistic ruler, notably in settling delicate issues with Parliament. It was during his reign that the skyline of London was irrevocably changed as plague, then fire devastated the City – witnessed by **Samuel Pepys** and transcribed in cypher in his diaries; Nell Gwynne; **Robert Boyle** (1627-91) who established the law of physics which states that the volume of a gas varies inversely to the pressure put on it, provided temperatures are constant; **John Locke** (1632-1704) the liberal philosopher and founder of empiricism, the doctrine that all knowledge is derived from experience; **Henry Purcell** (1659-95) the composer; **John Dryden** (1631-1700), a prolific poet and dramatist.

Charles' younger brother **James II** (1633-1701) – James VII of Scotland (1685-8) – was an honest and capable admiral; unable, however, to achieve reforms for his Catholic supporters, he was forced to flee in 1688.

The Later Stuarts (8): William III (1650-1702), the grandson of Charles I, and Mary II (1662-94), daughter of James II, acceded to the throne in 1688. Their joint rule brought tolerance to the kingdom, although the king was preoccupied with the threat of war from France. He is painted by Lely and she by Wissing. The portrait of **Queen Anne** (1665-1714), the second daughter of James II who succeeded her brother-in-law William in 1702, is from the studio of John Closterman.

The ivory medallion bearing the profile of Sir Christopher **Wren** (in the showcase) was sculpted by David le Marchand from Dieppe (1723); others pictured include **Isaac Newton** (1642-1727) who learnt how to split the spectrum, invented the calculus (separately from Leibniz) and established the concept of gravitation; **Grinling Gibbons**.

The last of the Stuarts are represented by the Old Pretender, **James Edward** (the son of James II by his second marriage) and his sons **Charles Edward** (the Young Pretender) and Henry Benedict. The throne, meanwhile, passed to the Hanoverian **George I** (1660-1727), Elector of Hanover and James I's great grandson, who was elected king by Act of Parliament: he is here represented by a fine terracotta bust (1720-35) by Rysbrack.

Sir Peter Lely (1618-80)

Pieter van der Fies was born in Germany of Dutch parentage. He served his apprenticeship in Haarlem and moved to London in the 1640s. He produced uncontroversial history pictures during the Commonwealth, tailoring his grand and influential manner for the Restoration, succeeding Van Dyck as Principal Painter to Charles II in 1661. Ladies of the Court were endowed with languid beauty (Nell Gwynne, the actress and king's favourite): victorious military leaders with masculine dignity.

Kit-Cat Club (9): The Kit-Cat Club attracted its distinguished members from political and literary circles. They used to meet for dinner in a tavern run by Christopher Cat and sup upon delicious mutton pies called 'Kit-Cats', while proposing toasts to the ladies. For over 20 years Kneller, himself a member, painted the faces of the members while his assistants filled in the rest of their persons; these were collectively nicknamed the "Whigs in wigs".

Early 18C Arts and Sciences (10): **Sir Godfrey Kneller** was Court Painter (self-portrait); **Sir Christopher Wren** was professor of mathematics and astronomy, but achieved fame as Surveyor of the Royal Works charged with rebuilding St Paul's Cathedral; **Nicholas Hawksmoor** was Wren's successor; **James Thornhill**, the decorator of St Paul's dome; **Edmond Halley** (1656-1742) predicted the return of the comets, furthered the studies of Newton on gravitation and published a map charting the winds around the globe; **Sir Hans Sloane** (1660-1756) left his huge personal library to the nation providing a foundation for the British Museum; **Jonathan Swift** (1667-1745) wrote *Gulliver's Travels*; other writers include Addison; Steele; Congreve; Vanbrugh; Pope...

Britain in the early 18C (11): *End room.* George II (1727-60) by Thomas Hudson; The Court of Chancery picture is interesting with the dogs in attendance; *A Conversation of Virtuosi* (1735) shows leading artists and architects of the 1730s by Gawen Hamilton; bust of the actor and dramatist Colley Cibber (1671-1757); **Horace Walpole** (1717-97); the Roman Catholic poet and author of *The Rape of the Lock* **Alexander Pope** (1688-1744); the beautiful Catherine Hyde 'who died from a surfeit of cherries'. Terracotta bust (1741) of Hogarth; marble bust of John Wesley.

18C Arts (12): Portraits by Sir Joshua Reynolds of himself; the writer Laurence Sterne (1713-68), author of *Tristram Shandy* and *A Sentimental Journey*; the compiler of the first English dictionary **Samuel Johnson** (1709-84) and his biographer James Boswell (1740-95); **David Garrick** and Eva, his wife; the Irish author of *She Stoops to Conquer* and *The Vicar of Wakefield* **Oliver Goldsmith** (1728-74); the musician and composer Handel (1685-1759); J C Bach; the musicologist and renowned organist Dr Charles Burney; Sir Lancelot (Capability) Brown (1769) by Nathaniel Dance; self-portrait of **Hogarth**, George Stubbs; Gainsborough.

Britain becomes a World Power (14): Masterpiece by Reynolds (1768) of Warren Hastings, who went to India in 1750 and became Governor General (1774-85); **Captain James Cook** (1728-79) at the Cape of Good Hope on his third voyage; Robert Clive of India (1725-74) who laid the foundations of English power in India. Chinese portrait of Joseph Collet (1673-1725), administrator of the East India Co.

Britain at War (1793-1815) (17): Two political rivals William Pitt (1759-1806) and Charles James Fox (1749-1806); Edmund Burke (1729-97), the Whig writer and political philosopher; Admiral Lord Nelson (1758-1805) and his beautiful mistress Emma, Lady Hamilton (c 1765-1815); the Duke of Wellington (1769-1852).

General James Wolfe (cast c 1760) who captured Quebec; portraits of **George Washington** (1732-99) by G Stuart and of George III (1738-1820) in gold and ermine by A Ramsay.

The Romantics *(18)*: The neo-Classical sculptor John Flaxman who worked for the pottery manufacturer J Wedgwood (c 1796); John Opie (self-portrait 1785); the essayist Charles Lamb (1775-1834); Mary Shelley, author of *Frankenstein;* the visionary poet and illustrator **William Blake** (1757-1827); **J M W Turner** (1775-1851), the good-looking Constable, Girtin, Bonnington *(see MARYLEBONE – Wallace Collection)*; the poets John Keats (1795-1821), John Clare (1793-1864), Wordsworth (1770-1850), **Coleridge** (1772-1837), P B Shelley (1792-1822), Robert Burns (1759-96), **Byron** (1788-1824) in his Greco-Albanian costume. Deathmasks of Keats and Wordsworth.

Science and the Industrial Revolution *(19)*: Portraits of inventors: John McAdam (road surfacing material), James Watt (steam engines), George Stephenson (railways), John Wilkinson (first iron ship), the Duke of Bridgewater (first canal); Josiah Wedgwood (famous potter); Humphrey Davy (miners' lamps in the Science Museum – *see KENSINGTON*): civil and mechanical engineers: I K Brunel, Telford, Sir Richard Arkwright, Robert Owen, Samuel Crompton.

The Regency (20): The House of Commons (1833) by Sir George Hayter. A series of portraits by Sir Thomas Lawrence: the **Prince Regent** (c 1814); his wife Caroline of Brunswick; Lord Castlereagh (1809-10); William Wilberforce (1828); George Canning. Portrait (1788) by Reynolds of Maria Fitzherbert who secretly married the Prince of Wales in 1795; William IV (1800) by Sir Martin Archer Shee; two portraits by Henry Perronet Briggs: Charles Kemble, actor, and Rev Sydney Smith (1840); portrait by Sir William Beechey of Sarah Siddons (1793), actress; Jane Austen (c 1810) by her sister Cassandra.

FROM THE VICTORIAN ERA TO THE MODERN AGE *First Floor*

Note: The 19C and 20C part of the National Portrait Gallery collection is so large that displays are regularly altered. Listed below are a selection of works available that may or may not be on show.

Victorian and Edwardian Eras – Statue (landing) of Victoria and Albert as ancient Saxons by William Theed (1868).

Statesmen's Gallery (22): Portraits and busts of leading statesmen and people of influence and power in politics such as Joseph Chamberlain, Lord Randolph Churchill, Sir Robert Peel and Arthur Wellesley, 1st Duke of Wellington.

Expansion and Empire (23): Britain as a world power and the personalities who secured its interests in remote parts of the world. Sir Richard Burton (1875), the African explorer, by Sir Frederic Leighton; Rudyard Kipling (1899) by Sir Philip Burne-Jones; portraits by Sir Hubert von Herkomer of 1st Earl Kitchener of Khartoum (1890) and Robert Baden-Powell (1903); Queen Victoria presenting a Bible (c 1861) by Jones Barker.

Early Victorian Arts (24): Artists, writers and performers who epitomised the Victorian age including Sir Edwin Landseer (1852) by Sir Francis Grant; portraits (1858) by Michele Gordigiani of Elizabeth Barrett Browning and Robert Browning; Alfred Lord Tennyson (1840) by Samuel Lawrence; Charles Dickens (1839) by Daniel Maclise; the Brontë sisters (1834) by Patrick Branwell Brontë.

Drawings by Sydney Prior Hall of the Parnell Commission. Portrait photographs by Barraud and Walery of W G Grace; Cardinal Newman; Ellen Terry; Alma Tadema; Robert Browning; Charles Kingsley; Anthony Trollope; Oscar Wilde; Wilkie Collins; Frederic Leighton. Portrait drawings by Daniel Maclise. Victorian portrait photography.

Portraits and Politics (25): Queen Victoria by Sir George Hayter; Prince Albert by Franz Xaver Winterhalter; 7th Earl of Shaftesbury (1862) by G F Watts; portraits by J E Millais of Gladstone (1879) and Disraeli (1881); caricatures drawn for *Vanity Fair*.

G F Watts (26) – Self-portrait; portraits by and of G F Watts: Ellen Terry (c 1864), future actress; her marriage at 16 to Watts, thirty years her senior, lasted barely a year.

Science and Technology (27): Luminaries such as Michael Faraday (1841-42); I K Brunel (1857); Charles Darwin (1881); Thomas Huxley (1883).

Later Victorian Arts (28): Theatrical and literary portraits including W S Gilbert; Sir Arthur Sullivan; Sir John Tenniel; William Holman-Hunt; William Morris; James Abbott McNeil Whistler; Walter Sickert; J K Jerome; Sir Henry Irving; Thomas Hardy; R L Stevenson (bust 1893) by Allen Hutchinson.

The Turn of the Century (29): The Edwardian Era is illustrated by Edward VII (1907); Queen Alexandra, replica by Sir Luke Fildes; their three daughters Victoria, Maud and Louise (1883); Joseph Conrad (bust 1924) by Sir Jacob Epstein; Rupert Brooke (1911); Henry James, an American who took British nationality (1913), by his friend John Singer Sargent.

20C

First World War (30) – The impact of industrial warfare and the balance of power in Europe were major issues. Several General Officers and Statesmen of the Great War (1922) by John Singer Sargent and Sir James Guthrie; **Sir Winston Churchill** (c 1911-15) and Sir John Alcock (1919) by Ambrose McEvoy; David Lloyd George by Sir William Orpen (1927).

The Armistice to the New Elizabethans (31): Post-war political developments, the communications revolution and the Depression brought about profound changes in British society. Influential figures featured are **Sir Winston Churchill** (1927) by Sir Walter Sickert; Stanley Baldwin (c 1933) by R G Eves; Viscount Montgomery (1945) by Frank Salisbury; Sir Oswald Moseley (1925) by Glyn Philpot.

The artistic environment reflected new ideas in painting, literature and music. Members of the **Bloomsbury Group** (Virginia Woolf by George Beresford and Vanessa Bell); E M Forster (1920s) by Dora Carrington; Dame Edith Sitwell (1927) by Pavel Tchelitchew, and (c 1923) by Maurice Lambert; D H Lawrence (1920) by Jan Juta; G B Shaw (1934) and T S Eliot (1951) by Sir Jacob Epstein; Bertrand Russell (c 1923) by Roger Fry; Laurence Olivier (bust 1950) by Peter Lambda.

Britain 1960-90 – *Balcony Gallery* **(32)**: Iconic figures from all walks of life portrayed in different styles to illustrate a period of social and political change. Sir Alec Guinness (bronze 1984) by Elisabeth Frink; Sir Michael Tippett (bronze 1966) by Gertrude Hermes; Richard Rogers (bronze 1988) by Eduardo Paolozzi; Henry Moore (bronze 1962) by Marino Marini; The Beatles by Norman Parkinson (1963) and by Michael McCartney (1960s); Sir Winston Churchill (sketch 1954) by Graham Sutherland; Elizabeth Taylor by Andy Warhol (1967); Harold Wilson (1974) by Ruskin Spear. Cartoons of political figures by Gerald Scarfe and Mark Boxer.

Peter Blake and Francis Bacon by Clive Barker; Dirk Bogarde by David Tindle; Philip Larkin and Paul McCartney by Humphrey Ocean; Margaret Thatcher by Helmut Newton; George Melly by Maggie Hamblyn...

Paul McCartney, *Sam Walsh*

The Royal Family (33): Portraits of the Queen throughout her reign, of the Prince of Wales and his sons as well as a family portrait to mark the 100th birthday of HM the Queen Mother.

Britain since 1990 – *Ground Floor* **(34-40)**: Portaits and photographs of people in the public eye from writers, royalty, sports personalities to people connected with the arts, business, science, technology and the media: Diana, Princess of Wales, Richard Branson, Ken Loach, Harold Pinter, Alan Bennett, Stephen Hawking, Rupert Murdoch.

Piccadilly★

This busy thoroughfare lined with stately buildings, elegant shops and hotels, is the dividing line between fashionable Mayfair and dignified St James's. To the east Piccadilly Circus, famous for the statue of Eros and the illuminated hoardings, is a major hub and a meeting place for visitors. At the west end is the quiet elegance of Apsley House set against the luxuriant greenery of Hyde Park.

Location

Map pp 5-6 (DEXY) and area map under MAYFAIR; Michelin Atlas London: p 61. ⊖ *Piccadilly Circus, Green Park, Hyde Park Corner.* Many thoroughfares converge on Piccadilly Circus which is a short distane west of Leicester Square and within easy access of Soho. It is a short walk through Green Park to Buckingham Palace and the Mall.
Adjacent Sights: ST JAMES'S; MAYFAIR; KNIGHTSBRIDGE – BELGRAVIA; SOHO; TRAFALGAR SQUARE – WHITEHALL; BUCKINGHAM PALACE.

Directory

Light Bite

The Studio Lounge – *203 Piccadilly, at Waterstone's (5th floor), W1V 9LE –* ⊖ *Piccadilly Circus –* ☎ *020 7851 2433 – searcys_waterstones@talk21.com – Open Mon-Sat 10am-10pm, Sun noon-5.30pm – £7.50.* The Studio Lounge café, on the 5th floor of London's largest bookstore, affords far-reaching views over the rooftops of Westminster, to the London Eye, Big Ben and beyond. Short eclectic menu features rare roast beef sandwiches, ciabattas and more.

Fortnum & Mason – Restaurants – *181 Piccadilly, W1A 1ER –* ⊖ *Piccadilly Circus –* ☎ *020 7734 8040 – restauranats@fortnumandmason.co.uk – Fountain: Open Mon-Sat 8am- 8pm. St James: Open 10am-5.30pm. – £8.95/21.* This internationally famous purveyor of fine products, established in 1707, operates several restaurants in which to savour the classic institution of afternoon tea. The lower ground floor "Fountain" and the 4th-floor "St James's" with piano music are most popular.

Taking a Break

Mô – *25 Heddon St, W1B 4BQ –* ⊖ *Piccadilly Circus –* ☎ *020 7734 3999 – www.momoresto.com – Open Mon-Tue 11am-11pm, Wed noon-11pm, Thu-Sat noon-midnight.* In this small peaceful alley looking onto Regent's Street, Mourad Mazouz's first Moroccan restaurant in London was opened in 1997. Mô, the small adjoining café, invites you for a stop in North Africa, with all the trappings, such as pouffes, shining metal trays, mint tea and honey pastries in a very relaxed atmosphere.

The Ritz – *150 Piccadilly, W1J 9BR –* ⊖ *Green Park –* ☎ *020 7493 8181 – enquire@theritzlondon.com – Tea served daily at 1.30pm, 3.30pm and 5.30pm; booking essential – Tea £29.* If you fancy joining the illustrious in afteroon tea – Chaplin, De Gaulle, King Edward VII – in the magical Louis XVI lounge, you must reserve six weeks in advance.

Shopping

Hatchards Booksellers – *187 Piccadilly, W1J 9LE –* ⊖ *Piccadilly Circus –* ☎ *020 7439 9921 – books@hatchards.co.uk – Open Mon-Fri 9.30am-6.30pm, Sun noon-6pm.* This large traditional bookshop is the official supplier to Her Majesty the Queen. The five floors cover all ranges except academic.

N Peal & Co.Ltd – *37 Burlington Arcade, W1J 0QD –* ⊖ *Piccadilly Circus –* ☎ *020 7493 5378 – www.npeal.com – Open Mon-Sat 9.30am-6pm.* Two elegant modern boutiques (one for women, one for men) in this stately arcade selling luxury goods – cashmere, pashminas, modern-cut tops, shawls, in a range of dazzling colours.

Tower Records – *1 Piccadilly Circus, W1J 0TR –* ⊖ *Piccadilly Circus –* ☎ *020 7439 2500 – piccadilly2@virginmega.co.uk – Open Mon-Sat 9am-midnight, Sun noon-6pm; closed 25 Dec and Easter Mon.* This record shop offers the widest selection of music anywhere in London including records from the 1960's.

Waterstone's Booksellers – *203-206 Piccadilly, W1J 9HA –* ⊖ *Piccadilly Circus –* ☎ *020 7851 2400 – www.waterstones.co.uk – Open Mon-Sat 10am-10pm, Sun noon-6pm.* Occupying 6 floors of an attractive listed 1930s building, Waterstone's is reputedly the largest bookshop in London and possibly in Europe. A good national and international press section. Pleasant café on 5th floor.

Burlington Arcade: The Finishing Touch

A. Taverner/MICHELIN

Background

In the early 16C, the area was owned by Eton College and the Mercers' Company. The name Piccadilly is derived from Pickadill Hall (c 1612), an imposing family mansion built on a plot of land adjoining Great Windmill Street, by a Somerset tailor who had made a fortune manufacturing frilled lace borders known as "pickadills" which fashionable Elizabethans attached to their ruffs and cuffs.

Walking About

Piccadilly Circus★

The circus, once considered the hub of the Empire, still draws the crowds. It was created by **John Nash** as part of his new road from **Carlton House** in St James's to Regent's Park. The statue of **Eros**, officially the Angel of Christian Charity, is a memorial (drinking) fountain erected in 1892 to the philanthropist, **Lord Shaftesbury**.

The south side of the circus, built on the site of the 17C St James's market, is occupied by the **Criterion,** a Victorian building from the 1870s with pavilion roofs containing a hotel and restaurant. The 19C mosaic ceiling is still visible in the Criterion Brasserie; 19C decorative tiles line the foyer of the **Criterion Theatre**, which was incorporated in the building largely underground in 1874 and was one of the first theatres to be lit by electricity.

On the southeast corner *(at the top end of Haymarket)* stands a four horse fountain by Rudy Weller: high above, three divers reach for the sky.

The north side is taken up by the **London Pavilion**, crowned by 13 sculptures of Victorian maidens, which was redeveloped in the 1980s to contain shops and restaurants.

J. Malburet/MICHELIN

The Winged Eros in Piccadilly Circus

Trocadero

Open Sun-Thu, 10am-midnight; Fri-Sat 10am-1am. Closed 25 Dec. Charges for individual attractions. ☎ *0906 888 1100 (premium rate)*

A place of gentle entertainment throughout the Victorian and Edwardian eras when waltzing to Strauss was all the rage, has been lavishly redeveloped to accommodate a futuractive theme park-cum-computer-age emporium of sound, virtual reality and special effects spread over seven storeys. Be prepared for launch up 100m with the Rocket Escalator (biggest and best of its kind) to access the ever-changing interactive rides (Mad Bazooka, Beast in Darkness, Aqua Planet, Ghost Hunt, Space Mission, James Bond 007).

Cross to the south side of Piccadilly (St James's Church is described in ST JAMES'S).

Piccadilly★

The shops here display their merchandise with flair: silk, leather, cashmere, tweed; wines and spirits, fruit and preserves; books; china, glass and kitchenware; military memorabilia; umbrellas and walking sticks; hairbrushes; rifles and guns...

Of the most traditional establishments, it is worth noting no **203** (formerly Simpson's, now Waterstone's) for its fine, elegantly proportioned, simple yet sophisticated building (1935); **Hatchard's** *(no 187)* established by John Hatchard in 1797 with a capital of £5 and still trading from its original 18C building with small-panelled windows on either side of the entrance. In **Fortnum and Mason's** (founded 1707) the tailcoats of the assistants once added to the sense of luxury; when the clock (1964) above the Piccadilly entrance chimes the hour Mr Fortnum and Mr Mason emerge and bow to one another. *(See Directory).*

Cross over to the north side.

The Albany

The harmonious building is named after Frederick, second son of George III, Duke of York and Albany. Compelled by substantial debts, the prince sold the 18C house designed by **Sir William Chambers** to a builder who converted it into 'sets' or 'chambers for bachelors and widowers' which remain to this day. The building, as altered by **Henry Holland** in 1804, is in the shape of an H; the front, with a forecourt on Piccadilly, is of brick with a central pediment and porch, while at the rear it forms a stuccoed court on Vigo Street enclosed by two lodges between neighbouring 18C houses. Distinction has always come to Albany through its residents who have included Gladstone, Macaulay, Byron, J B Priestley, Graham Greene, Sir Isaiah Berlin. To preserve the peace, trustees rule that occupants are not allowed to whistle or keep cats, dogs or children under the age of 13!

Burlington House★

In 1664 the 1st Earl of Burlington bought a plot on which to build a town house on the edge of courtly St James's; the 3rd Earl, an architect in his own right, together with **Colen Campbell** remodelled and refaced the house in the Palladian style (1715-16). In the 19C the house was altered again, the second time in 1867-73 to its present neo-Italian Renaissance appearance.

The rear of Burlington House was remodelled in 1869 in ornate Italian style with towers, an upper portico of giant columns and a colossal porch, and suitably decorated with more than 20 magisterial statues. On completion the building became for many years the headquarters of London University *(see BLOOMSBURY)* and until recent years housed the Museum of Mankind which has now transferred to the British Museum *(see BRITISH MUSEUM)*. This section now houses the Royal Academy School of Fine Art which provides training in drawing, painting and sculpture.

Today, besides the Royal Academy of Arts *(described in Worth a Visit)*, the adjacent wings of the complex accommodate the Geological Society, Royal Astronomical Society and the Society of Antiquaries.

Burlington Arcade

The arcade along the west side of Burlington House, is delectable with traditional purveyors of luxury goods: table linen, fine antique jewellery, cashmere knitwear, leather and shoes are enticingly presented in bright shopwindows. It was built in 1819 and is patrolled by beadles; the gates are closed at night and on Sundays.

Near Old Bond St (see MAYFAIR) cross to the south side.

William Curtis-Green (1875-1960) designed no **160** as a car showroom (1922) for Wolseley Motors and later transformed the interior into a banking hall. The building *(now a restaurant)* is in the 'Big Bow-Wow style of Corinth USA' on the outside and inside, decked in the most sumptuous red, black and gold exotic decoration.

Ritz Hotel

The 130-bedroom hotel was opened on 24 May 1906 by César Ritz, a Swiss waiter turned entrepreneur, at the height of the Edwardian era. It was an immediate success, bordering on the decorous and the decadent with single rooms costing 10s 6d a night (52?p)! Externally, the early frame structure was fashioned by Mewès and Davis to the French Classical style, while inside all was gilded Louis XVI decoration and marble. Regular patrons have included royalty (the future Edward VII, the Duke of Windsor and Wallis Simpson, Queen Elizabeth the Queen Mother), the rich (the late Aga Khan, Aristotle Onassis), the glamorous (Rita Hayworth) and the plain famous (Noel Coward, Charlie Chaplin, Winston Churchill)... During the 1970s and 1980s a selection of spare jackets and ties was supplied so that 'pop' stars might conform with the strict dress code.

Walk on past Green Park towards Hyde Park Corner.

The ornamental gates on the north side of Green Park *(see ST JAMES'S)* were designed by Robert Bakewell of Derby to grace the entrance to Devonshire House.

The west end of Piccadilly is lined by late Georgian houses occupied by a growing number of hotels, following the demise of the gentleman's clubs. No **94,** a modest townhouse of 1756-60, two storeys high, with a Venetian window beneath the central pediment, was formerly the residence of George IV's son, the Duke of Cambridge (1829-50), and from 1854-65 of Lord Palmerston. No 128 harbours the **Royal Air Force Club.**

On the south side of Piccadilly, by the Hyde Park Corner underpass stands a **porters' rest**, a solid plank of wood at shoulder height on which porters could rest their back-packs without unloading them.

Worth a Visit

Apsley House★

(♿) Open Tue-Sun and Bank Hol Mon, 11am-5pm. Closed Good Fri, May Day Hol, 24-26 Dec, 1 Jan. £4.50; no charge 18 June: Waterloo Day. Soundguide (4 languages). ☎ 020 7499 5676; Fax 020 7493 6576; www.apsleyhouse.org.uk

Apsley House stands on the former site of a public house, and later, the old lodge of Hyde Park. As the first house beyond the turnpike, it became known in the 19C as No 1, London.

Apsley House, a mansion fit for a national hero overlooking the green acres of Hyde Park

The present house was purchased by Wellington in 1817, having been designed nearly 40 years before by **Robert Adam** for Baron Apsley: topographical views painted on porcelain in the Plate and China Room show Adam's house as being small, square and built of brick. It was subsequently altered by the duke and his architect Benjamin S Wyatt: the exterior was given a pedimented portico and refaced entirely in golden Bath stone; the interior, meanwhile, was rearranged (save the Portico and Piccadilly Drawing Room) and in 1812, extended. The transformation was such as to befit the town residence of the victorious general and national hero (later prime minister). On the ground floor it provided for the Muniment or Plate and China Room to house a priceless collection of treasures and on the floor above, the splendid Waterloo Gallery. In 1947 the 7th Duke presented the house to the nation.

Wellington Museum★ – Most of the objects displayed have significant associations with Wellington himself: orders and decorations include the silver Waterloo Medal, the first ever campaign medal, and 85 tricolours paraded on 1 June 1815 in Paris. The museum includes his highly personal collection of objects selected as supreme examples of quality and artistry: porcelain and silver, beautiful jewellery, orders of chivalry, field marshal's batons and snuffboxes. Of the paintings by English, Spanish, Dutch and Flemish masters, more than 100 had been appropriated from the Spanish royal collection by Joseph Bonaparte and acquired from him in 1813 following the Battle of Vitoria. The chandeliers are 19C English.

Plate and China – Exquisitely painted Meissen porcelain complements contemporary taste in the exotic and the topographical that was promoted by Napoleon following his major military campaigns in North Africa and Northern Europe. The opulent splendour of the Egyptian (Sèvres: 1810-12), Prussian (Berlin: 1819), Saxon and Austrian porcelain services compares well with the glorious gold and silver plate (Wellington Shield, solid silver candelabra), silver and gilt services (most of several hundred pieces) that would be used for lavish celebratory banquets. Meanwhile, the rich gold, enamelled and jewelled snuffboxes evidently reflect a more personal appreciation for quality.

In the basement are displayed the **Duke's death mask**, his uniforms and garter robes, his and Napoleon's swords from Waterloo, a panorama and a programme, printed on silk, of his remarkable funeral and a commentary on his political career by newspaper cartoonists of the day (1852).

Standing in the staircase vestibule is a Carrara marble (11ft 4in/3.5m) likeness of the Emperor Napoleon Bonaparte, posed like the god Apollo, sculpted by **Canova** – not something that Wellington could very easily hide away! Other portraits of *Napoleon* by Lefèvre and Dabos, of the *Empress Josephine* and *Pauline Bonaparte* by Lefèvre hang upstairs.

On the first floor, formal portraits line the walls – notable works include those by Wilkie (William IV), Reynolds and Lawrence. In the Piccadilly Drawing Room and Portico Room are beautiful examples of interior Adam decoration. The most striking room, however, is the **Waterloo Gallery**. The early Waterloo Day (18 June) reunion dinners, with only the generals present, used to be held in the dining room: but by 1829, with Wellington now premier, the guest list had grown to such an extent that he added the gallery (90ft/27m long). This he had decorated in 18C French style which set a fashion favoured until the end of the Edwardian era: on the ceiling the Wellington arms are combined with the George within the Garter collar. The windows that once would have had a rural view, are fitted with sliding mirrors which would have enhanced still further the already glittering gold decoration, flickering candles, glistening chandelier, silver centrepiece and plate, the blue and red uniforms with gold buttons and braid...

The **paintings** are dominated by the portraits of Charles I after Van Dyck, and the Goya portrait of the duke himself in the standard Spanish heroic pose on horseback – recent x-rays have revealed that it was painted somewhat prematurely and the head of Joseph Bonaparte had to be overpainted with that of the ultimate victor. Other major masterpieces hung here include works by **Murillo**, **Rubens**, Reynolds, Ribera, Mengs, Brueghel, **Velazquez**, notably *The Water Seller of Seville* and *A Spanish Gentleman* and the Duke's favourite, *The Agony in the Garden* by Correggio. Many of these were seized from Joseph Bonaparte in 1813, who had in turn stolen them from the King of Spain. The Yellow Drawing Room is hung with yellow damask resembling that originally in the Waterloo Gallery, while the striped drawing room is devoted to ***The Battle of Waterloo*** by Sir William Allan (about which the Duke commented 'Good; very good; not too much smoke').

Dining Room – The amazing portrait of George IV in Highland dress by Wilkie overlooks the banqueting table set with the silver centrepiece (26ft/8m) from the Portuguese service.

Royal Academy

Burlington House. ♿ Open daily, 10am-6pm (10pm Fri-Sat). Closed 24-25 Dec. £6-£10 according to the exhibition. Restaurant; cafe. Shop. ☎ 020 7300 5760 (recorded information), 020 7300 8000 (switchboard); Fax 020 7300 8001; www.royalacademy.org.uk

The Academy, founded in 1768, was first accommodated in Somerset House *(see STRAND – TEMPLE)*. When it moved to Burlington House the interior was drastically modified to provide a grand central staircase and exhibition galleries. The light and versatile Sackler Galleries, designed by Sir **Norman Foster** RA were opened in 1991 by the Queen. The academy's treasures, usually exhibited in the Private Rooms, include paintings by members (Reynolds, Gainsborough, Constable, Turner), 18C furniture, Queen Victoria's paintbox, **Michelangelo**'s unfinished marble tondo of the *Madonna and Child (in the sculpture section outside the entrance of the Sackler Galleries)*, and the famous copy of **Leonardo da Vinci**'s *Last Supper*.

Regent's Park★★★

The harmonious composition of the park bounded to the north by the Regent's Canal and around which are strung out dazzling terraces and splendid villas is a unique achievement combining nature and artistic flair. Visitors young and old enjoy the attractions of the Zoo. The fragrant rose garden, the spirited performances at the open-air theatre and band music in the park are highlights of the summer season. The superb amenities also include a boating lake and tennis courts.

Location

Map p 11 (CDV, St John's Wood: BCV, Little Venice: BVX); Michelin Atlas London: pp 90-92, 88-89 (St John's Wood), 72 (Little Venice). ⊖ Regent's Park or Portland Place. Regent's Park can also be reached by boat or bus from Camden Town *(⊖ Camden Town)* famous for its markets and by boat from Little Venice *(Bloomfield Rd, ⊖ Warwick Avenue)*. To the north and west are the desirable residential areas of Primrose Hill and St John's Wood.
Adjacent Sights: MARYLEBONE; ST PANCRAS – CAMDEN TOWN.

Background

The Proposal – It was a superb plan: the government needed something done with Marylebone Fields (which had been enclosed by **Henry VIII**and divided under the Commonwealth into manor farms of which the leases reverted to the crown in 1811) and a direct route from north central London to Westminster. **Nash** devised a tree-landscaped park with a serpentine lake bounded by a road along which, on all except

19C vision of urban living – Nash Terraces in the Outer Circle of Regent's Park

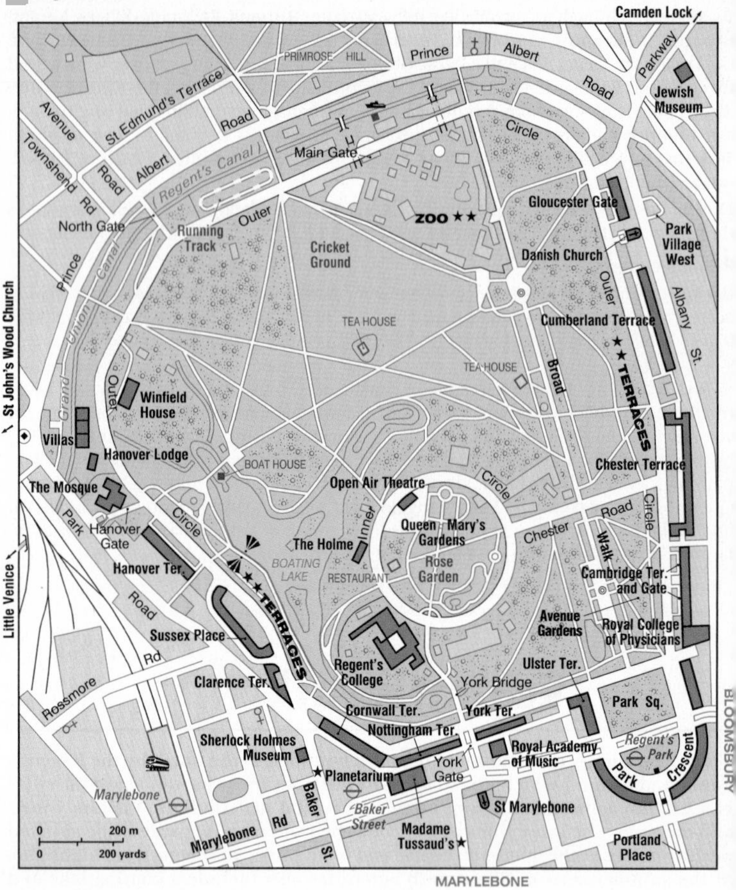

the north side, which was to be left open for the view of Primrose Hill and the heights of Hampstead and Highgate, there would be a series of terrace-palaces, providing three-bay town houses for the noble and fashionable. Within the park would be a circus, ringed by houses facing both in and outwards and, surmounting the upraised centre, a valhalla; elsewhere there would be a *guinguette* or summer pavilion for the Prince of Wales, which would be approached along a wide avenue (the Broad Walk) on an axis with Portland Place. Numerous other villas were planned to nestle, half-hidden, among the trees, while the central feature would be the proposed Regent's Canal. All in all, the park would become the most exquisite garden suburb.

The Constraints – Portland Place, a most successful speculation begun by the Adam brothers in 1774 consisted of a private road lined by substantial mansions and closed at the south end by Foley House, whose owner insisted on an uninterrupted view thereby dictating the street's 125ft/38m width. Between the place and park ran New Road (Marylebone Road), a psychological barrier that bisected the area into two – the junction would be transformed into a circus around St Marylebone Church (not then built). Portland Place, which Nash greatly admired would be extended due south across Oxford Street and Piccadilly by means of circuses, to arrive at Carlton House. The section south of Oxford Circus would be lined with a continuous arcade of shops sheltered by colonnades with balconied houses above; below would be excavated a much needed new sewer system for central London.

The Realisation – In essence the plan survived considering that it was subject to government commissions and the hazards of land purchase. The *guinguette*, all but seven villas and the would-be double Bath Crescent did not materialise but an Inner Circle was laid out as a botanic garden, now transformed into **Queen Mary's Gardens**. The approach from Portland Place was modified to the open-armed Park Crescent and Park Square. The extension south from Portland Place was given a pivoted turn by the construction of the circular porch of All Souls, and the angle at the south beautifully swept round by means of the Quadrant. The project took eight years to achieve (1817-25): New Street, as it was called at first, was a fashionable and glittering success clinched by the social promenaders and followers of Beau Brummel; the houses along the park were snapped up; meanwhile, the Prince, by now George IV, had unfortunately tired of **Carlton House** but it remained a worthy focal climax until 1829 when it was demolished and replaced by Waterloo Place and Carlton House Terrace *(see ST JAMES'S)*.

Nash himself probably designed only a few of the **terraces★★**, houses and shops, but he set the style sufficiently explicitly for different architects, among them Decimus Burton, to draw up plans, which subject to approval by Nash to ensure homogeneity could be executed. Giant columns, generally Ionic or Corinthian, are used throughout to articulate the centre and ends of the long façades which, in addition, were usually advanced and sometimes pedimented or given an attic screen decorated with statuary. Columns, of a different order, formed arcades or were adapted to frame doors or ground floor windows; balustrades and continuous first floor balconies of iron or stucco ran the length of the long fronts uniting them into single compositions.

In 1828 London Zoo opened on the north side of the Park beside the canal.

Walking About

Terraces★★

Start from Regent's Park Station and walk round clockwise.

The **terraces** are named after the titles of some of George III's 15 children. Park Crescent was designed by Nash to link Portland Place to Regent's Park.

Park Crescent (1821) is characterised by paired Ionic columns in a continuous porch, a balustrade and a balcony which emphasise the classical curve of **Park Crescent** (1821). The Doric Lodges once flanked iron gates closing off the crescent and the square from the main road. The **East and West** (1823-24) buildings which flank **Park Square**, are embellished by single Ionic columns.

Next in line is **Ulster Terrace** (1824); the idiosyncrasy appears in two closely positioned pairs of bay windows at either end.

York Terrace (1821; west end now named **Nottingham Terrace**), which is 360yds/329m long or nearly half the width of the park, comprises two symmetrical blocks, York Gate in the axis of St Marylebone Church *(see MARYLEBONE)* and some detached houses. The sequence of column orders is giant Corinthian in the mansions at either end, Ionic above Doric colonnades in the pedimented main blocks and Ionic in the houses at York Gate.

The attractive **Cornwall Terrace** (1822) has a 187yd/170m front, marked at either end and the centre by Corinthian columns and divided into a number of receding planes. Note through the trees the modest 18C brick houses and old pub on the far side of Baker Street/Park Road, also the lodge with rounded windows and pitched slate roof.

Clarence Terrace (1823) boasts a heavily accented Corinthian centre and angles above an Ionic arcade.

Notable features of **Sussex Place** (1822; **London Graduate School of Business Studies**) include the most surprising, finialled, slim, octagonal cupolas, in pairs, crowning the ends and framing the pedimented centre of the curved terrace; below the domes are canted bays and, between, a continuous line of Corinthian columns (the far side from the park was rebuilt in a modern buttressed style in brick in 1972).

The **Royal College of Obstetricians and Gynaecologists** (1960) is a four-storey brick building with a stone wing at right angles encompassing the low recessed entrance and over it, the hall.

Hanover Terrace (1822-23) is marked by pediments coloured bright blue as a background to plasterwork and serving as pedestals for statuary silhouetted against the sky. Hanover Gate has a small, octagonal lodge with heavy inverted corbel decoration and niches with statues beneath a pitched slate roof and central octagonal chimney.

The **Mosque** (1977), marked by its minaret (140ft/43m high), white with a small gold coloured dome and finial crescent, stands on the site of one of Nash's villas (Albany Cottage) and was designed by **Sir Frederick Gibberd**. The mosque itself has a pale grey façade pierced by tall arched windows of five lights arranged in groups of four; blind arcades support the drum which rises to a huge, gilded copper dome. Other new buildings accommodate a school and the Islamic Cultural Centre.

Hanover Lodge, one of the 18C villas, has a large modern brick addition. The row of three modern villas alongside (1989) are named **Ionic Villa, Veneto Villa and Gothick Villa**.

The neo-Georgian house of 1936, **Winfield House**, now the residence of the US ambassador, was built on the site of St Dunstan's Lodge where the organisation for blinded ex-servicemen was founded in 1915. The lodge was designed by **Decimus Burton** in 1825 for the 3rd **Marquess of Hertford** *(see index)* who, it is said, used it as a harem.

The **boating lake** which curves picturesquely around the Inner Circle is a popular spot for sport and recreation. There are boats and deckchairs for hire and band music throughout the summer.

Inner Circle

The **Open Air Theatre** presents a summer season of open-air performances of plays by Shakespeare and other playwrights. **The Holme** is one of the 18C villas.

Regent's College is on the site of South Villa and St John's Lodge, rebuilt and enlarged this century in red brick.

Queen Mary's Gardens were created out of the original Botanic Garden and are a delightful haven. The Rose Garden filled with heady perfumes in summer is very romantic.

Take Chester Rd and walk south down the Broad Walk to the Outer Circle.

Outer Circle

The southern section of the park is flanked by the **Avenue Gardens**, which have been relaid according to the designs prepared by William Andrews Nesfield in 1862.

A tesserae-faced building by Denys Lasdun, extends squarely forward to afford a recessed entrance encased in glass contrasting with a long polygonal construction of black brick to one side covering a hall. It is the home of the **Royal College of Physicians** (1964).

Cambridge Gate (1875), a totally Victorian, stone-faced block with pavilion roofs, stands on the site of the Coliseum, a large circular building with a portico and glazed roof used for exhibitions and panoramas (or dioramas). **Cambridge Terrace** (1825) and neighbouring buildings have been restored.

The longest unbroken façade (313yds/286m) of **Chester Terrace** (1825) has Corinthian columns rising from ground level to emphasise the ends, centre and mid-points between; at either end triumphal, named, arches lead to the access road to the rear.

The Ionic pillars of the façade (267yd/242m long) of **Cumberland Terrace** (1826) recur in the intervening arches. Britannia, the arts and science are represented in the central pediment behind squat vases.

Angle pediments with plasterwork against red-painted tympana and surmounting statues, mark the main terrace of **Gloucester Gate** (1827).

Pass through the gate and make a short detour to Albany St.

Park Village West – *Albany St.* This is the most attractive of the two dependent streets to the terraces. The small houses and modest terraces are in Nash's country cottage style, although not designed by him.

Worth a Visit

London Zoo★★

♿ *Open daily, 10am-5.30pm (4pm Nov-Feb); last admission 1hr before closing. Closed 25 Dec. £12. Restaurant, refreshments. ☎ 020 7722 3333; Fax 020 7449 6362; www.londonzoo.co.uk*

The foundation of a Zoological Society of London was spearheaded by Sir Stamford Raffles (of Singapore fame) and Sir Humphry Davy (1826) for "the advancement of Zoology and Animal Physiology and the introduction of new and curious subjects of the Animal Kingdom".

The first part of the original concept has been realised by a collaboration between the Zoological Society and the zoo staff who research into systematic anatomy – the Wellcome Institute of Comparative Physiology (f 1962) and the Nuffield Institute of Comparative Medicine (f 1964) have streamlined studies in reproductive physiology (including human fertility), biochemistry and disease as they affect diet, health and husbandry.

The second part of Sir Stamford's proposal to introduce "curious subjects of the animal kingdom", was realised in 1828 when the Society opened on a site (5 acres/2ha) in Regent's Park with a small collection of animals looked after by a keeper in a top hat, bottle green coat and striped waistcoat. The first big cats came from the menagerie at the Tower of London (closed by William IV); the first giraffes, unloaded in the Docklands, had to be led all the way through the City to Regent's Park (May 1836). During the Second World War, the most dangerous animals were destroyed in case the zoo were bombed with devastating consequences.

Today, the major objective of the zoo is to conserve and breed endangered species and to pursue research into the biology of rare animals. A large proportion of the animals are bred in Regent's Park or at Whipsnade Wild Animal Park. Domestic animals are presented at close quarters in the **children's zoo**. The elephants have been transferred to Whipsnade.

Housing – The zoo gardens were originally laid out by **Decimus Burton** who also designed several buildings of which there remain the Ravens' Cage on the Members' Lawn, the Clock Tower, the Giraffe House and the East Tunnel.

Activities

The programme of **daily events** includes animal **feeding times**, bath time for the elephants, animals in the **Amphitheatre** and **animal encounters** in which the keepers introduce the animals in their charge. The Society's latest conservation, scientific and veterinary work is presented in the **Lifewatch Centre**, where the **London Zoo Experience** brings the history of the zoo to life. The **Discovery Centre** enables visitors "to walk like a camel, hear like an elephant, fly like a bird and see like a giraffe".

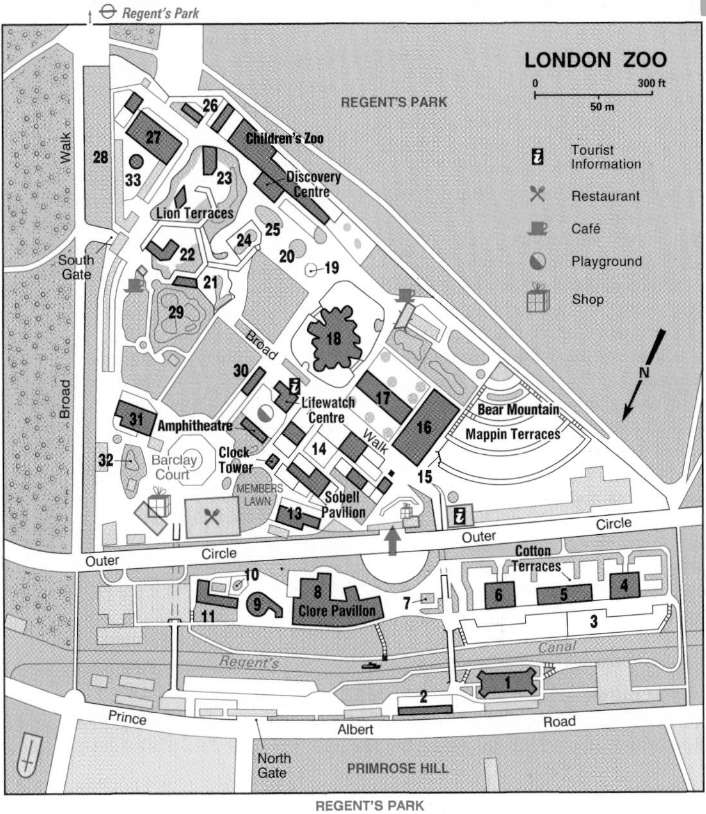

Regent's Park

LONDON ZOO

0 — 300 ft — 50 m

Tourist Information
Restaurant
Café
Playground
Shop

REGENT'S PARK — Children's Zoo — Discovery Centre — Lion Terraces — South Gate — Broad Walk — Broad Walk — Lifewatch Centre — Amphitheatre — Barclay Court — Clock Tower — MEMBERS LAWN — Sobell Pavilion — Bear Mountain — Mappin Terraces — Outer Circle — Cotton Terraces — Clore Pavilion — Regent's Canal — Prince Albert Road — North Gate — PRIMROSE HILL

REGENT'S PARK

African Aviary	13	Flamingos	32	Penguins	25
Alpes and Monkeys	14	Gibbons	30	Pheasants	26
Anoa, Okapi	4	Giraffe, Zebra	5	Reptiles	16
Aquarium	15	Invertebrates	11	Reptiliary (summer only)	7
Arabian Oryx	3	Leopards	22	Snowdon Aviary	1
Asiatic Lions	23	Mongooses	19	Sumatran tigers	21
Binturong	9	Moonlight World and small mammals	8	Tropical bird house	27
Birds	20	Otters	10	Water birds	24
Camels	6	Owls	2	Web of life	33
Cranes	17	Parrots	31	Wolves	28
Elephants and Black Rhinos	18	Pelicans	29		

The **Reptile House** (1902) displays crocodiles, snakes, lizards, constrictors, tortoises and alligators behind glass. A cluster of locusts attracts attention in the **Insect House** (1912). Houses for all animals from tropical climates used to be kept heated and closed until the end of the 19C when **Carl Hagenbeck** of Hamburg Zoo revolutionised contemporary practice by providing paddocks for tropical animals and surrounding enclosures not with bars but moats and ditches. His example led to the construction of the **Mappin Terraces** (1914) in London and to the creation of Whipsnade (1931) on derelict farmland (480 acres/194ha) in Bedfordshire.

The Zoo has commissioned some highly innovative architecture. Berthold Lubetkin designed the **Great Apes Breeding Colony** (1933) and the **Penguin Pool** (1934) with its intersecting spiral ramps for the penguins to parade 'like arctic supermodels', the first

J. Malburet/MICHELIN

Elephants enjoying a cooling shower at the Zoo

example of such use of pre-stressed concrete, now in standard use. The **Cotton Terraces** (1963) present giraffes and zebras, camels and llamas, horses and cattle, antelope and deer (Père David herd) in new pavilions and Burton's altered Giraffe House. The distinctively roofed **Elephant and Rhino Pavilion** (1965) is by Sir Hugh Casson. Lord Snowdon designed the **Snowdon Aviary** (1965) (150ft/46m by 80ft/24m high) which in summer contains as many as 150 birds in natural surroundings and through which the visitor passes on an elevated walkway. The **Charles Clore Pavilion** for Small Mammals (1967) contains the **Moonlight World,** where one sees animals active only at night.

In 1972 the **Michael Sobell Pavilion** for Apes and Monkeys was built. The **Lion Terraces**, several enclosures planted with trees and bushes from which the big cats survey all lesser mortals, date from 1976. The design for an energy-saving glass building housing the **Web of Life**, which opened in 1999, draws inspiration from a termite nest. The exhibits are devoted to biodiversity and conservation: invertebrates, evolution and extinction of species.

Favourite Denizens

Jumbo has given his name to cuddly toys, chocolate bars and airplanes: the African bull came to London zoo from the Jardin des Plantes in Paris as a sickly (4ft) calf in 1865; when he grew too tall (11ft/3m) and big to offer joy rides to the public, he was sold to the American Circus owner P T Barnum (1882) – his departure attracted such crowds that enough money was raised to fund a new Reptile House (now the Bird House). **Winnie the Pooh** (d 1934) was an American black bear from Winnipeg who was left at the zoo when her owner, Canadian Lieutenant Colebourne, went to the front in 1914; she was so tame that children were allowed to feed her condensed milk and golden syrup in her den – as did Christopher (Robin) Milne. **Guy** the Gorilla **Fawkes** (d 1978) arrived on 5 November 1947 – hence his name. Goldie the Golden Eagle found fame when she escaped (1965) and eluded her captors for a whole fortnight, hovering above the aviary as if in contempt. More contemporary personalities include Chi Chi and Chia Chia the pandas from China, and **Josephine** the elderly Great Indian Hornbill spinster (b 1945), who came from Cheshire!

Danish Church

Open Tue-Fri, 9am-1pm and 6.30-9pm (except Fri); Sat-Sun, 12-5pm. Keys available at 5 St Katharine's Precinct. ☎ 020 7935 7584; Fax 020 7487 4029; dankirkelondon@msn.com; www.danskekirke.org

A neo-Gothic church (1829) in stock brick was built for the **St Katharine Royal Hospital Community** *(see Outer London: DOCKLANDS)* but was taken over in 1950 by the Danish community whose own building in Limehouse had been bombed. Inside are a coffered ceiling, below the windows shields of English queens from Eleanor to Mary, and beside the modern fittings, John the Baptist and Moses, two of the four figures carved in wood by the 17C Danish sculptor **Caius Cibber** for Limehouse. Outside to the right is a replica of the Jelling Stone.

Excursions

ST JOHN'S WOOD

West of Regent's park (take Park Rd and St John's Wood Rd).

It developed rapidly in the first half of the 19C as a residential district following the expansion of Marylebone and Nash's development of Regent's Park. Its rural character was swept aside as Italian type villas, broad eaved and often in pairs, were erected. As it was within three miles of the City and Westminster, it was a perfect place for wealthy Victorians resident in Belgravia to keep their mistresses; by 1824 a colony of artists had begun to gather.

St John's Wood Church

Prince Albert Road. (♿) Open daily, 9am-5pm. Concerts. ☎ 020 7586 3864

The church is of the same date, 1813, and by the same architect, **Thomas Hardwick**, as **St Marylebone** Parish Church *(see MARYLEBONE)* and like it has a distinctive, cupola-topped turret.

Lord's Cricket Ground

St John's Wood Road. Guided tour (including museum) daily, at noon, 2pm; also on summer days at 10am. Telephone for exact schedule. Closed during test matches, cup finals, preparation days and certain public holidays. £6.50. Museum only: Open match days to match ticket holders only £2.50. Leaflet (3 languages). ☎ 020 7616 8595; Fax 020 7266 3825

Lord's is a private gentlemen's club. The best introduction to the ground, its history and its aura is by guided tour through the inner sanctum, the famous Long Room in the Pavilion (open to MCC – Marylebone Cricket Club – members only during matches), the 'real' tennis court, the adjacent **MCC Museum** founded in memory of all the cricketers who lost their lives in the First World War which displays the famous **Ashes**, portraits (talking head of Dr WG Grace) and cartoons, cricketing dress, memorabilia from batting lists to snuff boxes, the Lord's shop and the award-winning

Mound Stand. The Library is perhaps the world's most important Cricket archive – alas incomplete as the earliest records were destroyed by a fire in 1825.

A Valued Trophy

The Ashes urn contains the precious ashes of a pair of wicket bails. It is competed for in a series of test matches biennially between Australia and England but remains at Lord's irrespective of the winner. It was first awarded to the England captain the Hon Ivo Bligh in 1883 when on tour in Australia.

The club, originally at the White Conduit in Islington, moved to Marylebone and altered its name accordingly in 1787 when Thomas Lord leased a site in what is now Dorset Square. In 1811 Lord lifted the sacred turf first to a field, which proved to be in the course of the Regent's Canal, and then to what, by purchase, has become the permanent ground.

The first match MCC played at the original Lord's ground (Dorset Fields) was against Essex on 1 June 1787. The present ground was inaugurated with a match against Herts on 22 June 1814. The first test matches at Lord's were played in 1884. The main gates were erected in memory of **Dr WG Grace** (d 1915) in 1923; Father Time, removing the bails, was placed on the grandstand in 1926.

The much acclaimed **Mound Stand** combines various building techniques: the ground level 1898 brick stand designed by the Verity brothers is preserved below decks of cantilevered steel-framed units (1985/6) sheltered by a marquee-like PVC-coated roof (1986/7). In accordance with MCC stipulations, the architect Michael Hopkins has differentiated public terraces from privately sponsored corporate boxes (including one reserved for Paul Getty Junior who funded half the project) and an upper promenade section exclusively for club members and debenture ticket holders. The futuristic design of the Media Centre (1999), an elliptical aluminium structure, breaks new ground.

Just around the corner from Lord's and up Grove End Road beyond the junction with **Abbey Road** is the particular zebra crossing immortalised by the Beatles album called Abbey Road and recorded at the EMI studios nearby. Nostalgic fans continue to come here to read the penned inscriptions and graffiti.

LITTLE VENICE

Bloomfield Rd west of Edgware Rd. For access see Location above.

The attractive triangular canal basin, shaded by weeping willows and overlooked by Georgian houses, modern flats and the Canal Office (formerly a toll house) is known as Little Venice, for obvious reasons. *For canal cruises and the Waterbus service see PRACTICAL POINTS.*

In 1795 a Cornishman, William Praed, began the canal which was to link the Grand Junction Canal (from Brentford to Uxbridge) to Paddington. By 1801 it was in use carrying produce from the market town to London and taking vast numbers of passengers on outings (half-a-crown to Uxbridge).

The **Regent's Canal** *(towpath open 9am to dusk)* was begun in 1812 to provide a link with the Thames. It runs for eight miles/13km from Little Venice to Limehouse docks and the Lea Valley *(see DOCKLANDS)*, passing through Maida Tunnel – where the boat crews legged their barges along lying on their sides or backs and pushing against the tunnel roof with their feet, under Macclesfield Bridge – known as "Blow Up" Bridge after a cargo of gunpowder and petroleum exploded there in 1874 – between the animal houses of London Zoo, through **Camden Lock** lined in former times by wharves and stabling for the barge horses, and on to Islington Tunnel. A flight of 12 locks carries the canal down 86ft/26m to the Thames.

Picturesque houseboats moored on the Regent's Canal at Little Venice

St James's★★

St James's which boasts a royal palace, dignified mansions used as royal residences or for official functions, gentlemen's clubs, specialist shops, and theatres lives up to its reputation as an exclusive address. Wander through the warren of alleyways to discover traditional pubs or join office workers lounging on the grass or in deckchairs for a pause.

Location

Map pp 11-12 (DEXY); Michelin Atlas London: p 61. ⊖ Piccadilly Circus; Green Park; St James's Park. The area is conveniently hemmed in by Piccadilly, Haymarket and the Mall. Trafalgar Square and Leicester Square are also within easy reach. Mayfair and Belgravia are to the west.

Adjacent Sights: PICCADILLY; MAYFAIR; BUCKINGHAM PALACE; TRAFALGAR SQUARE – WHITEHALL; SOHO.

Background

St James's earned its name from a hospital for 'maidens that were leprous' founded, it is thought at the time of the Norman Conquest, and dedicated to St James the Less, Bishop of Jerusalem. The buildings were acquired by **Henry VIII** who subsequently built a palace there. The domain was later given by Charles II at the Restoration to his loyal courtier, Henry Jermyn, later Earl of St Albans, who speedily developed the empty fields into an elegant suburb for members of the re-established court.

The founder of the West End, as he has since been described, laid out his estate around a square from which roads led from the centre of each side (not, as became the custom, from the corners): to the east was a large market bordered by the Haymarket, to the north lay Jermyn Street, the local shopping street, and in the axis of Duke of York Street stood the church. The community was self-contained; within a railed enclosure in the square the fashionable residents could take a promenade.

At the end of the Stuart monarchy, vacated private houses were taken over by the clubs. The latter had originated in taverns and coffee and chocolate houses where men of similar calling or like interest, who enjoyed congenial company, made a practice of meeting regularly. Their gatherings developed into subscription groups with reserved quarters and finally they took over the houses in which they met, employing the owner or publican as manager and enhancing the amenities, particularly the food for which many became famous. In the period of **Beau Brummell** (1778-1840) and the Prince Regent, the clubs were known as the resort of the wealthy and the fashionable and as infamous gambling centres. Numbers grew until by the turn of the 19C-20C there were nearly 200 in the West End; now there are fewer than 30. Their character has also changed from 18C flamboyance, to 19C silence and reserve and now to a modified social function or gaming.

St James's has remained a masculine world of bespoke boot and shoemakers, shirtmakers and hatters, sword, gun and rod makers, antique and 18C picture dealers, wine merchants, cheese vendors, jewellers traditional and modern, fine art auctioneers. Although banking and property companies have invaded St James's Street it is still the address of eight of London's principal clubs, Pall Mall of five.

Walking About

St James's Church★

Open daily. Recitals: Mon, Wed, Fri at 1.10pm. Concerts: Usually Thu-Sat at 7.30pm. Market: Wed-Sat, 10am-6pm (craft market only); Tue, 10am-6pm (antiques also). Lectures, seminars. ☎ 020 7734 4511 Fax 020 7734 7449; www.st-james-piccadilly.org

Wren, the automatic choice of architect in 1676 for the new parish church, built a plain basilica of brick with Portland stone dressings and balustrade and a square tower. Plain glass windows, segmental below and tall and rounded above, line the north and south walls and a tripartite and superimposing Venetian window fills the east end. The original entrance was placed in the south wall looking down Duke of York Street to the square; in the 19C the local emphasis had changed and new entrances were made on both sides of the tower.

The galleried interior is roofed with a barrel vault and entablature, richly decorated with plasterwork, fashioned from mouldings made from bomb damaged fragments. The organ came from the Roman Catholic Whitehall Chapel, donated by Queen Mary, the daughter of James II; its case, surmounted by figures, is original as is the altarpiece of gilded wood with garlands of flowers and fruit, the pelican with her young all carved by **Grinling Gibbons**, and the marble font in the form of a tree of life with Adam and Eve on either side. Several artists including the two Van der Veldes are buried here (plaque in vestibule) in what is the parish church of the Royal Academy. The outdoor pulpit against the north wall dates from 1902.

Directory

Light Bite

Nero – *35 Jermyn St, SW1 6DT – ⊖ Piccadilly Circus – ☎ 020 7437 9419 – www.aroma-cafes.co.uk – Open daily 7am (9am Sat-Sun) to 7.30pm (6.30pm Sun) – ⊠ – £6.* This small café, attached to St James's Church and its craft market, is an ideal place for a quick sandwich, salad or coffee. In good weather, take a seat on the delightful brick-paved terrace.

Caper Green @ ICA Bar and Café – *Carlton House Terrace, The Mall, SW1Y 5AH – ⊖ Piccadilly Circus – ☎ 020 7930 8619 – ica@capergreen.co.uk – £8.* Located on the ground floor of the Institute of Contemporary Arts, this bustling café offers exceptional value. At lunchtime, queue at the servery displaying a tempting selection of carefully prepared seasonal dishes. Bar menu available throughout the evening.

Pubs

Golden Lion – *25 King St, SW1Y 6QY – ⊖ Green Park, Piccadilly Circus – ☎ 020 7925 0007 – Open Mon-Fri 11.30am-11pm, Sat-Sun noon-6pm.* This early 18C pub spread over five floors was the annexe of St James's Theatre before its demolition. It has preserved all of its charm owing to such features as the stunning black marble pillars and the glass and mahogany interior.

The Red Lion – *23 Crown Passage off King St, SW1Y 6PP – ⊖ Green Park – ☎ 020 7930 4141 – Open Mon-Sat 11am-11pm.* Behind a flowery façade, you will discover a small well-kept pub with a Victorian atmosphere replete with mirrors and mahogany panels. Upmarket clientele.

Shopping

Berry Bros & Rudd – *3 St James's St, SW1A 1EG – ⊖ Green Park – ☎ 020 7396 9600 – www.bbr.com – Open Mon-Sat 10am-6pm (4pm Sat).* One of the world's oldest wine merchants, founded 1698, and official suppliers to the Royal Family since 1760. Admire the fine early 18C façade. A wide selection of wines, from old Port to New World vintages.

Hilditch & Key – *73 Jermyn St, SW1Y 6NP – ⊖ Piccadilly Circus – ☎ 020 7930 5336 – nsb@hilditch.co.uk – Open Mon-Sat 9am (10am Sat) to 6pm.* Located in legendary Jermyn Street, a bastion of traditional British male fashion, this is the area's oldest shirt shop. Here you can shop for made-to-measure or ready-to-wear shirts. All items are of exceptional quality and have won the hearts of such figures as Karl Lagerfeld (women's section also).

Jermyn Street – *Jermyn St, SW1.* A street with a distinctly masculine flavour. Shops include bootmakers, saddlers, leather workers, hatters, tailors, shirtmakers, shoemakers, gunsmiths, and pipe and tobacco merchants (Dunhill's at no 50, Davidoff cigars). There is also Grima the jeweller's (no 80), Floris the perfumer's (no 89), established in 1730, and the well-known purveyors of cheese and Scottish products, Paxton and Whitfield (no 93).

John Lobb – *9 St James's St, SW1A 1EF – ⊖ Green Park – ☎ 020 7930 3664 – johnlobb@johnlobbltd.co.uk – Open Mon-Sat 9am-5.30pm(4.30pm Sat).* The crème de la crème in fine shoes. Leather, crocodile, ostrich – in all materials and every colour imaginable. If you opt for made-to-measure, expect to pay a minimum of £1850 and to wait a minimum of six weeks.

Paxton & Whitfield – *93 Jermyn St, SW1Y 6JE – ⊖ Green Park, Piccadilly – ☎ 020 7930 0259 – admin@paxtonandwhitfield.co.uk – Open Mon-Fri 9.30am-6pm, Sat 9am-5.30pm.* This venerable institution has been here since 1797, and sells only the finest cheeses. In particular you will find first-rate Stiltons, farmhouse Cheddars and a good selection of drinks to accompany the cheese (port, wine, champagne).

Music

St James's Church – Recitals: *Mon, Wed, Fri at 1.10pm.* Concerts: *Usually Thur-Sat at 7.30pm.*

Market

St James's Church – *Wed-Sat, 10am-6pm (craft market only); Tue, 10am-6pm (antiques also).*

A wrought-iron pub sign

R. Besse/MICHELIN

Jermyn Street★

The narrow street boasts shirtmakers, pipe makers, antique dealers, antiquarian booksellers, a chemist with real sponges, a provision merchant *(no 93)* selling countless varieties of cheese over a wooden counter, a perfumer *(no 89)* modern jewellery *(no 80)*, restaurants (including Wall's original sausage shop, *no 113*), bars, chambers and the Cavendish, a luxury hotel, on the site of the famous Edwardian rendezvous.

Piccadilly Arcade★

This arcade, bright with bow-fronted shops, links Piccadilly to Jermyn Street.

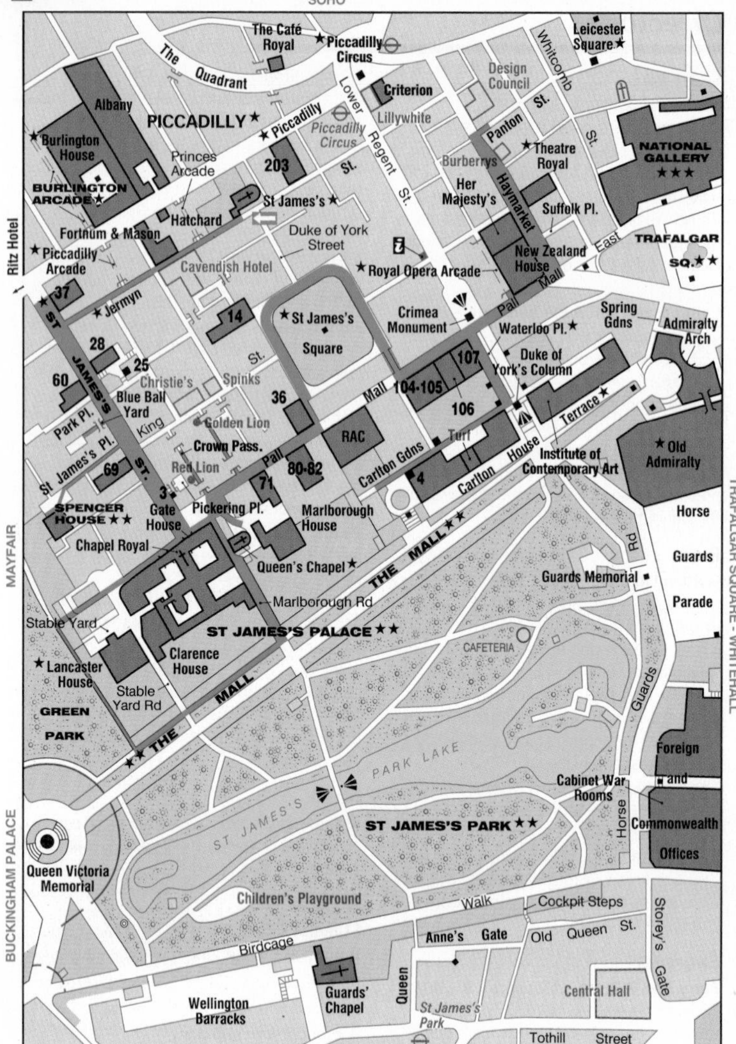

St James's Street★

The wide street, unnamed but clearly marked in early-17C maps as the approach from Piccadilly to St James's Palace, developed as part of the district and by the end of the century was lined on either side by town houses including those of merchants who fled the City after the **Great Plague** and Fire of 1665 and 1666. It retains an atmosphere of quiet elegance with individual shops, restaurants and clubs.

The most famous buildings (from north to south) include: **White's Club** (no **37**) established in 1693 from a coffee house of the same name. This club, the oldest and Tory in character, occupies a house of 1788 to which the famous bow window was added in 1811. The façade was renewed in 1852. **Boodle's Club** (no **28**) dates from 1762 and the building from 1765. Between identical porches is a bay window (1821) below a rounded Venetian style window. **The Economist** (no **25**) complex consists of three canted glass towers around a courtyard (1966-68) and provides the periodical with editorial offices as well as a space for exhibitions of contemporary art.

Brooks's Club (no **60** – *opposite The Economist*) was founded as the rival Whig club to White's in 1764 by the politician Charles James Fox and the Duke of Portland. The club occupies a house built of yellow brick and stone designed by **Henry Holland,** Robert Adam's rival, in 1778 in which year it took over the famous Almack's of Pall Mall.

Park Place

The narrow street is almost filled with the buildings and annexes of the **Royal Overseas League** (f 1910; 50 000 members). No 14 was formerly Pratt's Club.

Blue Ball Yard

The far end of the gaslit yard is lined by stables of 1742, now garages, but still with round niches in the walls where iron hay baskets once hung. Above are the old tiled cottage quarters and, in the corner, the Stafford Hotel.

St James's Place

The L shaped street is lined by 18C houses, some with decorative fanlights and continuous iron balconies. Castlemaine House (1959-60), a block of flats, strongly horizontal in line, was designed by **Denys Lasdun**. The Royal Ocean Racing Club *(no 20 – around the corner)* is a neat Georgian town house. At the far end is Spencer House *(no 27, description in Worth a Visit)*.

Return to St James's St and walk down.

The **Carlton Club** *(***no 69** *St James's St)*, which originated as 'Arthur's', was formed in 1832 by the Duke of Wellington. It is now in an early-19C Palladian stone building which incorporates rooms once part of White's Chocolate and Gaming House. No **74**, formerly the Conservative Club, was designed by **George Basevi** and **Sydney Smirke** in the mid 19C, in modified Palladian style including a canted bay window.

The Constitutional Club (1883), the Savage (1857), the National and the Flyfishers were formerly located at no 86 in a magnificent Victorian golden ochre stone building (1862).

On the opposite side of the street stands **Byron House** *(nos 7-9)*, built in the 1960s on the site of the house in which Byron awoke to find himself famous after the publication of his *Childe Harold* (1811). Long-established businesses in the vicinity include **Lobb's** the bespoke bootmaker *(no 9)*; **Lock's** the firm of hatters *(no 6)* since 1700 – the topper in the window is 19C and **Berry Bros & Rudd** (no **3**, the wine merchants 'established in the XVII century'. The half timbered passage beside the shop (note the wall plaque recording the stay of the Republic of Texas legation in an upstairs room 1842-45) leads to **Pickering Place,** a gaslit court of 18C houses, reputed to be the site of the last duel to be fought in London.

At the south end, echoing the corner opposite, are two buildings by **Norman Shaw** in terracotta brick and stone, with asymmetric gables, friezes and an angle tower.

A Traditional Establishment

Pickering's, later known as **Berry Brothers & Rudd Ltd,** has occupied this site, identified as Henry VIII's tennis court, since 1731. The sign of the coffee-mill hanging outside no 3 was put there by the Widow Bourne to mark her grocer's shop (1690s). As the shop was handed down through the generations, business, which had included 'arms painting and heraldic furnishings', moved into spices, smoking tobacco, snuff, fine teas and coffee, maybe claret and port, to become one of the best and most comprehensive grocer's of the day, judiciously placed for the 18C Beau Monde by St James's Palace. The variously fashionable commodities were carefully weighed from the great brass weighing beams, as were the more notable customers: indeed, a Register of Weights has been kept since 1765. The last remaining stocks of groceries were sold in 1896. The original dark panelling, oval table and Windsor chairs all date from the 18C.

St James's Palace**

In 1532 the 'goodly manor' built by **Henry VIII** was converted into a crenellated and turreted palace entered through the **Gate House** at the bottom of St James's Street, even then a regular thoroughfare. The original and early palace buildings, considerably more extensive before the fire of 1809 which destroyed the east wing, are of the traditional 16C Tudor red brick with a diaper pattern and stone trim along the line of the crenellations. With later additions they now surround only four courts: Colour, Friary, Ambassadors' and Engine which are lit at night by crowned wall standards.

Ph. Craven/PITKIN

A sentry stands guard outside the Tudor Gate House of St James's Palace

St James's Palace was the last royal palace to be built as such in the capital. Many kings and queens have been born or died in the palace. **Charles I** spent his last night in the guardroom, before walking across the park to his execution at the Banqueting House on 30 January 1649. After Whitehall Palace had burned down in 1698, St James's became the chief royal residence and, although no longer so, it remains the statutory seat – proclamations are made from the balcony in Friary Court and ambassadors are accredited to the Court of St James. The interior of the palace bears the imprint of successive architects and designers: **Wren**, **Grinling Gibbons**, **Hawksmoor**, **Kent** and **William Morris**. The splendid State Apartments are hung with full length portraits of Stuart and Hanoverian monarchs. Today the palace serves as the official residence of the Duke and Duchess of Kent and Princess Alexandra.

Chapel Royal – *Ambassadors Court. Open for services early-Oct to Good Fri, Sun at 8.30am (Holy Communion) and 11.15am (Choral Eucharist/Mattins); also Saints' Days for Evensong. ☎ 020 7839 1377*

The huge Tudor Gothic window, visible from the exterior to the right of the palace gateway, lights the Chapel Royal and its so-called Holbein ceiling. The choir is famous for its long tradition since the medieval period and the choristers wear scarlet and gold state coats at services. Besides several royal marriages conducted here including that of Queen Victoria to Prince Albert (1840), was the wedding of **Sir Christopher Wren** to his second wife Jane Fitzwilliam (1676).

For security reasons, access to this area is severely restricted.

Clarence House – *Stable Yard.* The distinctive white stucco mansion – the former home of Queen Elizabeth, the Queen Mother, and now the residence of the Prince of Wales – was built in 1825 by John Nash for the Duke of Clarence, the future William IV. It is best seen from the Mall. ♿ *Guided tours early-Aug to mid-Oct, 9am-7pm (6pm last admission). Timed ticket and advance booking only. £5. ☎ 020 7766 7303; www.royal.gov.uk*

Lancaster House

Stable Yard. The golden Bath stone mansion, designed by Benjamin Wyatt in 1825 for the Duke of York, who died in 1827, then became the town house of the Marquesses of Stafford and the Dukes of Sutherland. For many years in the 19C it was the setting for balls and soirées; today it maintains that function as the Government's hospitality centre. Inside reigns an opulent Baroque magnificence – painted plaster ceilings, vast pictures, gilding and chandeliers deck the state apartments.

DIANA, PRINCESS OF WALES (1961-97)

Following the tragic death of Diana, Princess of Wales in a car accident in Paris, her body was brought to the Chapel Royal, St James's Palace. On Friday 5 September the coffin was transferred to her private apartments at Kensington Palace before being carried in procession through Hyde Park, down Constitution Hill, along The Mall, through Horse Guards and Whitehall to Westminster Abbey for the funeral service, and thereafter north by road to her final resting place in Althorp Park, the Spencer family seat.

Green Park

The acres now known as Green Park were added to St James's Park in 1667 by Charles II, who in the early morning would regularly walk up a path to what is now Hyde Park Corner – hence '**Constitution Hill**'. From the east side of the park there is a fine view of Spencer House.

Follow left towards the Mall for a good view of Buckingham Palace, and continue round to Marlborough Road.

On the corner overlooking the Mall note the life-like relief by Reid-Dick of Queen Mary, consort of George V, and the gaslight lanterns crested with gilded crowns.

Queen's Chapel★

Past a large Art Nouveau bronze group in memory of Queen Alexandra (1926) is the entrance to the Queen's Chapel, intended for the Infanta Maria of Spain but completed for Charles I's eventual queen, **Henrietta Maria**, in 1625 by **Inigo Jones**. It was the first church in England to be designed completely outside the Perpendicular Gothic tradition. As a Roman Catholic foundation it was at first served by a friary of Capuchins and originally formed part of the palace; the road separating it from Friary Court dates from 1809.

The pedimented exterior of rendered cement with Portland stone dressings has three principal windows at the west end, of which the central one is arched above the unobtrusive, straight-headed door; at the east end is a broad Venetian window. The curved white coffered ceiling, framed by a richly detailed cornice, is picked out in gold above the chancel. The greyish-green walls are the original colour, the royal and other galleries, lower panelling, stalls and lectern are mid 17C; the organ loft is by Grinling Gibbons. The beauty of the small edifice lies in its perfect proportions (a double cube) and the simplicity of the interior decoration.

Turn right into Pall Mall.

Marlborough House

While John Churchill, **Duke of Marlborough**, was winning the final victories in the seemingly endless War of the Spanish Succession (Blenheim 1704, Ramillies 1706, Oudenaarde 1708) and the Duchess was appointed one of the Ladies of the

Bedchamber to Queen Anne and supervising the construction by Vanbrugh of Blenheim Palace (1705-24), Wren, in two years (1709-11), designed and completed Marlborough House. It was altered in 1771 by **William Chambers** and enlarged in the 19C.

Pall Mall

The ancient way from the City to St James's Palace is named after an avenue planted to its north which served as an alley for the game brought over from France early in the 17C and much favoured by the Stuarts. When St James's was developed, the avenue was cut down, the road lined with houses and renamed after the old alley.

Crown Passage *(opposite Marlborough House, under 59-60)* is a narrow alley leading past the 19C **Red Lion** pub *(see Directory)* and the back entrances to Locks' the hatters. The far end opens out into King Street where the two world-famous establishments have their headquarters *(see PRACTICAL POINTS)*: **Christie's** *(no 8)*, fine art auctioneers, founded in 1766 at the height of the fashion for doing the Grand Tour, and Spinks *(no 5)*, specialists in coins, medals and orders, as well as antiques of all kinds.

Angel Court leads back past the **Golden Lion** *(see Directory)*, a Victorian pub, gleaming with cut mirror glass and mahogany, to Pall Mall.

The **Oxford and Cambridge Club** (no **71**) was founded in 1830 by Lord Palmerston at the British Coffee-house in Cockspur Street.

The dark red brick exterior of **Schomberg House** (no **80-82**) dates from 1698; Nell Gwynne lived next door (no **79**), still the only freehold property on the south side of the street.

The **Army and Navy Club** (no **36**, founded 1839) was rebuilt in 1963 – not to be confused with the Naval and Military in St James's Square.

The **RAC** (Royal Automobile Club) is a vast building (1911) constructed by the builders of the Ritz.

Walk up the west side of St James's Square and round clockwise.

St James's Square★

The square, with a Classical equestrian statue of William III (1807) beneath very tall plane trees, is encircled by modern offices and 19C residences except on the north and west sides where there are still Georgian town houses. Of them the most notable are no 4 of 1676, remodelled in 1725 – Ionic porch, rich cornice and continuous iron balcony – and now the home of the Naval and **Military Club**; no 5 of 1748-51 with 18C and 19C additions; no 13 of 1740 with faked mortar uprights to give an all-header effect to the blackened brick wall; no 15, **Lichfield House**, of 1764-65 **James 'Athenian' Stuart**'s perfect Classical stone façade with its continuous iron balcony; fluted columns mark the doorway and embrace the upper floors beneath a pediment (the first house on the site was built in 1673 and occupied by Frances, Duchess of Richmond, a famed beauty in her day known as 'La Belle Stewart' who modelled as the Britannia featured on the old penny coin); and no 20 built by Adam in 1775 with no 21 its 20C mirror image. No 32 was the town residence of the Bishops of London from 1771 to 1919. No 31, Norfolk House, where George III was born, served as General Eisenhower's headquarters in 1942 and 1944.

No 14 (of 1896) is the **London Library**, no 12 with a stucco front and Tuscan pillared porch is possibly by Cubitt (1836) and nos 9-10, Chatham House, the Royal Institute of International Affairs (f 1920). The houses date from 1736 and no 10, in its time, has been residence of three Prime Ministers: William Pitt 1757-61, Edward Stanley 1837-54 and William Ewart Gladstone, 1890.

Return to Pall Mall and continue east.

The **Reform Club** (nos **104-105**), which was established in opposition to the Carlton by Whig supporters at the time of the Reform Bill in 1832, is housed in a 19C Italian palazzo building, on the renumbered site of the house where **John Julius Angerstein** lived.

The **Travellers' Club** (no **106**), also an Italian palazzo building (19C), was founded in 1819 with a rule that members must have travelled a minimum of 500 miles (now 1 000) outside the British Isles in a straight line from London.

Waterloo Place★

Pall Mall is intersected by Waterloo Place designed by John Nash as a broad approach to Carlton House, the southern end of his grand route linking the royal residence to Regent's Park; it lost its climax when the house was demolished in 1829 but gained a vista across St James's Park *(see BUCKINGHAM PALACE)*. In the northern half stands the **Crimea Monument**. The beginning of the southern half is marked by two clubs, planned by Nash, which face each other across the place. The **Athenaeum** (no **107**), designed by Decimus Burton, is a square stucco block (1829-30) with Classical touches: torches, Roman Doric pillars supporting the porch, the gilded figure of Pallas Athene and the important Classical frieze in deference to the membership of the club which was founded as a meeting place for artists, men of letters and connoisseurs.

Carlton Gardens is a small grass plot shaded by plane trees and surrounded by four grand houses. Kitchener lived at no 2 and Palmerston at no 4 (demolished and rebuilt in 1933): between 1940 and 1945 it served as the headquarters of the Free French

The Classical Façade of the Athenaeum in Waterloo Place

Forces. A tablet is inscribed with **General de Gaulle**'s famous call to arms to the French people broadcast on 18 June 1940. The statue (1993) of the general is by Angela Conner.

At the west end of the Carlton House terrace overlooking the Mall is a slim bronze statue of **George VI** by William McMillan.

Carlton House Terrace*

In 1732 Frederick, Prince of Wales purchased **Carlton House** (1709) which stood on the south side of Pall Mall backing on to St James's Park. The house had been refaced in stone when it was taken over in 1772 by the Prince Regent, who commissioned Henry Holland to make further alterations. At a cost of £800 000, it was transformed into the most gorgeous mansion in the land. In 1825, however, five years after his accession to the throne, **George IV** grew tired of the house and transferred his attention to Buckingham Palace.

Carlton House was demolished in 1829 and the government commissioned Nash, who had just completed the development of Regent's Park, to design similar terraces for St James's Park; only two were built.

The entrances, on the north side, have porches, sometimes in pairs, flanked by Tuscan or Ionic pillars and capped by balconies; Lord Curzon once lived at no 1. Between the two terraces, at the top of the steps leading down to the Mall is the **Duke of York's Column**, a pink granite column just tall enough, according to his contemporaries to place the Duke out of reach of his creditors; this is the same 'Grand Old Duke of York, who had ten thousand men; he marched them up to the top of the hill and marched them down again'.

The south side of the terrace, facing onto St James's Park is more majestic: each block is 31 bays wide with central pediments and angle pavilions, giant Corinthian columns and balconies, resting on squat, white-painted fluted cast-iron columns.

Turn back up Waterloo Place on the east side to Pall Mall past the Duke of Wellington's mounting block.

At no 116 stands a building of similar size and style to the Athenaeum opposite, designed by Nash but remodelled by Burton in 1842; formerly the United Services Club, it now houses the Institute of Directors.

Cross Pall Mall.

Royal Opera Arcade*

The delightful row of bow-fronted shops was designed by **Nash** and **Repton** in 1817 as one of three arcades surrounding the then Royal Opera House to harmonise with other buildings opposite in the Haymarket and Suffolk Place. It presently accommodates a number of branches of Farlow's who specialise in equipment for hunting, fishing, shooting and other country pursuits.

New Zealand House

Haymarket. Since 1963, the 15-storey tower above a 4 storey podium, 225ft/68m in all, has stood sentinel at the bottom of the street. It is glazed overall, banded in stone, recessed at ground level to provide a canopy.

The bronze statue of George III on horseback in Cockspur Street completes the scene – the future king was born in St James's Square.

Walk up Haymarket.

Haymarket is named for its market which in the 17C supplied the Royal Mews on what is now Trafalgar Square.

Her Majesty's (The King's)

On the corner of Charles II Street, is the fourth theatre on the site, a Victorian, French pavilioned, building with an ornate but efficient interior plan, constructed by Beerbohm Tree as his own theatre in 1895-97. Originally home to the Italian Opera in London, the theatre now stages major musicals.

Theatre Royal, Haymarket*

When **John Nash** designed the theatre in 1821 with a great pedimented portico, he resited it to stand, unlike its predecessor of 1720, in the axis of Charles II Street and so enjoy a double aspect. The interior (remodelled) is most elegantly decorated in deep blue, gold and white.

Panton Street recalls Colonel Panton, a notorious card-player and gambler, who of an evening in 1664 won enough money to purchase "a parcel of ground at Piccadilly."

Worth a Visit

Spencer House**

♿ *Guided tour (1hr) Sun (except Jan and Aug), 10.30am-4.45pm every 20min. £6. Children must be accompanied by an adult; no child under 10yrs. Guided tour (7 languages) by arrangement. No photography. No smoking. ☎ 020 7499 8620 (for recorded information); Fax 020 7409 2952; www.spencerhouse.co.uk*

Spencer House is, today, the city's only great 18C aristocratic town house to survive intact. The house was built in 1756-66 for John, 1st Earl Spencer who initially employed the Palladian architect John Vardy; the external elevation and ground floor rooms reflect the Palladian style. In 1758 Vardy was replaced by James "Athenian" Stuart who was responsible for the accurate Greek detail of the interior decoration (first floor rooms); the house is one of the pioneer examples of the Neoclassical style. The 2nd Earl, who succeeded in 1783, invited Henry Holland, son-in-law of 'Capability' Brown, to make various changes to the ground floor.

In 1942 the house was stripped of original fixtures with chimney-pieces, panelling, mouldings and architraves being removed to Althorp – providentially as it turned out for the house suffered some war damage. Spencer House has now regained the full splendour of its late 18C appearance after a ten-year programme of restoration. It is now partly used as offices and as a place where entertainments can be held in the historic setting of the eight State Rooms complemented by a magnificent collection of paintings and furniture: *(ground floor)* Morning Room or Ante Room; Library; Dining Room; the Palm Room, designed by Vardy with carved and gilded palm trees framing the alcove; and *(first floor)* the Music Room, Lady Spencer's Room, the Great Room and the Painted Room decorated in Stuart's Greek style. An excellent illustrated brochure provides more information.

St Pancras – Camden Town

On the edge of Bloomsbury, St Pancras which is a rail hub with three major stations serving the Midlands and the North of Britain, has been given a boost by the siting of the British Library in Somers Town and by the long-term plan to make King's Cross the terminus for Eurostar. The tourist infrastructure is improving with the opening of moderately priced hotels, a trendy club scene and some interesting small museums. Camden Town with its markets, clubs, restaurants and Irish pubs and its Bohemian atmosphere is enormously popular, especially at weekends

Location

Map p 12 (EV); Michelin Atlas London: pp 93-94. ⊖ King's Cross-St Pancras. St Pancras is north of Bloomsbury and Euston Road is a major thoroughfare busy with traffic. Camden Town – ⊖ *Camden Town* – to the north of St Pancras is also well served by buses and accessible from Regent's Park.
Adjacent Sights: BLOOMSBURY; REGENT'S PARK.

Background

The area contains three of London's six mainline railway terminals situated as near the city centre as was permitted in the 19C. To the east stands **King's Cross** (1852), the Great Northern terminus, built by Lewis Cubitt; the clock in the tower was displayed at the 1851 Exhibition *(see SOUTH KENSINGTON)*; the front is largely masked by an advanced single-storey hall providing covered access to the platforms at the rear. **St Pancras** (1864), the Midland terminus, medieval Gothic in brick with Italian terracotta, was designed by Sir George Gilbert Scott. **Euston** (1837), the London and North Western terminus, was rebuilt in 1968; exposed plain black piers support glass panels; the interior is recessed west of the centre to provide a colonnade; a statue of Robert Stephenson, chief engineer of the London Birmingham line (1838) stands in the forecourt.

Pinnacles, turrets and gables of the ornate Victorian building at St Pancras Station

R. Garrat Design

Directory

Pub

The Camden Brewing Company – *1 Randolph St, Camden, NW1 0SS – ⊖ Camden – ☎ 020 7267 9829 – Open daily noon-11pm (midnight Sat).* Formerly the Camden Arms, this friendly pub, slightly off the beaten track, has undergone a nice renovation. Its cherry red and white façade, large sofas and open fire in winter make it a good stopping point during your visit to Camden.

Markets

Camden Market – *Corner of Camden High St and Buck St. Open Thur-Sun, 9am-5.30pm.See PRACTICAL POINTS – Shopping).*

Camden Lock Market – *Chalk Farm Rd. Open Sat-Sun, 10am-6pm; indoor stalls Tue-Sun, 10am-6pm .*

Stables Antique Market – *off Chalk Farm Rd. Open Sat-Sun, 8am-6pm. See PRACTICAL POINTS – Shopping)*

Worth a Visit

ST PANCRAS

British Library

96 Euston Road. ♿ *Exhibition Galleries: Open Mon-Sat, 9.30am-6pm (8pm Tue; 5pm Sat), Sun, 11am-5pm. Reading rooms: Open only to readers with a Readers Pass.* ☎ *020 7412 7332 (Visitor Services); visitor-services@bl.uk; www.bl.uk*

Eight years behind schedule and three times over budget, the new red-brick premises have earned few compliments, described by the Prince of Wales as "a dim collection of sheds groping for some symbolic significance." In the forecourt stands a powerful statue of Sir Isaac Newton by the British sculptor Eduardo Paolozzi.

In contrast the entrance hall in light Portland stone rises the full height of the building and the eye is drawn to the stacks of the King George III Library. The reading rooms which boast computerised catalogues are quiet havens. Three exhibition galleries present the library's treasures – advanced technology enables visitors to turn the pages of rare books at the touch of a finger; the story of book production from the Middle Ages to the present time and temporary exhibitions on related themes.

The British Library collections include rare manuscripts, Books of Hours, examples of early printing (Caxton and Wynkyn de Worde's books), famous works (Lindisfarne Gospel, Codex Sinaiticus, Gutenberg Bible), handmade books, children's books, postage stamps, George III's library, Henry Davis' Gift (fine bindings). Among the broad range of historical documents (early maps, musical scores, modern calligraphy) are copies of the Magna Carta, Essex's death warrant, Nelson's last letter, Shakespeare's signature and first folio (1623). The core collection is stored on site while books less in demand are kept at different locations.

The new precincts now also accommodate the **National Sound Archive** for discs and tape recordings of music, oral history, documentary material, spoken literature, language and dialect.

St Pancras Parish Church

Upper Woburn Place, Euston Road. Open Sun, 7.45-11.30am and 5-7pm, Mon-Fri 9am-2pm and 3-5pm, Sat, 9am-11am. Brochure (6 languages). Concert: Thur at 1.15pm; no charge. ☎ *020 7388 1461; st.pancras@lineone.net; www.stpancraschurch.org*

The church was built in 1819-22 at the time of the Greek Revival and William Inwood's design, selected from 30 submitted in response to an advertisement, echoes the Erechtheon on the Acropolis in Athens in the caryatids supporting the roofs of the square vestries, north and south. The columned two-stage elevation of the octagonal steeple and front Classical colonnade are modelled on the Tower of the Winds in Athens. Too tall to fit, the caryatid figures had to have their trunks shortened – hence their air of malaise.

Camley Street Natural Park

Camley St. Overlooked by the Victorian gas-holders at King's Cross, a wildlife haven has been created in a 2 acre park on the banks of the Regent's Canal including ponds, a marsh and reed beds with the aim of attracting insects, butterflies, birds and wildfowl.

London Canal Museum

12-13 New Wharf Road. (♿) Open Tue-Sun and Bank Hol Mon, 10am-4.30pm (3.45pm last admission). Closed 24-26 Dec. £2.50. ☎ *020 7713 0836; Fax 020 7689 6679; info@canalmuseum.org.uk; www.canalmuseum.org.uk; www.canalmuseum.org.uk/wap /index.wml*

The museum is housed in an old ice house beside the Battlebridge basin on the Regent's Canal which once supplied Carlo Gatti, Victorian London's leading ice-cream maker with natural ice from Norway. An old film, *Barging through London*, illustrates canal life in 1924. The display records the building of canals in England, the construction of the Regent's Canal, the various methods of towing or propelling the barges (horsepower, legging, poling, steam tug, towpath tractors), 20C decline and conversion to leisure use: towpath walk (1970); boating, canoeing, fishing.

CAMDEN TOWN

From the tube station walk up Chalk Farm Rd past the markets (see PRACTICAL POINTS, Shopping).

In spite of appearances, Camden Town, which is on the edge of Regent's Park and near Primrose Hill with its delightful village atmosphere and vast green expanses as well as on the way to leafy Hampstead, has pockets of large, elegant houses which are in great demand by artists, writers, actors and media people.

In stark contrast to the local terraced houses, the Post-Modernist **TV-AM building**, in Hawley Crescent *(near Camden Lock)*, designed by T Farrell, is of some interest. From Camden Lock it is possible to board a boat for a sedate trip upstream to the Zoo and Little Venice or downstream to Limehouse.

Roundhouse

Chalk Farm. Ambitious plans to turn the 1840s former locomotive shed, a listed building, into television, radio and recording studios and to create large and small theatre spaces, a glass-covered restaurant and landscaped garden are in hand. In the meantime successful shows draw the crowds.

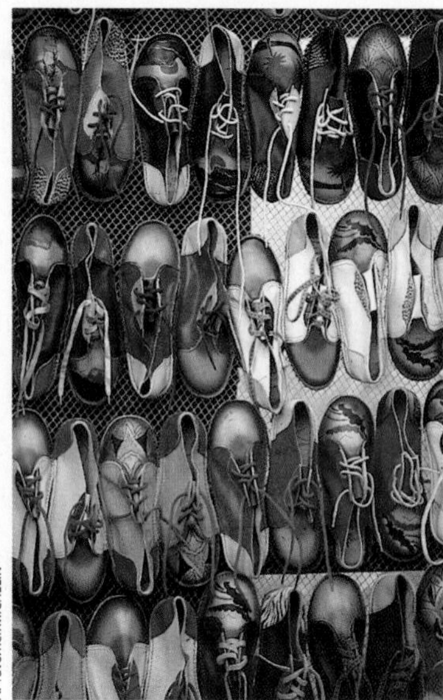

Footwear from Camden Lock Market

Camden Lock Market

Facing onto the canal, the former timber wharf was renovated in the late 1980s and offered at low rents to young artisans for use as workshops. At weekends, endless ethnic food stalls open up to cater to the crowds of browsers.
The **Regent's Canal Information Centre** presents historical displays relating to the canal development.

Stables Market

The Stables, as their name suggests were built in the 1840s to accommodate the horses that hauled the barges along the Regent's canal. The present buildings put up in the 1950s provide spacious premises for a large market *(see Directory)* for dealers in collectables (Art Deco artefacts, 1950s and 1960s clothing, period fixtures and fittings) and antiques. Outside, the cobbled yard has more stalls and dealers.

Jewish Museum

129/131 Albert Street, near Parkway, Camden Town. ♿ Open Sun-Thr, 10am-4pm (5pm Sun). Closed Fri-Sat, Jewish Festivals, Bank Hols. £3.50. ☎ 020 7284 1997; Fax 020 7267 9008; admin@jmus.org.uk; www.jewishmuseum.org.uk

The museum at Raymond Burton House provides an introduction to the history of London's Jewish community with coins, silver and artefacts. Portraits (17C-19C) record the faces of successful individuals while painted porcelain figures (Bow, Minton, Derby and Rockingham) illustrate the more familiar sight and character of the rag trader. The Alfred Rubens Ceremonial Art Gallery *(upstairs)* displays a fabulous collection of ritual objects including a 16C Venetian Ark of the Law, Torah scroll holders of beaten silver and mantles of embroidered silk; exquisitely crafted silver receptacles from the Continent. Prayer books and intricately painted parchment marriage contracts emphasise the importance of ceremony and devotional tradition in Jewish culture.

St Paul's Cathedral★★★

The imposing dome of St Paul's dominating the skyline is one of the enduring sights of London. The grandeur of the edifice combined with the harmonious proportions and spaciousness inspires a sense of wonder. There are many surprises in store: discover the Whispering Gallery and its amazing acoustics; climb up to the dome for a close-up view of the frescoes and for wonderful perspectives of the interior as well as for bird's-eye views of the city; explore the crypt with its remarkable monuments to famous men and women; pause for refreshment in the café and restaurant.

Location

Map pp 11-12 (FX) and area map under The CITY; Michelin Atlas London: p 81. ⊖ St Paul's. For the sights outside the immediate vicinity, turn to the section entitled The CITY.
St Paul's in the City of London is a focal point from which to explore the environs; the Barbican and the Tower of London are within easy access and it is a short walk to the south bank over the Millennium Bridge or Blackfriars Bridge.
Adjacent Sights: The CITY; STRAND – TEMPLE; TOWER OF LONDON.

Background

St Paul's Cathedral is the mother-church of the Diocese of London which embraces some 500 parishes north of the Thames. It was here on 19 July 1981, that the marriage of HRH Prince Charles to Lady Diana Spencer was celebrated with pomp and glory. Ever since the dome of St Paul's first rose out of the ashes of the Great Fire (1666) among a host of elegant church spires it came to be a talisman for Londoners. In December 1940 when the whole City and docks were set ablaze, the dome soared above the smoke and flames, a symbol of hope appearing each morning serene against the pale dawn sky (specific orders for its protection were given by Churchill).

After nearly three centuries this glorious dome has lost none of its majesty although it is now surrounded by towering office blocks.

Old St Paul's – The present cathedral of St Paul is probably the fifth or even the sixth to stand on the site. Records document a church founded here in AD 604. A second edifice may have been built under the aegis of St Erkenwald, Bishop of London (675-685); it or its successor was burnt down by the Danes in 962. A subsequent building was then devastated by fire in 1087.

The next cathedral was planned on a grand scale with a nave of 12 bays, far-flung transepts and a shallow, apsed chancel; in 1221 the massive tower above the central crossing was embellished with a lead-covered 514ft/156m steeple (in 1561 this was struck by lightning and caught fire – despite the evidence of some contemporary engravings, it was never replaced); work lasted until 1240. In 1258-1314 the chancel was replaced by a longer decorated choir so that the building measured 620ft/189m from east to west.

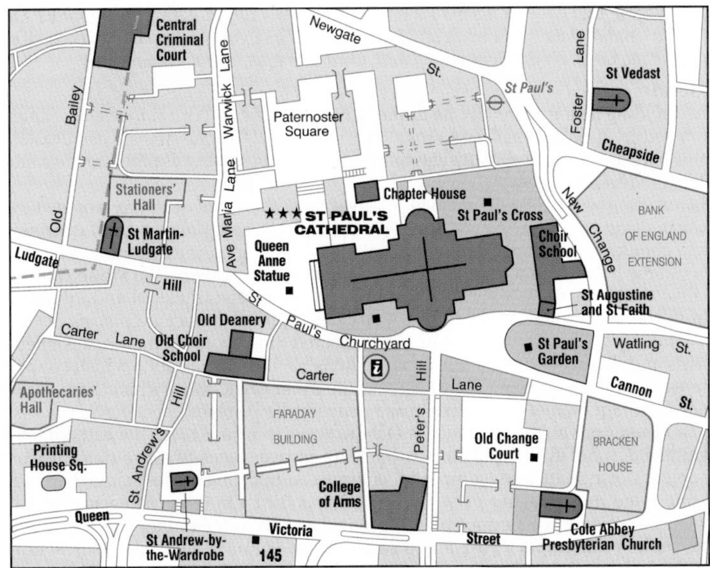

During the 14C the building was allowed to suffer neglect and even desecration: the west towers were used as prisons, relics and shrines were looted, according to a Bishop of Durham of the time "the south aisle" was used "for popery and usury and the north for Simony, and the horse fair in the midst for all kinds of bargains, meetings, brawlings, murders, conspiracies and the font for ordinary payments of money".

Royal commissions under the first two Stuarts on the "decayed fabric" resulted in repairs to the choir screen, the refacing of the nave and west transept walls and in the addition at the west end of an outstanding Classical portico with columns (50ft/15m high) designed by **Inigo Jones**.

The Civil War brought, in Carlyle's words, "horses stamping in the canons' stalls" and mean shops squatting in the portico. A new commission (1663) was selected and included **Christopher Wren**, then 31 and untried as an architect though reputed as a geometer, astronomer and Fellow of the Royal Society (FRS). On 27 August 1666 his fellow commissioner John Evelyn noted in his diary: "I went to St Paul's church with Dr Wren... to survey the general decays of that ancient and venerable church;... we had a mind to build it with a noble cupola." Ten days later, the Great Fire was over, he wrote "St Paul's is now a sad ruin and that beautiful portico now rent in pieces..."

Facts and Figures

The cost of the cathedral, recorded as £736 752 3s 3 1/4d, was met, together with the cost of rebuilding the City churches, by a tax levied on all sea coal imported into the Port of London. Wren was paid £200 a year during the construction of the cathedral.

The cathedral's overall length is 500ft/152m; height to the summit of the cross 365ft/111m; height of the portico columns 40ft/12m; height of the statue on the apex of the pediment 12ft/3.7m; length of the nave 180ft/55m, width of the nave, including the aisles, 121ft/37m; width across the transept 242ft/74m; internal diameter of the dome 110ft/33.5m; height of the nave 92 1/2ft/28m; height to the Whispering Gallery 100ft/30.5m; height to the apex of the internal dome 218ft/66.5m; total surface area approximately 78 000 sq ft/7 200sq m.

Wren's Cathedral – Within six days of the end of the Fire, Wren had submitted a plan for rebuilding the City; it was not accepted. For two years the authorities dallied with the idea, opposed by Wren, of patching up the cathedral fabric. At last in 1668 they invited him to submit designs for a new building; he produced the First Model, the Great Model and the Warrant Design but each, in turn, was rejected by the church authorities. Having been appointed Surveyor General to the King's Works in 1669, Wren resolved to submit no more plans but to go ahead "as ordered by his Majesty".

The foundation stone was laid without ceremony on 21 June 1675. In 1708, after 32 years of unceasing work, Wren saw the final stone, the topmost in the lantern, set in place by his son; Wren was 75. 15 years later (1723) he died and was buried within the cathedral walls.

Café and Restaurant in the Crypt

Take a short break or enjoy a fine meal in this unusual venue. Fresh pastries and good fare at reasonable prices.

Highlights

♿ *Open for visitors Mon-Sat, 8.30am-4pm (last admission); Sun for services only. Galleries: 9.30am-4pm, £6. Guided tours (90-120min) at 11.30am, 1.30pm, 2pm. Organ recitals: Sun, at 5pm. Audio guide (6 languages). Leaflets (9 languages). Guide book (6 languages).* ☎ *020 7246 8348; chapterhouse@stpaulscathedral.org.uk; www.stpauls.co.uk*

Exterior

The building is dominated by its **dome**, which rises from a drum to a stone lantern crowned by a golden ball and cross. The lantern, 21ft/6.5m across, has detached columns projecting on all four sides and a small cupola serving as plinth to the golden ball (6 1/2ft/2m diameter).

The exterior of the drum is divided into two tiers; the lower storey is crowned by a balustrade and encircled by columns which are punctuated (for structural reasons) at eight points by a radiating wall containing a decorative niche; the upper tier is recessed behind the balustrade so as to provide a circular viewing gallery, the **Stone Gallery**.

Unlike the dome of St Peter's Basilica in Rome which so fascinated and influenced Wren, the dome of St Paul's is not a true hemisphere. In fact it consists of three structures *(see illustration)*: the outer lead-covered timber superstructure designed to satisfy purely esthetic considerations, an invisible inner brick cone which supports the weight of the lantern (850 tons); and the inner brick dome which opens at the apex (20ft/6m diameter) into the space beneath the lantern.

At the **west end**, beyond a statue of Queen Anne, in whose reign the cathedral was completed, a broad flight of steps sweeps up in two stages to a two-tier portico of coupled Corinthian and composite columns supporting a decorated pediment surmounted by the figure of St Paul by Francis Bird. On either side rise the west towers, Wren's most Baroque spires, designed as foils to the dome.

The shallow **transepts** terminate in semicircular, columned porticoes surmounted by triangular pediments crowned by statues.

The double portico and twin towers of St Paul's Cathedral

The **north and south sides and the east end** are enclosed within a two-storey wall articulated by coupled pilasters against the rusticated stone. The lower storey beneath the cornice frieze is pierced by round-headed windows with segmental hoods, garlanded and decorated with cherubs. The upper storey (111ft/34m) is punctuated by blind windows, designed as niches; except at the east end and the south and north end of the transept, the upper storey forms an advanced screen, enclosing the structural buttressing and supporting the dome.

The carving and texture of many features are particularly emphasised if floodlit, animating the statues, reliefs, figures by **Caius Cibber** and Francis Bird; garlands, swags, panels, cherub heads in stone by Grinling Gibbons.

Interior

The greatest impact is the size and scale of the building, its almost luminescent stone flattered by gold and mosaic. Wren's church was designed to have no extraneous monuments but in 1790 the figures of four national benefactors Joshua Reynolds, the penal reformer John Howard, Dr Johnson and the orientalist Sir William Jones were placed by the dome piers. Since then marble statuary has proliferated.

Nave – At the west end of the aisles are the chapels of St Dunstan *(left)* and St Michael and St George *(right)*, each preceded by a finely carved wooden screen (17C-18C) rising to a crest incorporating broken pediments and coats of arms. The square pillars dividing the nave and aisles are faced (on the nave side) with fluted Corinthian pilasters which sweep up to the entablature, wrought-iron gallery railing, clerestory and garlanded-saucer domes.

The **Wellington** monument **(1)**, which occupies the entire space between two piers in the north aisle and ascends from a recumbent bronze effigy at the base to a full-size equestrian statue of the duke at the apex, was the lifework of Alfred Stevens and completed only in 1912 long after the sculptor's death in 1875.

The bronze gasoliers date from the late 19C. In the pavement are the Night

The Light of the World

"Behold I stand at the door and knock: if any man hear my voice, and open the door, I will come into him, and will sup with him, and he with me."
Revelations (3:20)

Holman Hunt's best known religious painting **(2)** hangs in the north transept. This large Pre-Raphaelite **Brotherhood** painting is one of three versions of the same subject (Keble College, Oxford and Manchester City Art Gallery) for which Hunt built an outdoor straw hut where he might settle to study and paint the light of a full moon between the hours of 9pm and 5am. It was described by Ruskin as *"one of the very noblest works of sacred art ever produced in this or any other age."*

Watch memorial stone (cathedral guardians 1939-45) and the inscription commemorating the resting of Sir **Winston Churchill's** coffin in the cathedral during the state funeral on 30 January 1965. Beneath the dome is Wren's own epitaph in Latin: "Reader, if you seek his monument, look around you."

Crossing and Transepts – The space beneath the dome is emphasised by the giant supporting piers which flank the entrances to the shallow transepts. The north transept serves as a baptistery and contains a dish-shaped font carved in 1727 by Francis Bird. The south transept includes the exceptional portrait statue of **Nelson** by **Flaxman (3)** and the beautiful wooden door-case with fluted columns made up in the 19C from a wood screen designed by Wren and decked with garlands carved by Grinling Gibbons, while in the north transept stands a statue of Reynolds **(4)**.

Dome – *Entrance in the south transept.* From the **Whispering Gallery** *(259 steps)* there is an impressive, unusual perspective of the choir, arches and clerestory far below, and a closer view of the dome frescoes painted by **Thornhill**. A hushed word uttered next to the wall can be heard quite clearly by a person standing diametrically opposite. The **Stone Gallery** *(530 steps)* provides a good but less extensive **view***** than that perceived from the **Golden Gallery** at the top of the dome over the present day City rooftops.

Choir and Ambulatory – The east end is filled by the marble high altar set below a massive post-war baldachin, which was carved and gilded according to drawings by Wren. Gilding also offsets the glass mosaics (19C-20C) above which continue in the chancel aisle vaulting (note the Christ in Majesty in the domed apse).

In the foreground, warm in the light of red-shaded candle lights, pillared beneath a crested canopy, are the dark oak **choir stalls** (6)**, the exquisite work of **Grinling Gibbons** and his craftsmen. Each stall is different from the next – see how the cherubs' expressions vary as do the flowers, leaves and fruits that make up the wreaths and garlands; even the stall backs are carved forming a screen between the choir and the chancel aisles.

The **organ (5)**, a late-17C Smith instrument, together with its Gibbons case, has been divided and now towers on either side of the choir opening.

The iron railing adapted from the original altar rail, the gates to the chancel aisles and the great gilded screens **(7)** enclosing the sanctuary, are the work of **Jean Tijou**, wrought-iron smith extraordinary.

In the north aisle, the graceful marble sculpture of the Virgin and Child **(8)** is by **Henry Moore** (1984). Before the Chapel of modern martyrs, a 14C Graduale, a "Breeches" Bible (16C) and mementoes of thanksgiving services from Queen Anne to Elizabeth II are on display.

In the south chancel aisle, against the first outer west pillar, is a statue of **John Donne (9)** carved by **Nicholas Stone**: the metaphysical poet and Dean of St Paul's (1621-31) is shown wrapped in his shroud, standing on an urn in the up-ended coffin (which he kept in his house), but, from his expression, very much alive.

Crypt – *Entrance in the south transept.* At the east end, simply decorated with royal banners, is the Chapel of the Order of the British Empire (OBE). Grouped in bays, formed by the massive piers which support the low-groined and tunnel vaulting, are the tombs, memorials and busts of men and women of all talents, of the 18C, 19C and 20C, of British, Commonwealth or foreign origin, who contributed to the national life; not all those commemorated are buried in the crypt.

– In south aisle, east of the staircase, is **Artists' Corner** honouring John Rennie *(2nd recess)*; Sir Max Beerbohm and Walter de la Mare *(north and west faces of pillar)*; Christopher Wren, beneath a plain black marble stone with above him the inscription: *Si monumentum requiris circumspice.* There are also monuments to George Dance the Younger, William Blake, Ivor Novello, Sir Edwin Lutyens, Sir Edwin Landseer, Sir Thomas Lawrence, Benjamin West, Lord Leighton, Sir John Everett Millais, JMW Turner, Sir Joshua Reynolds and Holman Hunt.

- In the north aisle are commemorations of Sir Arthur Sullivan, Sir Hubert Parry, William Boyce *(on the floor)*, John Singer Sargent – beneath a relief by himself *(choir face of dividing wall)*, Wilson Steer, Sir Alfred Munnings, John Constable, Sir Alexander Fleming and Sir Stafford Cripps – bronze bust by Jacob Epstein (1953).

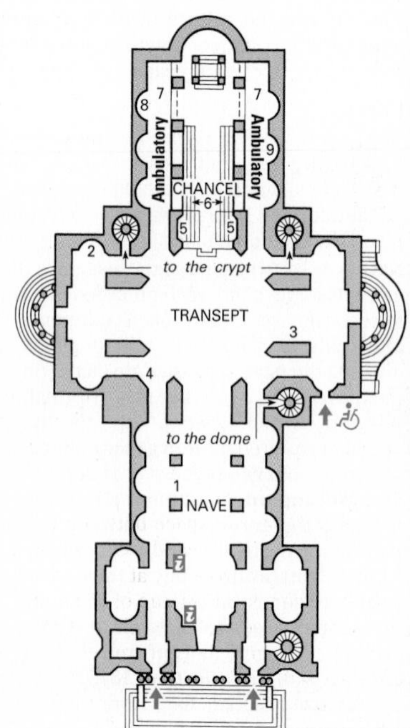

– Down the steps: **Wellington** occupies the Cornish porphyry sarcophagus; memorials to ten of the great soldiers of the Second World War are a more recent addition; beyond, to the south, is a plaque to Florence Nightingale.
Below the dome: at the centre of a circle of Tuscan columns lies **Nelson** beneath a curving black marble sarcophagus (originally intended for Cardinal Wolsey and subsequently proposed but rejected for Henry VIII). Beneath the arches to the south are Admirals Beatty, Jellicoe and Cunningham, and a bronze bust of WE Henley by Rodin (1903). Opposite on the north side are more military figures including TE Lawrence by Epstein. Only a handful of effigies were rescued from Old St Paul's in which were buried John of Gaunt, Thomas Linacre (c 1460-1524), founder of the Royal College of Physicians, teacher of Greek to Thomas More and Erasmus, Sir Philip Sidney and Sir Anthony van Dyck *(modern plaque)*.
North transept: the **Treasury** displays plate and vestments belonging to the Cathedral and on loan from parishes in the London Diocese.
West end: models showing the construction of the Cathedral and dome.

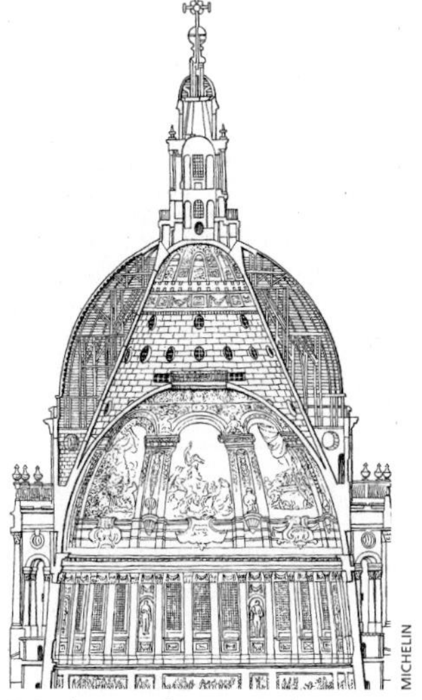

St Paul's Dome (cross section)

Chapter House
This perfectly proportioned red-brick building, with a crowning parapet and stone quoins marking the angles and centre, was built by Wren (1710-14). The iron hand pump *(west)* was erected in 1819 by the parishioners of St Faith's *(see below)*.

St Paul's Cross
The cross *(site marked on the pavement north of the apse)*, which is known to have been in existence as a preaching cross in 1256, became the centre and symbol of free speech and so was removed by the Long Parliament in 1643. The monument in the garden with St Paul at the top dates from 1910.

Choir School
The modern buildings of the choir school abut the tower of the church of **St Augustine and St Faith** (1680-87) which was built by Wren and destroyed during the Second World War. The square tower of newly hewn stone ends in a pierced parapet quartered by obelisk pinnacles; above rise an almost black, tulip-shaped dome and lead spire, rebuilt since the war to Wren's original design.

St Paul's Garden
The garden is complemented by a sculpture, *The Young Lovers* by George Ehrlich, and a pond.

Walking About

Old Deanery
Deans Court. The house (1672-73) was built by Wren.

Old Choir School
Corner of Carter Lane. The building (now a youth hostel) was built in 1873 and is decorated with *sgraffito* ornamentation in the spandrels and a terracotta inscription from Galatians IV, 13.
Take Carter Lane.

Old Change Court
The modern piazza is adorned by a statue *Icarus* (1973) by Michael Ayrton. In the northwest corner is the circular City Information Centre.
Walk up New Change east of the Cathedral to Cheapside.

Cheapside
Cheapside, a wide commercial street originally known as West Cheap, takes its name from the Anglo-Saxon word *ceap* meaning to barter. The names of the side streets, Milk Street, Bread Street, Honey Lane, indicate the commodities sold there, first from stalls, later in shops; other streets were inhabited by craft and tradesmen.
The street was also the setting for many a medieval tourney with contests being watched from the upper windows by householders and royalty alike; the Lord Mayor and aldermen watched from a balcony in the tower of St Mary-le-Bow which records such scenes in a window. Of the three churches in Cheapside during the Middle Ages, only St Mary-le-Bow was rebuilt after the Fire; three communal fountains served the area: Lesser Conduit at the west end, the Standard before St Mary-le-Bow (a place of public execution) and the Great Conduit, east of Ironmonger Lane.

St Vedast's

Foster Lane. Open Mon-Fri, 8am-6pm. Closed Bank Hols. Services: Sung Mass Sun at 11am; Mon-Fri at 12.15pm. Guide book (3 languages). www.vedast.net

The church (1670-73) dedicated to the beatified Bishop of Arras was designed by Wren. The **tower and spire★** consist of a square stone tower with an overhanging entablature on which Wren later (1697) set a lantern with advanced triple pilaster at the corners through three stages, below the ribbed stone spire surmounted by a ball and vane.

The exterior, with a pre-Fire curving southwest wall which Wren retained when he rebuilt the church for £1 853 15s 6d (the cheapest of all the City churches), is almost unnoticeable from Foster Lane. (The street's name is a corruption of Vedast, 6C Bishop of Arras, to whom the church was dedicated in the 13C.) The interior is entirely new: the floor has been marbled in black and white; pews are aligned collegiate style beneath the **ceiling★**, reinstalled to Wren's design with a central wreath, cornice and end panels in moulded plasterwork, highlighted in gold and silver – St Vedast's is the Goldsmiths' Church. The wooden altarpiece and the ornate octagonal pulpit are also of interest.

Soho★

Soho, which lies to the north of Piccadilly Circus and Leicester Square, is at the hub of London's advertising and film industry during the day, while at night the place takes on a new life as lights flicker in the windows of the various clubs, bars, restaurants (French, Italian, Greek and Chinese), jazz venues, nightclubs, cinemas and theatres thronged with night owls. There is also a louche side to Soho with risqué shows and shops but it has a solid core of loyal residents as well as a transient population; its Bohemian appeal has always attracted artists, writers and foreign immigrants. It is also the centre of the book trade with famous bookshops lining Charing Cross Road, immortalised in Helene Hanff's novel *84 Charing Cross Road*.

Location

Map pp 11-12 (DEX); Michelin Atlas London: pp 61, 76-77. ⊖ Leicester Square; Piccadilly Circus; Tottenham Court Road; Oxford Circus. The area is bounded by Oxford Street, Charing Cross Road, Regent St and is to the west of Covent Garden. It is the theatre and cinema heartland.

Adjacent Sights: COVENT GARDEN; PICCADILLY; BLOOMSBURY; TRAFALGAR SQUARE – WHITEHALL.

Background

In the Middle Ages Soho was a chase, named after the cry of the medieval hunt which was often found in the vicinity of St Giles'-in-the-Fields *(see COVENT GARDEN)*.

Early maps show a windmill marking Great Windmill Street, two breweries in Brewer Street, a bottle glass factory in Glasshouse Street and several big houses of which only their names survive: Newport House (built c 1634, demolished 1682), Monmouth House (the residence of the **Duke of Monmouth** from 1682 until his execution on Tower Hill in 1685), Karnaby House corrupted to becoming Carnaby Street.

By the mid 19C, through piecemeal development, Soho included the worst slums in the capital. The building of Regent Street divided the West End from its disreputable neighbour and three new streets were built to penetrate the foetid tangle: Charing Cross Road (1880), Shaftesbury Avenue (1886) and Kingsway (1905).

People of All Nations – The indigenous Londoners of Soho have always been artisans (tapestry weavers, furniture and violin makers), cottage industry workers, and, until planning regulations eliminated local factories, craftsmen in labour-intensive manufacture. Refugees began to arrive in the 17C, settling where their skills and labour would find a market: Greeks fleeing the Ottoman Turks; persecuted Huguenots after the revocation of the Edict of Nantes (1685); Frenchmen hounded by the Revolution and later by political changes – these established French restaurants and cafés (Wheeler's at **19 Old Compton Street** was founded by Napoleon III's chef; the York Minster pub at 49 Dean Street, run by two generations of French landlords, became known as the French Pub). Waves of Swiss, Italian, Spanish immigrants followed. Then came the Chinese from Hong Kong, Singapore and the docks to transform Gerrard Street into a Chinatown.

Directory

Light Bite

Bar Italia – *22 Frith St, W1D 4LF – ⊖ Leicester Square – ☎ 020 7437 4520 – £5/10.* A veritable Soho institution open around the clock. Regulars and visitors of all styles spill onto the pavement terrace sipping first-rate espresso or munching a filled ciabatta. It's all fiercely old-fashioned Italian as exemplified by the poster of Rocky Marciano behind the congested counter.

R. Besse/MICHELIN

The Empire, Leicester Square

Café Bohème – *13-17 Old Compton St, W1D 5JQ – ⊖ Leicester Square – ☎ 020 7734 0623 – info@cafeboheme.co.uk – Open Mon-Sat 8am-3am, Sun 8am-10.30pm.* A warm and friendly place for a snack, in the very heart of Soho.

Wagamama – *10A Lexington St, W1R 3HS – ⊖ Piccadilly Circus – ☎ 020 7292 0990 – lexington@wagamama.com – ⚟ – £7/15.* Despite Wagamama's success, this stylish Japanese eaterie remains London's best bet for fast food. It's healthy, cheap and delicious. Don't be discouraged by the long queues; the friendly and efficient service keeps things moving. Smart minimalist decor in a basement space. Other central locations: Harvey Nichols *(see KNIGHTSBRIDGE)*, 1 Tavistock St *(see COVENT GARDEN)* and 4A Streatham St in Bloomsbury.

Mezzo Café – *100 Wardour St, W1F 0TN – ⊖ Leicester Square – ☎ 020 7314 4060 – marcelos@conran-restaurants.co.uk – £12/16.* Next door to its sprawling big brother, this bright and warmly decorated restaurant provides a more tranquil atmosphere. The menu has a distinct Middle Eastern flavour, ranging from mezze to assorted skewers and dips.

York Minster (French House) – *49 Dean St, W1D 5BG – ⊖ Leicester Square – ☎ 020 7437 2799 – Pub: Open daily noon-11pm (10.30pm Sun). Restaurant: Open until midnight; closed bank hols.* Which London bar serves the most wine, champagne and beer? The French House of course! This true Parisian bistro was founded by Frenchman Victor Berlemont, at the beginning of the 20C. During the war, De Gaulle made it the Free France House. Maurice Chevalier, George Carpentier and Salvador Dalí were regular customers. Today it is under British management and is a popular haunt for a mixed crowd of regulars and tourists. Always a lively atmosphere.

Pub

Argyll Arms – *18 Argyll St, W1F 7TP – ⊖ Oxford Circus – ☎ 020 7734 6117 – Open Mon-Sat 11am-11pm, Sun noon-10.30pm.* Almost 300 years old, this very popular pub, laid out on two floors, is a typical Victorian gin palace with decorative mirrors.

Going out for the Evening

Milroy's of Soho – *3 Greek St, W1D 4NX – ⊖ Leicester Square – ☎ 020 7437 9311, 2385 – shop@milroys.co.uk – Open Mon-Sat 11am-11pm; closed bank hols.* London's most reputed whisky shop with some 700 malt whiskies and many international whiskies as well as bottles for collectors. 300 varieties of whisky for sampling in the cellar as well as hundreds of fine wines from around the world which can be drunk at shelf price.

The Lab Bar – *12 Old Compton St, W1D 4TQ – ⊖ Leicester Square, Tottenham Court Road – ☎ 020 7437 7820 – info@lab-bar.com – Open daily 4pm-midnight (10.30pm Sun).* The Lab has a reputation for excellent and original cocktails prepared by true specialists. Sit back and enjoy them in a 1970s leather and Formica atmosphere, spread over two floors (look out for the transparent glass floor). Young and mixed crowd in the heart of London's gay area.

Shopping

Algerian Coffee Stores – *52 Old Compton St, W1D 4PB – ⊖ Leicester Square – ☎ 020 7437 2480 – fcrocet@btconnect.com – Open Mon-Sat 9am-7pm.* The name honours the first foreign owners who opened the shop in 1887. Choose from 100 different types of the best coffees and 140 types of teas, not to mention the designer teapots and coffee makers.

Berwick Street – *Berwick St, W1 – ⊖ Piccadilly Circus.* Berwick Street is reputed for its market and many specialist record shops (new and old). At nos 26 and 30, the famous Reckless Records.

Borders Books & Music – *120 Charing Cross Rd, WC2H 0JR – ⊖ Tottenham Court Road – ☎ 020 7379 8877 – saggion@bordersstores.com – Open Mon-Sat 9am-11pm, Sun noon-6pm.* A large book-shop owned by an American

chain. An airy room with more than 150 000 publications, magazines, many American titles and a café.

Foyles – *113-119 Charing Cross Rd, WC2H 0EB – ⊖ Tottenham Court Road – ☎ 020 7437 5660 – orders@foyles.co.uk – Open Mon-Sat 9.30am-8pm, Sun and bank hols noon-6pm.* The world's greatest bookshop celebrated its centenary in 2003 with a massive refurbishment but still specialises in rare books as well as maintaining a comprehensive general list. Over the years it has become an institution, famous for its past eccentric practices and its continuing literary lunches.

Hamley's – *188-196 Regent St, W1R 6BT – ⊖ Oxford Circus – ☎ 0870 332 2455, 020 7494 2000 – customerservices@hamleys.co.uk – Open Mon-Fri 10am-8pm, Sat 9.30am-8pm, Sun noon-6pm.* London's toy kingdom, occupying 7 floors with teddy bears, electric trains, office gadgets and the latest in electronic games.

Ray's Jazz Shop – *113-119 Charing Cross Rd, WC2H 0EB – ⊖ Tottenham Court Road – ☎ 020 7440 3205 – rays@foyles.co.uk – Open Mon-Sat 9.30am-8pm, Sun noon-6pm; closed 25-26 Dec.* Popular with jazz enthusiasts, Ray's has diversified into blues and folk recordings and world music. Lunchtime and evening live events and talks.

Top Shop – *214 Oxford St, W1C 1DA – ⊖ Oxford Circus – ☎ 020 7636 7700 – oxford.circus.reception@arcadiagroup.co.uk – Open Mon-Fri 9am-8pm (9pm Thu), Sun 11.30am-6pm.* Billing itself as the "biggest fashion shop" in the world, this reasonably priced store is a treasure trove for men and women fashion hunters. You will find casual clothes, lots of accessories, plus a nail bar and a café.

Virgin Megastore – *14-16 Oxford St, W1D 1AR – ⊖ Tottenham Court Road – ☎ 020 7631 1234 – www.virgin.com/megastores/uk – Open Mon-Sat 10am-8.30pm (9pm Thu), Sun noon-6pm.* This is the largest of the famous Virgin stores. An astounding selection of music as well as books, videos and mobile phones.

Zwemmer – *80 Charing Cross Rd, WC2H 0BB – ⊖ Leicester Square – ☎ 020 7240 4157 – sales@zwemmer.com – Open Mon-Sat 10am-6.30pm (7pm Thu).* Specialising in art publications, Zwemmer has several locations in London, this one being devoted solely to fashion, photography and cinema.

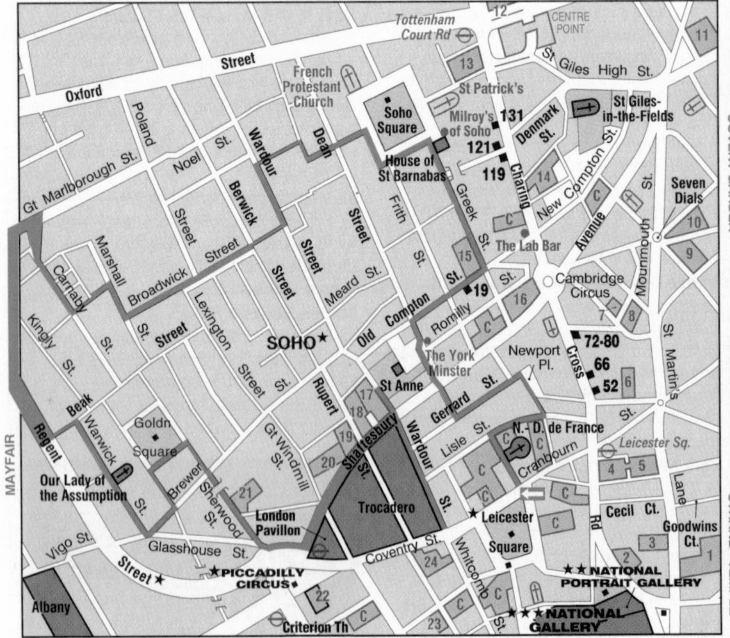

C : CINEMA

THEATRES

Albery	5	Cambridge	9	Lyric	20
Ambassadors	7	Comedy	23	Palace	16
Apollo	19	Criterion	22	Phœnix	14
Arts Theatre	6	Dominion	12	Piccadilly	21
Astoria	13	Donmar Warehouse	10	Prince Edward	15
		Duke of York's	3	Prince of Wales	24
		Garrick	2	Queen's	17
		Gielgud	18	St Martin's	8
		London Coliseum	1	Shaftesbury	11
				Wyndham's	4

Commerce – Today Soho survives on the various trades associated with entertainment. The southern end of Shaftesbury Avenue is known for its theatres; the area around Golden Square is dominated by the film industry, television production companies, cinema advertisers, photographers; sleazy parts boast peep-shows and sexshops below lurid neon signs and blackened windows; this is also the home of London's mainstream jazz – instruments, specialist music shops and clubs pepper Shaftesbury Avenue, Charing Cross Road, and Denmark Street.

A Roll-Call of Luminaries

William Blake was born in Soho (1757), Hazlitt died there (1830); Edmund Burke, Sarah Siddons, Dryden, Sheraton lived there; Marx, Engels, Canaletto, Haydn lodged there; Mendelssohn and Chopin gave recitals at the 18C house in Meard Street of Vincent Novello, father of Ivor and founder of the music publishers. J L Baird first demonstrated television in Frith Street in 1926...

Walking About

Leicester Square★

The square is now a pedestrian precinct surrounded by cinemas and eating houses. At the centre stands the Shakespeare Memorial Fountain (1874) facing a statue of **Charlie Chaplin** *(north side)* by John Doubleday (1980). On the circumference of the inner paving are plaques identifying the direction and distance of the capital cities of the Commonwealth countries, while around the railings sit busts of famous local residents – Reynolds, Newton, Hunter, Hogarth; panels tell the history of the square from Leicester Fields, common ground where people dried their washing, to the building of the Alhambra (1854), Daly's Theatre and the **Empire**, which established the reputation of the square as a centre for light entertainment.

On the south side of the central garden is **tkts** (the Half-Price Ticket Booth, *see PRACTICAL POINTS – Going out for the Evening, Theatres*), while in the northeast corner of the square stands the former Swiss Centre (now an entertainment centre) and its **Glockenspiel**. *Plays Mon-Fri at noon, 6pm, 7pm, 8pm; Sat-Sun and Bank Hols at noon, 2pm, 3pm, 4pm, 5pm, 6pm, 7pm, 8pm.*

Cross Cranbourn St to Leicester Place.

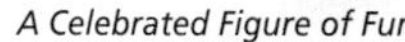

J. Malburet/MICHELIN

A Celebrated Figure of Fun

Notre Dame de France

Open daily, 9.30am-8pm. Brochure (2 languages). ☎ 020 7437 9363; Fax 020 7437 9364; information@notredame.fsnet.co.uk; www.notredame.fsnet.co.uk

The circular Roman Catholic church was erected from the ashes of a 19C predecessor. Inside, an Aubusson tapestry hangs above the altar, mosaic ornaments a side altar and paintings by **Jean Cocteau** adorn the walls.

Turn right into Lisle St, then left into Newport Pl to Gerrard St.

Chinatown

Gerrard Street is the centre of this colourful area marked by oriental gates and other exotic street furniture, which abounds in restaurants, supermarkets selling exotic foodstuffs, oriental medicine centres, travel agents etc. It is the scene of great festivities at Chinese New Year (a moveable feast in Jan or Feb) celebrated in traditional fashion.

Walk up Gerrard Pl, across Shaftesbury Ave, up Dean St past the York Minster (see Directory) to Old Compton St.

Old Compton Street

At the heart of Soho, this street which is lined with pubs, eating places, wine merchants, pastry shops and Italian foodstores, is frequented by a spirited gay crowd.

Proceed east and turn left into Greek St.

House of St Barnabas

Greek Street. Open First Sun of the month (if Bank Hol then Tue), 10am-4pm, Wed at lunchtime and at 5.30pm (service). Check times before visiting. Closed Easter and Christmas. Donation. ☎ 020 7434 1846; houseofstb@hotmail.com

The House of Charity, a temporary home for women in need, was built c 1750. The exterior is plain except for two obelisks at the entrance; the interior, one of the finest in Soho, has beautiful plasterwork ceilings and walls, and an unusual crinoline staircase. The proportions of the small chapel, built in 1863 in 13C French Gothic style, are unique.

Soho Square

The pleasant square laid out in 1680 to the north of the manor built by the Duke of Monmouth on land between Greek Street and Frith Street, is adorned by a fountain topped by a statue of Charles II by Caius Cibber. Two churches stand to the east and northwest of the square.

Leave by Carlisle St west, cross Dean St, continue to Great Chapel St and turn left into Sheraton St to Wardour St.

Wardour Street

The street and its immediate vicinity (Beak Street, Dean Street and Soho Square) conjure up the **film industry** from the creators of blockbuster movies and catchy commercials.

Walk south and past St Anne's Ct turn right into Broadwick St cutting across Berwick St.

Many of the houses along Berwick Street are 18C. The **Berwick Street Market**, which dates from 1778, is the only fresh produce market in central London.

Continue past Marshall St to Carnaby St.

Carnaby

The largely pedestrianised area around Carnaby St (Foubert's Place, Kingly St, Beak St...), which was a high spot of the Swinging 60s before succumbing to crass commercialism, has now reinvented itself as a centre of stylish shops, trendy bars, eateries and clubs.

Walk up to Great Marlborough St and turn left towards Regent St (For the beginning of Regent St, see map under MARYLEBONE).

Regent Street*

Dickins and Jones, Liberty's, Jaeger, Hamley's Toyshop, Aquascutum, the Café Royal, Austin Reed all line this elegant street sweeping southwards to Piccadilly Circus and the heart of the West End.

Liberty & Co was founded by Arthur Liberty, the son of a draper, in 1875 with a loan of £1 500 from his future father-in-law: it soon acquired the dignified title of 'Emporium' stocking broad ranges of exotic silks imported from the East, Japanese porcelain – wallpapers and fans followed, and when it introduced a costume department it was quick to become associated with the Aesthetic Movement. Furniture, made in workshops in Soho supplemented the imported ranges. Own brand fabrics were made to different weights (from lawn to furnishing and upholstery materials) after traditional Indian prints so familiar already to colonials and from designs commissioned from CFA Voysey, Butterfield, Arthur Silver – sympathetic to the Aesthetic and Arts and Crafts Movements. The Liberty jewellery resulted from dealings with the Continent where Art Nouveau was flourishing and from where furniture was imported. An affiliation with a Birmingham firm of goldsmiths (WH Haseler) was consolidated in the Cymric range of silver and enamel pieces, the pewter Tudric range followed. The distinctive spirit of the Liberty Style was modelled on Celtic entrelacs and flowing organic asymmetrical designs. Emphasis was placed upon craftsmanship and applied to contemporary ceramics from factories in Germany and Hungary as well as at home: Wedgwood, Poole, Royal Doulton and glassware. The success of the Art Nouveau Style lasted until the outbreak of war in 1914, after which furniture manufacture reverted to Queen Anne and Tudor styles. Liberty fabrics and jewellery, however, continue much in the same traditional vein.

Note the splendid **pediment** on the Regent Street façade, dominated by the great figure of Britannia, with three stone ladies behind overlooking the parapet! The **Tudor Building** (1922-24) in Great Marlborough Street, was designed by Edwin T and Stanley Hall, and built from oak and teak timbers taken from the Royal Navy's last two sailing ships.

Proceed down Regent St, turn left into Beak St and right into Warwick St.

Tucked away off Regent Street, stands **Our Lady of the Assumption**, a plain church, originally the chapel of the Portuguese, rebuilt in 1788 after the Gordon Riots with only a pediment as decoration.*Open daily, 7am (10am Sat) to 7pm. ☎ 020 7437 1525*

Turn left into Brewer St and left again into Lower John St.

Golden Square

The attractive square with gardens enclosed by railings is the preserve of the media and fashion industries.

Walk down Lower St James St and Sherwood St and turn left into Shaftesbury Avenue past the theatres and proceed to the bottom end of Wardour St.

St Anne's

The church, consecrated in honour of Anne, Princess of Denmark as Soho's Parish Church (1686) was bombed in the war. The tower, now occupied by the Soho Society, was restored, together with the clock, in 1979. Beneath it are buried the ashes of Dorothy L Sayers, churchwarden and detective-story writer, while Hazlitt and the legendary 18C Theodore, King of Corsica, lie in the churchyard.

Continue down Wardour St past the Trocadero (description in PICCADILLY, Walking About) and back to Leicester Sq or Piccadilly Circus.

An Exotic Quarter

"Of all quarters in the queer adventurous amalgam called London, Soho is ... untidy, full of Greeks, Ishmaelites, cats, Italians, tomatoes, restaurants, organs, coloured stuffs, queer names, people looking out of upper windows, it dwells remote from the British Body Politic."

John Galsworthy

South Bank★

The new image of the South Bank as a tourist hot spot is well borne out by the crowds of visitors thronging to the new attractions built to mark the third millennium. It is a success story which will be further enhanced by the transformation of the South Bank Centre which offers first class entertainment and the improvement of pedestrian access when work on Hungerford Bridge is completed. Amble along the leafy riverside walkway affording superb views, browse at the book stalls under Waterloo Bridge, stop for a bite at Gabriel's Wharf or Oxo Tower and if time permits, take in a show at the National Theatre or the National Film Theatre or enjoy a concert at the South Bank venues – the choice is yours!

County Hall dwarfed by the huge wheel of the London Eye

Location

Map pp 11-12 (EFY); Michelin Atlas London: pp 62-63. ⊖ Waterloo; Westminster. The area known as the South Bank lies opposite Westminster and Charing Cross and past Waterloo Bridge to Blackfriars. The Millennium Mile (or Queen's Walk) starting from Westminster Bridge to Southwark, Tower Bridge and Bermondsey runs past most of the attractions of the South Bank. There are several piers for those arriving by boat.

Adjacent Sights: BANKSIDE – SOUTHWARK; LAMBETH.

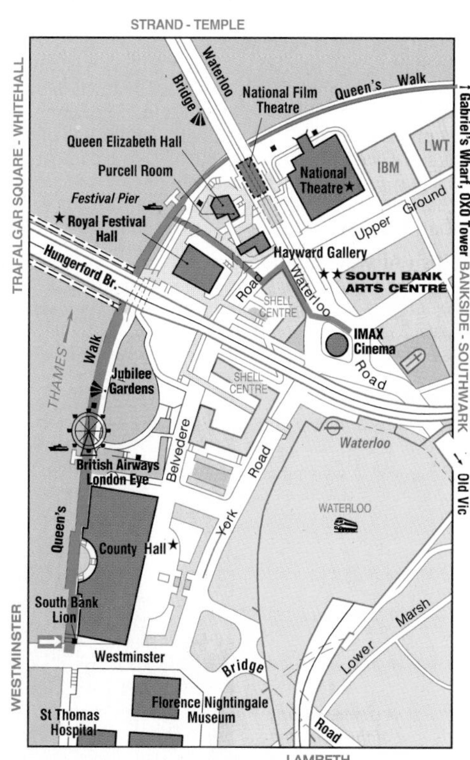

Background

The area on the south bank remained rural until the construction of Westminster and Blackfriars Bridges and their approach roads in the mid 18C. The evolution of public transport developed the area from village to town and spa, where the modestly wealthy such as **Henry Thrale** built out-of-town residences. Finally the area became a suburb where squares and terraces were erected by **Thomas**

Cubitt and lesser men, which agglomerated in a network of small streets between the major roads.

Victorian Industrial Works – Benefiting from an ample workforce and easy transport by river, and later by railway, this area has boasted a long list of works and plants: an ordnance factory (Charles II's reign), the Vauxhall Plate Glass Works (1665-1780), the Coade Stone Factory (late 18C), Doultons, lead-shot foundries (a shot tower stood at the centre of the 1951 Festival of Britain), Price's candle works (Battersea), vinegar, basket, brush factories, boatyards, breweries, distillers, specialist workshops and potteries including one producing Lambeth delft. Bombing during the war devastated acres of Victorian streets, slums, the Lambeth Walk and factories, making it possible for the authorities to rebuild on a vast scale.

LIGHT BITE

Konditor & Cook – *66 The Cut, Southwark, SE1 8LZ – ⊖ Southwark – ☎ 020 7620 2700 – Open Mon-Sat 8.30am (10.30am Sat) to 11pm – £5/12.* Photographs from past performances at the adjacent Young Vic line the walls of this unpretentious little cafe. From the counter you can choose homemade cakes and pastries or soups and salads and vegetarian dishes.

THE FESTIVAL OF BRITAIN

The theme *The Land and the People* was presented in pavilions designed in new contemporary styles and materials by a team of young and untried architects and embellished by sculptors and painters. The small site (27 acres/11ha) on the South Bank was dominated by the Skylon, a cigar-shaped vertical feature which appeared to float in mid-air, and the Dome of Discovery (diameter 365ft), a circular pavilion made of steel and aluminium. Between May and September 8.5 million people visited the Festival where they learned about British achievement in arts, sciences and industrial design and enjoyed themselves at the **Pleasure Gardens** in Battersea Park: fireworks, Music Hall shows, a vast single pole tent as a dance pavilion, sticks of Festival rock, the tree walk, the crazy Emmett railway and a Mississippi Showboat on the river.

Walking About

Start from Westminster Bridge (description in WESTMINSTER).

South Bank Lion

The lion (13ft/4m long, 12ft/3.5m high), carved out of Coade stone, gazes speculatively from a plinth at the foot of Westminster Bridge. Painted red, it was the mascot in the 19C of the Lion Brewery until placed at the bridgefoot in 1952.

County Hall★

Belvedere Road. County Hall was the headquarters of the London County Council and its successor, the Greater London Council until 1986. It now houses two hotels, and restaurants and several attractions.

The hall, a colonnaded arc 700ft/213m in diameter and still, amid all the new constructions, one of London's most distinctive buildings, was designed in 1908 by a 29-year-old architect, Ralph Knott. The stone pile with Renaissance-inspired, steeply pitched, dark tile roof with a multitude of dormers, only completed in 1922, has since been trebled in size but always in compatible style. The County Hall houses an aquarium and the Saatchi Gallery *(descriptions in Worth a Visit).*

Other attractions include an amusement arcade with the latest electronic games and a **Dali Universe** exhibition *(description in Worth a Visit).*

British Airways London Eye

♿ *Open Jul-Aug, daily, 9.30am-10pm; June, daily, 9.30am-9pm (10pm Fri-Sun); May and Sep, daily, 9.30am-8pm (9pm Fri-Sun); late-Jan to Apr and Oct-Dec, daily, 9.30am-8pm. Closed 25 Dec and 3 weeks in Jan. £11. ☎ 0870 5000 600; 0870 990 8886 (group bookings); customer.services@ba-londoneye.com; www.ba-londoneye.com*

A London mascot at the south end of Westminster Bridge

The giant Ferris wheel, which is a triumph of engineering, is a spectacular new landmark on the Thames. Sightseers (trip 30min) accommodated in closed pods, enjoy unparalleled **views★★★** of London extending 12mi/20km in all directions as the wheel rotates to its apex.

Jubilee Gardens

The gardens, on the site of the 1951 Festival and incorporating the flagpole from British Columbia, were opened in 1977 to celebrate the 25th anniversary of the Queen's accession. A bronze sculpture by I Walters (1985) is dedicated to the International Brigade (1936-39). Nearby is the Jubilee Oracle, a smooth bronze by Alexander (1980). The whole area is scheduled for redevelopment.

South Bank Arts Centre★★

After the war, the LCC, under Herbert Morrison, cleared bomb-damage debris from the riverside to make way for the 1951 Festival of Britain and a future arts centre. The arts complex, connected by elevated walkways (shown in grey on plan) has been described as "a sterile concrete wasteland disastrously out of character and contact with the rest of London" – in an attempt to rectify this, plans for extensive redevelopment of the entire riverside precinct have been approved.

Royal Festival Hall★ – The building was planned by the architects Sir Leslie Martin and Sir Robert Matthew, who worked, it was said, from the inside. Design began with the hall: its acoustics, the visibility of the stage capable of holding a choir of 250, comfortable seating for an audience of 3 000 – in that order. They succeeded both aesthetically and practically in the design of foyers, staircases, concourses, bars and restaurants, managing the space to avoid crowding, and afford views of the river and inner perspectives of the building itself; finally the whole edifice was insulated against noise from nearby Waterloo Station. In 1954 an organ was installed. In 1962-65 the river frontage was redesigned to include the main entrance, and faced with Portland stone. There are good facilities for refreshments, book and record shops and all kinds of free entertainment in the foyer.

The Oxo Tower lends an exotic note to the South Bank Skyline

Queen Elizabeth Hall and Purcell Room – In 1967 a second smaller concert venue with seating for 1 100 was opened with a third, the Purcell Room providing a recital room for 370 planned in the second phase of building. The exterior is in unfaced concrete; the interior acoustics are superb.

For the Hayward Gallery, see descrption in Worth a Visit. Pass down the east side of the Royal Festival Hall, cross Belvedere Road, bear left and walk by the Shell Centre for access to IMAX Cinema.

IMAX Cinema – Rising at a busy roundabout at the southern end of Waterloo Bridge, the circular structure houses a state-of-the-art cinema screening 2D and 3D films. The auditorium has 482 seats. Be prepared for exciting adventures as the camera explores distant horizons and new worlds!

Return to the riverbank.

National Film Theatre – The NFT, which opened in 1951, was rebuilt in 1957 and enlarged in 1970 so that it now comprises two cinemas (seating 466 and 162). The NFT, one of the world's leading cinematheques, organises the London Film Festival in November each year.

In front of the **National Theatre** *(description in Worth a Visit)* stand a pleasing stone sculpture, *Arena,* by J Maine (1983/84) and a bronze of *London Pride* by **F Dobson**, a sculpture commissioned for the 1951 Festival.

Waterloo Bridge

The sleek five-arched concrete structure faced in Portland stone was designed by GG Scott in 1945; it replaced the original by Rennie that was opened on the second anniversary of the **Battle of Waterloo** (18 June 1817). From the bridge is a fine view: east of the National Theatre stands the IBM building, faced in concrete and granite and designed by Sir Denys Lasdun (1983) to harmonise in scale and structure with the National Theatre. Next in line is the London Weekend Television building dominated by tall towers.

On the waterfront is the lively **Gabriel's Wharf,** a workplace for craftspeople which has evolved alongside the gardens and low-cost housing of the Coin Street development. *Open Tue-Sun, 11am-6pm (later bars and restaurants).* ☎ *020 7401 2255; fatbeehive.com; www.gabrielswharf.co.uk*

Bernie Spain Gardens is a pleasant sunken green space from which to enjoy the spectacle on the river and the north bank.

Stamford Wharf is marked by the **OXO tower**, a former beef-extract factory and now housing restaurants, stylish designer studios. The **Bargehouse**, an old warehouse, is an unusual but successful venue for temporary off-beat exhibitions.

Walk round to Upper Ground to view colourful banners strung along the street.

The distinctive river façade of Sea Containers House with its gilded decorative elements lies beyond.

Worth a Visit

National Theatre★

♿ *Backstage tour three times daily, (75min) Mon-Sat. £5.00. Booking in advance by telephone or in person at the Lyttelton Information Desk (10am-11pm). 'Platforms' (early evening discussions, readings, interviews, debates: 45min) as advertised. Bookshop. Restaurant; refreshments. Free concerts in Lyttelton foyer: daily except Sun before matinee and evening performances.* ☎ *020 7452 3400; www.nationaltheatre.org.uk*

The theatre opens the third phase in the South Bank scheme, both by its position downstream from Waterloo Bridge and, more importantly, by its design. The architect, **Denys Lasdun**, has incorporated three theatres: the Lyttelton, with proscenium stage and seating for 890; the Olivier, with large open stage and audience capacity of 1 100 and the Cottesloe, a studio theatre with a maximum of 400 seats; workshops, bookshops, bars and buffets, within a spacious construction in which the external height is bisected by strata-like cantilevered terraces which parallel the course of the river outside and 'release' the beautiful view of Somerset House and St Paul's beyond.

Aquarium

In the County Hall, Belvedere Road. Open daily, 10am-6pm (5pm last admission). £8.75. ☎ *020 7967 8000; Fax 020 7967 8029; info@londonaquarium. co. uk; www.londonaquarium.co.uk*

Open daily, 10am-6pm (5pm last admission). £8.75. ☎ *020 7967 8000; Fax 020 7967 8029; info@londonaquarium.co.uk; www.londonaquarium.co.uk*

"A fish cathedral", a monumental aquarium has been built in the basement of the County Hall, reaching two floors below the Thames water level. Highlights include moon jellyfish and friendly flatfish.

Dali Universe Exibition

Open daily, 10am-5.30pm (last entry). Closed 25 Dec. £8.50. ☎ *020 7620 2720; Fax 020 7620 3120; info@daliuniverse.com; www.daliuniverse.com*

Dedicated to the Spanish Surrealist artist who worked in diverse artistic media and techniques, the fascinating exhibits provide an insight into his creative genius range from sculpture, graphics, jewellery to furniture and watercolours.

Saatchi Gallery

Open daily, 10am-6pm (10pm, Fri-Sat). £8.50. Refreshments. ☎ *020 7823 2363 (infoline) or 020 7823 2332 (administration); Fax 020 7823 2334; www.saatchi-gallery.co.uk*

Housed in the ornate formal rooms of County Hall, the gallery showcases works from the Saatchi Collection of Modern Art, with a focus notably on young British artists (Damien Hirst, Marc Quinn, Rachel Whiteread, Richard Wilson, Tracey Emin, Gary Hume, Sarah Lucas, Jenny Saville etc). The gallery also presents exhibitions from other international collections and museums.

Hayward Gallery

♿ *Open daily, 10am-6pm (8pm Tue-Wed). £7. Cafe/bar, shop.* ☎ *020 7261 0127 (recorded information),* ☎ *020 79604242 (advance booking); hgenquiries@hayward.org.uk; www.hayward.org.uk*

The gallery, purpose-built to house temporary exhibitions of painting and sculpture was opened in 1968. The building, a terrace-like structure of unfaced concrete, in fact 'works' successfully to provide on two levels five large gallery spaces and three open-air sculpture courts.

Strand – Temple★★

Bordering Covent Garden and on the edge of the city, the area holds many attractions despite the relentless traffic. Lined with ornate buildings recalling its aristocratic past, it boasts elegant hotels which offer every refinement, lively theatres and fabulous art galleries at Somerset House in keeping with its reputation as a place of entertainment. Fleet Street and Temple are part of different traditions: the former is linked with the written press and the latter with the law.

Location

Map pp 11-12 (EFX); Michelin Atlas London: pp 3, 62-64. ⊖ *Temple, Charing Cross.* Strand is adjacent to Covent Garden, Trafalgar Square and Leicester Square. Waterloo Bridge and Hungerford Bridge provide direct access to the South Bank. At the top of Fleet Street are Ludgate Circus and St Paul's Cathedral *(for this part of the walk, see map under The CITY).*
Adjacent Sights: The CITY; COVENT GARDEN; TRAFALGAR SQUARE - WHITEHALL.

Fountains playing in the courtyard of Somerset House

Background

The Strand was an ancient track, midway between the Thames, London's main thoroughfare, and the highway leading west out of the City. Only the churches have survived from the medieval period. From Plantagenet to Hanoverian times it was a street of great mansions and law students' hostels (inns). The south side was particularly favoured by provincial bishops for their town houses. After the Dissolution of the monasteries, the palaces and mansions were purchased by the nobility. Several of these are recorded for posterity in local street names: Essex Street and Devereux Court record the site of Essex House owned by Robert Devereux and later by another Elizabethan favourite, Robert Dudley, Earl of Leicester. Arundel Street recalls the great house of the Howards.
In 1624 **James I** presented York House, one-time palace of the Archbishop, to George Villiers, Duke of Buckingham; Of Alley has been renamed York Place but the rest of the Duke's name is perpetuated in the streets east of Charing Cross railway station. Hungerford Lane recalls the 15C house of a notorious family who replaced it with a market to pay off gambling debts and even built a footbridge (1854) to attract customers, before selling the site for the construction of the railway station.
Between the big houses and down the side lanes were hundreds of small houses, ale houses, brothels, coffee houses and shops. The **New Exchange** (1609 to 1737) was an arcade of shops of which 76 of the 150 were milliners and mercers, patronised by James I and his queen, by **Charles I** and later by **Pepys** who recounts how he bought gloves, linen, lace, garters, stockings and even books there. The Grecian, later the Devereux public house and a favourite with Addison, is now the Edgar Wallace with an Edwardian decoration and interesting mementoes.
In the late Victorian and Edwardian era the Strand was known for its restaurants and hotels – the Cecil (now Shell-Mex) had 1 000 bedrooms, the Metropole, the Victoria and the Grand, and for its theatres: a popular 19C music hall song was *Let's all go down the Strand.*

Temple – The Order of the Knights **Templars** was founded in 1118 to protect pilgrims on the road to the Holy City of Jerusalem, and welcomed to England by **Henry I**. They settled first at the north end of Chancery Lane before moving to a preferred site by the river where they began building their church in 1185. In 1312 the Templars were suppressed and their property assigned to the **Hospitallers** who, in turn, were dispossessed by **Henry VIII**. The church reverted to the crown; the outlying property remained with the lawyers to whom it had previously been leased by the Hospitallers and to whom it was granted, together with the safekeeping of the church, by **James I** in 1608. The lawyers early formed themselves into three Societies: the **Inner Temple** (being within the City; emblem a Pegasus), the **Middle Temple** (emblem a Pascal lamb) and the **Outer Temple**, which was on the site of Essex Street but has long since disappeared. Today the area is abuzz with lawyers through the week and a haven of peace at weekends; at night, it is lit by gaslight.
According to Shakespeare, the origin of the Wars of the Roses derives from the plucking of a red and white rose from the Temple Gardens in 1430.

Walking About

Start from Charing Cross Station and walk down Villiers St to view the railway viaduct.

STRAND★

Today the Strand links Trafalgar Square to Fleet Street and the City and is in the process of redevelopment. The elegant open glazed building of **Coutts Bank** *(no 440)* was designed by **Sir Frederick Gibberd** to be sympathetic to its 19C neighbours in the style of John Nash. The bank was transferred to this address in 1904 by Thomas Coutts.

Directory

Pubs

Cock Tavern (or Ye Olde Cocke Tavern) – *22 Fleet St, EC4Y 1AA – ⊖ Blackfriars – ☎ 020 7353 8570 – Open Mon-Fri 11am-11pm.* The decor is in the 17C style with a panelled bar counter. The restaurant rooms on the first floor were used for meetings of the Dickens and Thackeray Associations.

Punch Tavern – *99 Fleet St, EC4Y 1DE – ⊖ Blackfriars – ☎ 020 7353 6658 – Open Mon-Fri noon-11pm.* The drawings decorating the walls remind us that this was the birthplace of the celebrated satirical magazine. Admire the superb mosaics in the entrance. Excellent beer.

The Devereux – *20 Devereux Court, Essex St, Strand, WC2R 3JJ – ⊖ Temple – ☎ 020 7583 4562 – Open Mon-Fri 11am-11pm.* The Devereux, one of the best pubs in the area, with a flower-decked façade, excellent beer and a restaurant upstairs, is always packed at peak times.

The Sherlock Holmes – *10-11 Northumberland St, WC2N 5DA – ⊖ Embankment, Charing Cross – ☎ 020 7930 2644 – sherlock.WC2N@Laurel pubco.com – Open Mon-Sat 11am-11pm, Sun noon-10.30pm.* The former Northumberland Hotel was renamed The Sherlock Holmes in honour of author Sir Conan Doyle. Upstairs you can also see a reconstruction of the Holmes and Watson study and a host of objects associated with the detective. It is less touristy than you might think, a pleasant pub with a regular clientele.

Ye Olde Cheshire Cheese – *145 Fleet St, EC4A 2BU – ⊖ Blackfriars – ☎ 020 7353 8570 – Open Mon-Fri noon-11pm, Sat noon-3pm and 5.30-9.30pm, Sun noon-3pm.* A huge labyrinthine 17C pub with small beamed rooms and coal fires on three floors; three rooms are restaurants. A Fleet Street institution.

Taking a Break

The Savoy Hotel – *Strand, WC2R 0EU – ⊖ Charing Cross – ☎ 020 7836 4343 – www.the-savoy.com – Open Mon-Fri 2.30-5.30pm, Sat-Sun 2-4pm and 4-6pm – Tea £24/£27; Champagne tea £31.50-£34.50.* Listen to the pianist in the elegant Thames Foyer, where Noel Coward performed, Caruso sang and Pavlova dance, as you take afternoon tea – delicious sandwiches, pastries and cakes and scones with clotted cream and strawberry preserve; for a very special occasion ask for a champagne tea.

Going out for the Evening

American Bar-Savoy Hotel – *Strand, WC2R 0EU – ⊖ Charing Cross, Embankment – ☎ 020 7836 4343 – www.the-savoy. com – Open Mon-Sat 11am-1.30pm.* The American Bar has been a stylish meeting place since it opened in the 1890s. Listen to the pianist and enjoy the tradition of new cocktails invented for special occasions which was started in the 1920s by the famous American barman, Harry Craddock, inventor of the White Lady and Dry Martini.

Gordon's Wine Bar – *47 Villiers St, WC2N 6NE – ⊖ Embankment – ☎ 020 7930 1408 – simon@gordonswinebar.com – Open Mon-Sat 11am-11pm, Sun noon-10pm; closed 25 Dec.* A bar with a soul! ! A narrow staircase leads to the bar and the smoky dusty place is always packed with Londoners. Wine has been served here since 1364. As you savour the bouquet, enjoy excellent cheese and good food at reasonable prices.

Shopping

R Twining & Co – *216 Strand, WC2R 1AP – ⊖ Temple, Charing Cross – ☎ 020 7353 3511 – www.twinings.com – Open Mon-Fri. 9.30am-4.45pm.* Two Chinamen flanking the Twining lion over the door identify the very narrow shop. The famed tea merchant has been located here since 1706. It offers a large selection of teas; there is also a small museum which traces the history of Twining.

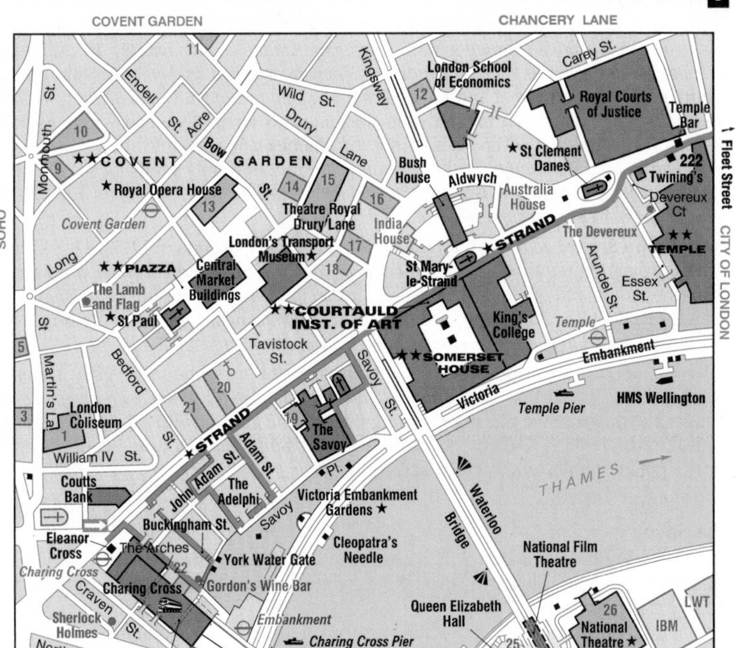

THEATRES

Theatre	No.
Adelphi	21
Albery	5
Aldwych	16
Cambridge	9
Donmar Warehouse	10
Duchess	18
Duke of York's	3
Fortune	14
London Coliseum	1
National Theatre	26
New London	11
Players	22
Playhouse	23
Queen Elizabeth Hall	25
Royal Opera Covent Garden	13
Royal Festival Hall	24
Royalty	12
Savoy	19
Strand	17
Theatre Royal Drury Lane	15
Vaudeville	20

In the station forecourt stands a reproduction, designed by EM Barry, of the original **Eleanor Cross** which stood in Trafalgar Square.

Charing Cross Station

The street frontage is scaled to pleasing proportions appropriate to the Strand site, alongside EM Barry's neo-Gothic **Charing Cross Station Hotel** (1863-64). The modern station buildings conceived by Terry Farrell (1990) as part of a larger all-encompassing design project spanning both banks of the Thames, feature a great white arch over and beyond the station viaduct. This giant glazed railway "hangar", lodged between four granite-faced corner service towers, boldly occupies its strategic position in the riverside panoramic profile.
Down by the river, beneath the viaduct is held the **Charing Cross Collectors Market** *(see PRACTICAL POINTS, Markets)*.

Hungerford Bridge

A footbridge runs parallel to the east side of the plain lattice girder structure (1862) which carries the railway. It replaced a suspension bridge (1845) by Brunel which was later incorporated into Clifton Suspension Bridge. It is undergoing a major facelift as part of the redevelopment of the South Bank.

Take Savoy Pl off Villiers St to Buckingham St.

Buckingham Street

(River side). 17C and 18C brick houses with pilastered, hooded and corbelled doorways still line both sides (nos 12, 17, 18, 20 date from the 1670s) down to Victoria Embankment Gardens. Pepys lived at no 12 in 1679-88. At the south end stands **York Water Gate**, a triple arch of rusticated stone, decorated with the Villiers arms and a scallop shell, built in 1626 at the water's edge by Nicholas Stone, master mason to George Villiers, 1st Duke of Buckingham.

Return to the Strand to view the ornate façades on both sides of the street, then go down the steps to John Adam St and walk round.

The Adelphi

The river front retains the name although the massively ungraceful stone and brick block with cumbersome angle statues could scarcely be more remote from the Royal Adelphi Terrace erected by Robert Adam in 1768-72 (demolished 1937). The Adam brothers – *adelphi* is the Greek word for brothers – transformed the area by the construction along the foreshore of a towering embankment arcade, the Adelphi Arches, supporting a terrace of 11 houses. The row was framed by John (now John Adam) Street, Robert Street and Adam Street, the end houses in the two latter, which overlooked the river, pedimented and decorated to form advanced wings to the terrace. It was the first and possibly finest of Thames-side concepts but the expense was exorbitant and doomed it to be a financial failure; now only a few houses remain to give an idea of how the quarter must have looked in the 18C. At no 10A lived George Bernard Shaw (1896-1927).

John Adam Street: no 8 was built for the **Royal Society of Arts** in 1772-74 by Adam with a projecting porch surmounted by a giant order of fluted columns framing a Serlian window and graces with refined and delicate ornamentation. The RSA was founded in 1754 "to embolden enterprise, to enlarge science, to refine art, to improve our manufacture and extend our commerce."

Adam Street: the east side has a run of houses beginning with no 10, Adam House, neat and compact with a rounded corner and curved ironwork; 9 and 8 are the street's standard with attractive pilastered doors; no 7, in the axis of John Adam Street, is a typical example of the Adam decorative style including his favourite acanthus leaf motif applied to pilasters, cornice and ironwork.

Return to the Strand.

The Savoy

The Savoy is now a precinct which comprises a chapel, a **theatre**, the first public building in the world to be lit throughout by electricity and a grand **hotel** built by D'Oyly Carte in 1889.

The name dates from 1246, when Henry III granted the manor beside the Thames to his queen's uncle, Peter of Savoy. On the acres extending from the Temple to the Adelphi he built a palace which by the 14C had passed to the Dukes of Lancaster and as "the fairest manor in England" became, until his death, the "lodging" of King John of France, captured by the Black Prince at Poitiers (1356). The last owner was John of Gaunt who, however, was forced to flee to Ely Place *(see CHANCERY LANE)* in 1381 when the palace was sacked by Wat Tyler's Kentish rebels. The manor was annexed in 1399 by Henry IV.

Walk down Savoy Hill to Savoy Pl and Victoria Embankment Gardens.

The Queen's Chapel of the Savoy (Chapel of the Royal Victorian Order) – *Savoy Hill. Open (services permitting) Oct-Jul, Tue-Fri, 11.30am-3.30pm. Guided tour by arrangement. ☎ 020 7836 7221*

The chapel, largely rebuilt after the war, dates back to a bequest by Henry VII for the construction of a hospital for 100 "pouer, needie people" and the erection of a dependent place of worship in 1510-16. The hospital was dissolved in 1702 but the chapel and burial yard survived to be made into the Chapel of the Royal Victorian Order in 1937.

Savoy Hill is famous as the site of the BBC's first studios and offices from 1923 to 1932 (plaque on the Embankment façade of no 2 Savoy Place).

The ever burning light in Carting Lane is fuelled by sewer gas.

Victoria Embankment Gardens★

The gardens, complete with their bandstand for summer concerts, were created in 1864. Opposite the gardens on the river front, flanked by great bronze lions stands **Cleopatra's Needle**, erected after a long saga in 1878: one of two needles uncovered at Heliopolis (c 1450 BC), it was first offered to George IV by Mehemet Ali of Egypt. Similar obelisks stand in Paris (Place de la Concorde) and New York.

The dolphin lamp standards and decorated bench ends are appropriate to their riparian location.

Walk back to the Strand and cross Lancaster Pl.

The restaurant **Simpson's in the Strand**, replaces a coffee house – The Grand Cigar Divan founded by Samuel Reiss in 1828. The association with John Simpson came some twenty years later. *See PRACTICAL POINTS, Where to Eat.*

Somerset House★★

The present building was erected enduringly in Portland stone in 1776-86 to the designs of **Sir William Chambers** and housed the Navy and Navy Pay Offices, the, then small, Tax and Excise offices and three learned societies.

The 18C building stands on the site of the palace begun by Protector Somerset in 1547 and still incomplete when he was executed in 1552. He achieved a palace of entirely new appearance, which extended from the Strand to the river and which, on his execution, passed to the crown and was given by each Stuart to his queen: Anne of Denmark (when it was known as Denmark House), Henrietta Maria, who returned to it at the Restoration, and Catherine of Braganza.

The Building – The narrow Strand façade of Somerset House, inspired by Inigo Jones' Palladian riverside gallery designed for Henrietta Maria, has a triple gateway and giant columns beneath a balustrade decorated with statues and a massive statuary group by Bacon.

Through the arch is a vast courtyard surrounded by ranges of buildings treated like rows of terrace houses round a square. A continuous balustrade punctuated by vases unites the fronts. The riverside front stands on a continuous line of massive arches which in the 18C were at the water's edge.

The Strand block of Somerset House, the most elaborate, has two advanced wings and contains the so-called **Fine Rooms**, notable for their pleasing proportions and handsome plasterwork. This was originally designed for three learned societies: the Royal Society, the Antiquaries and the Royal Academy, now in Burlington House *(see PICCADILLY)*.

Somerset House now houses major art collections *(descriptions in Worth a Visit)*. Fountains adorn the piazza which is used for public entertainment and fine **views**★★ of the Thames may be enjoyed from the riverside façade.

St Mary-le-Strand

Open Mon-Fri, 11am-4pm; Sun, 10am-1pm. Leaflet (5 languages). Recital: Wed at 1pm. ☎ 020 7836 3126 (Church), 020 74051929 (Parish office)

This compact, Baroque miniature (1714-24) was the first commission to be undertaken by **James Gibbs**. It is sober and ordered: a simple apsed space that is light and harmoniously proportioned.

The tower rises in four tiers over the rounded porch and first floor pediment to a gilded weather vane. Two superimposed orders, Ionic and Corinthian on the outside and Corinthian and Composite inside, articulate the walls of the single storeyed interior: solid at ground level and the large windows above – intended to lessen the constant noise of traffic over the cobbles. Fine carvings decorate the exterior, but it is perhaps the Italianate plasterwork ceiling which is particularly worthy of note: executed by English craftsmen, the stylised flower heads are especially delicate. It is known as the "Cabbies church"

King's College

King's College, founded in 1829, was housed from its earliest days in the east extension of Somerset House, built in accordance with Chambers' designs; the Strand front (1970s) is in an unrelated, modern style. The courtyard, long and narrow, is terminated by the colonnaded pavilion which completes the Somerset House river front.

Aldwych

The sweeping semicircle was laid out in 1905. The huge half-moon island on the Strand is occupied by massive buildings: Australia House, India House (reliefs) and, in the centre, the 1925-35 **Bush House**, base of the BBC External Services.

St Clement Danes★

Oranges and Lemons carillon: Operates daily at 9am, noon (except Sun), 3pm (except Sun), 6pm. Leaflets (6 languages). ☎ 020 7242 8282, Fax: 020 7404 2129

St Clement's, designed by **Wren** in 1682, with the open spire in three diminishing pillared stages – the steeple was added by **James Gibbs** (1719) – was burnt out on 10 May 1941 and rebuilt as the RAF church in 1955-58. The dark oak panelling, first floor galleries beneath a richly decorated vault and plasterwork Stuart coat of arms conforms to Wren's original design, now embellished with Air Force mementoes that include badges carved in Welsh slate and inlaid in the pavement, memorials of the Commonwealth air forces and the Polish squadrons, a USAAF and other shrines. The grand pulpit is the original one by Grinling Gibbons.

Tradition has it that the original 9C church of St Clement Danes was built by Danish merchants married to Englishwomen; St Clement, Bishop of Rome and patron of seafarers, was martyred under Trajan. "Oranges and lemons say the bells of St Clement's" refers to the boats that came up the Thames to land fruit for sale in Clare Market (on the site of Kingsway) and paid a tithe in kind to the church and although the association is disputed with St Clement Eastcheap *(see CITY – Monument)*, the carillon rings out the **nursery rhyme**.

At the east end stands a statue of Dr Samuel Johnson, a worshipper at the church who lived near by.

No 216 **Twinings** is a very old tea shop *(see description in Directory)*. Several generations have witnessed changes in tea trading: the Commutation Act almost cancelled the hefty tax imposed by the Treasury (1784); in 1839 the clipper *Calcutta* landed Indian tea from Assam thereby breaching the Chinese monopoly; new supplies were imported from Ceylon in 1879. Today Twinings manufacture over 150 blends of tea, herb and fruit infusions.

Lloyd's Law Courts Branch

No 222. The **Palsgrave Tavern**, as frequented by the dramatist Ben Jonson, was named after Frederick Palsgrave, later King of Bohemia, who married Elizabeth, daughter of James I. All three figures are commemorated in the singular glazed earthenware decoration supplied by Royal Doulton. In 1883, the premises were refurbished as a restaurant complete with electric lighting generated by steam engines and dynamos, an elaborate ventilation system and its own Artesian well to provide elaborate fountains, but the business failed. Inside, the building, a branch of Lloyds bank since 1895, is panelled with American walnut and sequoia, inset with tiles.

Wig and Pen Club

229/230 Strand. The building, which survived the **Great Fire** (1666) dates from 1625. It now comprises two narrow 18C town houses with dark wood panelling. The club, which is the home of the London Press Club, draws its members from journalism, business and the law.

Royal Courts of Justice

The Law Courts date from 1874-82 when the Perpendicular design of GE Street was constructed to replace the ranges erected around the courts' original seat in Westminster Hall. The centrepiece inside is the Great Hall, a vaulted arcade decorated with foliated doorways, blind arcades, diapering and a seated statue of the architect. The early courtrooms, the majority (there are still more than 20) lead off the hall which is marked outside by a needle spire, off setting the long arched façade, the heavy tower and polygonal west end. There is a small exhibition of legal costumes.
At this point, the Strand gives way to Fleet Street enclosed within the confines of the City of London: the boundary is marked by the Temple Bar.

TEMPLE BAR TO LUDGATE CIRCUS

Area map under CITY **(AY)**

Fleet Street

Named after the **River Fleet** which flows south from Hampstead to drain into the Thames at Blackfriars, Fleet Street links the City with Westminster – the obvious place between centres of commerce and government for journalists to congregate. The 'Street of Ink', once synonymous with the press, has changed in character since the age of technology has ousted many of the most famous major newspaper publishers to offices in Docklands *(Daily Mail, Times, Daily Telegraph)* or south of the river *(Daily Express Financial Times, Observer).* The main thoroughfare and royal route is lined with imposing buildings in a variety of styles.

Temple Bar

It has been the City's western barrier since the Middle Ages; the sovereign pauses here to receive and return the Pearl Sword from the Lord Mayor on entering the City. The present memorial pillar with statues of Queen Victoria and the future Edward VII surmounted by the City griffin, dates from 1880. It replaced the "bars" which had developed from 13C posts and chains and at various times constituted a high, arched building, a prison (thrown down by **Wat Tyler** in 1381) and finally an arch of Portland stone designed by Wren in 1672 and used in the days of public execution as a spike for heads and quarters. It was dismantled in 1870 and removed to Theobald's Park near Waltham Cross.

Child & Co

No 1 Fleet Street. One of the country's oldest banks *(now Royal Bank of Scotland)* "at the sign of the Marigold" *(see OSTERLEY PARK)* has also been known as the Devil Tavern.

Pass through Inner Temple Gateway (between nos 16 and 17 Fleet Street).

Temple★★

See Background above.

Inner Temple – The Tudor **Inner Temple Gateway**, gabled, half timbered, 3 storeys high, each advanced on the one below so that the tunnel arch and pilastered stone ground floor are in shadow, dates from 1610 (reconstructed 1906). It leads into the lane, past 19C buildings and the house *(right)* where Dr Johnson lived from 1760 to 1765, to the church.

Temple Church★★ – *Open Wed-Sun, 11am-4pm. Guide book. verger@templechurch.com; www.templechurch.com*

This special church survived the Great Fire but was badly damaged in the Blitz (1941). "The two learned and honourable Societies of this House" are the four Inns of Court, the Inner and Middle Temples; it is a private chapel under the jurisdiction of the Sovereign as Head of the Church, who appoints the Master of the Temple.
It is largely built of soft-coloured stone. At the west end, the wall sweeps in a great curve reaching up to a square crenellated roofline. The round-headed west doorway into the round church of 1160-85 is Romanesque, protected from weathering by a rib-vaulted porch added later.
The round church is modelled on the Church of the Holy Sepulchre in Jerusalem: six composite piers of Purbeck marble support an arcade of transitional pointed arches, a triforium articulated by interlacing blind arcading and tall clerestory windows. Above the door is a Lombard-style radiating window. Laterally, this open space is ringed first by an ambulatory, then by a continuous stone sill that provides seating before being enclosed by a wall decorated with blind arcading and crisply carved grotesque heads.

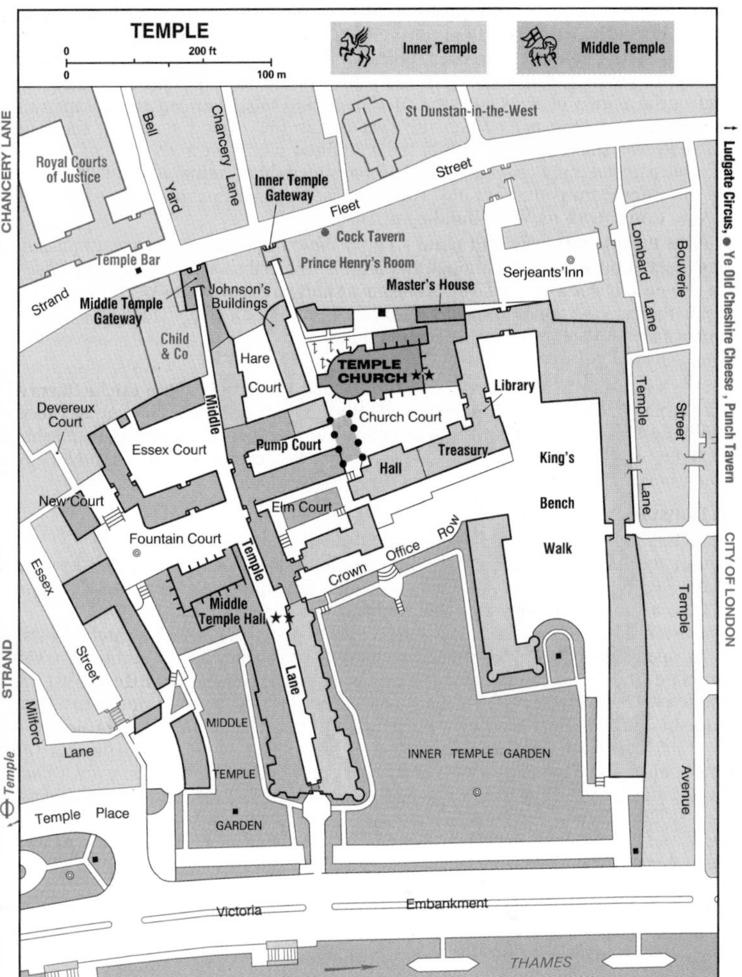

A sense of clarity and order is enhanced by the stylised capital decoration and the polished ringed shafts of Purbeck marble, that soar up to the conical roof. On the stone floor lie ten 10C-13C effigies of knights in armour. The traditional flexed posture may indicate that the knights took part in the crusades. The font is a replica, carved with St George and a hunting scene preceded by playing dogs.

Level with the beginning of the hall-church chancel (1220-40) are placed two 16C monuments "repaired and beautified in 1687" – behind that on the north side (Edmund Plowden d 1584) is the penitential cell dating back to Templar times (door in chancel).

In the chancel, slender Purbeck columns rise to form the ribs of the quadripartite vaulting. The oak reredos designed by Wren was carved by **William Emmett** in 1682 for £45. Note in passing the heraldic floor brass (half way down the nave) with a Latin scroll winding between 29 shields.

In the graveyard (north side) lies **Oliver Goldsmith**, a contemporary of Dr Johnson. To the northeast of the church stands the **Master's House** rebuilt in 17C style.

The **Inner Temple Hall**, Treasury and Library were all rebuilt after the war.

Pass through the passageway to the east.

King's Bench Walk – The northern of the two ranges, in the largest Temple court, dates from 1678 and is by **Wren** (no 1 rebuilt). Below the east gate are two houses of especial note, no 7 of 1685 and no 8 of 1782.

Retrace your steps and follow the route through passageways to the west.

Middle Temple – In **Pump Court** the cloisters (from Church Court) and the south side have been rebuilt (Edward Maufe); the north (except for the 19C Farrar's Building) is late 17C.

Middle Temple Hall★★ – (♿) *Open Mon-Fri, 10am-11.30am and 3-4pm. Closed Bank Hols and during Law Vacations. library@middletemple.org.uk; www.middletemple.org.uk* The Elizabethan great hall has ancient oak timbers, panelling and fine carving, heraldic glass, helmets and armour: the roof (1574) is a double hammerbeam, the finest of the period. The small panels in the high wainscot are bright with the arms of readers who instructed the medieval law students who not only ate but attended lectures and even slept in the hall (100ft/30.5m ? 40ft/12m). At the west end above the high table are royal portraits (Charles I after Van Dyck, Charles II by Kneller, and Queen Elizabeth). According to tradition, Elizabeth watched the first performance of Shakespeare's *Twelfth Night* (1602) here in the company of the benchers in the hall. When the spectacular 16C carved screen at the hall's east end was shattered by a bomb, the splintered pieces were dug out of the rubble and painstakingly reassembled. The roof, incredibly, remained unharmed.

Up the steps from Fountain Court (immortalised by Dickens in *Martin Chuzzlewit*) is **New Court** with its Wren building of 1676.

Middle Temple Gateway and Lane – The pedimented gateway with giant pilasters was erected only in 1684 although the lane is referred to as early as 1330 since it used to end in stairs on the river, affording a short cut by water to Westminster. Just inside the gate are two houses of 1693, their ground floors overshadowed by jutting timber-faced upper storeys with 17C windows.

Return to Fleet St and proceed east.

On the south side of Fleet Street stands the **Cock Tavern (Ye Olde Cocke Tavern)** *(see Directory)*. At no 17 is **Prince Henry's Room**: its upstairs tavern room has Tudor panelling with ornate strapwork, a Jacobean ceiling with a centre decoration of Prince of Wales' feathers and the initials PH. It is now crammed with Samuel Pepys mementoes. *Open Mon-Sat, 11am-2pm. Closed Bank Hols.*

St Dunstan-in-the-West

Open Tue, 10am-4pm, otherwise by appointment. ☎ 020 7405 1929

Within the City boundary stands this church which was built in 1833 by John Shaw, slightly to the north of a site on which previous churches had stood since 1237 so as not to jut out onto Fleet Street. It was badly bombed in 1944.

The exterior, apart from the neo-Gothic tower which rises from an arched porch to an openwork octagonal lantern, is chiefly remarkable for the additions which associate the church with Fleet Street: the bust of **Lord Northcliffe** (1930), the public **clock** complete with its giant oak jacks (the first with a minute hand was made by Thomas Harrys in 1671 for the handsome sum of £35); the **statues** from the 1586 **Lud Gate** include that of Queen Elizabeth I modelled during her lifetime and originally on the gate's west face (in a pedimented niche over a doorway), while to the right stand the figures of the mythical King Lud and his two sons (1586). Corbels at the main door are carved with the likenesses of Tyndale *(west)* and John Donne *(east)* who were both associated with St Dunstan's as were **Izaac Walton** (the *Compleat Angler* was printed in the churchyard as was Milton's *Paradise Lost*) and the Hoares banking family.

St Dunstan's, dedicated to the patron of goldsmiths, jewellers and locksmiths, is octagonal in plan with a high, star vault. The main altar, oriented to the north, is set in 17C "choice panelling", Flamboyant Flemish in style.

Fetter Lane

Beyond, yet still off the north side of Fleet Street is a series of narrow alleys known collectively as **"the Courts"**: alas these have been substantially redeveloped, their names providing the sole vestige of interest: Crane, Red Lion, Johnson's, St Dunstan's, Bolt, Three Kings, Hind, Wine Office, Cheshire and Peterborough.

Turn into Johnson's Court to Gough Sq.

Dr Johnson's House★★

17 Gough Square. Open Mon-Sat, 11am-5.30pm (5pm winter). Closed Bank Hols. £4. Guide book (4 languages). Guided tour (50min) £3 by appointment. ☎ 020 7353 3745; curator@drjohnsonshouse.org; www.drjohnsonshouse.org

This unremarkable house so typical of the late 17C, was home to the great scholar and lexicographer between 1749 and 1759. Modest in size and proportion, it was chosen by **Johnson** (1709-84) almost certainly for its large, well-lit garret, where he worked with his five secretaries to complete his *Dictionary* published in 1755. The small rooms on each floor are sparsely furnished with 18C oak gate-leg tables and chairs, period prints, mementoes and a collection of books on the impecunious essayist's life and times, including his biography by James Boswell. The work completed, he moved to chambers in the Temple, in 1765 to no 7 Fleet Street (known purely coincidentally as Johnson's Court), and finally to Bolt Court where he died in 1784.

Return to Fleet St, past Shoe Lane then cross to the south side.

In Wine Office Court is the **Cheshire Cheese** pub and restaurant *(see Directory)*. Nestling between the first floor windows of the gable-fronted Gothic no **143** is a 19C statue of Mary Queen of Scots.

The **Reuters and Press Association** is located at no 85 in premises designed by Lutyens in 1935; the somewhat dilapidated **Express** group building at nos 121-8 remains a landmark, its bold 1931 black and clear glass panels set in chromium, with straight lines throughout except for the corner on Shoe Lane; at no 135 stands the **Daily Telegraph** building (1928) built in a ponderous mixture of styles.

St Bride's★

Open Mon-Sat, 8am (9.30am Sat) to 4.30pm. Closed Bank Hols. Recitals: certain days (except Aug, Advent, Lent) at 1.15pm. Brochure. ☎ 020 7427 0133; Fax 020 7583 4867; info@stbrides.com; www.stbrides.com

The famous white **spire★★** of St Bride's (dedicated to the 16C Irish Saint Bridget), Wren's tallest and most floating steeple, rises by four open octagonal stages to a final open pedestal and tapering obelisk which terminates in a vane (226ft/69m above ground). When the spire was newly erected a baker used it as a model for wedding cakes; he made a fortune and inaugurated a lasting tradition; his wife's silk dress is in the museum in the crypt.

The wedding-cake steeple of St Bride's Church

J. Malburet/MICHELIN

In 1940 Wren's church, described as "a madrigal in stone", was gutted by fire leaving only the steeple and calcined outer walls standing. During rebuilding the crypt was opened; it had been used for burials from c 1720 until it was closed after the cholera epidemic of 1853. Subsequent excavations have revealed a Roman ditch, walls, a pavement and the outlines of church buildings on the site dating to Saxon times at least.

The exterior was restored by Godfrey Allen to Wren's design with tall rounded windows between pedimented doors surmounted by circular windows; above is a line of oval clerestory windows; at the east end a tripartite window beneath a pediment.

The interior has been re-arranged to enclose the nave, now set with collegiate-style pews, and to fill the east end with a massive 17C style reredos against a *trompe-l'œil* painting. Wren's design of a barrel-vaulted nave and groined aisles has been retained. The decoration is 17C.

The nationally famous **St Bride Printing Library** and Bridewell Theatre are located nearby as is the **Punch Tavern** *(see Directory)*, named after the magazine which had premises there.

Continue along Fleet St to Ludgate Circus.

Associations

It is St Bride's associations, however, rather than its architecture, that make it unique to many: **Thomas Becket** was born close by; **King John** held a parliament in the church in 1210; **Henry VIII,** advised by **Thomas Wolsey,** built Bridewell Palace nearby between the church and the river, and received Charles V there in 1522; high ranking churchmen unable to pay for lodgings within the City walls, built town houses in the neighbourhood (Salisbury Square) and since the clergy were the largest literate group in the land it was only natural that when **Wynkyn de Worde** acquired his master's press in 1491, he should remove it from Westminster to St Bride's and Fleet Street (Caxton had been wealthy enough not to have to depend upon the press for his livelihood, unlike his apprentice). By the time Wynkyn died in 1535 (he was buried in St Bride's), the parish boasted several printers, including Richard Grafton who printed the first English Language Bible in 1539. The church was the first to use the Book of Common Prayer, while its neighbouring taverns and coffeehouses were frequented by Chaucer, Shakespeare, Milton, Lovelace, Evelyn, Pepys (born nearby and like all his family christened in the church), Dryden, Izaac Walton, Edmund Waller (poet), Aubrey, Ashmole, John Ogilby (mapmaker), Thomas Tompion (father of English clock and watchmaking), Addison; in the 18C by Johnson and Boswell, Joshua Reynolds, Goldsmith, Garrick, Burke, Pope, Richardson (coffin in the crypt) and Hogarth; in the 19C by Charles Lamb, Hazlitt, Wordsworth, Keats, Hood, Leigh Hunt, Dickens. Today modern pew backs are labelled with the names of contemporaries, for St Bride's remains the printers' church, the Cathedral of Fleet Street.

Worth a Visit

Courtauld Institute of Art★★

♿ *Open daily, 10am (noon Sun) to 6pm. Closed 24-26 Dec, 1 Jan. £5. Coffee shop. ☎ 020 7848 2526; Fax 020 7848 2589; galleryinfo@courtauld.ac.uk; www.courtauld.ac.uk*

The foundation of an institute dedicated to art connoisseurship, the teaching of art history on the lines of the Harvard University – Fogg Museum, and the preservation of art was largely initiated by Viscount Lee of Fareham (1868-1947). This extremely fine collection is drawn from several major bequests and is complemented by long-term loans.

Samuel Courtauld began collecting Impressionist and Post-Impressionist paintings in 1922. His perceptive eye and discerning taste selected some of the most famous expressions of the modern masters.

Count Antoine Seilern (The Princes' Gate Collection – 1978) was Austrian by extraction but British by birth. As he had undertaken research into the Venetian sources of Rubens's ceiling pictures while in Vienna, 32 paintings and over 20 drawings by the master make up the bulk of his important donation which includes works from early Netherlandish (*Entombment* by Master of Flémalle) and Italian Schools (Bernardo Daddi triptych, Tiepolo oil sketches), and several pieces by modern masters Cézanne, Kokoschka, Pissarro, Renoir. There is also a large number of important drawings.

Viscount Lee of Fareham, having given his first collection and Elizabethan manor house "Chequers" to the Nation in 1917 for use as a country retreat for Prime Ministers in office, began building his second collection in the early 1920s. Italian Renaissance painting (Botticelli *Holy Trinity;* Giovanni Bellini *Assassination of St Peter Martyr,* Paolo Veronese *Baptism of Christ*) complements the Flemish and English portraits (Dobson, Lely, Gainsborough, Romney, Raeburn).

Sir Robert Witt donated his extensive collection of old master drawings collected for their exceptional quality and individual worth (Gainsborough sketchbooks) in the early 1920s. The documentary photographic archive was acquired in 1952. His son, Sir John Witt (1907-82) also left a number of important British watercolours.

Thomas Gambier-Parry (1816-88) collected 14C Italian Primitives (Bernardo Daddi – Crucifixion polyptych, Lorenzo Monaco – *Coronation of the Virgin,* three Fra Angelico predella panels.

Roger Fry (1866-1934) was an art historian, critic and painter who collected contemporary works by Duncan Grant, Vanessa Bell associated with the **Bloomsbury Group** and the Omega Workshop during the 1930s *(see INTRODUCTION – Painting)*. His personal taste was for Bonnard, Derain, Friesz, O'Connor, Rouault, Sickert and Seurat.

GALLERIES

Allow about 1 hr. Paintings are hung chronologically or for contrast and comparison: displays are therefore subject to change. Interior colour schemes conform where possible, to William Chambers' original specifications.

Gallery 1: Royal Academy Teaching Room – Exquisite examples from the Early Italian and Low Countries Schools have a jewel-like quality that is emphasised by their size, gold background and pious devotional purpose. Rare pieces by the Tuscan Bernardo **Daddi** show the artist tentatively breaking away from Byzantine iconography by animating his figures with emotion – the choir of angels chatter together, the Virgin recoils from the Angel of the Annunciation. Lorenzo **Monaco** endows his elegant figures with weight and volume (*Coronation of the Virgin* – c 1395). The Northern artists developed a far more detailed style facilitated by oil painting, but drawn from observation: draperies fall into brittle folds and plants are minutely documented. Intense expression pervades the religious subjects, as a tear is wiped away or the angels resigned to Fate bear the symbolic crown of thorns and nails of the cross (**Master of Flémalle** *The Entombment* Triptych – c 1420). In the 16C landscape and architectural features are introduced in sacred painting (*The Madonna with Child and Angels* by Q Massys).

The showcases display English and French ivories carved with religious scenes; Limoges enamels; Venetian and Bohemian glass; Islamic metalwork.

Gallery 2: Royal Academy Ante-room and Library – The main panel depicting the *Theory of Art* by Reynolds has been replaced by a copy. The panels dedicated to Nature, History, Allegory and Fable are by Cipriani.

Botticelli's *Holy Trinity* would probably have been the central panel of an altarpiece commissioned for the Augustinian convent of Sant' Elisabetta delle Convertite, a sanctuary for reformed prostitutes, which would explain the prominence given to John the Baptist (patron saint of Florence) and a penitent Mary Magdalene in the barren landscape. The Archangel Raphael holding the hand of Tobias is often portrayed to represent Redemption – as his name means 'God has healed'.

The culture of the Italian city states in the 15C is exemplified by the combination of secular interests and religious subjects (Perugino). In *The Creation and The Fall of Man* by Albertinelli, scenes are shown chronologically in a harmonious composition. The gentle landscape reveals a Flemish influence while the figures are reminiscent of antique statuary.

Gallery 3: Royal Society Meeting Room – The strong colour scheme is based upon paint samples and surviving original documentation.

The incomplete panel of *The Holy Family* is attributed to **Perino del Vaga**: note how the warm ground pervades the painted figures with a golden hue and the Florentine artist's ability to suggest movement and alertness between the figures. Lorenzo **Lotto**'s *Holy Family with St Anne* is animated by the diagonal emphasis of the composition emphasising the youthful expressions of the fearful Virgin and loving Christ-Child. In *The Virgin and Child* by **Parmigianino** the elegance and poise of the Virgin is characteristic of the artist's refined idea of beauty. The naturalistic treatment of *The Adoration of the Shepherds* by **Tintoretto** reveals the symbolism attached to the Nativity (the Child on a patch of straw, peasant woman offering a basket of eggs). In *The Baptism of Christ* Veronese captures the tension among the protagonists and the play of light on the figures and landscape.

The Morelli marriage chests (*cassoni* – 1472), carved and painted, are notable: the front panels depict scenes taken from Livy's *Histories* while the end panels show the masculine Virtues, Justice and Fortitude.

Gallery 4: Royal Society and Society of Antiquaries Ante-room – The delicate stucco decoration is French in feeling; wreaths would have framed portrait medallions – now lost: the ceiling grisaille (monochrome) panels show putti playing with objects representing Earth, Air, Fire and Water; the central panel shows the head of Apollo surrounded by the signs of the Zodiac.

The early tradition of Netherlandish painting is represented by **Bruegel the Elder**: religious subjects set in vast landscapes, balanced composition, bands of colour to emphasise spatial recession *(Landscape with the Flight into Egypt)*, austere composition and monumental figures *(grisaille – Christ and the Woman taken in Adultery)*. *Adam and Eve* (1526) provides Lucas Cranach the Elder, friend and ally of Luther, with an opportunity to represent nude figures, markedly influenced by Italianate prototypes diffused by engravings and woodcuts. Many of the portraits are particularly striking (*Sir John Luttrell* by H Eworth).

Gallery 5: Society of Antiquaries Meeting Room – Several works by **Rubens** demonstrate the master's ability to treat historical and religious subjects, portraits and landscape with equal adeptness. Strong contrasts of light and texture, gesture and emotion characterise the colourful and restless compositions, exaggerated to some extent in the *modelli* or oil sketches produced for a large altarpiece. The portrait of Baladassare Castiglione is copied from an original painting by Raphael in the Louvre. The intimate scene *The Family of Jan Bruegel* has great impact. The *Landscape by Moonlight* is more contemplative in nature.

Gallery 6: Royal Academy Council and Assembly Rooms – The ceiling panels painted by Benjamin West and Angelica Kauffman were moved to Burlington House when the Royal Academy moved there in 1837.

Portraiture became an important genre in the 17C. **William Dobson** and **Sir Peter Lely** emerge as masters of a style pioneered by Van Dyck and providing modern viewers with a strong idea of contemporary dress and attitude.

Van Dyck also contributed to developments in English painting: his portraits are dignified yet informal, the eye of the sitter is often engaged by that of the onlooker. Rich painterly effects of fabric, fur, hair and skin are all detailed with energy and skill.

Gallery 7: Antique Academy – As with landscape painting, portraiture emerges in the 18C as uncontroversial subject matter in which English artists achieved new heights: **Gainsborough**, **Reynolds**, **Raeburn**, **Ramsay** preserve natural likenesses of the leading thinkers, intellectuals, leaders and gentry of the Age of Enlightenment. Sketches for altarpieces and ceiling frescoes in luminous colours reveal GB **Tiepolo**'s (1696-1770) technical mastery and deep, religious feeling.

The collection of silver was made by three generations of the Courtauld family, Huguenot refugees from western France; their work moved from the elegant Queen Anne style, through mid-century Rococo to the Neoclassical style in the late 1760s.

Galleries 8 and 9: Ante-room and Royal Academy Great Room – Light is the main preoccupation of the 19C French landscape painters at Barbizon and their followers the Impressionists. Bonnard, Boudin, Cézanne, Pissarro, Sisley, Seurat, Monet and Renoir all explored landscapes with stretches of water *(Deauville, Autumn Effect at Argenteuil, Boats on the Seine, Le Lac d'Annecy, The Bridge at Courbevoie)*.

Informality seems to pervade the early 20C collection. **Fry**'s collection of French pictures included **Bonnard**'s *Young Woman in an Interior*, a portrait of the artist's mistress and subsequent wife Marthe Boursin. Another key influence is **Derain** who painted simplified forms with bold colour.

Manet's *A Bar at the Folies-Bergère* is a late work presented as a bold portrait of a young working woman; the wealthier members of the audience reflected in the mirror behind her seem oblivious of the trapeze artist wearing green pumps suspended in the top left corner. The sketch for *Le Déjeuner sur l'Herbe* (final version in Musée d'Orsay – Galerie du Jeu de Paume) was intentionally controversial – while being "modern", Manet desperately hoped to earn respect from the Salon establishment – his figures, dressed in contemporary fashion, echo pictures from the Renaissance (Titian's *Concert champêtre* in the Louvre and Raimondi engraving after Raphael's *Judgement of Paris*). **Degas** was a close ally of Manet. He was particularly influenced by Japanese prints and photography, experimenting with viewpoints – down and across the stage in *Two Dancers on Stage* thereby leaving a large section of the picture plain empty. In *Woman at a Window*, the light source is behind the sitter thereby obscuring her features completely.

A Bar at the Folies-Bergères, *E Manet*

Toulouse-Lautrec uses paint as if it were pastel, faces are lit and even distorted by artificial light *(Tête-à-tête Supper)* and volumes are flattened: in *Jane Avril at the entrance to the Moulin Rouge* Jane's fur-collared coat is defined as economically as the hat and coat hanging on a peg behind. **Cézanne**, considered as the "father of modern art", builds a suggestion of space and depth into still-life *(Still-life with Plaster Cupid)* and landscape *(Montagne Ste Victoire)* by means of colour (blues and greens give depth whereas reds and oranges give relief) and form arranged in the foreground, middleground and background. His figures *(The Card-players)* meanwhile are strong and direct studies of personality.

In *Nevermore* and *Te Reriora,* painted at the height of **Gauguin**'s Tahitian period, naturally posed figures are shown in the intimacy of the home, in harmony with a more primitive way of life. **Van Gogh** also developed his own individual style: *Peach Blossom in the Crau* working in the mainstream Impressionist manner where fractured light is boldly captured by strong brushstrokes of thick paint. In his *Self-portrait with Bandaged Ear* the artist is dressed in a greeny-blue coat which gives his eyes a haunting look; behind, Van Gogh acknowledges the inspiration he derived from Japanese prints, here apparent in the blue doorframe and easel used to suggest the features of the picture space. Whereas Van Gogh, Degas and Monet use strokes of contrasting strong colour together, **Seurat** mechanically painted in dots of colour which if seen from a particular distance merge into tonal values. Comparative examples of pointillism are the dusty interior scene *Young Woman powdering herself* and the misty outdoor landscape *Bridge at Courbevoie.*

Galleries 10, 11: Private rooms – These rooms are now used for thematic displays drawn from the Institute's collection of Impressionist and Post-Impressionist works. Domestic interiors provide recurrent subjects for Walter Sickert, Roger Fry and Vanessa Bell, members of the Omega Workshops, an artistic faction of the **Bloomsbury Group** (*Lily Pond* four-fold screen by Duncan Grant). This collection of works by British artists should be considered as a selection made by discerning individuals for their own personal pleasure rather than for a major public museum, and as such modern art is presented as highly approachable.

Gallery 12: Royal Academy School of Painting – The room where the Royal Academy once presented its exhibitions is now used for special displays.

The Gilbert Collection★★

Open daily, 10am-6pm. Closed 24-25 Dec. £5. no charge after 4.30pm. Audio guide. ☎ 020 7420 9400; Fax 020 7420 9440; info@gilbert-collection.org.uk; www.gilbert-collection.org.uk

From the main entrance (Embankment) pass into the splendid vaulted rooms displaying richly ornamented mosaic cabinets, tables and decorative panels with at the far end superb gilded and silver gates. The magnificent array of **tableware** (mezzanine) in silver and silver gilt includes large platters and ewers made by De Lamerie and Storr among others from stately homes such as Althorp, Belton, Stowe and Powderham Castle and some solid gold vessels. Among the outstanding collection of gold boxes are six jewelled snuffboxes which belonged to Frederick II of Prussia. The micromosaics are remarkable. An 18C barge in the King's Barge House recalls a past era when the Thames was a busy waterway.

Hermitage Rooms

♿ *Open daily, 10am-6pm (5pm last admission). Closed 24-26 Dec, 1 Jan. £6. ☎ 020 7845 4630; Fax 020 7845 4637; info@hermitagerooms.org.uk; www.hermitagerooms.org.uk*

The gallery presents rotating exhibitions of art treasures from the prestigious State Hermitage Museum in St Petersburg offering a unique insight into Russian art and history. A video screen shows the live scene at the Russian museum.

Tate Britain★★★

Tate Britain enjoys a superb site overlooking the Thames. The imposing building is a splendid showcase for British Art and after extensive redevelopment, it boasts modern facilities for innovative displays of its fine collections. The gallery has a strong tradition of well-presented special exhibitions and public events; it also sponsors The Turner Prize, a prestigious award for the visual arts.

Location

Map p 12 (EZ); Michelin Atlas London: p 46. ⊖ Pimlico. The gallery is situated along the embankment running from Westminster to Chelsea and near Vauxhall Bridge. Victoria Station is to the west.

Adjacent Sights: WESTMINSTER; TRAFALGAR SQUARE – WHITEHALL.

Background

Tate Britain is the national gallery of British Art (16C to the present day). It is also entrusted with the Archive of Twentieth Century British Art for works of art, artist's writings, film, video, sound recordings and associated printed ephemera.

National Gallery of British Art – 50 years after the purchase of the Angerstein Collection and the founding of the National Gallery (1824), the nation had acquired a large number of works that were shuffled between the National Gallery, the Victoria and Albert Museum and Marlborough House: the **Chantrey Bequest** provided for the purchase of works by living artists; the **Vernon** and **Sheepshanks** Collections; the Turner Bequest (1856) included 300 oil paintings and 20 000 watercolours and drawings from the artist's personal estate.

In 1889 the initiative was taken by the sugar broker Henry Tate who was an astute collector of British art; he offered his collection of 67 paintings (including JE Millais's *Ophelia*) to the nation together with £80 000 for a purpose-built gallery dedicated to British art post 1790 on condition that the government provide a site for it. The Tate opened in 1897 on the site of the former Millbank Prison.

National Collection of Modern Foreign Art – In 1915, Sir Hugh Lane died when the *Lusitania* was torpedoed off the south coast of Ireland leaving 39 paintings, including some superb Impressionists, "to found a collection of Modern Continental Art in London" *(see NATIONAL GALLERY)*. Extensions to the original building were endowed by the son of Sir Joseph Duveen in 1926 and in 1937 to accommodate sculpture; further building was completed in 1979; the Tate then took over the former Queen Alexandra Hospital, before the Clore Wing was designed by James Stirling (1987) to accommodate the Turner collection. In 1954 the Tate Gallery became legally independent of the National Gallery.

The museum is devoted exclusively to **British Art from 1500 to the Present Day** illustrating the quality, diversity, character, originality and influence of British art over five centuries. The works are presented chronologically with rooms devoted to major artists. The text below traces the main trends and highlights significant paintings. As the contemporary collections are divided between Tate Britain and Tate Modern, the modern schools are dealt with under Tate Modern *(see BANKSIDE – SOUTHWARK)* where British movements are placed in the international context.

Practicalities – It is advisable to obtain a gallery plan from the information desks as the galleries are regularly re-hung.

The vulnerability of many works on paper to exposure to light means that they are displayed for short periods only (and then in subdued light) – while endeavours to represent paintings by each artist are made, it is impossible to ensure that a particular watercolour is on view; if you intend to visit the collection so as to see a particular work of art it is advisable to contact the Gallery first to check whether it is on display.

Duveen Sculpture Galleries – The lofty spaces of the central galleries, particularly the Sackler Octagon, make a superb setting for displays of modern sculpture taken from the gallery's collection or on temporary show.

Highlights

♿ *Open daily, 10am-5.50pm (5pm last admission to exhibitions). Closed 24-26 Dec. No charge for permanent collection; variable fee for temporary exhibitions. Guide book (6 languages). Restaurant: Open daily noon-3pm (4pm Sun). Self-service café: Open daily, 10am-5.40pm. Audio guide, £3. ☎ 020 7887 8008 (recorded information), 020 7887 8000; 7887 8687 (minicom); Fax 020 7887 8007; information@tate.org.uk; www.tate.org.uk*

PAINTING IN BRITAIN 16C – 19C

For more information on the evolution of the British School, see INSIGHTS AND IMAGES – Painting.

Image and Allegory: English Renaissance

John Bettes painted the earliest English work in the collection: his *Man in a Black Cap* betrays the influence of Holbein, highlighting the face against a background of mottled brown wall and fur collar, black cap and robe. **Hans Eworth** demonstrates a similar talent at rendering the exquisite details of an embroidered dress and a chalcedony cameo set in gold.

Nicholas Hilliard, the most famous Elizabethan miniaturist encapsulates an idealised vision of his gracious queen: flat, stylised, linear, exquisite, fragile... Elizabeth is shown holding a rose, a Tudor emblem, red for the House of Lancaster, thornless like that borne by the Virgin Mary, "the rose without thorn": a powerful image full of political allegory.

Other continental painters (Geerhardt, Mytens) attracted by royal patronage gently chart a change in climate from simple austerity to a celebration of status: the prolific **Van Dyck** paints his figures standing comfortably in space, poised in movement or gesture.

The unsigned portrait of *The Cholmondeley Sisters* is highly stylised but is nevertheless quite striking; it naively records in the bottom left corner that it depicts two ladies of the family who were born, married and gave birth on the same day.

William Dobson's portrait of *Endymion Porter (see INSIGHTS AND IMAGES – Painting)*, executed during Charles I exile in Oxford during the Civil War, shows the artist's concern for capturing the personality of his sitters.

Peter Lely adapted to the delicate political climate: his sitters are shown with elegant informality in uncontroversial poses. His biblical and mythological subjects *(Susannah and the Elders)* meanwhile, verge on the erotic, hitherto unprecedented in the Puritan age.

Hogarth and Modern Life

Hogarth was a perceptive portraitist *(Captain Coram)* and versatile painter, the patriotic author of "modern moral subjects" and humorous satires that make him the first great commentator of his era (*O The Roast Beef of Old England* or *Calais Gate; Scene from the Beggars Opera VI; The Dance* or *The Happy Marriage*). In *The Painter and his Pug,* the oval self-portrait rests upon three volumes labelled Shakespeare (comic and tragic theatre), Swift (acutely observed social and political comment in fiction) and Milton (epic poetry) – as if to confirm the complementary objectives of painting and literature; Trump, his pet pug, represents the private side of the sitter. The fashion for "conversation pieces", usually representing a domestic interior, were popular with his successors **Francis Hayman** and Joseph Highmore, who exploited the illustrative quality of the genre. Hayman was among the first to draw inspiration from Shakespeare *(As You Like It)* and the novels of Richardson *(Pamela)*; alas, little remains of the series of panels he produced for the supper-boxes or pavilions at the Vauxhall Pleasure Gardens, other than engravings which betray the influence of French Rococo painting (especially Watteau who visited London for medical reasons 1719-20) with its accent on playfulness set in pretty, idyllic landscapes.

Eighteenth Century: Courtly Portraiture

During the Age of Confidence the term "Grand Style" alluded to art in the manner of the great Italian Renaissance masters (Michelangelo, Raphael, Titian): subjects were usually drawn from the Bible, classical mythology or literature and thus qualified as 'high art'. The taste for this kind of painting was given a further stamp of approval when the Royal Academy was founded in 1768. **Reynolds**, its first president, was quick to recognise that English "history" pictures found little favour with English patrons, and therefore fashioned his own style of portraiture: sitters were flattered and posed as Classical gods *(Three Ladies Adorning a Term of Hymen – The Montgomery Sisters)*, actresses were painted in costume. In contrast, **Gainsborough**'s portraits are full of movement and gesture, colour, light and space. His patrons were largely country gentry (Sudbury, Suffolk; Bath; London) and his sitters often are depicted in Arcadian (imaginary) landscapes.

Landscape and Empire: Aspects of Naturalism, Sporting Art and Genre Painting

The man who most successfully painted landscape in the Grand Manner was **Richard Wilson**, having travelled in Italy for seven years. His topographical landscapes suggest admiration for Claude and the Venetians (Canaletto), and were popular among London-based merchants and businessmen *(Westminster Bridge Under Construction; On Hounslow Heath)*.

Benjamin West, an American-born artist who settled in London in 1763, succeeded Reynolds as President of the RA.

George **Stubbs** adapts the Grand Manner to sporting pictures, Joseph **Wright of Derby** to modern genre painting and portraiture, often celebrating scientific invention. *Sir Brooke Boothby* is shown inspired by his friend Jean Jacques Rousseau, the "Noble Savage" author and philosopher.

Subsequent developments in landscape painting overlap with its treatment in literature: Burke outlines a new kind of Beauty between the Sublime and the Beautiful, Jane Austen satirises **The Picturesque** in *Sense and Sensibility* (1811) and *Northanger Abbey* (1818), while Wordsworth composes pastoral poetry and Blake the words to *Jerusalem* (1804-20). Watercolour becomes the favourite medium of travellers to the Continent for recording impressions of lofty mountains, avalanches, sun-baked plains and erupting volcanoes.
This drama is perpetuated, meanwhile by **Loutherbourg** who settled in London in 1771: as scenery painter at Drury Lane, he conceived his pictures rather as a theatrical set, like Hogarth had before him, but now introducing dramatic natural phenomena like lightning and thunderbolts; one of his principal followers was Francis Danby.

Works on Paper: Watercolours and Prints 1680-1900

William Blake and his followers include his patron John Linnell and the visionary painters Samuel Palmer, Edward Calvert, George Richmond, known as the "Ancients". Blake (1757-1827) pioneered monotype printing methods for his limited edition illustrations of the Creation: pigment was applied to a hard board upon which sheets of paper were laid, each taking a different impression before the colour dried; this image was then worked up separately with pen, ink and watercolour. Romantic subjects were chosen from great literature (The Bible, Dante's *Divine Comedy,* Virgil's *Eclogues*) as his poetry explored the themes of Youth, Wisdom, Innocence, Guilt... Blake never tasted success in his own lifetime despite the exhibitions of his "tempera" pictures.
Palmer (1805-81) was profoundly impressed by Blake, not only in the use of woodcut and tempera on a relatively small scale (oil paint was identified with Rubens and Rembrandt and regarded as too sensuous and unctuous for the spiritual honesty of their work) but also in his mystical view of the English landscape, in Palmer's case around Shoreham in Kent. He was followed by **Richard Dadd** (1817-86) who produced highly individual illustrations (Shakespeare's *Midsummer Night's Dream*): in 1843, Dadd murdered his father and was condemned to Bethlem Hospital and Broadmoor Prison where he was able to explore his hallucinatory world of fantasy, visions, fairies and hobgoblins.
Realism and Idealism – The British interest in topographical drawings, coloured with ink or wash, is rooted in the 17C Dutch tradition. During the 1750s artists were employed by gentlemen-travellers on the Grand Tour to record sights, ruins, monuments much as we might today use photography; draughtsmen were charged with making meticulous studies that might allow their patrons to have facsimiles made on their return home. In the 19C, Ruskin, Leighton and Lear were all supreme draughtsmen.
Girtin's *The White House in Chelsea* marks a new departure in watercolour painting from the stained, monochrome drawings of 18C to the luminous, atmospheric "impressions" of the 19C. Great swathes of delicate wash are applied to the absorbent white paper which he favoured, the low horizon a homage to the watercolours and etchings of Rembrandt.
John Constable: *Flatford Mill*; *The Lock*; *The Opening of Waterloo Bridge*; *Chain Pier, Brighton*; *Cloud Study*; David Cox: *A Windy Day*.

Art and Victorian Society

The Royal Academy School taught technique, its gallery displayed current artistic trends: Wilkie (1785-1841), Frith (1819-1909), Landseer (1802-73), Queen Victoria's favourite painter who had been an infant prodigy exhibiting his work at the RA from the age of 12 and who learnt to endow his animal subjects with human-like expressions.
Pre-Raphaelites and Symbolists – JE Millais encapsulated the ethic of the PRB in his painting *Christ in the House of His Parents (The Carpenter's Shop)*, exhibited in 1849, and full of meticulous realism and elaborate iconography: the carpenter's shop was based on premises in Oxford Street, Joseph's figure and hands are modelled upon those of a real carpenter, his head is a portrait of Millais' father, the sheep were drawn from two heads obtained by the painter from a local butcher's, the still life on the back wall is charged with the symbolism of the Crucifixion (Dove of the Holy Spirit, the triangle of the Trinity, the tools that represent the Passion)... The overall effect was new and precipitated controversy: to quote part of Dickens' diatribe "Wherever it is possible to express ugliness of feature, limb or attitude, you have it expressed. Such men as the carpenters might be undressed in any hospital where dirty drunkards, in a high state of varicose veins, are received. Their very toes have walked out of St Giles's."
Rossetti was the son of an Italian political refugee, living in London. He learnt to paint from Cotman and Hunt; from an early age he showed a fascination for Dante and the dreamy world of Romance, legend, pure love and chivalry that were also to inspire him to write poetry. In 1850 he met Elizabeth Siddal, she became his muse and eventually his wife (1860), only to die two years later from an overdose of laudanum, a derivative of opium. In the posthumous portrait *Beata Beatrix*, Rossetti includes two ephemeral but complementary (red and green) figures – these may be allegories of life and death, or allude to the ideal couple Eve and Adam, Beatrix the

Muse and Dante the artist joined by an arched bridge based on the Ponte Vecchio in Florence; the bird is the messenger of death; the white opium poppy the instrument; the sundial marks time. He later courted William Morris's wife Jane (1871), but bereft of his muse, Rossetti became a virtual recluse and eventually died a chloral addict.

Holman Hunt's *The Awakening Conscience* is set in St John's Wood and shows a "maison de convenance" where lovers have illicitly met (a wedding ring is missing from her bejewelled hand, the cat plays with a bird under the table).

William Frith's *Derby Day* was much admired when it was exhibited in 1858. It is a prize piece of Victorian genre complete with accurate portraits of recognisable people (young and old, rich and poor), realistic vignettes of such an occasion (the gambling, the entertainment, the social scene, lavish picnics and ragged beggary) all set against a meticulously rendered view of Epsom Racecourse, painted from specially commissioned photographs.

A Moral Dilemma

The delicate moral question of infidelity and prostitution was topical at a time when abandoned mistresses and high-society prostitutes used to flaunt themselves on horseback in Hyde Park: in literature the subject treated by Abbé Prévost *(Manon Lescaut)*, Marquis de Sade *(Justine, ou les Malheurs de la Vertu)*, Laclos *(Liaisons Dangereuses)*, Dumas *(La Dame aux Camélias)*, Flaubert *(Madame Bovary)* was worked in music by Mozart *(Don Giovanni)* Verdi *(La Traviata)*, Rossini and Massenet... In painting, the cause was publicised with realism by Frith, Millais, Tissot or condoned by the Aesthetes and Decadents with idealisations of exotic beauty (Leighton, Alma Tadema, Russell Flint).

Edward Burne-Jones (1833-98) is closely associated with William Morris. His idealised young subjects are bathed in a dreamy soft light; profiles and textures are carefully contrasted one with another (flesh tones, stone carving, embroidered fabric, metal armour, flora and foliage). A preference for tall compositions may reflect the contemporary use of paintings as decorative panels integrated into more complex interior schemes.

Aestheticism

The movement's call for "art for art's sake" evolved during the 1870s and found its manifesto in Walter Hamilton's *The Aesthetic Movement in England*, published in 1882. Whistler and Albert Moore imported their own ideas from Paris; at home, the handsome, intellectual, well-travelled and charismatic **Lord Leighton**, elected President of the Royal Academy in 1879, assumed the mantle. Alma-Tadema, Watts and Poynter, otherwise known as the Olympians, drew inspiration from Hellenistic Greece and the images evoked by the Elgin Marbles. Composition is simplified, colour is carefully blended into harmonious arrangements, form is precisely outlined and defined by texture or surface decoration, the fall of drapery, the perspective of a tiled floor...

British Art and France

The most original painter to digest the current influence and instigate Continental modernism was **Whistler** (1834-1903). Receptive to all the prevailing artistic movements in Paris, Whistler assimilated influences from the Impressionists (overall composition), imported Japanese prints (unusual perspective and muted colour), the writings of established art critics like the Romantic poets Baudelaire and Gautier as well as the spirit of his middle-class Parisian contemporaries Gustave Moreau, Marcel Proust, George Sand, Chopin, Gounod, Berlioz... In London, he painted *Nocturne in Blue and Gold: Old Battersea Bridge* which, in spirit, betrays all these influences: the scene was sketched from life and the impression transposed from memory; perspective has been distorted for the sake of the composition, realism has been forsaken to evoke atmosphere.

A Poetic Vision

"Just the other day a young American artist, JM Whistler, was showing a set of etchings, as subtle and lively as improvisation and inspiration, representing the banks of the Thames; wonderful tangles of rigging, yardarms and rope; farragoes of fog, furnaces and corkscrews of smoke; the profound and intricate poetry of a vast capital..."

Baudelaire: Painters and Etchers, 14 September 1862

John Singer Sargent (1856-1925), an American painter who had worked outdoors with Claude Monet and Camille Pissarro moved to London in 1885.

Monet *Poplars on the Epte;* Pissarro *A Corner of the Meadow at Eragny;* Degas: *Two Figures of Dancers;* Renoir: *Dancing Girl with Castanets; Dancing Girl with Tambourine;* Sargent *Carnation, Lily, Lily, Rose.*

The Modern Age

British artists reacted to the events of the early 20C in a particular way. **War and Memory** examines the impact of the First World War through the works of the futurist Nevinson and the sombre landscapes of Paul Nash. In the 1930s Henry Moore, Barbara Hepworth and Ben Nicholson were pioneers of modernism whereas extreme developments are traced in **An International Abstract Art**. Rotating exhibitions

Burning of the Houses of Parliament, *JMW Turner*

tell the story of British art from the Second World War through the haunting works of Francis Bacon, Graham Sutherland, the realism of the Kitchen Sink school and of the Independent Group (Richard Hamilton, Eduardo Paolozzi).

The period from 1960 to the present day is illustrated by changing displays: David Hockney, Peter Blake are leading exponents of **Pop art**; abstract painting (Bernard Cohen, Richard Smith) and sculpture (Anthony Caro, Phillip King) flourished. **Conceptual art** which is exemplified by artists such as Gilbert and George, the Living Sculptors and Richard Long, was rejected by the School of London formed by Howard Hodgkin, Lucian Freud and Kitaj. Sculpture became symbolic and allusive as in the works of Stephen Cox, Bill Woodrow and Richard Deacon. Contemporary art is marked by the **YBAs** (Young British Artists) whose leading figures are the controversial Damian Hirst and Tracey Emin. Other artists such as Tacita Dean, Steve McQueen, the Wilson twins explore different media such as film and video.

CLORE GALLERY: TURNER COLLECTION

Turner bequeathed a large proportion (100) of his finished paintings to the nation, with the request that they be hung in their own separate gallery. The will was subsequently challenged by his heirs and after much tribulation, the Tate received some 300 oil paintings together with 19 000 watercolours and drawings. The Turner Bequest is presently displayed in its purpose-built three temporary and six permanent galleries.

Much research has been undertaken to analyse Turner's genius: influences have been traced to Poussin, Claude, Vernet, 17C Dutch masters, Salvator Rosa, Wilson, Lambert as he switches from Historical subjects *(Hannibal and his Army crossing the Alps)* to Classical *(The Decline of the Carthaginian Empire)* and topographical ones *(London from Greenwich)*. Perhaps it is sufficient to admire them for their suggestive evocation of wind and sunshine *(Shipwreck)*, reality or imagination *(Norham Castle, Sunrise; Childe Harold's Pilgrimage)*, artistic talent and technique, and enjoy them for their colour, light, movement and poetic spirit.

Studies and Projects: *Self-portrait* (1800). Works produced during visits to Petworth and East Cowes: *Chain Pier, Brighton*. The Classical Ideal: works produced in admiration of Claude before Turner's first visit to Italy in 1819. Italy and Venice: *Bridge of Sighs, Ducal Palace and Custom House*. Later works: seascapes and whaling *(Shipwreck)*.

Tower of London★★★

The romantic outline of the Tower of London, which is an integral part of the country's history, is like a stage set although it is evocative of scenes of horror as well as royal pageantry. A visit to the tower is a must to admire the dazzling Crown Jewels and to be entertained by the dramatic tales of the Yeoman Warders in their traditional attire.

Tower Bridge is also a fascinating experience and the bird's-eye view enjoyed from the elevated walkway is memorable. Facing the tower are the riverside attractions of Bermondsey with fashionable restaurants and bars and interesting museums.

Location

Map pp 13-14 (HJXY); Michelin Atlas London: p 67. ⊖ *Tower Hill, DLR Tower Gateway.* The tower marks the boundary between the City and Wapping; it is well served by buses. Boats call at Tower Pier on the way from Westminster to Greenwich. Access to Bermondsey is by Tower Bridge.

Adjacent Sights: The CITY; DOCKLANDS.

Background

Tower of London – This royal residence was established by William I primarily to deter Londoners from revolt; additionally its vantage point beside the river gave immediate sighting of any hostile force approaching up the Thames. The first fortress of wood (1067) was replaced by a stone building (c 1077-97) within the Roman City Wall, of which a piece still stands (A). Norman, Plantagenet and Tudor monarchs extended the fortress until it occupied 18 acres/7ha. Excavations have revealed part

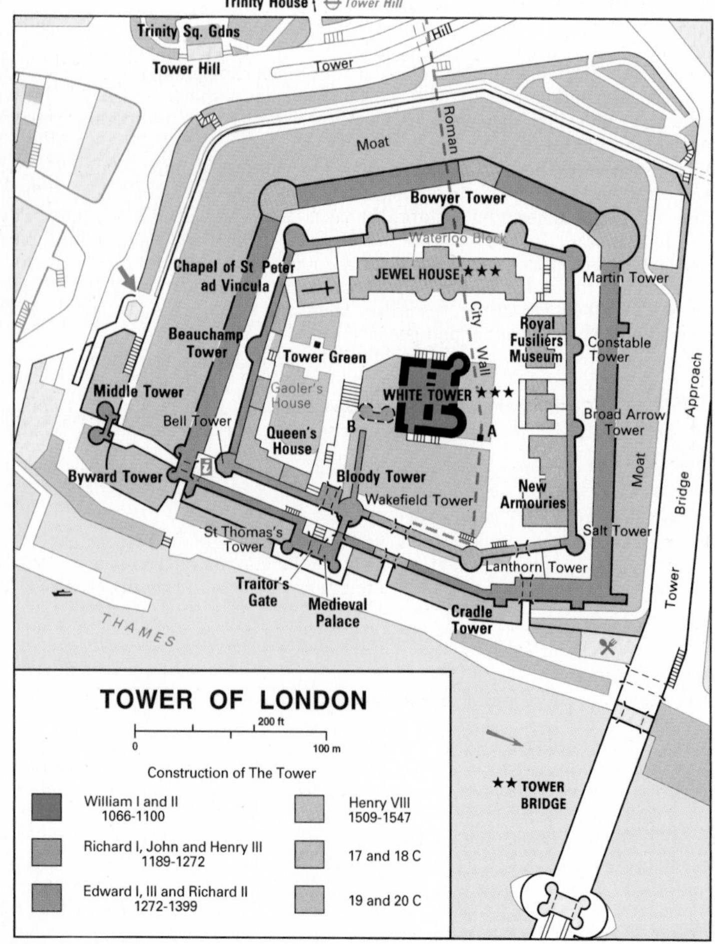

of a 13C perimeter wall and the Coldharbour Gate (B); St Peter's Church was incorporated within the Tower, a second fortified perimeter wall was built, the moat was excavated, barracks were erected; the royal residence was transferred to new (now demolished) palatial buildings against the south wall, where **Anne Boleyn** stood trial in the 16C. The last sovereign in residence was **James I**. The Tower was opened to the public in Victorian times, drawing large crowds intrigued by lurid tales from Romantic literature.

Royal Stronghold – The reputation of the Tower rests mainly on its role as a prison and place of execution for traitors rather than a centre of torture. Six hundred Jews accused of adulterating the coin of the realm were confined within its walls in 1282. Among later unwilling inmates were individuals captured in battle or suspected of intrigue: David, King of the Scots (1346); **King John of France** (1356-60) captured at Poitiers; **Richard II** (1399); **Charles Duke of Orleans** (1415-37) captured at Agincourt; **Henry VI** (1465-71); the Duke of Clarence, drowned in a butt of Malmsey (1478); the **Little Princes** (1483-85), Edward V and Richard of York, who according to legend, were murdered in the Bloody Tower and may have been buried in the White Tower where children's bones were discovered beneath an old staircase in the 17C, now in Westminster Abbey; Perkin Warbeck (1499); **Thomas More** (1534-35); **Anne Boleyn** (1536); **Thomas Cromwell** (1540); **Protector Somerset** (1552); **Lady Jane Grey**(1554); Robert Devereux, Earl of Essex (1601); **Sir Walter Raleigh** (1603-16); **Guy Fawkes** (1605); **James, Duke of Monmouth** (1685); Lord Lovat (1745-47); **Roger Casement** (1916) and Rudolf Hess (1941).

Following the restoration of the monarchy in 1660 when Charles IIreturned from exile, the Tower underwent major remodelling and a permanent garrison was posted within the precincts equipped with a full battery of weaponry.

From 1300 to 1812 the Tower housed the **Royal Mint** and, for a brief period, the Royal Observatory. Because of its impregnability it became the **Royal Jewel House** and it was used for a period as a bank by City merchants until 1640 when Charles I "borrowed" the commoners' deposits amounting to £130 000. From the 13C the **Royal Menagerie** was kept in the Lion Tower (demolished); it was closed in 1834 by the Duke of Wellington. For centuries the Tower served as an arsenal for small arms. The **Royal Armouries** collection was started by **Henry VIII** and augmented under **Charles II** when suits and accoutrements from Greenwich, Westminster and Hampton Court were redistributed between Windsor Castle and the Tower. A considerable part is now housed in the purpose-built Royal Armoury Museum in Leeds – *see The Green Guide GREAT BRITAIN*.

Ceremony and Tradition – The 40 **Yeoman Warders** (including Gaoler and Chief Warder) originally consisted of a detachment of the Royal Bodyguard founded by Henry VII on Bosworth Field (1485); it is now made up of former long-serving non-commissioned officers from the Army, Royal Marines or Royal Air Force holding the Long Service or Good Conduct Medal. It is unclear where the misnomer "Beefeater" comes from. They wear Tudor uniform (dark blue and red "undress" for every day – introduced in 1858, scarlet for ceremony), embroidered with the sovereign's monogram and may be seen on parade in the Inner Ward *(daily at 11am)*.

The **Ceremony of the Keys**, the ceremonial closing of the Main Gates, takes place every night *(at 10pm; admission on written application only)*. After the curfew a password, which is changed daily, is required to gain admission.

Every third year at Rogationtide (the three days before Ascension Day) the 31 boundary stones of the Tower Liberty are beaten by the choirboys of St Peter ad Vincula, armed with long white wands, the Governor and Warders in procession (1999, 2002, 2005...).

Royal Salutes are fired by the Honourable Artillery Company from four guns on the wharf *(at 1pm)*, 62 guns for the Sovereign's birthday, accession, coronation; 41 guns for the State Opening of Parliament, birth of a royal child...

Tower Hill– Over the centuries the area has preserved its traditional role as a place of free speech and rallying point from which marchers set out, nowadays, usually to Westminster. In 1380 **Wat Tyler** and the Kentish rebels summarily executed the Lord Chancellor and others outside the Tower.

Highlights

TOWER OF LONDON***

(♿) Open Mar-Oct, daily, 9am (10am Sun) to 6pm; Nov-Feb, daily, 9am (10am Sun-Mon) to 5pm; last admission 1hr before closing. Closed 24-26 Dec, 1 Jan. £11.50. Tickets are also available from London Underground stations. Guided tour (1hr) by Yeoman Warders from the Middle Tower (exteriors only). Chapel of St Peter-ad-Vincula: Guided tour Sun. Jewel House: queues tend to be shorter early in the day. Audio guide (Prisoners' Trail – 5 languages). Guide book and leaflet (7 languages). Royal Fuseliers Regimental Museum: 50p. ☎ 0870 756 6060 (recorded information), 020 7709 0765 (Tower of London); ☎ 020 7488 5611 (Regimental Museum); www.hrp.org.uk

The White Tower – William the Conqueror's stronghold on the edge of the City of London

Ph. Gajic/MICHELIN

Landward Entrance

The first element used to be the Lion Tower (demolished; position marked by stones in the pavement) which took its name from the Royal Menagerie introduced by Henry III (1216-72); it included an elephant donated by Louis IX of France in 1255, three leopards given by the German Emperor and a polar bear from the King of Norway. The **Middle Tower** (13C; rebuilt in the 18C) stood between the second and third drawbridges and was originally preceded by a causeway. The moat was drained and grassed over in the 19C. Pass through the **Byward Tower** (13C) where the portcullis and lifting machinery are still in position even if not visible; continue straight on before turning left through the Bloody Tower *(see below)* uphill into the main enclave.

Queen's House

Elizabeth I, among others, was confined in the **Bell Tower**, and took exercise on the ramparts beyond.

Beauchamp Tower

The three-storey tower, which served from the 14C as a place of confinement large enough to accommodate a nobleman's household, is probably named after Thomas Beauchamp, 3rd Earl of Warwick (imprisoned 1397-99). On the ground floor is displayed a fine crossbow; the main chamber *(first floor)* contains many graffiti carved by the prisoners.

Tower Green

The square was the site of the scaffold where executions took place; a new block was made for each victim (the last was in 1601 for the Earl of Essex). A plaque bears the names of the seven most famous victims who were privileged to be beheaded within the Tower; all were beheaded with an axe except Anne Boleyn, who was executed by the sword.

Beneath the lawn were interred the bodies not only of those executed on the green but also of many of those executed on Tower Hill where public executions took place; their heads were placed on pikes and displayed for all to see at the southern gateway to London Bridge.

Chapel Royal of St Peter ad Vincula

The chapel takes its name from the day of its consecration in the 12C: the feast of St Peter in Chains. It was rebuilt in the 13C and the 16C. It is the burial place of "two dukes between the queens, to wit, the Duke of Somerset and the **Duke of Northumberland** between Queen Anne and Queen Catherine, all four beheaded", to whom Stow might have added Lady Jane Grey, Guildford Dudley her husband, Monmouth and hundreds more. Note the Tudor font and the carvings by **Grinling Gibbons**.

Jewel House★★★

The antechamber, bearing the armorials of every ruling monarch from William the **Conqueror** to **Queen Elizabeth** IIserves as a rightful reminder of the long tradition associated with the Crown jewels. For the most part, the priceless gems are real, and the coronation regalia is still used for formal occasions such as the opening of Parliament.

> **Royal Economy**
>
> It must be noted, however, that in days of yore, it was common practice for stones to be 'rented' at a proportion of their real value for the singular occasion of a coronation: George IV's coronation crown was endowed with jewels worth £62 250 for the ceremony; the frames were then filled with paste for display purposes (Mary of Modena crown) or melted down.

The jewels are presented in the order in which they come in the coronation procession representing each individual stage: the bejewelled **Procession Sword** set with diamonds, emeralds and rubies in the form of roses, thistles and shamrocks, the emblems of England, Scotland and Ireland, and **St Edward Staff** are followed by the anointing objects (the engraved **Anointing Spoon** is the oldest piece of regalia having been made for Henry II or Richard I; the eagle **Ampulla** holds the holy oil with which the monarch is anointed). The **coronation ornaments** include robes, armills and spurs: the 22 carat Elizabeth II armills, made by the Royal jewellers Garrard & Co in 1953, were offered by the Commonwealth countries Australia, Canada, Ceylon, New Zealand, Pakistan, South Africa and Southern Rhodesia.

Most of the **Crown Jewels**, which consist of crowns, orbs and rings, date in fact from the Restoration (1660) as the earlier regalia was sold or melted down on the orders of Cromwell.

St Edward's Crown, so named because it may have belonged to Edward the Confessor, was remodelled for the coronation of Charles II; it weighs nearly 5lbs and is worn only at a coronation. The **Imperial State Crown** was made for **Queen Victoria** in 1838 and is worn on state occasions such as the Opening of Parliament *(see illustration in INSIGHTS AND IMAGES – Government)*. It contains a total of 3 733 precious jewels: the balas-ruby is the one said to have been given to the Black Prince by Pedro the Cruel after the Battle of Najera in 1367 and to have been worn by Henry V at Agincourt; the diamond (incorporated centuries later) is the second largest of the Stars of Africa cut from the **Cullinan diamond**, mined in 1905 and presented to Edward VII in 1907. The **Koh-i-Noor diamond**, the stone found in 1655 and presented by the East India Company to Queen Victoria, is incorporated in the crown made for Queen Elizabeth the Queen Mother for the coronation in 1937. The **Royal Sceptre** contains the **Star of Africa**, the biggest diamond (530 carats) in the world.

On a more modest scale note Queen Victoria's small crown familiar to every stamp collector.

Of the large gold and silver vessels that fill the subsequent cases (banqueting plate, altar plate and christening fonts) the **punchbowl and ladle** are perhaps the most impressive: the main vessel was supplied to George IV in 1829 – it weighs over a quarter of a tonne (257kg) and will hold up to 144 bottles of claret; the ladle came later.

Crowns and Diamonds – In the Martin Tower is arranged a display of additional royal crown frames that would have been temporarily fitted with cut diamonds and precious stones – these include the Imperial State Crown of George I (1715) and the Coronation Crowns of George IV (1821) and Queen Adelaide (1831).

White Tower★★★

The White Tower, one of the earliest fortifications on such a scale in western Europe, was begun by William I in 1078 and completed 20 years later by **William Rufus**. The high walls (100ft/30m) of Kentish rag stone (Blue stone) dressed with Portland stone, form an uneven quadrilateral, defended at the corners by one circular and three square towers. It became known as the White Tower in 1241 when **Henry III** had the royal apartments and exterior whitewashed. In the 17C repairs were made and the windows were enlarged on all but the south side. The interior is divided on every floor by a wall into two unequal chambers.

Chapel of St John the Evangelist★★ – *Entrance from south side.* The second floor Caen stone chapel (55 1/2ft/17m long and rising through 2 storeys) has changed little since its completion in 1080 although the interior painted decoration and rood screen have gone. The nave is divided from the aisles and ambulatory by an arcade of 12 great round piers (known as the 12 Apostles) with simply carved capitals rising to typical Norman round-headed arches, a tribune gallery and tunnel vault. Medieval monarchs, accompanied by their chosen Knights of the Bath passed the night in vigil in this chapel before riding to their coronation at Westminster; some also lay in state there, Henry VI in 1471, while **Mary Tudor** was betrothed there by proxy to Philip II in 1553.

The Royal Armouries Collection – The history of the White Tower is inextricably linked with the Royal Armouries Collection, for it has served as a depository of arms for centuries. Displays explore its role as a medieval castle – and later as a menagerie. The early organisation of a Royal Armoury begins with **Henry VIII**, his personal armours, his private arsenal and surviving pieces associated with the Stuart dynasty. Between the 15C and 19C, the nation's arsenal depended upon the Office of Ordnance which supervised the design, manufacture, and trial of arms for service on land and sea, while maintaining fortifications of the realm and its garrisons. Besides arms and armour, a large number of paintings, engravings and documentation are used to complete the exhibitions.

The collection also includes a large selection of smaller arms, several more gruesome weapons allegedly captured from the Armada (1588), larger trophies retrieved from various battlefields such as cannon and mortar, wooden carvings and miscellaneous artefacts, along with instruments of torture of foreign manufacture imported to the Tower for display purposes in the 19C, and an executioner's axe and block.

The **Line of Kings** reunites a series of 17C life-size portraits of the kings of England dressed in personal attire or suits of armour.

Royal Armour

Henry VIII had one suit of armour made in 1520, when the Tudor king was 29, and weighed 49lbs; a larger suit was made in 1540, silvered and engraved for the king and his horse. Some suits were made in Greenwich including examples tailored to Robert Dudley (c 1575) and for Worcester (110lbs). Note also the armour made in France in 1598 for the Earl of Southampton (1573-1624), the only acknowledged patron of William Shakespeare; a 3/4 gilt suit with helmet and cuirass, probably made for **Charles I**as a boy (c 1610); the ornate Stuart royal armours (c 1625-30).

Royal Fuseliers Regimental Museum

Separate entrance charge. The history of the regiment is presented from its formation in 1685 to the present day. Banners, documents, paintings, medals and paraphernalia.

Bloody Tower

The former Garden Tower acquired its lurid name only in the 16C, probably because the Little **Princes**were last seen alive there or after the suicide of Henry Percy, 8th Earl of Northumberland. It was once the main watergate and the portcullis can be seen in the lower storey. The study, which is paved with the original tiles (protected by matting), is furnished as in the time of **Sir Walter Raleigh**, the longest and most famous "resident" who wrote his *History of the World* while imprisoned there (1603-16).

Traitor's Gate

The gateway (13C) served as the main entrance to the Tower when the Thames was London's principal thoroughfare. Only later, when the river was used as a less vulnerable and more secret means of access than the road, did the entrance acquire its chilling name.

The Medieval Palace

St Thomas' Tower contains the Great Chamber where King Edward I would have slept. Meticulous archaeological research has allowed this Magna Camera to be re-created. **Edward I**ruled as an absolute monarch from here, subduing the Welsh tribes (nominating his son the Prince of Wales – a title conceded traditionally thereafter to the Monarch's eldest son) and extended English power across to France. Modifications to the 13C building were made by Henry VIII. The end room or Aula was where the king would have played chess and taken his meals.

The octagonal Throne Room in the **Wakefield Tower** (1240) would have served as the main official government chamber: it is furnished with reproductions of a throne based upon the Coronation Chair in Westminster Abbey, a German corona, candelabra, French oak chests and a chapel screen appropriate to the period; the corner turret accommodates a small oratory where Henry VI is thought to have been murdered while at prayer on the orders of Edward IV.

The **Lanthorn Tower** (13C, demolished in 1776 and rebuilt in 1883), contains a display of rare objects from the domestic life in the age of Edward I, accompanied by 13C music.

The Ravenmaster

The Ravens

Ravens are usually regarded as birds of ill-omen, feeding as they do on carrion and dead flesh: it is their absence from the Tower, however, that is feared, as legend has it that this would portend disaster. The practice of having six ravens at all times was decreed by Charles II, two extra are kept in reserve. To prevent them from flying away, they have one wing clipped by the Raven Master: this is a painless operation and by imbalancing their flight, the birds do not stray far. Each is identified by a coloured leg ring. The oldest resident, Jim Crow lived to the great age of 44, and occasionally ravens have been dismissed for "unbecoming behaviour" – Raven George was sent to the Welsh Mountain Zoo for consistently perching up on TV aerials. Since 1987 several clutches have successfully been reared.

Henry III's Watergate

A private entrance for royalty arriving by river was built east of the Wakefield Tower in the 13C.

East Wall Walk

The walk starts in the **Salt Tower** (1240), passes through the **Broad Arrow Tower** (1240) furnished as a knight's lodging in the 13C, through the **Constable Tower** (1240, rebuilt in the 19C) and ends in the **Martin Tower** which at one time was used as a Jewel Tower.

Cradle Tower

A watergate was created here (1348-55) as a private entrance for the king.

Walking About

Start at Tower Hill Station.

Trinity Square Gardens

The gardens include the site *(railed area)* of the permanent **scaffold and gallows** erected in 1455; the last execution took place in 1747.

On the north side stands **Trinity House**, the seat of the Corporation of Trinity House (1514), guarded by twin cannon. The principal business of the Corporation is the safety of shipping and the welfare of seafarers. It was founded in the 13C and its main responsibilities include the maintenance of automatic lighthouses, lightships, navigation buoys and beacons. The elegant two-storey building relieved by plain Ionic pillars and capped by a fine weathervane, was rebuilt after the war.

On the south side are the **Mercantile Marine Memorials** (1914-18) designed by Edwin **Lutyens**and (1939-45) by Edward Maufe.

Further east are a section (50ft/15m) of the **City Wall**, part medieval and part Roman, a monumental Roman inscription (original in the British Museum) to the procurator who saved London from Roman vengeance after the City had been sacked by **Boadicea**in AD 61, a statue presumed to be of Emperor Trajan (AD 98-117) and the remains of a 13C gate tower.

Walk up Cooper's Row and turn left into Pepys St.

St Olave's*

Open Mon-Fri, 9am-5pm. Concerts: Wed and Thu at 1.05pm. ☎ 020 7488 4318; Fax 020 7702 0811; www.sadds.demon.co.uk/hartst

Three parish churches have been built on this site: in wood (c 1050) and stone (c 1200; enlarged to present size c 1450). The church was restored in 1953 after severe bomb damage in 1941. Throughout, associations have been kept alive: the dedication to **St Olaf**, who in 1013 helped **Ethelred** against the Danes remains vivid in the new Norwegian flag; a bust (19C) of Samuel **Pepys**, diarist and founder of the modern Navy, appropriately blocks the former south doorway (inscription outside) which used to be the entrance to a gallery where Pepys had the Navy Office pew.

The churchyard gateway on Seething Lane, decorated exclusively with skulls is dated 1658; opposite is the site, now a garden, of the Navy Office of Pepys' day (burned down 1673). The square medieval ragstone tower's upper brick section is 18C; it is crowned with a lantern and weathervane. A round-faced clock projects back over the nave.

The church porch, into which one descends, is 15C like the major part of the church. The interior is divided into a nave and aisle of three bays by quatrefoil marble pillars, probably from a former, 13C, church; the clerestory and roof are post-war, as is the glass, except for the late-19C heraldic panels which had been removed for cleaning in 1939. Furnishings have been donated: the **pulpit**, made reputedly in Grinling Gibbons' workshop for St Benet Gracechurch (by Wren; demolished 1867); Jacobean altar rails; four 18C sword rests. The monuments, which incredibly, survived the fire, include tablets, brasses, natural and polychrome stone effigies: **Elizabeth Pepys** who married at 15 and died aged 29 (17C bust in an oval niche high on the sanctuary north wall), the 17C kneeling Bayninge brothers (below); Sir James Deane (17C kneeling figure with three wives and children; south wall over 15C vestry door); Sir Andrew Riccard, Chairman of East India and Turkey Companies (17C standing figure north aisle).

The **crypt** *(steps at west end)* of two chambers with ribbed vaulting, is built over a well and is a survival of the early-13C church.

Take Hart St west and walk up Mark Lane.

When the church of **All Hallows Staining** (1671) was demolished in 1870, the 15C battlemented ragstone tower was retained; it is now dwarfed by overshadowing office blocks.

Proceed down Mark Lane to Tower St and cross the busy main road.

All Hallows-by-the-Tower

Open Mon-Fri, 9am-5.45pm; Sat-Sun, 10am-4.30pm. Undercroft museum and audiotour: Mon-Sat, 11am (1.30pm Sun) to 4.30pm (donation). Organ recital: Thu, 1.10pm. Guide book. Brass rubbing. ☎ *020 7481 2928; mail@allhallowersbythetower.org.uk; www.allhallowsbythetower.org.uk*

The square brick tower dates from the 17C. The lantern, encircled by a balustrade and supporting a tapering green copper spire, was added after the Second World War making it the only shaped spire to be added to a City Church since Wren. The tower is the one climbed by Pepyson 5 September 1666 when he "saw the saddest sight of desolation that I ever saw."

The church, that time, was saved by Sir William Penn, whose son William, founder of Pennsylvania, had been baptised there on 23 October 1644. Four churches have stood on the site: in the late 7C, a chapel erected soon after its parent house, Barking Abbey, 12C and 14C churches, and finally 20C rebuilding. Inside, the south wall of the tower is pierced by the only Anglo-Saxon arch (AD 675) still standing in the City; modern sculpture has been grouped in the south aisle; in the baptistery is an exquisite wooden **font cover★★**, attributed to Grinling Gibbons for whom, obviously, no cherub was anonymous, 18 exceptional **brasses★** dating from 1389-1591 (of which eight may be rubbed – *by appointment only*), wall tablets, sword rests, model ships in the Mariners' Chapel. The **Toc H**association chapel and lamp, give the church a distinctive atmosphere despite its inevitable "newness".

In the undercroft are tessellated Roman pavement fragments, pottery, 11C Saxon stone crosses, memorials of Archbishop Laud, William Penn's baptism record and the marriage lines of John Quincy Adams (1794), Sixth President of the USA who was married here.

Walk down Tower Hill towards Tower Bridge and cross to the east side.

Old Royal Mint

Tower Hill. The neo-Classical stone building, converted into offices, was the home of the Royal Mint from 1811 to 1968 when the operation was transferred to Llantrisant near Cardiff. The Master Worker and Warden of the Mint is the Chancellor of the Exchequer. The first mint in London was set up by the Romans; by the 11C there were 70 in various parts of the country; by the 14C there were only two, which under Henry VIII amalgamated into one; in the mid 16C it was located in the Tower of London.

Excavations on the site have revealed the remains of St Mary Graces Abbey, a Cistercian convent (c 1350).

Walk south past the tower to Tower Bridge (description in Worth a Visit) and Bermondsey.

Bermondsey

Until the Reformation Bermondsey was known for its famous Cluniac monastery. Bermondsey Abbey, founded in 1082, was located between Abbey Street, Tower Bridge Road and Grange Road. At Bermondsey Priory in Rotherhithe, the monks brewed beer. In the 18C the area became fashionable as a spa famous rather for its spring water. Several street names – Leathermarket, Tanner, Morocco – recall the activities of Elizabethan tradesmen working the calf-skins and hides landed there from Southern Ireland.

New Concordia and China Wharves

Situated on the south bank of the Thames extending east of Tower Bridge, the area has undergone extensive redevelopment and the riverfront is alive with people enjoying the restaurants and bars while gazing at the river traffic and wonderful views.

For details of the famous Friday Bermondsey or New Caledonian Market, see PRACTICAL POINTS – Shopping.

Walk down the steps past Tower Bridge Experience.

Butler's Wharf

Presently listed as a conservation area, this part of London is slowly developing its own resident population and commercial interests; fine restaurants and designer bars line the waterfront and there are interesting specialist shops. *Description of the Design Museum in Worth a Visit.*

Church of St Mary Magdalen

Junction of Tower Bridge Rd and Long Lane. ♿ Open by appointment. ☎ 020 7357 0984
The parish church founded in 1290 was rebuilt in 1691 and twice restored in the 19C. It retains 12C carved capitals (from Bermondsey Abbey, once on the same site), 17C woodwork, boards inscribed with 18C charity donations, three hatchments vividly painted with armorial bearings and tombstones in the aisle pavements giving a sad insight into 18C infant mortality.

China Wharf

Beyond the Design Museum, **Cinnamon Wharf** (the first residential warehouse conversion on Butler's Wharf) and **St Saviour's Wharf**, stands China Wharf facing conspicuously onto the river. Completed in 1988, this striking, orange-red, scalloped building sitting in the river has won its architects CZWG several awards. The unit consists of 17 two-bedroom apartments designed to fill a gap between the existing **New Concordia** and **Reed** Wharves. Note the front entrance balcony named The Great Harry.

Other inventive warehouse conversions include: the glazed design-studio-cum-residential **David Mellor Building** *(22-24 Shad Thames)*, the modernist **Saffron Wharf** *(18)* and the untreated Iroko timber-clad **Camera Press** *(21/23 Queen Elizabeth St)*. The four gently curved blocks that make up **The Circle** *(Queen Elizabeth St)*, faced with glazed cobalt-blue tiles, replace the Courage Brewery stables; its balconies swirl in a great spiralling sweep – a far cry from Jacob's Island, the inspiration for Bill Sykes' abject den of vice and poverty described in Charles Dickens' *Oliver Twist*.

Worth a Visit

Tower Bridge★★

♿ Open daily, 9.30am-6pm (5pm last admission). Closed 25 Dec. £4.50. Guide book (5 languages). Parking at Tooley Street and Lower Thames Street. ☎ 020 7940 3985; Fax 020 7403 4477; enquiries@towerbridge.org.uk; www.towerbridge.org.uk

The bridge was designed by Sir John Wolfe Barry and Horace Jones to harmonise with the Tower of London. The familiar Gothic towers are linked by high-level footbridges, encased in steel lattice-work, which provide **panoramic views★★★** of London and a comprehensive display entitled the Tower Bridge Experience; the changing skyline is demonstrated by compact disc interactive terminals.

R. Besse/MICHELIN

Tower Bridge – a traditional symbol of London

Visitors pass from the North-west to the South-east Tower guided by an animatronic figure called Harry, who, aided by films and models, explains the construction of the bridge (1886-94); the design had to allow for the passage of road traffic without impeding the river traffic in the Port of London, hence the bascules (1 100 tons) which lift to allow the passage of a ship; in 1952 a bus failed to heed the lights and signals and was caught on the bridge as it opened but successfully "leaped" the gap of several feet.

In the Power House beneath the southern approach to the bridge are the original steam engines, now operated by electricity, which until 1976 drove the hydraulic pumps that raised the bascules.

The royal opening of the bridge by Edward, Prince of Wales, is re-created using traditional 19C theatre techniques in a reconstruction of a small Victorian theatre.

Design Museum

Shad Thames. ♿ Open daily, 10am-5.45pm (last entry 5.15pm) £6. Cafe ☎ 020 7940 8790; Fax 020 7378 6540; enquiries@designmuseum.org.uk; www.designmuseum.org

The museum opened in 1989 to popularise, explain, analyse and criticise design of the past and present and speculate about design in the future. True to the ethic of the Conran empire, the complex has been summed up as "modest, clean, spacious and white".

The **Review Gallery** on the first floor displays a selection of state-of-the-art products from around the world.

The main space is dedicated to temporary (six monthly) exhibitions of product or graphic design and architecture: early designs and manufacture are compared and contrasted with current fads and fashions produced by different industrial processes. Experimental projects are presented with concept foam or painted MDF prototype and test models, and visuals.

The airy top-floor space is reserved for the museum collection of household appliances, television sets, cameras, spectacles, furniture, office equipment, cars, bicycles... VDUs are available for access to a database.

Trafalgar Square – Whitehall★★

This landmark with its famous statue and fountains and with the National Gallery closing the vista, is the culmination of Whitehall, the avenue leading from the Palace of Westminster, and is well known all over the world. It is here that people congregate in times of strife or celebration: for political rallies, at Christmas around the Norwegian Christmas tree, or on New Year's Eve pending the chimes of Big Ben...

Location

Map p 12 (EX); Michelin Atlas London: pp 2-3, 62, 46. ⊖ Charing Cross, Westminster. Several main arteries radiate from Trafalgar Square with buses running to St Paul's and the City, to Waterloo and the South Bank, to Oxford St and Marble Arch, and to Victoria and Chelsea. Leicester Square, Covent Garden, the Mall and Buckingham Palace are easily accessible.

Adjacent Sights: STRAND; COVENT GARDEN; BUCKINGHAM PALACE; SOHO; WESTMINSTER.

Background

Trafalgar Square – The square celebrates Britain's naval prowess following Nelson's victory at Trafalgar (20 October 1805), and the full glory of her Colonial Empire.

To the north stretches the length of that glorious institution, the **National Gallery** *(see NATIONAL GALLERY)*; to the east stands **South Africa House** designed by Herbert Baker in 1933 where pickets rallied for the release of Nelson Mandela and an end to apartheid; opposite sits **Canada House**, a neo-Classical building of golden Bath stone (1824-27) conceived by Sir Robert Smirke in fact for the Royal College of Physicians.

In the immediate vicinity of the square stand a myriad of other Commonwealth High Commissions (Australia House in the Strand, New Zealand House in Haymarket, Nigeria in Northumberland Avenue...).

Another celebration of British power is embodied by **Admiralty Arch**, built across the Mall (the central gateway being the Sovereign's Gate) on the site of the Spring Gardens frequented in the 17C by Pepys. This massive curved structure by Sir Aston Webb in 1906-11 takes its name from the Admiralty buildings on the south side of the square.

A Noble Emblem

In the south-east corner was the early 17C Northumberland House (demolished in the 19C to make way for Northumberland Avenue), identified by the magnificent Northumberland lion, now at Syon *(Outer London: SYON HOUSE)*, which stood above the gate.

Directory

Light Bite

Café in the Crypt – *Duncannon St, St Martin-in-the-Fields, WC2N 4JJ – ⊖ Charing Cross – ☎ 020 7839 4342 – www.stmartin-in-the-fields.org – Open daily 10am (noon Sun) to 8pm (11pm Thu-Sat) – £10/16.* The self-service installed in the lovely 18C vaulted crypt is one of the best places in the area to have a quick inexpensive snack in an uncommercial setting; all proceeds go to the famous church.

Concerts

St-Martin-in-the-Fields – *Evening concerts: Thur-Sat at 7.30pm; tickets available from the Crypt box office (Mon-Sat, 10.00am-5pm) or by telephone. ☎ 020 7839 8362; Fax 020 7839 5163.* Candle-lit concerts make for a romantic experience. *See PRACTICAL POINTS – Going out for the Evening, Classical Music.*

Palace of Whitehall – Henry VIII's confiscation of Cardinal Wolsey's London palace in 1529 was a matter of convenience as well as convetousness. The property dated back to the mid 13C when it had passed by bequest to the See of York; in 1514 Wolsey made it his personal property, rebuilding, enlarging and enriching it, adding to the grounds until they occupied 23 acres/9ha. Henry VIII continued building and increased the royal precinct until it extended from Charing Cross to Westminster Hall, from the river to St James's Park. In 1996 archaeologists confirmed the discovery of a sophisticated type of Turkish bath, fitted with a 12ft/3.5m stove and lined with British-made tiles, located below the Ministry of Defence.

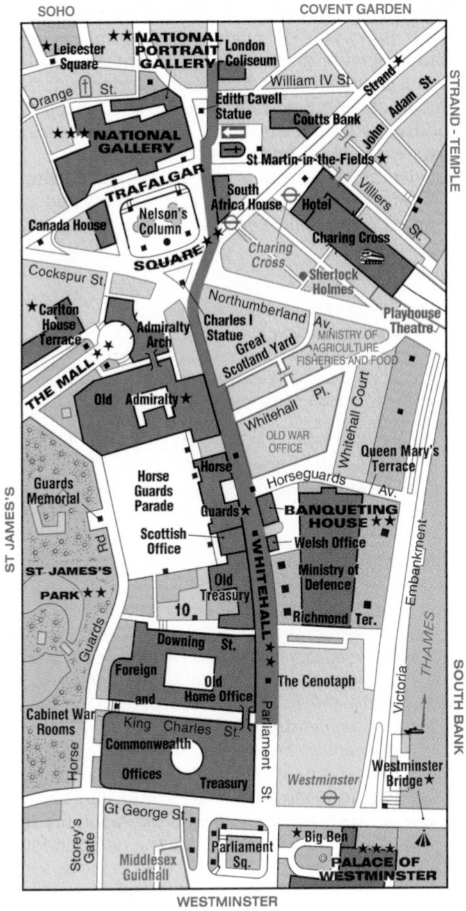

The early owners of Whitehall had shown respect for a parcel of land known as Scotland, which until the 16C had been the site of a Scottish royal palace. When it was eventually built over, the streets were named Little, Great **Scotland Yard** etc. The newly formed Metropolitan Police, given an office there in 1829, became known by their address and retained it when they moved in the 1890s along the Embankment and later, in 1967, to Victoria Street.

Tudors and Stuarts continued after Henry to live in and alter Whitehall Palace, but William and Mary disliked it and bought Kensington and, after a disastrous fire in 1698, did nothing to restore it. All that remains are Tudor walls and windows behind the Old **Treasury** *(visible from Downing Street)*, the end of Queen Mary's Terrace, a riverside quay and steps built in 1661 by Wren *(NE corner of the Ministry of Defence)* and the highly decorative Banqueting House *(see below)*.

Walking About

Trafalgar Square★★

The square was laid out by **Nash** in 1820 as part of a proposed north-south route linking Bloomsbury to Westminster across open space on the edge of **Charing Village** *(ceirring* from the Anglo-Saxon word for a bend): here the Strand, running west from the City, turned south to meet King Street (Whitehall). Pall Mall East was built, St Martin's Lane was straightened and Charing Cross Road was laid out in the 1880s. Twenty years later, the square was completed by **Sir Charles Barry** who also constructed the north terrace in front of the National Gallery – formerly the Royal Mews.

As Trafalgar Square traffic has been re-routed and major improvement plans have created a majestic piazza with grand steps sweeping down from the National Gallery.

A National Hero

Horatio Nelson, 1st Viscount (1758-1805), was the son of a Norfolk clergyman. He went to sea aged 12 and rose through the ranks to become captain in 1793. During various French revolutionary actions, he lost his right eye (1794) and his right arm (1797) before defeating the French at Aboukir Bay (1798), and destroying their fleet at Trafalgar. It was during this final campaign that he died from a musket wound to the shoulder (the ball is conserved at the National Maritime Museum in Greenwich, as are many letters, personal possessions and memorabilia).

Monuments – Nelson, a small man in life, is here three times life-size in a sculpture 17ft 4 ins/5m tall. The monument rises from a pedestal, decorated with bronze reliefs commemorating the Battles of St Vincent, Aboukir, Copenhagen and Trafalgar cast from French cannon, via a fluted granite column (98ft/30m), to a bronze Corinthian capital supporting the admiral – a full 185ft/56m overall.

Landseer's bronze lions (20ft/6m long, 11ft/3m high) were mounted in 1867, 25 years after the column was erected.

Against the north terrace wall are **Imperial Standards of Length** and busts of 20C admirals; the north-east pedestal is occupied by a bronze equestrian figure of **George IV**, originally commissioned by the king for Marble Arch and installed here in 1843; on the south corner plinths are mounted two 19C generals *(due to be moved in the near future)*. The two lamps are from or modelled after those on the *Victory*, the east one on a police observation post.

On the outside of the square, before and behind the National Gallery are figures of **James II** by Grinling Gibbons, **George Washington** after Houdon (marble original in Richmond, Virginia) and Henry Irving. On the island (NE) is Nurse **Edith Cavell**.

Eleanor Cross

In 1290 Edward I erected 12 crosses to mark the route taken by the funeral cortege of his queen on its journey to Westminster. It was here, in Trafalgar Square that the last of the solid-looking octagonal structures of marble and Caen stone was placed; it was destroyed by the Puritans but a 19C reproduction now stands in the forecourt of Charing Cross Station. A mural in the Underground station (Northern Line) shows the medieval cross being built.

St Martin-in-the-Fields★

♿ *Open daily, 8am-6pm. Brochure (6 languages). Choral services: Sun at 10am, 12noon, 5pm; Wed at 1.05pm, 5pm. Lunchtime recitals: Mon-Tue and Fri at 1.05pm; no charge. Evening concerts: Thu-Sat at 7.30pm; tickets available from Crypt box office (Mon-Sat, 10am-5pm) or by telephone. Café in the Crypt: Open daily, 10am (noon Sun) to 8pm (10.30pm Thu-Sat). Crypt Bookshop: Open daily, 10am (noon Sun) to 7.30pm (7pm Sun). Outdoor market: daily. ☎ 020 7766 1100 (church office); ☎ 020 7839 8362 (ticket office); ☎ 020 7839 4342 (Crypt café); ☎ 020 7766 1122 (bookshop); Fax 020 7839 5163; clergyoffice@smitf.co.uk; boxoffice@smitf.co.uk; cafeinthecrypt@smitf.co.uk; www.stmartin-in-the-fields.org*

The church is famous not only for its architecture – particularly its elegant spire – and, since the 1930s, as a shelter for the homeless, but also for giving its name to the world-famous chamber orchestra the **Academy of St Martin-in-the-Fields**, which maintains the church's long-standing tradition for classical music with recitals and concerts *(see Directory)*. Records confirm the existence of a church on the site in 1222 and its rebuilding in 1544 before the present edifice was designed by Gibbs in 1722-26. The steeple, which then towered above the surrounding slums, rises in five stages to a pillared octagonal lantern and concave obelisk spire. Before the west door is an outstanding Corinthian portico crowned by a triangular pediment bearing the royal arms justified by the fact that Buckingham Palace stands within the parish boundary. The spacious galleried interior is barrel vaulted; the stuccowork by the two Italians Artari and Bagutti; the pulpit is by Grinling Gibbons.

H. Le Gac/MICHELIN

Nelson on his column looks down on Trafalgar Square, a rallying point

In the vaulted crypt are accommodated a shop, an inexpensive café *(see Directory)* and the **London Brass Rubbing Centre** which has replicas of brasses from churches in all parts of the country and from abroad, including some Celtic engravings. *Open daily, 10am (noon Sun) to 6pm. Closed Good Fri, 25 Dec. Brass rubbings including all materials £2.90 to £15 according to size. ☎ 020 7930 9306*

In the courtyard flanking the northern side of the church is a lively arts and crafts **market**, and in the alley behind the market, a bronze head with flowing locks crowning a granite slab in the shape of a sarcophagus commemorating **Oscar Wilde** is by Maggie Hamblyn (1998).

Walk up to St Martin's Lane.

Beyond the Post Office stands the striking Edwardian **Coliseum**, home to the English National Opera *(see PRACTICAL POINTS – Going out for the Evening)*.

Retrace your steps, continue past the grand buildings between Strand and Northumberland Ave to the top of Whitehall and cross to the west side noting Charles I's statue on the island.

Hubert Le Sueur's equestrian statue of **Charles I** *(south side of square)* was cast in Covent Garden in 1633 (date and signature on the left forefoot); in 1655 it was discovered in the crypt of St Paul's by Cromwell's men who sold it "for the rate of old brass, by the pound rate" to a brazier who made a fortune from its supposed "relics". Eventually it was purchased for £1 600 by Charles II and set up in 1675 overlooking the execution site (wreath-laying 30 January at 11am by the Royal Stuart Society). From this point are measured mileages from London *(plaque in pavement behind statue)*.

WHITEHALL★★

Whitehall, formerly known as King Street, and Parliament Street are lined by government offices. Whitehall is synonymous with the executive as Westminster is a synonym for the legislature *(see INSIGHTS AND IMAGES – Historical Perspective, Westminster, Centre of Government)*.

Old Admiralty★

The Old Admiralty of 1722-26 was, in Horace Walpole's phrase "deservedly veiled by **Mr Adam's** handsome screen" in 1759-61, a single storey, blind porticoed wall with angle pavilions and a central arch crowned by a low balustrade between winged seahorses. In the 1890s vast terracotta brick additions were made to the rear.

Horse Guards★

Ceremonial mounting of the Queen's Life Guard daily by the Household Cavalry at 11am (10am Sun) on Horse Guards Parade; dismount ceremony daily 4pm in the Front Yard of Horse Guards. The Cavalry rides along the Mall between Horse Guards and their barracks in Hyde Park. ☎ 020 7414 2353. www.army.mod.uk

The low 18C stonefaced edifice, designed symmetrically by **William Kent** around three sides of a shallow forecourt, is pierced by a central arch and marked above, like its mid-17C predecessor on the same site, by a clock tower. The plain building acts as the official entrance to Buckingham Palace and as such is where all dignitaries on State visits to London are greeted – only holders of an "ivory" pass may use the entrance. To this end it is guarded by mounted sentries: when the Queen is in London this comprises an officer, a corporal major to bear the standard, two non-commissioned officers, a trumpeter and 10 troopers (Long Guard); otherwise there are two non-commissioned officers and 10 troopers only (short guard). Sentry duty by statue-still members of the Household Cavalry Mounted Regiment alternates between the Life Guards in scarlet tunics and white plumed helmets, and the Blues and Royals in blue with red plumes. The west front *(through the arch)* overlooks the parade ground where the Colour is Trooped in June.

Ph. Gajic/MICHELIN

Sentry duty at Horse Guards

Among the statues and memorials is a huge French mortar from Cadiz (1812) mounted on the back of a winged and scaly dragon *(against the west front)*, and the **Guards' Memorial** (1926) *(on the far side)* backed by St James's Park *(see BUCKINGHAM PALACE)*.

Cross to the east side for the Banqueting House (description in Worth a Visit).

Scottish Office and Welsh Office

The 18C **Dover** and **Gwydyr Houses**, both named after 19C owners are, in the latter case, open to the street, the only ornament a Venetian window above a tripartite door and in the former, a tall screen with an advanced porch designed by Henry Holland for the then owner, Frederick, Duke of York, in 1787.

Ministry of Defence

In front of the monolithic building stands the small, jaunty, bronze of **Sir Walter Raleigh**, who was beheaded nearby. Next to him stands **'Monty'**, a 10ft/3m solid bronze statue of Field Marshal Lord Montgomery of Alamein by Oscar Nemon, unveiled in 1980.

Richmond Terrace

The terrace was designed by Thomas Chawner in 1822. The façade has been restored to its original design and the Fine Rooms reinstated.

Cross the street again to the west side.

Old Treasury

Treasuries have stood on the site since the 16C. The present one of 1845 by Barry, using the columns from the previous building by Soane, was the first of the phase of government building which has continued to the 20C.

Downing Street

No 10 has been the residence of the Prime Minister since 1731 when Sir Robert Walpole accepted it *ex-officio* from George II. The "four or five very large and well built houses, fit for persons of honour and quality, each having a pleasant prospect of St James's Park", were erected in the 1680s by Sir George Downing, diplomat, courtier and general opportunist of the Commonwealth and Restoration. The speculation was successful. The row was rebuilt in the 1720s. No 10 contains the **Cabinet Room** and a staircase, on which hang portraits of each successive resident.

The Cenotaph

The slim white monument by **Lutyens** (1919) is without any effigy; the horizontal lines are very shallowly arced, the verticals converge 1 000ft/300m up in the sky; flags stir in the wind on either side.

On Remembrance Sunday *(November)* a service is held at which those who died in battle are remembered.

Old Home Office, Foreign and Commonwealth Offices and Treasury

The two Victorian-Italian palazzo style buildings of 1868-73 and 1898-1912 are best known for the Treasury door on Great George Street, from which the chancellor goes to the House on Budget Day, and the former Home Office balcony, from which members of the Royal Family watch the Remembrance Day service.

To the far end of Charles St there's the Cabinet War Rooms (description in Worth a Visit). For Parliament Sq see WESTMINSTER.

Worth a Visit

Banqueting House★★

♿ *Open (Government functions permitting; check by phone) Mon-Sat, 10am-5pm. Closed Bank Hols, 24 Dec to 1 Jan. £4 (including audio guide).* ☎ *0870 751 5178 (Mon-Fri, 9am-5pm), 020 7930 4179 or 020 7839 8919; val.jarvis@hrp.org.uk; www.hrp.org.uk*

The hall, the third on the site, has been called a memorial to the Stuarts: it was commissioned by James I (1619-22); Charles I had the sumptuous ceiling paintings done by the Flemish diplomat and artist PP Rubens in 1629 and stepped on to the scaffold in Whitehall through one of its windows on 30 January 1649; Charles II received the Lords and Commons in the hall on the eve of his restoration on 29 May 1660; after James II's flight in 1689, William and Mary received within it the formal offer of the crown.

Banqueting houses served many purposes: as a setting for court ceremonial and revelry, for the reception of royalty and embassies, state banquets, the distribution of Royal Maundy, touching for the King's Evil, for dancing, music-making and courtly masques.

Inigo Jones, King's Surveyor and famous masque designer, constructed for James I at the centre of the Tudor palace, a Palladian-inspired building. It was conceived as a double cube but made the exterior appear as a two-storey palazzo. The use of pedimented windows, swags and delicate rustication are borrowed directly from Palladio. Although the exterior has been refaced in Portland stone (1829 by Soane) and a new north entrance and staircase were added by Wyatt in 1809

Death of a King

After his defeat by Cromwell and the Parliamentary troops Charles I had been brought to trial on 20 January in Westminster Hall on a charge of high treason and "other high crimes against the realm of England" before a specially constituted high court of justice, which he refused to recognize on the grounds that "a King cannot be tried by any superior jurisdiction of earth." He maintained that he stood for "the liberty of the people of England" and refused to plead. On 27 January he was sentenced to death as a "tyrant, traitor, murderer and public enemy." He claimed that he was a martyr for the people. He was buried a week later at Windsor.

The Palladian splendour of the Banqueting Hall – a fine setting for an evening function

(lead bust of Charles I over the door and bronze of James I by **Le Sueur** inside) and although the interior was used as a chapel and a museum from the 18C to the 20C, it now looks as splendid as it might have done in the 17C and still serves superbly beneath the chandeliers for occasional official functions.

Exterior – The building stands two storeys high above a rusticated basement with an open balustrade at the crest. Note how the windows are alternately pedimented and, above, straight hooded; four columns with projecting entablatures give the side elevation a central feature, while pilasters articulate the side bays.

Interior – Inside it is a single empty space, a gilded stage awaiting players. It has the distinction of being a double cube 110ft/33.5m x 55ft/17m x 55ft,17m with a delicate balcony, supported on gilded corbels on three sides; above, richly decorated beams quarter the ceiling decorated with Rubens' flamboyant **paintings** in praise of James I. In Stuart times the lower walls would have been hung with Mortlake and other tapestries.

Sir Winston Leonard Spencer Churchill (1874-1965)

Churchill was perhaps Britain's most charismatic leader: his speeches – broadcast worldwide by the BBC – rallied military troops in action, civilians at home and in occupied Europe, prisoners, spies, friends and foes... He is still remembered for his bursts of anger and impatience by those who knew him, but is respected rather for his brilliance, staunch patriotism and remarkable use of the English language. His school report (aged nine) describes him as "very bad... a constant trouble to everybody and is always in some scrape or other" – a far cry from the man who was to rise through Harrow, soldiering, to the war premiership, and become an elder statesman through the Cold War crisis.

He was a creature of habit: on the whole, he would wake at 8.30am, hold court from his bed throughout the morning until it was time for his bath (mid/late morning); he would then lunch, take a nap and maybe another soak before going out to dinner and dealing with business late into the night; meals were preferably accompanied by champagne, and punctuated by a dozen or so cigars smoked throughout the day. His presence lives on in the Cabinet War Rooms while his distinctive silhouette holds guard over the House of Commons from Parliament Square.

Cabinet War Rooms

Clive Steps, King Charles Street. ♿ Open daily, 9.30am (10am Oct-Mar) to 6pm (5.15pm last admission). Closed 24-26 Dec. Audio guide (8 languages). £5.80. Cafeteria. ☎ 020 7766 0120, 0121 (general enquiries); Fax 020 7839 5897; cwr@iwm.org.uk; www.iwm.org.uk

The underground emergency accommodation provided to protect **Winston Churchill**, his War Cabinet and the Chiefs of Staff of the armed forces from air attacks was the nerve centre of the war effort from 1939 to 1945. The 19 rooms on view include the Cabinet Room prepared for in-camera discussions on national security and action; the Transatlantic Telephone Room – a secretive alcove for one-to-one strategic discussions, for direct communication with the White House; the Map Room decked with original maps from a pre-computer age marked with pins and coloured strings, and a bar chart of sticky paper, three distinctive figures representing the different armed forces (Navy, Air Force and Army); the Prime Minister's Room, and the room from which Churchill made direct broadcasts to the nation. Other paraphernalia so typical of the contemporary bureaucratic civil services includes "the beauty chorus" of coloured telephones, functional kneehole desks and iron beds, detailed notices and printed instructions. Also in situ are the wedged wooden supports which were installed by the Naval team assigned to reinforce the premises against collapse during shelling and the tunnel to the map room annexe which had to be drilled through concrete poured into the Camp Commandant's cramped quarters located below a staircase in the main building.

Victoria and Albert Museum★★★

A treasure house of art objects – masterpieces from every period and from all over the world – affords great enjoyment to visitors ambling through the labyrinth of corridors and galleries of this museum which is famous for its expertise in many fields. Connoisseurs have their own favourites but there are many discoveries to be made by those who love beautiful things and are willing to explore the recesses of the museum.

Location

Map p 11 (CY) and area map under KENSINGTON; Michelin Atlas London: p 41. ⊖ *South Kensington*. The museum, located in the South Kensington area with its many famous restaurants and bars, is within walking distance of the Brompton Oratory and the shops in Knightsbridge. Chelsea and King's Rd are also easily accessible by Underground to Sloane Sq.

Adjacent Sights: KENSINGTON; KNIGHTSBRIDGE – BELGRAVIA.

Background

Museum of Manufactures

The Victoria and Albert Museum, Britain's National Museum of Art and Design, was created to accommodate the contemporary works manufactured for the 1851 Exhibition *(see KENSINGTON)*. In 1857 the collection was moved from Marlborough House to the South Kensington Museum housed in a building known as the Brompton Boilers; later (1899) the museum was renamed in honour of the Queen, who laid the foundation stone of the present idiosyncratic brick-fronted building, and Prince Albert, the museum's instigator. The original disparate collection was soon extended to include various items accumulated by the Government School of Design in Ornamental Art at Somerset House; subsequent gifts, bequests and purchases have since transformed the collections through time (over 4 million objects; 7mi/11km of galleries) to encompass "the fine and applied arts of all countries, all styles, all periods." The **Henry Cole Wing** (1867-71) on Exhibition Road which commemorates the eminent civil servant who conceived the Great Exhibition comprises the former Huxley Building designed by General Henry Scott as lecture halls for a variety of scientific educational institutions. Besides the premises in South Kensington, the V & A is also curator to the Wellington Museum at Apsley House, the Museum of Childhood at Bethnal Green and the Theatre Museum in Covent Garden.

A proposed extension, an amazing Cubist-inspired structure of inclined planes forming a self-supporting spiral clad in ivory-coloured tiles, designed by Daniel Libeskind, is scheduled to be completed by 2004.

Note – This vast establishment maintains its prime educational and didactic purposes by providing important study collections for specialists, historians, artists, collectors and connoisseurs. Its conservation department was set up in 1960. For the one-time visitor its sheer size may at first be overwhelming: it is advisable therefore to make for the departments that might be of personal interest and then to meander back through the other sections. For this reason, the departments have been presented here to echo the central organisation of the museum and allow the visitor to seek advice or assistance relative to their interest from the appropriate curators.

Highlights

♿ *Open daily, 10am-5.45pm (10pm Wed and last Fri of month). Closed 24-26 Dec. Brochure/map (26 languages). Guided tours (1hr; no charge): daily at 10.30am, 11.30am, 12.30pm. 1.30pm, 2.30pm and 3.30 (also Wed at 4.30pm and 7.30pm) from the Main Entrance. Gallery talks daily, 1pm (no charge). Demonstrations Sat, 2-5pm (no charge). Photography permitted (no flash, no tripods). Restaurant (Open daily till 5.30pm or 9.45pm). Entrances in Cromwell Road and Exhibition Road. Print Study Room: Tue-Fri, 10am-4.30pm. ☎ 020 7942 2000; ☎ 020 7942 2197 (info for families); 020 7942 2209 (info on course, study days and lectures); vanda@vam.ac.uk; www.vam.ac.uk*

WESTERN WORKS OF ART

Sculpture

The National Collection of European post-Classical sculpture spans the ages from Early Christian times to 1914 – pieces thereafter are displayed at Tate Britain and Tate Modern *(see separate listings)*.

Ivories – *Level A: 43; Lower level B: 62.* An early artform that provided precious, portable images and mascots during times when people undertook long, arduous and hazardous journeys. Ivories might be carved from the tusk of an elephant, walrus or moose, hippopotamus, or rhino horn. Amulets, early Christian religious icons, Carolingian caskets and pyxes, decorative panels set into manuscript bindings were followed in the 13C by exquisite Gothic figures. The art of ivory carving in France reached great heights in the 1300s (secular toilet articles), before declining in the mid 15C, it enjoyed a brief revival in the 17C notably for portraits, only to revert to incidental detailing inlaid or adorning furniture.

Renaissance Sculpture – *Level A: 12-20; Lower level B: 63-64.* Many important Italian masters are represented using different media (wax, terracotta, bronze, marble): Giovanni Pisano (*Crucified Christ* c 1300), **Donatello** (*The Chellini Madonna* 1456; *The Ascension of Christ with the Giving of the Keys to St Peter* c 1430 – *Gallery 16*) Ghiberti, Rossellino, della Robbia (*Adoration of the Magi* early 16C), Sansovino, **Cellini**, Torrigiano, Lombardo, Riccio *(Shouting Horseman)*, Giambologna (*Samson and the Philistine* c 1562), **Bernini** *(Neptune and a Triton)*... Perhaps the most highly prized is **Michelangelo**'s *Slave*, a wax preparatory model for a figure intended for the tomb of Pope Julius II.

It is interesting to compare the stylistic differences in modelling, gesture, expression, texture, perspective, scale, and canons of beauty between the Italian, French, Flemish, German and Spanish Schools. This is particularly pertinent in religious compositions and portraiture (De Fries, Bernini, Le Sueur, Roubiliac). Later works include those by Canova, Barye, Flaxman *(Level A: 50)*; Rodin *(Henry Cole Wing 419)*.

Medals also form part of this large department with notable examples by the eminent Renaissance medallist Pisanello.

Cast Courts – *Level A: 46a (Italy) and 46b (Northern Europe).* The architecture of the courts (1868-73) is typically Victorian. The casts were made (1860-80) for the benefit of art students who could not afford to travel abroad; they still serve a useful purpose as the originals have in many cases suffered from the damaging effects of pollution: *Trajan's Column* (AD 113); bronze doors of the Baptistery in Florence by Ghiberti; statue of St George by Donatello; *David* and *Moses* and *Dying Slave* by Michelangelo.

Highlights★★★ – German amber altarpiece; Henry VII bust by Torrigiano; Michelangelo's *Slave*, Donatello's *The Ascension of Christ with the Giving the Keys to St Peter*; Bernini's *Neptune*; Houdon busts (Voltaire); Roubiliac's *GF Handel* from Vauxhall Gardens.

British Collection

Art and Design 1500-1750 *Lower level B: 52-58*
Art and Design 1750-1900 *Level C: 118-126*
Art and Design 20C *Level B: 70-74*

European Collection

Italian Art 1400-1500 *Level A: 11-20*
European Art and Design 1500-1600 *Level A: 21*
Northern Europe: Art and Design 1100-1450 *Level A: 22-24*
Spanish Art *Level A: 25*
Northern Europe: Art and Design 1450-1550 *Level A: 26-29*
European and American Art and Design 1800-1900 *Lower level A: 8-9*
20C Study Collection *Level B: 103-106*
European Dress *Level A: 40; Lower level B: 52*
European Folk Dress *Level B: 96 and 99*
European Ornament Gallery *Henry Cole Wing: 217-221*
European Painting *Henry Cole Wing 403, 417-421*
European Prints *Henry Cole Wing 207-209*
Fakes and Forgeries *Level A: 46*
National Art Library *Level B: 77-78*

Eastern Collection

Chinese Art *Level A: 44*
Indian Art Nehru Gallery *Level A: 41*
Islamic World 700-1800 *Level A: 42*
Japanese Art Toshiba Gallery *Level A: 45*
Korean Art Samsung Gallery *Level A: 47g*

Prints, Drawings and Paintings

Besides the well-established media of printmaking and watercolour, this collection includes other commercial graphic material: drawings, wallpaper samples, fashion plates, posters, photographs, packaging; caskets, painted furniture and banners decorated or designed by the likes of Botticelli, Crivelli, Tintoretto, Beccafumi...

Prints – *Henry Cole Wing 207-209 and 503.* The print collection includes narrative illustrations (woodcuts, engravings, etchings, linocuts, lithography, silkscreen prints) and design pattern book plates for all the decorative arts (armour, ceramics, furniture, silver, jewellery). Artists range from Rembrandt *(Virgin and Child with Cat and Snake)* to the post-Impressionist Kitaj.

National Collection of Watercolours – *403, 417-421.* Topographical, architectural studies and drawings (Sir John Vanbrugh, Frith, Henry Fuseli, Landseer, CFA Voysey, Henry Moore, Paul Nash, Stanley Spencer, the Bauhaus teacher Joseph Albers, Helen Chadwick).

National Collection of Portrait Miniatures – Since the foundation of the Tate Gallery for British Art, the V & A has limited itself to acquiring miniatures: Hans Holbein *(Anne of Cleves)*, Nicholas Hilliard, Isaac Oliver *(Girl aged Four Holding an Apple; Girl aged Five Holding a Carnation)*.

VICTORIA AND

LEVEL B

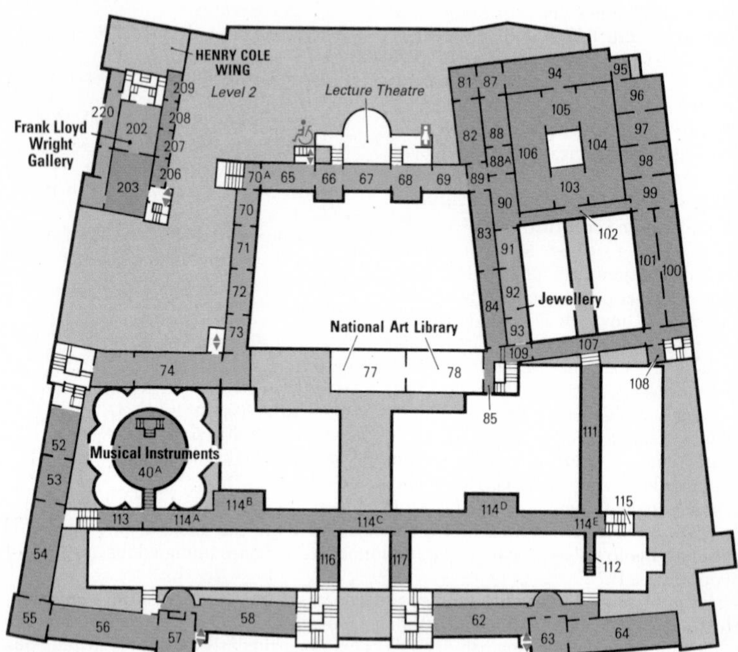

LEVEL A

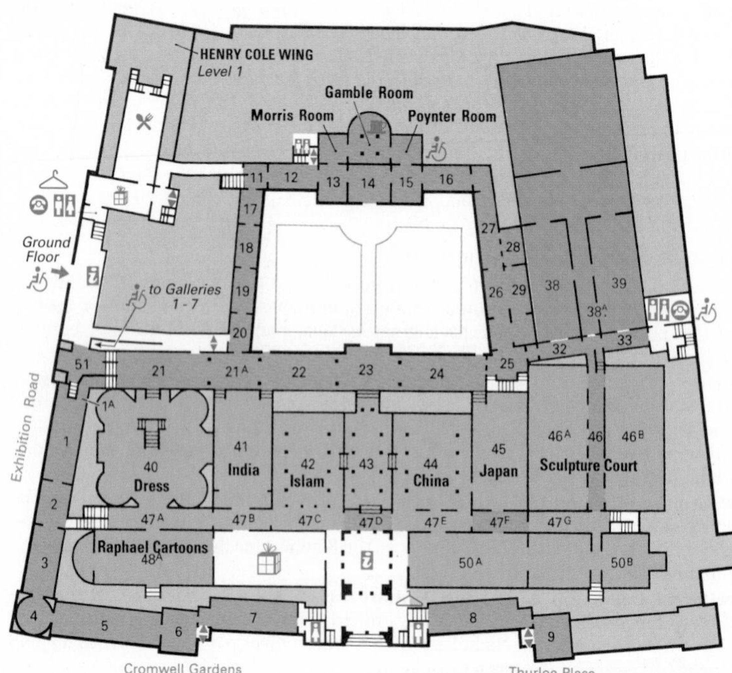

ALBERT MUSEUM

LEVEL D

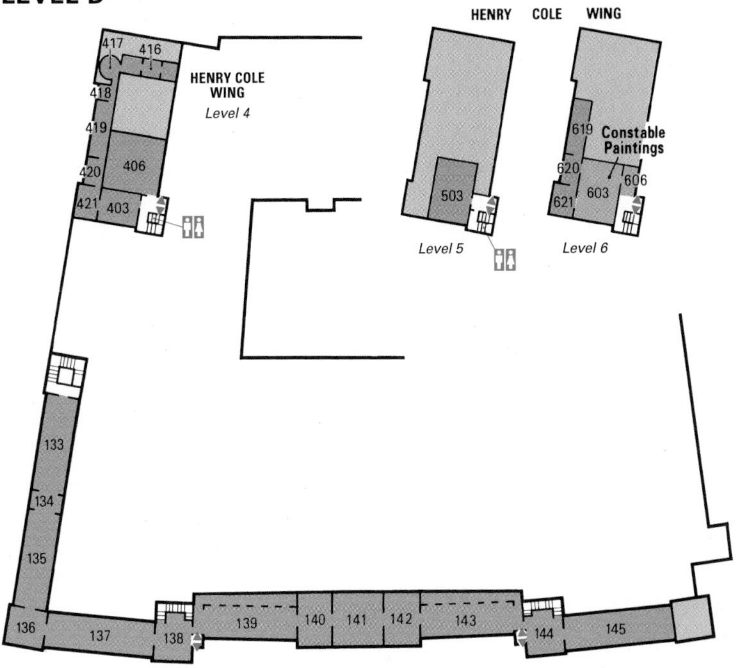

HENRY COLE WING

417 416 418 419 406 420 421 403

HENRY COLE WING
Level 4

503
Level 5

619 620 621 603 606
Constable Paintings
Level 6

133 134 135 136 137 138 139 140 141 142 143 144 145

LEVEL C

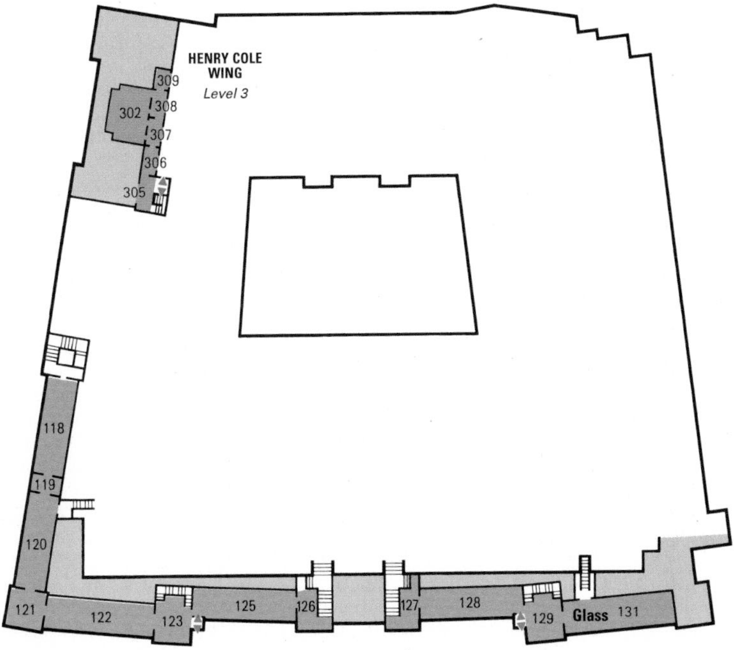

HENRY COLE WING
Level 3

309 302 308 307 306 305

118 119 120 121 122 123 125 126 127 128 129 Glass 131

Bequests – The **Sheepshank Gift★★** *(Henry Cole Wing: 419)*, one of the earliest bequests of paintings (1857) comprised contemporary works in oil and watercolour – Turner, Blake, Palmer, Waterhouse. These attracted great crowds to the museum when on Monday evenings the galleries were gaslit. Later, the bequest of Constable paintings and drawings (1888) was made by the same benefactor's children *(see below)*. Pieces in the collection by Continental artists are largely due to the bequests of such collectors as **John Jones** *(Lower level A: 1-7)* – 18C French Rococo: Boucher's portrait of *Madame de Pompadour*, Rev CH Townsend – mid 19C Swiss, **CA Ionides** – 18C-19C French: Ingres, Delacroix, Courbet, Daumier, Barbizon School, Degas... *(Henry Cole Wing 403, 417-421)*.

Raphael Cartoons – *Level A: 48a.* These were commissioned in 1515 by Pope Leo X for the Sistine Chapel and illustrate incidents from the lives of the Apostles St Peter and St Paul. Since 1864, the seven tapestry patterns from a series designed by Raphael were purchased by Charles I in 1623 and used at Mortlake Tapestry workshops; in 1699 they were framed by Sir Christopher Wren and hung at Hampton Court; they are presently owned by HM the Queen who has entrusted them to the V & A.

John Constable Collection – *(Henry Cole Wing: 603, 606, 620, 621.)* The largest collection in the world of works by Constable, presented in 1888 by the artist's daughter, Isabel, includes paintings exhibited at the Royal Academy summer exhibitions and demonstrates the artist's technique through sketches in pencil, watercolour and oil from which the finished oil paintings were created: *Dedham Lock, Salisbury Cathedral, Boat-building*.

Hierarchy of Artistic Subjects – The Great Staircase in the Henry Cole Wing is hung with 300 paintings arranged according to the hierarchy of artistic subjects defined by Sir Joshua Reynolds, first President of the Royal Academy, beginning at the bottom with life studies and copies of Old Masters, the basis of academic art training and therefore the least important, and mounting through landscape and genre painting to historical and religious subjects at the top.

Highlights★★★ – Raphael Tapestry Cartoons; John Constable Collection of paintings and watercolours; Boucher's portrait of *Madame de Pompadour*.

Shows

Temporary exhibitions are mounted in the Print Room *(Henry Cole Wing: 503)*: check on arrival what is on display from the information desk before deciding whether to include a visit to this section of the museum.

Furniture and Woodwork

The collection ranges from the Middle Ages to the present day and is drawn from an area that embraces Europe, the Middle East and America.

Many fabulous items from the collection are loaned to other museums and country houses where they might be seen in their original period interiors (Apsley House – *see PICCADILLY*).

British Furniture 1500-1900 – *Lower level B: 52-58; Level C: 118-126.* Little pre-16C furniture survives other than chests and odd chairs. Perhaps the most remarkable single piece from this period is the **Great Bed of Ware** of carved oak: mentioned by Shakespeare, the bed has become legendary since it was made as a tourist attraction for the White Hart Inn, a popular hostelry on the way from London to Cambridge.

Of particular interest is the **18C Collection**, as pieces by the great furniture designers **Chippendale**, **Sheraton**, Hepplewhite *(see INTRODUCTION – Furniture)* and the architects-cum-interior designers and decorators **William Kent**, **Robert Adam** *(Kimbolton Cabinet)*, **William Chambers** may be compared and contrasted to appreciate the variety and craftsmanship prevalent at that time. Important re-created interiors include the Clifford's Inn Room (c 1687); Henrietta Place Room (c 1725) by James Gibbs; Hatton Garden Room (c 1730); Norfolk House Music Room (1756); Wotton-under-Edge Room (provincial Rococo); Croome Court Library (1760) and Glass Drawing Room from Northumberland House (1700s); Lee Priory Room (1785, Gothic Revival).

The 19C section is one of the strongest of the furniture collection as it shows the various styles presented and exhibited at the different European International Exhibitions (London: 1851; Paris: 1867, 1900); many of these pieces were made specially for show and as such, were not intended for everyday use, however, they demonstrate the eclectic tastes of the Victorians and the high quality of cabinetmaking prevalent at that time. Notable pieces include **Pugin**'s armoire; a Medieval Revival painted cabinet by **Burgess**; a cabinet by Ernest **Gimson**; a painted screen by **Vanessa Bell** reflecting the influence of Matisse; a very fine rectilinear Japanese-inspired ebonised mahogany sideboard signed **EW Godwin**; Art Nouveau oak chair designed by the architect **CFA Voysey**.

European Furniture – This collection is divided into two sections spanning the years 1400-1600 *(Level A: 12-27)* and 1600-1800 *(Lower level A: 1-7)*. Room 21 is dedicated to remarkable 16C Italian pieces including a series of very fine carved and painted chests. Note the fabulous bone-inlaid portable German writing desk c 1600; a fine ebony cabinet with silver mounts from Augsburg c 1600; a cabinet made by Jacob, one of Napoleon's favourite cabinetmakers.

American and European 1800-1900 – *Lower level A: 8-9.* The 19C Collection items displayed here were all bought new by the museum. These include the **Hoffmeister** throne; Louis Majorelle Art Nouveau walnut armchair; striking pre-Art Deco marquetry desk and chair... The Art Nouveau objects were for the most part purchased from the Paris Exhibition of 1900.

Morris, Gamble and Poynter Rooms – *Level A: off 13-15.* Three refreshment rooms (in use as such until 1939) added from 1866 onwards with tile panels and an iron brass grill by Sir Edward Poynter, stained glass and ceramics by Gamble, wallpaper and stained glass by William Morris and Burne-Jones, furniture by Philip Webb. Other Morris & Co furnishings are displayed in Level C: 118-119.

Frank Lloyd Wright Gallery – *Henry Cole Wing: 202.* F L Wright (1867-1959) was described as "the greatest American architect to date" by Pevsner. He was responsible for the conception of the Prairie House and the Larkin Building, complete with correspondingly appropriate furnishings, and his importance as an interior designer stems from his association with the Chicago Arts and Crafts society (f 1897), which closely echoed the ideas and objectives of the British Arts and Crafts movement.

V&A Picture Library

Panel from the Morris Room
by E Burne-Jones

The gallery displays examples of furniture, metalwork, stained glass, prints, books and graphic designs; the office interior he tailored for the Pittsburg department store chief Edgar J Kaufman (25ft/8m x 22ft/7m) in 1936-37, a great admirer and patron of Wright in the last years of his long career.

20C Study Collection – *Level B: 70-74; 103-106.* Pre-1960 British furniture is on view in Room 74. A changing display of furniture from the period 1960-1991 is permanently housed in galleries 103-106. This might include pieces designed by Le Corbusier, Koloman Moser, Eileen Gray and Frank Lloyd Wright.

William Morris (1834-96)

Morris epitomises the Victorian age as a well educated, middle class, talented and successful designer, craftsman, poet, conservator (founder of the Society for the Protection of Ancient Buildings) and political (Liberal then Socialist) theorist, endowed with enormous vision, imagination and energy. Morris went to Oxford to study theology; there he came across the teachings of Ruskin and met members of the Pre-Raphaelite Brotherhood (DG Rossetti, Burne-Jones, Ford Madox Brown). He commissioned his friend Philip Webb to design a house in Bexleyheath; when trying to furnish The Red House, Morris discovered how "all the minor arts were in a state of complete degradation" (1860) and set about improving the situation. Morris, Marshall, Faulkner & Co quickly proved successful; major projects included reception rooms at St James's Palace and a new refreshment room for the South Kensington Museum (V & A); in 1875 the company was re-formed as **Morris & Co**, and manufacturing was moved to Merton Abbey in 1881 where production continued until 1940. He employed the services of other like-minded talented technicians and draughtsmen: Webb, Burne-Jones (figurative tapestries and stained glass), George Jack (furniture including the famous Morris chair), **William de Morgan** (ceramics including lustreware); from embroideries he moved on to wallpapers, stained glass, printed and woven textiles, carpets, rugs, tapestries, furniture, light fittings, ceramics... In 1890 he founded the **Kelmscott Press** for the specialist production of exquisitely printed books modelled on Medieval manuscripts including Morris's own translation of Icelandic myths. Morris upheld the importance of good craftsmanship in the face of mechanisation and industrial processes, the use of the most appropriate materials for functional objects, and the need for good design in even the most lowly, domestic things; his lasting reputation and example have inspired the ethic of 20C industrial design.

Musical Instruments – *Level B: 40a; Lower level B: 52.* It is to be noted that the large range of Western instruments has been collected here for their applied decoration rather than their value as musical instruments, for this reason some may be displayed with other contemporary furniture as part of an interior display.

Highlights★★★ – Great Bed of Ware; musical instruments: Queen Elizabeth's virginals; Grinling Gibbons' reliefs *(Crucifixion, Stoning of St Stephen)*; Jones Collection: 18C French commode, secretaire, bed; Mme de Serilly's boudoir (Marie-Antoinette's music stand and work-table); Taskin harpsichord, Riesener jewel casket; 18C Italian cabinet of mirrors; Italian oval room (c 1780); five lapis lazuli columns illustrating the five orders of architecture made for Marie-Antoinette; William Morris Room; Frank Lloyd Wright study.

Textiles and Dress

This is one of the world's most extensive collections of textiles spanning 5 000 years from Europe, the Near, Middle East and Central Asia. The Dress Collection (late 1500s-1990) consists of trendsetting European designs. The models also show the underwear and foundation garments and the influence of new technology.

Woven Fabrics – *Level B: 100.* The earliest samples are Pharaonic linens retrieved from excavated Egyptian tombs; later examples include Classical, early Christian, Coptic styles, silk from Byzantium and the dawn of the Islamic Near East. Woven silks from Italy (13C-15C) show developments in patterns; sumptuous vestments from the Renaissance in silk and velvet; ravishing 17C furnishing fabrics echo paintings of Titian and Veronese. France begins her own silk-weaving industry in Lyons (1650s). The principal factories in England were located at Spitalfields (London), Manchester, Macclesfield and Norwich – *Lower level B: 57; Level B: 100, Level C: 125.*

The 19C is well documented with important items from the 1851 Great Exhibition (William Morris fabrics and hangings; shawls from Paris, Norwich, Paisley).

Embroidery – *Level B: 101.* English medieval ecclesiastical embroidery was so renowned (13C-14C) as to have its own name "**opus anglicanum**" (Clare chasuble; Syon cope); it earned particular recognition in 1246 when Pope Innocent IV noticed the vestments of visiting English bishops and commissioned some for himself. The ground is usually silk or satin; couched gold thread is used for background; figures are worked in silk in fine split-stitch; designs are drawn from contemporary manuscript illustration. In the mid 14C decoration begins to dominate the figures, pre-empting a subsequent decline in standards of craftsmanship; elements become increasingly stylised; production dwindles at the Reformation.

Of the post-1500 embroideries from Western Europe, English examples still dominate – the most popular being the **Oxburgh hangings** with its exotic animals and birds, flowers and beasts worked by the likes of Mary Queen of Scots, Bess of Hardwick and their entourage (linen canvas embroidered in silk cross-stitch) and the **Bradford table carpet** with its fabulous border illustrating contemporary late-16C life (linen canvas embroidered in silk canvas-stitch).

Lace – *Level B: 96.* The art of lacemaking from Italy and Flanders (late 15C) is well represented as lace was applied to vestments, collars and ruffs, church and domestic linen. Lacemaking machinery was invented by John Heathcote (1808-9), but it was unable to rival the best hand-made designs.

Tapestries – *Level B: 94; Level A: 22-24.* The Dukes of Devonshire 15C **Gothic Hunting tapestries** are among the masterpieces of the collection, woven probably at Arras in wool (c 1430). Examples from the London factories at Mortlake, Soho, Lambeth and Fulham – set up by an ex-employee of the Savonnerie Factory (1750-55) and purchased by Claude Passavant, an associate of Thomas Whitby of the Axminster carpet factory fame. Works also include pieces from the Continent like the Gobelins and Aubusson factories (Alexander Calder: *Autumn leaves* 1971).

Carpets – *Level A: 42 and 33 stairs.* The highlight of this section is undoubtedly the Ardabil mosque carpet, the largest Persian carpet in the world (1540; 30 million knots, woollen pile on silk weft – *Level A: 42*): other pieces (9C-20C) illustrate styles from Iran, Turkey, Turkestan, India, North Africa, America and Europe (English Turkey work).

Printed Fabrics – *Level B: 100-101.* Cotton was imported from India in the 16C in the form of chintz (five-colour, block-printed) and calico (painted, printed or stencilled) but subjected to taxes in order to protect the native wool and silk industries. Early woodblock printing with madder dyes (black, reds, purple and brown) evolved with the use of indigo (blue) and weld (yellow) in the 1750s. Naturalistic organic designs were introduced in the mid 1750s. In 1752 copperplates began to be used in Ireland, with use spreading to England in 1756 and to France in 1770 (with Oberkampf at Jouy); this facilitated complicated designs in monochrome (reds, sepia and indigo) on white. In 1783, a Scotsman patented metal roller-printing which simplified production still further; garish modern colours and designs were checked by William Morris and the Arts and Crafts movement, which prescribed good design and craftsmanship in industrial textile production.

Patchwork is displayed in Level B: *102.*

Dress – *Level A: 40.* This wonderful collection charts developments in men's, ladies' and children's wear from the 16C. Displays start with a rare linen shirt from the 1540s. Items from the 17C include the most expensive outfits: heavy cloaks, jackets, bodices... The 18C includes items familiar from contemporary portraiture: hooped skirts, embroidered silk or velvet court suits; Neo-Classical gowns with the most complicated trimmings and contrivances deemed fashionable in this age of eclectic taste (1740s court mantua, 1770s polonaise, 1790s shawl-dress).

The late 19C and early 20C is predominantly represented by Miss Heather Firbank's collection (1905-20) and that accumulated by the famous fashion photographer Sir Cecil Beaton (post-1920s). More recent designs (1960-90) have been donated or acquired by a special committee. From the gorgeous to the weird, designers represented include Fortuny (Delphos dress) Worth, Poiret, Schiaparelli, Dior, Chanel,

Norman Hartnell, Balenciaga, Balmain, Saint-Laurent, Galliano, Versace, Mary Quant, Karl Lagerfeld, Zandra Rhodes, Caroline Charles, Vivienne Westwood, Issey Miyake, Rifat Ozbek. Accessories include: Shilling (millinery), Vuitton (luggage), Ferragamo (shoes), Montblanc pens, Sony Walkman, Filofax organisers, besides the gloves, fans, umbrellas and parasols, canes and sticks, socks and stockings, bags and pouches, handkerchiefs and ties, haircombs and hatpins...

Highlights★★★ – For general interest, the Fashion Galleries will provoke a smile on the face of anyone remotely interested in the tides of fashion; the Textile Study Collection is a haven for embroiderers, dressmakers and design professionals.

M. Kitcatt

Chelsea factory: The Music Lesson

Ceramics and Glass

The foundations of the collection were laid in the 19C with objects selected for the improvement of contemporary British design: examples from the rest of Europe, China and Islam have been acquired since.

The Ceramic Galleries chart the evolution of pottery and porcelain worldwide. Greek and Roman pottery; pieces from the Near East, the discovery of tin-glaze; from Moorish Spain; Renaissance Italy, maiolica; Germany; Turkey; Persia. Chinese and Japanese pottery and porcelain prompted the Europeans to copy not only the elegant shapes of these exotic wares but also to replicate the delicate white texture of porcelain into their soft and hard-paste equivalents.

Porcelain – *Level D: 139-145.* Gallery 139 displays a fabulous bequest made by Lady Charlotte **Schreiber** (1884) including pieces from the Chelsea, Bow, Derby, Worcester porcelain factories and Staffordshire pottery. British porcelain is displayed in Level D:*139-140*; European porcelain in Level D: *142*, French factories Lower level A: *4*; Far Eastern ceramics in Level D: *143-145*.

Pottery – *Level D: 134-138.* **Tin-glazed earthenware**: the application of a white glaze to biscuit-fired pottery was inspired by Chinese porcelain and perfected in the 9C in Baghdad from where its use spread to Spain and Italy (13C). Once dipped in glaze (tin and lead oxide mixed with silicate of potash) high temperature resistant colours may be applied as decoration, additional gloss may then be achieved by applying a lead glaze. Variations include maiolica from Italy, faience from France, delft from Holland and England.

Stoneware: this very hard, dense, resonant, opaque grey or red, non-porous material is contrived from clay and fusible stone (feldspar) fired at very high temperatures (1200-1400°C). Pioneered in China, the technique developed in Europe in the Rhineland. Early types of salt glaze were achieved by throwing salt onto the kiln fire during firing: the heat breaks the chemical compound releasing the chlorine as a gas while the sodium combines with the silicates in the pottery to provide a thin glaze.

Perhaps the most important English potter before Wedgwood was **John Dwight** (c 1635-1703) who established his pottery in Fulham and perfected the use of stoneware for figures (very fine portraits of his dead daughter and Prince Rupert) and practical vessels (bottles, teapots). **Josiah Wedgwood** (1730-95) produced broad ranges of vessels in response to changing tastes and demand from the rising middle classes; he pioneered the mass-production of Neoclassical shapes and decoration (Etruria ware, jasper ware and black basalt ware aped Roman designs of pots excavated in Italy; cream coloured earthenware was called Queen's ware once royal approval had been secured – *Level C: 121, 123*), his first factory (1759) was soon supplemented with others, thereby establishing the famous Staffordshire potteries for all time.

Art pottery evolved at the end of the 19C at the tail-end of the Arts and Crafts movement; exploiting various techniques were William de Morgan and the Martin Brothers. From this developed the English **Studio Pottery** *(Level D: 137)* epitomised by Bernard Leach and Lucie Rie, which spread to Scandinavia (Stig Lindberg), America (Rudy Autio) and into the industrial mainstream of today.

All the **tiles** save the Spanish and Islamic collection, are displayed in drawers for convenient comparison *(Level D: 141)*.

Faience and French porcelain are displayed on the floor below in galleries 127 and 128.

Enamels – *(Level A: 43; Level B: 89)* from Limoges are cased alongside the French collection.

Glass – *Level C: 131.* Just as artists copied one another, so did craftsmen: the impact of Venetian blown glass reached the Low Countries and England, generating an important lead glass industry at Nailsea, Newcastle-upon-Tyne, that culminated with George Ravenscroft (1632-83), the most famous of the English glassmakers and inventor of flint glass as an indigenous alternative to Venetian glass.

POTTERY

Iznik, in Turkey, produced the finest quality pottery of the Islamic world.
Hispano-Moresque was made in Islamic Spain (8C-1492): colours include green, yellow, white, black and manganese; shapes include albarello drug or water jars.
Delftware or Dutch tin-glazed earthenware was inspired by Italian maiolica (Antwerp c 1584). The commonplace use of underglaze blue was a direct response to Chinese wares imported through the Dutch East India Company founded in 1609.
Lustre is the name given to the iridescent metallic finish: silver oxide provides a brassy yellow colour, copper for a rich red. Pioneered in Baghdad, developed in Spain (Malaga, Valencia) and Italy (Deruta, Gubbio), revived by William de Morgan (19C). Other, less durable gilding methods adopted by Wedgwood included the use of platinum salts for silver, gold for pink, purple lustre.
Cream ware consists of lead glazed stoneware with a cream-coloured body containing flint (silica). Cheap to produce, hard wearing and a lighter alternative to porcelain, it also facilitated intricate open basket work. Its colour was ideally suited to transfer printing.
Slipware suggests the use of diluted clay (slip) for trailed or dripped decoration, sealed with clear glaze.

European glass remained essentially functional until the mid 19C after which came cameo cutting, acid etching, moulding, iridescent and lustre texturing (Lalique, Tiffany, Dale Chihuly). More recently, the Gallery has acquired a number of contemporary studio pieces from home and abroad.

The Story of Glass, a history combining information from the Corning Museum of Glass in New York is available on computer in the gallery.

Stained Glass – *Level B: 111 and 117.* English and European stained glass, medieval to 19C, notable display of 15C-16C German stained glass. A rare panel designed by Frank Lloyd Wright is displayed in the Henry Cole Wing.

Highlights★★★ – Meissen goat modelled by Kaendler for the Japanese Palace at Dresden; supreme and rare pieces commissioned by the Medici Grand Duke of Tuscany (1570s). Delftware charger made by Christian Wilhelm, the founder of the Pickleherring pottery in Southwark. Palissy and St Porchaire pottery. Examples of glass by the Venetian Verzelini, active in London in the 16C.

Metalwork and Jewellery

This is perhaps the most diverse and eclectic national collection ranging from the 2C BC to the 20C AD and encompassing a broad selection of items (jewellery, watches, cutlery, plate, ormolu, mortars, British biscuit tins) made of different materials: platinum, gold, silver, copper, brass, bronze, iron, tin, lead, alloy and plastic. Only items since the 9C are now actively acquired.

Medieval Treasury and Church Plate – *Level A: 43; Level B: 83-84.* From the earliest times, supreme craftsmanship has been dedicated to liturgical objects (12C Gloucester candlestick, Eltenberg reliquary, Ramsey Abbey censer, Studley bowl, Swinburne pyx); many pieces disappeared at the Reformation when a market developed for domestic objects (Valence casket).

Silver – *Level B: 65-69.* England boasts an important silver tradition, sustained in London by the Worshipful Company of Goldsmiths *(see CITY)*. Note the intricate workmanship of the **Howard Grace cup** (also known as the Thomas-a-Becket cup) set with pearls and garnets and the Vyvyan salt with its panels of *verre eglomisé*. In the national collection designs by Paul de Lamerie (sumptuous Newdigate centrepiece), Robert Adam (elegant sauce boats), AWN Pugin, William Burgess, Christopher Dresser, CR Ashbee, Harold Stabler mark high points in patronage and aesthetic movements. The development of Sheffield plate as an alternative to solid silver achieved high standards of quality of its own *(Level B: 82)*.

Important 15C-17C European secular pieces (German and Spanish) come from the bequest made by Dr Hildburgh. Rare examples of French silver include the 14C Rouen treasure and 1528 Burghley nef showing Tristan and Iseult playing chess on their journey from Ireland to Cornwall: designed to carry salt, its position on the high table at a banquet would mark the guests of honour "above the salt." The Bergamo cross is perhaps the most exceptional Italian piece (c 1390). Russian enamelled silver.

The art of goldsmithing is explored and celebrated in Lower level A: *7*; Level B: *91-93*.

Iron – *Level B: 113-114.* Fine range of locks, wrought-iron grilles, railings, firebacks and shopsigns illustrate the rich variety and skill of the blacksmith through the ages. Other items in the collection are clocks (displayed in the Musical Instruments Gallery), pewter receptacles and cutlery *(Level B: 81)* arms and armour *(Level B: 88a and 90)*.

Jewellery Gallery – *Level B: 91-93.* Beyond the Saxon brooches, gold and silver set with enamels and gemstones, are sets of exquisite Prussian iron jewellery and psychedelic modernist plastic costume pieces. Note the particularly fine Armada jewel of enamelled gold, set with diamonds and rubies enclosing a miniature painting of Elizabeth I on vellum.

Simon Costin's fishhead brooch (1988) is made from a real red bream head dried and preserved in formaldehyde, lined in 18ct gold, decorated with a taxidermist's glass (puma) eye, Venetian glass beads, enamel paint and watercolour and glazed with

polyurethane varnish; the original was eaten by rats in the artist's studio – this therefore, strictly speaking is a replica! *(Level B: 102).*
Oriental jewellery is exhibited with other indigenous artefacts – *see below.*

Highlights★★★ – Jewellery galleries; Burghley nef; Nuremberg beaker; Collection of clocks, sundials, watches displayed with the Musical Instruments *(Level B: 40a).*

National Art Library – *Level B: 77-78.* The reference collection comprises some 300 000 publications on architecture, sculpture, topography, theatre, fashion, heraldry, printing, binding, manuscripts and autographs.

EASTERN WORKS OF ART

Far Eastern

Sixty thousand artefacts from China, Korea and Japan make up this collection.

T T Tsui Gallery of Chinese Art – *Level A: 44.* The oldest artefacts (5000-1700 BC) have been retrieved from burial sites: these include ritual items, seals, cylinders and jade discs bearing the most intricate designs given the basic technology and tools available at the time. The first historic culture of China is associated with the Bronze Age **Shang** state (1700 BC) when metal signified the greatest wealth and luxury.
The **Han** dynasty (206 BC-AD 220) was evidently a period of sophistication celebrated in naturalistic tomb paintings and extensive reliefs; funeral items include pottery and carved jade. The ensuing period was marred by war and strife.
The **Tang** dynasty (618-906) enjoyed another flowering of the arts: lavish objects found in tombs include beautifully carved animals (camels and horses), elegant silver and gold receptacles, incense burners, funerary jars, head rests, early examples of white porcelain.
Between 960 and 1278 the **Song** period witnessed the development of new forms of ceramic including the Ru and Guan imperial wares, and specific styles of embroidered ritual robes. Then followed the **Yuan** dynasty of the Mongols (1279-1368); political ambition is echoed in bolder technique and style in painting and ceramics; this is when underglazed blue was perfected. The **Ming** dynasty (1368-1644) is remembered for the building of the Forbidden City in Peking furnished with plain but "designer" furniture (canopied bed 1650), ornaments, writing and painting materials, fabulous silk textiles and intricate tapestries embroidered with exotic birds and beasts, dragons and flowers.
Chinese items of 20C urban and rural dress from the Valery Garrett Collection are shown in Level B: *98.*

Gallery of Chinese Export Art – *Level A: 47e and 47f.* Under the **Qing** dynasty (1644-1911), trade with the west flourished and goods were manufactured specially for the European market: topographical views of coastal towns, lacquered furniture, exquisite fancy goods of carved ivory, porcelain objects (barber's shaving bowl), painted silk cloth and decorative fans.

Samsung Gallery of Korean Art – The main collection dates from the Koryo dynasty (918-1392) when the arts were already highly developed (bronze vase inlaid with silver wire; gold and colour depiction of the Buddha Samantabadhra on silk). The greatest sense of perfection probably emanates from the ceramics: simple pure forms, restrained decoration, harmonious colours and delicate glazes. After the devastation wrought by the Mongol invasions (13C) the new **Choson** dynasty (1392-1910) emerged and the arts flourished once more, almost in defiance of the Chinese threat.

Toshiba Gallery of Japanese Art – *Level A: 45.* The most important single factor in the development of Japanese art was the introduction of Buddhism to the Asuka court (552-645) from Korea. The following **Nara** dynasty (645-794) maintained relations with China, assimilating Tang influences into ceramic designs and metalwork. The **Heian** court (794-1185), based in Kyoto, patronised the arts and culture; this was continued by the **Kamakura** rule (1185-1333) during which time paintings and sculptures of Buddha become increasingly more refined.
The famous rituals enacted at tea ceremonies crystallised during the 16C and 17C, just as Japan evolved her own porcelain factories and the art of "japanning" furniture for the export markets in Europe (**Van Diemen Box** and the **Mazarin cabinet**). Supreme levels of craftsmanship were attained during the Edo period (1615-1868) in the production of porcelain and woodblock printing (collected during the 1860s by the likes of Monet, Degas and Whistler), lacquerware for domestic use (picnic set, incense ceremony utensils, writing utensils); folk craft; textiles; dress and accessories. The museum's present policy is to boost its historic collection with important contemporary works selected from the various modern Japanese studio crafts.

Note: the Momoyama period (early 17C) six-fold screen depicting the arrival of European traders in Japan.

Indian and South-east Asian

Artefacts from India, Pakistan, Bangladesh, Sri Lanka, Tibet, Nepal, Bhutan and the Himalayas, Burma, Thailand, Cambodia, Vietnam, Malaysia and Indonesia are all collected together in an overview of the South-east Asian continent.

Nehru Gallery of Indian Art 1550-1900 – *Level A: 41*. The Indian subcontinent, as large and culturally diverse as Europe, has produced an immense range of folkloric, religious, imperial art through the ages. The V & A collection is the largest and most complete, assembled from the end of the 18C when Indian decorative arts became appreciated by Europeans. Sculpture in terracotta (most ancient female figurines), stone (*yakshan* nature spirits), bronze, wood, stucco and ivory has been crafted to the glory of Hindu, Buddhist and Jain deities, eclipsed at times by Islam from the north and the Deccan (13C).

In the 16C the Mughal established their court and fostered a great flowering of the finest arts. As their empire crumbled, regional kingdoms were subjugated by European trading companies like the English East India Company. In 1857 British power transferred to government with the institution of the Raj until independence was granted in 1947.

The exhibits are presented in seven sections, pre- and post-Mughal: **Hindu, Buddhist and Jain India**. Highlights include stylised figurative works: an exceptionally refined 11C-12C gilt bronze Buddha from the heart of Buddhism introduced into Southern India in the 3C BC; his handsome head crowned like a monarch or conforming to a strict iconography (forehead *urna*, elongated earlobes, high hair knot); a smiling *yakshi* tree spirit; Siva's sacred bull Nandi, ascetics, dancers.

Mughal, Rajput and British India (Mughal Age, Sultanates of the Deccan, Rajput Courts, India and Europe, Regional Courts, Britain and India 1850-1900). Northern India was dominated by Muslim sultans from the 13C. In 1526 Prince Babur invaded Delhi and founded the Mughal empire; successive generations nurtured peace, extended their territories and patronised the fine, decorative and applied arts (fabulous illuminated manuscripts: *The Akbarnma*, Jahangir's *Memoirs, Bhagavata Purana, Harivamsa*, wonderful carvings, introduced carpet weaving from eastern Persia), their naturalism prompted by European influences (Jesuit missionaries, Portuguese, Dutch, English traders). Exhibits range from arms and armour to garments, carved screens, Bidri ware, cotton chintz and muslin, carpets, embroideries in gold and silver thread and exquisite jewellery set with enamel, gems and semi-precious stones.

A Gory Image

Tipu's painted wood tiger represents an Indian tiger mauling a British officer. The tiger's body contains a miniature (possibly French) organ which ingeniously simulates its roar as well as the groans of its victim. Captured in 1799 at the fall of Seringapatam, during which Tipu the ruler of Mysore was killed, it became a favourite exhibit in the East India Company's London museum; it is also mentioned in Keats' satirical poem *The Cap and Bells*.

Highlights★★★ include the Sri Lankan Robinson Casket, a Gujarati travelling box set with mother of pearl, Tipu Sultan's Tiger, the golden throne of Maharaja Ranjit Singh (1780-1839) who reputedly united the Sikh community until war forced the British to annex the Punjab after his death.

Nepal and Tibet – The Himalayan regions boast a long and vital link with Buddhism: Buddha is alleged to have been born in Lumbini (southern Nepal) and the religion was nurtured in Tibet with influences from India (8C-13C) alongside a complicated indigenous animistic religion (Bön) which it slowly assimilated. The arts of the region, meanwhile, blended Indian and Chinese, Kashmiri, Nepalese and Central Asian designs.

Nepal was sustained more directly by eastern India (Gupta, post Gupta and Pala Styles span 4C-12C AD). The finest artists and craftsmen seem to have come from the Newar community which served Hindu and Buddhist patrons alike. This duality is translated into a distinctive artform where imagery and iconography are synchronised.

M. Kitcatt

Tipu's Tiger

South-east Asia – The area described by Ptolemy (2C AD) as "India beyond the Ganges" was united by a Sanskrit Brahman culture promoted by the educated priesthood and ruling class. Regional traditions were evolved from Indian practices. The artistic legacy is that of Angkor in Cambodia, Pagan in Burma, Sukhothai in Thailand and the complex temple communities of central and east Java. Religious tolerance prompts a variety of styles: Indian cults of Siva, Vishnu and Harihara;

Mahayana Buddhism; Hinduism. The revival of Hinayana Buddhism, as practised today, was prompted by Sri Lankan monks who regarded themselves as the guardians of the true cult and worked as missionaries. Iconography is embellished and complicated by influences brought by the trade routes between China and Persia.

Islamic Collection

Level A: 42. The faith of Islam is rooted in the 7C teachings of the Arab Prophet Mohammed (d 632), later recorded in the Koran. From Mecca and Medina, where it united various tribal factions, the Islamic armies undertook to conquer Syria, Egypt, sections of the Byzantine and Sassanian empires that included Iraq and Iran: from Spain to Central Asia lands were united under Islam, their arts subjugated to rigorous rules (the mosque's orientation towards Mecca, the prohibition of human or animal representations, the emphasis on the word of God) that encouraged alternative embellishment in the form of superlative calligraphy, painted tiles, carpets, lamps, carved and inlaid wooden furniture: in more secular contexts, the rules are less formally applied. Objects, however, are always functional (lustre and slipware pottery, carved boxes and writing sets, carpets and hangings, brass furnishings or receptacles).

Highlight★★★: the **Egyptian rock crystal ewer** (c 1000) carved from a single block of rock crystal, must surely be the most supreme example of craftsmanship. The **Luck of Edenhall**, a Syrian glass goblet with enamelled decoration would have come to Europe with the crusaders; the **Ardabil carpet** *(see Carpets above)*, and the elaborate, classical Persian **Chelsea carpet**.

Westminster★★★

Westminster is resonant with royal and political history: the Coronation ceremony and other prestigious royal events at Westminster Abbey, the state opening of Parliament with elaborate pageantry, and state visits when royal personages and other dignitaries process in glittering carriages with the mounted cavalry in attendance. The Palace of Westminster, Big Ben and Westminster Abbey are the undisputed highlights but there are also elegant enclaves to admire.

Location

Map pp 11-12 (DEY); Michelin Atlas London: pp 45-46 ⊖ Westminster, Victoria. The South Bank is a short walk over Westminster Bridge and for Tate Britain follow the river upstream on the north bank. St James's and Buckingham Palace are within walking distance. For excursions on the Thames visit Westminster Pier.

Adjacent Sights: TRAFALGAR SQUARE – WHITEHALL; ST JAMES'S; BUCKINGHAM PALACE; TATE BRITAIN; SOUTH BANK.

Background

Westminster embodies two important institutions of state: Westminster Abbey *(listed separately)*, where coronations and royal weddings are held, and the Palace of Westminster, the seat of both Houses of Parliament.

The district acquired its name meaning "the minster in the west", as opposed to St Paul's Cathedral, "the minster in the east", when Edward the Confessor rebuilt the abbey church on Thorney Island; he also built a royal palace and the parish church of St Margaret next to the abbey precincts.

Royal Palace – "**King William I** built much at his palace, for, according to Stow, he found the residence of **Edward the Confessor** "far inferior to the building of princely palaces in France." Unlike the Tower, William's palace at Westminster was never strongly fortified but remained intact for centuries. It was never deliberately demolished but gradually disappeared beneath frequent rebuilding occasioned by fires, the most devastating occurring in 1298, 1512 and 1834. Hemming in the palace on all sides were houses for members of the court, knights and burgesses, who, as representatives of local communities or commons, began from 1332 to meet apart as the House of Commons.

Early Parliaments – The opening ceremony of Parliament took place then, as it does now, in the presence of the monarch but in those days it was held in a richly ornamented hall known as the Painted Chamber. The Lords then adjourned to the White Hall, while

The riverside front of the Palace of Westminster

the Commons remained or adjourned to the Westminster Abbey Chapter House *(see WESTMINSTER ABBEY)* or to the monks' refectory. After the fire of 1512 the old palace was not rebuilt and **Henry VIII** had no royal residence in Westminster, until he confiscated York House from Wolsey in 1529.

In 1547 St Stephen's Chapel, the king's domestic chapel, was granted by **Edward VI** to the Commons as their chamber. It was while they were in St Stephen's Chapel that King Charles I came to arrest and impeach Hampden, Pym and three others (1642) and it was there that they continued to sit until the 19C. The Lords, so nearly blown up in the **Gunpowder Plot** (1605), continued to meet in the White Hall until the night of 16 October 1834 when cartloads of notched tally sticks (old Exchequer forms of account) were put into the underground furnace, which overheated. In hours the buildings had burnt almost to the ground; the only ones to survive were Westminster Hall, St Stephen's Crypt, the two-storey St Stephen's cloister (1526-29) and the Jewel Tower.

Houses of Parliament – In 1835 a competition was held for new Parliament buildings which, it was decided, should conform to an English style, preferably Tudor or Gothic. The winners were both Gothicists **Charles Barry** by necessity and **Augustus Pugin** by innermost fervour. The foundation stone was laid in 1840, the Victoria Tower completed by 1860; there were over 1 000 rooms, 100 staircases and 2mi/3km of corridors spread over 8 acres/3mi. In 1852 Barry was knighted and Pugin died in Bedlam, the asylum for the insane.

Highlights

Palace of Westminster***

Guided tour (75min) Aug-Sep (Summer Recess) starting from The Victoria Tower. £7; £2 surcharge on language tours. Firstcall 0870 906 3773; www.firstcalltickets.com

When Parliament is in session it is well worth queueing for the Visitors' Gallery to catch a glimpse of the interior and to watch the proceedings in the House of Commons.

Barry's ground plan is outstandingly simple: two chambers are disposed on a single, processional north-south axis so that the throne, the Woolsack, the bars of the two chambers and the Speaker's chair are all in line. At the centre is a large common lobby, which the public enter through St Stephen's Hall. Libraries, committee rooms and dining rooms, parallel to the main axis, overlook the river. Above the central lobby rises a lantern and slender spire (originally part of the ventilation system); each end is marked by a tower: the Victoria Tower over the royal entrance, the other housing a clock. The external design is equally remarkable – symmetrical and yet asymmetrical, as the ends of the complex are marked by two quite dissimilar towers, and the St Stephen's turrets do not match; the long waterfront is entirely regular, articulated from end to end with Gothic pinnacles and windows and decorated with medieval tracery, carving, niches and figures, individually designed by Pugin in Perpendicular Gothic. The stone used was Yorkshire

A. Taverner/MICHELIN

limestone (badly quarried and in constant need of repair). Hundreds of painters, sculptors and craftsmen combined in the realisation of Barry's plan and Pugin's décor.

Westminster Hall★

The hall was added to William I's palace by his son, **William Rufus**, in 1097. Throughout the Middle Ages it was used for royal Christmas feasts, jousts, ceremonial and as a place of assembly. It was repaired by **Thomas Becket**, flooded in the 13C "when men did row wherries in (its) midst" and re-roofed by command of **Richard II** in 1394. In 1401, however, before the work was complete, the king was arraigned there before parliament and deposed. **Sir Thomas More** (1535), **Somerset** (1551), **Northumberland** (1553), Essex (1601), **Guy Fawkes** (1606) and **Charles I** all stood trial in the hall.

When peripatetic courts following the king were abandoned, Westminster Hall was appointed the permanent seat of justice until the Royal Courts of Justice *(see STRAND)* moved to the Strand in the 1870s; the floor space was divided between courts of Common Pleas, Chancery and King's Bench, bookstalls and shops. This century monarchs and Churchill have lain in state there.

The superb **hammerbeam roof★★★**, probably the finest timber roof of all time, was constructed by Henry Yevele, master mason, and Hugh Herland, carpenter, at the command of **Richard II** in 1394. The upper walls were rebuilt and buttresses added to the exterior to support the weight (over 600 tons). The roof rises to 90ft at the crest and depends on projecting hammerbeams (21ft/6m long x 3ft 3in/1m x 2ft 1in/0.7m thick), supported on curving wooden braces resting on carved stone corbels. The beams, now reinforced with steel, which support the vertical posts on which the superstructure rests, are carved with great flying angels.

The hall (238ft/69.5m x 70ft/21m) is lit by nine-light Perpendicular windows at each end. The south window was removed to its present position in the 19C by Barry; beneath the resulting arch, now flanked by six 14C statues of early English kings, Barry inserted a dramatic flight of steps rising from the hall to **St Stephen's Porch**.

The Gunpowder Plot

Robert Catesby, Thomas Winter, Thomas Percy and John Wright intended to blow up the House of Lords, the king and queen and heir to the throne. They rented a cellar extending under Parliament and enlisted **Guy Fawkes**, a little-known individual from abroad, to plant the explosive in the cellar: at least 20 barrels of gunpowder camouflaged with coal and faggots. Seeking to recruit additional support, Catesby approached Francis Tresham, who warned Lord Monteagle, his brother-in-law, not to attend Parliament on the fateful day. Monteagle alerted the government and Guy Fawkes was discovered in the cellar late on 4 November. Under torture on the rack he revealed the names of his fellow conspirators. Catesby and Percy were killed while resisting arrest. The others were tried and executed on 31 January 1606.

St Stephen's Crypt (St Mary's Chapel)

The domestic chapel built (1292-97) by Edward I was on two levels, the upper being reserved for the royal family. After St Stephen's had been granted to the Commons, the lower chapel was used for secular purposes until the 19C when the medieval chamber was redecorated as a chapel.

St Stephen's Hall

The long narrow hall, the public entrance to the Central Lobby, was constructed by Barry with ribbed vaulting springing from clustered piers to look like the 14C St Stephen's Chapel, where the Commons had met. At the end are two superimposed arches, the upper filled with a mosaic of St Stephen between King Stephen and Edward the Confessor. The brasses on the floor mark the limit of the old Commons chamber (60ft/18m x 30ft/9m).

Central Lobby★

The octagonal lobby (75ft/23m high) is the hub of the building, where constituents waiting to see their MP may spot many well-known political figures. Every element of the design is by Pugin: Perpendicular arches framing the windows and entrances, decorated with English sovereigns, life-size 19C statesmen, mosaics over the doors, gilded and patterned roof ribs and the chandelier.

Commons Lobby

When the lobby, destroyed in an air raid in 1941, was reconstructed, stones from the original fabric were incorporated in the **Churchill Arch**; it is flanked by his statue in bronze by Oscar Nemon and a statue of Lloyd George.

House of Commons★

The chamber, also destroyed in the 1941 raid, was rebuilt simply, without decoration. The roof is a plain Gothic timber structure. The parallel benches in the traditional green hide provide seating for 437 of the 651 elected members. At the end is the canopied Speaker's chair; before it are the seats of the Clerks and the table of the house bearing the mace and the bronze-mounted despatch boxes. The red stripes on either side of the green carpet mark the limit to which a member may advance when addressing the house; the distance between the stripes is reputedly that of two drawn swords. The government sits on the Speaker's right, the Prime Minister opposite the despatch box. When a division is called, members leave for the tellers' lobbies past the Speaker's right for Aye and through the far end for No.

Libraries – The libraries, overlooking the river, are oases of silence. The Lords' library, which is the more remarkable owing to the decoration by Pugin, contains the warrant for the execution of Charles I signed by Cromwell and the council.

Terrace – The terrace is reserved for Members of Parliament and their guests, a very special place to take tea.

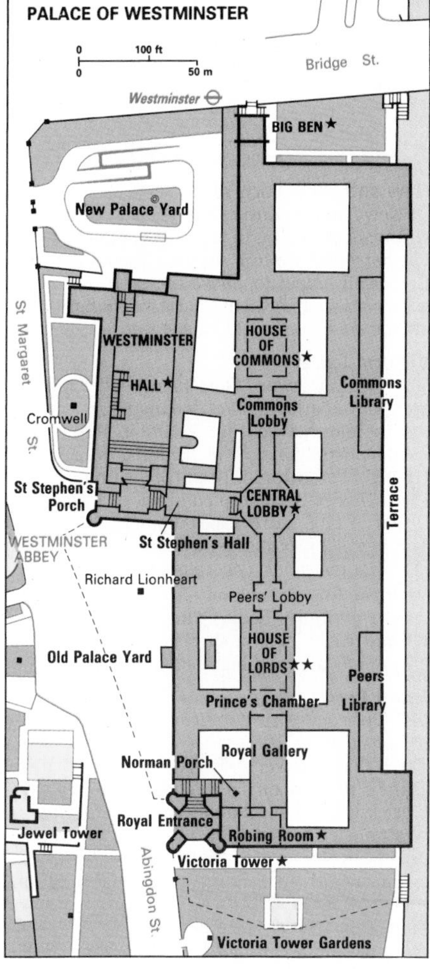

House of Lords★★

The "magnificent and gravely gorgeous" chamber is the summit of Pugin's achievement; a symphony of design and workmanship in scarlet, gilding and encrusted gold. At one end of the chamber on a stepped dais stands the throne beneath a Gothic canopy, decorated with niches and finials, mounted on a wide screen, all in gold. The ceiling is divided by ribs and gold patterning. The Woolsack, symbol of England's medieval wealth, is said to be "most uncomfortable". The benches are covered in red buttoned leather; the one with arms is for the bishops (possibly to retain those who have dined too well). The cross benches are between the clerk's table and the bar of the house, behind which the members of the House of Commons stand when summoned by Black Rod to hear the speech from the throne at the State Opening of Parliament in November. Between the windows are statues of 18 barons who witnessed King John's assent to the ***Magna Carta***. When the Lords divide on an issue they vote Content or Not Content.

Royal Gallery – The gallery (110ft/33.5m), the sovereign's processional way, is decorated with frescoes by Daniel Maclise, gilt bronze statues of monarchs from Alfred to Queen Anne and portraits of all the sovereigns and their consorts since George I. In the following **Prince's Chamber** are representations of the Tudor monarchs and their consorts, including all six wives of Henry VIII.

Robing Room★ – Here the sovereign assumes the Imperial State Crown and crimson parliamentary robe. The room, like the Lords' Chamber, presents Pugin's most remarkable concentration of decorative invention; the panelled ceiling is ornamented with sovereigns' badges, patterned and gilded, coloured, carved; the walls are hung with flocked paper and pictures or decorated with frescoes depicting the legend of King Arthur.

Royal Entrance and Staircase – On ceremonial occasions, such as the Opening of Parliament, the sovereign is met by high officers of state at the entrance to the Victoria Tower; members of the Household Cavalry line the flight of stairs leading up to the **Norman Porch**, which is square in shape and Perpendicular in style with gilded vaulting.

Big Ben's Clock Tower★

St Stephen's clock tower (316ft/97m) was completed by 1858-59, thereby replacing another that stood close to the site of the old palace clock tower (1288-1707), which at one time had the staple or wool market at its foot. Inside is a luxurious

Facts And Figures

Measuring 9ft/3m in diameter and 7ft/2m in height, **Big Ben** weighs in at 13tons 10cwts 3qtrs 15lbs, it also has a 4ft/1m crack which developed soon after being installed.

The **clock** mechanism weighs about 5 tons. The dials of cast-iron tracery (diameter 23ft/7m) are glazed with pot opal glass; the figures are 2ft/60cm long; the minute spaces are 1ft/30cm square; the 14ft/4m long minute hands are made of copper, weigh 2 cwts and travel 120mi/193km per year.

prison cell in which the leader of the militant movement for women's suffrage, Emmeline Pankhurst, was detained in 1902.

The name **Big Ben**, probably after Sir Benjamin Hall, First Commissioner of Works and a man of vast girth, applied originally only to the bell which was cast at the Whitechapel Foundry. The clock with an electrically wound mechanism has proved reliable, except for minor stoppages, for 117 years until it succumbed to metal fatigue in 1976 which required major repairs. Big Ben was first broadcast on New Year's Eve in 1923. The Ayrton light above the clock is lit while the Commons is sitting.

New and Old Palace Yards

In **New Palace Yard** is the Jubilee Fountain of heraldic beasts, sculpted in iron and inaugurated by the Queen in May 1977.

Further south a plinth supports the telling statue by Hamo Thorneycroft of **Oliver Cromwell**; opposite, above the small north-east door of St Margaret's Church *(see below)* is a small head of Charles I. **Richard the Lionheart** meanwhile patiently sits astride his horse in Old Palace Yard.

Victoria Tower★

The Victoria Tower (336ft/102m), taller than the clock tower, was designed as the archive for parliamentary documents, previously kept in the Jewel Tower *(see below)* and therefore saved from the fire in 1834. The **House of Lords Record Office** now contains 3 million papers including master copies of acts from 1497, journals of the House of Lords from 1510 and of the Commons from 1547, records of the **Gunpowder Plot**, Charles I's attempted arrest of Hampden, Patents of Nobility, the Articles of Union of 1706 etc. ♿ *Open Mon-Fri, 9.30am-5pm; preferably by appointment. Closed certain public hols and last two weeks of Nov. Leaflet. ☎ 020 7219 3074; Fax 020 7219 2570; hlro@parliament.uk; www.parliament.uk*

Victoria Tower Gardens – The statuary in the gardens includes a cast of the great bronze group by Rodin, **The Burghers of Calais**, who ransomed themselves to Edward III in 1347, a slim statue of the suffragette **Emmeline Pankhurst** and a bronze medallion of her daughter, Christabel.

Jewel Tower

(EH) Open daily, Apr-Sep, 10am-6pm (5pm Oct, 4pm Nov-Mar). Closed 24-26 Dec, 1 Jan. £2. ☎ 020 7222 2219

The L-shaped tower with a corner staircase turret, dates from 1365 when it was built as the king's personal jewel house and treasury and surrounded by a moat. There is a brick vaulted strongroom on the first floor with a later iron door (1612). When Westminster ceased to be a royal palace, the tower, with window renewed in 1718, became the archive for parliamentary papers *(see below)* and subsequently the weights and measures office. Standards of Weight and Length are displayed in the top chamber. In the vaulted lower chamber are the tower's rediscovered ancient wooden foundations, bosses from Westminster Hall and capitals.

Adjoining the Jewel Tower in Abingdon Garden stands the sculpture *Knife Edge to Edge* by Henry Moore (1964).

Walking About

Start from Westminster Bridge, then cross to Parliament Sq.

Westminster Bridge★

The stone bridge (1750), where Wordsworth composed his sonnet (1807), was the first to be built after London Bridge. It was replaced in 1862 with a flat stone structure by Thomas Page comprising seven low arches. From the bridge there is a fine view of the terrace and river front of the Houses of Parliament. At the bridge foot is a sculpture of **Boadicea** heroically riding in her chariot in her campaign against the Romans.

Parliament Square

The square and Parliament Street, which were laid out in 1750 at the time of the building of the first Westminster Bridge, were redesigned in 1951. The bronze statues are of **Churchill** by Ivor Roberts Jones, **Jan Smuts** by Jacob Epstein, **Lord Palmerston**, Lord Derby (note the pedestal reliefs of the old Commons in 1833), **Benjamin Disraeli**, **Robert Peel**, **George Canning** and Abraham Lincoln. On the west side stands **Middlesex Guildhall** (1905), described as Art Nouveau Gothic, richly embossed with figures beneath a turreted tower.

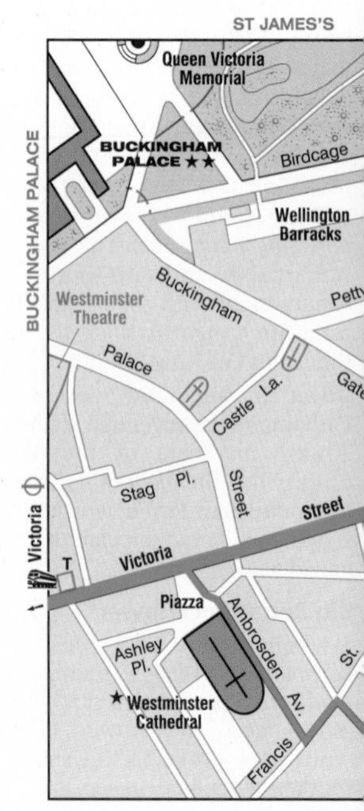

Cross the square to the south and walk past St Margaret's Church (description in Worth a Visit) and Westminster Abbey (see WESTMINSTER ABBEY).

The Sanctuary

In the monastery's day, the right of sanctuary extended over a considerable area. The quarter became so overbuilt with squalid houses and the right was so abused by vagabonds, thieves and murderers that it was first restricted and finally abolished, in all but name, under James I.

The Gatehouse in which **Sir Walter Raleigh** spent the last night before his execution and **Richard Lovelace** penned the line "stone walls do not a prison make nor iron bars a cage" was demolished in 1776; on the site stands a red granite column erected in memory of former pupils of Westminster School *(see below)* who died in the Indian Mutiny and the Crimean War.

Opposite the Sanctuary buildings, designed by Sir Gilbert Scott with an archway through to the Dean's Yard *(see WESTMINSTER ABBEY)*, are in marked contrast with the 1970s **Queen Elizabeth II Conference Centre** and **Central Hall**, designed as a Wesleyan church with the third largest dome in London by Rickards and Lanchester in 1912 and now used as an examination hall or hired out for public events.

An Innovator

Nearby, on the opposite side of Great Smith Street, stood the almonry where the well-to-do cloth merchant **William Caxton** set up his press in 1476 using as his imprint William Caxton in the Abbey of Westminster (publishing **Chaucer**'s *Canterbury Tales*, Malory's *Le Morte d'Arthur* and Aesop's *Fables*).

Walk up Storey's Gate and turn left into Old Queen St.

Old Queen Street is incomplete but contains several 18C houses, one *(no 28)* with a rounded hood on corbels.

Cockpit Steps now lead to Birdcage Walk and St James's Park *(see BUCKINGHAM PALACE)* but in the days of Whitehall Palace they led down to a cockfighting pit.

Flanked by the Home Office buildings on the left, is **Queen Anne's Gate**, an L-shaped street of substantial three-storey terrace houses built of now darkened brown brick that date from the reign of Queen Anne (1704) – a statue of the queen as a very young woman stands between blind windows in an end wall *(no 15, south side)*. The sash windows are square beneath continuous eaves and wide stone courses; in several instances, the pilastered doorways are protected by flat wooden hoods, decorated with rich carving and hanging pendants. The street's hall-mark is the white satyr's mask set in place of a tablet stone above the ground and first floor windows of every house.

Take Broadway and Tothill St to the top of Victoria St.

Victoria Street

The street was cut through the Georgian slums to link Parliament to Victoria Station in 1862. It is now lined with 20C buildings – tower blocks in steel and brown glass, faced in marble, stone and concrete, providing offices for government ministries and international companies.

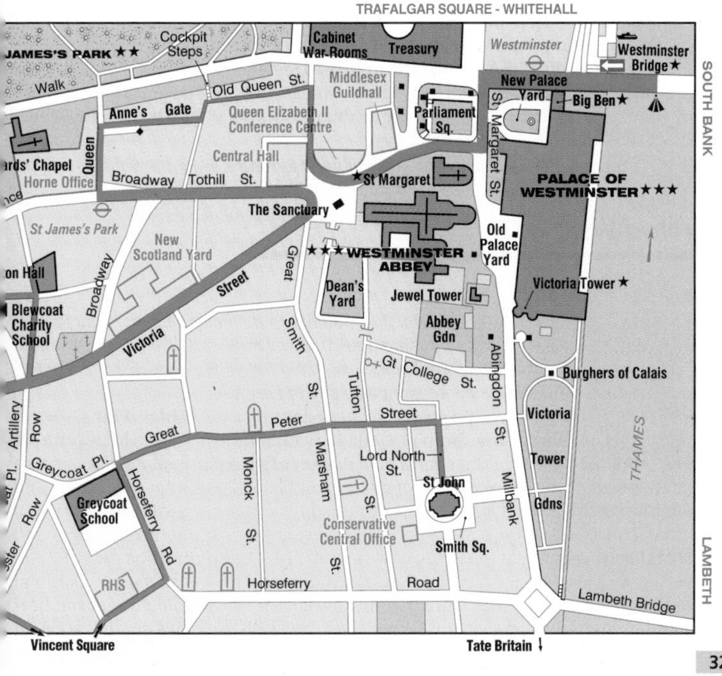

On the north side in an old churchyard, shaded by plane trees, is a monument to the suffragette movement by E Russell (1974). Among the neighbouring buildings are: **New Scotland Yard** (1967); **London Transport**'s headquarters (1927-29) by Charles Holden with decorative statuary groups by **Jacob Epstein** and reliefs by **Eric Gill**, **Henry Moore** and others; **Caxton Hall** (1878), once famous for register office weddings; the old **Blewcoat Charity School** *(Buckingham Street)*, a delightful square red brick building erected in 1709 to house the school, which was founded in 1688 and is now the property of the National Trust *(shop). National Trust Shop and Information Centre: Open Mon-Fri, 10am-5.30pm.(7pm Thu); Nov, Sats; Dec, Sats, 5, 13, 20. Closed 25 Dec to 1 Jan and Bank Hols. ☎ 020 7222 2877*

At the west end of the street stands **Little Ben**, a model (30ft/9m high) of Big Ben. **Victoria Railway Station** was built in the 1870s on the site of the Grosvenor Canal; the present buildings date from the turn of the century. The Grosvenor Hotel (1860-61) was designed by JT Knowles. In Stag Place, a great bronze stag marks the site of the Stag Brewery (closed 1959).

Walk back to Westminster Cathedral (description in Worth a Visit) piazza, turn right into Ambrosden Ave, walk up Francis St and make for the north side of Vincent Sq.

Vincent Square

The large square was laid out in 1810 on part of the old Tothill Fields to provide playing fields for Westminster School *(see WESTMINSTER ABBEY)*. On the north-east side is the **Royal Horticultural Society** (f 1804), a square brick building with the New Horticultural Hall (1923-28) at the back where monthly flower shows are held *(open to non-members)*. Its library, the Lindley Library, was founded in 1886 and boasts some 50 000 volumes dating back to 1514,and rare botanical drawings.

Proceed along Elverton St and take Horseferry Rd.

Greycoat School

Greycoat Place. The grey uniform of this Westminster Charity school, founded in 1698, can be seen on the small wooden figures in niches contrasting puritanically with the brilliantly coloured royal coat of arms set between them on the pedimented stucco; it is now a girls' school. There was a green-liveried school (1633) nearby in Greencoat Place.

Proceed along Great Peter St and turn right into Lord North St.

Smith Square

The square itself, the four streets which enter midway along each side and the streets to the north include many of the original Georgian houses: nos 6-9 Smith Square, all Lord North Street except at the northern end and at the south end of Cowley Street (occasional date stones 1722, 1726).

Today, the square is associated with politics; in the south-west corner is **Conservative Central Office** whilst many properties all around accommodate MPs' offices or lodgings.

At the centre stands **St John's**, **Smith Square**, a tall Baroque church which now serves as a concert hall. The church (1714-28), designed by Thomas Archer, is lit by Venetian windows (east and west) and has great porticoes (north and south) composed of colossal pillars beneath open pediments. Its four ornate corner towers having been compared by the queen to an upturned footstool gave rise to its nickname "Queen Anne's Footstool." It was badly bombed during the Second World War but the interior has been restored with giant Corinthian columns beneath a deep cornice and an 18C chandelier.

Take Dean Stanley St east and turn left into Millbank to return to Parliament Sq.

Worth a Visit

Westminster Cathedral★

♿ Open daily, 7am-7pm (5.30pm Bank Hols). Audio tour. Pocket guide (7 languages). Belltower: Mar-Nov, daily, 9.30am-12.30pm and 1-5pm; Dec-Feb, Thu-Sun, same hours. ♿ entrance at southwest side of Cathedral. ☎ 020 7798 9055; Fax 020 7798 9090; barrypalmer@rcdow.org.uk; www.westminstercathedral.org.uk

Set back from Victoria Street and graced by a modern piazza, **Ashley Place**, towers the remarkable neo-Byzantine Roman Catholic cathedral. In 1884 when Cardinal Manning purchased the site, the land was in disuse: early records show it as a marsh before the Benedictines of Westminster Abbey established a market and fairground there; following the Reformation it was occupied by a maze, a garden, a bullring, a house of correction and then a prison which during the Commonwealth detained 1 500 Scots taken prisoner at the Battle of Worcester (1651), pending their deportation. Despite the fashion for neo-Gothic, Cardinal Manning and his successor Cardinal Vaughan, determined on early Christian inspiration for the architecture of the new cathedral, in part perhaps because they had no wish to emulate the style of

Westminster Abbey. The architect **JF Bentley**, travelled widely in Italy before producing (1894) plans for an **Italianate-Byzantine** building; construction started promptly in 1895 and was completed so far as the fabric was concerned by 1903. The building (360ft/109m long x 156ft/47m wide) is composed of 12.5 million bricks and distinguished by a domed **campanile** (273ft/83m high).

Interior – The initial impression is of vastness and fine proportions. The nave, the widest in England, is roofed by three domes. The decoration is incomplete; above the lower surfaces and piers, which are faced with coloured marble and granite, rise unpointed bare brick walls, awaiting mosaics. The eye follows the successively raised levels of the nave, chancel and apse. The altar, beneath its baldachin supported on yellow marble columns, is dominated by a suspended crucifix. On the main piers are the 14 Stations of the Cross, distinctive low reliefs over beautifully incised lettering by **Eric Gill**, sculptor and type-face designer.

The body of the English martyr, John Southworth, hanged, drawn and quartered at Tyburn in 1654, lies in the second chapel in the north aisle. The south transept contains an early 15C alabaster statue of the Virgin and Child, carved by the Nottingham school, which originally stood in Westminster Abbey but was removed to France in the 15C and returned in 1955; there is also a bronze of St Teresa of Lisieux by Giacomo Manzù and a Chi-Rho, executed in flat-headed nails, by David Partridge. The cathedral has its own choir school and is known for its music.

St Margaret's Church*

Open Mon-Sat, 9.30am to 3.45pm (1.45pm Sat); Sun 2-5pm.

The Parish and Parliamentary Church was built by Edward the Confessor to serve local parishioners. In the mid 14C the wool staple (market) was established at Westminster, close to the site of the clock tower; the subsequent increase in prosperity enabled the church, by then dilapidated, to be rebuilt. A third reconstruction (1488-1523), scarcely completed at the time of the Reformation, would have been demolished and the stone used to build Protector Somerset's palace in the Strand had not the parishioners "with bows and arrows, staves and clubs and other such offensive weapons... so terrified the workmen that they ran away in great amazement." Much of the church's present late Perpendicular appearance derives from the radical restoration undertaken by Sir George Gilbert Scott in the mid 19C. St Margaret's is the church of the House of Commons, not only because the Palace of Westminster lies within the parish but by a tradition inaugurated on Palm Sunday 1614 when the Commons met for the first time for corporate communion and, being mostly Puritans, preferred the church to the abbey.

Each year in November a **Garden of Remembrance**, composed of commemorative Flanders poppies, blossoms in the churchyard.

Interior – The interior presents a rich assemblage of Tudor monuments: sympathetic old Blanche Parry, Chief Gentlewoman of Queen Elizabeth's privy chamber (to the right side of the porch on entering), the figures of Thomas Arnway (d 1603) and his wife, who left money to be loaned to the young to set up in business, a Yeoman of the Guard (d 1577 at 94), Richard Montpesson, kneeling by his wife's tomb. There are two plaques *(by the east door)* and fragments of a window *(north aisle)* as memorials to **Caxton**, buried in the old churchyard; **Walter Raleigh** executed in Old Palace Yard on 29 October 1618 and buried beneath the high altar is commemorated in a tablet near the east door and in the west window, presented in the late 19C by citizens of the USA. The carved lime-wood reredos (1753) is based on Titian's *Supper at Emmaus*. The east window is special having been made in Flanders in 1501 at the behest of Ferdinand and Isabella of Spain to celebrate the marriage of their daughter Catherine to Prince Arthur; by the time it arrived Arthur was dead and the princess affianced to the future Henry VIII. The window was despatched outside London and retrieved only in 1758 when the House of Commons purchased it for 400 guineas and presented it to the church.

Westminster Abbey★★★

The splendour of the abbey, the pageantry of royal ceremonies and the potent historical associations make this a glorious monument which is the focal point of the English nation and of British national life. The abbey has a strong musical tradition and the carol concerts are an enjoyable feature of the Christmas period.

Location

Map p 11 (EY) and area map under WESTMINSTER; Michelin Atlas London: p 46. ⊖ *Westminster.* The abbey, which is at the heart of Westminster, is in the vicinity of many important tourist sites. The area is on several bus routes from Victoria Station and Trafalgar Square.

Adjacent Sights: WESTMINSTER; ST JAMES'S; BUCKINGHAM PALACE; TRAFALGAR SQUARE – WHITEHALL; TATE BRITAIN; SOUTH BANK.

Background

Westminster Abbey was a royal mausoleum for many centuries and became a national shrine owing to its situation next to the Palace of Westminster, once the sovereign's residence and now the seat of Parliament. Since the coronation of William I in 1066, all but two of the kings and queens of England have been crowned in the Abbey. In more recent times, it has hosted the marriage of the future George VI to Elizabeth Bowes-Lyon (1923), Prince Andrew to Sarah Ferguson (1986) and the funeral of Diana, Princess of Wales (1997).

Monastery Church – Sebert, 6C king of the East Saxons is credited with building the first church and monastery on Thorney Island, a triangle of land formed by the twin outflows (700yds/640m apart) of the Tyburn into the Thames.

Intending to make the church his sepulchre, **Edward the Confessor** "built it of new" in the Norman style and indeed died and was buried in it within a week of the dedication on 28 December 1065. It was in this abbey church that William I was crowned on Christmas Day in 1066.

In 1220, inspired by the Gothic style of Amiens and Rheims, the Plantagenet king, **Henry III**, began to rebuild the church, starting with the Lady Chapel to provide a noble shrine for **Edward the Confessor** who had been canonised in 1163. By the late 13C, the east end, transept, choir, the first bay of the nave and the chapter house were complete; work then came to a halt and another two centuries passed before the nave was finished.

When **Henry VII** constructed his chapel (1503-19), Perpendicular Gothic was the fashionable ecclesiastical style; Henry VII's Chapel is the jewel of its age, more delicate, with finer niches and pinnacles than any other part of the abbey.

Later additions, notably the upper parts of the west towers (1722-45) by **Wren** and **Hawksmoor**, and repairs by Sir George Gilbert Scott and others have echoed the Gothic theme: heavenward vaulting, soaring windows between slender buttressed walls, flying buttresses, gabled transepts surmounting rose windows with delicate tracery and doors with enriched coffering. Recent additions (1998) on the west front are limestone statues of modern Christian martyrs (Grand Duchess Elizabeth of Russia, Maximilian Kolbe, Martin Luther King, Oscar Romero among others) placed in niches above figures depicting truth, justice, mercy and peace.

Royal Peculiar – When Henry VIII ordered the Dissolution of the monasteries in 1540, the abbey's treasures were confiscated and its property forfeited but the buildings were not destroyed. The 600-year-old Benedictine community of some 50 monks was disbanded; the abbot, who enjoyed both temporal and spiritual power and his own lavish household, was dismissed; so too were those who supervised the widespread property or served on missions abroad. In 1560 Elizabeth I granted a charter establishing the Collegiate Church of St Peter, with a royally appointed dean and chapter of 12 prebendaries (canons), and also the College of St Peter, generally known as Westminster School, which replaced the monastic school.

Bells – There are 12 bells which ring out, generally between 12noon and 1pm, on great occasions and on some 25 days of festival and commemoration including 25, 26 and 28 December, 1 January, Easter and Whit Sundays and the Queen's official birthday.

Statistics

The abbey dimensions are: internal length from west door to east window 511ft 6in/156m; length of nave 166ft/50m; length of Henry VII's Chapel 104ft 6in/32m; width of the nave including the aisles 72ft/22m; height of the nave 102ft/31m; overall external height to the top of the pinnacles on the west towers 225ft/68m; height to the top of the lantern 151ft/46m. The fabric is Caen and Reigate stone.

Highlights

♿ *Open Mon-Sat, 9.30am-3.45pm (1.45pm Sat). £6. Leaflet (8 languages). Audio-guide (£2; 7 languages). ☎ 020 7222 5152; Fax 020 7233 2072; press@westminster-abbey.org; www.westminster-abbey.org*
Enter by the north door.

Interior

The **monuments** to national figures, which crowd the abbey, date from the early Middle Ages. The older monuments, the figures on the ancient tombs, are mostly in the chapels east of the high altar; some are derived from death masks and are revealing in expression; others make no pretence of portraying the living. In the 18C it became the practice, when a famous man was interred in the abbey, to erect memorials to others of equal standing in his field. This resulted in a surfeit of monuments in the 18C and 19C sculpted by the great artists of the day: Roubiliac, the Bacons, Flaxman, Le Sueur, Westmacott, Chantrey. Permission to be buried in the abbey or for a memorial to be erected is granted by the Dean.

Nave – The soaring vaulting retains the beauty of its original conception; the carving is delicate, often beautiful, sometimes humorous.

At the west end of the nave is the memorial to the **Unknown Warrior (1)**, set in the pavement and surrounded by Flanders poppies.

Against the first south pier is the **painting of Richard II (2)**, the earliest known painting of an English sovereign. In the north aisle, low down, is the small stone which covered the upright figure of the playwright "O rare Ben Johnson" **(3)** (misspelt).

Musicians' Aisle – The graves and memorials of famous musicians include Orlando Gibbons, John Blow and Henry Purcell, all organists of the Abbey.

North Transept – The transept is also known as the Statesmen's Aisle as it contains many graves and memorials of famous national figures.

Choir – The choir screen, which faces the west door, is a 13C structure of stone, with lierne vaulting under the arch; it was richly redesigned with gabled niches in the 19C when the choir was re-embellished.

Sanctuary – This is where the monarch is crowned and receives the peers' homage in the **coronation** ceremony. The area is approached by a low flight of steps, flanked *(left)* by a gilded and black wood 17C pulpit. The floor is laid with a 13C Italian pavement of porphyry and mosaic. Behind the altar is the gilded blaze of the 19C high altar screen. To the right hangs a 16C tapestry behind a large

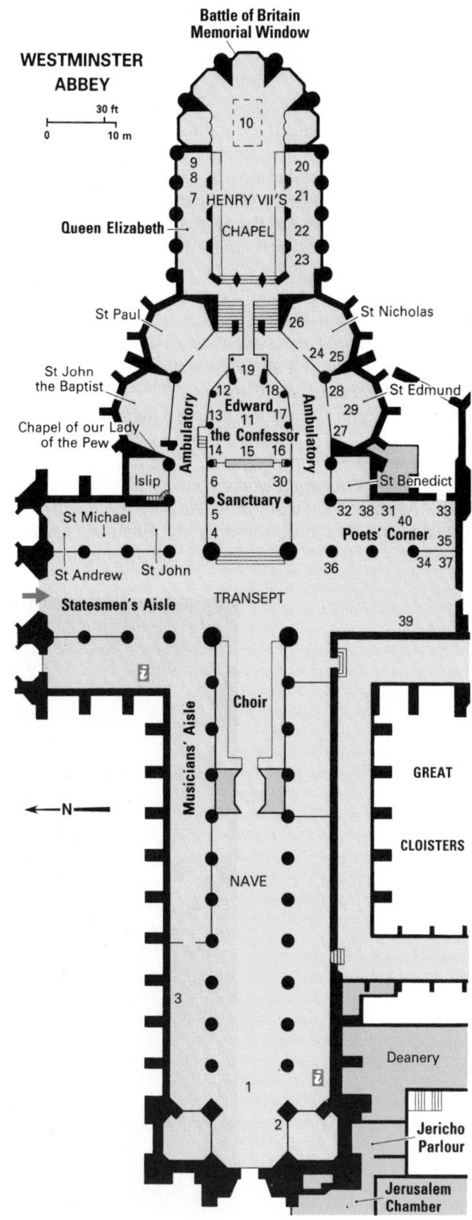

15C altarpiece of rare beauty. Beyond is an ancient 13C sedilia painted with full length royal figures (Henry II, Edward I and a bishop). On the left are three tombs, each a recumbent figure on a chest beneath a gabled canopy: Aveline of Lancaster (**4**; d 1274), a great heiress of renowned beauty; Aymer de Valence, Earl of Pembroke (**5**; d 1324), cousin to Edward I; Edmund Crouchback (**6**; d 1296), youngest son of Henry III, husband of Aveline.

North Ambulatory – On the right are visible the small gilded kings and queens on the tomb of Edmund Crouchback **(6)**. Opposite is the chantry chapel of Abbot Islip, known for its rebus – an eye and a slip or branch of a tree clasped by a hand, also a man slipping from a tree.

The **Chapel of Our Lady of the Pew**, in the thickness of the wall, contains a modern alabaster Madonna and Child, modelled on the original which is now in Westminster RC Cathedral. The chapels of St John the Baptist and St Paul contain elaborate gilded wall memorials crested with helms and medieval tombs with highly coloured effigies in decorated recesses or beneath ornate canopies.

Queen Elizabeth Chapel – In the north aisle of Henry VII's Chapel is the tomb of **Queen Elizabeth I (7)** in white marble, ruffed and austere, the only colour being the regalia, lions and the overhead canopy; beneath is the coffin of Mary Tudor without any monument. At the east end are memorials to two young daughters of James I, Princess Sophia and Princess Mary **(8)** and in a small sarcophagus, the bones found in the Tower of London presumed to be those of the Little Princes **(9)**.

Henry VII's Chapel★★★ – The eye is directed first to the superb fan-vaulted roof, then to the banners of the Knights Grand Cross of the Order of the Bath, hanging still and brilliant above the stalls, which are crowned with pinnacles, helmets and coifs, and ornamented with the heraldic plates of former occupants and their esquires; the witty and inventive misericords date from the 16C to 18C. The chapel was first used for the knights' installations in 1725 when George I reconstructed the order.

At the east end is the tomb of Henry VII and Elizabeth of York **(10)**. Beyond, in the RAF Chapel, is the **Battle of Britain Memorial Window** (1947), a many-faceted, brightly coloured screen containing the badges of the 68 Fighter Squadrons which took part.

The great double gates at the entrance are made with wooden frames in which are mounted pierced bronze panels of the royal emblems of Henry Tudor and his antecedents: the roses of Lancaster and York, the leopards of England, the fleur-de-lys of France, the falcon of Edward IV, father of Elizabeth, Henry's queen.

Chapel of Edward the Confessor★★ – The chapel, also known as the Chapel of the Kings, contains the tombs of five kings and three queens around the **Confessor's Shrine (11)**.

The shrine itself is in two parts; the lower, prepared by Henry III, is Purbeck marble, the upper is a stepped wooden construction made to replace the original which had been looted at the Dissolution. Against the north wall are **Queen Eleanor of Castile** (**12**; d 1290), in whose memory the Eleanor crosses were erected *(see TRAFALGAR SQUARE – WHITEHALL)*, slender and serene, in gilded bronze by the master goldsmith

Fan-vaulting and emblems of chivalry in Henry VII's Chapel

William Torel; Henry III (**13**; d 1272), in gilded effigy, builder of the chapel who spent more than all the money he possessed in constructing the abbey; **Edward I**, Longshanks (**14**; d 1307), the first king to be crowned in the present abbey (1272) and the Hammer of the Scots, who brought south the Scottish regalia and the stone of Scone in 1297. The carved **stone screen**, which closes the west end of the chapel, was completed in 1441. At the centre stands the **Coronation Chair (15)** made of oak and once brightly painted and gilded with the Stone of Scone beneath the seat (now removed to Scotland); for coronations the chair is moved into the sanctuary.

Against the south wall are Richard II **(16)** who married Anne of Bohemia in the abbey in 1382 and raised her tomb there in 1394; the gilt bronze figure of Edward III (**17**; d 1377) on an altar tomb of Purbeck marble, surrounded in niches at the base by the bronze representations of his children, of whom six remain (facing the ambulatory) including the Black Prince; carved in white marble, once painted and gilded, his queen, Philippa of Hainault (**18**; d 1369) who interceded for the Burghers of Calais. At the east end on a Purbeck marble tomb is the oak figure, once silver plated, of the young Henry V (**19**; d 1422); above is the king's chantry chapel in which Katherine de Valois is now buried.

South Aisle of Henry VII's Chapel – Here are buried, without sculptured memorials, in a royal vault **(20)**, Charles II, William III and Mary, Queen Anne and her consort, George of Denmark. Three grand tombs occupy the centre, all effigies upon tomb chests: Lady Margaret Beaufort (**21**; d 1509), mother of Henry Tudor, in widow's hood and mantle, her wrinkled hands raised in prayer, her face serene in old age, a masterpiece by **Torrigiano** in gilt bronze; **Mary Queen of Scots (22)** in white marble like Elizabeth I but beneath a much grander canopy and with a crowned Scottish lion in colour at her feet; Margaret Douglas, Countess of Lennox (**23**; d 1578), niece of Henry VIII, mother of Darnley and grandmother of James I, a beautiful woman carved in alabaster.

South Ambulatory – St Nicholas' Chapel contains the tomb of Philippa, Duchess of York (**24**; d 1431) with wimple and veil about her expressive head; the vault of the Percys **(25)**; the tomb of Anne, Duchess of Somerset (**26**; d 1587), widow of the Protector. In St Edmund's Chapel are the tomb of William de Valence (**27**; d 1296), half brother of Henry III, the figure remarkably carved with clothes and accoutrements powdered with crests, and the marble effigy of John of Eltham (**28**; d 1337), second son of Edward II. In the centre, on a low altar tomb, is the abbey's finest **brass** of Eleanor, Duchess of Gloucester (**29**; d 1399) beneath a triple canopy. On the north side of the ambulatory are Sebert's tomb **(30)** and the sedilia painting of the Confessor.

Poets' Corner★ – This famous corner of the abbey in the south transept contains the tomb of Chaucer **(31)**, who as Clerk of Works was associated with the abbey and the palace; statues of the court poets Dryden **(32)** and Ben Jonson **(33)**, William Shakespeare **(34)** (a "preposterous monument" in Horace Walpole's opinion), John Milton **(35)**, William Blake **(36)** (bust by Epstein, 1957), Robert Burns **(37)**, Longfellow **(38)**, Joseph Addison **(39)** who observed at the time (18C): "In the poetical quarter I found there were poets who had no monuments and monuments which had no poets." Plaques and stones are now more the order of the day: WH Auden, Thomas Hardy, Gerard Manley Hopkins, Dylan Thomas and Lewis Carroll **(40)**. Oscar Wilde, who died in Paris, is honoured with a window.

Great Cloisters

Preserved in the abbey's precincts are a number of historical buildings.

Chapter House – The octagonal chamber (1248-53), used at one time as a royal treasury, measures 60ft/18m in diameter, its fine vault supported by an elegant central pier braced with shafts of Purbeck marble. On the outside, eight marble columns diffuse the weight borne by the lierne ribs to the tiled floor (1255). In between, set back from the ledge, marble shafts crowned with trefoiled blind arcading encircle the house. The walls are further decorated in parts with medieval paintings of the Last Judgement and the Apocalypse. The large windows date from the transitional period not followed in the body of the church as it would have spoilt the architectural unity: each bay rises (nearly 40ft/12m) to quatrefoils and cusped circles. In 1257 the King's Great Council, under Henry III, met in the chapter house indicating that it was intended from the first to accommodate secular assemblies as well as the 60-80 monks of the abbey. Under Edward I it became the **Parlement House of the Commons** and continued after the Dissolution, when the hall passed into the direct ownership of the Crown. By the 19C it had become an archive for the state papers; the floor had been boarded over and a second storey inserted. In 1865 the building's condition necessitated complete restoration. A century later, when the damage caused during the Second World War was repaired the windows were reglazed with clear glass, decorated with the coats of arms of sovereigns and abbots and the devices of the two medieval master masons, Henry de Reyns, who designed Henry III's abbey, and Henry Yevele, who built the nave (south-west and south-east windows).

Chapel of the Pyx – The chamber built between 1055 and 1090 as a monastery chapel and retaining the only stone altar in its original position, was converted into the monastery treasury in the 13C to 14C. At the Dissolution it passed to the Crown and was used as the strongroom in which gold and silver coins were tried against standard specimens kept there in a box or pyx. Today it is used to display church plate from the abbey and from St Margaret's Church *(see WESTMINSTER)*, notably a 17C cloth of gold cope and a late medieval oak cope chest.

Westminster Abbey Museum – The museum is housed in the low Norman undercroft; two of the several pillars in its length (110ft/33m) are still decorated with 11C carving. It contains historical documents, gold plate, reproductions of the coronation regalia, a number of unique wax and wood funeral effigies. Edward III and Katherine de Valois, both full length, are of wood. Of the 11 wax effigies, the contemporary figure of **Charles II** in his Garter robes is unforgettable though not carried at his near-clandestine funeral. Among the women are Catherine, Duchess of Buckingham, natural daughter of James II and wife of John Sheffield, builder of Buckingham House, who had her effigy made during her lifetime, and Frances, Duchess of Richmond and Lennox who was the model for Britannia on the old penny piece.

Nelson, of whom it was said by a contemporary "it is as if he was standing there", was purchased by the abbey in 1806 in an attempt to attract the crowds away from his tomb in St Paul's Cathedral.

Abbey Garden

The garden, 900 years old, is an oasis of quiet at the heart of Westminster, surrounded by the buildings of Westminster School.

Jericho and Jerusalem Chambers

Closed to the public. Both are in the lodgings, formerly of the abbot, now of the Dean. The Jericho Parlour has early-16C linenfold panelling on the walls and is 150 years older than the Jerusalem Chamber where Henry IV died in 1413 *(Henry IV, Part II: 4 iv)*.

Dean's Yard

The yard, once the heart of the Abbey precinct, is now a tree-shaded lawn. The eastern range of buildings, some medieval, some Georgian, contains a low arch, the entrance to **Westminster School** *(private)*, which extends eastwards from Little Dean's Yard to the Palladian College, the mid-17C brick Ashburnham House, incorporating part of the Prior's Lodging (12C to 13C), and the Great Hall (known as School), which is part of the monastic dormitory (late 11C) and until 1884 was the school's only classroom, now rebuilt and again emblazoned with the arms of former headmasters and pupils; College hall, formerly the abbot's state dining hall, serves as the school refectory.

The south side of Dean's Yard is filled by **Church House** (1940), containing the large circular Convocation Hall, where the General Synod of the Church of England meets, and the Hoare Memorial Hall, where the Commons sat during the war.

On the west side are parliamentary offices and Westminster Abbey Choir School.

The North Gate is flanked by the Sanctuary buildings, designed by Sir George Gilbert Scott, and leads into the Sanctuary *(see WESTMINSTER)*.

Pagoda, Kew Gardens

Outer London

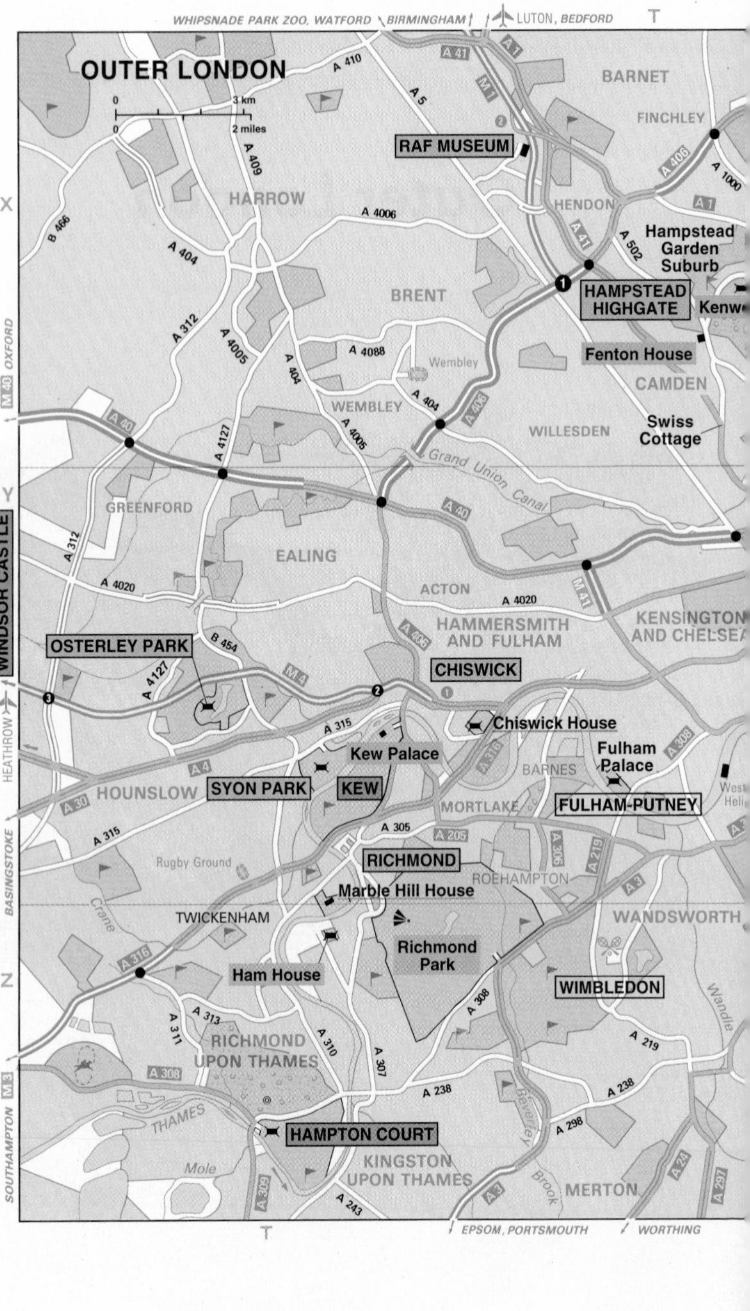

OUTER LONDON

Many houses or other buildings in London are marked with a Blue Plaque giving the name, dates and claim to fame of well-known residents – scientists, artists, soldiers, politicians, sociologists but few women – who deserve recognition, have been dead for 20 years, have contributed to human welfare and happiness. The first plaque was affixed in 1867 to 24 Holles Street, Westminster where Lord Byron was born.

The early plaques erected by the Royal Society of Arts were not always round with white lettering on a dark blue ground as they are today. Between 1901 and 1985 the names of those to be commemorated were chosen by the LCC and then the GLC. Responsibility for this selective task now rests with English Heritage.

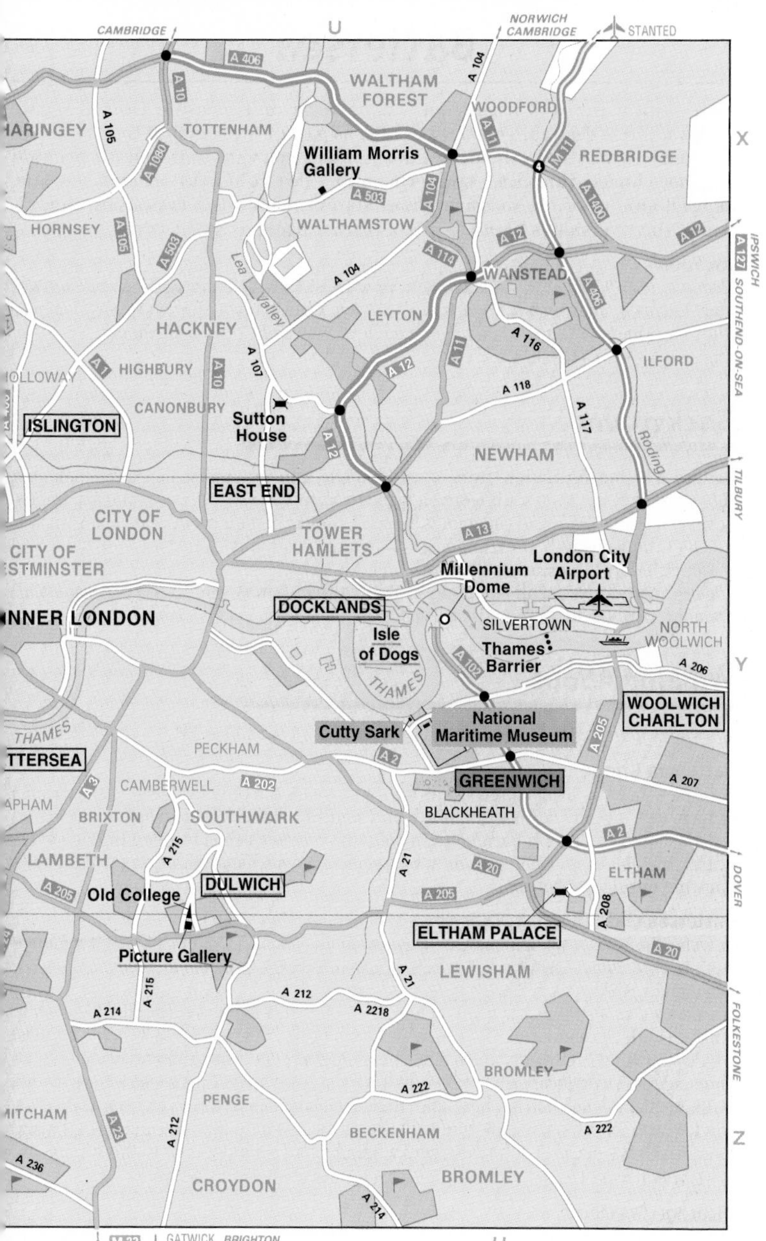

Cockney Rhyming Slang

Traditionally people born within earshot of Bow Bells pealing from St Mary-le-Bow had the right to call themselves a cockney. So that the many immigrants into the East End of London would not be able to understand their exchanges, market porters and barrow boys developed their own style of speech which makes no sense to the uninitiated.

On my jack jones (alone)
To get me barney cut (Barney Fair = hair)
Sorry (sorry and sad = bad) state, mate !
Take a butcher's (butcher's hook = look) at this !
A sexy jam jar (car)
Go for a ball of chalk (walk)
Haven't heard a dicky bird (word)
Me trouble (trouble and strife = wife) 'll 'ave me tucker (tommy tucker = supper) ready...

Battersea

Battersea on the south bank has changed beyond measure from a sedate backwater to a desirable residential area as part of the overspill from Chelsea. The park, which has a boating lake, gardens, playgrounds and an oriental pagoda, hosts funfairs, concerts and the colourful Easter parade. Redevelopment of the massive power station, which is a famous landmark, and of the riverside is likely to give a further boost to the district.

Location

Map p 11 (CDZ); Michelin Atlas London: pp 9-11 and 26-28. Overground: Battersea Park from Victoria; Queenstown Road from Waterloo. Chelsea is a short hop on foot over Chelsea, Albert or Battersea Bridge. Excellent views of Chelsea Harbour.
Adjacent Sights: CHELSEA.

Background

Battersea's transformation from a rural town into an industrial town took just 100 years. In 1782, 2 160 souls were engaged in cultivating strawberries and asparagus, herbs (Lavender Hill) and vegetables for seed; they sent their produce to Westminster: by 1845 the railway had extended to Clapham (originally Battersea) Junction and the population explosion had begun.
Local street names recall the St John Bolingbroke family and their successor, Earl Spencer, Lord of the Manor since 1763.

Walking About

Start from Battersea Bridge and turn right into Battersea Church Rd.

Battersea Bridge

Battersea Railway Bridge (1863) was for many years the only bridge which carried a railway line directly connecting north and south England. The present construction was designed by Joseph Bazalgette in 1890. Its predecessor, a wooden bridge (1771) lit first by oil lamps (1799) and then by gas (1824), was the inspiration for Whistler's painting entitled *Nocturne*.

Battersea Old Church, St Mary's

♿ *Open Tue-Wed, 11am-3pm (ask at the Parish Office); or by appointment. Services: Sun at 8am, 11am, 6.30pm. Guide book (English). ☎ 020 7228 9648; office@stmarysbattersea.org.uk; www.stmarysbattersea.org.uk*
Since Saxon times there has been a church well forward at the river bend. The current building with a conical green copper spire dates from 1775 (portico 1823); the 14C east window encloses 17C tracery and painted heraldic glass. The aisle windows commemorate famous people with local connections: the 18C botanist William Curtis who is buried here, **William Blake** who married here and **Turner** who sketched the river from the vestry window and whose chair now stands in the chancel. There are amusing epitaphs and memorial busts of the St John Bolingbroke family, lords of the manor in the 17C to 18C.
For Old Battersea House see Worth a Visit. Continue along Vicarage Cres.

Vicarage Crescent

Devonshire House is an early-18C stucco house of three storeys with a Doric porch, small curved iron balconies and a contemporary wrought-iron gate. St Mary's House is a late-17C mansion.
Old Battersea House (no 30) is a 2-storey brick mansion with a hipped roof and pedimented doorway, built by Sir Walter St John in 1699.
At the end of Vicarage Cres, turn left into High St.

High Street

The Raven, with curving Dutch gables, has dominated the crossroads since the 17C. **Sir Walter St John School**, founded in 1700, was rebuilt in the 19C-20C on the original site in Tudor Gothic style. Note the St John motto surmounted by helm and falcon at the entrance.
Continue along High Street to Battersea Sq and take a bus along Westbridge Rd and Parkgate Rd to Albert Bridge Rd.

Albert Bridge★

The cantilever suspension bridge, which is most attractive when lit up at night, was designed by RW Ordish in 1873; it was modified by Joseph Bazalgette and reinforced with a central support in the 1970s; spare bulbs are stored in the twin tollmen's huts at either end.
Take a walk through the park.

Battersea Park
The marshy waste of Battersea Fields was popular in the 16C for pigeon shooting, fairs, donkey racing and duels; by 1828, however, when Wellington and Lord Winchelsea exchanged shots over the Catholic Emancipation Bill, they had become ill famed. In 1843 **Thomas Cubitt** *(see index)* proposed that a park be laid out; a bill was passed in 1846 and 360 acres/145ha purchased. The site was built up with land from the excavation of the Victoria Docks.
The park includes a boating lake, a garden for the handicapped, sculptures by **Henry Moore** and Barbara Hepworth, and sports facilities.
A **Japanese Peace Pagoda** (1985), complete with gilded wind bells and seated Buddhas, is one of several instituted by an organisation dedicated to world peace.
East of the park is Queenstown Rd.

Chelsea Bridge
The 1934 suspension bridge by Forest and Wheeler, replaces an earlier one from 1858.

Marco Polo House
The bold building on Queenstown Road to the east of the park, has been compared to something from a packet of liquorice allsorts or from Legoland: clad in hi-tech Japanese panels of Neo-Paries, a synthetic-looking light and finely finished material, and Pilkington glass, the building's simplified classical lines are pleasing.
Continue south to Battersea Pk Rd and turn left.

Battersea Power Station
Battersea Pk Rd. The completion of this familiar landmark, largely built in 1932-34, was overseen by Giles **Gilbert Scott** after the Second World War. He extended the chimneys to 337ft/102m and endowed the colossus with surface detailing – fluting and ridging to lessen its bulk. The power station shut down in 1983; plans to convert the massive structure and its 31 acre/12ha site into a shopping and entertainment centre, while retaining the fine Art Deco interiors of the two turbine halls and control room, are still under review.

Four tall chimneys identify a familiar landmark beside Battersea Park

Worth a Visit

De Morgan Foundation
38 West Hill. (♿) Open Mon-Wed, noon-6pm, Fri and Sat, 10am-5pm. £2. ☎ 020 8871 1144
An imposing white brick building with original Arts and Crafts roof houses a collection of ceramics by **William de Morgan** who was associated with the Arts and Crafts movement, and paintings and drawings by Evelyn de Morgan Spencer Stanhope, JM Strudwick and Cadogan Cowper.

Battersea Dogs' Home
4 Battersea Park Rd. Open daily except Thu, 10.30am-4.15pm (3.15pm Sat-Sun and Bank Hols). £1. ☎ 020 7622 3626; Fax 020 7622 6451; info@dogshome.org; www.dogshome.org
The home, established in 1860, moved to its present site in 1871. The number of dogs and cats brought in annually runs into thousands.

Chiswick★★

The beautiful scenery of Chiswick which nestles into a deep loop of the Thames is a delight in spite of the thundering traffic of the busy motorway. Along the riverside walk which stretches to Hammersmith Bridge are delightful pubs affording fine views of the activity on the river where keen rowers are out in all weathers. Chiswick boasts many artistic and historic associations and a magnificent mansion with splendid gardens.

Location

Map p 336 (TY). ⊖ Turnham Green and Bus no 190 or overhead train to Chiswick from Waterloo Station. Chiswick is to the west and off the A4 motorway.
Adjacent Sights: KEW; FULHAM – PUTNEY.

Background

Chiswick retains something of the country village which it was until the 1860s; by the 1880s the population had increased from 6 500 to 15 600; in the 20C the motorway (M4) and its feeder flyover divided the riverside from the rest.
Georgian houses survive, however, in Church Street and other parallel roads to the river and in Chiswick Mall overlooking the river and the Eyot.

Directory

Pubs

Black Lion – *2 South Black Lion Lane, W6 9TJ – ☎ 020 8748 2639 – Open noon-11pm (10.30pm Sun).* The pub is set back from the river behind a garden with a brick arcade from an old riverside factory.

Blue Anchor – *13 Lower Mall, W6 9DJ – ☎ 020 8748 5774 – Open Mon-Sat 11am-11.30pm, Sun noon-10.30pm.* A bustling pub by the river, which attracts a good crowd.

Old Ship Inn – *25 Upper Mall, W6 9TD – ☎ 020 8748 2593 – www.oldshipW6.co.uk – Open 10am-midnight.* An old pub by the river.

Rutland – *15 Lower Mall, W6 9DJ – ☎ 020 8748 5586 – Open Mon-Sat 11am-11pm, Sun noon-10.30pm.* A Victorian pub in an attractive riverside location; good atmosphere.

The Dove – *19 Upper Mall, W6 9TA – ☎ 020 8748 5405 – Open Mon-Sat 11am-11pm, Sun noon-10.30pm.* In the 18C it was a coffeehouse where James Thomson is said to have written the words of Rule Britannia in the upstairs room; from 1900 it housed the Dove Press and Bindery. Now it claims to have the smallest bar in the country.

Walking About

From the station or bus stop walk to Chiswick House and Hogarth House (description in Worth a Visit) then cross Burlington Lane and proceed to Church St near the Hogarth roundabout.

Chiswick Square

Burlington Lane. Low two-storey houses (1680) flank a forecourt in front of the three-storey **Boston House** (1740) where, in the novel *Vanity Fair* by **Thackeray**, Becky Sharp threw away her dictionary. *For description of Fuller, Smith and Turner Griffin Brewery see Worth a Visit.*

St Nicholas Parish Church

Open Sun, 2.30-4.30pm; Tue and Thur, 10am-noon; otherwise key available from the Vicarage. ☎ 020 8995 4717; Fax 020 8995 8536; www.chiswickparishchurch.org
The site was mentioned in 1181 and the list of vicars traces incumbents, with a few gaps, by name from 1225. This deceptively broad church has a buttressed and battlemented west tower (1436); the rest dates from the 1880s as do the highly decorative windows; the chancel ceiling has been blackened by fire. The ring of eight bells includes five hung in 1656, reputedly because of the intervention of the parishioner Lady Mary Fauconberg, daughter of Oliver Cromwell: in the family vault below the chancel are three coffins, the shortest possibly holding the headless body of **Cromwell**, exhumed from Westminster Abbey and rescued from Tyburn in 1661. In the churchyard lie **Hogarth** (enclosed with railings) – under David Garrick's epitaph "Farewell, Great Painter of Mankind"; Lord **Burlington**; **William Kent**; **JM Whistler**; **Philippe de Loutherbourg**; the Italian poet Ugo Foscolo (disinterred and reburied in Florence).

Chiswick Mall★★

Elegant 18C-19C houses, with bow windows and balconies, overlook the river. **Morton House** (1730) is built of brick with red-brick surrounds to the windows of its three storeys. **Strawberry House** (1735) has six bays, two floors surmounted by attic dormers, a wide central balcony supported on iron pillars and slender fluted pillars outlining the porch. **Walpole House**, begun in the 16C and enlarged in the 17C, presents an irregular advanced brick face preceded by a fine iron gate and railings; in the 18C it was the residence of Barbara Villiers, Duchess of Cleveland (and mistress of Charles II), in her latter days (d 1709); in the 19C it became a school with Thackeray among its pupils.

Hammersmith Riverside

The most attractive part of Hammersmith is along the waterfront. Upstream from the bridge the embankment developed gradually from the early 18C with modest houses built singly or in terraces, adorned with balconies or festooned with wistaria; in the past the view included sailing barges making for harbour; now there are yachts or oarsmen in training.

Hammersmith Terrace – The very urban terrace of 17 almost identical brick houses of three and four storeys, built as a single unit facing the river, dates from the mid 18C when all around were fields, market gardens, vineyards and famous strawberry fields. Philippe de **Loutherbourg**, artist and scenic designer at the Drury Lane Theatre *(see COVENT GARDEN)* in the 18C, lived at no 13; Sir Emery Walker, antiquary and typographer, who collaborated with Morris at the Kelmscott Press, lived at no 7; for more than 50 years Sir Alan Herbert (APH) (1890-1971), writer, lover and ardent protagonist of the Thames, occupied nos 12 to 13.

At the west end of the Mall are two pubs: the **Old Ship Inn** and the **Black Lion** *(see Directory)*.

The **London Corinthian Sailing Club** is housed in Linden House, which has Ionic pillared doorways and dates from the 18C (much refurbished); opposite, above the riverside wall, looking like a glassed-in crow's nest, is the race officers' box.

Rivercourt House (now a school) dates from the early 19C.

Make a short detour up South Black Lion Lane to view St Peter's Church.

North of the Great West Road the focal point of St Peter's Square with its substantial houses adorned with bay windows and pillared porches, is **St Peter's Church** (1829), a yellow stock-brick landmark with pedimented portico and square clock tower; before it is a sculpture of a reclining woman by Karel Vogel (1959).

Return to the riverside.

Upper Mall – Kelmscott House, a plain three-storey house with five bays and dormers behind the brick coping, dates from the 1780s. In the 19C it became home to **William Morris** and his family until his death in 1896. There Morris drew the illustrations and designed founts for the fine books he printed in the nearby no 14 and published under the imprint of the **Kelmscott Press** *(see VICTORIA & ALBERT MUSEUM)*.

The **Dove** pub has had a licence for 400 years, although the present building goes back only a couple of centuries *(see Directory)*. Sussex House (1726) has stone urns at the corners of the brick coping and segmentally pedimented doorways flanked by Doric pilasters.

Lower Mall – Near the pier is a plaque which indicates the site of the creek and "harbour where the village began." Westcott Lodge *(Furnival Gardens)* consists of two storeys beneath a plain brick coping, embellished with a canopied balcony supported by an Ionic pillared porch protecting the front door in the last of the six bays. Among the 18C-19C buildings are the **Blue Anchor** pub; the **Rutland**, a Victorian pub *(see Directory)*; Kent House *(no 10)*, which is late 18C with symmetrical bay windows, yellow brickwork decorated with medallions after Adam and contemporary ironwork; the Amateur Rowing Association *(no 6)*, which has a canopied balcony and a bow window supported on slender iron columns over the entrance to the boathouse.

Hammersmith Bridge – The present suspension bridge (1884-87), designed by Joseph **Bazalgette**, replaced the first Thames suspension bridge (1827).

Two big houses once stood on the riverbank below the bridge. **Craven Cottage** was an 18C cottage *orné* with Egyptian-style interiors, which burnt down in 1888; its name is now perpetuated in the name of Fulham football ground *(Stevenage Road)*. **Brandenburgh House** (17C) was the residence of Queen Caroline of Brunswick when she attempted to claim the rights of consort on the accession of her husband as George IV; it was demolished after her death in 1821.

Worth a Visit

Chiswick House★

Burlington Lane. (EH) (♿) Open late-Mar to Oct, daily, 10am-6pm (5pm Oct); house may close Sat, 3.30pm, ring for details. £3.30. Guided tour by appointment. Audio guide (3 languages). Parking. Tearoom, picnic area. ☎ 020 8995 0508; www.english-heritage.org.uk

In 1682 the first Earl of Burlington purchased a Jacobean mansion set in extensive acres at Chiswick. During the 18C the house was altered and extended by Richard Boyle, the

Classical symmetry at the heart of Chiswick House

3rd **Earl of Burlington** (1695-1753), connoisseur and generous host and patron to Kent, Rysbrack, Campbell, Pope, Swift, Gay, Thompson, Handel... Burlington designed a Palladian villa (1725-29) in which to display his works of art and entertain his friends. In plan, it strictly adheres to Palladio's principles: main front, garden façade, two identical lateral elevations; symmetrical arrangement of rooms along the main axis.
Much of the interior decoration and the gardens – complete with temples and a canal – were the work of his protégé **William Kent** (1686-1748). The villa still stands but nothing remains of the Jacobean mansion nor of additions made in the 18C and 19C by Georgiana, Duchess of Devonshire and queen of society, and her successors, who entertained leading Whigs, Edward VII and the czars.

Exterior – An avenue of terms approaches the villa endowed with all the grace of Classical proportion. Paired dog-leg staircases overlooked by statues of Palladio *(left)* and Inigo Jones *(right)* lead up to a portico; behind the pediment is a raised octagonal dome, flanked by obelisks, which contain the chimney flues.

Interior – The lower floor octagon hall (with wine cellar below), lobbies and library now display drawings and other material about the design and restoration of the house and garden. From the library the pillared link building leads to the Summer Parlour (1717), originally connected to the Jacobean mansion. The grisaille paintings are by Kneller (1719).
On the first floor or "piano nobile" *(staircase to the left of the library)* public function rooms follow a square plan of intercommunicating rooms arranged around a central octagon. The central **Dome Saloon** has eight walls punctuated alternately by Classical busts and pedimented doors with gold highlights; the coffered cupola rises from an ochre-coloured entablature to a windowed drum. The Red, Green and Blue Velvet Rooms have richly gilded coffered ceilings, Venetian windows and pedimented door casings, carvings, chimney-pieces. The roundels in the Blue Room are of Inigo Jones (by Dobson) and Pope (by Kent). Along the west front runs the **gallery** which consists of three rooms: the apsed, oblong central room communicates through arches to circular and octagonal end rooms, their space and sparkle exaggerated by being reflected and refracted by mirrors. From the octagonal room a passage leads north into the upper storey of the link building which is adorned with Corinthian columns.

Gardens – The gardens were landscaped mostly by Kent who planted the giant cedars and modified Burlington's earlier geometrical plan of avenues and formal vistas; the canal was adapted into a series of serpentine curves, while temples, obelisks and statues were strategically placed so as to catch the stroller unawares. Georgiana made the design even less formal and commissioned Wyatt to build a bridge across the water. The greenhouse was probably the work of Joseph Paxton from Chatsworth. Italian formal gardens were laid out providing a brilliant pattern of colour. The Inigo Jones Gateway *(north-east of the house)* was erected in 1621 outside Beaufort House in Chelsea and presented to the 3rd Earl of Burlington by **Sir Hans Sloane** in 1736.

Around the corner stands Hogarth's House, the very antithesis of William Kent's Italianate taste.

Hogarth's House★

Immediately on the left down the west carriageway of the Great West Road after the Hogarth Roundabout. (♿) Open Tue-Fri, 1-5pm (4pm Nov-Mar); Sat-Sun, 1-6pm (5pm Nov-Mar). Closed Good Fri, 25-26 Dec, all Jan. Parking. ☎ 020 8994 6757

William Hogarth was 52 and well established when he acquired the three-storey brick house which he called his "little country box by the Thames", and to which he added

William Hogarth (1697-1764)

Born the son of a bankrupted author near Bart's Hospital, Hogarth started work apprenticed as an engraver to a silversmith while living in Leicester Fields (now Leicester Square). Recognising the need for a formal training he enrolled at St Martin's Lane Academy but failed to grapple academic figurative painting in the grand manner. Instead, he developed the "conversation piece" (1729), a more informal type of portraiture representing his middle-class sitters in domestic interiors. For these uncontroversial representations of contemporary life, which he described as his "moralities" – *Rake's Progress* (1735), *Marriage à la Mode* (1743-5), Hogarth must have drawn inspiration from the theatre of John Gay *(The Beggar's Opera)*. His acute powers of observation, innate humour and sharp wit animate his narrative pictures which found a large audience when copied and reproduced as engravings. Admirers recognised their contemporaries lampooned by caricatures and sympathised with the artist's patriotism as a defender of things "English". Aware and sensitive to the hardship of life in London as portrayed in his prints (child mortality, alcoholism, prostitution and corruption, cruelty to animals), Hogarth was appointed governor of Captain Coram's charitable institution, the Foundling Hospital in Bloomsbury. His paintings are exhibited at the National Gallery, Tate Britain and Sir John Soane's Museum *(see CHANCERY LANE)*.

a hanging bay window above the front door. The mulberry tree in the small garden was there in his day. He spent not only the summer but ever longer periods at Chiswick, entertaining such contemporaries as David Garrick.
Hogarth found fame as a commentator on 18C London life and the house displays several "Conversation pieces" collected by contemporaries who recognised in them personalities of the day: *The Election, London Scenes, The Harlot's Progress, Marriage à la Mode* and many more.

Fuller, Smith and Turner Griffin Brewery

The Brewery stands across the Hogarth roundabout. and it was relocated from Bedford House in Chiswick Mall. *Guided tour Mon, Wed-Fri at 11am, noon, 1pm, 2pm. £5 (including full tasting session); no admission to children under 14 yrs. Book in advance. ☎ 020 8996 2063; Fax 020 8996 2079; julie.knight@fullers.co.uk; www.fullers.co.uk*

Docklands★

Along the Thames where it describes a great loop opposite Greenwich, the cityscape from Tower Pier down to the Thames Barrier has undergone a radical change with Canary Wharf as a shimmering landmark dominating other award-winning schemes. It is worth arriving by the overhead train for the views which give an insight into the scale of the redevelopment of the docks marking an extension of London to the east.

Location

Map pp 14-15 (HJKL-XYZ). Docklands stretches east from Tower Bridge to the Royal Docks in North Woolwich. The area is accessed by an efficient automated overground light transport facility, the Docklands Light Railway, which extends to Lewisham south of the river, and the Jubilee Line of the Underground network.
Adjacent Sights: EAST END; TOWER OF LONDON; The CITY.

Background

"Docklands" stretches across a great swathe of land south of the East End between the Tower of London and Woolwich. Under the Docklands Joint Committee established in the 1970s, and its successor the London Docklands Development Corporation (LDDC) established in 1981, the redundant London docks have been transformed into a modern annexe to the City, thus regenerating the riverside communities: Wapping, Isle of Dogs and Silvertown – some 5 000 acres/2 000ha extending 8mi/5km east of Tower Bridge on the north bank and Bermondsey and Rotherhithe on the south bank.

Walking About

WAPPING

⊖ *Tower Hill, Wapping, Shadwell; DLR: Tower Gateway, Shadwell*
The Romans built a signal station at Wapping, which was just a village beside the Thames until the 16C when a continuous riverside sprawl began to develop; in 1598 Stow was describing the riverside, east from St Katharine, as a "continual street... or filthy strait passage, with alleys of small tenements or cottages inhabited by sailors, victuallers almost to Radcliffe and Radcliffe itself hath been also increased in building eastward (to) Limehouse."

Directory

Pubs

Prospect of Whitby – *57 Wapping Wall, E1W 3SP – ⊖ Wapping – ☎ 020 7481 1095 – Open Mon-Sat 11.30am-11pm, Sun noon-10.30pm.* Built in 1520, this is one of the oldest port-side pubs where mariners came before sailing to New World. It is also one of the most romantic, with a balcony terrace beside the Thames. The pub is nevertheless a victim of its success and you may see coaches dropping off tourists for lunch and dinner.

The Grapes – *76 Narrow St, Limehouse-Docklands, E14 8BP – ⊖ Westferry DLR – ☎ 020 7987 4396 – Open Mon-Fri noon-3pm, 5.30-11pm, Sat noon-11pm, Sun noon-10.30pm; closed 25-26 Dec and 1 Jan.* Charles Dickens described this 18C pub under the name of *The Six Jolly Fellowship Porters* in *Our Mutual Friend*. Well-kept real ales; fish-led bar meals and snacks. Small speciality fish restaurant; booking essential. Tiny outside deck for spectacular views over the River Thames in a slightly out-of-the-way area near Canary Wharf.

The Gun – *27 Cold Harbour, E14 9NS – ⊖ Blackwall DLR – ☎ 020 7987 1692 – Open Mon-Sat 11.00am-11pm, Sun noon-10.30pm.* This large pub looking onto the Thames is named after the neighbouring foundry that produced canons during Nelson's era. The view from the terrace is magnificent.

The Town of Ramsgate – *62 Wapping High St, E1W 2PN – ⊖ Wapping – ☎ 020 7481 8000 – Open daily noon-11pm (10.30pm Sun).* This historic pub, which takes its name from the home town of fishermen who unloaded their catch here, sits by Execution Dock where the bodies of pirate and thieves condemned to death by hanging (Captain Kid in 1701) were left for the tide to wash over them three times.

Radcliffe was well known for shipbuilding and repairs; **Samuel Pepys** took the boat at Radcliffe Stairs to cross to Deptford. In the past there were many stairs (landing places) along the densely populated waterfront cut by alleys, steps, stages and docks, where **Charles Dickens** set several of his novels.

Commercial Docks

The first docks to be built in Wapping were the **London Docks** (1805) which handled imports of tobacco, rice, wine and brandy; they consisted of the West Basin, the East Basin and the Shadwell Basin. The **St Katharine Docks**, built in 1828, consisted of two basins surrounded by warehouses (25 acres/10ha) designed by **Thomas Telford**. The two enterprises eventually amalgamated; they were damaged by bombing during the war and finally closed in 1969. The London Docks were infilled and redeveloped as the offices of News International (1986) responsible for publishing ***The Times*** and ***Sunday Times***. The radical move into using computers for newspaper production and distribution irrevocably emancipated the industry from Fleet Street working practices. St John's Wharf and Gun Wharf warehouses on the waterfront have been converted into luxury flats.

St Katharine Dock★

The dock take its name from the **Hospital of St Katharine by the Tower**, a medieval community founded in 1148 by Queen Matilda, the first of an unbroken succession of royal patrons, and which traded from its own wharves. Located as it was outside the City, within which no immigrant might live, it soon had its own hospital, travellers' hostel and refugee settlement. Among the first to be sheltered were the English, forced to quit Calais in 1558: Flemings, Huguenots and others soon followed. By the 18C the

St Katharine Dock

R. Pérousse/MICHELIN

overcrowded settlement numbered nearly 3 000. When the site was sold in the 19C, the Community moved to Regent's Park but returned to Wapping in the 1920s. In 1968 the 19C dock basins were converted into a **yacht marina**; Telford's Italianate building, renamed **Ivory house**, was transformed into residential units and arcades of shops; part of a pre-1820 timber brewery built of European redwood and discovered within the brick cladding of one of the old cooperage and sugar-crushing house, was re-sited and converted into a three-storey restaurant and pub, the **Dickens Inn**; other warehouses were demolished; the **Coronarium Chapel** which was consecrated in June 1977 to commemorate the medieval hospice, consists of seven Doric metal columns from a former warehouse arranged in a circle around a plastic sculpture of an irradiated crown.

New buildings on the dockside accommodate the **World Trade Centre** *(east side)*, the **London Commodity Exchange** *(north side)*, which trades in commodity futures (cocoa, coffee, sugar, pork bellies, etc), and the **International Petrol Exchange**.

Take St Katharine's Way and Wapping High St.

Wapping Pier

The two parallel terraces of 18C houses, which originally flanked the entrance to the London Docks were built for dock officials.

River Police Boat Yard

The modern building houses the 33 craft of the **Metropolitan Special Constabulary** (Thames Division), which patrols the last 54mi/87km of the River Thames. The original River Police were established in 1798.

Old Pumping Station

The attractive old building, which was originally a pumping station providing hydraulic power (1892-1977), is used as a rehearsal hall and recording studio by the Academy of St-Martin-in-the-Fields *(see TRAFALGAR SQUARE – WHITEHALL)*.

Retrace your steps and take Wapping Lane to the Highway.

Tobacco Dock★

The Highway. Redevelopment in progress. Open Mon-Sat, 9am-4/5pm (2pm Sat). ☏ 020 7702 9681

The beautiful brick vaults and cast-iron superstructure of the Skin Floor (1811-13) of the London Docks are of interest.

At the rear on the canal are moored two historic ships. The *Sea Lark* is an American-built schooner which ran the blockade from 1810 to 1814, ceased trading in 1885, and now tells the classic adventure of *Kidnapped* by RL Stevenson. The *Three Sisters*, a replica of the original which traded from 1788 to 1854, traces the history of piracy, on three decks.

St George-in-the-East

Cannon Street Road or Cable Street. Open usually Mon-Fri, 9am-1pm; telephone for confirmation. ☏ 020 7481 1345; Fax 020 7680 0665

The church, which was designed by **Hawksmoor** and consecrated in 1729, was severely damaged in 1941; after the war a modern church (1964) was built within the 18C shell. The **tower**, comprising a two-tier octagonal lantern squarely buttressed and crowned with a balustrade and flat-topped sculptured drums, is the most distinctive in the East End.

Proceed east along the Highway.

Waterfront Pubs

A few of the once numerous riverside pubs have survived. **The Town of Ramsgate, The Prospect of Whitby**, possibly the oldest riverside public house in London. Both are in Wapping. **The Grapes** (Limehouse) dates back to the 18C and appears in a novel by **Charles Dickens**. *See Directory*

St Paul's Church

During refurbishment in 2003 phone for an appointment. Key usually available from The Rectory, 298 The Highway, Shadwell. ☏ 020 7488 4633 (Parish office)

In the 17C and 18C it was known as the Church of the Sea Captains, one of whom was **Captain Cook.**

St Katharine

Butcher Row. In the 1920s the St Katharine **Community** *(see above)* returned from Regent's Park to the Thames and settled in new buildings in Limehouse next to St James's Park.

LIMEHOUSE

DLR: Limehouse

Limehouse was named after its lime kilns and became a shipbuilding centre. Its exotic street names and some fine Chinese restaurants are a reminder that Chinese immigrants first settled here in the 18C. In later years the area gained notoriety owing to its gambling and opium dens.

A Fearsome Rascal

Captain Kidd was dispatched by **William III** (1700) to curtail increased pirate activity on the high seas. Bored by long periods offshore his crew began rioting on board; the captain ended up murdering a man, for which he would have to face the death penalty. He therefore decided to turn his own hand at piracy and raised the Jolly Roger. Captured and repatriated, he was tried on 3 May 1701 and hanged at Execution Dock; the first time the rope stretched and broke, the second time he was less lucky.

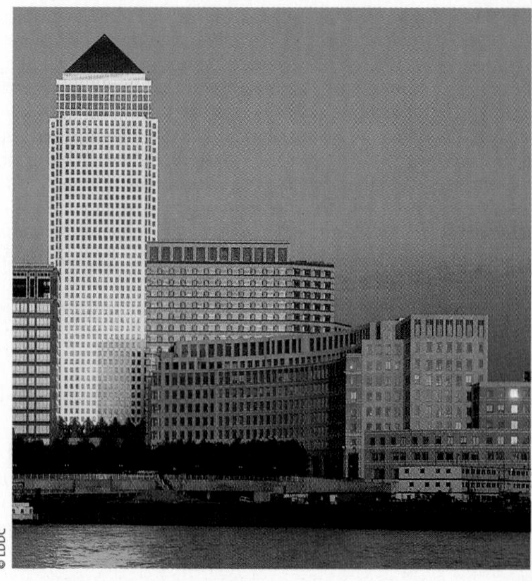

Canary Wharf – modern architecture in Docklands

Limehouse Basin
From Dunbar Wharf, India Pale Ale, brewed locally, was shipped to India and Australia. **Regent's Canal Dock**, built in 1820 and enlarged in 1836, 1852 and 1865, used to acccommodate barges coming down the Regent's Canal to the Thames, or into the Lea Navigation canal system via the Limehouse Cut (1 mile long).

St Anne's Limehouse
Open Sun, 10.30am-12.30pm and 6-7.30pm; Thur, 1-2pm. ☎ 020 7987 1502; cpsalm19@aol.com
A distinctive square tower marks Hawksmoor's first church in the East End of London (1712-24).

ISLE OF DOGS*
DLR: West India Quay, Canary Wharf, Crossharbour, Island Gardens
The Isle of Dogs is a tongue of land round which the Thames makes a huge loop south from Limehouse to Blackwall, dominated today by the slick outline of Canary Wharf tower. Some say the Island acquired its name from the loud howling and baying of hounds kennelled on the north bank when "the Queen" or "her Dad", alluding to Elizabeth I and Henry VIII, were in residence at Greenwich. For centuries the marshy pastures were used to fatten cattle for the City; a single track led south to the Greenwich ferry. In the 19C the Island developed into a densely populated industrial district with three dock systems. In the 50 years from 1850 to 1900 the population grew from 5 000 to 21 000. Since the docks were closed to shipping in 1980, the area, a designated "Enterprise Zone" has been transformed under the auspices of the LDDC into a high-tech commercial alternative to the City.

West India Docks
Extensive development of the Island began early in the 19C when the **West India Docks** (Import Dock 1802 and Export Dock 1806) were built to receive rum and sugar from the West Indies. They were the first commercial wet docks built in London, enclosed by a high brick wall and patrolled by their own police force; warehouses and other buildings were designed by George Gwilt. The **City Canal** (1805), built to provide a direct passage for ships from Blackwall to the London Docks in Wapping, was transformed into a dock in 1870.

Canary Wharf**
This ambitious project was sponsored entirely by private funding. Development was managed in phases, initiated with the construction of the seven buildings suspended in part over water, enclosing **Cabot Square**. As intended, these buildings conceived to exude corporate power are dominated by Cesar Pelli's tower block **1 Canada Square** (800ft/244m, 50 floors), which he described as "a square prism with pyramidal top in the traditional form of the obelisk, which is the most archetypal way of creating a vertical architectural sign... this is the essence of the skyscraper.". The tallest towerblock in London, it is also the first to be clad in stainless steel to reflect light like a beacon visible for many miles across the flat riverside landscape.
Ships belonging to the **Maritime Trust** are sometimes moored in the docks. The development also houses a concert hall, restaurants, pubs and shops and open spaces. The blue-glass South Quay Plaza shimmers with reflections from the still waters.

Peterborough House houses the **Daily Telegraph** editorial offices. In January 1996, this area was severely damaged by an IRA bomb. By 1999 eleven buildings in the scheme had been completed with seven under construction. Canary Wharf has attracted many prestigious firms including investment banks.

Old West India Dock Buildings

At the west end of the old import (north) dock stand the **Cannon Workshops**, so called because a cannon once stood at the entrance, now occupied by a number of small businesses; they were formerly the Quadrangle Buildings (1824), built to provide offices, stores, a cooperage and engineering shops. To the north stands the old **Dockmaster's House** (now a pub). The north quay of the dock is lined by two **warehouses** (1802), designed by George Gwilt, the earliest multi-storey warehouses surviving in London.

The **Museum in Docklands**, housed in Warehouse No 1, celebrates the impact of the port activity on the social and economic life of the country from Roman times to the present day. Displays illustrating working methods and equipment, restored cranes, tugs and barges as well as interactive exhibits make for a fascinating experience.

New Billingsgate Market

The wholesale fish market moved from Old Billingsgate *(see CITY – Monument)* in the City to its new tent-like building in 1982.

Millwall Docks

The name Millwall recalls the windmills which once lined the west bank of the peninsula. The **Millwall Docks** (1868) were built on the site of earlier shipyards: Napier's Yard where Brunel's *Great Eastern* was launched in 1858, and Yarrows which moved to the Clyde in 1904. Their 30ft/9m draft was required in order to accommodate the larger ships bringing cargoes of grain and timber.

Mudchute Park

Park: Open daily. Farm: Open daily, 10am-4pm. ☎ 020 7515 5901; Fax 020 7538 9530; info@mudchute.org

The open space by the banks of a stream supports a riding stables and small urban farm. Earlier in the 20C the park was divided into allotments. The name Mudchute recalls how silt dredged from the Millwall docks was deposited here by a special machine.

Island Gardens

The riverside garden, which was opened in 1895 by the Commissioners of the Royal Naval Hospital at Greenwich, provides a famous **view★★★** south to Greenwich and the Royal Naval College which laid out the garden to improve its own view north.

Footway Tunnel

Open daily. In the round domed building beside the river a lift (or 100 steps) leads down to a foot tunnel beneath the Thames *(10min)* to Greenwich.

Cubitt Town

Little remains of the community developments financed by the property speculator Sir **William Cubitt** in 1843 for Irish labourers, save **Christ Church (Manchester Road)**, a Victorian Gothic church (1857).

Island History Trust

Island House, Roserton Street. Open Tue-Wed and 1st Sun of each month, 1.30-4.30pm. ☎ 020 7987 6041; eve@islandhistory.org.uk; www.islandhistory.org.uk

The Trust, which is mainly of interest to people with a local connection, maintains an extensive archive of photographs about living on the Island and organises open days and bi-annual festivals of local history, recollection and reunion.

Glengall Bridge

The blue Dutch-design lifting bridge (1969) marks the eastern entrance to the City Canal *(see above)*.

The Gun pub *(see Directory)* dates from the 15C and from time to time Lady Hamilton stayed in the upper room. It is rumoured that her ghost haunts the building, which people say is connected by a passage to a house occupied by Nelson.

BLACKWALL

DLR: All Saints

When in 1600 Queen Elizabeth granted a charter to the **East India Company**, it established a shipbuilding and repair yard at **Blackwall** where it landed its cargoes – although excavations have since found traces of far earlier ships, notably of Roman and Viking origins. Its offices were in the city on the site now occupied by Lloyd's *(see CITY)*. Houses and inns developed on either side of Poplar High Street, an important thoroughfare busy with traffic between the City and Blackwall, where some passengers would disembark to complete their journey to London more quickly by coach. In 1776 the company built **St Mathias Church** (now a nursery) with seven mighty masts to support the roof. Brunswick Dock was built by the company in 1789 and equipped with a mast house, seven storeys high, which was an important landmark until it was demolished in 1862; in 1806 this dock was incorporated into the new **East India Docks**.

A Philanthropist

The statue by W Wyon (1865) on East India Dock Road shows **Richard Green** seated with his dog and scenes of 19C shipbuilding on the west side of the base. The Green family owned the Blackwall shipyard and were local benefactors.

Early-17C emigrants to America and later mid-19C emigrants to Australia and New Zealand sailed from Blackwall. In 1812 the congestion in Poplar High Street was so great that the East India Dock Road and Commercial Road were created.

The Blackwall yard made its name with fast clipper ships and later with iron ships; in 1943 the East India Import Dock was used for the construction of the Phoenix units of the floating Mulberry harbour used in the D-day Normandy landings in 1944. Today, just above the Blackwall Tunnel, impressive modern buildings alongside the *Financial Times* printworks accommodate the Town Hall.

Blackwall Tunnel

The Old Tunnel (1897) was built for vehicles and pedestrians; it has carried only northbound traffic since the New Tunnel (1963) was built for vehicles travelling south.

Financial Times Printworks

240 East India Dock Road. The award-winning building (1988) was designed by **Nicholas Grimshaw** for housing offices, platemaking rooms and printing presses, visible through the Pilkington Planar glass front.

Alongside stands **Telehouse**, a blind stronghold for communication technology.

Whitebait Dinners

Blackwall was associated with the 19C political whitebait dinners. The Brunswick Hotel and Tavern, built in 1835 by the East India Company at Blackwall, was patronised by the Fox Club, followers of **Charles James Fox** *(see index)*; their political opponents, William Pitt the Younger, Gladstone and their Whig followers dined at Greenwich where the tradition of whitebait dinners still thrives (Trafalgar Tavern).

Reuters Docklands Centre

Blackwall Yard. In this building designed by **Richard Rogers**, function dominates aesthetic considerations: black glass preserves anonymity and ensures security. As with the Lloyd's Building, the austerity of the architecture is relieved by coloured service ducts.

Bow Creek

This is the name given to the estuary of the **River Lea**. In the 18C it was the site of the famous Thames Ironworks which was also a shipbuilding yard from 1846 to 1912.

For details of the Royal Docks and the Thames Barrier, see Outer London: WOOLWICH - CHARLTON.

Dulwich★

The highlights of Dulwich are its pretty village, fine museum, handsome weatherboarded buildings and elegant houses, and a vast park filled with exotic species.

Location

Map p 337 (UYZ). Overground: West Dulwich from Victoria, North Dulwich from London Bridge. Dulwich lies to the south of Southwark and is accessible by A 23, A 215 and A 205 (South Circular).

Background

King Edgar bestowed the manor of Dilwihs on one of his thanes in AD 967. It was then owned by **Bermondsey Abbey** until the Reformation and in the 17C was acquired by Edward Alleyn *(see below)*.

Dulwich's glory lies in its leafy setting. The houses reflect the transition from 17C manorial village to small country town where 18C-19C city merchants and gentlemen chose to reside (a low triangular milestone on Red Post Hill *(north of railway station)* indicates that it is 4mi/6.5km to the Standard in Cornhill or the Treasury in Whitehall). Commuter trains and cars have transformed it into a south London suburb; yet it remains rural in character, the main street, known as Dulwich Village, dividing at the green where Alleyn built his school.

Walking About

Start from Dulwich College opposite the Art Gallery (description in Worth a Visit).

Dulwich College★

Edward Alleyn: Man of the Theatre, Founder of God's Gift, born in 1566 the son of a City innkeeper, was by common consent one of the greatest actors of his day although **Shakespeare** disagreed and voiced his dislike in Hamlet's counsel to the Player King. His marriage in 1592 to the stepdaughter of **Philip Henslowe**, theatrical businessman, leaser of plays, costumes and theatres, builder of the **Rose Playhouse** (1587), extended Alleyn's interests so that by 1605 he had virtually retired from the theatre and for £5 000 bought Dulwich manor. Having no heir, he established in 1613 a charity for '"six poor men and six poor women and the education of twelfe poor children", which he named the Chapel and College of God's Gift (1619).

Old College and Chapel – The buildings on the triangular site, where the main street divides, are entered through 18C iron gates surmounted by the Alleyn crest. Between the much altered two-storeyed white building which still serves as almshouses, stands the central wing including the clock tower and door to the chapel where Alleyn is buried.

Dulwich Village

Pond House, Village Way, at the opening of the Village, is a three storey house with spanking white trims, a delicate balustrade edging the roof at the rear and a round-headed door complemented by the curving lines of the porch, steps and balustrades. Nos 60, 62 – **The Laurels, The Hollies** – date from 1767. In the 18C the ironwork canopy on iron pillars over the pavement shaded the fare of the village butcher. Nos 93 and 95 – North and South Houses – are of a later date. Nos 97-105 form an 18C terrace, the last two houses daate from the mid 1700s.

College Road

On the pair, nos 13 and 15, built c 1765, note the early Sun Insurance fireplate. The small house at no 31, Pickwick Cottage, is said to be where **Dickens** envisaged Mr Pickwick retiring. Bell Cottage *(no 23)* is a rare example of the once common small, white, weatherboarded local cottages; by contrast the Bell House dating from 1767 is brick built.

Dulwich College, now nearly 1 400 strong, is housed in buildings of 1866-70 designed by Charles Barry in Italian Renaissance style, complete with a stout campanile. Great crested iron gates mark the entrance in College Road.

Pond Cottages (beyond the main road, Dulwich Common) is an 18C group overlooking the Mill Pond, several wholly or partly weatherboarded. The **Toll Gate** is the last in use in the London area: charges at one time were registered as 6d (2 1/2p) or 10d (4p) for "a score of beasts"...

Kingswood House

Seeley Drive. The castellated house built of ragstone in 19C baronial style, was known, when the owner was the founder of the meat extract firm, as Bovril Castle! The Jacobean style interior now serves as a library and community centre.

Worth a Visit

Dulwich Picture Gallery★

Open Tue-Wed and 1st Sun of each month, 1.30-4.30pm. ☎ *020 7987 6041; eve@islandhistory.org.uk; www.islandhistory.org.uk*

Dulwich Gallery, which opened in 1814, is the oldest public picture gallery in the country. Edward Alleyn bought pictures as a man of substance rather than a connoisseur: in 1618 he paid £2 for six royal portraits and later £2 13s 4d for a further eight crowned heads! His final collection of 39 pictures, including his own full length portrait, probably painted from a death mask, was later increased by 80 likenesses of contemporary authors and players: Michael Drayton, Richard Lovelace, **Burbage**, Nat Field (now mostly in the East Room).

In 1811 a double legacy of 400 pictures necessitated the construction of a special gallery. This gift originated with a Frenchman, **Noel Joseph Desenfans**, an unsuccessful language teacher, who changed his profession to become the richest picture dealer of his day. Among his patrons was King Stanislaus of Poland who commissioned a gallery but abdicated in 1795 before paying for the paintings which Desenfans incorporated in his own collection and left to his widow and his friend, **Sir Francis Bourgeois**, who chose Dulwich as the gallery site. Mrs Desenfans contributed £6 000, suggested **Sir John Soane** as architect and presented the furniture still on display.

K. Brett/MICHELIN

The distinctive interior of the Dulwich Picture Gallery

The Building – Sir John Soane was given a free hand in 1811 and three years later the gallery, much as it is today, was opened. The plain exterior belies the skilful inside plan: facing the central entrance, on the far side of two adjoining square galleries is the small domed mausoleum of the founders, Sir Francis Bourgeois, Noel Desenfans and his wife: symmetrically dependent on this central suite are oblong and final square galleries of subtly varied dimensions. The rooms are ingeniously lit by skylights, and the walls have been restored to their original red colour. An extension (1999) comprises an elegant cloister in glass and bronze linking the gallery to a new wing which provides more display space and better facilities.

The Pictures – Several landscapes by **Aelbert Cuyp**, three superb **Rembrandts** including *The Girl at a Window* and *Titus,* 17C and 18C landscapes and pastorals by **Poussin**, Claude, Watteau and Lancret; **Gainsborough** portraits of the Linley family, a **Reynolds** self-portrait and portrait of *Mrs Siddons* are among the highlights of the collection, which also includes works by **Van Dyck**, Teniers the Younger, Raphael, Tiepolo, Canaletto, **Rubens**, Murillo (peasant boys and *Flower Girl*), Reni, Rosa, Lebrun, Guercino and Veronese – although some may be on temporary loan to other galleries. Secondary pictures hang high above the Old, or modern (Francis Bacon) Masters.

East End

The East End prides itself on its Cockney tradition which is enriched with the culture of waves of immigrants. The vast tract stretches east from the City to Stratford, West Ham and beyond. The vibrant multicultural scene is in sharp contrast to the business atmosphere of the City to the west and to modernistic Docklands to the south and west. Visitors who explore the area will gain a greater insight into the complexity of the East End, which is an integral part of London.

Location

Map pp 14-15 (HJKL-VX) and p 337 (UX); Michelin Atlas London: pp 82-83, 98-99. ⊖ *Aldgate East, Whitechapel, Mile End, Stratford, Bow Road.* Major arteries cut across the East End: A 11, A 12, A 406 and A 13. The Docklands Light Railway and the extension of the Jubilee Line have opened up many areas of the East End which were previously only accessible by bus.

Adjacent Sights: The CITY; DOCKLANDS; CLERKENWELL.

Background

The East End of London includes the riverside communities on the north bank *(see Outer London: DOCKLANDS)* and the districts to the north, into which the population spread in the 17C, 18C and 19C as commercial and industrial activity increased: Spitalfields, Whitechapel, Stepney, Mile End and Bethnal Green, names which became synonymous with overcrowding and poverty.

Urbanisation – The odd manor was recorded in the **Domesday Book**; by the 12C the population east of the City, grouped in small communities, had grown to 800, and the area east as far as the **River Lea** and north to **Hackney Downs** was entrusted to the Constable and named Tower Hamlets (a name revived under the 1965 Local Government Act).

In the first instance, the population was swelled by the arrival of English craftsmen: woodworkers, boatbuilders and masons, then 10 000 freed slaves who fled to the waterside to work as dockers. In the 16C Dutch traders and craftsmen began to settle: leatherworkers, nail- and locksmiths. The overcrowding was further exacerbated by many waves of refugees: Dutch and French **Huguenots** (13 000 French arrived in 1687), Irish, Jews, Chinese – the latter settled near Limehouse Causeway.

From the 16C to the 19C houses were used as workshops, factories and dwellings; families moved on as soon as they had the means to leave the appalling conditions, which were starkly described by **Mayhew** in his *Survey of the London Poor* (1850). In the 20C many of the slums were demolished and replaced by more modern low-cost housing, inhabited by immigrants from the West Indies, India, Pakistan and Bangladesh...

Institutions – Several national or famous philanthropic institutions were born in the East End of London. These include **Dr Barnardo's** first children's home (1874) in Stepney; **Toynbee Hall** *(Commercial Street)*, the first **university settlement**, instituted in 1884; the **Salvation Army**, founded in 1765, began on Trinity Green in the Mile End Road.

The **London Hospital**, which now operates on three sites, was founded in 1740 by John Harrison, a young surgeon, with six others in a tavern in Cheapside; it started as the London Infirmary in a house near **Bunhill Fields** *(see CLERKENWELL)*, soon removed to Prescot Street in Wapping and thence to Whitechapel in 1757. A display of archive material is accommodated in the crypt of the former hospital church St Augustine with St Philip.

Queen Mary College, which was incorporated in the University of London in 1905, originated in the mid 19C as the Philosophical Institute in a grand building and library; it was taken over by the Drapers' Company which re-conceived it as a **People's Palace** combining education with gymnastics, swimming, music etc., taking its present name in 1934 upon receiving a Royal Charter. Later it merged with the Bromley and Bow Institute to form the **East London College** and become part of London University. The College is housed in a terracotta brick and stone building (1885), fronted by a wide forecourt on the Mile End Road, and in additional buildings of glass, brick and concrete (1950s).

Jewish Community – The Jewish community in the East End, which in 1850 consisted of a ghetto round Petticoat Lane, grew rapidly in the 1880s with the influx of 100 000 Russian and Polish Jews and about 20 000 German, Austrian, Dutch and Romanian Jews (Synagogue at 48-50 Artillery Lane in 1896). By 1914 the East End of London contained the largest Jewish community in England.

As they became more affluent, they moved away to the outer suburbs of London or abroad; as numbers dwindled their synagogues disappeared as did the Jew's Free School (founded about 1821) and Jewish Care, the successor to the Jewish Board of Guardians *(plaque: 129 Middlesex Street)* founded in 1859 to help the poorer immigrants by offering evening classes in English, sewing classes, apprenticeships and interest-free loans. Among the few landmarks that have survived is the **Brady Street Cemetery** (1761-1858) where **Nathan Mayer Rothschild** *(see p 173)* is buried.

Directory

Going out for the Evening

Great Eastern Dining Room – *54 Great Eastern St, Shoreditch, EC2A 3QR – ⊖ Liverpool Street, Old Street – ☎ 020 7613 4545 – www.greateasterndining.co.uk – Open Mon-Sat noon (6.30pm Sat) to midnight.* Undoubtedly the smartest bar in the area with its black walls and floors, red leather sofas and designer chandeliers. Frequented by a thirty-something crowd drawn by the atmosphere and excellent cocktails.

The Light – *233 Shoreditch High St, E1 6PJ – ⊖ Liverpool Street – ☎ 020 7247 8989 – info@thelightE1.com – Open Mon-Sat noon-midnight (2am Thu-Sat), Sun noon-10.30pm; closed at Christmas and bank hols.* Five minutes from Liverpool Street Station, this reconverted electric generating station will surprise you by its sheer size and the impressive industrial decor of exposed beams and bricks. When it becomes unbearably noisy, head out onto the terrace.

Walking About

SHOREDITCH

⊖ *Old Street*

In the reign of Elizabeth I, when theatrical performances were disapproved of and frequently banned by the City authorities, many theatre folk lived in and around Shoreditch. The first English playhouse, **The Theatre**, was founded within the precincts of the former Holywell Priory in Shoreditch in 1576 by **James Burbage** (d 1597) a joiner by trade who became head of Lord Leicester's players; he also founded the **Little Curtain** named after the curtain wall of the enclosure. In 1597 The Theatre in Shoreditch was pulled down, on the orders of the Privy Council, and the materials were used by James' son **Cuthbert** (d 1635) to build the **Globe** *(see BANKSIDE – SOUTHWARK)* on the South Bank in 1599; his other son **Richard Burbage** (d 1619) was the first actor to play Shakespeare's *Richard III* and *Hamlet* – all three Burbages lie buried in St Leonard's Church.

Proceed east along Old St to the junction with Kingsland Rd (Geffrye Museum described in Worth a Visit) and Hackney Rd.

St Leonard's Church

119 Shoreditch High Street. ♿ Refurbishment in progress. Open by appointment only. Open previously Sun, 10am-noon, Mon-Fri, 10am-5pm; Sat by request. ☎ 020 7739 2063 (Vicar)
The mid-18C building with its 192ft/58.5m spire replaces another earlier church. Within its precincts were buried: one of Henry VIII's court jesters William Somers (d 1560); one of Queen Elizabeth's players, Richard Tarleton (d 1588); **James Burbage** (d 1597) and his sons **Cuthbert** and **Richard**; Gabriel Spencer (d 1598), a player at the Rose Theatre who was killed by **Ben Jonson** *(see WESTMINSTER)*; William Sly (d 1608) and Richard Cowley (d 1619), players at the Globe on Bankside.

Hoxton Square

This working-class district has gained a certain notoriety as artists, musicians and other creative types move in and set up their studios. Consequently there are now several bars and restaurants, a cinema and art galleries which attract a Bohemian crowd.

HACKNEY

Overground: Hackney Central; Hackney Downs.

In the 16C Hackney was a country village where wealthy city merchants established a second country residence away from the congestion and plague of the City. In the following century it was famous for its many schools; there were so many girls' boarding schools that Hackney was dubbed the "Ladies University of Female Arts" and **Pepys** records attending Hackney Church in order to admire the young ladies.

Hackney Town

The ragstone tower is all that remains of the medieval Church of St Augustine: the present church, **St John-at-Hackney**, dates from the 1700s.

Hackney Empire *(Mare St)* was designed by Frank Matcham (1901) and is a fine example of the variety palaces which were popular at the turn of the century. The Rococo auditorium has excellent acoustics.

For Hackney Museum see description in Worth a Visit.

Dalston

Holy Trinity Church (1849) in Beechwood Road is the Clowns' Church as it holds an annual memorial service for Joseph Grimaldi (1779-1837) on the first Sunday in February. The tradition of clowns meeting once a year in church was started in the days of **Grimaldi**, the most famous British clown, the first to paint the face, who lived in Islington and is buried in the churchyard of St James' Church in Pentonville. When St James' Church was demolished, the clowns' service moved to Dalston. ♿ *Memorial service: first Sun in Feb at 4pm. Otherwise open by appointment.* ☎ *020 7254 5062 (Vicarage)*

Bring On The Clowns

Clowns International is a charitable organisation set up by clowns for clowns: its aims are to provide these special entertainers with an annual festival that celebrates their historical art and organises a convention at which to meet, exchange ideas, support others and encourage the talented young and hopeful, worldwide. It maintains a small gallery and archive at 1 Hillman Street which is open to all, the curious, the interested, the circumspect and its professional and amateur members. Museum curator ☎ 020 7723 3877.

SPITALFIELDS

⊖ *Aldgate East, Shoreditch.*

The market (fruit, vegetables and flowers) was granted a royal charter by Charles II in 1682 and acquired by the City Corporation in 1902; in 1991 London's largest wholesale depot was moved to Leyton. Food shops abound, but the best market is held on Sundays. Look out for the mechanical railway sculpture...

Walk up Commercial St.

Christ Church

♿ *Restoration in progress until spring 2004: telephone for opening times. Open usually Mon-Fri, 12.30-2.30pm. Annual Music Festival: Jun and Dec (☎ 020 7377 0287). ☎ 020 7247 0790; christchurch@fsnet.co.uk*

Hawksmoor's spire still dominates the area almost as it did when built in 1714-30, although now more starkly having been rebuilt in the 19C without the original dormers on each face, corner crockets and stone finial. It rises above a Classical west portico through an interplay of ascending circular bays and arches, dramatically cut by the horizontal lines of the entablature and cornice. At the east end a Venetian window is framed by paired niches beneath a pediment.

Take Fournier St to Brick Lane.

Fournier Street contains a series of handsome Georgian houses (1718-28), which were once occupied by silk weavers and merchants when **Spitalfields silk** was famous in the late 17C to mid 19C *(see VICTORIA & ALBERT MUSEUM)*.

Brick Lane

The history of the **mosque**, which was built as a Christian chapel in 1743 and later became a synagogue, reflects the successive waves of immigrants who have lived in the district. On Sunday mornings, a bric-a-brac and second-hand clothes **market** spreads through the district around Bethnal Green Road, Cheshire Street.

The spacious glass-fronted reception area of **Truman's Brewery**, founded 1666, reveals older buildings round a cobbled yard.

WHITECHAPEL

⊖ *Aldgate East*

The gleaming white **Sedgwick** Centre (1986) houses a conference centre, sports complex and the Chaucer Theatre.

Walk east along Whitechapel Rd.

J. Malburet/MICHELIN

Whitechapel Art Gallery – a rare example of the Arts and Crafts Movement in the East End of London

Whitechapel Art Gallery

♿ *Open Tue-Sun, 11am-6pm, (9pm Thu). Charges for certain exhibitions. Talks, tours and film screenings: telephone for details. Café.* ☎ *020 7522 7878 (recorded information), 020 7522 7888 (general enquiries Mon-Fri); Fax 020 7377 1685; info@whitechapel.org; www.whitechapel.org*

The gallery provides exhibition facilities for modern and contemporary art by non-established artists; Barbara **Hepworth** and David **Hockney** first showed their work here. The building (1901) was designed by **CH Townsend**; it is decorated with contemporary Arts and Crafts reliefs and surmounted by twin-angle turrets.

Passmore Edwards Library

The library was built in the Arts and Crafts style. In the entrance is a panel composed of decorated tiles depicting the Whitechapel Hay Market which flourished for over three hundred years until it was abolished in 1928 as an obstruction.

Whitechapel Bell Foundry

The foundry has been on its present site since 1738; its records go back to 1570 but it may be 150 years older. It has cast and recast, owing to fire in 1666 and the Second World War, the bells of St Mary-le-Bow, St Clement Dane's and Big Ben.

East London Mosque

The mosque was built in 1985 by the most recent immigrants who came from the Indian subcontinent.

Mile End Road

⊖ *Whitechapel.* The Trinity Almshouses, built by the Corporation of Trinity House in 1695 for "28 decay'd Masters and Comanders of ships" or their widows, form a terrace of basement and ground floor cottages around three sides of a tree-planted quadrangle.

On Trinity Green stands a statue (1979) of General William Booth erected on the 150th anniversary of his birth to mark the site where he began the work of the Salvation Army.

The London Blitz

During the eight-month bombardment, which ceased in May 1941, 190 000 bombs were dropped; 43 000 civilians died, 61 000 were seriously injured; 404 firemen were killed on duty and 3 000 were injured; 1.25 million houses in the London region were damaged. At first people took refuge in Anderson shelters, which were effective but damp and crowded; later they spent the hours of darkness in the Underground stations, where bunks and sanitary facilities were installed; only three Underground stations received direct hits resulting in deaths. St Paul's Cathedral was hit twice: on 12 September a 1 000lb bomb lodged in the clocktower; it was removed by sappers (Royal Engineers) who were awarded the first George Crosses and exploded on Hackney marshes where it created a crater 100ft/30m in diameter; on 16-17 April 1941 a bomb fell through the north transept and exploded in the crypt.

BETHNAL GREEN

⊖ *Shoreditch, Bethnal Green*

St Matthew

The parish church of Bethnal Green was built (1743-46) by George Dance the Elder and the interior remodelled (1859-61) by Knightly. The **Watch House** (1826) stands in the south-west corner of the churchyard.

The west tower of **Sir John Soane**'s **St John's Church** (1825-28), though not high, is an easily distinguished landmark as it rises from a square clock stage, through a drum with blind arches to a vaned cupola. *Open at Mass times and Sat, 10am-11am. Key available at the Rectory, 30 Victoria Park Square; alan.green@virgin.net*

Walk up Cambridge Heath St to visit the Museum of Childhood at Bethnal Green (description in Worth a Visit).

WEST HAM

⊖ *Bromley By Bow*

West Ham early developed into a manufacturing town owing to its position near the confluence of the navigable River Lea and the Thames and its proximity to London, where noxious industries were banned by the City authorities. As early as the 11C the **Domesday Book** recorded eight mills on Bow Creek. From the 17C onwards industrial activity diversified into calico and paper making, distilling and the manufacture of gunpowder at Congreve's rocket factory. In the 18C Bow Pottery was the largest porcelain factory in England; to its original blue and white pieces copied from Chinese porcelain, it added figures taken from mythology and natural history. At the end of the 19C there were about 300 companies in the area engaged in various industries: chemicals, engineering and metals, food, drink and tobacco, textiles, leather and clothing, timber and furniture, brick, pottery, cement and glass.

Take the subway towards a supermarket, then turn right into Abbey Mill Lane.

Three Mills

♿ Open Mar-Dec, 1st Sun in the month, 11am-4pm; also early-May to late-Oct, other Sun, 2-4pm; also early-Jun to late-Sep, Sat, 2-4pm. £3. Leaflet. ☎ 020 8980 4626; www.housemill.com

At the north end of Bow Creek there is an attractive group of early industrial buildings. The **House Mill**, built in 1776 by Daniel Bisson, spans two waterways and four mill-races and as such is the largest tide mill known in the country. It still contains six pairs of mill stones and four undershot water-wheels which were driven by releasing the head of the water impounded at high tide. Some of the more modern equipment was removed in 1941 when work ceased because of the war. The original **miller's house** (demolished in the 1950s) has been reconstructed as part of the restored Georgian street front.

Granite setts and flagstones mark the path across to the **Clock Mill** which dates from 1817. The ornate clock tower, which is earlier, is surmounted by an octagonal turret, containing a bell and a weathervane. The conical caps of the two **drying kilns** are Victorian. Barge stands are visible in the river at low tide; they prevented the grain barges from being trapped in the mud at low water.

Abbey Mills Pumping Station – The impressive cruciform building, which houses sewage pumping machinery, was designed (1865-68) by **Sir Joseph Bazalgette** and Vulliamy in the Venetian Gothic style with an octagonal lantern above the crossing.

Worth a Visit

Geffrye Museum★

Kingsland Road. ♿ Open Tue-Sun and Bank Hol Mon, 10am (noon Sun and Bank Hol Mon) to 5pm. Closed Good Fri, 24-26 Dec, 1 Jan. Guided tour by appointment. Herb garden and period garden rooms: Open Apr-Oct. Restaurant. Shop. ☎ 020 7739 9893, 020 7739 8543 (recorded information); Fax 020 7729 5647; info@geffrye-museum.org.uk; www.geffrye-museum.org.uk

The almshouses and chapel were erected around three sides of an open court planted with plane trees (1712-19) by the Ironmongers' Company with a bequest left by Sir Robert Geffrye, Lord Mayor. The two-storey brick buildings are decorated with continuous modillioned eaves; at the centre, marking the chapel, is a pediment and niche in which stands the periwigged figure of the founder.

Inside, a series of rooms displays furniture and furnishings from Tudor times to the 1950s: including John Evelyn's Closet of Curiosities, several Georgian shopfronts and a woodworker's shop with bench and tools and, at the back, an open hearth kitchen. A distinctive horseshoe extension comprising two brick warehouses with pitched roofs and simple gable ends curves around a central light stairwell, an inspired architectural device. In the upper gallery, the new rooms take the collection to the present day and include a minimalist loft. In the grounds there is a large walled herb garden and other historic gardens.

Museum of Childhood at Bethnal Green

Cambridge Heath Road, Bethnal Green. (♿) Open daily except Fri, 10am-5.50pm. ☎ 020 8980 2415 (recorded information); Fax 020 8983 5225; bgmc@vam.ac.uk; www.museumofchildhood.org.uk

The museum houses the Victoria & Albert Museum's collection of toys, dolls, doll's houses, games, puppets, toy theatres and toy soldiers, as well as a collection of children's clothing, furniture, paintings, prints, photographs, books and other artefacts of childhood.

The building, the oldest surviving example of the type of pre-fabricated iron and glass construction utilised by **Paxton** (now with a brick encasement) was originally erected to contain items from the **1851 Exhibition** *(see VICTORIA & ALBERT MUSEUM)*; it was re-erected and opened on the present site in 1872.

Hackney Museum

1 Reading Lane. Open Mon-Tue and Thu-Sat, 9.30am (10am Sat) to 5.30pm (8pm Thu, 5pm Sat). ☎ 020 8356 3500, Fax 020 8356 2563; www.hackney.gov.uk

The chief exhibit of this museum of local history is an **Anglo-Saxon longboat** hollowed out from the trunk of an oak tree (c AD 900) abandoned during a Viking invasion.

Sutton House

2, 4 Homerton High St. ⊖ Bethnal Green. (NT) (♿) Open early-Feb to late-Dec, Fri-Sun and Bank Hol Mon, 11.30am (1pm Fri-Sat) to 5.30pm (5pm Bank Hols). Art Gallery: Open early-Jan to late-Dec, Wed-Sun, 1.30am-5pm. £2.20. No photography. No dogs. Braille Guide. Café. ☎ 020 8986 2264; suttonhouse@nationaltrust.org.uk; www.nationaltrust.org.uk

The house, which was probably built for Ralph Sadleir, who later became Principal Secretary of State to Henry VIII, dates from c 1535; it had gable ends and mullion windows and was originally known as the "bryk place" as most buildings then were timber-framed structures. Early in the 18C the gable roofs were cut back to make room for the parapet, the present sash windows were inserted and a second entrance was made to the west wing. The cement rendering on the east wing dates from about 1870 and the porches from 1904.

The interior contains one of the **original Tudor transom windows**, now in the Lobby. The Parlour is entirely lined with **oak linenfold panelling** dating from the early 16C and has retained its original stone fireplace, surmounted by an overmantel with typical Renaissance fluted pilasters. The **painted staircase** is decorated with coloured oil painting directly on to plaster showing coats of arms, animals on pedestals bearing shields and a frieze with *trompe-l'œil* work. The Little Chamber is lined with **Baltic oak panelling** dating from the late 16C.

The house was named in 1951 after Sir Thomas Sutton (d 1611), founder of Charterhouse School *(see CLERKENWELL)*, who lived in the neighbouring Tanhouse but had been thought to have lived in Sutton House.

Eltham Palace★

The vision of discerning art lovers has preserved remains of Eltham Palace while creating a refined residence. The wonderful Art Deco interior has been lavishly restored.

Location

Map p 337 (UY). Overground: Eltham or Mottingham from London Bridge. Eltham to the south-east is accessible by the South Circular (A 205) and A 20.

Adjacent Sights: WOOLWICH – CHARLTON; GREENWICH.

Background

South of Eltham and off Court Yard nestles a historical country retreat, a house of radical contrasts. Nine miles/14km as the crow flies from London Bridge stands Eltham Palace, which is documented as being in the possession of Odo, Bishop of Bayeux and half-brother of William the Conqueror in 1086. From 1295 it was owned by Bek, Bishop of Durham who ceded it to Edward Prince of Wales (later **Edward II**) – the first of several monarchs to live there, preferring it to Windsor which they found to be draughty by comparison, especially at Christmas time. By all accounts it would have been quite a large complex in the 14C, set among well-stocked mature forest described by the chronicler Froissart as "a very magnificent palace". In 1390, under **Richard II**, **Geoffrey Chaucer** was Clerk of the Works here. **Edward IV** added the Great Hall in 1479-80; only foundations of **Henry VI**'s royal apartments still remain; **Henry VIII** met **Erasmus** there, happy to live there until his interest in ships spurred him to move to Greenwich. During the Commonwealth, according to **John Evelyn**, it fell into "miserable ruins" and was finally valued only as building material (£2 754). During the late 18C and 19C the place was more or less abandoned – painted as a Romantic folly by **Turner** and Girtin.

In 1931, it was leased to **Sir Stephen Courtauld** who restored the Great Hall and built his own distinctive 1930s country residence. When the Courtaulds moved to Scotland, the place was occupied by the Royal Army Corps (1945-92). It is now in the hands of English Heritage.

Highlights

Eltham Palace★

Open Wed-Fri, Sun and Bank Hols, 10am-6pm (5pm Oct; 4pm Nov-Mar). House and gardens £6.50; gardens £4. Audiotour (3 languages). Guidebook. No dogs. Parking 200m from entrance. Tearoom. ☎ 020 8294 2548; www.english-heritage.org.uk

The house is approached over a fine stone bridge straddling the fish-filled moat. To the right of the Tudor House would have stood the chapel and "My Lord Chancellor's lodging" *(34-38 Courtyard)* or the occasional residence of **Cardinal Wolsey**, who was installed as Lord Chancellor in the palace chapel.

The **Great Hall** (101ft/31m long, 36ft/11m wide and 56ft/17m to the roof apex) is built of brick, faced with stone. Its chief glory, in all but the technical sense since the posts are tenoned, is the sweet-chestnut hammerbeam roof with a central hexagonal louvred section that once would have served to expel smoke from the large open hearth. Earlier than the roof at Hampton Court, Eltham's narrowly predates that of Crosby Hall in Chelsea, and was almost certainly constructed by the king's master mason Thomas Jordan and carpenter Edmund Gravely. The windows are placed high in the wall, allowing for heavy tapestry hangings to insulate the lower sections. The wooden reredos was installed in the 1930s. Beyond the dais, reached via the oriels or bay windows, once lay the king's and queen's separate apartments.

Courtauld House – The task of redeveloping the site fell to the architects John Seely and Paul Paget. The five principal entertainment rooms with the bedrooms above, are accommodated in the south wing, extending eastwards in line with the Great Hall. The service wing meanwhile is orientated at an angle pivoting on the entrance hall.

All "mod cons" pervade the house: soft American-style uplighting, a centralised vacuum cleaner in the basement that collected dust from hoses fitted in every room, underfloor heating boosted in the bedrooms with single bar electric fires, synchronised clocks and a loud-speaker system that worked throughout. It is, however, the unique quality of the 1930s internal decoration that is particularly remarkable: fine wooden veneer (flexwood) panelling is fitted in all the main bedrooms, stylishly fashioned like the inside of a Cunard cruise liner – golden-satin coloured aspenwood, weathered sycamore, bird's-eye maple, Japanese chestnut, Indian mahogany...

Notable peculiar features of the house include the entrance-hall inlaid panels of Venice and Sweden (Roman gladiator and Scandinavian Viking) and the Alice in Wonderland reliefs set between the windows; Lady Courtauld's legendary lemur's centrally-heated cage; her personal bathroom furnished with an onyx basin surround, gold-plated taps and gold-leafed mosaic alcove (designed by the then ever-so-fashionable Peter Malacrida); the locally made leather patchwork map in her sitting room that features London's first airport at Croydon and the cardinal points as an Eskimo, Chinaman, African warrior and Red Indian chief; the dining room fitted with its square-coffered silver-leafed ceiling, distinctive doors – with panels commissioned from Narini who studied the animals at London Zoo – and 1930s black marble fireplace set with mother-of-pearl ribbon bands and polished Art Deco grate.

Discerning Patrons

Sir Stephen Courtauld (1883-1967), brother of Samuel the benefactor of the Courtauld Institute, was an avid horticulturalist. He and his wife, Virginia (1885-1972) – Ginnie for short – moved from 47 Grosvenor Square, taking their famous art treasures and favourite fittings (fireplace, grilles, doors) with them to Eltham. In 1944 they moved to Scotland as the war continued, and emigrated finally to Rhodesia where Stephen might study his beloved orchids.

The house has been lovingly furnished in Art Deco style based on photographs of the interiors and on a detailed inventory; there are replicas of carpets, furniture and some of the paintings as well as fabrics in the style.

Gardens – Lovingly landscaped and planted by the Courtaulds, the gardens boast beautiful mature trees and beds of fragrant flowers (syringa, wistaria, honeysuckle, roses), a perfect pleasure ground for visiting guests welcomed with warm hospitality to the house (hence the relief figure over the front door of the house).

Well Hall

Well Hall Road; 1 mile north. The Well Hall estate was the home of the Roper family, descendants of **Thomas More** *(see CHELSEA)*, until 1733. All that now remains are the site of the medieval house surrounded by a moat and reached by a 16C bridge, a Tudor barn *(restaurant and art gallery)* and the Pleasaunce – a garden surrounded by old red brick walls.

Fulham – Putney

These fine residential areas linked by a bridge enjoy a pleasant riverside location. Fulham has become an offshoot of fashionable Chelsea while Putney with its leafy common land has a rural atmosphere. It is well worth taking a stroll to visit the picturesque pubs and enjoy the scenery.

Location

Map p 336 (TY) – ⊖ Putney Bridge. Fulham and Putney which lie to the south-west are bisected by A 308 and A 219 which merge and lead to A 3 and M 25.
Adjacent Sights: CHELSEA.

Background

Fulham, Parsons Green, Walham Green, all within a wide loop of the river were once separate riparian villages with the odd large mansion in its own grounds which ran down to the water's edge. Market gardens covered the fertile marshlands. The Bishop of London was the lord of the manor, a property of vast extent, a mere four miles/6.5km from Hyde Park Corner. Urbanisation came within a period of 50 years: in 1851 the population numbered 12 000; in 1901, 137 000.
The **Charing Cross Hospital** *(Fulham Palace Road)* moved from the Strand in 1973 into more modern cruciform premises equipped with state-of-the-art facilities.

Directory

PUBS

Boat and Dragon – *180 Lower Richmond Rd, SW15 1LY – ⊖ Putney Bridge – ☏ 020 8788 0925.*

Duke's Head – *8 Lower Richmond Rd, SW15 1JN – ☏ 020 8788 2552 – Open Mon-Sat 11am-11pm, Sun noon-10.30pm.*

Spencer Arms – *237 Lower Richmond Rd, SW15 1LY – ⊖ Putney Bridge – ☏ 020 8789 5126 – Open Mon-Sat noon-11pm, Sun noon-10.30pm.*

Walking About

FULHAM

Start from the north side of Putney Bridge.

Downstream from the bridgehead, **Hurlingham House**, an 18C mansion in its own wooded grounds, is the last of the big houses which once lined the river bank. It is now a private club with extensive tennis courts.

Walk up Fulham Palace Rd and turn left into Bishop's Av.

Fulham Palace

Bishop's Avenue. The **palace**, which retains the appearance of a modest Tudor manor, was the official summer residence of the Bishop of London from 704 to 1973. The gateway, a low 16C arch with massive beamed doors, leads through to the courtyard (1480-1525) graced by a large central fountain (1885). The two-storey red-brick walls,

K. Brett/MICHELIN

Fulham Palace – a charming example of domestic Tudor architecture

Oxford and Cambridge Boat Race, Putney

except in the south range (restored), are strongly patterned with a black diaper design. The chapel (1866), added on the south side, was designed by William Butterfield in mock Tudor style. *For description of Fulham Palace Museum see Worth a Visit.*

The **grounds** consist of lawns shaded by a copper beech and an ancient evergreen, possibly planted by Bishop Grindal who sent grapes to Elizabeth I. The first magnolia to be grown in Europe and several other exotic species were planted here by Bishop Compton. The old walled kitchen garden contains beech hedge screens, a herb garden and a **wistaria walk**, enclosing the old vinery and clipped box hedges. The remains of a moat (1 mile long), filled in the 1920s, may date from the Roman period. Traces have been found of prehistoric and Roman settlements. *Open daily.*

Fulham Pottery

At 210 New King's Road, one disused bottle kiln still stands on the site of the seven- or nine-kiln pottery established by John Dwight in 1671 by special permission of Charles II and soon known for its stoneware – vulgarly called Cologne ware, and salt-glazed earthenware so suited to modelling commemorative busts and statuettes.

Return to the bridge and turn right into Church Gate.

All Saints Church

♿ *Open Mon-Fri, noon-3pm. Guide book. ☎/Fax: 020 7736 6301; info@allsaints-fulham.co.uk; www.allsaints-fulham.co.uk*

Fulham parish church has been a landmark at this bridging point of the river since the 14C, its square Kentish stone tower a twin to Putney church on the south bank, although the vessel was rebuilt in Perpendicular style in the 19C.

Inside there is a rich collection of monuments and brasses: note the tombstones in the chancel floor to William Rumbold, standard-bearer to Charles I in the Civil War, and Thomas Carlos, whose coat of arms, an oak tree and three crowns, was granted to his father after he had hidden in the oak tree at Boscobel with Charles II after the Battle of Worcester, 1651. Fourteen Bishops of London are buried in the yew-shaded churchyard.

Close to the church note the 19C **Powell Almshouses** with steep pitched roofs over a single storey, forming an L-shaped building around a quiet garden.

PUTNEY

The area's transformation was precipitated by the arrival of the railway in the mid 19C. In its wake came the builders. Evolution previously had been gradual, from settlement beside the ford to substantial village where **Oliver Cromwell** held a council of war round the communion table in St Mary's in 1647. Even the erection of a wooden toll-bridge in 1729 – the first above London Bridge – had little effect.

The early association with the river remains: rowing clubs still line the Surrey bank, oarsmen practise in midstream; the **Boat Race** between Oxford and Cambridge Universities is rowed each spring over the 4 1/2mi/7km course to Mortlake, as it has been ever since 1845.

Putney Bridge

The bridge, which marks the beginning (just upstream in line with the Universities' Stone by the Star and Garter pub) of the Oxford and Cambridge boat race, was designed in Cornish granite by **Joseph Bazalgette** in 1884 and replaced a wooden toll-bridge of 1729.

St Mary's Parish Church

Open Mon-Fri, 9.30am-3pm. Leaflet. ☏/Fax 020 8788 4414 (Parish offices), 020 8788 4575 (Vicar), 020 8788 7164 (Curate)

The church at the approach to Putney bridge was burnt out in 1973 and reopened after restoration in 1982. The 16C chantry chapel and 15C tower were preserved when the church was rebuilt in 1836.

Take Lower Richmond Rd west.

Lower Richmond Road

Near the bridge-foot, low lying between the Lower Richmond Road and the river bank road which serves the club boat houses, is 18C **Winchester House**, dwarfed by the surrounding buildings.

Lower Richmond Road itself winds upriver past a straggling line of village and antique shops and small Victorian houses, punctuated by pubs of varying vintage: the **Duke's Head**, late Georgian overlooking the river and, just before the common, the Georgian **Boat and Dragon** and the 19C gabled **Spencer Arms** *(see Directory)*.

On the Lower Common is **All Saints Church** (1874), notable for its Burne-Jones windows *(open for services only)*.

Return to the bridge and walk south.

Putney High Street, Putney Hill

The bustling High Street with, halfway along, a Tudor style, gargoyle decorated pub, the **Old Spotted Horse**, still includes tall 19C house-fronts. At the start of Putney Hill, near the crossroads, are to left and right, no 11, The Pines, a monstrous tall grey attached Victorian House where **Swinburne** lived and no 28A, a pink-washed Georgian villa with a firemark set like a beauty patch on its pale wall.

Worth a Visit

Fulham Palace Museum

Grounds: Open daily. Museum: ♿ Open Mar-Oct, Wed-Sun, 2-5pm; Nov-Feb, Thu-Sun, 1-4pm. Children under 16 must be accompanied by adult. Guided tour: 2nd and 4th Sun in the month at 2pm, otherwise by appointment; £3. ☏ 020 7736 3233; fulhampalace@waitrose.com

Housed in the east wing, in the Dining Room and Library (formerly a chapel); it traces the history of the site, the buildings and the gardens: archaeological finds, souvenirs and portraits of past bishops, the ecclesiastical and political role of the Bishop of London, ecclesiastical vestments, stained glass.

Greenwich★★★

The glories of Greenwich are various: a wonderful riverside setting, a vast park, an attractive town with antique shops and a busy market and famous museums. A pleasant stroll along the riverside walk runs past historic pubs and affords superb views of the majestic royal buildings and of the modernistic skyline on the north bank. The regenerated Greenwich Peninsula now boasts the Millennium Village; however the Dome, an exciting technical success, has gained notoriety. The harmonious architecture of Blackheath village on the far side of the heath is noteworthy.

Location

2 Cutty Sark Gardens, Greenwich, SE10 9LW. Open daily, 10am-5pm. ☎ 0870 608 2000, Fax 020 8853 4607; tic@greeenwich.gov.uk; www.greenwich.gov.uk

Map p 15 (KLZ) and p 285 (UY). ⊖ North Greenwich; Overground: Greenwich from Charing Cross, Waterloo, London Bridge or Cannon Street; DLR: Cutty Sark; by boat from Westminster, Tower Bridge. Greenwich is located on the south bank of the Thames opposite Canary Wharf and the Isle of Dogs. Access by road is by A 206 or A 2.

Adjacent Sights: DOCKLANDS; WOOLWICH – CHARLTON.

Background

The small town beside the Thames has a worldwide reputation owing to the Greenwich Meridian and Greenwich Mean Time. The Royal Observatory stands on a hill overlooking an attractive park sloping down to the river. Greenwich has many associations with the Royal Navy and British maritime history and its days as a royal residence are recalled in the delightful Queen's House.

The **antique market** *(see PRACTICAL POINTS – Shopping)* is well known and there are other shops selling antiques and second-hand books.

A **footway tunnel** *(lift or 100 steps)* leads under the Thames *(10min)* to the Isle of Dogs, from where there is a fine **view**★★ of Greenwich Palace, as painted by **Canaletto** in 1750 and now in the National Maritime Museum Collection.

Bella Court – Greenwich has been in the royal domain since King Alfred's time. It was Humphrey, Duke of Gloucester, brother of Henry V, who first enclosed the park and transformed the manor into a castle, which he named Bella Court; it was he also who built a fortified tower upon the hill from which to spy invaders approaching London up the Thames or along the Roman road from Dover. On Duke Humphrey's death in 1447, Henry VI's queen, **Margaret of Anjou**, annexed the castle, embellished it and renamed it **Placentia** or Pleasaunce.

Tudor Palace – The Tudors preferred Greenwich to their other residences, and **Henry VIII**, who was born there, enlarged the castle into a vast palace with a tiltyard and a royal armoury where craftsmen produced armour to rival the Italian and German suits *(see TOWER OF LONDON)*.

Henry also founded naval dockyards upriver at Deptford and downstream at Woolwich which he visited by sumptuous royal barge to inspect his growing fleet. The docks were also accessible by a road skirting the wall which divided the extensive and quite magnificent royal gardens from the park. Overlooking the thoroughfare was a two-storey gatehouse which, legend has it, **Queen Elizabeth** was approaching one day in 1581 when **Walter Raleigh**, seeing her about to step into the mire, threw down his cloak so that she might cross dryshod.

Palladian House and "Pretty Palace" – Rich as the Tudor palace was, in 1615 **James I** commissioned **Inigo Jones** *(see INSIGHTS AND IMAGES – The Changing Face of London)* to build a house for his queen (**Anne of Denmark**) on the exact site of the gatehouse, straddling the busy Woolwich-Deptford road. Jones, then aged 42 (b 1573), was known rather for his revolutionary stage settings, but he proved equally inventive in his design for the Queen's House. Based on the principles of the Italian architect, **Palladio** (1508-80), it is a compact and well proportioned house despite its "bridge room" over the road. Work stopped on Anne's death and was resumed only when **Charles I** offered the house to his queen, **Henrietta Maria**, whose name and the date (1635) appear on the north front; her initials are also inscribed over the fireplace in the queen's presence chamber, so "furnished, that it far surpassed all other of that kind in England."

During the Commonwealth the Tudor palace was despoiled, cleared for use as a barracks and prison while its collections were sold. At the Restoration, the Queen's House alone emerged relatively unscathed, allowing Henrietta Maria to return there to live from time to time until her death in 1669 (in France). Charles II meanwhile, disliked the derelict palace, finding the Queen's House too small for his court: in 1665 he commissioned a King's House to be built by **John Webb**, a student of Inigo Jones. This resulted in what is now known as the King Charles Block of the Old Royal Naval College, endowed with groups of four giant pilasters at either end and at the centre where they are crowned by

Directory

Pubs

Cutty Sark Tavern – *4-6 Ballast Quay, Lassell St, SE10 9PD* – ⊖ *Greenwich* – ☎ *020 8858 3146* – *Open Mon-Sat 11am-11pm, Sun noon-10.30pm.* The Union Tavern, built in 1804, was an important meeting place for fishermen. It was renamed the Cutty Sark Tavern in memory of the famous clipper moored at Greenwich. A truly charming, picturesque pub with great views of the Thames from the Georgian panelled interior and the terrace.

Plume of Feathers – *19 Park Vista, SE10 9LZ* – ⊖ *Greenwich, Island Gardens* – ☎ *020 8858 1661* – *Open 11am-11pm, Sun noon-10.30pm.* An old fashioned pub.

The Yacht – *5 Crane St, SE10 9NP* – ⊖ *Greenwich, Island Gardens* – ☎ *020 8858 0175* – *Open 11am-11pm, Sun noon-10.30pm.* A quaint traditional pub serving bar food.

Trafalgar Tavern – *Park Row, SE10 9NW* – ⊖ *Greenwich, Island Gardens* – ☎ *020 8858 2437* – *www.trafalgartavern.co.uk* – *Open Mon-Sat 11.30am-11pm, Sun noon-10.30pm.* Since the middle of the 19C the Trafalgar has overlooked the Thames from its location next to Greenwich Palace. Dickens himself immortalised this pub in his novel "Our Mutual Friend". The interior is disappointing – the decor lacks warmth and the atmosphere is quite subdued except when there is jazz at the weekend.

a pediment. With the exception of the Observatory, however, all construction had to cease for lack of funds long before Charles' "pretty palace" was complete.

Royal Hospital to Royal Naval College – Work at Greenwich was resumed in 1694 when **William** and **Mary**, who preferred Hampton Court as a royal residence, granted a charter for a Royal Hospital for Seamen at Greenwich founded on the lines of the Royal Military Hospital in Chelsea, appointing **Christoper Wren** as Surveyor of Works. Wren, as usual, submitted numerous plans before proposing the one we know today: at Queen Mary's insistence this incorporated the Queen's House and its 150ft/46m wide river vista (acquired only when the Tudor palace was demolished), the King Charles Block alongside the construction of three additional symmetrical blocks, the King William (SW), Queen Mary (SE) and Queen Anne (NE, below which exists a crypt, sole remnant of the Tudor palace; *closed to the public*). To complete the scheme emphasis was focused by projecting cupolas before the refectory and chapel and the course of the Thames was modified and embanked – the only major vista design by Wren to be properly realised. The project took more than half a century to complete and involved **Vanbrugh**, **Hawksmoor**, **Colen Campbell**, Ripley, "Athenian" Stuart... **John Evelyn** recorded in his diary that on 30 June 1696 he "laid the first stone of the intended foundation at five o'clock in the evening... Mr Flamsteed the King's Astronomer Professor observing the punctual time by instruments." By June 1704 he observed that the hospital had begun "to take in wounded and worn out seamen... the buildings now going on are very magnificent", but as treasurer he also noted that by 1703 the cost already amounted to £89 364 14s 8d (the list of donors in the entrance to the Painted Hall shows that the King gave £6 000, the Queen £1 000, Evelyn £2 000).

Old Royal Naval College and Queen's House, Greenwich

In 1873 when the buildings were transformed into the Royal Naval College, a centre of scientific instruction, steam and steel had just replaced wood and sail. In 1998 the naval university moved out and most of the premises have now been taken over by the University of Greenwich.

The Queen's House, extended by colonnades and two wings in 1807, first accommodated the Royal Hospital School before becoming part of the National Maritime Museum (1937).

Walking About

EAST OF THE MUSEUM 1

Start at Greenwich Pier and walk east along the river past The Old Naval College (description in Worth a Visit) and proceed to Park Row.

Riverside Downstream

The area has preserved its historic heritage.

The **Trafalgar Tavern** *(see Directory)* of 1837 recollects the personalities and events of Nelson's time. It overlooks the river from cast-iron balconies resembling the galleries of a man o'war. In the early 19C the tavern was the setting for the Liberal ministers' '**whitebait dinners**' *(see Outer London, Blackwall)*. **Dickens** used to meet there with Thackeray and Cruikshank. Also overlooking the river and backing onto the old and narrow Crane Street, is **The Yacht** *(see Directory)* which is at least a century older.

The **Trinity Hospital** (f1613) is a small white, gabled and crenellated charity building. **Ballast Quay** is a terrace of neat 17C early Georgian houses (note the 1695 Morden estate marks).

The **Cutty Sark Tavern** was rebuilt with a great bow window in 1804 on the site of earlier inns *(see Directory)*, while at the end stands the four-square Harbourmaster's Office *(no 21)* which for 50 years, until the 1890s, controlled colliers entering the Pool of London.

For Thames Barrier see Outer London: WOOLWICH - CHARLTON.

Walk back and turn left into Maze Hill.

Vanbrugh Castle

The castle, a caricature of a medieval fortress with Gothic towers, turrets, high walls, crenellations and all, stands at the top of Maze Hill. It was built and lived in by the architect and playwright, Sir John Vanbrugh, himself, from 1717-26 while he was Surveyor to Greenwich Hospital.

Cross into the park, then return downhill to Park Vista.

Millennium Dome

Riverside walks, parkland and lakes to attract wildlife have transformed the Greenwich peninsula where the site of a former gas works has been extensively redeveloped to include roads, housing, stores and other amenities for the local population. However, the focal point of the regenerated area is the Millennium Dome, a vast domed structure with a spectacular glass-fibre roof designed by Lord Richard Rogers, built to mark the third millennium. Owing to the lack of success of the Millennium Experience exhibition, the Dome has aroused much controversy and its future use is still uncertain.

A. Taverner/MICHELIN

In the park west of the castle, beyond the Roman Villa and Great Cross Avenue are a **flower garden**, in front of ancient cedars of Lebanon, a pond with wild fowl and a Wilderness with a small herd of fallow deer.

In Park Vista are the early-18C plain two-storey **Manor House (no 13)**, the **Vicarage (no 33)**, a rambling 18C house incorporating Tudor fragments, and the 18C public house, the Plume of Feathers.

Greenwich Park

The Old Royal Observatory and the Planetarium are described in Worth a Visit.

Greenwich Park, palisaded in 1433 and surrounded by a wall in Stuart times, is the oldest enclosed royal domain. It extends for 180 acres/73ha in a great sweep of chestnut avenues and grass to a point 155ft above the river crowned by the Royal Observatory and the **General Wolfe** monument. On the slope below the Observatory there are traces of the giant grass steps designed by Le Nôtre in 1662.

SOUTH OF THE MUSEUM 2

Greenwich Pier

A rounded pavilion, echoed by another on the north bank of the Thames, provides access to the **foot tunnel** to the Isle of Dogs *(10min)*.

Cutty Sark★★ – (♿) *Open daily, 10am-5pm. Closed 24-26 Dec. £3.95. Leaflet (22 languages); guide book (3 languages). ☎ 020 8858 3445; Fax 020 8853 3589; info@cuttysark.org.uk; www.cuttysark.org.uk*

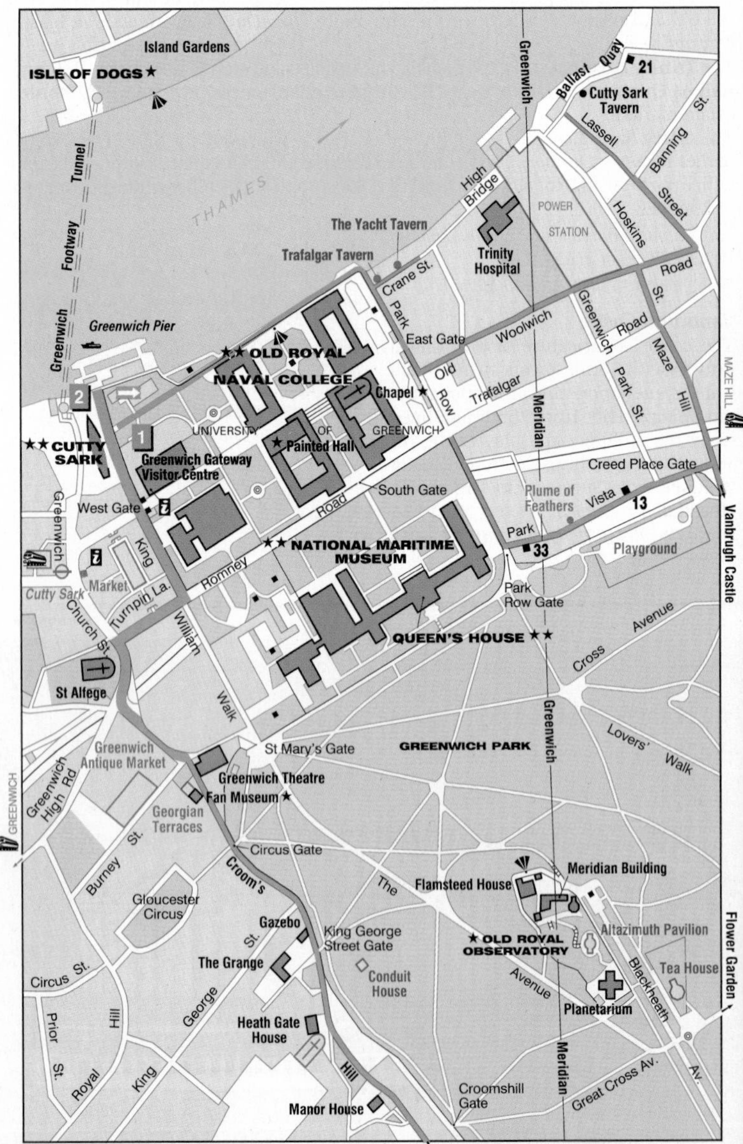

Launched at Dumbarton in 1869 for the China tea trade, the *Cutty Sark* became famous as the fastest clipper afloat: her best day's run with all 32 000 sq ft/2 975sq m or ? acre/0.2ha of canvas fully spread was 363mi/584km. In her heyday she brought tea from China and later wool from Australia, chasing before the wind like the cutty sark or short chemise of the witch Nannie, "a winsome wench" in Robert Burns' poem *Tam O'Shanter*, hence the boat's distinctive figurehead. In 1922 she was converted into a nautical training school and transferred to dry dock at Greenwich in 1954. In her hold are papers, charts, mementoes and models, illustrating the history of the clipper trade *(see also BANKSIDE – SOUTHWARK – Bramah Museum of Tea and Coffee)* and her own story in particular. In the lower hold is a lively collection of boldly coloured 19C figureheads.

Continue down King William Walk, turn right into Romney Rd passing near the market to Church St.

A Famous Name

Cutty Sark is also the name of a pale, most delicate blend of Scotch whisky branded by **Berry Bros & Rudd** of St James's. The name was suggested by the clipper which had just returned to British waters having traded under the Portuguese flag: the whisky meanwhile, was especially blended for the export market – destined for America and supplied throughout Prohibition (1920-33) via Nassau in the Bahamas; 'the real McCoy', a certain Captain William McCoy, was one such boot-legger there. Today the Cutty Sark Tall Ships' Race organised annually by the Sail Training Association is sponsored by the wine and spirit merchants.

J. Malburet/MICHELIN

Cutty Sark – the fastest tea-clipper of her time

St Alfege Church

Open Mon-Sat, noon (Sun 1pm) to 4pm. Leaflet (22 languages). Lunchtime recitals: Thu at 1pm.

The somewhat gaunt church (1718) with an elegant Doric portico is by **Nicholas Hawksmoor**, the superimposed tower by John James. Inside there are no pillars, although the span measures 65ft/20m by 90ft/27.5m. The murals *(east end)* are by Thornhill and the carving by **Grinling Gibbons**.

On the site where Alfege, Archbishop of Canterbury, suffered martyrdom at the hands of Danish invaders in 1012, churches were erected which witnessed **Henry VII** and his queen at worship, the baptism of **Henry VIII**, heard the father of English church music **Thomas Tallis** playing the organ for 40 years (console in SW corner) and saw his burial and also that of **General Wolfe**, parishioner and Commander of the British Army at the capture of Quebec (d 1759). Two other parishioners were Lavinia Fenton, the original Polly Peachum in *The Beggar's Opera* and **John Julius Angerstein**. The registers which date back to 1615, vividly portray the large families, child mortality, the decimation of plague years, and contrasting but usual, people's longevity.

Croom's Hill

The winding lane was already an established local thoroughfare in the 15C, when the park was enclosed, and thus became its natural western boundary.

At the bottom of Croom's Hill, on the corner, is the **Greenwich Theatre**, built in 1968 in the shell of a Victorian music hall.

The Georgian terrace *(nos 6-12)* dates from 1721-23. The Poet Laureate, C Day Lewis lived at no 6 from 1968 to 1972.

Continue past the Fan Museum (description in Worth a Visit).

Gloucester Circus *(side turning)*, designed by Michael Searle in the 1700s, has retained some of the original houses on the east and south sides.

The Grange, an early-17C building with 18C additions, stands on a site recorded as having been given to Ghent Abbey in 818 by a daughter of Alfred the Great; overlooking the road and the park is a small square **gazebo** (1672) with a pyramid roof and carved plaster ceiling.

On the east side is a row *(nos 3-11)* of modest 17C tenements, weatherboarded at the rear.

Heath Gate House is a relatively low brick mansion with large gabled dormers and pilasters on brackets supporting the upper floor. The house (1630s) is a rare example of so early a domestic building with its exterior unaltered.

The **Manor House**, two storeys of red brick, is typical of 1697, even to the hooded porch with a finely carved shell motif.

Macartney House *(private flats)*, a large rambling building of mellow brick and stone, with a roof balustrade and tall rounded windows overlooking its own garden and Ranger's House, was built by Andrew Snape, Serjeant Farrier to Charles II and, according to Evelyn, "a man full of projects", who in 1674 filched the land from the royal domain.

Croom's Hill leads to Ranger's House (description in Worth a Visit) and Blackheath.

Worth a Visit

National Maritime Museum**

Tour: 2hr. ♿ Open daily, 10am-5pm (6pm summer); 31 Dec, 1 Jan, 13 Apr, restricted hours. Closed 24-26 Dec. Licensed café- restaurant. Play area. ☎ 020 8312 6565 (24hr recorded information); 020 8858 4422 (administration); www.nmm.ac.uk

The fabulous historical collection of things maritime (fine art, precious prizes, rare instruments, treasures and mementoes) is proudly displayed by this large and beautifully organised museum. After the redevelopment of Neptune Court with a large free-span glass roof, 16 new galleries have been created.

The development of Britain's might as a sea power is traced from Henry VIII's early Tudor fleet through voyages of discovery (**Captain Cook**'s travels in the South Seas and Pacific Islands, Sir John Franklin's Polar exploration) to 20C naval warfare in the Falklands and in the Gulf. Attention is also focused on the impact of modern life (travel, cargoes, pollution) on the sea.

A yacht, a 1930s speedboat, a gilded barge, a figurehead set the scene at the entrance. The theme of **Explorers** is the quest of early navigators and the exploits of intrepid men in search of new frontiers. The depths of the sea, the polar regions and space provide further challenges. Migration, tourism and transport of goods and mail brought about the age of cruise liners presented in **Passengers**. **Cargoes** examines the profound effect of sea transport, a cheap and efficient way of moving energy products, raw materials and finished goods round the world (container ships, oil tankers), on industrial activity and trade patterns. The style of uniforms and functional outfits (diving and survival suits) is dictated by climate and rank as illustrated in **Rank and Style**. Oceans influence climate and help to sustain life on earth. **Planet Ocean** (opening 2002) focuses on environmental change, biodiversity and sustainable development, and exhibits range from oceanographical, meteorological and navigation instruments to deep-sea exploration equipment.

Attractions for Children

All Hands Gallery: interactive exhibits on diving, propulsion, signalling etc, model of 74-gun ship.
The Bridge: ingenious solutions to navigation problems.
Ship of War: exquisite models of warships.
It is best to visit the Royal Observatory at the top of the hill first.

Maritime London has held a prominent place in Britain's economic and social development: financing of trading ventures, chartering and insurance of ships and cargoes, setting up of Lloyd's, the Bank of England, the Stock Exchange and commodity exchanges. The city grew with the thriving docks, warehouses and related industries. Modern issues include safety standards at sea. The British Empire spread to the four corners of the world; the complex story of balances of power and cultural influences unfolds in **Trade and Empire**: slave trade, opium wars, American independence, transportation of convicts, reverse emigration from Asia and the Caribbean. Maritime rivalry between France and Britain in 18C-19C, world conflicts and nuclear-powered vessels and missiles are the themes of **Sea Power**. Banks of video monitors illustrate the conditions on modern ships; screens show how pilots use computerised navigation information picked up from automated lighthouses and buoys.

Horatio **Nelson**'s military campaigns during the French Revolutionary wars, battles with Napoleon are illustrated with contemporary paintings, portraits, uniforms, logs, guns, maps and navigational instruments, models and a large collection of decorated china memorabilia. Personal artefacts include his bullet-pierced uniform worn at Trafalgar, his cabin furniture and items from his house at Merton.

There are also presentations on the story of the water cycle, the fragile ecology and the future of the sea, and exhibitions of paintings and photographs.

In the gardens at the rear are a **Dolphin Sundial** and the mast of the **Great Britain** (1863).

Queen's House** – ♿ *Open daily, 10am-5pm (6pm summer); 31 Dec, 1 Jan, 13 Apr, restricted hours. Closed 24-26 Dec. ☎ 020 8312 6565 (24hr recorded information); 020 8858 4422 (admin); bookings@nmm.ac.uk; www.nmm.ac.uk*

This elegant white Palladian villa (1616), the first Classical building in England, was designed by **Inigo Jones** *(see above)*. Distinctive features included its colour, the beautiful horseshoe-shaped staircase descending from the terrace on the north front and the loggia on the south front facing the park.

The ground floor rooms illustrate the architecture of the house, famous associations and its historical importance in the context of Greenwich. On the first floor are displayed naval portaits and paintings from the museum's collections.

Royal Observatory Greenwich★ – *Tour 45min. (♿) Open daily, 10am-5pm (6pm summer); 31 Dec, 1 Jan, 13 Apr, restricted hours. Closed 24-26 Dec. Leaflet (6 languages). Café and restaurant. ☎ 020 8312 6565 (24hr recorded information), 020 8858 4422 (admin); astroline@nmm.ac.uk (astronomy enquiries); www.rog.nmm.ac.uk*

In 1675 **Charles II** directed **Sir Christopher Wren** to "build a small observatory within our park at Greenwich, upon the highest ground, at or near the place where the castle stood" for "the finding out of the longitude of places for perfecting navigation and astronomy". Wren, who was a former astronomer as well as an architect, designed a house of red brick with stone dressing, an upper balustrade and miniature canted cupolas "for the Observator's habitation and a little for pompe"; it is named Flamsteed House after John Flamsteed the first Astronomer Royal, appointed in 1675.

The **Meridian Building**, a mid-18C addition of the same brick, was built to house the observatory's growing **collection★★** of instruments.

At the main gate are clocks showing world time, the 24-hour clock and **British Standard Measures**. The **tour** begins in the Meridian courtyard where visitors may record the exact time at which they stand on the Greenwich Meridian, the brass meridian of zero longitude linked in a straight line to the north and south poles.

On the south face of Flamsteed House are sundials. The red time ball on the roof was erected in 1833 to serve as a time check for navigation on the Thames; the ball rises to the top of the mast and drops at exactly 13 00 hours GMT.

A PIONEERING CLOCKMAKER

John Harrison (1693-1776) was born the son of a carpenter; little otherwise is known of his early life until 1713 when he completed his first pendulum clock made entirely of wood: oak for the wheels and box for the axles (Worshipful Company of Clockmakers Museum – *see CITY – Guildhall)*.

In 1722 Harrison installed a unique clock at Brocklesby Park made from lignum vitae, a tropical hardwood; this continues to keep accurate "mean" time today. His next important invention was the bi-metallic gridiron-grasshopper pendulum (1725-27); the grasshopper mechanism provided a friction-free means of clocking the units of time.

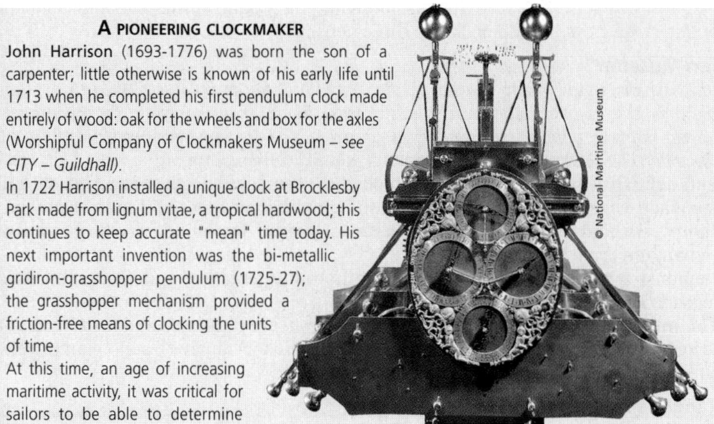

J Harrison's Marine Timekeeper No 1

At this time, an age of increasing maritime activity, it was critical for sailors to be able to determine longitude in order to chart the oceans that divided land masses accurately. In 1730 Harrison journeyed to London with drawings and calculations for a reliable clock that would be seaworthy: pendulum-less, resistant to corrosion or rust and resilient to extremes in weather. There he met the astronomer Dr Edmund Halley. Harrison's No 1 (H-1) was tried on a journey to Lisbon in 1737, the clock proved itself accurate and the Board of Longitude convened for the first time. Described by **Hogarth** in his *Analysis of Beauty* as "one of the most exquisite movements ever made" (1753) H-1 equipped the English with the technology to begin their colonisation of the high seas.

Within **Flamsteed House** the first rooms trace the foundation and purpose of the Observatory, the various interpretations of the stars invented by early civilisations and the evolution of man's understanding of the heavens. Some of the usual small 17C rooms are furnished as they were in Flamsteed's day. The lofty and beautifully proportioned **Octagon Room** has been restored to its original 17C appearance, when, according to John Evelyn, it was equipped "with the choicest instrument."

The other displays trace the discovery of latitude and longitude: Parliament's prize (£20 000) offered to anyone who might invent a reliable way of charting a ship's position at sea; its award in 1773 to John Harrison for the H-1; the early practice of map and chart makers who fixed the zero meridian where they chose (Greenwich, Paris, the Fortunate Islands); the gradual adoption of the British reading with the inauguration in 1767 of the annual publication, *The Nautical Almanack*, which in combination with the marine chronometer and sextant enabled navigators to find longitude in relation to the Greenwich meridian; the standardisation of the meridian in 1884 at the Meridian Conference in Washington. The development of the railways and the telegraph had produced anomalies and even legal disputes: the time lag between London and Plymouth was 16 minutes. The six-pip time signal was introduced in 1924.

The **Meridian Building** contains the **Quadrant Room**, the Airy Transit Circle through which the meridian passes *(video)*, a collection of **telescopes** of all sizes and the Telescope Dome which contains Britain's largest (28in/50cm) refracting telescope *(video of the moon landing)*.

A variety of lectures on the moon and stars are given *(up 42 steps)* in the **Planetarium** at different times.

Old Royal Naval College★★

Painted Hall and Chapel and Greenwich Gateway Visitor Centre: Open daily, 10am (Sun 12.30pm) to 5pm. ☎ 020 8269 4791; Fax 020 8269 4757; info@greenwichfoundation.org.uk; www.greenwichfoundation.org.uk

The college now accommodates the campus of the University of Greenwich. The King Charles block is now occupied by the Trinity College of Music and buildings overlooking the Thames house the offices of the Greenwich Maritime Institute. The former Dreadnought Hospital designed in 1764 by **James "Athenian" Stuart**, has been restored as the university library.

Painted Hall★ – Wren's domed refectory designed as a pair with the chapel, was completed in 1703. In 1805 it was the setting for Nelson's lying in state before his burial in St Paul's. The hall and upper hall were painted in exuberant Baroque by Sir **James Thornhill**: William and Mary, Anne, George I and his descendants celebrate Britain's maritime power in a wealth of involved allegory. The artist portrayed the current monarch as he worked through each new reign (1708-27) and was paid £3 a sq yd for the ceilings, £1 for the walls.

Chapel★ – Wren's chapel was redecorated after a fire in 1779 by "Athenian" Stuart and William Newton in Wedgwood pastel colours. Delicate Rococo swags and panelled rosettes cover the upper walls and ceiling; corbels and beams are masked by a lacework of stucco. Set up across the apse is *St Paul after the Shipwreck at Malta* by Benjamin West (1738-1820) who also designed the **Coade stone** medallions for the pulpit made from the top deck of a three-decker.

Fan Museum★

10-12 Croom's Hill. Open Tue-Sun, 11am (noon Sun) to 5pm. Closed 24-26 Dec, 1 Jan. £3.50 (no charge for senior citizens Tue after 2pm). Fan-making workshop: by appointment 1st Sat in every month. Audio guide. Brochure. Leaflet (2 languages). ☎ 020 8305 1441; Fax 020 8293 1889; www.fan-museum.org; admin@fan-museum.org

This delightful museum owns some 2 000 fans. Permanent displays explain how fans are made, the different materials used and the different types and sources of fans. Temporary shows are organised by theme – children, feathered fans, flowered fans – changing three times a year.

Demonstrations on fan-making, construction, conservation and restoration take place in the craft workshop.

The museum occupies two Georgian terrace houses (1721), scrupulously restored; the garden is laid out with a fan-shaped terrace, a pool, Japanese style planting and a reproduction of a Georgian orangery.

Ranger's House★

Chesterfield Walk, West Parkside. (EH) (♿) Open Jun-Oct, Wed-Sun and Bank Hols, 10am-6pm (5pm Oct; 4pm Nov to late-Dec and early to late-Mar). £4.50. Audiotour. Parking. ☎ 020 8853 0035; www.english-heritage.org.uk

The mansion was originally a small brick villa with a stone balustrade lining the roof and steps leading up to an elegant stone frontispiece decorated with a mask. Rounded wings in pale yellow brick were added during the house's ownership by Philip, 4th Earl of Chesterfield (1694-1733), politician, diplomat and wit. The resultant south gallery, 75ft/23m in length with a compartmented ceiling and three fine bow windows commands, its satisfied owner declared, 'three different, and the finest prospects in the world'; the gardens are still as beautiful.

The panelled rooms on the ground and first floor provide a splendid setting for the outstanding **Wernher Collection** of European Art, which reflects the eclectic taste of Sir Julius Wernher (1850-1912), a mining magnate and philanthropist, who was instrumental in the founding of Imperial College *(see KENSINGTON)*. His London home, Bath House in Piccadilly, was demolished in 1960 and he had a large country house, Luton Hoo, in Bedfordshire.

The collection includes rare early religious paintings (Filippo Lippi, Hans Memling) and paintings by Dutch painters (Metsu, Van Ostade, de Hooch), exquisite Renaissance jewellery, precious medieval ivories, Renaissance bronzes, and wrought silverware. Also on view are Maiolica ceramics, Limoges enamel plates, Sèvres porcelain and Meissen pottery figures as well as fine French furniture, tapestries and portraits by the British artists, Sir Joshua Reynolds, George Romney among others.

Environs

BLACKHEATH★

Overground: Blackheath from Cannon Street or London Bridge

The heath has always been an open space bisected by major roads; the course of the Roman Watling Street between the south coast and London is marked by Blackheath Road, Blackheath Hill and Shooters' Hill, which were notorious for highwaymen in the 18C.

Rebel forces have used the heath as a rallying ground: **Wat Tyler** (1381), the Kentishmen under **Jack Cade** (1450), the Cornishmen under Audley (1497). In more joyful mood, in 1415 the people greeted **Henry V** on his victorious return from Agincourt; in 1660 **Charles II** was welcomed by the Restoration Army and in 1608, so it is said, while in residence at Greenwich, **James I** taught the English to play golf on Blackheath. Today, it provides an ideal site for a traditional fairground during Bank Holiday weekends.

Morden College, St German's Place

The college *(closed to the public)*, founded as a "refuge for discrete merchants" who had fallen on hard times, stands in an 18C landscaped park. The attractive, low, two-storey building in mellow brick with stone dressings, was designed by **Sir Christopher Wren** in 1695. The figures of the founder, Sir John Morden, a city merchant, and his wife, stand in a double niche above the central stone gateway which leads to an inner quadrangle.

The heath is ringed by stately **terraces** and **houses★** mostly built of brick relieved by dressings of stone or of sparkling white painted stucco. They date in the main from the 18C and early 19C when merchants, newly rich from the expanding docks, began to build in the vicinity.

On the south side stands All Saints Church, a neo-Gothic oddity by Furley, built of Kentish ragstone, with the tower unusually placed on the south side.

Overlooking the heath from the **south side** is an almost unbroken line of buildings: **Colonnade House** *(South Row)* is a large early-19C house with a Tuscan portico extending the full width of the front; **The Paragon**, a late-18C shallow crescent by Michael Searles, consists of 14 semi-detached brick villas linked by Tuscan colonnades; Lindsey House *(Lloyds Place)* is in brick with white trims; Grotes' Buildings is a mid-18C terrace; Heathfield House, a stucco building, with a Tuscan-columned, paired bow window, dates from the early 19C.

On the **west side** in Dartmouth Row are the early-18C Spencer House and Perceval House with 11 bays, several Georgian houses and a few of the original houses (1680-90).

Blackheath Village – The main street and Tranquil Vale, which despite its name is full of noisy traffic, lead off the heath southwards to modern estates by Span and other architects.

DEPTFORD

Overground: Deptford from London Bridge

The riverside village expanded during the reign of **Henry VIII** as a shipbuilding yard; later several Deptford-built vessels numbered among the fleet which defeated the Armada (1588). It was in Deptford Creek that **Queen Elizabeth** boarded the ***Golden Hinde*** in 1581 to dub **Francis Drake** knight for his circumnavigation of the globe and where Christopher **Marlowe** was stabbed to death in a tavern brawl (1593). In the 17C the diarist John **Evelyn** lived at Sayes Court where he cultivated a fine garden and which briefly, in 1698, and to his regret since the Russian was a bad tenant, he leased to **Peter the Great** while the latter learnt the art of shipbuilding in the yards. The dockyard closed in 1869.

St Paul's Church

East of Deptford High Street. Closed until 2004. ☎ 020 8692 0989 (Rectory)

Thomas Archer's church (1712-30) has a lofty semicircular stone portico supporting an impressive steeple; inside, great columns with gilded Corinthian capitals uphold a richly sculpted plaster ceiling above an extensive gallery. Nearby, in Albury Street, some 18C houses with elaborately carved doorcases have been preserved.

St Nicholas' Church

Corner of Deptford Green and Stowage Lane. Open Mon-Fri, 9.15am-2pm; Sat-Sun, by arrangement with vicar. Guided tour by appointment (☎ 020 7639 4048 Don Price). ☎ 020 8692 2749 (Vicar); wgcorneck@tesco.net

St Nicholas' stands on a site occupied by Deptford parish churches since Saxon times. Of particular interest in the post-war reconstructed interior are the extended reredos by the church's 17C parishioner **Grinling Gibbons** *(see INSIGHTS AND IMAGES – The Changing Face of London, Sculpture)*, with swags of leaves, flowers and fruit, a peapod, the ciphers and coat of arms of William and Mary. There is also a weird carved relief, an early work by Grinling Gibbons, known as the *Valley of Dry Bones*. The Jacobean pulpit is supported on a cherub believed to have been a ship's figurehead.

The laurel-wreathed skulls on the gateposts were originally above crossed bones, and since so many privateers sailed from Deptford, it is claimed that the carvings inspired the traditional skull and crossbones flag. More honourably, the church so long associated with **Sir Francis Drake** and his descendants, and steeped in naval history, has the privilege of flying the White Ensign. It is here that **Christopher Marlowe** lies buried "slaine by Francis Frezer, the 1 June 1593" (tablet on west wall).

Hampstead★★ – Highgate

High up on a hill is the picturesque village of Hampstead with its maze of alleyways and passages, its smart shops and a plethora of bars and restaurants frequented by affluent residents. However its glory lies in the rolling woodland and meadows of the Heath enjoyed by walkers for its rural aspect; swimming in the ponds is a favourite recreation of the locals. Concerts and funfairs are seasonal features.
Highgate which is also full of character has some fine houses and pubs.

Location

Map pp 284-285 (TUX). *⊖ Hampstead.* Hampstead lies to the north of Regent's Park and Highgate is slightly to the north-east.

Background

Hampstead Village developed from a rural area with a few substantial houses, manors and farms into a fashionable 18C spa when the chalybeate springs were discovered in what became Well Walk. It was 4mi/6.5km only from the centre of London and, by the time enthusiasm for taking the waters had subsided, builders had begun the erection of houses and terraces, which continues to this day. In 1907 came the Underground. Throughout its history this pleasant district has attracted writers, artists, architects, musicians, scientists.

The village, irregularly built on the side of a hill, has kept its original street pattern; main roads from the south and south-east meet and continue north; between is a network of lanes, groves, alleys, steps, courts, rises, places... At the foot of the hill lie Hampstead Ponds. On the north side of the Heath is Kenwood *(see separate listing)*.

Old Brewery Mews

Off Hampstead High Street on the east side, the former brewery building overlooking a well protected by a wrought-iron cage, has been converted into offices and a row of modern town houses.

Directory

Light Bite

Coffee Cup – *74 High St, Hampstead, NW3 1QX – ⊖ Hampstead – ☎ 020 7435 7565 – ⊭ – £2.50/8.50.* Recognisable by its red and white canopy, the Coffee Cup makes the ideal pit stop. Inside it's all wood panelling and red leather but the outside seats provide people watchers with a good vantage point.

Pubs

Bar Room Bar – *48 Rosslyn Hill, Hampstead, NW3 1NH – ⊖ Hampstead – ☎ 020 7435 0808 – www.brbhampstead@spiritsgroup.com – Open daily noon-11pm (10.30pm Sun).* This bright pub often exhibits (and sells) paintings by young artists and operates as a peaceful café by day. Three evenings a week, a DJ livens the atmosphere. Beautiful terrace at the rear and pizzas cooked in a wood oven.

Bull and Bush – *North End Rd, Hampstead, NW3 7HE – ⊖ Hampstead – ☎ 020 8905 5456 – Open daily noon-11pm (10.30pm Sun).* A 1920s building with a modern inn sign and turn of the 19C/20C paintings of Florrie Forde.

Gate House – *1 North Rd, Highgate, N6 4AA – ⊖ Highgate, Archway – ☎ 020 8340 8054 – Open Mon-Sat 10am-11pm, Sun noon-10.30pm.* A busy pub with elaborate decor and historic associations.

Spaniard's Inn – *Spaniards Rd, NW3 7JJ – ⊖ Hampstead – ☎ 020 8731 6571 – Open Mon-Sat 11.00am-11pm, Sun noon-10.30pm.* Historic tavern founded in 1585. In 1780, when Gordon's wild anti-papal rioters were heading for Lord Mansfield's residence to ransack it, they stopped at the inn to ask the way. The landlord plied them with drinks and held them up until the militia were able to arrive or so the story goes. Worth a trip out in summer. Take time to read the display of humorous sayings such as: "When a woman marries, she loses the attention of all men and gains the inattention of one".

The Flask – *14 Flask Walk, Hampstead, NW3 1HE – ⊖ Highgate, Archway – ☎ 020 7435 4580 – Open Mon-Sat 11am-11pm, Sun noon-10.30pm.* A quaint pub with a roaring fire in winter, where Karl Marx was a frequent visitor.

Ye Olde White Bear – *Well Rd, Hampstead, NW3 1LJ – ⊖ Hampstead – ☎ 020 7435 3758 – Open Mon-Sat 11.00am-11pm, Sun noon-10.30pm.* In a picturesque area of Hampstead, this old pub has been carefully preserved. Comfortable club atmosphere with wooden floorboards and wooden and panelling in the two bars. Quiz every Thursday evening.

Walking About

HAMPSTEAD VILLAGE – WEST SIDE 1

Flask Walk, which begins as a pedestrian street with a Victorian pub and tea merchant, continues east past Gardnor House, built in 1736, with a full height rounded bow window at the rear, to New End Square.

It was at **no 40** Well Walk that **John Constable** lived from 1826 to his death in 1834.

HAMPSTEAD RESIDENTS – OLD AND YOUNG

In the cemetery lie Kate Greenaway, the illustrator of children's books, and Laszlo Biro, the inventor of the ball-point pen. Temporary residents of the neighbourhood have included John Constable, John Keats, Ian Fleming, Agatha Christie, Sid Vicious, Sting, Boy George, Elizabeth Taylor, Tom Conti, Emma Thompson, Rex Harrison, Peter O'Toole, Jeremy Irons...

Christchurch Hill with its Georgian cottages leads to the mid-19C Church with a soaring spire visible for miles.

Downshire Hill going west to the foot of Hampstead High Street has some good Regency houses.

Walk back to the top of Fitzjohn's Ave.

One flank of **Church Row** is lined by a fine 1720 terrace of brown brick houses with red dressings, tall windows, straight hoods on carved brackets shading the Georgian doors. The range along the north pavement, older, younger and more varied, includes cottages, a weatherboarded house with oversailing bay, full style town houses of 3 storeys with good ironwork...

The Parish Church of **St John** at the row's end, obscured in summer by the trees, was built boldly on an ancient site in 1744-47 with a spire rising from a battlemented brick tower, banded in stone. The interior, with giant pillars supporting arches in the tunnel roof, galleries on three sides and box pews, was twice enlarged in the 19C to accommodate Hampstead's rapidly growing population: 4 300 in 1801, 47 000 in 1881.

Make a short detour to Frognal via Frognal Way.

Frognal

The district to the west, once a manor, hence all the roads of similar name, presents some distinctive buildings: University College School, large and neo-Georgian with Edward VII in full regalia standing above the entrance door; **Kate Greenaway**'s house (no **39**) designed in 1885 by **Norman Shaw** in true children's story book appearance with rambling gables and balconies; and the Sun House *(no **9** Frognal Way)* by **Maxwell Fry** at his 1935 best, in stepped horizontals in glass and gleaming white.

Retrace your steps and turn into Holly Walk.

Holly Walk

The path north from the church, bordered by the 1810 cemetery extension crowded with funeral monuments, rises to the green- and pink-washed, three-storey houses of Prospect Place (1814) and delightful cottages of Benham's Place (1813).

Holly Place, 1816, is another short terrace flanking **St Mary's**, one of the earliest RC churches to be built in London, founded by Abbé Morel, refugee from the French Revolution who came to Hampstead in 1796. From the top of the hill a maze of steps and alleys leads down to Heath Street.

Mount Vernon Junction

The triangular junction of Windmill Hill, Hampstead Grove and Holly Bush Hill, weighed down by the late-19C National Institute for Medical Research, is redeemed by **Romney's House** (plaque), picturesquely built of brick and weatherboarding in 1797, and a tall 18C group: Volta, Bolton, Enfield and Windmill Hill, all of brown brick.

Walk up Hampstead Grove Hill past Fenton House (description in Worth a Visit) and turn left.

Admiral's Walk

The road leads to Admiral's House, built in the first half of the 18C and given its nautical superstructure including, in his time, a couple of cannon with which to fire victory salutes, by the colourful Admiral Matthew Burton (1715-95) after whom the house, now resplendent in "tropical whites", is named. It was the home of **Sir George Gilbert Scott** from 1854 to 1864, who made no alteration. The adjoining Grove Lodge, also white, probably older, was **Galsworthy**'s home from 1918 until his death in 1933 where he wrote all but the first part of the *Forsyte Saga*. Lower Terrace, at the end of Admiral's Walk, is where **Constable** lived from 1821 to 1825 before moving to Well Walk.

Continue up Lower Terrace to Heath St and the Whitestone Pond.

Hampstead Heath

Hampstead Heath was the common of Hampstead Manor, an area where laundresses laid out washing to bleach in the 18C and, since earliest times, a popular place of recreation (vast one-day fairs; *Easter, Spring and Summer holiday Mondays*).

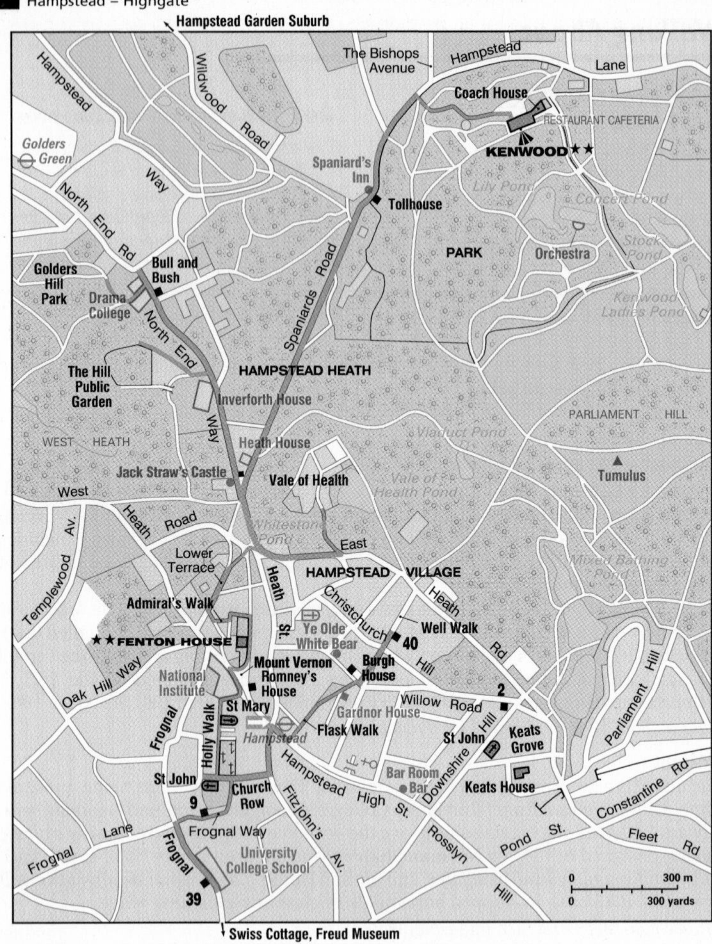

Whitestone Pond – The pond and the milestone ("Holborn Bars 4 1/2" in the bushes at the base of the aerial) from which it takes its name, are on London's highest ground (437ft/133m). The flagstaff is thought to stand on the site of an Armada beacon, the link with the signal south of the river on Shooter's Hill, Blackheath, visible on a clear day, and even more distinct at night. In the 18C and 19C, military and admiralty telegraphs stood on Telegraph Hill (west).

Jack Straw's Castle – It was first mentioned in local records in 1713. The name is thought to be derived from the possibility that supporters rallied on the spot before going to join Straw in Highbury and **Wat Tyler** in central London in the Peasants' Revolt of 1381. The weather-boarded building is now being redeveloped as part of a residential scheme.

Standing on its own at the junction of the two roads, Heath House, a plain early-18C mansion of brown brick, is chiefly remarkable for its commanding position and the visitors received by its 18C-19C owner, the Quaker abolitionist, **Samuel Hoare**: **William Wilberforce**, Elizabeth Fry and the leading politicians of the day.

Make a short detour down East Heath Rd.

Vale of Health – The Vale, a cluster of late-18C to early-19C cottages, mid-Victorian and now a few modern houses and blocks, built in a dip in the Heath and connected by a maze of narrow roads and paths, has at various times been the home of Leigh Hunt, the Harmsworth brothers, Rabindranath Tagore, DH Lawrence, Edgar Wallace, Compton Mackenzie. The origin of the Vale's name is said to derive from the fact that the area was unaffected by the plague in 1665; until 1677 it was a marsh; the houses began to be named from 1841.

Walk back and proceed to North End Way.

To the west of North End Way stands Inverforth House, rebuilt in 1914 and formerly an annexe to Manor House

Hampstead Garden Suburb

The suburb was conceived by **Dame Henrietta Barnett,** living in what is now Heath End House, as a scheme for rehousing London slum dwellers in the early 20C. Raymond Unwin, the principal architect, designed an irregular pattern of tree-lined streets and closes converging on a central square with its Institute and two churches (one Anglican and one Nonconformist) by Sir Edwin Lutyens. The houses are in varied architectural style. It is now an affluent area.

hospital; it is now a residential development. Lord Leverhulme's extensive newly restored pergola, sweet with wistaria, rambling roses, clematis and honeysuckle, now forms part of **The Hill Public Garden**, formally laid out on a steeply sloping site and framed by the natural beauty of the trees of the West Heath. Nearby on the northern edge of the West Heath lies **Golders Hill Park**, its landscaped lawns and shrubberies sweeping down to two ponds past bird and animal enclosures.

Bull and Bush – The pub *(see Directory)* reputedly stands on the site of a 17C farmhouse. In the 18C it became for a brief time **Hogarth** 's country retreat, then a tavern, patronised by the painters **Joshua Reynolds**, **Gainsborough**, **Constable**, **Romney**... Opposite is the gabled brick house (now a speech and drama college) where **Anna Pavlova** lived from 1921-31.

Continue along Spaniards Rd east of the pub.

Spaniards Inn and Tollhouse – The inn and tollhouse have slowed traffic on Spaniards Road into single file since they were built in the early 18C. The small brick tollhouse marks an entrance to the Bishop of London's Park; the white painted brick and weatherboard pub stands on the site of a house said to have been the residence of a 17C Spanish Ambassador. *See Directory.*

Kenwood is described in Worth a Visit.

HIGHGATE 2

⊖ *Archway; Highgate*

The area began to be developed in the 16C-17C when one or two decided it was the place to build their country seats; in the 17C rich merchants built mansions there; in the 18C the prosperous constructed their houses... Highgate remains a village in character, centred on Pond Square and the High Street.

SPAS

In the 18C a number of **London spas** developed round mineral springs where people could take the waters in rural surroundings. They were frequented by the less wealthy, who could not afford the elegance of Bath. Among the most popular were Hampstead and Islington and also Sadler's Wells, which offered dancing, pantomimes and rope dancing, accompanied by the consumption of cold meat and wine.

Start from the top of Highgate High St and take North Rd for a short distance.

The tree-lined **North Road** runs past the 19C red-brick buildings of Highgate School (f 1565) on the right and opposite a late Georgian terrace, nos 1-11, followed by individual houses of the same period *(nos 15, 17 plaque to AE Housman, 19)*, and at 47, 49 another early Georgian group. Beyond stand the clean-lined buildings. Highpoint One and Two, designed by **Lubetkin** and Tecton in 1936 and 1938; the first has two Erechtheon caryatids supporting the porch, one facing front, but the other (bored perhaps?) at the half turn!

Walk back and up Hampstead Lane and turn right into The Grove.

The Grove

This wide tree-planted road, branching off to the north, presents behind open railings late-17 to early-18C terrace housing at its satisfying best; rose brick in colour, of dignified height, with segment-headed windows and individual variations.

The poet and critic **ST Coleridge** lived at no 3 from 1823 till his death in 1834 and is buried in **St Michael's Church**, discernable by its tapering octagonal spire (1830) overlooking Highgate Cemetery.

The Flask (1721) on Highgate West Hill corner is a period country pub *(see Directory)*.

South Grove is lined with various houses: the early-18C Church House *(no 10)*, the Highgate Literary and Scientific Society *(no 11)* and Moreton House *(no 14)*, a brick mansion of 1715. The late-17C **Old Hall**, built in plain brick with a parapet, has a great bow window, topped by a pierced white balustrade at the back. **Bacon's Lane** honours the philosopher Francis Bacon, who was a frequent guest (and died) at Arundel House which used to be where Old Hall now stands.

Pond Square

Small houses and cottages line three sides of the irregularly shaped Pond Square – from which the ponds disappeared in the 1860s. On the south side **Rock House** *(no 6)* retains its overhanging wooden bay windows (18C).

Continue down the High St.

Highgate High Street

The **Gate House Tavern** *(see Directory)* stands on the site of a 1386 gate house to the Bishop of London's park (18C house at the rear); no 46, with a small-paned bay window, dates from 1729; no 23 opposite, Englefield House with straight-headed windows and modillion frieze, and nos 17, 19 and 21 are all early 18C.

AN ANCIENT LAND

Highgate Wood *(north of Archway and Muswell Hill junction)* comprises 70 acres/28ha and is classified an ancient woodland, a remnant of the larger Ancient Forest of Middlesex, mentioned in the **Domesday Book**. Archaeological surveys have revealed that potteries were active in the area around the time of the Roman conquest (AD 43). Between the 16C and 18C hornbeam would have been coppiced, while oak would have been grown to provide the Crown with timber for shipbuilding. In 1885, under threat of development, the wood was acquired by the Corporation of London. Today it is protected by an active conservation policy and equipped with children's recreation facilities.

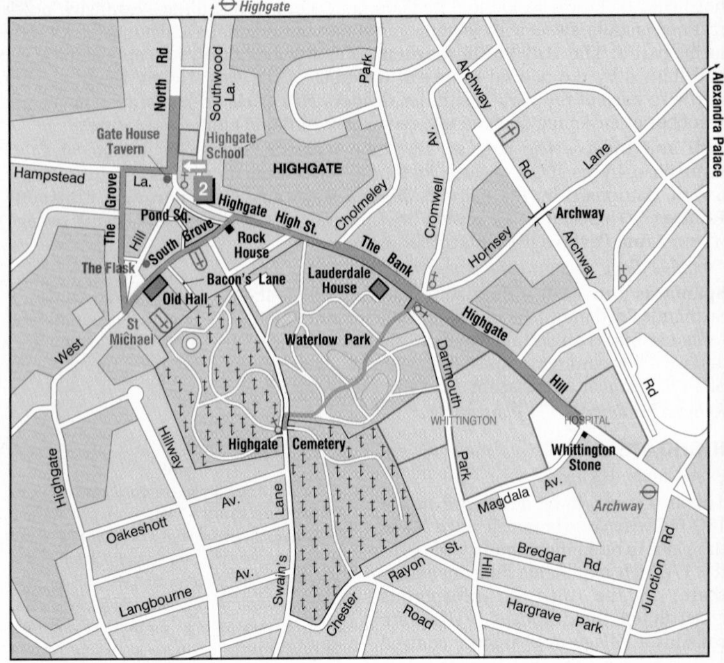

Highgate Hill

Just inside **Waterlow Park** stands **Lauderdale House**, 16C in origin but remodelled in the 18C in small country house style. This is the house about which the tale is told that in 1676, **Nell Gwynne**, not yet successful in obtaining titled recognition for her princely six-year-old son, dangled him out of a window in front of his father the king, threatening to drop him, whereupon Charles called out "Save the Earl of Burfor" (the future Duke of St Albans). It is now used as a cultural and educational centre.

Highgate Cemetery – *Swain's Lane. East cemetery: Open daily, 10am (11am Sat-Sun) to 5pm (4pm winter); £2. West cemetery: Guided tour only, Sat-Sun, 11am-4pm (3pm winter), every hour; Mon-Fri at 2pm (except Dec-Feb); £3. Hand-held cameras only permitted; permit £1. ☎ 020 8340 1834; www.highgate-cemetery.org*

The Eastern Cemetery is still in use; here lie **George Eliot** (1819-80) and **Karl Marx** (d 1883) – bust (1956) by Laurence Bradshaw. The Western Cemetery (opened 1838) contains some remarkable 19C monumental masonry and the tombs of **Michael Faraday** (1791-1867), Charles Cruft who started the dog shows in 1886, and **Dante Gabriel** and Christina **Rossetti** *(see TATE BRITAIN)*.

Walk back to Highgate Hill

Opposite, high above the road, is **The Bank**, a row of brick houses; nos 110, 108 and 106, Ireton and Lyndale Houses are early 18C, no 104, Cromwell House (so called for uncertain reasons since 1833), of now mellow red brick with a solid parapet, is 16C and has an octagonal domed turret (1638).

West of Highgate Hill is the **Archway**, a viaduct built to allow the road north (A1) to pass through the hill 80ft/24m below Hornsey Lane. The original structure by John Nash was replaced in 1897 by a metal construction designed by Alexander Binnie.

Whittington Hospital has grown out of the original "Leper spytell" of 1473. The **Whittington Stone** (1821), a marble cat sitting on a stone, marks the spot where according to tradition **Dick Whittington** *(see index)* heard Bow bells telling him to "turn again."

Worth a Visit

Fenton House★★

(NT) (♿) Open late-Mar to early-Nov, Wed-Sun and Bank Hol Mon, 2pm (11am Sat-Sun and Bank Hol Mon) to 5pm; early to mid-Mar, Sat-Sun, 2-5pm. £4.50. Guide book (4 languages). Braille guide. No photography. ☎/Fax 020 7435 3471; 01494 755 563 (infoline); fentonhouse@nationaltrust.org.uk

An iron gate (1707) by **Tijou** gives access to a red-brick house, built in 1693; it is Hampstead's finest besides being one of its earliest and largest. The east front, with a recessed porch, is less attractive than the south front of seven bays beneath a hipped roof with a central pediment.

In the original design a self-contained closet was attached to every room but the dividing walls in all but one have now been removed. The original main pine staircase, with its twisted balusters and wide handrail, has survived as well as some doorcases, panelling and chimney-pieces. In 1793 the house was bought by a Riga merchant, Philip Fenton, after whom it is still named; in 1952 it was bequeathed to the National Trust.

Collection – The furniture and pictures form a background to 18C porcelain – English, German and French – and the Benton-Fletcher collection of early **keyboard instruments**, some 18 in number ranging in date from 1540 to 1805, plus an early-17C Flemish harpsichord lent by HM the Queen Mother, an Arnold Dolmetsch clavichord (1925) and some stringed instruments. The instruments are for the most part kept in good playing order and are accessible to students. There are frequent concerts.

On the ground floor are harpsichords (1770 English, 1612 Flemish), the most important part of the English porcelain collection (Bristol, Plymouth, Chelsea, Bow, Worcester), some of the German figures, and an Oriental room (porcelain, lacquer pierglass, enamelled ware); on the landing Staffordshire figures and a Trubshaw grandmother clock.

On the first floor are German figurines, teapots, Worcester apple green porcelain in satinwood cabinets, the most important piece of English porcelain in the collection, a Worcester pink-scale vase and cover probably decorated in London (Drawing Room), 17C-18C Chinese blue and white porcelain, 18C English harpsichords, a 16C Italian and an early-18C English spinet, and a 17C virginal; on the top floor 18C square pianos, 17C and 18C harpischords, 17C and 20C clavichords, and a 17C spinet and virginal. The 17C needlework pictures (Rockingham Room), the bird and flower pictures by the 18C artist Samuel Dixon (Porcelain Room) and the works of Sir William Nicholson (Dining Room) are noteworthy.

Kenwood**

(EH) (♿) House: Open daily, 10am (10.30am Wed and Fri) to 5.30pm (5pm Oct; 4pm Nov-Mar). Closed 24-26 Dec, 1 Jan. ☎ 020 8348 1286 for details. Audio-guide (hire charge). Grounds: Open daily, 8am-dusk. Gypsy caravan: ☎ 020 7973 3893. Lakeside concerts: Jul to early-Sep, Sat evenings (occasionally Sun). Parking. Restaurant, picnic area. ☎ 020 8348 1286; Fax 020 7973 3891 Access: by bus 210 (from Golders Green or Archway)

"A great 18C gentleman's country house with pictures such as an 18C collector might have assembled" – William Murray, younger son of a Scottish peer, acquired Kenwood, then a 50-year-old brick house, in 1754, two years before he was appointed Lord Chief Justice and created Earl of Mansfield. He intended Kenwood as his country retreat, where he could relax and entertain, and in 1764 invited his fellow Scot, Robert Adam, to enlarge and embellish the house. The architect transformed it both outside and in and left so strong an imprint that all subsequent additions were in his style.

Iveagh Bequest – Kenwood was purchased by Lord Iveagh in 1925 and bequeathed to the nation in 1927. The house's contents, including much Adam furniture, had previously been sold and he filled it instead with the remarkable collection of pictures he had formed at the end of the 19C. Efforts to recover the original furnishings (Adam sidetable and pedestals of 1775 in the Parlour) have been painstaking. The **Suffolk Collection** of portraits is also on display on the first floor.

Exterior – The pedimented portico with giant fluted columns, frieze and medallion was Adam's typical contribution to the north front; on the south front, from which there is a splendid view down to the lake, Adam raised the central block to three floors (decorating the upper floors in his own style with pilasters and stucco), refaced the existing Orangery and designed the Library to the east to balance the façade.

Interior – The house has been refurbished to a high standard with original colour schemes. Of the rooms on either side of the hall, the most remarkable are the Music and Dining Rooms (cornice and doorcase related in motif to the preceding enriched columns and entablatures), the Adam Library and Orangery.

Adam Library** – The "room for receiving company" as Adam described it, is richly decorated with Adam motifs and painted in blue and old rose, picked out in white and gold. The oblong room, beneath a curved ceiling, leads into two apsidal ends, each lined with bookcases and screened off by a horizontal beam supported on fluted Corinthian columns. Arched recesses, fitted with triple mirrors, flank the fireplace and reflect the three tall windows opposite.

Paintings** – A **Rembrandt**, *Self-portrait in Old Age*, the lusty *Man with a Cane* by Frans Hals, the ringletted young girl *Guitar Player* by Vermeer, and works by Bol, Rubens, Cuyp and Crome hang in the Dining Room. **Van de Velde** seascapes and a Turner, *The Iveagh Seapiece* are found in the Parlour; the Vestibule is mostly hung with Angelica Kauffmann. Portraits by the English school people other rooms: beautiful **Gainsborough** women, including *Mary, Lady Howe* in pink silk with that special flat hat, *Lady Hamilton* by **Romney**; children – sentimental, patient, delighted – by Raeburn *(Sir George Sinclair)*, Reynolds *(The Brummell Children, The Children of JJ Angerstein)* and Lawrence *(Miss Murray)*. Gainsboroughs of unusual character hang in the Breakfast Room and Orangery: *Going to Market, Two Shepherd Boys with Dogs*

The Library, Kenwood – a fine example of interior décor in the Adam Style

Fighting and the dramatic *Hounds coursing a Fox*; the portrait of *J Merlin* is also noteworthy. A portrait of special interest is that by John Jackson of the *Earl of Mansfield, Lord Chief Justice,* creator of Kenwood.

Coach House – The restaurant contains the 19C family coach capable of carrying 15 people.

Burgh House

New End Square, Highgate. Open Wed-Sun, noon-5pm; Sat by appointment; Bank Hols, 2pm-5pm. Closed, Good Fri, Easter Mon, Christmas to New Year. Licensed Buttery: Wed-Sun, 11am-5.30pm. ☎ 020 7431 0144, 020 7431 2516 (Buttery); Fax 020 7435 8817; burghhouse@talk21.com

This dignified house, with its south-facing terrace, was built, probably by Quakers, in 1703 when Hampstead was becoming popular as a spa. The local physician, Dr William Gibbons, lived there in the 1720s; the wrought-iron gates bear his initials. The house takes its name from the Revd Allatson Burgh, vicar of St Lawrence Jewry in the City, who was so unpopular that his parishioners petitioned Queen Victoria to have him removed. A frequent visitor from 1934 to 1937 was Rudyard Kipling whose daughter and son-in-law rented the house.

The panelled rooms, still served by the original oak staircase, are now used for poetry and music recitals, exhibitions by local artists and the Hampstead Museum; one room is devoted to the artist John Constable *(see index)*; information on the history, architecture and natural history of Hampstead and the Heath is available from the bookstall.

2 Willow Road

(NT) Guided tour (1hr) by timed ticket early-Mar to early-Nov, Thu-Sat, noon-5pm (Mar and Nov, Sat only); tours at noon, 1pm and 2pm; unguided visits, 3-5pm. £4.50. ☎/Fax 020 7435 6166; 01494 755 570 (infoline); 2willowroad@ntust.org.uk; www.nationaltrust.org.uk

Erno **Goldfinger** (1902-87) was born in Hungary; in 1920 he went to Paris and studied architecture at the École des Beaux Arts; five years later, he and a number of fellow students persuaded Auguste Perret, a pioneer in the use of reinforced concrete and "structural rationalism", to set up a studio. In Paris he met and married the striking Ursula Blackwell (of the Crosse & Blackwell family), who then began painting under Amédée Ozenfant, a former collaborator of Le Corbusier.

A Romantic Poet

John Keats (1795-1821) was the eldest of three sons. From an early age he showed a keen talent for poetry by translating Virgil's *Aeneid* into prose when still at school. In 1810, after losing both his parents (his father in a riding accident and his mother to consumption), he was apprenticed to a surgeon; four years later he transferred to St Thomas' and Guy's Hospitals in Southwark. By 1817, then living in the City, Keats decided to devote himself to the study of Elizabethan literature and to writing poetry, adopting the free form of the heroic couplet. When his brother and sister-in-law resolved to sail for America, Keats travelled to Liverpool to see them off and onwards on an extensive tour of the north (Lancaster, Lake District, Carlisle, Dumfries, Ireland, Ayr, Glasgow...); spent by the exertion and exposure, Keats began to display the symptoms of his fatal malady. His other brother died that December and Keats returned to Hampstead where he met Fanny Brawne not long before he too was to die in Rome.

The three houses they built replaced a run-down terrace, but despite causing early controversy, their discreet, modern, functional design is sympathetic to the Georgian brick houses around. Inside, the central block is spacious, airy, light, practical, homely and full of individual mementoes, art collected by the couple (Ernst, Penrose, Miller, Picasso) and personal possessions (including a particularly long bath!). A central stairwell provides the main axis and access to the three floors; partition walls allow space to be transformed to accommodate large parties or enclose the warmth of intimate gathering; colour and texture are also significant.

St John's Church

Downshire Hill. Itmarks the Keats Grove fork, white and upright with a small domed bell turret, Classical pediment, large name plaque and square portico, a chapel of ease dating from 1818. *Open Mon-Sat, 7.45am (9am Sat) to 6pm; Sun, 8am-7pm. ☎ 020 7794 5808; vestry@hampsteadparishchurch.org.uk; www.hampsteadparish.church.org.uk*

Keats Grove is lined by early-19C houses and cottages irregular in height, detached and terraced, bay windowed, balconied with canopies, many with flowered front gardens.

Keats House

(♿) Open (from 19 Apr 2003) Tue-Sun, noon-5pm (4pm Nov-Mar). Guided tour, Sat-Sun, at 3pm. Closed 25-26 Dec, 1 Jan. £3. ☎ 020 7435 2062; Fax 020 7431 9293; www.cityoflondon.gov.uk/keats

Two small semi-detached Regency houses with a common garden, known as Wentworth Place, were erected in 1815-16 by two friends with whom Keats and his brother, in lodgings in Well Walk, soon became acquainted. In 1818, Keats came to live with his friend Brown in the left-hand house; shortly afterwards Mrs Brawne and her children became tenants of the right-hand house. He wrote poems, including the *Ode to a Nightingale*, in the garden; he became engaged to Fanny Brawne but, after falling ill with tuberculosis, in September 1820 he left to winter in Italy and in February 1821 he died.

"His short life" in Edmund Blunden's words "was of unusual intensity; it insisted on being recorded in many ways." These records are now assembled, chiefly in the Chester Room added in 1838-39 when the second house was acquired. The original rooms are furnished much as Keats and Fanny Brawne must have known them.

The **Keats Memorial Library** *(available to students by appointment only)* is in the local library next door.

K. Brett/MICHELIN

Keats House, Hampstead celebrates a young poetic genius

Freud Museum

20 Maresfield Gardens. ⊖ Swiss Cottage. (♿) Open Wed-Sun, noon-5pm. Closed Easter Bank Hols, 24-26 Dec and at New Year (telephone for details). £5. Brochure (5 languages). Limited parking. Shop. ☎ 020 7435 2002; Fax 020 7431 5452; freud@gn.apc.org; www.freud.org.uk

The house to which Sigmund Freud escaped from Nazi persecution in Vienna in 1938 and where he lived until his death in 1939, has been turned into a museum devoted to Freud's life and work and to the history and development of psychoanalysis. On the ground floor are his study and working library with his famous couch and collection of books, pictures and **antiquities★★**, kept intact by his daughter Anna.

Hampton Court★★★

In a romantic setting by the Thames, the royal palace was the perfect rural retreat for many sovereigns. The glorious buildings in contrasting styles and the splendid gardens are enduring symbols of royal power and wealth.

Location

Map p 336 (TZ). Overground: Hampton Court from Waterloo. Boat: Hampton Court (see PRACTICAL INFORMATION). Hampton Court is to the south-west of London at the junction of A 308 and A 309.

Adjacent Sights: RICHMOND.

Background

Hampton Court Palace was begun in the 16C, an age of splendour and display, which is reflected in the magnificent and extensive Tudor buildings. It was extended in the late 17C with two ranges of handsome state apartments designed by **Sir Christopher Wren** for **William** and **Mary**.

Wolsey's Mansion – In 1514 the manor of Hampton was sold by the **Knights of St John** of Jerusalem to **Thomas Wolsey**, the son of an Ipswich butcher. While still in his early thirties, Wolsey was appointed to a chaplaincy in the household of **Henry Tudor**; under **Henry VIII** he rose to be Archbishop of York (1514), Lord Chancellor (1515), Cardinal (1515) and Papal Legate (1518). He celebrated his wealth and position with his houses in Whitehall, at Moor Park in Hertfordshire and at Hampton-on-Thames, which he chose for its "extraordinary salubrity" attested by eminent English physicians and doctors from Padua.

In 1515 he enclosed the estate (1 800 acres/728ha) and began to construct a fine mansion according to the usual Tudor plan of consecutive courts bordered by buildings: Base Court, Clock Court, Carpenter's Court, hall and chapel (300ft/91m by 550ft/168m overall). The mansion was richly furnished throughout with painted and gilded ceilings and panelling and tapestries on the walls. It was staffed by the cardinal's personal household of 500 and contained some 1 000 rooms of which 280 were kept prepared for guests. Spring water was brought from Coombe Hill 3mi/5km away and carried under the Thames in leaden pipes. The palace was well supplied with water closets and great brick sewers which drained into the Thames and lasted until 1871.

Wolsey's wealth, it was said, exceeded the king's; the magnificence of his mansion outshone the royal palaces and attracted the eye and envy of the king. After 15 years Wolsey fell from power; within months of his disgrace he died (1530).

Tudor Palace – Despite its magnificence, **Henry VIII** enlarged and rebuilt much of the palace. He added a moat and drawbridge and wings to either side of the central gateway. He constructed the Great Hall, the Great Watching Chamber, the annexes around the Kitchen Court, including the Haunted Gallery, the Fountain Court, the tennis court wing and the south front overlooking the Pond Garden. A painting of this palace seen from the Thames, now in the Renaissance Picture Gallery *(see below)*, shows a forest of pinnacles and turrets and chimneys. Henry also built a tiltyard and planted a flower garden, kitchen garden and two orchards.

Edward VI, who was born and christened (1537) at Hampton Court, his two sisters, Mary and Elizabeth, and the early Stuarts resided at the palace in fine weather or when the plague was rife in London.

Unlike other royal residences, Hampton Court was reserved for **Cromwell** and was therefore preserved with its contents, particularly the woodcarvings and paintings. When **Charles II** was restored to the throne he initiated the modern garden layout but the buildings remained largely unaltered and unmaintained until the late 17C.

Renaissance Reconstruction – Hampton Court entered its third and last phase of construction in the reign of **William and Mary**, who wished to make Hampton Court their main residence outside London. They engaged the talents of an unrivalled team of artist-master-craftsmen: **Grinling Gibbons**, **Jean Tijou**, **Antonio Verrio**, **Morris Emmett**, **CG Cibber**, **Daniel Marot**, the king's Dutch architect, and the great gardeners, George London and **Henry Wise**.

Initial schemes for the total demolition of the Tudor palace were discarded. Instead Wren rebuilt the east and south ranges of the Fountain Court to provide two suites of State Apartments, each comprising a guardroom, presence and audience chambers, drawing room, state bedroom and closet. The King's Side was in the south range overlooking the Privy Garden and the Queen's Side was in the east range overlooking the Fountain Garden. Wren also rebuilt the smaller informal royal apartments facing into the **Fountain Court★** and added a colonnade and a new south range to the Clock Court. The buildings were executed in brick in the classic

Renaissance style of the 17C with stone centrepieces, enrichments and window surrounds; the long rows of tall, circular or square windows emphasise the horizontal lines of the building and the roof-level balustrade. The Banqueting House overlooking the river was built in the last years of William's reign after the death of Mary.

The decoration and furnishing of the State Apartments was begun under **Queen Anne** and completed under **George II**, the last monarch to reside at the palace, who also commissioned **William Kent** to decorate the Cumberland Suite. When the Great Gatehouse was rebuilt (1771-73), it was reduced in height by two storeys.

In 1838 **Queen Victoria** opened the State Apartments, the gardens and Bushy Park to the public.

Highlights

20 Maresfield Gardens. ⊖ Swiss Cottage. (♿) Open Wed-Sun, noon-5pm. Closed Easter Bank Hols, 24-26 Dec and at New Year (telephone for details). £5. Brochure (5 languages). Limited parking. Shop. ☎ 020 7435 2002; Fax 020 7431 5452; freud@gn.apc.org; www.freud.org.uk

PALACE★★★

The **Trophy Gates** were built as the main gates in the reign of George II with lion and unicorn supporters.

The **moat and bridge** were constructed by Henry VIII; the bridge, buried by Charles II when the moat was filled in, was excavated in 1910 when the parapet was renewed and fronted by the King's Beasts.

The **Great Gatehouse** built by Wolsey was flanked in the reign of Henry VIII with wings decorated with 16C diapered brickwork. The **stone weasels** on the battlements date from the same period.

The **Arms of Henry VIII** appear in a panel *(renewed)* beneath the central oriel in the Great Gatehouse and also on Anne Boleyn's Gateway *(see below)*. The **terracotta roundels** depicting Roman emperors, which appear on the turrets and elsewhere, were bought by Wolsey for Hampton Court in 1521; they cost 6 guineas each and were originally painted and gilded.

Anne Boleyn's Gateway is so called because it was embellished by Henry VIII during her brief period as Queen; the bell turret is 18C. The Base Court side bears Elizabeth I's badges and initials, dating from 1566; on the other side are Wolsey's arms in terracotta (restored) and his cardinal's hat.

Caius Cibber carved the window surrounds in the Fountain Court, as well as many of the palace's finest window and arcade ornaments.

The interior of the palace is divided into six separate tours, each with a different theme (site plan below).

A Curiosity

The **Astronomical Clock** was made for Henry VIII in 1540 by Nicholas Oursian; on the dial (8ft/2.5m) are indicated the hour, month, date, signs of the zodiac, year and phase of the moon. It predates the publication of the theories of Copernicus and Galileo and the sun therefore revolves round the earth. It was transferred in the 19C from St James's Palace to its present site in the Clock Court which was the main Court of Wolsey's house.

Tudor Royal Lodgings

30min; entrance in Anne Boleyn's Gateway. The **Great Hall (1)** (106ft/32m x 40ft/ 12mx 60ft/18m), used by Henry's men for dining and sleeping, was built in five years (1531-36): Henry VIII was so impatient to see it finished that work continued by candlelight. The magnificent hammerbeam roof is ornamented with mouldings, tracery, carving and pendants relieved with gilding and colours. The walls are hung with 16C Flemish tapestries made by Van Orley to illustrate the *Story of Abraham*. At the west end is the Minstrels' Gallery.

The **Horn Room (2)**, from which the stairs led down to the kitchens, was the serving place for the upper end of the hall: it takes its name from the deer antlers which were hung there for many years.

The **Great Watching Chamber (3)** was built in 1535-36 at the entrance to the Tudor State Rooms *(demolished)* with an elaborately panelled ceiling set with coloured bosses displaying Tudor and Seymour devices between ribs which curve down to form pendants. The 16C Flemish tapestries depicting the *Vices and Virtues* were possibly purchased by Wolsey in 1522; three others illustrate scenes from Petrarch's *Triumphs*.

The **Haunted Gallery (4)**, which is said to be haunted by the ghost of Catherine Howard (condemned because of her infidelity), looks on to the Round Kitchen Court. The Flemish tapestries are probably from Queen Elizabeth's collection.

The **Royal Pew (5)** was designed for Queen Anne with a ceiling by Sir James Thornhill.

The **Chapel Royal (6)** was built by Wolsey but lavishly transformed by Henry VIII who inserted the fan-vaulted wooden ceiling and gilded pendants. The reredos, a wreath of cherubim above drops on either side of a framed oval, is by **Gibbons**; it is framed by Corinthian pillars and a segmental pediment by **Wren**.

HAMPTON COURT PALACE

FIRST FLOOR

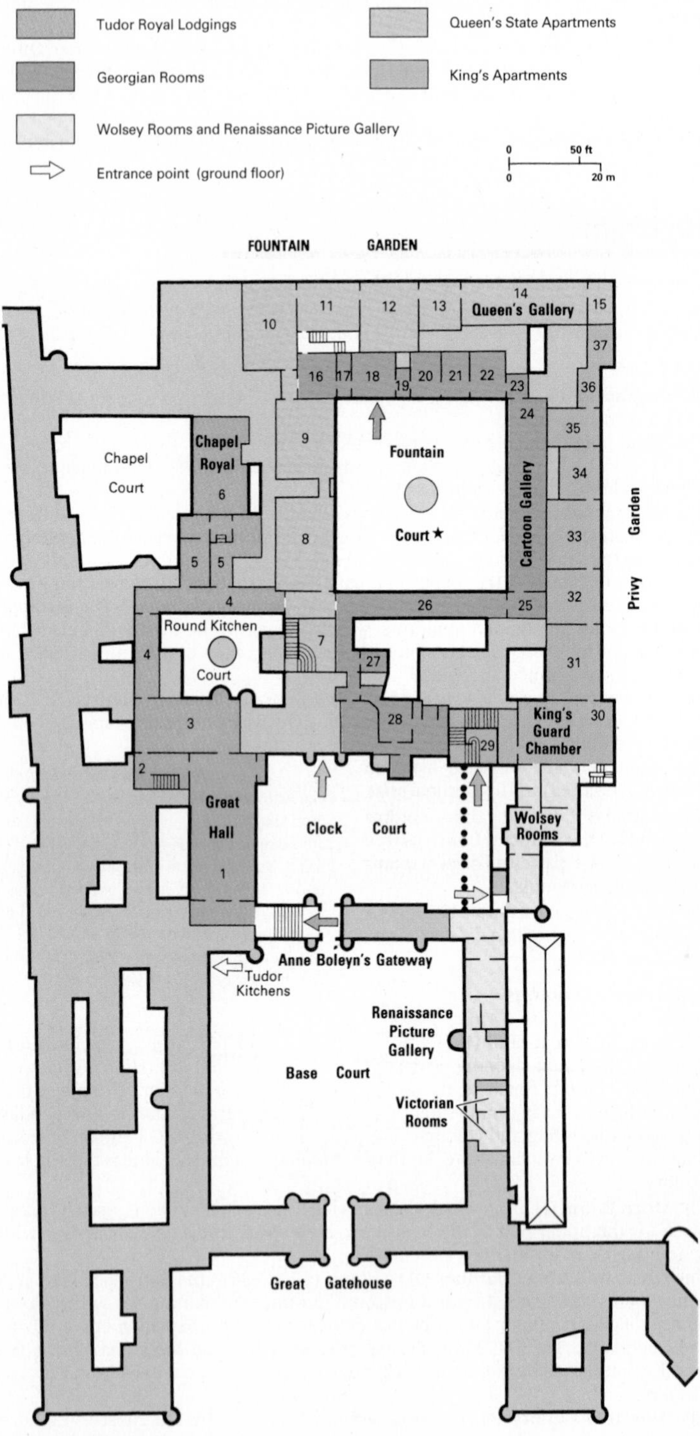

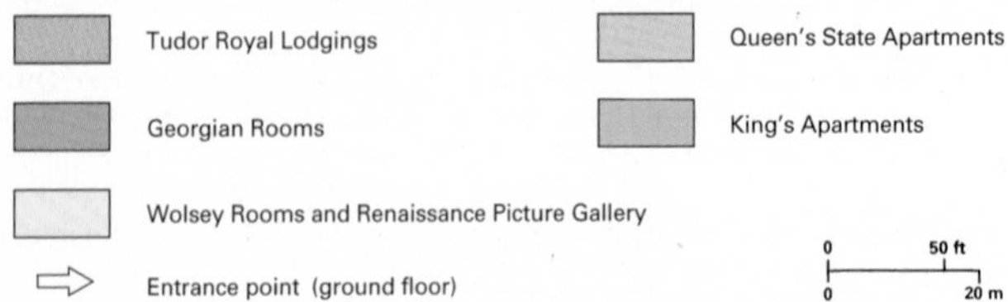

Queen's State Apartments

45min; entrance in Clock Court. The **Queen's Staircase (7)** was the ceremonial approach to the Queen's State Apartments. The beautiful wrought-iron balustrade is by **Tijou** and the lantern by Benjamin Goodison (1731). The walls and ceiling were decorated by Kent (1735); on the west wall is an allegorical painting by Honthorst (1628) depicting Charles I and Henrietta Maria as Jupiter and Juno, and the Duke of Buckingham as Apollo.

The **Queen's Guard Chamber (8)** contains a monumental chimney-piece carved by Grinling Gibbons.

The **Queen's Presence Chamber (9)** contains a bed and furniture made for Queen Anne (1714). The elaborate plaster ceiling is by Sir John Vanbrugh, carvings by Gibbons and the paintings by Tintoretto *(The Nine Muses)*, Gentileschi and Vasari.

The **Public Dining Room (10)** was decorated by **Sir John Vanbrugh** c 1716-18 for the future George II and Queen Caroline. The cornice and royal arms above the fireplace were carved by Grinling Gibbons. The paintings are by Sebastiano Ricci, Pietro Liberi and G Knapton *(Augusta, Princess of Wales with her family)*.

The **Queen's Audience Chamber (11)** is hung with a 16C tapestry illustrating the *Story of Abraham and* contains the canopied Chair of State. Portraits of the *Duke and Duchess of Brunswick* and of *Anne of Denmark*.

The **Queen's Drawing Room (12)** is decorated with wall and ceiling paintings by Verrio (1703-05) commissioned by Queen Anne: *The Queen as Justice* (ceiling), *The Queen receiving homage* (west wall), *Prince George of Denmark as Lord Admiral* (north wall), *Cupid drawn by sea-horses* (south wall).

From the central window there is a splendid **view★** of the Fountain Garden *(see below)*.

The **Queen's Bedroom (13)** contains a state bed, chair and stools (1715-16) in crimson damask; portrait of *Queen Anne as a child* by **Sir Peter Lely**. The ceiling by **Sir James Thornhill** (1715) contains medallions of George I, the Prince and Princess of Wales.

The **Queen's Gallery (14)** is hung with five early-18C tapestries depicting the history of Alexander the Great and two cartoons by Carlo Cignani (1628-1719). The Tulip vases were made for William and Mary. The mantelpiece was designed by John Nost and the carvings are by Grinling Gibbons.

The adjoining chamber **(15)** is decorated with embroidered wall coverings.

Georgian Rooms

30min; entrance in Fountain Court. In contrast with the public state rooms, these private apartments are more intimate and comfortable. Most have been restored to recreate interiors from 1737.

The **Queen's Private Chapel (16)** has a domed ceiling with a lantern. Religious paintings by Fetti surmount the doors here and in the following rooms.

The **Bathing Closet (17)** has no locks, instead a curtained screen would have been used. Note how the wooden bath is lined with linen to safeguard against splinters.

The **Private Dining Room (18)** is hung with works by Pellegrini. The large silver service is on loan from a private collector.

The next room is a second **Closet (19)**.

The **Queen's Private Chamber (20)** is hung with paintings by Ruysdael, Brueghel and Van de Velde. The painting of *Friars in a Nunnery* was a particular royal favourite.

The **King's Private Dressing Room (21)** contains a small early-18C bed.

George II's Private Chamber (22) is notable for its 1730 flock wallpaper and a portrait of Cardinal Richelieu by Philippe de Champaigne. There follows a small **lobby (23)**.

The **Cartoon Gallery (24)** was designed by Wren (1699) to display seven of the ten tapestry cartoons drawn by **Raphael** (1515) and depicting scenes from the lives of St Peter and St Paul; they were purchased by **Charles I** in 1623 and are now displayed in the Victoria and Albert Museum. The cartoons hanging here are copies. The four doorcases and the very long drops framing the tapestry over the fireplace were carved by Grinling Gibbons. The panel below the mantelshelf is by John Nost.

Royal Etiquette

Etiquette dictated that the king visit the queen rather than vice-versa as she had fewer servants liable to be listening at the keyhole. In order to protect privacy, a special lock was contrived: a silk cord within reach of Queen Caroline's bed.

The **lobby (25)** is hung with a view of Hampton Court in George I's reign and a 17C hunting scene.

The **Communication Gallery (26)**, which links the King's and Queen's Apartments, is hung with the famous ***Windsor Beauties*** of Charles II's court by Lely; originally it was hung with Mantegna's cartoons which are now in the Orangery *(see below)*.

Wolsey's Closet (27) contains its original furnishings: linenfold panelling *(restored)*; painted wall panels; frieze with Tudor badges, mermaids and Wolsey's motto as a running motif; ceiling of timber with plaster and lead mouldings, a coloured and gilded combination of Tudor roses, Prince of Wales' feathers and Renaissance ornament.

The **Cumberland Suite (28)** was designed by **William Kent** (1732) for George II's third son: elaborate plasterwork and chimneypieces; portraits of some of the royal children; paintings by Ricci, Carracci, Allori *(Judith with the head of Holofernes)*, Giordano, Vouet *(Diana)*, Balestra, Strozzi and Le Sueur.

King's Apartments

45min; entrance in Clock Court. The **King's Staircase (29)**, the ceremonial approach to the King's Side, is decorated with allegorical scenes painted by Verrio c 1700 and stylised wrought-iron balustrade by Tijou.

In the **King's Guard Chamber (30)** the upper walls are decorated with over 3 000 **arms** arranged by John Harris, William III's gunsmith.

The **First Presence Chamber (31)** contains William III's canopied chair of state. The oak doorcases and limewood garlands are by Grinling Gibbons. A picture of the king by Kneller (1701) hangs in its original place; the portrait of *The Marquess of Hamilton* is by Mytens.

The smaller **Second Presence Chamber (32)** sometimes served as a dining room. Note the pier-glasses and the portrait of *Christian IV of Denmark* over the fireplace.

The **King's Audience Chamber (33)** contains the state canopy and 17C chair. The portrait of *Elizabeth of Bohemia* is by Honthorst. Note the pier glasses and carving. View of the Privy Garden.

In the **King's Drawing Room (34)** note the elaborate carved frame above the fireplace, headed by a crown of fruit and flowers and descending in drops including garlands, *putti* and birds.

In the **King's State Bedroom (35)** the ceiling was painted by Verrio. The tapestries are from the 16C Abraham series. The state bed was used only for the formal *levée* and *couchée*.

The king slept in the **King's Dressing Room (36)** which is furnished in yellow taffeta; the ceiling by Verrio depicts *Mars in the Lap of Venus*.

The **King's Writing Closet (37)** was used for formal business, signing important documents. The mirror over the fireplace provides a view through the whole suite of rooms.

The **King's Private Apartments** on the ground floor are panelled and hung with portraits of courtiers by Kneller, Lely and Rigaud; they display architectural drawings of the Palace, a silver-gilt toilet service (c 1670) by Pierre Prévost, Dutch and Italian paintings, furniture.

The **Orangery** provided winter accommodation for the orange trees which grew in tubs and stood out of doors in summer.

The **Oak Room** is furnished with bookcases and a writing table.

The **King's Private Dining Room** is hung with portraits of the ***Hampton Court Beauties*** (Queen Mary's Court) by Kneller; the table is laid with pyramids of fruit and meringues; gold plate is on display in the alcove.

Wolsey Rooms and Renaissance Picture Gallery

30min; entrance in Clock Court. The Wolsey rooms, which were probably used by guests rather than by the cardinal himself, are ornamented with 16C linenfold and later plain panelling and an elaborate ceiling decorated with Wolsey's badges. The Renaissance paintings, from HM the Queen's collection, include a family group of *Henry VIII and his children* including a posthumous portrait of *Jane Seymour* after Holbein, portraits of *Charles I and Henrietta Maria*, and *Charles I as Prince of Wales* by Mytens; *Charles V*; *The Field of the Cloth of Gold*; mid 17C view of Hampton Court; *Elizabeth I, Henry VIII, François I, Edward VI* attributed to William Scrots.

There are also paintings by Tintoretto, Titian, Savoldo, Lotto, Bronzino, Bassano, Dosso Dossi, Correggio *St Catherine*, Salviati *The Virgin and Child with an Angel;* Bellini, Parmigianino, Raphael; Quentin Massys *Erasmus;* Cranach *Judgment of Paris;* Breugel the Elder *Massacre of the Innocents;* Joose van Cleeve; Hans Baldung.

The two **Victorian Rooms** are furnished in the style of the 1840s.

Tudor Kitchens

45min; entrance in Clock Court; sound guide available. The 16C kitchens are the largest and most complete to survive from this period. When the court was in residence they served two meals a day to some 600 people and employed about 230 staff. They are laid out as

Hampton Court

for the preparation of the feast served on Midsummer's Day in 1542. The tour begins in the cellar beneath the Great Hall (**model** of the kitchens), proceeds to the main gates, where the produce entered the palace, and passes through the **Butchery**, the **Boiling House**, the **Flesh Larder** and the **Fish Court** to the **Great Kitchens**, where the meat was cooked on spits, turned by boys known as gallopines, and sauces were prepared over charcoal stoves; the dishes were then dressed or transferred directly to the **Servery**. The Wine Cellar is one of three in which home-brewed ale and imported wine were stored.

GARDENS***

The gardens (50 acres/20ha) bear the imprint of their creators: the Tudor, Stuart, Orange monarchs, their designers and great gardeners. Over the years features have been raised and levelled; 17C and 18C box-edged parterres have been converted into lawns or woodland in line with fashion; new species have been introduced.
Wolsey planted a walled flower garden between the south front and the river; under Henry VIII the area was converted into the Pond Garden and Privy Garden. The Privy Garden began as squares of grass, coloured brick dust and sand, dotted with heraldic beasts on poles and topiary; a gazebo was erected on a raised mound by the river, with a spiral approach flanked by gaudily painted King's Beasts; there was a watergate to welcome visitors who usually travelled by river in those days. Between 1599 and 1659 the heraldic garden was replaced with four simple grass plots containing fine statuary; the beasts were transferred to stand in the court before the main entrance and the mound was levelled and the soil used to construct the terraces which now flank the Privy Garden.
Under Charles II the land overlooked by the east front was laid out in the fashionable French style practised by Le Nôtre; a vast semicircle of lime trees enclosed three radiating avenues, laid out in a giant goosefoot *(patte d'oie)*; the central claw was represented by a canal, the Long Water, which pierced the rows of lime trees.
The layout of the gardens today has been restored to that of 1702, designed largely by William III, a "Delighter" in gardening, and Mary, his queen, who was "particularly skill'd in Exoticks", for which she sent botanists to Virginia and the Canary Islands.

South Side

The **Knot Garden**, a velvety conceit of interlaced ribands of dwarf box or thyme with infillings of flowers, was replanted this century within its walled Elizabethan site. The royal cipher **ER 1568** appears on the stonework of the bay window in the **South Front** overlooking the Knot Garden; the lead cupola and octagonal turret date from the 16C.
The **Lower Orangery**, a plain building by Wren, now houses the **Mantegna Cartoons** (c 1431-1506), possibly the earliest pictures on canvas to survive, which were bought by Charles I early in the 17C. *The Cartoons of the Triumph of Caesar* consists of nine giant paintings, showing a triumphal procession, ending with the portrait of an ashen withered Caesar, high in his chariot.
The **Great Vine*** produces an annual crop of 500-600 bunches of Black Hamburg grapes *(on sale late August to early September)*; it has a girth of 78 in/2m and was planted in 1768 by **Capability Brown** for **George III**.
The massive wistaria, near the Vine House, dates from 1840.
The **Banqueting House** *(for access, see plan)*, attributed to William Talman under William III, contains an important Baroque interior, the Painted Room by Verrio.
The **Privy Garden** was reserved for the monarch and his guests; each monarch altered the layout to conform with contemporary fashion. The last major redesign took place under William and Mary when Queen Mary's Bower, a hornbeam alley, and the Queen's Terrace were built; the Tudor Water Gallery was demolished and the garden extended to the river; it was screened from the towpath by 12 delicate wrought-iron panels with English, Welsh, Scottish and Irish emblems designed by **Jean Tijou**; the centre was laid out to a sophisticated "broderie" design with pyramidal yews and clipped round-headed hollies. In the late 18C informal planting was introduced, the statuary was removed and the trees were allowed to grow unclipped. The gardens have now been restored to their former glory, complete with the bowered walkway.

East Side

The entablature (1694-96) of the east front of the palace was carved by Caius Cibber combining the William and Mary cipher with crown, sceptres, trumpets.
The **Broad Walk** was planned by Wren and Queen Caroline to separate the Privy Garden from the Fountain Garden.
The **Fountain Garden** was created under William III by retaining the radiating avenues created by Charles II and reducing the Long Water to its present length (3/4 mi/1.2km); 13 fountains were installed in a formal scrollwork setting of dwarf box hedges (a Dutch fashion), obelisk-shaped yews and globes of white holly. Under Queen Anne eight fountains at the circumference were removed, the box hedge arabesques were replaced by grass and gravel; in Queen Caroline's time the fountains were reduced to the present singleton. In the late 20C the yews, which grew as they would in the 19C, were trimmed to their present conical shape to make room for flower beds and to reveal spectacular vistas from the east front. The double semicircle of lime trees was replanted in the 1980s.
The **Tudor Tennis Court** *(for access, see plan)* for real tennis, which is still played on regularly, was built by Henry VIII; the windows are 18C.

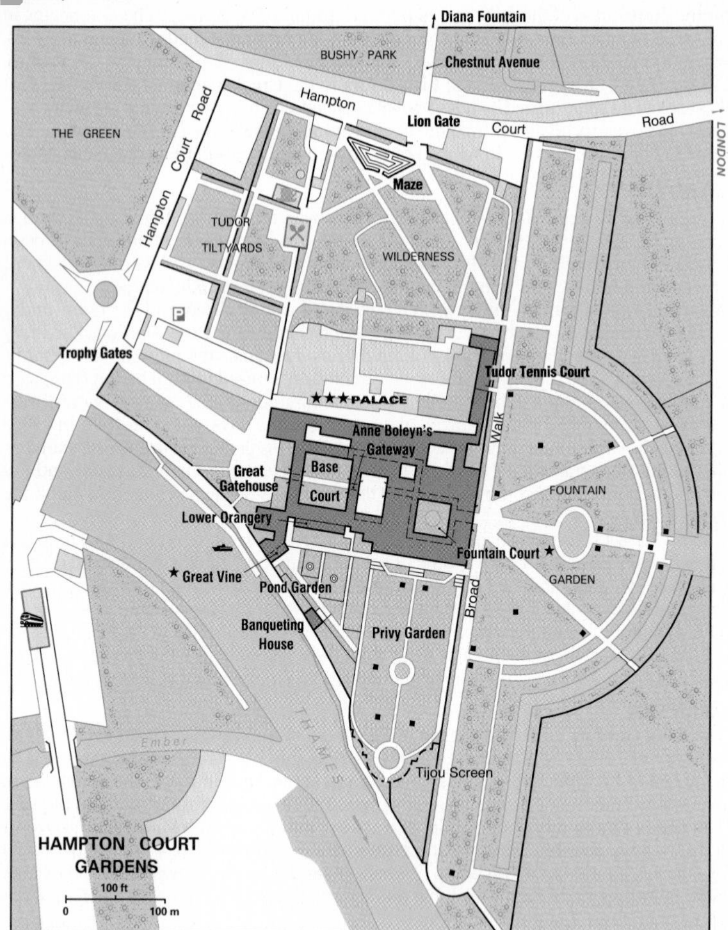

North Side

The **Tudor tiltyards**, surrounded by six observation towers, of which one remains, are now walled rose gardens – roses cost four pence for 100 bushes in Tudor times. The **Wilderness**, now an area (9 acres/4ha) of natural woodland, includes a triangular **maze** *(access see plan)* which dates from 1714. The site, originally occupied by Henry VIII's orchard, was formally laid out by William III with espaliers, clipped yews, hollies, box hedges and a circular maze.

The **Lion Gates** were part of Wren's grand design for a new north entrance and front to the palace.

The **Chestnut Avenue** in Bushy Park is another feature of Wren's plan. Four rows of lime trees flank the double row of chestnut trees (274 trees planted 42ft/13m apart extending for over a mile/2km) which are particularly striking when they are in flower in mid May. The **Diana Fountain** was commissioned by Charles II from Francisco Fenelli for the Privy Garden. North-west of the fountain is a **Woodland Garden** (100 acres/40.5ha) where rhododendrons and azaleas of every hue flourish beneath the trees on either side of the stream which is home to waterfowl and a black swan. **Bushy Park** was first enclosed by Charles I as a deer park; he also had a tributary of the Colne River diverted to form the Longford River (9mi/14.5km).

HAMPTON COURT GREEN

Opposite the palace gates and along the south side of the green are houses associated with the court, particularly in the late 17C and 18C: early 19C hotel on the bridge road, Palace Gate House, The Green, **Old Court House**, the home (1706-23) of Sir Christopher Wren, Paper House, Court Cottage, **Faraday House** (18C with a bow window) where **Michael Faraday** lived in retirement (1858-67), and Cardinal House behind a high fence. Hidden behind the last two houses are Old Office House, with a hipped roof, and small, square **King's Store Studio**, with white weatherboarding (George III plaque). Facing the Green is the long brick range of the Tudor **Royal Mews**, built round a courtyard.

Islington

The proximity of Islington to the City of London and its elegant Georgian squares and Victorian terraces ensure its popularity as a residential area. It is a curious mix of gentrification and dilapidation; this is reflected in its smart restaurants, bustling bars, antique shops, art cinema and avant-garde theatres which do a roaring trade next to its street market and social housing schemes. There are plenty of pleasant discoveries to be made as one strolls about the district.

Location

Map p 337 (UX) *⊖ Angel; Highbury; Islington.* Islington is to the north of the City of London with the mainline stations King's Cross, St Pancras and Euston to the west and merges with the East End. The main highway is A 1.

Adjacent Sights: CLERKENWELL; ST PANCRAS – CAMDEN TOWN; EAST END.

Background

In the 19C the cartoonist **Cruikshank**, who lived in Highbury Terrace, was commenting graphically in *London going out of Town* or the *March of Bricks and Mortar* on the new builder-developers, among them Thomas Cubitt, who were laying out squares, terraces and "meaner streets" which were soon inhabited by workers from the new light industries invading the neighbourhood (pop 1801 – 10 000; 1881 – 283 000; 1901 – 335 000). By the 20C Islington and Angel in particular had become a synonym for slums, grime and grinding poverty, raucous children, rough pubs, the Caledonian Market (Cally Market), the gaslit glories of Collins Music Hall.

Since the Second World War restoration and repainting have returned terraces and squares to their precise well-groomed lines – notably **Duncan Terrace**, **Colebrooke Row**, built in 1761, and **Charlton Place**, with their Tuscan column framed front doors and lanterns, or rounded doorways and ground floor windows and shallow iron balconies; slums have been largely replaced by four- to eight-storey blocks of brick, reminders of the locality's past as a major London brickfield.

Walking About

Start from Angel station, walk a short distance west along Pentonville Rd.

Angel

Five main thoroughfares converge on the ancient crossroads – named after the Angel Inn which once stood on the corner.

Crafts Council Gallery

44a Pentonville Road. ♿ Open Tue-Sun, 11am (2pm Sun) to 6pm. Closed 25 Dec to 1 Jan. Telephone to check exhibition programme. ☎ 020 7278 7700; Fax 020 7837 6891; reference@craftscouncil.org.uk; www.craftscouncil.org.uk

The Crafts Council is a government-funded body dedicated to sustaining and encouraging a strong tradition in the decorative and applied arts. Besides publishing a magazine, it holds major exhibitions of contemporary (Chelsea Craft Fair) and historical work in its own collections. Further information is provided through its bookshop and slide index. It is housed in a deconsecrated Dissenters' Chapel known as Claremont Hall (1818-19).

Return to Angel and proceed along the High St.

ISLINGTON

"A pleasantly seeted country town" as it was styled by John Strype (1643-1737), became a suburb in the 17C when people fled the City after the plague (1665) and the Great Fire (1666); the better-off removed to Islington while the poor, numbering some 300 000, erected shacks and tenements on Finsbury and Moorfields. Islington became fashionable: tea gardens were set up around the **wells** (Clerkenwell, Sadler's Wells etc); taverns marked the stages on the old well-trodden roads from the north, which had been used for centuries, until the coming of the railways, by farmers and herdsmen driving cattle, sheep and swine south, resting them in fields and pens around the village which became known as one of London's dairies, before going on down St John Street to Smithfield or, in the 19C and 20C, to the Caledonian Market.

Camden Passage

Upper Street. Market days: Wed and Sat, 8am-5pm (4pm winter).
The quaint old alley is lined with small shops, arcades, restaurants, two Victorian pubs, and the newly built "Georgian Village". *See PRACTICAL POINTS, Shopping.*

Business Design Centre

Between Upper Street and Liverpool Road. The former **Royal Agricultural Hall** (1861-62) was used successively for cattle shows, military tournaments, revivalist meetings, bullfighting (1888) and Cruft's Dog Show (1891-1939). After many years of dereliction it has been restored and modernised for trade exhibitions.

Islington Green

The shaded triangular green is marked at its centre by a statue of Sir Hugh Myddelton *(see index)*. A plaque marks the site (north side) where from 1862 until the middle of the last century **Collins Music Hall** was boisterous with song.

ENTERTAINMENT

Little Angel Theatre – *14 Dagmar Passage, Cross St, N1 2DN* – ⊖ *Angel* – ☎ *020 7226 1787* – *info@littleangeltheatre.com* – *www.littleangeltheatre.com* – *Open Sat-Sun; telephone for programme* – *£6.* A former temperance hall, north of St Mary's Church, has since 1961 been a flourishing theatre devoted to puppetry. Marionettes, rod and shadow puppets, costumes and settings for the productions are made in the adjacent workshop.

CANONBURY

Canonbury is served by a network of streets and squares lined by early-19C terraced houses of which **Canonbury Square★**, one time home of George Orwell and Sir Francis Bacon, is the prime example since it is complete and beautifully proportioned. Minor connecting roads, such as Canonbury Grove with small country cottages overlooking a New River backwater *(towpath walks)*, and others, like Alwynne Road in which later-19C villas and semi-detached houses stand in the shade of tall plane trees, add to the atmosphere. *See description of Estorick Collection of Modern Italian Art in Worth a Visit.*

Canonbury Tower

A square dark red brick tower (60ft/18m high) is all that remains of the manor rebuilt in 1509 on land owned in the 13C by St John's priory. In 1570 Canonbury was acquired for £2 000 as his country residence by Sir John Spencer, Lord Mayor and owner of Crosby House in Bishopsgate who largely rebuilt his out-of-town house. Buildings which now abut the tower date from the 18C-19C. Of the five late-18C houses overlooking Canonbury Place, the most imposing is the pedimented two-storey **Canonbury House**, with a central door framed by slender Ionic pillars. Today the tower is leased to a repertory drama company, the Tower Theatre.

HIGHBURY

By the 19C Highbury had fallen into the hands of undistinguished developers except for **Highbury Place** (1774-79), Highbury Terrace (1789), Highbury Crescent (1830s), where detached and semi-detached villas had been erected for the more opulent.

Worth a Visit

Estorick Collection of Modern Italian Art

Northampton Lodge, 39a Canonbury Square. ♿ *Open Wed-Sat, 11am-6pm; Sun, noon-5pm. Library: by appointment. £3.50. Café. Shop. Garden.* ☎ *020 7704 9522, Fax 020 7704 9531; curator@estorickcollection.com; www.estorickcollection.com*
Giacomo Balla *(Rhythm of the Violinist)*, Umberto Boccioni *(Modern Idol)*, Carlo Carrà *(Leaving the Theatre)*, Gino Severini *(The Boulevard)*, Luigi Russolo *(Music)* together with the poet Filippo Tommaso Marinetti became fascinated with the concept of universal dynamism: in the words of the Futurist manifesto of 1910, "a clean sweep should be made of all stale and threadbare subject-matter in order to express the vortex of modern life – a life of steel, fever, pitch and headlong speed." Energy is boldly represented as electric light, cinematic movement and music: colour is irridescent, scintillating; space exists as a series of contrasted shadows. Besides the **Italian Futurists**, Estorick collected works by De Chirico (*The Revolt of the Sage*, 1916), Rosso, Modigliani, Morandi, Marini...

William Morris Gallery

Map p 297 (UX) ⊖ *Walthamstow Central.* (♿) *Open Tue-Sat and 1st Sun of each month, 10am-1pm and 2pm-5pm. Leaflet.* ☎ *020 8527 3782; Fax 020 8527 7070; www.lbwf.gov.uk/wmg*
The museum is accommodated in a house that was home to the Morris family between 1848 and 1856, built c 1750 and named Water House after the moat which still exists in the grounds.

The displays are connected with the work of **William Morris** (1834-96) and of the firm Morris & Co (1861-1940) which he co-founded under the definition: "Fine Art Workmen in painting, carving, furniture and the metals." Although destined for the church, Morris tried architecture and painting under the influence of **Ruskin** and the **Pre-Raphaelites**, before finding expression for his talents in the decorative arts.

The career of the designer and the history of the firm are traced in parallel and illustrated by examples of stained glass, tiles, furniture, wallpapers, fabrics and embroidery; Morris' own work includes his poetry and books published by the **Kelmscott Press** : Folio Edition of the Works of Geoffrey Chaucer (1896).

Two smaller rooms display work produced by members of the **Arts and Crafts Movement** *(ground floor)* and the work of the **Century Guild** *(first floor)*, founded by Arthur MacMurdo, who was influenced by Ruskin and Morris. Etchings and oils by **Sir Frank Brangwyn** are exhibited *(first floor)* with paintings and drawings by the Pre-Raphaelites and their contemporaries.

For additional information see VICTORIA & ALBERT MUSEUM and Outer London: CHISWICK.

Kew★★★

The Thames describes a great loop around Kew, an affluent residential area with a village atmosphere. An ideal day excursion out of town brings much enjoyment as one strolls through the splendid gardens with their rare and exotic species, great glasshouses and picturesque dells.

Location

Map p 336 (TY) ⊖ *Kew Gardens.* Access to Kew to the south-west of London is by A 4 or A 316 and A 205 (South Circular).

Adjacent Sights: RICHMOND; CHISWICK; SYON PARK; OSTERLEY PARK.

Background

Royal Residence – The Old Deer Park, which belonged to Richmond Palace *(see Outer London: RICHMOND)*, was guarded by a keeper's lodge, built on the site occupied since 1769 by Kew Observatory. In 1721 the lodge, which had been rebuilt, was sold to the future **George II** and his consort, Queen Caroline, who laid out around the renamed **Richmond Lodge** elaborate gardens in which she included typical 18C ornamental statues and follies.

In 1730, Frederick, Prince of Wales, although on unfriendly terms with George II, leased a house only a mile away. The residence, the **White House**, "an old timber house" built in the late 17C, was redeemed in the diarist **Evelyn**'s eyes only by the "garden (which) has the choicest fruit of any plantation in England." Frederick and his wife Augusta rebuilt the house (known also as Kew House) on a site now marked by a sundial, in which the princess continued to reside after Frederick's death in 1751, devoting herself particularly to the garden.

King George III (1760-1820) and Queen Charlotte found, with a growing family of 15 children, that Richmond Lodge was too small, and on Princess Augusta's death in 1772 moved into the White House. This also rapidly proved too small and, in 1773, the **Dutch House** was leased for the young Prince of Wales (the future George IV) and his brother as well as other houses on Kew Green. Not satisfied, however, George III commissioned **James Wyatt** to design a new "Gothic" enterprise to be sited on the riverbank. The **Castellated Palace**, as it was known, was never completed, but like the White House was demolished, leaving alone of all the cousinhood of royal residences, just the Dutch House or Kew Palace *(see below)*, which was occupied by Queen Charlotte until her death in 1818. In 1899 it was opened as a museum.

Light Bite

Browns – *3-5 Kew Green, TW9 3AA–⊖ Kew Gardens– ☎ 020 8948 4838– www.browns-restaurant.com– £7.95.* A popular brasserie-style restaurant not far from Kew Gardens.

Highlights

ROYAL BOTANIC GARDENS★★★

♿ *Open daily, late-Mar to Aug, 9.30am-6.30pm (7.30pm Sat-Sun and Bank Hol); Sep-Mar 9.30am-4.15pm (5.30pm early-Feb to late-Mar). Closed 25 Dec, 1 Jan. Glasshouses, museum and galleries close earlier than the Gardens. £7.50. Visitor Centre at Victoria Gate. Guided tour from Victoria Gate: daily at 11am and 2pm. Maps available (5 languages). Restaurants. Shops.* ☎ *020 8332 5655; info@kew.org; www.kew.org*

Kew Gardens are pure pleasure. Colour and the architecture of the trees, singly like the weeping willow and the stone pine, or in groups, delight at all seasons. The layman will spot commonplace flowers and shrubs and gaze on delicate exotics, gardeners check their knowledge against the labels, for this 300 acre/120ha garden is the superb offshoot of laboratories engaged in the identification of plants and plant material from all parts of the world and in economic botany.

The curatorship of the biggest herbarium in the world, a wood museum, a botanical library of more than 100 000 volumes and the training (thre year course) of student gardeners are also within the establishment's province.

The botanical theme of the gardens, as opposed to the purely visual, began under Princess Augusta who was personally responsible for the inauguration of a botanic garden south of the Orangery and the enlargement of the gardens from seven to more than 100 acres. On moving into the White House *(see below)*, Prince Frederick had employed **William Kent** not only to rebuild the house but to landscape the garden. On the prince's death in 1751, the Dowager Princess of Wales, guided by the Earl of Bute, a considerable botanist if no politician, appointed William Aiton as head gardener (1759-93) and **William Chambers** as architect (1760). Under Aiton, a Scot who had worked at the Chelsea Physic Garden, his son who succeeded him (1793-1841), and **Sir Joseph Banks** (d 1820), voyager, distinguished botanist, naturalist, biologist and finally director, plants began to be especially collected from all parts of the world for research and cultivation. By 1789, 5 500 species were growing in the gardens.

In 1772 on the death of Princess Augusta, George III combined the Kew and Richmond Lodge gardens and had them landscaped by **"Capability" Brown**. The Palace, Orangery, Queen's Cottage, Pagoda remain as colophon to the royal epoch.

Gardens

Major plantings and flowering seasons are indicated on the map overleaf, colour keyed to draw your attention to flowers in outlying areas. Many fine specimens of trees, some over 200 years old, were uprooted in the storm in October 1987 but most of the damage has been repaired.

Palm House★★

The house was designed by **Decimus Burton** and the engineer, Richard Turner, as a purely functional building (362ft/110m long, 33ft,10m high in the wings and 62ft/19m at the centre). It is constructed entirely of iron and glass, has curved roofs throughout, took four years to erect (1844-48). Inside are tropical plants both useful (coffee, cocoa) and ornamental. The Chilean runner lizards in residence were given to Kew by Customs and Excise after having been smuggled into Britain. Outside *(west)* is a semicircular rose garden; the pond *(east)* is watched over by the Queen's Beasts (stone replicas of those designed by James Woodward to stand outside Westminster Abbey at the coronation in 1953).

Temperate House★

The house, again by Burton, but 20 years later and including crested ridges, octagons, wings, ornamentation, epitomises Victorian conservatory construction. The **Evolution House** recreates the climate of change affecting the Earth.

Alpine House

Beneath a glass pyramid, built in 1981, from which rainwater drains into the surrounding moat, is a rock landscape including a refrigerated bed.

Other specialist houses (Aroid, Fern, Tropical Waterlily and Australian) present creepers from rainforests, cacti, gourds and wattles, mimosas and eucalyptus.

Princess of Wales Tropical Conservatory

In this modern steel and glass diamond-shaped structure are recreated ten different tropical habitats ranging from the extremes of mangrove swamp to desert – from ferns and orchids to carnivorous and stone plants *(Lithops)*, cacti and succulents set against a Mohave desert diorama. In 1996, a titan arum or "corpse flower", which blooms every 30-odd years, attracted great attention: the Sumatran native has flowered at Kew in 1889, 1926 and 1963.

Marianne North Gallery

In a building (1882) specially designed by her architect friend, James Ferguson, are exhibited paintings by Miss North of plants, insects and general scenes from the many countries she visited between 1871 and 1884.

KEW GARDENS

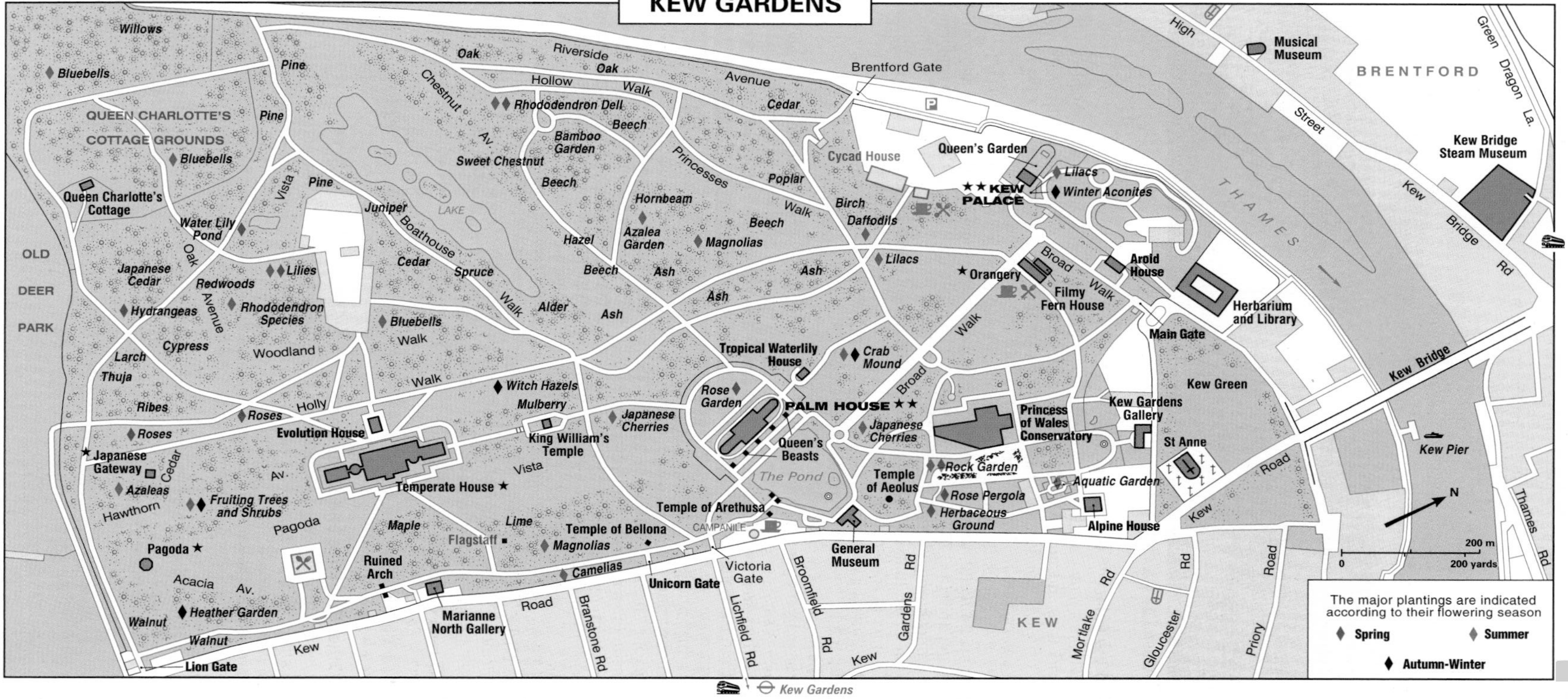

The major plantings are indicated according to their flowering season

◆ Spring ◆ Summer

◆ Autumn-Winter

0 200 m
200 yards

N

BRENTFORD
THAMES
KEW
OLD DEER PARK
QUEEN CHARLOTTE'S COTTAGE GROUNDS

Musical Museum
Kew Bridge Steam Museum
Brentford Gate
Queen's Garden
Cycad House
★★ KEW PALACE
Lilacs
Winter Aconites
Arold House
Herbarium and Library
Main Gate
Kew Green
St Anne
Kew Gardens Gallery
Kew Pier
Kew Bridge
★ Orangery
Filmy Fern House
Princess of Wales Conservatory
Aquatic Garden
Alpine House
Rock Garden
Rose Pergola
Herbaceous Ground
Temple of Aeolus
General Museum
PALM HOUSE ★★
Queen's Beasts
The Pond
Japanese Cherries
Crab Mound
Tropical Waterlily House
Rose Garden
Temple of Arethusa
CAMPANILE
Victoria Gate
Unicorn Gate
Temple of Bellona
Camelias
Magnolias
Flagstaff
Lime
King William's Temple
Mulberry
Witch Hazels
Temperate House ★
Evolution House
Maple
Ruined Arch
Marianne North Gallery
Pagoda ★
Heather Garden
Fruiting Trees and Shrubs
Azaleas
Japanese Gateway
Lion Gate
Queen Charlotte's Cottage
Water Lily Pond
Lilies
Rhododendron Species
Bluebells
Hydrangeas
Japanese Cedar
Redwoods
Willows
Rhododendron Dell
Bamboo Garden
Sweet Chestnut
Azalea Garden
Hornbeam
Daffodils
Birch
Lake
Boathouse Walk
Riverside Avenue
Hollow Walk
Princesses Walk
Broad Walk
Woodland Walk
Holly Walk
Pagoda Vista
Cedar Vista
Chestnut Av.
Oak Avenue
Acacia Av.
Cedar Av.
High Street
Green Dragon La.
Kew Bridge Rd
Thames Rd
Kew Road
Priory Road
Gloucester Rd
Mortlake Rd
Kew Gardens Rd
Broomfield Rd
Lichfield Rd
Branstone Rd
Kew Gardens

Ph. Gajic/MICHELIN

Palm House, Kew

Kew Palace★★ (Dutch House)

The terracotta brick building complete with Dutch attic gables and notable for the richness and variety of the brick laying, cutting and moulding, was built by Samuel Fortrey, a London Merchant of Dutch parentage, who commemorated his house's construction in a monogram and the date 1631 over the front door.

At the rear is the **Queen's Garden**, a formal arrangement of pleached alleys of laburnum and hornbeam, parterres (formal symmetrical beds), a gazebo and plants popular in the 17C. The nosegay garden which dates from the 17C has been replanted with contemporary herbs.

Inside, the house reflects the standard features of a small George III country house. The rooms downstairs are all panelled: the King's Dining Room in white 18C style, the Breakfast Room in early 17C style and the Library Ante-Room in re-set 16C linenfold. Upstairs, apart from the white and gold Queen's Drawing Room, formally set out with lyre-back chairs for a musical evening, the rooms are wallpapered with new paper printed from the delightful original blocks, and intimate with family portraits by Gainsborough and Zoffany. In the King's rooms note the embossed terracotta paper in the Ante-room and in the bedroom a russet red paper patterned in dark green with matching hangings. Downstairs in the Pages' Waiting Room, is an exhibition of minor royal possessions: silver filigree rattles, alphabet counters, snuffboxes, lists of Prince Frederick's gambling debts, the Queen's code of bell pulls...

Pioneering work

Kew has practised biological control (Integrated Pest Management) throughout its premises tailored to 40 000 txa (specific species) of plant and 750 000 specimens of fungi since 1991. Efforts to save some of the world's rarest orchids have led scientists at Kew to evolve a way of germinating plants from seed without the symbiotic fungus required in more natural habitats. Some 5 000 species (about 20% of the total known number) are now propagated at Kew, having been accumulated over the last 200 years. The seed bank, founded to provide scientists and conservationists with the practical means of research, will expand at Wakehurst Place in West Sussex courtesy of the National Lottery.

Queen Charlotte's Cottage

The two-storeyed thatched house, typical of "rustic" buildings of the period (1772) was designed by Queen Charlotte as a picnic house: the cottage is furnished including tea for two upstairs.

Other Buildings and Monuments

Under Princess Augusta, **William Chambers** set about constructing typical 18C garden follies: temples, a ruined arch, an **Orangery**★ (1761) and a **Pagoda**★ (1761), a garden ornament 163ft/49m and 10 storeys high, still the climax to a long vista: now alas without its gilded dragon finials, this folly had its floors pierced by the RAF during the Second World War to give them a 100ft/30m vertical drop to test model bombs.

The **Main Gates** are by Decimus Burton (1848, the lion and unicorn on the original gate are now above gates in Kew Road). By the pond stands the **Museum of Victorian Plant Oddities**, formerly the General Museum, which dates from 1857-58, when it replaced the original Museum of Economic Botany, the first in the world in 1847. The **Japanese Gateway**★ was imported for the Anglo-Japanese Exhibition of 1912.

Walking About

Kew Village

The most attractive houses on the green are those by the main gates to the gardens. Dominating the north (river) side are Kew Herbarium (collection of 5 million dried plants and library – *open to specialists*), a three-storey Georgian house and extensive annexe, followed by an irregular line of 18C-19C houses of brick with canted bays, canopied balconies, rounded doors and windows in arched recesses... *(nos 61-83)*. On the far side of the gates backing onto the gardens, are a line of one-time royal "cottages", including, at no 37, Cambridge Cottage, now the **Wood Museum** and **Kew Gardens Gallery** *(enter from inside the gardens)*.

St Anne's Church – The west end is adorned by a triangular pediment and peristyle and crowned by a bell-turret. The nave and chancel were constructed of brick in 1710-14 on the site of a 16C chapel once frequented by Tudor and Stuart courtiers. In 1770 the church was lengthened and a north aisle built on; books and furnishings were presented by George III, who in 1805 added the royal gallery (note the fine Queen Anne arms and hatchments). In the rose-filled churchyard lie **Gainsborough** (d 1788) and Zoffany (d 1810).

Public Record Office

Ruskin Avenue. Open Mon-Sat, 9am (9.30am Sat, 10am Tue) to 5pm (7pm Tue and Thu). Closed public hols, Bank Hol weekends, Christmas, New Year and Easter. ID required for admission. ☎ 020 8876 3444

The **Domesday Book**, **Shakespeare**'s will, **Guy Fawkes**'s confessions, **Captain Cook**'s charts, Bligh's accounts of the mutiny on the Bounty are just a few of the precious historic charters, accounts, maps, seals, reports, registers, government papers and old chests (including the Million Bank with multiple locks) entrusted to the PRO, founded in 1838 and formerly in Chancery Lane. In their new premises, fragile papers are kept in temperature, and humidity-controlled environments.

Kew Bridge

The 18C bridge, also known as King Edward VII's Bridge, was replaced in 1903 by the present structure of three spans of stone by Wolfe Barry and Brereton.

The Domesday Book

The famous register of lands of England, named after *Domus dei* – where the volumes were originally preserved in Winchester Cathedral, was commissioned by order of William the Conqueror so that he might ascertain the dues owed to him by his subjects, thereby setting the rules by which the monarch, later the government, might levy tax nationwide. As a result we have a comprehensive idea of how the kingdom was divided in 1085-86 both in terms of land holding and popular employment. Lords of the manor held the bulk of the land on a freehold basis, which they tenanted or leased to a complex hierarchy of dependents, villeins or freemen. Land was allocated to agricultural functions (meadow, pasture) in proportion to hunting (woodland) and fishing (ponds and rivers)...

The **Little Domesday** (384 pages) records estates throughout latter-day Essex, Norfolk and Suffolk, while the **Great Domesday** (450 pages) surveys the rest of the kingdom with the exception of Northumberland, Cumberland, Durham, parts of Lancashire and Westmorland which lay outside the king's jurisdiction. The City of London is also omitted as the conquering king could not have been certain of brokering his rights over the shrewd and powerful business community. A facsimile is displayed at the Public Record Office in Kew.

Environs

Kew Bridge Steam Museum

Brentford. Entrance in Green Dragon Lane. (♿) Open daily, 11am-5pm. Closed Good Fri, 20 Dec to 2 Jan. Sat-Sun (engines in steam) £4.60; Mon-Fri (engines static) £3.60. Children under 13 must be accompanied by an adult. Guide book and brochure (6 languages). Large print guide available. Parking. Café (Sat-Sun). ☎ 020 8568 4757; group@kbsm.org; www.kbsm.org

This museum of water supply demonstrates the development of James Watt's basic idea through over a century of improved efficiency and increased scale. There are six Cornish Beam Engines – the Boulton and Watt (1820), the 90" (1846), the Easton and Amos (1863), the Dancers End (1867), the Maudslay (1938), the Hathorn Davey Triple (1910) – and the Waddon Engine, the last steam-powered water pumping engine used commercially until 1983. A variety of smaller steam engines, traction engines and steam lorries, a narrow-gauge railway, a water-wheel (1702), a forge, machine shop and a collection of relics connected with London's water supply complete the display. Buildings in the 19C were, for the most part, erected round the engines with no provision for bringing in replacement parts so confident were our forefathers that their engines would last indefinitely. Exteriors were functional, the interiors dominated by giant columns, slender pillars and staircases enabling one to climb to cylinder and beam levels. The standpipe tower outside is a local landmark nearly 200ft/61m high.

Musical Museum

368 High Street, Brentford (150yds/137m west of Kew Bridge). ♿ *Closed in 2003 for local relocation. Open previously Apr-Oct, Sat-Sun, 2-5pm; also Jul-Aug, Wed, 2-4pm. £3.20. Guide book, recordings available.* ☎ *020 8560 8108; enquiries@musicalmuseum.co.uk; www.musicalmuseum.co.uk*

Inside an acoustically rewarding neo-Gothic church (19C) is a collection of some 200 mechanical music-makers – pianolas, organs, a Wurlitzer...

Boston Manor

⊖ *Boston Manor. Grounds: Open daily. House: Closed for refurbishment during 2003. Open previously early-Apr to late-Oct, Sat-Sun and Bank Hol Mon, 2.30-5pm.* ☎ *020 8560 5441*

The red-brick house was begun in 1623 by Lady Mary Read who had acquired the property by settlement from **Sir Thomas Gresham** through marriage to his stepson; the magnificent moulded plaster ceiling in the State Room is dated 1623; the staircase with its *trompe-l'œil* balustrade is also original.

In 1670 James Clitherow bought the property for £5 136 17s 4d, adding the bold entablature, window architraves and garden door, and landscaped the grounds with cedars and a lake.

Osterley Park★★

A magnificent country mansion surrounded by parkland on the outskirts of London is well worth a visit. The rooms are elegantly furnished and decorated to reflect the tastes of wealthy and discerning owners. It is an easy excursion by public transport.

Location

Map p 336 (TY). ⊖ *Osterley.* Osterley Park is situated to the west of London, by A 4 (north side) and near the M 4 (Exit 2).

Adjacent Sights: SYON PARK; KEW.

Background

Osterley Park is the place to see **Robert Adam** interior decoration at its most complete. Room after room is as he designed it: ceilings, walls, doorcases, doors, handles, carpets, mirrors and furniture down to chairs standing in the exact positions for which they were designed.

A Country Seat for City Gentlemen – Sir Thomas Gresham bought Osterley Manor in 1562 and immediately began to build a country house adjoining the old manor house, a late-15C Tudor brick building surrounding three sides of a courtyard. When Gresham's mansion was complete, **Queen Elizabeth** honoured her financier and merchant adventurer by a visit to the "house beseeming a prince" (1576), which on his death in 1579, passed to his stepson Sir William Read, husband of Lady Mary of Boston Manor *(see Outer London: KEW – Environs).*

In 1711 the mansion was purchased by another City grandee **Francis Child**, although the old banker never lived there. His grandchild, namesake and heir, began transforming the place in 1756, work which was to continue for more than 20 years by which time the house was owned by Francis Child's great-niece, Sarah Sophia who in 1804 married the future 5th Earl of Jersey.

In 1773 Horace **Walpole**, visiting from nearby **Strawberry Hill**, wrote: "The old house is so improved and enriched that all the Percies and Seymours of Sion must die of envy... There is a hall, library, breakfast room, eating room, all *chefs d'œuvre* of Adam, a gallery 130ft long, a drawing room worthy of Eve before the Fall."

Osterley was presented to the nation by the 9th Earl in 1949.

An Astute Financier

Francis Child, a clothier's son from Wiltshire, came to seek his fortune in London in the 1650s, had found it, been knighted, elected Lord Mayor (1698) and become banker to Charles II, Nell Gwynne, Pepys, John Churchill, future Duke of Marlborough, King William and Queen Mary... He had started as a goldsmith's apprentice; moved to a second house where he married the owner's daughter, inherited the family fortune and business which he transformed to suit the times. Gold coinage was accumulating rapidly through increased trade in Tudor and Stuart times but was easily stolen; after finding that even deposits in the Tower were vulnerable (Charles I seized £130 000 from the vaults in 1640!) merchants placed their bullion with goldsmiths usually for a fixed time; the smiths with Francis Child as a forerunner began to lend the cash out at interest and became the City's first bankers. **Child's Bank** (now Royal Bank of Scotland) "at the sign of the Marigold" after the premises they occupied when there were no street numbers, can still be seen at no 1 Fleet Street *(see STRAND – TEMPLE – Fleet Street).*

Highlights

(NT) House: ♿ Open early-Apr to early-Nov, Wed-Sun and Bank Hol Mon, 1-4.30pm; early to late-Mar, Sat-Sun, 1-4.30pm. £4.50, £11.20 family ticket. No photography. Park: Open daily, 9am-7.30pm/dusk/early during major events. Dogs on lead. Parking £3 (closed 25-26 Dec). Tearoom. Braille guide; sympathetic hearing scheme. ☎ 020 8232 5050 (visitor services), 01494 755 566 (infoline); Fax 020 8232 5080; osterley@ntrust.org.uk; www.national.org.uk

Exterior

The square form with corner towers of Sir Thomas Gresham's house remains, though enlarged and encased by new bricks and stone quoins in the 18C by the first of the two architects employed on the transformation. Sir William Chambers in addition reduced the courtyard to provide a hall and continuous passage round the house and completed the Gallery and Breakfast Room before being superseded in 1761 by the more fashionable Robert Adam. The latter made two contributions to the exterior, the grand, theatrical six-columned portico at the front and, at the rear, a horseshoe staircase with delicate wrought-iron and brass work (1770).

Interior

The wide **Hall** is apsed at either end, the fine ceiling filled with floral scrolls is echoed in the two-tone marble pavement. Distinctive relief panels with trophies of war fill the spaces between pilasters, Classical statues nestle in niches on either side of the curved fireplaces and grisaille paintings. Each detail, save the statues and elegant marble urns on pedestals after the Antique, is designed by Adam, including the door handles.

Leave the Hall by the north door – on the right when entering the house – and follow past a cabinet filled with fine porcelain, to the far end of the passage.

The **Breakfast Room** is painted in a strong lemon yellow contrasted with touches of blue to highlight the delicate ornamental detailing. The ceiling is by Chambers; tables and pier glasses, however, were designed by Adam and the lyre-back mahogany armchairs probably by Linnell.

The distinctive feature of the **Library**, painted in creamy-white to emphasise the leather-bound books and set off the painted panels, is the furniture: the lyre-back armchairs, a pedestal desk veneered with harewood (stained sycamore) and inlaid with motifs matched in the side tables are all made in about 1775 by John Linnell, the leading cabinet maker of his day, probably to his own designs under Adam's supervision.

The **staircase**, begun by Chambers, has a fine iron balustrade, and delicate stucco decoration added by Adam who also designed the three lamps hanging between the Corinthian columns. The ceiling painting is particularly Rubensesque.

At the top, turn right.

The **State Bedroom** or Yellow Taffeta Bedchamber is furnished with painted taffeta curtains and bed hangings, and ornate gilded mirrors. The bed, surmounted by cupped acorns, was designed by Adam (1779).

Beyond the stairhead is the suite of less extravagant rooms designed by Chambers for Mr and Mrs Child. None of the furniture in his **dressing room** is original but most pieces date from the mid 18C. The **bedchamber** has window curtains and bed valances made of cotton imported from India in the 1760s. The lacquer dressing-table and French ebony cabinet on a stand were among the furniture in the 1760s. The cornice, doors and shutters of her **dressing room** are the distinctive work of Chambers. The chimney-piece and mirror were designed by Linnell; the portrait is Robert Child's daughter, Sarah Anne, who eloped with the 10th Earl of Westmorland. The only original pieces are the 17C Japanese lacquer cabinet and the 18C Chinese porcelain.

Return downstairs; turn right.

The exhuberant splendour of the State Bed at Osterley Park designed by Robert Adam

The **Eating Room** is an all Adam room: motifs from the pink and green ceiling decoration, notably the honeysuckle and pineapples are most typical. According to 18C custom the carved mahogany lyre-back chairs are set against the wall when not in use, gateleg tables would be brought in for dining.

The light and airy **gallery** boasting a fine view of the garden across the width of the house, was designed by Chambers. Marble chimney-pieces, Classical doorcases and 18C Chinese pieces and lacquered furniture are contrasted by the delicate Rococo-style frieze against the ochre and green colour scheme introduced by Adam. As in the 18C the room is sparsely furnished and hung with pictures. Other fixtures, including the five-seater sofas, are by Adam; the pier glasses and girandoles, garlanded and supported by nonchalant mermaids, represent the Scotsman in his lightest vein.

The somewhat over gilded **Drawing Room** is dominated by the low, heavy coffered ceiling studded with flowering paterae and ostrich feathers. Pale pinks and greens, gold and red are picked out in cornice and carpet (made at Moorfields) while motifs from the doorcases are echoed in the fireplace, the inlaid design and ormolu decoration of the two harewood veneered commodes. The serpentine sofas and chairs are after the early French neo-Classical style. The pier glasses and perfume burners are French.

In the **Tapestry Room**, the Adam motifs for ceiling and fireplace fade into insignificance beside the richness of the Gobelins' tapestries woven for the room, signed and dated by (Jacques) Neilson, 1775, an artist of Scots origin in charge of the works in Paris from 1751 to 1788. On a rich crimson ground, framed in gold, is the Boucher series, *The Loves of the Gods,* and between are flower-filled urns, garlands, cupids at play... Chairs and sofa are in the same style.

The **State Bed Chamber** is decked in cool green. The Child crest of an eagle with an adder in its beak features on the eight-poster valance. The gilded chairs, their oval backs supported on reclining sphinxes, are one of Adam's most graceful designs (1777). The chimney-glass, surmounted by the Child crest, is declared in the house inventory of 1782 to have been the "first plate made in England." The walls would originally have been covered in green velvet.

The **Etruscan Dressing Room**, which helped to launch a fashion for the Antique, demonstrates Adam's application to an 18C interior of what he took to be Etruscan decorative themes, derived in fact from Ancient Greek pottery; even the chairs are made to conform to the theme in colour and patterning, though not in shape. According to surviving inventories from 1782, it was here that the japanned Chippendale 1773 lady's writing desk was situated – a decorative mix that would not have offended or jarred 18C tastes or sensibilities.

The Demonstration Room is hung with plans and drawings of house and garden by Adam and others. The two 18C views of Osterley by Anthony Devis *(in the corridor to the hall)* are the only works from the original picture collection.

The **Stables**, built in 1577 by Sir Thomas Gresham were altered and refitted early in the 18C.

The **Pleasure Grounds** *(west of the house)*, which are being restored according to old maps and prints, contain Chambers' Doric temple to Pan and Adam's semicircular garden house (c 1780). The cedar trees on the south lawn were planted in the 1760s. The chain of lakes was created in the 1750s.

Richmond★★

In an attractive riverside location,the vibrant town of Richmond is complemented by a rural atmosphere with its leafy parks, woodland and golf courses. Together with neighbouring Twickenham, the home of English rugby, it is a highly desirable area. Fine mansions recall past aristocratic associations when Richmond Palace was a favourite residence of the Tudor monarchs. Richmond has all the amenities of an affluent town: historic pubs, pleasant restaurants, antique shops, select boutiques.

Location

Old Town Hall, Whittaker Avenue, Richmond TW9 1TP. Open Mon-Sat, 10am-5pm; also May-Sep, Sun, 10.30am-1.30pm. ☎ 020 8940 9125; Fax 020 8940 6899; information.services@richmond.gov.uk; www.richmond.gov.uk

The Atrium, Civic Centre, 44 York Street, Twickenham TW1 3BZ. Open Mon-Fri, 9am-5.15pm (5pm Fri). ☎ 020 8891 7272; m.coles@richmond.gov.uk; www.richmond.gov.uk

Map p 336 (TYZ) ⊖ Richmond; Overground: Richmond from Waterloo Station and by North London Line. Richmond lies to the south-west of London between the main axes to A 3 and M 3. It is also accessible by boat from Westminster Pier.

Adjacent Sights: KEW

Background

Richmond, possessing what has been called the most beautiful urban green in England, grew to importance between the 12C and 17C as a royal seat and, after the Restoration, as the residential area of members of the court: Windsor, Hampton Court and Kew are easily accessible. In the courtiers' wake followed diplomats, politicians, professional men, dames and their schools, and with the coming of the railway in 1840, prosperous Victorian commuters.

Richmond Palace: **Royal Residence Through Six Reigns** – The first residence, a manor house, erected in the 12C, was extended and embellished by **Edward III**, who died in it in 1377, was favoured by **Richard II**, his grandson while his queen, Anne of Bohemia, was alive but demolished at her death in 1394. A new palace, the second, was begun by **Henry V** but completed only 40 years after his death in the reign of **Edward IV** who gave it with the royal manor of Shene to his queen, Elizabeth Woodville, from whom it was confiscated by **Henry VII**; in 1499 it burned to the ground. Henry VII, parsimonious where his son was prodigal, nevertheless, "rebuilded (the palace) again sumptuously and costly and changed the name of Shene and called it Richmond because his father and he were Earls of Rychmonde" (in Yorkshire). This palace, the third on the site, was to be the last.

The new Tudor palace conformed to standard design: service buildings of red brick, preserved today in the gateway, enclosed an outer or Base Court, now Old Palace Yard, from which a second gateway led to an inner or Middle Court, lined along one side by a Great Hall of stone with a lead roof.

The Privy Lodging, which included the state rooms, surrounded another court. Domed towers and turrets crowned the construction, which covered 10 acres/4ha and was by far the most splendid in the kingdom. **Henry VII** died in his palace; **Henry VIII** and Catherine of Aragon frequented it; **Queen Elizabeth** held court in it, particularly in springtime, and died there; Prince Henry, James I's son, resided there and added an art gallery to house the extensive collection of royal paintings, increased after the prince's death (in the palace) by the future **Charles I** who also resided there, notably during the plague of 1625. At the king's execution the palace was stripped and the contents, including the pictures, were sold. By the 18C little remained and private houses – the Old Palace, Gatehouse, Wardrobe, Trumpeters – were constructed out of the ruins on the site.

Directory

Pubs

Prince's Head – *28 The Green, TW9 1LX – ⊖ Richmond – ☎ 020 8940 1572 – Open Mon-Sat 11am-11pm, Sun noon-10.30pm.* A pleasant local pub with a good atmosphere.

The Cricketers – *The Green, TW9 1LX – ⊖ Richmond – ☎ 020 8940 4372 – Open Mon-Sat noon-11pm, Sun noon-10.30pm.* Situated beside Richmond Cricket ground, this pub is the perfect place to unwind in the sun.

The White Swan – *Riverside, Twickenham, TW1 3DN – ⊖ Twickenham rail – ☎ 020 8892 2166 – whiteswan@massivepub.com – Summer Mon-Sat 11am-11pm, Sun noon-10.30pm; winter Mon-Thu 11am-3pm, 5.30-11pm, Sun noon-10.30pm.* This three hundred-year-old pub, overlooking the Thames and only 10 minutes from Twickenham stadium, has a rich history. Today rugby paraphernalia cover the walls, the exterior terrace looks onto Eel Pie Island, and the landlord prepares barbecues for match days. A visit to this charming pub is really well worth the detour.

Walking About

Take a stroll through the town.

Town Centre

On the east side of the main road are reminders of the growing village in the parish **Church of St Mary Magdalene** with its 16C square flint and stone tower, early brasses and monuments (actor Edmund Kean), 18C houses (Ormond and Halford Roads), 19C cottages (Waterloo Place), the Vineyard dating back in name to the 16C-17C when local vines were famous, and the rebuilt almshouses of 17C foundation – Queen **Elizabeth's**, **Bishop Duppa's** and **Michel's**. In Paradise Road stands Hogarth House built in 1748, where Leonard and **Virginia Woolf**, who lived there from 1915 to 1924, founded the **Hogarth Press**.

Cross the High St and pass through charming alleyways to Richmond Green.

Ph. Gajic/MICHELIN

Richmond Theatre

Richmond Green

The Green, once the scene of Tudor jousting, has been a cricket pitch since the middle of the 17C.

Richmond Theatre, which overlooks the Little Green, was designed by Frank Matcham in 1889 and refurbished in 1991 more or less in accordance with its original appearance.

Along the east side of the Green are 17C and 18C houses and two narrow lanes opening into George Street. In the south corner in Paved Court are two pubs, the **Cricketers** and the **Prince's Head** *(see Directory)*; behind are narrow lanes with small shops.

Along the west side is **Old Palace Terrace** (1692-1700), six two-storey brick houses with straight hooded doorways, built by John Powell (who lived in no 32 which he also built).

Oak House and **Old Palace Place** date back to 1700. **Old Friars** (1687 date on a rainwater head) is so named as it stands on part of the site of a monastery founded by Henry VII in 1500; the house was extended in the 18C to include a concert room for the holding of "music mornings and evenings."

Maids of Honour Row★★★ – The famous row dates from 1724 when the future George II gave directions for "erecting a new building near his seat at Richmond to serve as lodgings for the Maids of Honour attending the Princess of Wales." There are four houses in all, each three storeys high with five bays apiece, pilastered, with friezed doorcases, and small gardens behind 18C wrought-iron gates and railings. The brick is mellow, the proportions perfect.

The Old Palace and the Gatehouse – On the south side are two houses: the first – castellated, bay-windowed and with a central doorway incorporating Tudor materials, notably brickwork, from Henry VII's palace; the second is the original outer gateway of the palace (note the restored arms of Henry VII over the arch).

The Wardrobe – *Old Palace Yard.* Note the blue diapered Tudor walls incorporated in the early 18C building, and the fine 18C ironwork.

Trumpeters' House★ – *Old Palace Yard.* The main front of this house converted c 1701 from the Middle Gate of Richmond Palace, overlooks the garden and can be seen through the trees from the riverside path. The giant pedimented portico of paired columns was formerly guarded by stone statues after which the house is still named. For a brief period in 1848-49 it was occupied by Metternich.

Walk down Old Palace Lane.

Richmond Riverside

Old Palace Lane, lined by modest, wistaria-covered 19C houses and cottages, leads from the south-west corner of Richmond Green to the river.

Asgill House★ – Standing at the end of the lane overlooking the river from a site once within the palace walls, is a house that was built c 1760 as a weekend and summer residence for the City banker and sometime Lord Mayor, Sir Charles Asgill. In pale golden stone with strong horizontal lines and a central bay advanced and canted for the full three storeys, it was one of the last of its type to be built overlooking the Thames.

Take the towpath upstream past Trumpeters' House and Friars Lane to Whittaker Avenue. The Old Town Hall houses the Museum of Richmond *(description in Worth a Visit).*

Flanking the Old Town Hall is a new complex of offices, shops and restaurants (1988), designed by Q Terry to complement the neighbouring buildings.

Richmond Bridge★★ – The bridge, a classical, stone structure of five arches and parapet designed by James Paine, was built in 1774 to replace the horse ferry and widened in 1937; tolls were levied until the 19C. There is a milestone-obelisk at the north end.

The towpath continues beyond the bridge as a riverside promenade below Terrace Gardens (between Petersham Road and Richmond Hill).

From Richmond Bridge walk up Richmond Hill.

Richmond Hill

The **view**★★ gets ever better as one climbs the steep road lined by balconied terraces, immortalised through the ages by many artists including Turner and Reynolds.
The **Wick** and **Wick House** on the west side of the road, built in 1775 and 1772 – the latter by **Sir William Chambers** for **Sir Joshua Reynolds** – both enjoy views across the bend in the river towards Marble Hill.
At the top, overlooking the park stands **Ancaster House**, a brick mansion with big bow windows, built in 1722 principally to designs by **Robert Adam**. The house is now attached to the **Star and Garter Home** for disabled sailors, soldiers and airmen opposite, which stands on the site of an inn famous in the 18C and 19C and was opened in 1924. (The British Legion poppy factory is at the Richmond end of Petersham Road.)
The park gates which mark the hilltop are dated 1700 and are attributed to **"Capability" Brown**.

A Ditty

This lass so neat, with smiles so sweet,
Has won my right good-will,
I'd crowns resign to call thee mine,
Sweet lass of Richmond Hill.
Leonard Macnally (1752-1820)

Richmond Park★★

The countryside had been a royal chase for centuries when **Charles I** enclosed 2 470 acres/494ha as a park in 1637. It is the largest of the royal parks, and is famous for its varied **wildlife** – most notably its herds of almost tame red and fallow deer, its majestic **oak trees** and the **spring flowers** (rhododendrons) of the Isabella Plantation.
On a fine day from the top of the Henry VIII mound (said to have been raised to allow the king to survey the field) there is a dramatic **panoramic view**★★★ extending from Windsor Castle to the dome of St Paul's – look out for Telecom Tower, Battersea Power Station, Canary Wharf...
Among the houses in the park are **Pembroke Lodge** *(cafeteria)*, a rambling late-17C-18C house at the centre of colourful walled and woodland gardens adapted by **John Soane** from a molecatcher's cottage and later used by Lord John Russell (Prime Minister 1846-51 and 1865-66) and his grandson, the philosopher **Bertrand Russell**; Thatched House Lodge, the home of Princess Alexandra; and **White Lodge**, built by George II in 1727 as a hunting lodge and since 1955 the junior section of the **Royal Ballet School**.

TWICKENHAM

Map p 336 (TYZ) Overground: Twickenham, St Margaret's from Waterloo Station

Twickenham nowadays draws visitors rather to its rugby matches than to its riverside *(see PRACTICAL POINTS – Sports)*. In the 19C, **Louis-Philippe**, cousin of Louis XVI and future King of France (1830-48), three of his five sons, several descendants and a number of sympathisers all lived in as many as nine houses in Twickenham. Of these, three remain: **Bushy House** was the home of the Duke of Clarence, later William IV who lived there first with his mistress **Dorothea Jordan** *(see index)* and their 10 illegitimate children, and later with his wife, the future Queen Adelaide, until her death in 1849; it is now leased by the Crown Estates to the National Physical Laboratory (Teddington). The other two are **Morgan House** on Ham Common which is now part of the Cassel Hospital, and York House. In the grounds of Upper Lodge is the most complete 18C water garden in London.

Description of Marble Hill House in Worth a Visit.

York House

Richmond Road. The Yorke family lived on and worked a farm on the site in the 15C and 16C; successors, who from 1700 altered and rebuilt the house, retained the name including, in the 19C, members of the exiled French royal family and, this century, an Indian merchant prince. Today, the house accommodates Council offices.
The house has a terrace at the rear overlooking the walled garden. A footbridge leads to a cascade and rose garden preceding a shrubbery and grass terrace beside the Thames.

Sion Road

The road leading down to the river is joined halfway down, at the rounded Waterman's Lodge, by Ferry Road, a close of "two down, two up" cottages. Beyond is **Sion Row**, a terrace of 12 three-storey houses built in 1721, in ordered lines with a uniform cornice, three lights and off-centre entrances, personalised by individual doorways.
At the end, parallel to the river, is a straggling line of houses of all periods: a pub, all corners and balconies, the Ferry House, three floors of white stucco with a slate roof, and Riverside House (1810), a rambling two storeys beneath broad eaves. There is a passenger ferry to Ham House *(description in Worth a Visit)*.

Worth a Visit

HAM HOUSE**

Map p 296 (TZ) Overground: Twickenham from Waterloo. (NT) ♿ House: Open early-Apr to early-Nov, Sat-Wed and Good Fri, 1-5pm. Garden: Open Sat-Wed, 11am-6pm/dusk. Closed 25-26 Dec, 1 Jan. £6. Braille guide; sympathetic hearing scheme. Parking. Refreshments. ☎ 020 8940 1950; Fax 020 8332 6903; hamhouse@nationaltrust.org.uk; www.nationaltrust.org.uk

Ham House was at its prime under Elizabeth Dysart, **Duchess of Lauderdale**, "a woman of great beauty but greater parts... a wonderful quickness of apprehension and an amazing vivacity in conversation... (who) had studied... mathematics and philosophy; but... was restless in her ambition, profuse in her expense and of a most ravenous covetousness; she was a violent friend, and a much more violent enemy." She lived in dangerous times – her father, William Murray first Earl of Dysart, had literally been youthful "whipping boy" for Prince Charles, future Charles I. Elizabeth, it was said, became for a time the Protector's mistress.

Her first husband, Sir Lyonel Tollemache, was the first in the line of Earls of Dysart, who remained owners of Ham House until it was presented to the National Trust.

Her second husband, the Earl, later Duke of Lauderdale, favourite of the Stuart restoration, was a learned, ambitious, vicious character. A double portrait, *Both ye Graces in one picture,* by **Sir Peter Lely** in the Round Gallery, presents them graphically; the toll of years is clearly evident in the duchess of whom there is an earlier portrait on the same wall.

The Lauderdales, according to their contemporaries, "lived at a vast rate." They enlarged the house, which had been built to the conventional Jacobean plan in 1610, and modified the front to give a continuous roof line with a horizontal emphasis. A family idiosyncrasy for making inventories and for hoarding furniture, paintings, hangings and bills for structural and decorative alterations, has enabled the house to be returned to its 1678 appearance when it was described by **John Evelyn** as "furnished like a great prince's." The gardens have been relaid to the 17C plan.

Exterior – The fabric is brick with stone dressings; the building, three storeys beneath a hipped roof with a five-bay centre *(north side)* recessed between square bays and typical, canted Jacobean outer bays. The fine iron gates and piers date from 1671; previously the house had been approached by a tree-lined canal from the river to a watergate near the main door; the present forecourt, with the **Coade stone** figure of **Father Thames** by John Bacon, was laid out in 1800.

Interior – Paintings, in this house, bring to life the period of Charles II, the Cavalier generals, the women at court – young, fair, delicately complexioned and far from innocent. Furniture, doors, doorcases, fireplaces and ceilings display the craftsmanship of the period, frequently Dutch for Dutch craftsmen were well established long before the accession of William III. The remarkable ceilings show the progress from geometrical type plasterwork to garlands and spandrels (compare the original, north and later, south rooms).

Ground Floor – The house has an impressive entrance in the Great Hall, increased above by the Round Gallery with a decorated plaster ceiling by Kinsman (1637). **Lely** portraits adorn the gallery; below are portraits of Dysarts (17C-18C) by **Kneller and Reynolds**.

The most notable features of other rooms on the ground floor are the gilt leather wall hangings and the 1679 cedar side tables in the Marble Dining Room (parquetry replaced the marble paving in the 18C), the artificially grained and gilded panelling, fashionable in the 1670s, the chimney furniture of silver, considered very ostentatious

The panelled interior of the Long Gallery, Ham House

by contemporaries. In the Duchess's Bedchamber are damask hangings; in the Yellow Bedroom or Volury Room the bed (note the carved cherub feet) is hung with purple and yellow; in the White Closet are an oyster work veneered writing desk and picture of the south front of the house in 1683 *(fireplace)*. The altar cloth of "crimson velvet & gould & silver stuff" in the chapel is original.
The **Great Staircase** of 1637, built of oak round a square well and gilded, has a singularly beautiful balustrade of boldly carved trophies of arms.

Upper Floor – Lady Maynard's suite contains 17C Flemish tapestries after Poussin below a wooden frieze and family portraits.
The Museum Room displays examples of the original vivid upholstery, an 18C toilet set, a prayer book of 1625, ledgers and bills of the alterations to the house and the 1679 inventory which has enabled the rooms to be arranged as in Elizabeth Dysart's day. The Cabinet of Miniatures presents a collection of miniatures by **Hilliard**, **Oliver** and Cooper.
The North Drawing Room is sumptuous, epitomising the Lauderdale passion for luxury and display in a plaster frieze and rich ceiling (1637) above walls hung with English silk tapestries (woven by ex-Mortlake workers in Soho), carved and gilded wainscoting, doorcases and doors; furniture is carved, gilded and richly upholstered; the fireplace is exuberantly Baroque...
Equally opulent is the Queen's Suite, rich with late-17C garlanded plaster ceilings, grained wainscoting and carved wood swags above the fireplaces; the furniture includes then fashionable Oriental screens, English japanned chairs, a small Chinese cabinet on a gilded stand and 18C tapestries.
In the heavily ornate closet with painted ceiling and the original satin brocade hangings, note the carved "sleeping chayre."

Marble Hill House★

(EH) (♿) Open late-Mar to Oct, daily, 10am-6pm (5pm Oct). £3.30 Audiotour. Guided tour (1hr) by appointment. Dogs on leads. Parking. Restaurant (summer), picnic area. ☎ 020 8892 5115; www.english-heritage.org.uk

Marble Hill House was built in 1729 by Henrietta Howard (a mistress of the Prince of Wales, later George II), with monies settled on her by her royal lover. She acquired a parcel of land beside the river; plans were sketched by **Colen Campbell**, Architect to the Prince of Wales. It was 1731, however, before Henrietta, now **Countess of Suffolk** and Mistress of the Robes, could "often visit Marble Hill" and several years more before she took up residence there with her second husband, George Berkeley. She was an active hostess and received politicians, lawyers, and men of letters, including **Alexander Pope** and **Horace Walpole**. The most famous of later residents was another royal mistress (of the Prince Regent), Mrs Fitzherbert, who lived there briefly in 1795.
The gardens, now disappeared but in the 18C considered integral to the house's design, were, from 1724, the preoccupation of **Alexander Pope** whose adages included "in all let Nature never be forgot", a near neighbour at Crossdeep: of his house and gardens nothing remains save a grotto.

The House – The Palladian style, stucco house is three storeys high with the centre advanced beneath a pediment and an insignificant 18C entrance.
From the small hall, the square mahogany staircase leads directly to the Great Room, a 24ft/7m cube splendidly rich in white and gold with carved decoration and copies of Van Dyck paintings upon the walls. Lady Suffolk's bedchamber *(left)*, divided by Ionic pillars and pilasters to form a bed alcove, is completed, like the other rooms, by a rich cornice and ceiling decoration. Though the actual furniture and furnishings were dispersed, an almost exact reconstruction has been achieved from a detailed inventory made on her ladyship's death in 1767. Some original items have been successfully traced: overmantel and overdoors by Panini and carved table in the Great Room. There is a fine collection of 18C paintings (Hogarth, Wilson, Hayman, Kneller).
A stone staircase leads to the restored second floor *(access on conducted tours only)* where is displayed a collection of chinoiserie.
The stable block *(north-east)* dates from 1825-27. Close by is an 18C terrace, Montpelier Row.

Museum of Richmond

Old Town Hall. ♿ Open Tue-Sat, 11am-5pm; also May-Sep, Sun, 1-4pm. ☎ 020 8332 1141; Fax 020 8948 7570; musrich@globalnet.co.uk; www.museumofrichmond.com

Displays relate to the local history of Richmond, Ham, Petersham and Kew: model of Richmond Palace in 1562.

Orleans House Gallery

Riverside, Twickenham. Garden: Open daily, 9am-dusk. House: ♿ Open Tue-Sun, 1pm (2pm Sun and Bank Hols) to 5.30pm (4.30pm Oct-Mar). Parking. Guide dogs welcome. Ramp access and toilet facilities for visitors using wheelchairs and pushchairs. ☎ 020 8892 0221; Fax 020 8744 0501; r.tranter@richmond.gov.uk; m.denovellis@richmond.gov.uk; www.richmond.gov.uk

Orleans House itself was demolished in 1926, only the **Octagon**, added in 1720, 10 years after the house was first built, remains. This wing by **James Gibbs** has a brick exterior and splendid plasterwork, including fireplace, door pediments, figures and ceiling.

Royal Air Force Museum★★

Magnificent flying machines and simulators inform and entertain enthusiasts and laymen alike at this well-presented museum which is undergoing extensive redevelopment. Events throughout the year help to give an understanding of history to the younger generations.

Location

Map p 336 (TX), Grahame Park Way. Buses: 226 along Edgware Road. ⊖ Colindale. Colindale is situated to the north-west of London off A 5 or A 41.

Background

Affiliated to the Imperial War Museum *(see LAMBETH)*, this museum is dedicated to the history of aviation and of the RAF and is presented in several hangars on the historic site of Old Hendon Airfield, where Grahame-White established his flying school before the First World War.

R.A.F. Museum

A Lancaster Bomber – A decisive force in mid-20C conflict

Highlights

♿ *Open daily, 10am-6pm. Closed 24-26 Dec, 1 Jan. No charge; flight simulator £2. Guided tour. Parking. Licensed restaurant. ☎ 020 8205 2266; Fax 020 8200 1751; info@rafmuseum.org; www.rafmuseum.org*

Historical Galleries

First floor. The displays recount the history of the Air Force: early experiments with balloons and biplanes; early trophies including the two British Empire Michelin Trophies awarded to the British pilot flying the greatest distance in a British plane: No 1 was awarded to Moore-Brabazon in 1910 for a distance of 19mi/16km; Von Richthofen's flying helmet; uniforms worn by Lord Trenchard, Chief of Air Staff; VCs and GCs won in combat; escape equipment; ejector seats; audio-visual display on life in the RAF today.

Main Aircraft Hall

The World War I hall presents a unique collection of aircraft in chronological order from a Blériot monoplane and a Sopwith Camel through a Supermarine Stranraer flying boat, a Westland (Bristol) Belvedere helicopter and a Sikorsky hoverfly to a Lightning Mach 2. The **Flight Simulator** offers three programmes: flying with the Red Arrows in a Tornado; an aircraft carrier strike; a 1918 dog-fight in which the cockpit pitches and rolls as if at the mercy of the elements.

Visitors can sit in the cockpit of a **Jet Provost Trainer** and try the controls.

Bomber Command Hall

This hall contains a Lancaster, a Heinkel He 162A-2, a Handley Page Halifax, a Vickers Valiant, Vimy and Wellington, a B17 Flying Fortress, Mosquito and a Vulcan. There are static displays on the USAAF in Britain and the history of the RAF Factory at Farnborough and a replica of the office of Sir Barnes Wallis who invented the bouncing bomb.

Battle of Britain Experience

The Battle is announced by tableaux on the Munich Crisis, the Declaration of War and Evacuation.

The forces involved are represented by an impressive array of aircraft: Junkers 87 and 88, Heinkel 111, Messerschmitt against Gloster Gladiators, Tiger Moths, Spitfires and Hurricanes. In addition to the machines are an operations room, uniforms, medals, documents, relics and other memorabilia. The far end of the hall presents a V2 Rocket, Short Sunderland V, Westland Lysander and a Supermarine Seagull.

The museum is undergoing extensive redevelopment to turn it into a state-of-the-art exhibition area with new galleries and more planes on view as well as interactive displays.

Syon Park★★

The prospect of this splendid mansion, set in a vast park by the Thames and opposite Kew Gardens, is enchanting. It has been the seat of an aristocratic family since the 16C and is a prime example of the Robert Adam style. Take a stroll through the fragrant rose garden, admire the great conservatory and enjoy the many other attractions in the grounds.

Location

Map p 336 (TY). Overground: Syon Lane from Waterloo Station. Syon Park is south of the A 4 and near M 4 (Exit 2).

Adjacent Sights: KEW, OSTERLEY PARK, RICHMOND.

Background

Artistic Patronage – On the walls inside are portraits of the men and women who built up the house and their royal patrons by **Gainsborough**, **Reynolds**, **Van Dyck**, Mytens, **Lely** and by unknown artists of the English 16C school. Two men were principally responsible for the construction: the Lord Protector, **Duke of Somerset**, brother of Henry's queen, Jane Seymour, in the 16C, and Hugh Percy, 1st Duke of **Northumberland** in the 18C. Somerset was given the former monastery site in 1547 by his nephew **Edward VI** and erected a Tudor mansion in the plan of a hollow square, dined his monarch there in 1550, laid out gardens, including the first physic garden in England... but in 1552 he was charged with conspiracy and executed.

For the next two centuries Syon was a political storm centre as the owners intrigued, conspired and often died brutally: John Dudley was beheaded (1553) for promoting his daughter-in-law, **Lady Jane Grey**, as Queen; Percys, Earls of Northumberland, were executed for supporting **Mary Queen of Scots** (1572), were found dead in the Tower (1585) and imprisoned for association with the **Gunpowder Plot**... With the marriage in 1682 of Elizabeth Percy to Charles, 6th Duke of Somerset, Syon returned to a descendant of its earlier owner, who also held office under the Crown. In the 18C the new heirs, the Duke and Duchess of Northumberland, considered the house and grounds were in urgent need of remodelling: they commissioned **Robert Adam** and **Capability Brown** to produce designs.

Pub

London Apprentice – *62 Church St, Isleworth, TW7 6BG – ☎ 020 8560 1915 – Open Mon-Sat 11am-11pm, Sun noon-10.30pm.* The pub is said to be named after one of the apprentices who from the 16C to 19C rowed up the river on their annual holiday and made the inn their own for a day.

Highlights

Gardens: Open daily, 10am-5.30pm/dusk. House: (♿) Open late-Mar to early-Nov, Wed-Thu, Sun and Bank Hols, 11am-5pm. Audio-guide. Guide book. Leaflet. Closed 25-26 Dec. House and gardens £6.95; gardens £3.50. ☎ 020 8560 0882; Fax 020 8568 0936; www.syonpark.co.uk

The House

The colonnaded east front of Syon House is visible across the river from Kew Gardens, the Northumberland Lion with outstretched tail silhouetted against the sky; a second beast, also from the model by Michelangelo, crowns the Lion Gate and graceful Adam screen on the London Road (A 315). The plain castellated main front gives no hint of the rich ornamentation within.

In the **Great Hall**, Adam is at his most formal: the high ceiling echoes the patterns laid into the black and white marble pavement; in the apses at either end nestle copies of Classical statues – the *Apollo Belvedere* and the *Dying Gladiator*.

The **Ante-room**, by contrast, gleams darkly with heavy gilding, reds, blues, yellows, in the patterned *scagliola* floor, and green marble and *scagliola* pillars (dredged from the Tiber), which line the walls on three sides and stand forward from the fourth to "square" the room. Gilded statues gaze down from the entablature.

State Dining Room – The long apartment with column screened apses at either end was the first to be remodelled by Adam: deep niches with copies of antique statues along the left wall were reflected in pier mirrors; frieze, cornice, ceiling, decorated half domes, beautiful doorcases and doors afforded a perfect setting for the banquets given by the Duke and Duchess in the late 18C.

Red Drawing Room – Scarlet Spitalfields silk, blooming with pale gold roses, on the walls and at the windows, a carpet, signed and dated 1769, woven at Moorfields, door pilasters with ivory panels covered with ormolu, gilded ceiling studded with Cipriani painted medallions provide great richness; the room is, however, dominated by its

K. Brett/MICHELIN

Great Conservatory, Syon Park

Stuart portraits: Charles I (Lely); his queen, Henrietta Maria (Van Dyck); his sister Elizabeth of Bohemia (Van Honthorst); his elder brother who pre-deceased him, Prince Henry (Van Somer); his daughter, Princess Mary of Orange (Hanneman), Henrietta, Duchess of Orleans (Mignard), Princess Elizabeth (Lely), his sons, Charles II and his wife Catherine of Braganza (Huysmans) and James II as Duke of York (Lely). The elegant mosaic-topped side tables are noteworthy.

Long Gallery – The long gallery of the Tudor house was transformed by Adam into a ladies' withdrawing room (far enough away from the dining room not to hear any masculine after dinner ribaldry!). It is 136ft/42m long, 14ft/4m wide and has a crossline decoration on the ceiling, grouped pilasters, wall niches, pier mirrors, so arranged as to disguise the length. Much of the furniture was designed, as throughout the house, by Adam, notably the veneered chest of drawers made by Chippendale.

The furniture in the **Print Room** includes two remarkable walnut, marquetry inlaid cabinets of the late 17C; the walls are again hung with family portraits.

Gardens★

Capability Brown assisted in designing the gardens, which extend to the river and maintain a tradition begun by Protector Somerset who planted many rare and imported trees; two of his mulberries still survive. In 1837 the gardens, world famous for their botanical specimens, were opened to the public. A vast **rose garden** *(separate entrance south of the house)* is in bloom from May to August.

The **Great Conservatory**, a beautiful semicircular building of white painted gun metal and Bath stone, with a central cupola and end pavilions was designed by Charles Fowler in 1820-27. Inside are cacti and an aquarium.

London Butterfly House – ♿ *Open daily, 10am-5pm (3.30pm winter). Closed 25-26 Dec. £3.30. Parking. ☎ 020 8560 7272 (recorded information), 020 8560 0378; Fax 020 8560 7272; www.butterflies.org.uk*

In a tropical greenhouse visitors may stroll among many varieties of brilliant butterflies. All stages of breeding may be observed. Another section displays live spiders and insects: locusts, crickets, ants and scorpions.

Riverside

The **Isleworth Parish Church of All Saints** on the south outskirts of Syon Park has a square crenellated west tower of ragstone dating back to the 15C. The church was bombed and on the site since 1970 has stood a well-proportioned modern building of brick, wood and plain glass, with only small brasses rescued from the fire.

The London Apprentice pub *(see above)* dates back centuries although the present building is a mere 200 years old.

Wimbledon

In addition to its thriving village perched on a hilltop, vast common land including meadows, woods, ponds, a windmill and a golf course, Wimbledon takes great pride in its acclaimed tennis championship which draws international stars every summer. Two theatres and a stadium offer other kinds of entertainment; a Thai Buddhist temple is an unusual feature in the town.

Location

Map p 336 (TZ). ⊖ Wimbledon, Southfields, Wimbledon Park; Overground Wimbledon. The busy suburb of Wimbledon to the south-west of London is accessible by A 3, the main thoroughfare to the south.

Adjacent Sights: FULHAM – PUTNEY.

Background

The earliest known inhabitants of Wimbledon occupied the Iron Age hillfort on the south-west side of the Common, known erroneously as **Caesar's Camp**. The village developed in Saxon times along the High Street and around the church, first coming to prominence in 1588 when Thomas Cecil, **Lord Burghley**, then Lord of the Manor, built a mansion with turrets and gables, set amid terraced gardens on a slope north-east of the church. Before its destruction in 1720 it was visited by **Queen Elizabeth** and **King James I**. The only building surviving from this period is **Eagle House** (1613) in the High Street which was built by Robert Bell, a native of Wimbledon and a founder of the **East India Company**. The Manor subsequently passed to **Queen Henrietta Maria**, to Sir Theodore Janssen, a financier who built a new house west of the church but was ruined in the South Sea Bubble, and then to Sarah, **Duchess of Marlborough**, who also built a new house linked to detached servants' quarters by an underground passage.

Directory

Pubs

Crooked Billet – *11 Crooked Billet Rd, SW19 4RQ – ⊖ Wimbledon – ☎ 020 8946 4942 – Open Mon-Sat 11am-11pm, Sun noon-10.30pm.*

Dog and Fox – *24 High St, SW19 5DX – ⊖ Wimbledon – ☎ 020 8946 6565 – Open Mon-Sat 11am-11pm, Sun noon-10.30pm.*

Hand-in-Hand – *6 Crooked Billet Rd, SW19 4RQ – ⊖ Wimbledon – ☎ 020 8946 5720 – Open Mon-Sat 11am-11pm, Sun noon-10.30pm.*

Rose and Crown – *55 High St, SW19 5DX – ⊖ Wimbledon – ☎ 020 8947 4713 – Open Mon-Sat 11am-11pm, Sun noon-10.30pm.*

Entertainment

Polka Theatre for Children – *240 The Broadway, SW19 1SB – ⊖ Wimbledon – ☎ 020 8543 4888 (box office) – boxoffice@polkatheatre.com – Open late-Sep to early-Aug Tue-Fri 9.30am-4.30pm, Sat 11am-5.30pm.* A full programme of performances and workshops for children, supplemented by exhibitions of puppets etc; also playground, shop and café.

Walking About

Wimbledon Common

In 1871, after seven years of legal dispute with Earl Spencer, Lord of the Manor, who wanted to enclose the Common and develop some 300 acres/120ha for housing, Wimbledon Common was transferred to the Conservators to preserve in its natural state. Whereas Lord Spencer asserted that the land was boggy with noxious mist and fogs arising from it, Leigh Hunt wrote of the "furze in full bloom making a golden floor of all that fine healthy expanse." The horse racing, duelling and drilling of soldiers of earlier days have given way to horse riding, cricket, rugby and golf. "Every person playing golf" is required by the Conservators "to wear a red outer garment." From 1860 the National Rifle Association held their annual shooting competitions on the Common, even setting up a horse-drawn tramway for the spectators, before moving to Bisley in 1889.

The 18C saw several large mansions rise round the Common; **Lauriston House** (1724; destroyed 1959), home of **William Wilberforce**; **King's College School** (1750) with adjoining Great Hall in Gothic Revival style (note the hexagonal pillar-box of

1872); **Southside House** (1776) *Woodhayes Rd. Guided tour (1hr 15min) Sat before Easter to early-Oct, Wed, Sat-Sun and Bank Hol Mon at 2pm, 3pm, 4pm. £5. ☎ 020 8946 7643*

Access: by bus 93 to Wimbledon War Memorial; Putney Bridge, Wimbledon

Gothick Lodge (1760) *Woodhayes Rd*, was owned by the writer of adventure stories Captain Marryat in the 1820s; **Crooked Billet** and **Hand-in-Hand** are 17C public houses *(see Directory)*; **Chester House** (1670) was famous for the Sunday parties of the Revd John Horne Tooke, whose election to Parliament in 1801 provoked the Act which made the clergy ineligible; **Westside House** (1760). **Cannizaro** (1727, rebuilt in 1900) was owned by Viscount Melville from 1887 who laid out the gardens and entertained William Pitt, **Edmund Burke** and **Richard Sheridan**. *Open daily, 8.30am-dusk (9.30pm at latest). ☎ 020 8946 7349*

Also of interest are **Stamford House** (1720) and **The Keir** (1789). The **Round** or **Old Central School** *(Camp Rd)*, an octagonal building, was built in 1760 to educate 50 children of the deserving poor and is now incorporated in a primary school.

Wimbledon Village

Stage coaches set out from the **Rose and Crown** and later from the **Dog and Fox** in the High Street, although the road over Putney Heath was infested with highwaymen. *(See Directory)*.

The **Well House** in Arthur Road dates from 1761.

St Mary's Church

Church Rd. ♿ Open usually Mon-Sat, 9am-4pm. Closed sometimes during school holidays. ☎ 020 8946 2605; Fax 020 8946 6293; church@stmaryswimbledon.fsnet.co.uk; www.zyworld.com/wimbledonchurch/stmarys.htm

Wimbledon church was mentioned in **The Domesday Book**; parts of a 13C rebuilding remain in the chancel. The present nave, tower and spire were designed in 1843 by Sir George Gilbert Scott. Several famous people – **William Wilberforce**, Sir Theodore Janssen and **JW Bazalgette** *(see index)* – are buried in the churchyard. To the north stands the **Old Rectory** (1500) the oldest house in Wimbledon and probably a priest's house until the Reformation. Near the churchyard entrance stands a small white house, **Stag Lodge**, with the hinges on which the gate to the later Manor House was hung still visible on a post at the side.

Worth a Visit

Wimbledon Lawn Tennis Museum

Church Rd. ♿ Open daily 10.30am-5pm. Closed Sun during and Monday following The Championships, 24-26 Dec, 1 Jan. £5.50. Leaflet (6 languages). Parking. Tea room. ☎ 020 8946 6131; Fax 020 8944 6497; museum@aeltc.com; www.wimbledon.org/museum

Displays depict the development of tennis and include sections on dress, equipment and the Wimbledon Champions from the early days in Worple Road to the modern era.

A Summer Event

The **All England Lawn Tennis Open Championships** are usually held at the end of June. The Centre Court is exclusively reserved for the Championships; use of the No 1 court is limited to special events such as the occasional Davis Cup match.

Wimbledon Museum

Ridgway. Open Sat-Sun, 2.30-5pm. ☎ 020 8296 9914; mail@wimbledonmuseum.org.uk; www.wimbledonmuseum.org.uk

The local history museum is housed in the **Village Club**, which was built in 1858 to provide the working and middle classes with enjoyment and improvement through a reading room, library, lectures and instruction.

Wimbledon Windmill Museum

Windmill Rd. (♿) Open Easter or Apr-Oct, Sat-Sun and Bank Hols, 11am (2pm Sat) to 5pm. £1. Parking. Café. ☎/Fax 020 8947 2825

The windmill, a hollow post mill built on the Common in 1817, has been converted into a museum illustrating the story of windmills in pictures, models and the machinery and tools of the trade.

In the neighbouring miller's house **Lord Baden-Powell** began to write *Scouting for Boys* in 1907.

Woolwich – Charlton

Woolwich has many interesting features besides the spectacular Thames Barrier: imposing buildings, a lively market and shopping precinct, green spaces and an attractive riverfront. It has a strong naval and army tradition. The old part of Charlton to the south has a certain rural charm with its 17C mansion and church.

Location

Map p 337 (UY). Buses: 51, 177, 180. Overground: Charlton from Waterloo. Boat: Thames Barrier from Westminster Pier, Greenwich. The Woolwich Ferry plies between Woolwich and North Woolwich. A new pier will give river access to the Royal Arsenal. A 205, the South Circular, terminates near Woolwich. Access from Greenwich is by A 206. *Adjacent Sights: GREENWICH; ELTHAM PALACE.*

Background

The fishing village of Woolwich began its naval and military career in the Tudor period. In those days it was the most important naval dockyard in the country. The *Great Harry*, built in 1512 during the reign of Henry VIII, was the first four-master to be launched in England; it had square sails on the fore and main masts, topsails on all four masts and topgallants on the first three. In 1717 the gun casting works were transferred from Moorfields and became the **Royal Arsenal** which reached its maximum output during the First World War when it extended over 1 200 acres/480ha and employed 80 000 men and women.

Walking About

WOOLWICH

Following the regeneration of the Royal Arsenal site with residential, business and leisure schemes and better transport facilities, the character of the former army town is changing. Take a stroll along the Riverside Walk linking Greenwich to Thamesmead to admire the views.

Royal Artillery HQ

The grandiose home of the RA comprises the arcaded buildings of the former **Royal Military Academy** (founded in 1741 and amalgamated with Sandhurst in 1964) and its regimental barracks (720ft/219m long). The grand buildings, including The Old Military Academy, are being restored to their full glory. *Description of Firepower! The Royal Artillery Museum in Worth a Visit.*

Thames Barrier

Unit Way. ♿ Open Apr-Sep, daily, 10.30am-4.30pm (11am-3.30pm, Oct-Mar). Closed 24 Dec to 1 Jan. £1; tickets available from the cafe area. Parking. Cafeteria. ☎ 020 8305 4188; Fax 020 8855 2146; www.environment-agency.gov.uk

The construction of the barrier at Woolwich was undertaken in 1972-82 to protect central London from the threat of inundation by a surge tide. London is sinking on its bed of clay and Britain itself tilting: Scotland and the north-west are rising, the south-east is dipping by about a foot a century; tide levels have risen by 2ft/60cm at London Bridge in the last 100 years. The barrier is composed of four falling radial gates (three to the north and one to the south) and 6 rising sector gates, the four larger being 200ft/61m long and weighing 3 300 tonnes and the two smaller being

The gleaming cowls of the Thames Barrier

K. Brett/MICHELIN

103ft/31.5m long and weighing 900 tonnes. Each sector gate is raised, rotating through 90° from its concrete sill in the riverbed, by two arms projecting from the barge-shaped piers in which the lifting machinery is housed beneath huge stainless steel cowls. Further information is provided in an audio-visual presentation in the Visitor Centre.

A Tradition

The **Woolwich Free Ferry** dates from the 14C and is the last regular service of the hundreds which once crossed the Thames. It is now operated by three roll-on roll-off vessels each capable of carrying 1 000 passengers and 200 tonnes of vehicles on the 5min crossing.

Charlton

From the station walk down Charlton Church Lane.

The Village

The parish church, the big house, the **Bugle Horn Inn**, a rebuilt post-house, the 18C White Swan mark the length of the main street, still characteristically rural and appropriately named.

St Luke's Church

Charlton Church Lane. The brick church with its square tower and Dutch gable doorway, dates, in the main, from 1630 when it was rebuilt by Sir Adam Newton *(see below)*. Inside are a memorial tablet to Master Edward Wilkinson (d 1567), Yeoman of the Mouth to Henry VIII and Edward VI and Master Cook to Queen Elizabeth, a 17C heraldic north window, the hatchment (west wall) of the Spencer Percevals and Spencer Wilsons, who in the 18C owned Charlton House, the royal arms of Queen Anne and the tablet and bust of Spencer Perceval, assassinated in the House of Commons when prime minister in 1812. The church, a landmark from the Thames, served as a navigational aid in the early 18C and still flies the white ensign on St George's and St Luke's days.

Cross The Village. Description of Charlton House in Worth a Visit.

Worth a Visit

Firepower!

(♿) Open Apr-Oct, Wed-Sun, 11am-5.30pm; Nov-Mar, Fri-Sun, 11am-5pm. £6.50. Parking. ☎ 020 8855 7755; Fax 020 8855 7100; info@firepower.org.uk; www.firepower.org.uk

Field of Fire, an amazing multi-media presentation, is the centre-piece of this museum devoted to the history of artillery. The dramatic story of the brave gunners who served in recent conflicts is related using authentic footage and to the sounds of shell and gun fire. Heavy guns and vehicles are displayed in the Gunnery Hall; the History Gallery traces the development of artillery from the Middle Ages. After viewing medals and orders visitors are given the opportunity to use real equipment in the Real Weapons Gallery. Missiles, guns, vehicles and other large equipment are also on view in Monster Bits.

The Rotunda houses the reserve collections. This most elegant of small museums, began as a campaign tent designed by **John Nash** for the somewhat premature celebration of the defeat of Napoleon organised by the allied sovereigns in St James's Park in 1814. In 1819 the Prince Regent ordered the tent's re-erection at Woolwich "to house military curiosities."

Charlton House

(♿) Open by appointment Mon-Fri, 9am-10pm; Sat, 9am-5pm (library only). Leaflet. Refreshments. ☎ 020 8856 3951; Fax 020 8856 4162; www.greenwich.gov.uk

The house, the finest extant example of Jacobean architecture in London, was built between 1607 and 1612 for Adam Newton, Dean of Durham and tutor to Prince Henry, eldest son of James I. Characteristically of deep red brick with stone dressings, it has a shallow H shaped plan with symmetrical bays at the end of each wing and balustrades lining the crest and terrace. At the centre is the door with a surround dated 1607, and two-storey bay above in stone, exuberantly decorated in an unusual German style.

Features inside include the plaster work, particularly the ceiling with pendants in the Grand Saloon over the two-storey hall, the fireplaces, Long Gallery and typical staircase with square well and carved newel posts. The gateway, stranded on the front lawn, is the original Tuscan pillared entrance with an added 18C crest. In 1608 at James I's request a mulberry tree was planted in the north-east corner of the garden near the gazebo.

Windsor Castle★★★

On a steep bluff and in a beautiful park setting, the romantic turrets and the massive tower of Windsor Castle rise above the bustling town in the Thames valley. It is a fascinating example of a medieval castle which has evolved into a sumptuous royal residence.
The royal association gives great cachet to the pretty town which boasts a thriving theatre, fine shops, restaurants and tearooms. Over the bridge are the fine buildings of Eton College which are of great interest.

Location

24 High St. ☎ 01753 652 010. Overground from London Waterloo. Windsor is to the west of London and is easily accessible by M 4. Leave the motorway at Junction 6.

Background

Windsor Castle is the oldest royal residence to have remained in continuous use by the reigning monarchs, and the largest castle in England. It was originally intended by **William the Conqueror** (c 1080) as one of several defensive strongholds built around London, and as such was constructed on the only elevated point in that stretch of the Thames valley. Norman castles conformed to a standard plan with a large tower or keep dominating the complex from an artificially raised earthen mound or *motte*; at Windsor this is flanked by the Upper and Lower Wards. The castle covers an area of 13 acres/5ha.

Royal Residence – As early as 1110 **Henry I** is known to have had quarters in Windsor to which he would retire after a day's hunting in the forest (now Windsor Great Park). His successor **Henry II** began building the stone castle as a royal residence equipped with state apartments in the Lower Ward and with more intimate, private lodgings on the north side of the Upper Ward for use by his close family (1165-79). Further expansion was undertaken by **Henry III** (reigned 1216-72) and by **Edward III** (reigned 1327-77) a century later.

Royal Residents – Used by the Parliamentarians during the Civil War as a prison for Royalist supporters it became **Charles II**'s favourite (defensible) home outside London. In 1673 the architect Hugh May was appointed to manage a series of ambitious renovations that included the reconstruction of St George's Hall and the King's Chapel: he turned his attention not so much to changing the exterior appearance and crenellated walls but to the interior. He turned the draughty rooms into sumptuous apartments befitting a king: walls were insulated with oak wainscoting and festooned in **Grinling Gibbons** carvings, the ceilings decorated by the Italian painter **Verrio** (much of whose work was unfortunately destroyed by Wyatville in 1829) and gilded by a French master-craftsman René Coussin.

William III preferred Hampton Court to Windsor, but this situation was reversed with the accession of **George III** who had the Queen's Lodge (1777) designed by **William Chambers**; he modernised Frogmore in Home Park as a retreat for Queen Charlotte and revived the formal institution of the Order of the Garter in 1805. Additional plans for major improvements to other domestic apartments were laid after his first bout of illness, but work was halted as the king suffered a relapse in 1811.

Alterations to provide ever greater comfort were begun by **George IV** who appointed Jeffrey de Wyatville to oversee the transformations: mock Gothic renovations were implemented that included the addition of turrets, chimney-stacks and battlements and the heightening of the Round Tower by 33ft/10m, while extensions were remodelled to accommodate the large and complicated extension of the royal family. For this reason, Windsor was popular with **Queen Victoria** who received endless visits from her extended family in Europe and chose to receive heads of state there (**King Louis Philippe** in 1844; Emperor Napoleon III in 1855; King Victor Emanuel I of Italy; Emperor William I of Germany). She started the "dine and sleep" practice maintained by Queen **Elizabeth II** where guests might be invited to spend an evening and stay overnight.

The principal change made by Victoria was the creation of a private chapel in honour of **Prince Albert** who died at Windsor on 14 December 1861.

With the turn of the century came a change in spirit: **George V**'s Queen Mary began careful restoration of the castle which became the childhood home of HRH The Princesses Elizabeth and Margaret during the war, since which it has remained the Royal Family's principal home. The Court is in official residence throughout April and for Ascot Week in June when the annual Garter Day celebrations are held.

20 November 1992

The devastating fire which broke out in the Queen's Private Chapel at the north-east angle of the Upper Ward is thought to have been caused by a spotlight on a curtain high above the altar. Major losses included the wooden ceiling of the St George Hall and Grand Reception room. Work was completed in November 1997, six months ahead of schedule, to coincide with the Queen's 50th wedding anniversary. It was the largest project of its kind this century, costing in excess of £37 million and calling on the skills of some of the finest craftsmen in the country.

Highlights

♿ *Open daily, 9.45am-5.15pm (4.15pm Nov-Feb). Last admission Mar-Oct 4pm; Nov-Feb 3pm. Closed 2 Apr, Good Fri, 16 June, 25-26 Dec. St George's Chapel: Open (functions permitting) Mon-Sat, 10am-4.15pm (4.05pm last admission). £11.50 (Queen Mary's Dolls' House, State Apartments and St George's Chapel); reduced rate when the State Apartments are closed; telephone in advance to check. Changing of the Guard: Takes place (weather permitting) Apr-Jul, Mon-Sat at 11am; Aug-Mar, alternate days. Frogmore House, Gardens and Royal Mausoleum: Open May, certain days; Aug Bank Hol Sat-Sun; admission charge. ☎ 020 7321 2233 (ticket sales and information office), ☎ 01753 865 538 (St George's Chapel); ☎ 020 7799 2331 (Frogmore); information@royalcollection.org.uk; www.royal.gov.uk*

PRECINCTS

Enter from Castle Hill and proceed into the Upper Ward.

Round Tower

Henry II built this impressive section as a main defence feature surrounded by a dry (chalk) moat in c 1170; it was later heightened by Wyatville (1828-39). In fact oval (103ft/31.5m x 94ft/28.5m), it now houses the Royal Archives *(closed to the public)*. From the North Terrace there is a fine **view** over Eton and the River Thames.

Queen Mary's Doll's House

Conceived by Sir Edwin Lutyens as an accurate record of contemporary domestic design on a scale of 12:1, it was presented to Queen Mary in 1924. The contents include standard amenities in working order (water system, electric lights and two lifts), a gramophone, vintage bottles of wine (supplied by Berry Bros in St James's), vintage cars, original paintings, leather-bound books including works by Kipling, GK Chesterton, Sir Arthur Conan Doyle, Thomas Hardy and JM Barrie.

Wall cases also display another time capsule comprising a remarkable travelling "trousseau" of designer fashion-wear provided by the French and presented to the Princesses Elizabeth and Margaret after King George VI's official visit to France (1938). This includes hand-stitched kid gloves and a suite of period suitcases.

State Apartments**

When the apartments were remodelled by George IV, Gothic was used for processional spaces (lobbies, halls, staircases) and an eclectic form of Classicism for the main reception rooms.

The **Gallery**, a vaulted undercroft designed to serve as the principal entrance hall to the State Apartments, was cut off when the Grand Staircase was remodelled during the reign of Queen Victoria. Today it accommodates temporary exhibitions of prints, drawings and books from the Print Room and Royal Library. The **China Museum** displays fabulous pieces from services in the Royal Collection: Sèvres, Meissen, Copenhagen, Naples, Rockingham, Worcester... still used occasionally at banquets. The **Grand Staircase** leads up to the first floor. The full-size statue is of King George IV. On the walls is arranged a collection of trophies, arms and armour (fine suit made

Windsor Castle from the Long Walk

for Henry VIII at Greenwich) as an introduction to the array in the fan-vaulted **Grand Vestibule**. In the cases are displayed various 18C and 19C trophies acquired after the Battle of Seringapatam (1799) and the Napoleonic Wars (the lead shot that killed Lord Nelson in the Battle of Trafalgar).

The **Waterloo Chamber**, used to celebrate the anniversary of the **Battle of Waterloo** on 18 June, is hung with a series of portraits commissioned from Sir Thomas Lawrence by George IV; these depict the Allied leaders, political and military, who assisted in defeating Napoleon. Today the chamber is used for the annual luncheon given by the Queen for her Knights of the Garter and their consorts, for balls, receptions and concerts. The carved limewood panels (c 1680) from the workshop of Grinling Gibbons were retrieved from the King's Chapel.

The **Garter Throne Room** and the **Ante-Throne Room** is used by the Queen to confer upon her newly chosen knights the Order of the Garter (echoed in the plaster ceiling) before they adjourn to St George's Chapel. The **Grand Reception Room** particularly reflects George IV's personal francophile taste. The ceiling and walls, badly damaged in the 1992 fire, have been fully restored as well as the four huge chandeliers.

Public Rooms – The **King's Drawing Room** was once used by Queen Victoria for private theatrical performances, for which a stage was built up in the window alcove. Note the finely carved dado rail and Grinling Gibbons cornice; the five paintings by **Rubens** and his followers; the beautiful boulle kneehole desk reputedly acquired by William III; the carpet presented to Edward VII by the Shah of Persia in 1903. The porcelain is all Chinese.

The **King's Bedchamber** has been considerably altered through history. The marble fireplace was designed by William Chambers and transferred from Buckingham Palace; the grandiose *"polonaise"* bed is attributed to the French furniture designer George Jacob and given its furnishings for the occasion of a visit from Emperor Napoleon III and his wife Eugénie in 1855, whose initials appear at the foot of the bed. The early-19C Aubusson carpet was presented to HM The Queen by President de Gaulle in 1960. Note the Canaletto views of Venice.

The **King's Dressing Room** is lined in red damask as intended by George III; the ceiling bears the initials of William IV; the carved cornice and panelled dado, however, survive from the times of Charles II. On the walls hang a number of **masterpieces★★**: works by Dürer *(Portrait of a Young Man)*, Hans Memlinc, Jean Clouet, Hans Holbein, Andrea del Sarto, Rembrandt *(The Artist's Mother)*, Rubens *(Portrait of the Artist)*, Jan Steen, Van Dyck *(Charles I in Three Positions)*. The boulle marquetry bureau (c 1680) and cabinet (c 1695) are noteworthy.

The **King's Closet** is similarly furnished with exquisite pieces, mainly French, made of exotic woods (mahogany or satinwood) set with Japanese lacquer panels and bronze mounts.

The **Queen's Drawing Room** was substantially altered by Wyatville in 1834, the plate-glass windows being some of the first to be installed in England. The room is adorned with early-16C and 17C paintings (Holbein: *Sir Henry Guildford*, Mytens, Van Somer, Dobson: *Charles II*, Lely: *Mary II*) and furniture.

The **Octagon Lobby** is panelled in oak with splendid oval garlands by Gibbons. The **King's Dining Room** retains much of the character imparted to it by Charles II: Verrio's ceiling depicts a banquet enjoyed by the gods, while below, lovely still-life panels illustrate fruit, fish (lobster) and fowl; intricate limewood garlands of fruit and flowers carved by Grinling Gibbons and Henry Phillips tumble down the oak panelling. There is an interesting portrait by Sir Godfrey Kneller entitled *The Chinese Convert.*

The **Queen's Ballroom** or Queen's Gallery serves as a meeting room in which visiting heads of state may greet members of their diplomatic staff. Three English cut-glass chandeliers made for George III hang from Wyatville's plaster ceiling. The 17C silver pieces of furniture between the windows are rare vestiges of contemporary taste – similar pieces once made for Louis XIV had to be melted down to pay for military campaigns. On the walls hang a number of portraits by **Sir Anthony van Dyck** – the most notable being *Charles I in Robes of State.*

The **Queen's Audience Chamber**, together with the **Queen's Presence Chamber** next door, preserve the skilled artistry of craftsmen employed by Hugh May during the reign of Charles II. On Verrio's ceiling Queen Catherine of Braganza crosses the heavens in a chariot drawn by swans; Gibbons' crisply carved surrounds highlight the portraits; carved oak frames set off the Gobelins tapestries acquired by George IV in Paris in 1825. Note the fine sculpted bust by Roubiliac (Handel) and Coysevox. In the second chamber, now used by the Knights of the Garter as robing room, Charles II's queen is seated below a canopy as Justice banishes Envy and Sedition from the kingdom.

The **Queen's Guard Chamber** was remodelled at the behest of George IV as a museum of British military achievement: replica French banners, the tricolour and the gold fleur-de-lys are presented each year to the Queen by the current Duke of Wellington and the Duke of Marlborough as quit-rents for their estates at Stratfield-Saye and Blenheim, granted to their ancestors on perpetual leases by the grateful nation.

St George's Hall – This long room (180ft/55m) formed by remodelling Charles II's chapel and hall, was decorated by Wyatville in the neo-Gothic style inspired by the novels of Sir Walter Scott so admired by George IV. Completely gutted in the fire, the hall has been magnificently restored with a hammerbeam oak roof (instead of previous painted plaster ceiling), complete with the 700 coats of arms of past Knights of the Garter.

Quadrangle

The equestrian statue is of Charles II. In the south-east corner is the Sovereign's Entrance which leads directly to the private royal apartments.

Lower Ward

Much of this section of the Castle precincts is given to the **College of St George** founded on 6 August 1348 by Edward III and comprising a dean, twelve canons, thirteen vicars and 26 "Poor Knights" on whom was conferred the Order of the Garter. On the left are the mid-16C lodgings of the Military Knights built by Queen Mary. At the bottom stands the Guard House (1862). To the right sits St George's Chapel and beyond, a maze of cloisters and buildings attached to the chapel and choir school; the brick and timber-framed Horseshoe Cloister is reserved for the lay clerks (adult choristers).

St George's Chapel***

The spiritual headquarters of England's prime order of chivalry, the Most Noble Order of the Garter, is also the final resting place of 10 sovereigns including Charles I brought here after his execution at Whitehall in 1649.

The building was initiated by Edward IV (1475); the choir was finished in 1484; the stone-vaulted nave had been added at the death of Henry VII (1509); work was completed in 1528 in the reign of Henry VIII: a glorious expression of Perpendicular Gothic architecture *(see INSIGHTS AND IMAGES – The Changing Face of London)*. On the outside, the **Royal Beasts** (modern replacements) above the flying buttresses of the west end trace the royal descent from Edward III – the Lancastrians on the southside, the Yorkists on the north.

Interior – The 1790 Gothic-style Coade stone **organ screen** by Henry Emlyn was installed at the same time as the Samuel Green organ presented by George III. The splendid 75-light **west window** (36ft/11m high and 29ft/9m wide) survives in part from 1479, 1503, 1509 and 1842.

George VI Memorial Chapel was built in 1969, the first structural addition to the Chapel since 1504. The windows were designed by John Piper.

Quire – So called at Windsor to differentiate it from the body of choristers or choir, the Quire is separated from the nave by John Tresilien's magnificent wrought-iron gates (1478). The glorious east window (30ft/9m high, 29ft/8.5m wide; 52-lights) commemorates Prince Albert with incidents from his life illustrated in the lower tier, below the *Resurrection* (painted by Benjamin West) and the *Adoration of the Kings*. The carved alabaster reredos was also given by the Dean and Canons in memory of Prince Albert.

The woodwork executed largely by English and Flemish craftsmen dates from 1478-85 and includes a fine set of misericords or mercy seats and *popeyes* illustrating incidents from the lives of Christ (north side); the Virgin and St George (south side). The desk fronts of the front row are 19C.

Garter Stalls – On installation each knight is granted a stall marked with a numbered enamel nameplate (North 1 marks the Prince of Wales' stall), over which he/she will display their banner (5ft/1.5m square of heavy silk bearing the arms approved by the College of Arms in the City of London), crest, helm, mantling and sword (made of cloth or wood and depicted half drawn in readiness to defend the sovereign) and which they will keep until death when the accoutrements are all removed.

Order of the Garter

The highest order of chivalry in the land is also the oldest to survive in the world. It was established by Edward III in 1348 when England was engaged in the 100 Years War with France and may have been modelled on the legendary story of the 5C King Arthur and his Knights of the Round Table: not only was the order to reward men who had shown valour on the battlefield, but also to honour those who manifested the idealistic and romantic concept of Christian chivalry. Tradition relates how at a ball fêting the conquest of Calais in 1347, the king retrieved a fallen garter and returned it to its rightful owner, the young and beautiful Joan of Kent, Countess of Salisbury, with the words *"Honi soit qui mal y pense"* 'Shame on him who thinks evil of it' – the emblem and motto of the Order. A more likely derivation is a strap or sword-belt from a suit of armour to denote the bond of loyalty and concord. At its initiation, Edward III nominated 25 English **Companion Knights**, including the Heir Apparent (the Black Prince): thereby providing himself with his own jousting team and one with which to do battle! Today there are still 25 Companion Knights including the Prince of Wales and at least one representative of each force (Navy, Army, Air Force). Additional **"Royal Knights"** may also be appointed by the sovereign following amendments made to the statutes by George I. Stranger, Foreign or **"Extra Knights"** may also be appointed; since 1905 this has been conferred upon regents or monarchs only (not necessarily Christian as they have included two Sultans of Turkey, two Shahs of Persia, four Emperors of Japan).

Other stalls are reserved for the Military Knights of Windsor (formerly the 24 Poor Knights appointed by Edward III, impoverished by ransoms paid to the French for their freedom) and the Naval Knights of Windsor (now dissolved).

Memorials – Emperor **Napoleon III** and his wife Eugénie of France, the close friends of Queen Victoria who withdrew from the international scene in 1870 when the Third Republic was born. He died at Chislehurst in 1873. Statue of **Leopold I**, King of the Belgians, the uncle of both Queen Victoria and Prince Albert – his first wife, **Princess Charlotte Augusta**, who would have succeeded her father George IV had she not died in childbirth, is commemorated by a sculptural group in the Urswick Chapel where the tomb of **George V** (d 1936) and Queen Mary (d 1953) by Lutyens is situated. In the Rutland Chapel *(open by special permission only)*, founded in 1481, lies the particularly fine early-16C alabaster tomb of George Manners, Lord Roos, and his wife Anne, the daughter of the founders of the chapel. In the north aisle, but despoiled of its effigy and jewels during the Commonwealth, is the tomb of **Edward IV** and Queen Elizabeth Woodville (when the pavement was relaid in 1789, the vault was broken by accident revealing the two coffins: that of the king revealed that he had been 6ft 4in/2m tall!).

The **Royal Vault**, excavated by order of George III (1804-10) extends from the High Altar to the Albert Memorial Chapel; in it rest George III, George IV, William IV and many of their direct descendants. In a second vault (memorial stone inserted by William IV in 1837) lie **Henry VIII**, Jane Seymour, **Charles I** (his embalmed body having been exposed to public view for at least a week at St James's Palace) and one infant of 17 children borne by Queen Anne (1702-14). In the south aisle are the tombs of Edward VII (d 1910) and Queen Alexandra (d 1925) with their dog Caesar; Henry VI, founder of Eton College and King's College, Cambridge.

Albert Memorial Chapel

Built by Henry III (1240), this was the original chapel of the Order of the Garter at its foundation; left to decay, it was renovated by Henry VII as a mausoleum for Henry I and intended by **Cardinal Wolsey** as his ultimate resting place; fragments carved by Benedetto da Rovezzano were subsequently integrated into Lord Nelson's memorial in St Paul's Cathedral. It was given its magnificent Victorian embellishment by Sir George **Gilbert Scott** after the death of Albert, the **Prince Consort**, at the age of 42; it stands as a supreme expression of the 19C revivalist age complete with Venetian mosaics, inlaid marble panels and statuary. Note the four elaborate bronze candlesticks intended originally for the tomb of Henry VIII. Prince Albert's tomb was later removed to Frogmore.

Home Park

This section outside the Castle precincts but within the private grounds of Windsor Castle includes **Frogmore House** which was built in 1684 and used by various members of the Royal household, most notably by Queen Charlotte and her unmarried daughters; today it is furnished largely with possessions accumulated by Queen Mary (black papier maché furniture, wax and silk flowers).

Other buildings nearby consist of follies (Gothic ruin, Queen Victoria's Tea House and an Indian kiosk built of white marble) and the **Royal Mausoleum**, purpose built (1862) by Queen Victoria after the untimely death of her husband Prince Albert. In the **Royal Burial Ground** *(closed to the public)* at Frogmore rest the Duke (Edward VIII) and Duchess of Windsor.

WINDSOR GREAT PARK*

Open daily, dawn-dusk. ☎ 01753 860 222

A 4 800 acre/1 942ha park, once the hunting ground of Saxon leaders and medieval knights, is today linked to the castle by the **Long Walk** (3mi/5km) planted by Charles II with elms in 1645 and substantially replanted with planes and chestnuts in 1945. At the top of the hill stands the **Copper Horse**, an equestrian statue of George III (1831).

Nestling in the park are two additional secluded former royal residences: **Royal Lodge** used by George IV as a retreat and now by Queen Elizabeth, the Queen Mother; and **Cumberland Lodge** where George II's son William Duke of Cumberland resided while charged with landscaping the park.

Smith's Lawn is a stretch of lawn reserved for polo matches, while beyond stretch the **Valley Gardens**, planted by the Duke of Cumberland with shrubs and trees that extend to **Virginia Water**, an area of 130 acres/53ha arranged around an artificial lake. *Open daily, 8am-7pm (4pm/dusk in winter) via local (paying) car park. ☎ 01753 847 518; Fax 01753 847 536; savillgarden@crownestate.co.uk; www.savillgarden.co.uk; www.crownestate.co.uk*

On the far side of the lake stand the **Ruins** which consist of Roman fragments brought in 1817 from Leptis Magna in Libya.

Savill Gardens are another, independent set of landscaped wooded gardens laid in 1932 and endowed with a fine Temperate House in 1995. Glorious show in the spring when rhododendrons, azaleas, camellias and magnolias burst into symphonies of colour; highlights include many varieties of lilies and roses in summer. ♿ *Open daily, 10am-6pm (4pm Nov-Feb). Closed 25-26 Dec. £5.50 (Apr-May); £4.50 (Jun-Oct); £3.25 (Nov-Mar). No dogs. Parking. Licensed restaurant, picnic area. Plant and gift shop. ☎ 01753 847 518; Fax 01753 847 536; savillgarden@crownestate.co.uk; www.savillgarden.co.uk; www.crownestate.co.uk*

ETON COLLEGE★★

School Yard, Chapel, Cloister Court and Museum of Eton Life: Open during summer term time. Closed 28 May and 17 Jun; Chapel closed Mon-Sat, 1-2pm, Sun, 12.30-2pm. £3.70. Guided tour (£4.70; 1hr) daily at 2.15pm, 3.15pm. ☎ 01753 671 177; Fax 01753 671 265; visits@etoncollege.org.uk; www.etoncollege.com

Royal Antecedent – "The King's College of Our Lady of Eton beside Windsor" was founded by **Henry VI** in 1440; a year later he founded King's College Cambridge where the young men might continue their studies. In 1443 accommodation was provided along the north side of the **School Yard** (now dominated by a statue of the founder and the 16C **Lupton's Tower**) comprising a classroom (**Lower School**) and a dormitory (**Long Chamber**) where boys would have slept two or three to a bed; College Hall was built as a refectory for priests, headmaster and scholars.
Henry's grand intentions for an almshouse and pilgrimage church were thwarted when he was deposed by his Yorkist rival **Edward IV** who promptly withdrew funding; the existing choir building was roofed and completed in 1482, a fine example of Perpendicular Gothic. Henry's provision for 70 scholars however was left intact.

Chapel★★

At the heart of the college (originally meaning a community of priests rather than an educational establishment) is the chapel, endowed with many significant works of art.
The oldest are the Flemish-style wall paintings (1479-87), executed by at least four masters. On the north side are scenes associated with the chapel's patron the Virgin Mary, the south side ones depict the medieval story of a mythical empress.
In 1940 a bomb landed on the Upper School thereby destroying all the glass in the chapel save that above the organ. The east window was designed by Evie Hone in 1952 to complement panels designed by John Piper (four miracles on the north side and four parables on the south side). The modern roof is of stone-faced concrete, hung from steel trusses.
Famous pupils have included several kings including **George III**; statesmen, of whom 19 prime ministers, such as **Walpole**, **Gladstone**, **Pitt the Elder**, **Charles James Fox**, **Wellington**, Macmillan, Douglas-Home; the writers Fielding, Shelley, Thomas Gray, Aldous Huxley, George Orwell...

Collegers and Oppidans – Originally 70 scholars were to be entrusted to the care of a headmaster. In addition to the scholars, the school had a number of fee-paying Commensals who were lodged either in the Cloisters with the Fellows or in town. In the early 18C the system was reformed: accommodation was built to house such pupils who earned the name of "Oppidans" from the Latin *oppidum* meaning *of the town*. Today the 24 Oppidan houses are managed by a housemaster and assisted by a Dame. Rivalry is maintained by a traditional contest on St Andrew's Day when the Wall Game is played between the Oppidans and the Collegers.

School Dress – Tailcoats and pinstriped trousers are still the norm. Senior boys wear wing collars (stick-ups) and white bow-ties. Top hats survived to the 1940s. Scholars wear gowns as they have since the College's foundation.

Notes

Index

Charles I — *Names of people and events*
Westminster Abbey — Names of places, streets and buildings

The following subjects have been grouped together for easy reference: Almshouses, Churches and places of worship, Clubs (private), Guards, Hospitals, Markets, Museums and art galleries, Parks, Prisons, pubs and taverns (see Public houses), Registers, Theatres.

Notes

Notes

Notes